CRITICISM

Some Major American Writers

****

CRITICISM

Some Major American Writers

****

Selected by
LEWIS LEARY
University of North Carolina
at Chapel Hill

Holt, Rinehart and Winston, Inc.

New York   Chicago   San Francisco
Atlanta   Dallas   Montreal   Toronto

AN INTRODUCTION

Somewhat Personal

****

It is probably not good to read too much about writers. Nor is it always helpful to spend too much time reading what one reader has written about what he has read. Evaluation can, however, be a useful, compelling, and sometimes, strenuous intellectual enterprise. In whatever area it is exercised, in literature or art or athletics or morals, it is most often an index of taste, which to some degree is a matter of casual preference, but which in a larger sense depends on recognition of elements that transcend or expand personal expectations. The first purpose of any writing, it may be said, is to attract attention, to please or delight, or to arouse response that is angry or lustful or meditative. If it achieves one or several of these ends, it is likely to be called literature. One of literature's distinguishing characteristics is that, when successful, it moves a reader beyond where he was. Something new has been added, in thought, insight, or feeling. To determine what it was, why it had an effect, and how that effect was achieved are functions of that form of literary evaluation commonly called criticism.

And criticism can be a do-it-yourself process, or it may be found second hand in what other people have said about writers or writings. But when the answers are found in other people's words, something has come between the reader and what he has read. Someone else's response may be wiser or more perceptive; it may derive from larger experience in living or in reading; it may be better phrased, or it may be so utterly bad that it demands instant rejection. Whatever that response is, it requires reaction. It invites acceptance or dismissal, in whole or in part, and intrudes between the reader and the original work. Sometimes criticism becomes a thing of itself, attractive to people who care more for it than for the literature of which it speaks. Sometimes it becomes literature, an art which speaks of the experience of reading, and as such is difficult and demanding. Its first requirement is knowledge of literature. Its second is knowing how to talk about it.

Someone has said that there is no such thing as the teaching of literature, that literature, unlike mathematics or history, cannot be taught, only experienced. Reading can be taught, and what to look for in a poem or a book can be taught, but not literature. Strategies of presentation can be taught— the lulling deception of long words, the use of suspense, the necessity for honesty in description of scene or sentiment. Some of the mountebank tricks of inferior literature—the small, intrusive sentimentalities which can lull or mislead a careless reader—can be pointed out. The personal experiences of an author and the method by which these are woven into the texture of his writings often offer interesting hints to why he said what he did. The relation of the writing to the time in which it was written may provide instruction in social, economic, or moral history. Psychologists may probe for evidence of conscious or unconscious aberrations in the author or character.

Many things can be done with literature. This is one reason it continues to surprise, delight, and inform. It is an all-purpose art, adjustable to many uses. When it is good, it is very durable. However abused by the historian who reads it as history, by the psychologist who discovers it a laboratory of types, or by the sociologist or the moralist who finds it instructive as evidence, literature, when genuine, survives. It is tough and resilient and resists distortion when mishandled by people who explain exactly what it means. Most often it can be recognized as much for what it suggests as for what it says. Its purpose, it has been said, is to settle nothing, but to unsettle by intimation. One speaks of the aura, the afterglow, the shimmering quality of literature, its radiance, and its capacity for surprising a reader with insights which neither he nor the author had suspected. Because of what he is, has been, or has the potentiality of becoming, each reader discovers in some literature something which excites or amuses or inspires him. And he usually wants to tell someone about it, for, as Lionel Trilling has told us, "the literary experience is, of its very nature, communal—it asks to be shared in discourse."[1]

Even the most casual reader recognizes that everything which is written is not literature. Experience informs us all that much of the writing which is

[1] Lionel Trilling, *The Experience of Literature* (New York: Holt, Rinehart and Winston, Inc., 1967), p. x.

most widely read today will inevitably be forgotten completely within a few years. Almost everyone knows that certain writings which appeal to him do not appeal to everyone else. In my own case, I respond to what Richard P. Blackmur says in criticism on Herman Melville in his (to me) delightfully provocative gathering of essays called *The Lion and the Honeycomb*, but people who are perhaps better informed than I have convinced me that Blackmur's essay is too obtuse (I think they may mean too difficult) to be included in a collection such as this; I recommend it, however, and the other essays in that volume also, to anyone who wishes to discover examples of criticism so well done that it becomes literature itself. Many of my students tell me that Henry James is devious and tedious, but those few who like him, like him very much. Some people consider Mark Twain vulgar and often downright silly, though Ernest Hemingway once said that all American literature begins with *Adventures of Huckleberry Finn*. I myself think of Poe as a talented second-rate writer, a judgment for which many of my friends think me foolish indeed. Some people admire William Dean Howells, and Lionel Trilling in the essay included in this book explains why. In my judgment Ralph Ellison's *Invisible Man* is the best novel produced in America since World War II, and Theodore Roethke is the most interesting modern poet, but I have included only Ellison in this collection, in the hope that the reader will go directly to Roethke's poetry to discover it for himself. Some of my friends have thought that I should have included something about novelists John Updike or Philip Roth, or, among poets, e. e. cummings, Robert Lowell, or Allen Ginsberg, who seem to them more interesting and likely to survive. My wife tells me that she does not understand my enthusiasm for the rapid prose of Henry Miller. Many people tell me that I am wrong in preferring Nathaniel Hawthorne to Herman Melville.

This is not to say that the recognition of excellence in writing is only a matter of personal preference, nor is it to deny that those writings that have been considered truly great have reached that critical eminence because many people over the years have responded to them. Successful literature is what people like, but there is no way to avoid the thoroughly undemocratic attitude that suggests that the best literature is what people who know literature best most admire, just as the best violinist is the violinist whom people most knowledgeable about music and the technique of performance certainly recognize. A novel or a poem or an essay, or even a joke, may bring forth immediate response because it speaks of a situation or circumstance that is cherished or detested by a reader; to him it is good writing. It says something; it is pertinent; it requires a reaction, if only a chuckle. Why then is it, or is it not, literature? What is literature? What is it to me, to anyone else, to everyone?

Almost every reader has had the experience of being required to read a book, usually because it was on a class reading list, a book that was said by someone in authority to be a fine book, one that every well-read person should read, and then has discovered that for him it is not a fine book at all, but dull and tedious, concerned with people, who have no interest whatsoever for him. What it reveals has no relevance to what he knows of people and the way they act. However often he is told that reading can expand his knowledge of people, by allowing him to know more of them and to experience attitudes and adventures that he otherwise would not experience, he discovers nothing in it to which he can relate. Who in the world, in what antediluvian era, ever found reading that book worthwhile? or this poem whose feet never touch any ground his feet have touched?

Mark Twain once defined a literary classic as a book that everybody talks about but nobody reads. Most thoughtful readers have been tempted to acknowledge that certain "classics" of literature are enduring but not particularly rewarding; they merely have the momentum of reputation, and supply what one of my friends described as the penitential reading that every person well versed in literature must endure. Each reader has his own candidate for the most unreadable classic. According to a recent newspaper report, Bergen Evans, a popular expert on words and their usage, finds Dante's *Inferno* unreadable; publisher Bennett Cerf nominates John Bunyan's *Pilgrim's Progress;* novelist Max Shulman dislikes James Fenimore Cooper's *The Deerslayer*, and historian Bruce Catton finds Geoffrey Chaucer's *The Canterbury Tales* dull. Identifications of literary dropouts such as these probably say as much about the identifier as about the book. But it is often instructive to pause a moment to make a list of perhaps ten of the most overrated writings one has ever read. My list would start, I think, with Charles Dickens' *A Tale of Two Cities*, which was forced on me in the tenth grade and for which I have had an unreasonable revulsion ever since; it would include George Eliot's *Silas Marner*, which I understand has now, though belatedly, been removed from many compulsory reading lists; Mark Twain's *A Connecticut Yankee in King Arthur's Court* would be included for other reasons—it is sloppy with sentiment and bruised by brutality; William Faulkner's *A Fable* would be on my list, and Herman Melville's *Mardi*, for the reason that the input of effort required to read them seems to me too great in proportion to their output of enjoyment or almost any other advantage, and maybe, just maybe, if I were completely honest and dared risk the scorn of almost all my friends, *Moby-Dick* would be there also. To each his own.

"Books are like stars in the sky which seen innumerable," Ralph Waldo Emerson once told a lecture audience, "but begin to count them and they diminish apace. There are scarce a dozen of the first magnitude." Perhaps he is too severe, but he may seem to speak of our time as well as his own when he says, "we are born in an age when falsehood uses the press as freely as truth; when imitation is reckoned as good as nature; a book full of words is not discerned from a book full of things; and so literature degenerates, till it becomes the imitation of imitations, and losing all sterling value, loses presently all real hold of the hearts of men." Most experienced readers learn to distinguish between what is true because it is honest in literature, and what is spurious, made up of words that William Faulkner once said go up in the air like smoke instead of faithfully hugging the ground where people are. "All good books are alike," Ernest Hemingway explained, "in that they are truer than if they really happened and after you have finished one you feel that all that happened to you and afterwards it all belongs to you: the good and the bad, the remorse and sorrow. The people and the places and how the weather was."

For literature is about people and places and what natural forces can do to them. And people and places and nature seem various, in no two aspects alike. They are often so encrusted with veneers of pretension or self-indulgence, or decorated with artifice, or misread as menace, that relationships common to them all cannot easily be found. When a writer can plainly set these things forth, and give name or reason to something for which the reader formerly had no words, then he has done well. He is perceptive and skillful with words, but beyond that, he is honest. Because what he speaks is true, a reader who is honest will recognize it as true, for honesty is as much required of the reader and critic as it is of the writer, and it may be that honesty also cannot be taught, only encouraged.

If literature cannot be taught, there are many things about literature that can be examined. One becomes tired, perhaps, of such familiar undertakings as tracing plot or recognizing the value or the distraction of subplots, of discovering climax or anticlimax, or pointing to characters who are original creations and who are stock figures often presented. In reading verse it is easy to shrug off ventures in identification of rhyme schemes or rhythmical patterns, to notice alliteration or assonance or other subtly complicated arrangements of sound. Studies such as these have been called the finger exercises of criticism, but are of little merit in themselves. They have to do with the mechanics and classification of literature. It is possible to speak of the structure of a book, or, sometimes, of the skeletal outline of a poem; neither of these is of real significance until fleshed out toward suggestions of meaning. The fact that, in *The Scarlet Letter*, characters are presented in three scenes as standing on a scaffold—once at the beginning, once in the exact middle, and once at the close of the narrative—is interesting as an observation, but it only has relevance when it provokes answers to such questions as, "Who is present in which scene?" and "Why are they there?" and "What is the relation of their being there to what Nathaniel Hawthorne seems to be saying?" Sometimes structural investigation can be as disruptive as the search for symbols, as when it is decided that each peak on *The House of Seven Gables* is discovered to represent one of the seven deadly sins, or that Walt Whitman's *Song of Myself* is dismembered to seven, fifty-two, or three hundred and sixty-five calendar divisions, or even that it is revealed that Tom Sawyer spent three days and nights in a cave that might have been his tomb.

It is possible to make literature a playground for the exercise of ingenuity, as Philip Young in his critical remarks on Ernest Hemingway (included in this collection) is sometimes said to have done, by creating a pattern into which meanings may be too conveniently fitted. Yet literature may be thought of as a playground, and criticism as a kind of intellectual game. It should be remembered that Robert Frost often spoke of his poems as his little jokes; it is too often forgotten that literature, and talking about it, can be fun. It can be gay, and seriously engaged in play, by presenting not morality, but reality. Henry David Thoreau has told us that, when best, literature must be somewhat wild—and elusive, as wild things are. It can be other things also, of course, but no one should ever be worried about the danger of desecrating literature. If it is good, it is, as I have said, tough. It cannot be bent or smudged. It can be handled freely and turned this way and that to afford a better view, a wider and wiser understanding. Whatever is said about it can add to its essential force, increase its radiance, or dim a false shimmer. If it is not good, fun can find it out.

To me, the purpose of what is called the study of literature is to experience literature, and then to discover how to talk about it. To be able to explain why—not necessarily how, but why—some writing has been effective is not a simple task. There is a language of criticism, but it need not be a language of long words or of specialized terms and private understanding. If the criticism is to be worthy of the literature it discusses, it must be as free and honest, even as wild or gay or seriously committed as the literature is. It is a language that derives from close and continued reading and from careful attention to what is read, and then a putting into words, so that someone else can understand what the writer has done to enlarge the reader's understanding of life, or of himself, or of literature and what it can do. Sometimes a guide is helpful, as Virgil was to Dante, or as Sam Fathers was to Ike McCaslin in William Faulkner's *The Bear*, but a guide is only a guide and finally, like young Ike, the reader is on his own; the experience of literature is his alone, and the willingness or responsibility or desire to talk about it is his also.

For this collection I have chosen writers who are among those most often talked-about, and I have chosen, as people to talk about them, critics who seem to me sensibly perceptive, direct, and honest in what they have to say. Some are perhaps more discerning than others, but, in my judgment, all are guides who know the territories which they explore. Another person might have chosen other writers and other critics, and those who use this collection might well think that person's choice more correct than mine. I find no difficulty in admitting that, being me, and affected now and in the past by this or that or something else, I am perhaps inevitably directed toward a choice of which some others may not approve. One of the most heartening results of putting together such a book as this could be the reasoned conclusion of some reader that I am wrong, and why. There are other writers and there are other guides who might be chosen.

In my own reading about writers I have found, as I have said, Richard P. Blackmur's *The Lion and the Honeycomb* especially useful, as is almost everything in Allen Tate's *The Forlorn Demon*, another collection of essays. Leslie A. Fiedler's *Love and Death in the American Novel* may sometimes be tendentious, but it is invigorating and lively, and tough enough to be quarreled with, as is Richard Chase's *The American Novel and Its Tradition* and Daniel Hoffman's *Form and Fable in American Fiction*. A cornerstone for estimation of American writers has, for the past thirty years, been F. O. Matthiessen's *American Renaissance: Art and Expression in the Age of Emerson and Whitman*, from which have derived such influential and expansive estimates as R. W. B. Lewis's *The American Adam: Innocence, Tragedy, and Tradition in the Nineteenth Century* and Harry Levin's *The Power of Blackness*. Perry Miller's jaunty *The Raven and the Whale: The War of Wit and Words in the Era of Poe and Melville* must be read with the same caution that one applies to Van Wyck Brooks's gigantic five volumes, *Makers and Finders: A History of the Writer in America, 1800–1915*, for both are better for an overview than for detail. Many readers find Maurice Bewley's discussion of the American novel in *The Complex Fate* and *The Eccentric Design* stimulating; Tony Tanner's *The Reign of Wonder: Naivety and Wonder in American Literature* presents an Englishman's sympathetic view of writings done in his country's former colonies. I find that anything written by Philip Rahv, Lionel Trilling, Stanley Edgar Hyman, Richard Bridgman, or Quentin Anderson is worth careful reading. But about writers, writers themselves are sometimes best; no one puts aside D. H. Lawrence's *Studies in Classic American Literature* or Wright Morris's *The Territory Ahead* without feeling especially refreshed.

But any or all of these can be put aside when literature itself beckons. Each guide is expert in the experience of reading, and one may lead in one direction and another in another, for each guide is only partially reliable. The reading comes first, the talking about it or the listening to other people talking about it is a second, but not a final step. Further reading follows, and with it the discovery that each book or each poem comments on every other book or poem. It may be that Thoreau was right when he said that, unless a reader reads the best books first, he may find that he has no time to read them at all. The guides I have mentioned in this introduction or in headnotes to each selection may be of assistance in helping a reader discover which American writers are best, but determining why they are best, especially for him, is finally each reader's private responsibility.

September 1970   Lewis Leary

CONTENTS

****

An Introduction: Somewhat Personal   v

EDGAR ALLAN POE   1
    Richard Wilbur, *Introduction to Poe*   3

RALPH WALDO EMERSON   29
    Tony Tanner, *The Unconquered Eye and the Enchanted Circle*   31

HENRY DAVID THOREAU   49
    F. O. Matthiessen, *Thoreau*   51

NATHANIEL HAWTHORNE   73
    Richard Harter Fogle, *Hawthorne's Fiction: The Light and the Dark*   75

HERMAN MELVILLE   93
    Walter E. Bezanson, Moby-Dick: *Work of Art*   95

WALT WHITMAN   115
    Randall Jarrell, *Walt Whitman: He Had His Nerve*   117

EMILY DICKINSON   131
Albert J. Gelpi,   *Seeing New Englandly: From Edwards
to Emerson to Dickinson*   133

HENRY JAMES   165
Robert J. Reilly,   *Henry James and the Morality of
Fiction*   167

MARK TWAIN   193
James M. Cox,   *Southwestern Vernacular*   195

WILLIAM DEAN HOWELLS   217
Lionel Trilling,   *William Dean Howells and the Roots of
Modern Taste*   219

STEPHEN CRANE   239
Larzer Ziff,   *Outstripping the Event*   241

THEODORE DREISER   259
Alfred Kazin,   *Theodore Dreiser: His Education and
Ours*   261

T. S. ELIOT   269
Leonard Unger,   *T. S. Eliot's Magic Lantern*   271

ROBERT FROST   301
Lawrance Thompson,   *Robert Frost's Theory of
Poetry*   303

F. SCOTT FITZGERALD   323
Wright Morris,   *The Function of Nostalgia*   325

ERNEST HEMINGWAY   333
Philip Young,   *The Hero and the Code*   335

WILLIAM FAULKNER   351
Malcolm Cowley,   *Introduction to . . . Faulkner*   353

HENRY MILLER   369
Karl Shapiro,   *The Greatest Living Author*   371

RICHARD WRIGHT   389
Ralph Ellison,   *Richard Wright's Blues*   391

RALPH ELLISON   405
Earl H. Rovit,   *Ralph Ellison and the American Comic
Tradition*   407

SAUL BELLOW   417
Leslie A. Fiedler,   *Saul Bellow*   419

NORMAN MAILER   427
    James Baldwin,   *The Black Boy Looks at the White
    Boy*   429
JAMES BALDWIN   443
    Irving Howe,   *Black Boys and Native Sons*   445

EDGAR ALLAN POE

****

Much has been written about Poe, particularly on minor aspects of his life and art. Most perceptive remarks have been made by other poets—by W. H. Auden in his introduction to *Edgar Allan Poe: Selected Prose and Poetry* (New York, 1950); by T. S. Eliot in *From Poe to Valéry* (New York, 1948; reprinted in *Hudson Review*, II [Autumn 1949], pp. 263–274); by Allen Tate in "The Angelic Imagination: Poe and the Power of Words," *Kenyon Review*, XIV (Summer 1952), pp. 455–475, and "Our Cousin, Mr. Poe," *Partisan Review*, XVI (December 1949), pp. 1207–1219, both of which are reprinted in *The Forlorn Demon* (Chicago, 1953); and, perhaps most sensitively perceptive, by Richard Wilbur, as printed here. There is no completely satisfactory biography. Most detailed is Arthur Hobson Quinn's *Edgar Allan Poe: A Critical Biography* (New York, 1941); most sympathetic is Hervey Allen's *Israfel: The Life and Times of Edgar Allan Poe* (New York, 1934). Satisfying full-length critical studies include Edward H. Davidson's *Poe: A Critical Study,* Cambridge, Mass., 1957) and

Robert D. Jacob's *Poe: Journalist and Critic* (Baton Rouge, La., 1969). Patrick F. Quinn's *The French Face of Edgar Poe* (Carbondale, Ill., 1957) discusses Poe's reputation and influence in France. Perry Miller's *The Raven and the Whale: The War of Wit and Words in the Era of Poe and Melville* (New York, 1956) speaks of his relation to contemporaries. William C. Brownell's chapter on "Poe" in *American Prose Masters* (New York, 1909) reveals Poe as an artisan rather than an artist; Yvor Winters in *Maule's Curse* (New York, 1938) speaks of him as a poet of the second class.

INTRODUCTION TO POE

Richard Wilbur

***·

When Poe published *The Raven and Other Poems* in 1845, he described his verse productions as "trifles" and declared, "Events not to be
controlled have prevented me from making, at any time, any serious effort
in what, under happier circumstances, would have been the field of my
choice." Poe's low estimate of his verse is not now generally accepted. Still,
it was undoubtedly true that his mean circumstances forced him to slight his
poetry in favor of the criticism, editorial work and prose fiction by which he
got his bread. And most serious readers of Poe would say that his poems,
while by no means trifles, are on the whole inferior to his other work and
subsidiary to it.

The very young man who wrote the long poems "Tamerlane" and "Al
Aaraaf" was setting out, like Byron or Keats, to say his whole say in verse;
but "Al Aaraaf" was never finished, and from his twenty-first year onward

Reprinted from The Laurel POE edited and with an Introduction by Richard
Wilbur. Copyright © 1959 by Richard Wilbur and used by permission of the publisher, Dell Publishing Co., Inc.

Poe was but secondarily a poet. The philosophic and esthetic thought of "Al Aaraaf" was worked out thereafter in critical articles, in such prose "dialogues in heaven" as "The Colloquy of Monos and Una," and ultimately in the prose-poem "Eureka." The narrative impulse which had begotten "Tamerlane" was now directed toward the prose tale. The poems accordingly ceased to be efforts at full statement; they became in effect addenda to the prose pieces, embroideries, cryptic distillations.

Indeed, several of Poe's poems were conceived or used as interludes for the prose tales, and profit by being read in context. "Hymn," for example, was written as a part of "Morella," and can be quite misleading when read separately. "To One in Paradise" belongs to "The Assignation." "The Haunted Palace," though first published by itself some months before "The Fall of the House of Usher," was later incorporated in the tale, and offers a good opportunity to observe the relationship of poetry to prose fiction in Poe's mature period. As any attentive reader may perceive, the shape or plot of "The Haunted Palace" is the shape or plot of "Usher." Yet the poem is not a true epitome of the tale; it is a decorative and comparatively shallow treatment of material which the tale invests with a great deal of dark but discoverable point.

Poe contended that "Every work of art should contain within itself all that is requisite for its own comprehension." If that is so, then much of Poe's later verse is faulty. In order to grasp the ideas and intentions of the poems, and their implicit narrative basis, one has to go to the prose. I shall shortly attempt, in a quick and summarizing way, to do so.

II.

We can begin, however, with a poem—the "Sonnet—To Science" of 1829.

> Science! true daughter of Old Time thou art!
>   Who alterest all things with thy peering eyes.
> Why preyest thou thus upon the poet's heart,
>   Vulture, whose wings are dull realities?
> How should he love thee? or how deem thee wise,
>   Who wouldst not leave him in his wandering
> To seek for treasure in the jewelled skies,
>   Albeit he soared with an undaunted wing?
> Hast thou not dragged Diana from her car,
>   And driven the Hamadryad from the wood

To seek a shelter in some happier star?
   Hast thou not torn the Naiad from her flood,
The Elfin from the green grass, and from me
The summer dream beneath the tamarind tree?

This poem is unusual for Poe, because of its lucid logical progression and its air of being public speech. Most readers would assent to the following loose paraphrase: "The scientific spirit, now predominant, is like Time in that it destroys beauty: that is, Time destroys the objects in which we *find* beauty, while Science dispenses with the feelings and faculties through which we apprehend and create beauty. The poet, being committed to the praise and creation of beauty, has made a Promethean or Icarian resistance to the repressive spirit of the age, and like these heroes of myth has suffered for his presumption."

If we take the poem this way—and I think the paraphrase is correct so far as it goes—it may be read as a standard romantic protest against Cartesian dualism, against the exclusion of value from the world of fact, against the idea that the astronomer's star and the botanist's grass-blade are the only *true* star and grass-blade. So understood, the poem may seem a hyperbolic warning that if the age does not grant poetry its own kind of truth, it will deprive itself of the highest and fullest means of ordering and enhancing human experience.

But this is to accommodate Poe to our own prejudices. The poem is not hyperbolic; nor is the poet really asking that the subjective Elfin be restored to the objective grass. Poe means what he says, and what he says is this: that the scientific spirit and the universal prosaism which accompanies it have inherited the earth, outlawing the poetic imagination and exiling its subject-matter—the Beautiful—to "some happier star." In consequence, the poet is not concerned with the imaginative shaping of human life on the existing earth; his sole present recourse is to repudiate all human and mundane subject-matter, all "dull realities," and to pursue visions of those realms in which beauty was or is inviolate: the remote Earthly past, in which Naiad and Hamadryad went unchallenged, and the distant "happier star" to which they now have flown.

We are at present inclined to think of poetic composition as an effort to get our concerted faculties—our "whole souls"—to acknowledge and unify a maximum of diverse experience. Obviously Poe's outlaw poet cannot think of poetry in this way. He is allowed an absolute minimum of experience: his poetry is to consist of visionary gropings toward imaginary realms, and it will touch on the mundane only for the sake of negation. ("Oh! Nothing earthly. . . ." are the opening words of "Al Aaraaf," the poem to which "Sonnet—To Science" is a prelude.) A poetry so exclusive in subject-matter is also obliged to exclude, in its composition, certain faculties of the poet. Poe distinguishes in his criticism three divisions of mind—Intellect, Taste, and the Moral Sense—and bars the first and last from the poetic act on the ground that poetry has nothing to do with Truth or Duty. If the poet's object is to get away from Earth and men, he is plainly bound to disregard the Moral Sense, which is involved with the conduct and passions of men; and he must also degrade the Intellect (which defers to fact and "dull realities"), restricting its function to rationalization.

Poe's poetry, then, is not a protest against the separation of mind and world but an extreme assertion of that separation. It does not issue from a harmony of the faculties and a reconciliation of their provinces, but aspires rather to that isolate freedom of the imagination which we enjoy in dreams. Its declared subject-matter is Beauty—which in poetry, as Yvor Winters has observed, is not properly a subject at all, but a consequence of the treatment of a subject.

In his review of the poems of Joseph Rodman Drake and Fitz-Greene Halleck, Poe showed himself entirely aware of the extent to which he had contracted the scope and nature of poetry. "If," he said, "there be any one circle of thought distinctly and palpably marked out from amid the jarring and tumultuous chaos of human intelligence, it is that evergreen and radiant Paradise which the true poet knows, and knows alone, as the limited realm of his authority—as the circumscribed Eden of his dreams."

III.

The poetic principle, Poe tells us, consists in "the Human Aspiration for Supernal Beauty"; and of that beauty the most successful poem can give us only "brief and indeterminate glimpses." It follows that the Poe poem cannot possibly be a report on, or contemplation of, the realm of Supernal Beauty. The poet doesn't know enough about it. What he *can* give us is an account of the process of aspiration, and a rationale of the soul's struggle to free itself of earth and move toward the supernal.

This brings us to the two complementary "myths" which underlie Poe's work from beginning to end.

Poe's cosmic myth must be given very briefly and compositely here, without any analysis of its twenty years' development and revision. In the beginning, Poe asserts, God was a particle of non-atomic or "spiritual" matter, willed into being by Himself, and existing at the center of space in a state of perfect totality and unity. Then, through some inner necessity, this primordial particle was radiated into space in the form of concentric spheres. Thus the universe was established, and the original unity became diversity. The universe is now at the point of maximum diffusion, and, moved once again by inner necessity, is commencing to contract toward the original unity and final annihilation. At the present moment, according to Poe, God exists only in the diffused matter and spirit of the universe: from which it follows that each soul is in part its own God, and that nothing exists greater than the individual soul. Since "the source of all motion is thought," the universe must be reunited by means of the ever-increasing comprehensiveness of the thought of individual souls. In restoring the original unity of things, and so reconstituting God, every soul must logically absorb every other soul; hence every soul will become God.

How are the Earth and its poets related to this process of universal scattering and reunion? The Earth, in Poe's myth, is not only remote from that center of space where divine unity was and shall be; it has also "fallen," through human perversity, and must be purified (most likely by fiery cataclysm) before it can join the homeward journey or *nostos* of the other stars. The sin of Earth has been "intemperance of knowledge"; intellectual pride has led to the vain pursuit of a causative knowledge "not meet for man in the infant condition of his soul"; the race has become "infected with system, and with abstraction," and through practical science the Earth's face has grown "deformed as with the ravages of some loathsome disease." Inevitable corollaries are "the perversion of taste" and the "repression of imagination."

The poet dwells on this damned and diseased Earth as a prophet without honor, "living and perishing amid the scorn of the 'utilitarians.' " He alone of all Earth's souls can glimpse the original harmony in the present diversity, and so contribute, through the motive power of imaginative thought, to the reassembly of God. To this end, he "ponders piningly" on the Earth's paradisal beginnings, or dreams of "some happier star," employing a pure poetic intuition which is at once more exalted than scientific intellection and less presumptuous. It is more exalted and less presumptuous because the universe is a work of art—"a plot of God"—which men are intended to grasp esthetically rather than rationally.

Clearly Poe's cosmic myth is a justification of his kind of poetry, making it not only purposive but indispensable, and rendering the poet not only elect but Godlike. For if God-the-Artist is now diffused into the matter and spirit of His creation, it is doubtless the poet whose soul contains the most of divinity, and who can most effectually abet the universe in its contraction.

Since the poet's business is to help *undo* phenomena toward unity, dreaming the oak of the creation back to its original acorn, his negation of human and earthly subject-matter becomes in Poe's cosmic theory positive; his destructiveness becomes creative; his exclusiveness a condition of his inclusiveness; his vagueness a consequence of his unearthly subject-matter; his denial of Intellect a means to ultimate Truth. In short, Poe's myth of the cosmos presents his every apparent limitation as an advantage.

IV.

The second "myth" which permeates the poetry of Poe is a myth of the poet's life. Let me first offer it in simple outline, then mention a number of its allegorical embodiments.

In infancy and solitary boyhood, the poet enjoyed a continuance of that psychic integrity which he had possessed as a pre-existent soul. Mundane things and thoughts did not touch him; he was not yet of this corrupted Earth. His consciousness was unified, serene and intuitive; he was perfectly in key with the harmonies of nature and of the universe; his visionary spirit knew no restrictions of space or time.

Yet time betrayed him. Coming to young manhood, he came also to the world of men, and its banal complexities invaded his soul. Learning the social and "rational" language of men, he grew estranged from his former visionary self. His awakening passions wakened also the moral sense, and through the troubling conflict of desire and conscience his capacity for any purely "psychal" state of being became intermittent.

Now, as a grown man, Poe's poet feels himself a captive of the everyday world, and longs continually for that former condition in which his intact soul had an unbroken intuitive commerce with universal truth—apprehending it, however, as beauty. So different was that Edenic condition from his present "fallen" state that he cannot recollect it by means of the conscious memory: his only avenues to the blessed past are reverie and dream —which are, of course, at once means to and approximations of the former condition of intuitive wholeness and autonomy.

Sometimes the poet's intellect, that compromised part of him which embodies the practical and analytic spirit of the age, scorns and obstructs the imagination and its dreams; sometimes the conscience protests in favor of quotidian obligations; sometimes the dream becomes nightmare, or is disrupted by passion. Lacking its original simplicity, the poet's mind cannot easily deliver itself to pure vision: like Poe's universe, the poet's nature has been broken into fragments and in part corrupted by "science," so that the return to primal harmony is a struggle. Yet there are times when, the passions being quiet and intellect outwitted, the poet can annihilate his awareness of the world and move serenely through reverie into "the circumscribed Eden of his dreams." What he finds there are the dead past, his lost psychic unity, and a restored imaginative communion with the universal harmony.

What he foresees there are the simplification and restoration of his visionary soul in death, and its passage to a realm of true dreams. What he brings back are the materials of his poems and tales.

One of the fullest and clearest allegorical embodiments of this myth is the tale "Eleonora." The hero and narrator of that tale is born in a remote, inaccessible and paradisal valley, where all things in their strange and dream-like harmony speak "of the love and of the glory of God." His sole companion is a girl-cousin, Eleonora, from whose beauty that of the valley seems somehow to derive. The hero and his cousin roam their solitary domain, dreaming hand in hand, until in the hero's twentieth year they abruptly fall victims to Eros.

In accordance with this spiritual change, the valley now suffers a delirious transformation: the tint of the grass darkens; white daisies give way to "the ruby-red asphodel"; animal life appears for the first time, in the shape of garish birds and fish; the cloud-filtered light grows lurid. But Eleonora's delicate nature is unable to support the turbulence of passion, and she dies, promising to watch over her beloved in spirit, and if possible to "return to him visibly in the watches of the night." He in turn vows to be faithful to her memory, and never to transfer his love for her to any maiden "of the outer and everyday world."

With the death and burial of Eleonora, the valley suffers a second change: the fauna depart, the flora of passion wither to be replaced by dark and dew-encumbered violets; all is faded, still, and funereal. The hero, obsessed by grief, begins to lose his sanity. Though comforted by vague and fleeting visitations of Eleonora's spirit, he finds the valley painful now, and so forsakes it "for the vanities and the turbulent triumphs of the world." In time he comes to a "strange city," and dwells amid "the pomps and pageantries of a stately court," where despite all temptations, he keeps his vow to the dead Eleonora.

Quite suddenly, however, the visitations of her spirit cease; and at the same time there comes to the court, "from some far, far distant and unknown land," a seraphic and ethereal maiden named Ermengarde. Gazing down into "the depths of her memorial eyes," the hero yields his heart utterly, apparently forgetful of his pledge. But the infidelity is only apparent: shortly after his marriage to Ermengarde, the spirit of Eleonora pays him a last nocturnal visit, and assures him that "for reasons which shall be made known to him in Heaven," he is absolved of his vows to her.

The valley of "Eleonora," like all such valleys in Poe, represents the original isolate integrity of the poet's soul, and its attunement to universal harmony. Eleonora herself is the *genius loci,* the principle of beauty and harmony which the valley reflects; in a word, she is Psyche. The pure communion of the young poet and his Psyche is destroyed by Time and the advent of passion—passion being, as Poe so often observes, incompatible with the poetic faculty, and having "a tendency to degrade rather than to elevate the soul." In the death of Eleonora and the withering of the valley, Poe depicts the soul's loss of visionary self-sufficiency; the inevitable consequence is the abandonment of the Valley for the City—that is to say, the degraded soul's exposure to the "outer and everyday world" and its prosaic modes of apprehension.

Eleonora's ghostly visits to her lover are to be subjectively interpreted as moments of successful reverie, as fitful recoveries of imaginative power. The hero's faithfulness to Eleonora's memory is the poet's nostalgia for "Psyche," for his lost intuitive possession of all things. That is what all of Poe's dead and lamented ladies stand for: Ligeia, Lenore, Morella, the whole troop.

The Ermengardes are another matter. It is clear enough that Ermengarde somehow *is* Eleonora, and the latter's dying promise to "return visibly" may lead us to think that she has either managed a second incarnation or dispossessed Ermengarde of her body. Neither is the case: in a Poe fantasy whatever happens is the result of the hero's condition of mind, and the narrator-hero of Eleonora is "mad." What insanity, drug-addiction, myopia or drunkenness signifies in Poe's fiction is the ascendancy of imagination over intellect, the power subjectively to distort or annihilate the world in favor of reverie or vision. Ermengarde, then, is a young woman of the real world subjectively transformed or "Pythagorized" by the hero. He *sees her as* Eleonora. What this means, allegorically, is that the poet-hero has regained his complete imaginative independence of the world, that phenomena do not control his perceptions; he has recovered that psychic absolutism which was symbolized by Eleonora and the valley.

There are many Ermengardes in Poe's tales. The young daughter of Morella, under the obsessed and transforming gaze of her father, takes on more and more of the qualities of her dead mother. Finally, at the baptismal font, he gives her Morella's name. At that moment the identity of mother and daughter becomes complete, and the daughter, her very being usurped, dies. A living or "earthly" woman has been imaginatively destroyed that a dead or "ideal" one might briefly be reclaimed. Berenice, and Rowena in "Ligeia," are similarly deprived of their identities—dreamed out of existence, sacrificed to Psyche—by Poe's monomaniac heroes. And in "The Oval Portrait" a young bride, sitting for a portrait by her painter-husband (who "has already a bride in his Art"), wastes away in proportion as his exquisite painting grows more "lifelike," and dies as the last brush-stroke is applied.

The point is that imagination for Poe must be unconditioned; must utterly repudiate the things of this diseased Earth; must approach the ideal, not merely *through* the real, but by the negation of the real. Ermengarde and Rowena are mundane, physical creatures, daughters of the "outer and everyday world"; we will do them no violence if we see them as allegorical figures representing Earthly Beauty. Unhappily for them, the poet has once enjoyed, in and through Psyche (Eleonora, Ligeia), an acquaintance with Supernal Beauty, and therefore "nothing earthly" can satisfy his esthetic hunger. The poet may *use* Earthly Beauty as a means of reconceiving or remembering Psyche; the process, however, is not so much sublimation as it is an attritive negation. The images of Rowena and Berenice are *worn away* in the hero's mind by the action of his imagination, until they have grown so manageably indistinct that they may be supplanted by the images of Ligeia and of Egaeus' mother. Their supersession, though perhaps but momentary, is complete. For when the poet has imagined his way to Psyche, who either as Beauty (Eleonora) or as transcendental Knowledge (Ligeia, Morella) is a spiritual alcahest, or universal solvent, he finds himself on a plane of consciousness where the Earth, and Earthly Beauty, are in total eclipse.

We find this mechanism of destructive transcendence everywhere in Poe. For example, he ascribes it to Byron in his account of the latter's long attachment for Mary Chaworth. "It was," says Poe, "a passion (if passion it can properly be termed) of the most thoroughly romantic, shadowy, and imaginative character. It was born of the hour, and of the youthful necessity to love, while it was nurtured by the waters and the hills, and the flowers and the stars. It had no peculiar regard to the person, or to the character, or to the reciprocating affection of Mary Chaworth. Any maiden, not immediately and positively repulsive, he would have loved, under the same circumstances. . . ." This is Mary Chaworth playing Rowena, and supplying the poet Byron with a pretext for spiritual flights having no relation to her. Being attractive, female, and alive, she could, Poe says, "serve sufficiently well as the incarnation of the ideal that haunted the fancy of the poet." (Note that this last quotation, taken literally, sums up the entire closing action of "Ligeia.") Whatever of "soul-passion" was involved in the affair, Poe goes on to say, "is to be attributed entirely to the poet." Not only were Miss Chaworth's person, character and emotion irrelevant to the matter, but her physical absence—once the process of idealization had begun in Byron—was a positive advantage. "In absence, the bard bore easily with him all the fancies which were the basis of his flame—a flame which absence itself but served to keep in vigor. . . . She to him was the Egeria of his dreams—the Venus Aphrodite that sprange, in full and supernal loveliness, from the bright foam upon the storm-tormented ocean of his thoughts."

Poetic love, in this account, is a unilateral, visionary, creative act of the poet's, facilitated by but ultimately unrelated to the presumptive beloved. The real affair is between the poet and his soul, and the function of love is to produce visions. Similarly, Poe describes the art of poetry as commencing with earthly materials but finally annulling them. The essential impulse of poetry, he asserts, is "no mere appreciation of the Beauty before us, but a wild effort to reach the Beauty above. Inspired by an ecstatic prescience of the glories beyond the grave, we struggle by multiform combinations among the things and thoughts of Time to attain a portion of that Loveliness whose very elements, perhaps, appertain to eternity alone." The "combinations" by means of which the poet strives to create Supernal Beauty must above all be *novel;* they may be "novel combinations among those forms of beauty which already exist" or "novel combinations *of those combinations which our predecessors, toiling in chase of the same phantom, have already set in order."* (Poe makes the former kind of combination by establishing a City in the Sea; a subsequent poet might make the latter kind of combination by adding a third unexpected element to City and Sea.)

Poetry, then, builds upon earthly things, altering them by novel combination, or improves upon previous novel combinations of earthly things. However, as Poe explains in one of the most important of his "Marginalia," a poetic fusion of earthly things will when felicitous be not only superior in beauty to its original elements, but wholly dissociated from them:

> . . . as often analogously happens in physical chemistry, so not unfrequently does it occur in this chemistry of the intellect, that the admixture of two elements results in a something that has nothing of the qualities of one of them, or even nothing of the qualities of either.

We shall return later to the practical implications of this passage. For the present, suffice it to say that whether in fiction, in biographical essay or in criticism, Poe offered always the same account of the poetic process. Straining after a supernal beauty which might restore the unity of the diffused universe—and of his own shattered soul—the poet begins with earthly things (Rowena, Mary Chaworth, the City, the Sea), subverts their identities and accomplishes their imaginative destruction. The supposition is that a melodious and rhythmic destruction of the earthly must be heavenly.

V.

The "Eleonora" or "Ligeia" sort of story is an account by a "mad" hero of how, though dwelling among fallen creatures on a fallen planet, he has managed—at least momentarily—to blot out all consciousness of his environment and retrieve a state of mind unconditionally visionary. Another large class of stories tells the same tale in a different way: instead of "going mad" *in situ,* the hero of these stories goes on a journey to Dream-Land and revisits his Psyche. These stories are especially to the present purpose, because they offer a fairly clear contextual grasp of some of the imagery of Poe's poems.

Frequently these journey-narratives involve a division of the hero's personality into two or more characters, the fundamental duo corresponding to what Poe called the "Bi-Part Soul." I shall refer to these two egos as the Poet and the Dreamer: the Poet represents the hero's power to venture into and witness the dream, while the Dreamer represents the *moi intérieur,* the pure visionary self.

In Poe's story "The Domain of Arnheim" the Dreamer is a multimillionaire named Ellison, who has a genius for landscape-gardening and has devoted his fortune to the creation of a remote Eden, where he now dwells with a bride "whose loveliness and love envelop his existence in the purple atmosphere of Paradise." Ellison's theory is that Earthly nature has *fallen,* and no longer conveys to human eyes a sense of divine symmetry; he has proposed, in his gardening of Arnheim, to create a refined version of nature which would seem "the handiwork of the angels that hover between man and God."

The Poet of the tale is an unnamed friend of Mr. Ellison, and his narrative (once the character of Ellison has been described) consists of an account of the "usual approach" to Arnheim. He leaves the city one morning by river-boat. The shore scenery is at first "tranquil, domestic" and pleasantly ordinary, but "by degrees the idea of cultivation subsides into that of merely pastoral care." Later, an increasing sense of "retirement," and then of "solitude," accompanies the narrowing of the river, the heightening of the banks, and the coming-on of evening. The foliage grows more profuse and somber, and the river takes "a thousand turns," so that one can never see far ahead. At every instant, the vessel seems "imprisoned within an enchanted circle, having insuperable and impenetrable walls of foliage, a roof of ultramarine satin, and *no* floor—the keel balancing itself with admirable nicety on that of a phantom bark which, by some accident having been turned upside down, floats in constant company with the substantial one. . . ."

After a time, the river-channel develops into a "gorge" filled with "funereal gloom." And the visitor also begins to feel himself "enwrapt in an exquisite sense of the strange. The thought of Nature still remains, but her character seems to have undergone modification; there is a weird symmetry, a thrilling uniformity, a wizard propriety in these her works." At this point, the river widens into a circular basin, surrounded by steep hillsides which are capped with overhanging cloud; the gorgeously flowering slopes, perfectly reflected in the clear water, possess for the visitor's eye "a miraculous extremeness of culture that suggests dreams of a new race of fairies."

The visitor now leaves the river-boat and descends alone into a light ivory canoe, crescent-shaped and decorated with arabesques of scarlet. The river-boat and its passengers turn back toward the city, while the Poet's canoe is floated by the current, to the accompaniment of mysterious music, in the direction of the declining sun—now visible through the gorge—and of Arnheim. A bank of carpetlike emerald grass floats by, along with other evidences of a still increasing artificiality; the chiseled rock of the gorge-side has "the hue of ages," and vaguely suggests ruined architecture. With augmented velocity, and by way of vertiginous windings, the voyager comes at last to a great door of burnished gold, which reflects the light of the setting sun. This door is "slowly and musically expanded," and the canoe glides through, commencing a rapid descent into "a vast amphitheatre entirely begirt with purple mountains, whose bases are laved by a gleaming river. . . ."

> Meantime, the whole Paradise of Arnheim bursts upon the view. There is a gush of entrancing melody; there is an oppressive sense of strange sweet odor;—there is a dream-like intermingling to the eye of tall slender Eastern trees—bosky shrubberies—flocks of golden and crimson birds—lily-fringed lakes—meadows of violets, tulips, poppies, hyacinths and tuberoses—long intertangled lines of silver streamlets—and, upspringing confusedly from amid all, a mass of semi-Gothic, semi-Saracenic architecture sustaining itself by a miracle in mid-air; glittering in the red sunlight with a hundred oriels, minarets, and pinnacles; and seeming the phantom handiwork, conjointly, of the Sylphs, of the Fairies, of the Genii, and of the Gnomes.

After the discussion of "Eleonora," it hardly needs saying that this voyage from the City to the Valley is an allegory of the Poet's spiritual passage from the prosaic world into a realm of unbridled and ethereal imagination; it is a flight from Science and Old Time into Hamadryad-Land. The poet, as he moves toward Ellison and the complete visionary power he represents, watches a slow transformation in the character of Nature, a finely graduated transition from commonplace suburban farm-scenery to the unearthly magnificence of Arnheim. These alterations in the aspect of Nature correspond precisely to the gradual wasting-away, death, and supersession of Rowena, or of Morella's daughter, under the corrosive gaze of the Poe hero. Just as the much changed Rowena is altered, at the moment of death, into Ligeia or "Psyche," so earthly Nature in "The Domain of Arn-heim," having "undergone modification" during the voyage, yields at the tomb-door of the valley to a Nature patently supernal. The metamorphosis is caused, in "Arnheim" as in "Ligeia," by the progressive states of mind of the beholder: the Dreamer is a state of mind to which the Poet attains.

In "Arnheim," as in all of his dream-voyage tales, Poe deliberately de-rives his basic structure from the typical stages of the mind's approach to sleep. The beginnings of the mind's withdrawal into itself are represented, in this case, by the visitor's increasing sentiment of retirement and solitude, and by the darkening and narrowing of the river. The advent of day-dream, a condition in which semblance and reality are interfused, is represented by the equal clarity of the river-boat and its "phantom" reflection, as well as by the narrator's sense of being "enwrapt" or "imprisoned within an enchanted circle." The deepening of reverie, and the complete abstraction of the mind from the "outer and everyday world," are conveyed by the visitor's descend-ing alone into a canoe, while his fellow-passengers turn back to the City.

The clear circular basin, with its steep banks and its lid of cloud, is as claustral as—for example—the House of Usher, and indeed the visitor's mental condition while floating there is the one we associate with Roderick Usher. Staring down into that "inverted heaven" at "the duplicate blooming of the hills," the visitor affords an emblem of the hypnagogic state—that precarious threshold condition in which the conscious mind is conscious of the subconscious, and can, as it were, look down into the dream which is shortly to engulf it.

The relinquishment of the hypnagogic state involves the loss of all con-scious restraint, and therefore the visitor's canoe, once it leaves the basin, is swiftly and passively drawn toward the valley, through dizzy windings which express the dominance of the irrational and are prelusive of the plunge to come.

"By sleep and its world alone is *Death* imaged," said Poe in "The Col-loquy of Monos and Una"; and this should help to explain why the canoe is scarlet and white (Poe's color-symbol for physical dissolution), why the sun is dying in the west, why the chasm-walls suggest ruin and the golden door a tomb. What the visitor enjoys as the door of Arnheim swings open is "an ecstatic prescience of the glories beyond the grave," a glimpse of the vision-ary universe which he will inherit when death has purified him of everything earthly and reunited him with Psyche. Ellison and his bride represent that reunion.

When one understands the meaning and structure of one of Poe's dream-voyages, the others readily open up: for whatever their superficial differences, they are all one story of the mind's escape from corrupt mun-dane consciousness into visionary wholeness and freedom, the scenes and events being projections of a concatenation of mental states. The "humming noise" which precedes the storm in "MS. Found in a Bottle" corresponds to the mysterious music of "Arnheim"; the destruction of the ship and its crew to the turning-back of the river-boat; the transference of the narrator to a phantom ship to the visitor's descent into the canoe; the captain of the phantom ship to Ellison; the plunge into the whirlpool to the plunge into the valley. Poe often indicates or betrays the parallelism of his voyage-tales by coincidences not only of structure but of language: the valley of Arnheim is a "vast amphitheatre entirely begirt with purple mountains," and the ice-bound whirlpool of "MS. Found in a Bottle" is a "gigantic amphitheatre, the summit of whose walls is lost in the darkness and the distance." Similarly, the "intricate windings" of the river in "Arnheim" are identical to the "narrow and intricate windings" of Arthur Gordon Pym's path through the dark, crowded hold of the *Grampus,* or the "narrow and intricate" path of the two sailors through the plague-quarter in "King Pest." And all these windings (let the ostensible goal be treasure, drink, discovery, food, or any other) wind to the same end.

In those tales where the hero sits still and transforms his sense of the world by "going mad," the setting is frequently a hermetic and heavily draperied room representing the insulation of his mind. Its tinted windows stand for the exclusion of daylight fact; its tapestries, pictures and niched statuary are mental images, and can alter with the hero's moods; the eclectic luxury of the furnishings, which come from all lands and periods, indicates the richness of the dreamer's imagination and the idea that dreams are "out of SPACE—out of TIME." But in the dream-journey tales, where the process of "going mad" is expressed in movement through space, the room is too static to be serviceable, unless it becomes the car of a balloon ("Hans Pfaall"), the cabin of a ship ("MS. Found in a Bottle") or some such room-in-motion. It can, of course, serve as metaphor: the reader may have noticed, in my summary of "Arnheim," that Poe sometimes intensifies the ideas of artificiality and enclosure by describing natural scenes with such terms as "wall," "roof," "floor," or "carpet."

To sum up: the dream-journey tale makes its way through a series of scenes—each more solitary, begirt and enwrapt than the one before—and concludes in a descent into the "circumscribed Eden" of dreams. Poe's most frequent images of the mind's journey are the winding water-course, woods-path, canal, chasm, or nocturnal street; the ship's hold or cabin; and the basin, lake or tarn. These he modifies with darkness, narrowness, mist, overhanging cloud, sourceless music and the like, in such a way as to give the scenes their progressive strangeness and reclusiveness. At times, as in "Arthur Gordon Pym," Poe emphasizes the hero's isolation by staging the journey on an island; but the island, of course, is a symbol best suited to static treatment.

In "The Pit and the Pendulum," the last memorable stage of the mind's progress into unconsciousness is described as a "mad, rushing descent as of the soul into Hades." Hence the end of Poe's journey-tales is always, more or less obviously, a plunge. The canoe dives dizzily into the valley, the ship enters the whirlpool or the polar gulf on the way to Tartarus or the Earth's womb. Where the scenery and properties of the tale do not permit a giddy and plunging close, Poe *alludes* to the idea. At the end of "King Pest," to give but one of many possible examples, the intoxicated Hugh Tarpaulin is cast into a hogshead of ale and disappears "amid a whirlpool of foam."

"The Fall of the House of Usher" may now be seen, I think, as a blend of the "Ligeia" sort of tale with the dream-journey. Since it is Poe's best-known story, I shall not summarize it here. The narrator, as the reader will remember, has come to visit Usher from "a distant part of the country," but we are given only the last moments of his pilgrimage—those in which he surveys the crumbling Usher mansion and its tarn (experiencing a "rapid increase of . . . superstition"), then enters and proceeds through "dark and intricate passages" to Usher's shadowy room. Usher (like Ellison, or the captain of the phantom ship in "MS.") is the Dreamer of the tale, and represents the hero's true and inner self, his purely "psychal" aspect. At the same time, he is the fixation and personation of a moment of consciousness, of the state which one reaches in Poe by way of "dark and intricate passages." With his rapid fluctuations between lucidity and irrationality, Usher is an embodiment of the hypnagogic state, of that "brink of sleep" condition in which (as Poe describes it in his "Marginalia") "the confines of the waking world blend with those of the world of dreams."

The imminence of total dream is symbolized in two ways: by the physical decline of Usher's sister Lady Madeline, and by the relationship of house and tarn. Since Poe had already written "Berenice," "Morella," and "Ligeia," he did not present in "Usher" a full account of the process of "Pythagorization," but in the light of those earlier stories one knows how to take the information that Lady Madeline's disease involves "a gradual wasting away of the person." She is earthly, physical Beauty being immolated to Psyche, and the destruction of her identity is all but complete as the story opens. She dies on the evening of the narrator's arrival. We must wait some pages, in this case, for the resulting apparition of Psyche, because the main part of "Usher" is a prolongation of that "inappreciable point of time" during which the conscious mind totters on the brink of dreams—the incertitude of the hypnagogic state being presented as a struggle between madness and sanity.

The ruinous and fissured house, as Poe makes quite plain, symbolizes the tottering intellect of Roderick Usher. The tarn (a gloomy, stagnant version of "Arnheim's" "basin") is that into which Usher's intellect obsessively "looks down"—it is the subliminal mind, the "dim gulf" of the antememorial past, the lost valley become a Dead Sea. Together, mansion and tarn represent both a mind helplessly drawn to dreams of the past, and the advanced state of somnolence which immediately precedes the mind's "going under" into sleep.

Since sleep images death, and since dreams take us back through "the old time entombed" into a visionary world "all our own," Poe's journeys all move steadily away from the air, light, and sound of the living world, either into the stressed absence of these things or into a realm of oneiric counterparts. When the sun does shine into Poe's valleys, it is with a red and setting light, and there are clouds and mists to diffuse even that. The trees and flowers of the valleys do not sway in any breeze from the outer world: they "writhe" or "nod" on their own. When the valleys are not silent, they are filled with mysterious music of intramural or unearthly origin. What is true of the valleys is true of the cloud-veiled planet Al Aaraaf, and of all Poe's concretions or reverie or the dream-state. Hence it is no surprise to discover "Usher's" narrator approaching the mansion through a weather which is "dull, dark, . . . soundless," cloudy, and "oppressive," or to discover that "the whole mansion and domain" have "an atmosphere peculiar to themselves . . . an atmosphere which has no affinity with the air of heaven, but which reeks up from the decayed trees, and the gray wall, and the silent tarn. . . ." At the crisis of the story, the meteorological autonomy of the House of Usher becomes complete, indicating what Poe called elsewhere "the transition from the state of reverie to that of nearly total insensibility"; a whirlwind swaddles the mansion, just before its fall, in a dense, low mass of flying clouds, their undersides glowing with an "unnatural light" which emanates from the vapors of the tarn.

When Lady Madeline leaves her coffin, ascends to the turret apartment where Roderick awaits her, and falls expiring upon her brother's corpse, we know that she is no longer Lady Madeline but Psyche. We know also (through rather strong hints) that Roderick, by "going mad," has accomplished the transformation, and that the reunion of Roderick and his Psyche, though ostensibly horrible, represents two things: it is the end of one night's dream-journey, a short-term passport to the realms of supernal beauty; and it is also a foreview of the soul's reconstitution and purification in death.

The collapse of the Usher mansion into the tarn is simply another way of saying the same things; but the animation of the house, its *plunging* into the tarn, serves to round out the story as a journey. If the reader has a lively mind's-eye, he may already have thought of the general resemblance between the closing action of "Usher" and that of "Arnheim" or "MS." When the Usher mansion begins to split in two, the departing narrator observes the "full, setting, and blood-red moon" shining through the fissure, as the sun shone through the gorge of "Arnheim." "Usher's" whirlwind and tarn, taken together, are equivalent to the whirlpool of "MS.," or the intricate meanderings and final "rapid descent" of "Arnheim." As for what is engulfed, the Usher mansion has the "discoloration of ages," as the gorge-side of "Arnheim" had the "hue of ages"; like Arnheim's architecture, it "sustains itself by miracle in midair"; and its decayed condition, which reminds Poe of "the specious totality of old woodwork which has rotted for long years in some neglected vault," may remind us of the "worm-eaten . . . rottenness" of the phantom ship in "MS.," or of "Arnheim's" diseased canoe.

Here I had better call a halt. It would be possible to pursue this sort of analysis indefinitely, arguing that all of Poe's narratives (including the tales of *psychomachia* or soul-conflict and of detection, which I have not touched upon) are treatments of one theme, and that they disguise this fact by skillful mutations or recombinations of their fundamental symbols, as well as by the diversity of their ostensible subjects. But for the present purpose it suffices to have pointed out that Poe's stories do have detectable meaning, significant structure, and a fathomable symbolism. We may now return briefly to the poems.

VI.

In his review of Hawthorne's *Twice-Told Tales,* Poe makes a distinction between the poem and the prose tale:

> We have said that the tale has a point of superiority even over the poem. In fact, while the *rhythm* of this latter is an essential aid in the development of the poem's highest idea—the idea of the Beautiful—the artificialities of this rhythm are an inseparable bar to the development of all points of thought or expression which have their basis in *Truth*. But Truth is often, and in very great degree, the aim of the tale. Some of the finest tales are tales of ratiocination. Thus the field of this species of composition, if not in so elevated a region on the mountain of Mind, is a tableland of far vaster extent than the domain of the mere poem. Its products are never so rich, but infinitely more numerous, and more appreciable by the mass of mankind.

The tale, Poe holds, is essentially inferior to the poem, but is more capable than the latter of embodying "Truth." Since its function is less lofty than that of the poem (which seeks to excite the mind toward a sense of supernal beauty), the tale can afford to base itself more solidly in a world recognizable by the "mass of mankind"; it can indulge the intellect in the logical development of plot and idea; and it can proceed toward a definiteness of meaning not permissible in the poem. Poe's exclusion of such "Truth" from poetry—especially after 1829—is the reason why one must often refer to the tales in order to know what the poems are "about." Let me give one or two examples.

The "City in the Sea" was at one point entitled "The City of Sin." It makes mention of Babylon and clearly has in mind the engulfment (according to Flavius Josephus) of sinful Gomorrah in the Dead Sea. Moreover, the poem contains frequent allusions to *Revelation,* and the closing lines, as Professor Campbell points out, derive from Isaiah's prophecy of the fall of Babylon in XIV, 9: "Hell from beneath is moved for thee to meet thee at thy coming: it stirreth up the dead for thee, even all the chief ones of the earth; it hath raised up from their thrones all the kings of the nations." Overlooking certain inconsistencies (notably line 4) it is possible to see the poem as a fantastic picture of the wicked dead awaiting judgment during Jesus' thousand-year reign on earth. The final verse-paragraph would correspond to *Revelation* XX, 14–15, in which—after the Last Judgment—Death, Hell and the wicked are cast into the lake of fire.

But it is impossible to imagine that Poe's poem is merely a Gustave Doré illustration of certain apocalyptic passages in the Bible. To be sure, the poem itself does not forbid us to take it that way; but the evidence of the tales, and of the more explicit early poetry, is against it. And Poe's mind was not so submissively orthodox.

In the cosmic myth which I have outlined, Poe came to terms with deity at last by making God a poet and diffusing Him into His universal "poem"; poetic imagination and the poet became, in consequence, divine. But in the early work—"The City in the Sea" came out in 1831—this agreeable relationship of imagination to deity was not yet settled, and there is a frequent note of Satanism and Promethean defiance. It may be heard even in "Al Aaraaf" (1829), where Poe has consented to a conditional subservience of poetry to deity in order to certify the superiority of imagination to Science. One gets the impression, in "Al Aaraaf" and elsewhere, that God's "Truth," while not attainable by Science, is the same *kind* of bald truth that Science pursues, and that the poet proudly prefers his own dreams to both. The poet's refusal of Truth—whether earthly or divine—persists in afterlife: the poem "Dreams" (1827) asserts that, could one eternally prolong the reveries of boyhood, " 'T were folly still to hope for higher Heav'n." And the poetic spirits who dwell on Al Aaraaf, wishing to avoid that knowledge of His truth which God confers on the angels, have chosen instead

> no immortality—
> But sleep that pondereth and is not "to be."

The price of this choice, as Poe tells us in a note, is "final death and annihilation," but it is a price gladly paid: for the one truly paradisal state, to Poe's mind, is the suspended death-in-life or life-in-death of reverie, the contemplative "doze" of "The Island of the Fay," the "conscious slumber" of "The Sleeper" or "For Annie."

My suggestion is that "The City in the Sea" is simply a version of the star Al Aaraaf; that its residents are not the wicked dead but dreamers, poets and other refusers of "Truth"; that the main body of the poem represents their entranced afterlife, and the close their annihilation.

Poe's city obviously resembles much of the architecture of his tales; the same perilously poised spires and pinnacles are glimpsed in the final vista of "Arnheim," just before the plunge; Poe's dreamer-detective Dupin inhabits "a time-eaten and grotesque mansion . . . tottering to its fall"; the splendid visionary-hero of "The Assignation" is described as "squandering away a life of magnificent meditation in that city of dim visions, thine own Venice —which is a star-beloved Elysium of the sea, and the wide windows of whose Palladian palaces look down with a deep and bitter meaning upon the secrets of her silent waters." Most of all, one is reminded of the House of Usher, which corresponds to the City in the Sea in every salient respect: though time-eaten, it trembles not; it broods upon still waters below; it has its own stagnant atmosphere, and derives its own lurid lighting from the phosphorescent tarn; when it sinks into the tarn, as the City into its sea, there is "a long tumultuous shouting sound like the voice of a thousand waters," in which we hear *Revelation* XIV and the "voice of many waters" which precedes the proclamation of Babylon's fall.

Every time-eaten structure is occupied, in Poe, by a dreamer enwrapt in dreams of the past; the perpetual likelihood of its collapse or engulfment represents the mind's inclination to slip from somnolence into insensibility. Since "by sleep and its world . . . is *Death* imaged," Poe's conception of a poet's afterworld employs the same symbols as he uses elsewhere to project the life of reverie and dream. The City in the Sea is a whole metropolis of Arnheims and Usher mansions. Like Nesace's palace in "Al Aaraaf," it is an anthology of the architectural and sculptural glories of antiquity. And there the dead visionaries of the world "blandly repose," brooding on the salvaged beauty of the world's past in the seeming timelessness of dream.

The poem, if my reading of it is correct, employs Biblical material to present, and at the same time to disguise, an unorthodox or "Satanic" idea: the idea that the poet will refuse any heaven save that of his own dreams. In spite of its apparently uninviting and punitive aspects, the City in the Sea is a picture of Aidenn or Helusion, that special afterworld which Poe reserved for those devoted, in this world and the next, to "visions that the many may not view."

The poem is so thoroughly pictorial, so lacking in narrative or argumentative structure, that all evidence of Poe's true meaning must be drawn from external sources; largely from prose-pieces of later composition. The same is true of "The Valley of Unrest," which, taken by itself, yields no ideas and only the ghost of a story. In the earliest version of the poem, Poe alluded vaguely to a "Syriac tale" concerning the valley:

> Something about Satan's dart—
> Something about angel wings—
> Much about a broken heart—
> All about unhappy things. . . .

This served, at least, to tell the reader that the poem has to do with the heartbreaking loss of some sort of Eden through some sort of "sin"; but in his revision of this poem (as of many others) Poe pared down story and idea as far as he could. In order to make a confident guess at the poem's withheld "meaning," one must recall the significance of "going unto the wars" in "Tamerlane," and remember two descriptions of bereaved and "restless" nature. The first is that of "Eleonora's" valley after the heroine's death (with its "eye-like violets that writhed uneasily and were ever encumbered with dew"); the second is that of a sighing, unquiet Libyan landscape in "Silence—A Fable" (where the lilies nod and weep, and the underwood is agitated—though not by the wind—like "waves about the Hebrides"). One concludes that "The Valley of Unrest" is a condensed and obscured "Tamerlane": lines 1–8 are about the visionary soul before worldliness (going to the wars) corrupted it; the remainder portrays the fallen soul's enwrapment in mournful dreams of its former state and of its abandoned Psyche—who, like Eleonora, is buried in the valley.

"Dream-Land" differs from the two poems we have considered in that it forthrightly announces its subject in the title and proceeds to make a number of perfectly intelligible statements: we are told that the poet has just wakened from a dream; that in dreams one encounters the beloved dead; that, despite their terrors, dreams are a solace to melancholy and nostalgic natures; and that the living may, unfortunately, see dreamland only "through a glass darkly." Nevertheless, what Poe wrote and what we read are very dissimilar, unless we are quite steeped in his other works. A good half of the poem consists of a cascade of Poe's habitual symbols, *not* defined by significant concatenation, as in the prose dream-journeys, and *not* illuminated by the statements which the poem makes. For Poe, a "lone and dead" lake or a chasm would by 1844 have an instantaneous allegorical meaning as well as an aura of richness, a fetichistic value, deriving from long symbolic use. For his reader, however, the jumble of symbols which begins in line 9 will most likely resolve itself into a vague impression of sad strangeness.

And that, though one may not wholly approve, is undoubtedly what Poe primarily desired of the passage in question. Sharpness and fullness of meaning are, in Poe's theory, incompatible with poetry. In the critical passage cited above, he explains this incompatibility by arguing that poetic rhythms are a bar to the development of "Truth"; but this, as any reader of Andrew Marvell knows, is absurd. The real reason for Poe's exclusion of clarity from poetry may be found in almost any of his writings on the art, but is given most concisely in one of his "Marginalia" on Tennyson. There he praises his English contemporary for employing "a suggestive indefiniteness of meaning with the view of bringing about a definitiveness of vague and therefore of spiritual *effect*."

This, at any rate, is quite clear. Poetry does not offer "meaning," it offers "effect." What is more, the poem's "effect," its power to induce a certain "spiritual" state of mind in the reader, depends precisely on the obscuration of "meaning." Poe thinks of the poem, here and generally, not as an object of intellectual and emotional knowledge but as a sort of magic spell or mesmeric pass; it should move us not to contemplation but to a state of strange abstraction in which we seem, for a moment, to apprehend an unearthly beauty. The best of Poe's stories, though they, too, greatly aim at "effect," are masterly and trail-blazing realizations of psychic life. But the poem, for Poe, is not an effort to convert raw events into intelligible experience; it is a by-product of or stimulus toward the essential poetic activity, which is the enjoyment of "spiritual" excitement. So distinct, in Poe's mind, are the Poetic Sentiment and mere poetic composition, that the narrator of "Arnheim" can entertain the notion that the loftiest poetic genius is *above* writing—"that many far greater than Milton have contentedly remained 'mute and inglorious.' "

Story and idea have an ambiguous status in Poe's poetry: they are given, and they are taken away. Poe's subject-matter is always relevant to his peculiar concerns; yet very few poems ("Sonnet—Silence" is one) are in any sense exploratory of an idea, and few have "The Raven's" completeness of plot. It is as if the "content" of the poems were there mainly because something *must* be there; content seems less important, finally, than what is done *to* it, and what Poe does to it is to render it "indefinitive." That is, he obscures his subject-matter enough to prevent the reader from having a conclusive sense of the poem's meaning; such a conclusive understanding would contain the reader's mind within the poem, whereas what is desired is a sense of transcending tidy mundane thought-patterns in the direction of a "vague and therefore spiritual" realm where the closure of the mind on its material is impossible. Poe's whole magic consists in starting the imagination and then not stopping it.

Not only does Poe cut the poem loose from intellect by the withholding of meaning, but he makes a continual assault on the normal and factual senses of words. Consider as minor samples these lines from "Tamerlane" and "Annabel Lee":

> Nor would I now attempt to trace
> The more than beauty of a face
> Whose lineaments, upon my mind
> Are—shadows on th' unstable wind: . . .

> But we loved with a love that was more than love . . .

Some readers may find it simple to accept these lines as gallantry or passionate hyperbole; my own feeling is that Poe's use of "more than" is a device for exploding one's normal sense of the words "beauty" and "love," and propelling the imagination past them into the Wordless. We are asked to imagine a beauty which is not beauty as we know it, and which can only be indicated by the destruction of the concept "beauty." We are asked, in short, to conceive Ligeia by annihilating Rowena.

Poe's use of natural imagery is a good key to his treatment of the concrete in general. It hardly needs saying that no natural things in Poe's poetry seem securely rooted in the world of fact. At the very least, like the mist-hung trees of "Spirits of the Dead," they are infected with mysterious and otherwordly significance. Elsewhere, they die to the world as soon as mentioned, like the "bottomless vales" or "seas without a shore" of "Dream-Land." To be sure, Poe's local purpose in the second paragraph of the latter poem is to convey the idea that dreamland is beyond space and time, infinite and eternal; and of course the best device for conveying infinity is first to evoke the finite ("seas"), then to extend or transcend it ("without a shore"). But what happens to the vales, lakes, seas and mountains of "Dream-Land" is what happens to nature generally in the poetry. The juxtaposition of "bottomless" and "vales" is one of those "novel combinations," one of those "admixtures of two elements," by means of which Poe produces "a something that has nothing of the qualities of one of them, or even nothing of the qualities of either."

When Poe speaks of "cypress" in "Ulalume," or of "myrtles and roses" in "For Annie," we feel in the first instance a very slight denotative intention, in the second none. It is obvious that Poe is talking "the language of flowers," and means little or nothing more than "Mourning," in the first case, and "Love and Beauty" in the second. Because these meanings are conventional, we feel that Poe is using words in a poetic or symbolic way, but we have no feeling that the denotative sense of "cypress" or "myrtle" has been violently annulled. We do have that feeling when confronted with a "bottomless vale." Poe's strategy here is analogous to that of the Zen Buddhist who contemplates a logical contradiction in hopes of short-circuiting the intellect and so inviting a mystic illumination. The factual sense of the word "vale" is instantly blasted by the adjective "bottomless"; if Poe's vale has no bottom, it cannot mean what, in topographical language, is intended by the word "vale." Whatever meaning "vale" retains must be symbolic or ideal; but since it has no conventional meaning such as "Mourning" or "Beauty," and since the poem assigns it no definite contextual meaning, the word cannot be pinned down. Unballasted by factual or symbolic sense, the word rises *beyond* our imaginations, seeming to indicate a higher realm of spiritual significances unknown to us—a realm of unimaginable unities in which "bottomless" and "vale" are compatible. And this is exactly what Poe means it to do; in his view, the chief delight which poetry can confer is such an intimation.

Poetry has to do, Poe says in his review of Longfellow's *Ballads,* with physical rather than with moral beauty. But Poe's poetic process is not the conferring of beauty upon, or the discovery of beauty in, physical things. Rather it is the symbolic destruction of the physical. By estranging such words as "vale" and "lake" from their factual senses, and forcing them to seek their meanings in a transcendent realm of pure ideality, Poe is magically abolishing the physical world. The reader who responds to this magic finds himself *performing,* in imagination, that etherealization of nature which was described in "Arnheim."

Setting aside "The Bells," which is altogether a *tour de force,* I can think of only two poems—"Fairy-Land" and "The Raven"—in which Poe allows any dramatic or ironic variation of tone. This is because his poetry is out to express or induce, not the ordinary emotions of men, but a "psychal" excitement appropriate to the mock-destruction of this world and the dim glimpsing of another. This excitement sometimes masquerades as horror, sometimes as ravishment, but it is, in fact, not an emotion at all; it is hyperesthesia. The hero of "Morella" is ravished by the music of the heroine's voice, yet at the same time "shudders inwardly at those too unearthly tones": it is all one strange feeling—or sensation, rather. In "The Lake" (1827), Poe speaks of a feeling of "terror," but then goes on to say:

> Yet that terror was not fright
> But a tremulous delight—
> A feeling not the jewelled mine
> Could teach or bribe me to define—
> Nor Love—although the Love were thine.

Twenty-one years later, in a poem addressed to his benefactor Mrs. Shew, he flatteringly identifies that lady with Psyche, accords her the power to give him visions of Paradise, and writes:

> With thy dear name as text, though bidden by thee,
> I cannot write—I cannot speak or think,
> Alas, I cannot feel; for 't is not feeling,
> This standing motionless upon the golden
> Threshold of the wide-open gate of dreams. . . .

The psychal excitement appropriate to poetry can only be defined negatively as "not feeling" or paradoxically as delightful terror; with human emotion it has nothing to do, and it is facilitated, as we learn in "For Annie," by the death of the heart.

Since the rhythms of poetry derive in great part from the characteristic rhythms of the emotions, the supra-emotional nature of Poe's poetry would be sufficient explanation for its frequent metronomic regularity. One could also confidently attribute the regular rhythms (as well as the heavy assonance, alliteration, and rhyme) to Poe's desire to approximate music (the vaguest, hence most spiritual of the arts), and to secure the magical advantages of incantation. The taste for repeating whole lines and groups of lines, which grew progressively more conspicuous in Poe's verse, may be accounted for in the same ways. To repeat words or lines without (as in the modern sestina or villanelle) continually modifying their meaning is to shift the reader's attention from sense toward sound. If the sound is regular and sonorous, it may prove mildly hypnotic—as Coleridge found by endlessly repeating his own name—and so further the poet's effort to cast a spell.

But enough has been said elsewhere about Poe's readiness to "sacrifice sense to sound": the important thing is to see that, for better or for worse, such sacrifice is perfectly consistent with those extreme poetic purposes which Poe, in "Al Aaraaf" and "Eureka," moved heaven and earth to justify. By the refusal of human emotion and moral concern, by the obscuration of logical and allegorical meaning, by the symbolic destruction of material fact, by negating all that he could of world and worldly self, Poe strove for a poetry of spiritual effect which should seem "the handiwork of the angels that hover between man and God," and move the reader to a moment of that sort of harmonious intuition which is to be the purifying fire of Earth and the music of the regathering spheres. There has never been a grander conception of poetry, nor a more impoverished one.

RALPH WALDO EMERSON
****

Emerson has evoked various responses, from a most sympathetic acceptance to dismissal as an encumbrance and an embarrassment. His biography is completely detailed and his correspondence is edited by Ralph Leslie Rusk in *The Life of Ralph Waldo Emerson* (New York, 1949) and *The Letters of Ralph Waldo Emerson* in six volumes (New York, 1939). His thought is well and simply analyzed in Stephen E. Whicher's *Freedom and Fate: An Inner Life of Ralph Waldo Emerson* (Philadelphia, 1953). Matthew Arnold in *Discourses in America* (1885) calls him "the friend and aider of all who live in the spirit." John Jay Chapman speaks with discrimination of "Emerson Sixty Years After," in *Emerson and Other Essays* (Boston, 1898; reprinted 1909); George Santayana in *Interpretations of Poetry and Religion* (New York, 1900) identified him as, though not of first magnitude, "a fixed star in the firmament of philosophy"; John Macy in *The Spirit of American Literature* (New York, 1913) found him able to gather "the wisdom of twenty sages into one discourse"; but Yvor Winters in *Maule's*

Curse (New York, 1938) upbraids him as "a fraud and a sentimentalist." Perry Miller's "Edwards to Emerson," *New England Quarterly,* XIII (December 1940), pp. 559–618, links Emerson with his New England past; Robert Frost's "On Emerson," *Daedalus,* LXXXVIII (Fall 1959), pp. 712–718, is one poet's appreciative evaluation of another; and R. L. Cook's "Emerson and Frost: A Parallel of Seers," *New England Quarterly,* XXI (June 1958), pp. 200–217, is an appreciative evaluation of both. Walter Blair and Clarence Faust have written with authority on "Emerson's Literary Method," *Modern Philology,* XLII (November 1944), pp. 79–98, and F. T. Thompson has explained "Emerson's Theory and Practice of Poetry," *PMLA,* XLIII (December 1928), pp. 1170–1184. Hyatt H. Waggoner in *American Poets from the Puritans to the Present* (Boston, 1968) finds Emerson "the central figure in American poetry, essential both as spokesman and as catalyst."

THE UNCONQUERED EYE AND THE ENCHANTED CIRCLE

Tony Tanner

****

Emerson unquestionably played a key role in the shaping of the American imagination, and yet he seems to have had some trouble in defining his own role in his own times. Once he ceased to be a minister he did not start to become an artist; his work has neither the intense passion or still serenity of the true mystic nor the intellectual rigour of the philosopher. He experimented with various characters or projections of parts of his own uncommitted imagination—the Scholar, the Seer, the Man of Genius, the Contemplative Man, the Student, the Transcendentalist, even the Reformer and the Hero. Professor Henry Nash Smith is surely correct in referring to these as "a collection of embryos" and in going on to suggest that we should understand the essays and addresses in which Emerson deploys these characters as "rudimentary narratives rather than as structures of discursive reasoning." [1] In his work, therefore, it is wiser to seek the suggestive drift of the whole than to attempt to establish a consistently developed system of thought. In his many characters he canvassed many problems, but recurringly, insistently, he returned to the discussion of the relationship between man and nature, "the marriage of thought and things." He saw no basic hostilities in nature and no radical evil in man. When he does turn his attention to the problem of pain and suffering his tone remains suspiciously bland.[2] It is hard to feel that he has deeply registered some of the more rigorous paradoxes of existence; hard to feel that he ever experienced the chaos within. Evil was neither lasting nor real to Emerson. Thus the problem he addresses himself to is not how to restrain what is dark in man, but rather how to maintain a sense of the enveloping, involving divinity of the world. "What is life but the angle of vision"[3] he asserts, and much of his work is occupied with attempts to define the appropriate angle of vision. He felt that one of America's deepest needs was a "general education of the eye"[4] and it was just such an education that many of his essays and addresses attempted to give. I want to suggest that in the course of his "education" he procured special prestige for the angle of vision of the child.

In his diagnosis of what was wrong with contemporary attitudes towards the world, Emerson insisted that the fault was not in the world itself so much as in man's manner of regarding it. "The ruin or the blank that we see when we look at nature, is in our own eye. The axis of vision is not coincident with the axis of things, and so they appear not transparent but opaque. The reason why the world lacks unity, and lies broken and in heaps, is because man is disunited with himself."[5] If things appeared to lack unity that was because of some disorder in the eye: a new eye would unify the world in a new way—salvation is visual. Emerson shifts attention from environment to spectator. In one way he was merely continuing the tradition of neo-platonic thought among the romantics. When he writes: "Not in nature but in man is all the beauty and worth he sees"[6] we hear echoes of Blake and Goethe, and Coleridge. But in emphasizing the responsibilities and creative powers of "the eye of the beholder" he had a motive which the European romantics could not have had. For, as long as the interest of a locale was considered to be inherent in the place rather than the viewer, then Americans would be forever looking to Europe. By denying a hierarchy of significance among external objects he not only eliminated the special prestige of Europe (since everywhere is equally significant), he confronts the eye with an enormous, if exciting, task.

In the introduction to his earliest work he had written: "Why should not we also enjoy an original relation to the universe?"[7] and he had started out with the resolution: "Let us interrogate the great apparition that shines so peacefully around us."[8] Emerson wanted the eye to see the world from scratch, wanted to inculcate "the habit of fronting the fact, and not dealing with it at second hand, through the perceptions of somebody else." [9] But from the start we should alert ourselves to a doubleness which is inherent in almost everything Emerson says about man's visual relationship with nature. Briefly this doubleness consists of an emphasis which points both to the importance of particulars *and* the unmistakable presence of general truths. The world is full of isolated details which should command our equal attention and reverence, and yet ultimately it is all one vast simple truth: the world is both a mosaic *and* a unified picture which admits of no fragmentation. To pick up his own words the world is both opaque and transparent—it both resists and invites visual penetration. His complaint is that "as the high ends of being fade out of sight, man becomes near-sighted, and can only attend to what addresses the senses." [10] The senses bring us indispensable particulars but to limit knowledge to the "sensuous fact" is to be a Materialist: the Idealist, by a deliberate "retirement from the senses," [11] will discern truths of which material things are mere representations, truths of "the high ends of being."

> We live in succession, in division, in parts, in particles. Meantime within man is the soul of the whole; the wise silence, the universal beauty, to which every part and particle is equally related; the eternal ONE. . . . We see the world piece by piece, as the sun, the moon, the animal, the tree; but the whole, of which these are the shining parts, is the soul.[12]

Man must see all the shining parts of the world anew, as for the first time with his own uninstructed eye: but this is merely the prelude to his discerning "the ONE." Emerson's work would seem to prescribe an ascent from materialism to idealism and thence to mysticism—a passionate scrutiny of the minute particulars of a world which suddenly turns transparent and gives us an insight into "the background of being," "the Over-Soul," "the ONE." This duality of vision Emerson himself recognized, noting in his journal: "Our little circles absorb us and occupy us as fully as the heavens; we can minimize as infinitely as maximize, and the only way out of it is (to use a country phrase) to kick the pail over, and accept the horizon instead of the pail, with celestial attractions and influences, instead of worms and mud pies."[13] Emerson is not consistent in his advice for he is quite as likely to recommend that a man should scrutinize the pail rather than kick it over. But the passage describes very graphically one of his own habitual practices; for both visually and stylistically he moves from the pail (the discrete detail) to the horizon (the embracing generalization). Sherman Paul, who has written so well on Emerson, shrewdly adopts an idea from the work of Ortega y Gasset, and makes a similar point about Emerson. "The eye brought him two perceptions of nature—nature ensphered and nature atomized—which corresponded to the distant and proximate visual powers of the eye."[14] Emerson, seeking a sense of the unity and inter-involvement of all things, felt there was a great value in focusing the eye on "an unbroken horizon":[15] not only because the unbroken horizon offers an image of an unbroken circle, not only because at the horizon different elements meet and marry, but also because when the eye pitches its focus thus far, all things between it and the horizon fall into what Paul calls "a blur of relatedness." [16] Seen thus, individual things seem not to be discrete and unrelated but rather a part of one vast unifying process. The world appears as a concave container. On the other hand, when the eye fastens on to one single detail the rest of the world falls away and one is only conscious of the separateness and isolation of the thing: there is no hazy unity but only the encroaching fragment. The world becomes convex, thrusting out its differentiated particulars. The dangers of the close scrutinizing vision were clear to Emerson: "If you bury the natural eye too exclusively on minute objects it gradually loses its powers of distant vision."[17] The paradox is, I think, that Emerson himself effectively, if unintentionally, stressed the value of the close scrutinizing vision. In his case, of course, the detail seldom failed to reveal the divine spirit which rolls through all things. But Thoreau developed a habit of close scrutiny, a reverence for details, which occupied itself with "minute objects" to a degree never intended by Emerson. Thoreau was convinced that every fact, no matter how small, would flower into a truth, conveying to him a sense of the whole, the unity which maintained the details. Yet he seems to bear out Emerson's warning in a late melancholy complaint: "I see details, not wholes nor the shadow of the whole."[18] In such a phrase he seems to anticipate what could, and I think did, happen to subsequent writers. For many of them the eye got stuck at the surface, it was arrested among particulars. The mosaic stayed illegible with no overall, or underall, pattern discernible. Emerson himself gives intimations of such a possibility. "Nature hates peeping"[19] and, more forcefully, "Nature will not be a Buddhist: she resents generalizing, and insults the philosopher in every moment with a million of fresh particulars." [20] One of Emerson's natures is one divide unbroken process wherein all the teeming, tumbling details are seen as part of a flowing Unity, a Unity not described so much as felt, passionately, ubiquitously, empathetically. This is the nature that Whitman was to celebrate. But the other nature described by Emerson is a mass of discrete, clearly defined objects, a recession of endless amazing particulars —particulars which seem to quiver with hidden meanings but which never afford us the revealing transparency. This nature of clear contours and suggestive details is the nature of Anderson, Stein, Hemingway and many others.

As we noticed, the threat to the Transcendentalist lay precisely in the extreme generality of his assertions, his reliance on the all-explaining presence. For without a final mystical concept of nature Emerson confesses that he is left "in the splendid labyrinth of my perceptions, to wander without end." [21] Without the affirmed presence of the Over-Soul the world becomes a labyrinthine maze of perceptions which do not add up. The only way out of the maze was to look at it in a different way: this is why Emerson continually raises the question of how man should look at the world.

"Make the aged eye sun-clear"[22]—so Emerson appeals to Spring in one of his poems: it is an appeal which follows logically from his constant complaint that "we are immersed in beauty, but our eyes have no clear vision." [23] The age of an eye is presumably its sum of acquired habits, its interpretative predispositions, its chosen filter through which it sieves the world even while regarding it. Emerson thought that a person could become fixed in his ways of looking just as we talk of people getting fixed in their ways of thinking. Consequently he wants the eye to be washed clear of those selective and interpretative schemata which prevent us from "an original relation to the universe." As we now think, without these acquired schemata vision would be impossible: we have to learn to see and a "washed" eye would be an eye blinded by undifferentiated confusion. But the important thing is not that Emerson did not understand the mechanics of sight but that he thought it possible and desirable to start looking at the world as though one had never seen or heard of it before. What Emerson wanted from man was a renewed faculty of wonder. "All around us what powers are wrapped up under the coarse mattings of custom, and all wonder prevented . . . the wise man wonders at the usual."[24] "The invariable mark of wisdom is to see the miraculous in the common."[25] In this kind of visual relationship between the eye and the world, the eye stands completely passive and unselective while the surrounding world flows unbroken into it. Something like this was envisaged by Emerson when he described himself in the following way:

> Standing on the bare ground—my head bathed by the blithe air and uplifted into infinite space—all mean egotism vanishes. I am become a transparent eyeball; I am nothing; I see all; the currents of the Universal Being circulate through me; I am part or parcel of God.[26]

The notable aspect of this visual stance is its complete passivity, its mood of pious receptivity. Unfocusing, unselecting, the eye is porous to the "currents of the Universal Being." Rather similar is Emerson's description of the delight he receives from a fine day which "draws the cords of will out of my thought and leaves me nothing but perpetual observation, perpetual acquiescence, and perpetual thankfulness."[27] Thus relieved of the active will and conscious thought, Emerson could feel himself reabsorbed into the flowing continuum of unselfconscious nature.

Of course it was because of his optimistic mysticism that Emerson endorsed this mode of seeing, for he was convinced that if man could reattain a primitive simplicity of vision the ubiquitous divinity of the world would suddenly become clear to him. The wonder he advises is a form of visual piety: to see naively is to see religiously. This explains his interest in the animal eye and the child's eye—neither of which have been overlaid with the dust and dirt of custom and second-hand perception, both of which are free from the myopic interference of reason. The child sees better than the man. "To speak truly, few adult persons can see nature. Most persons do not see the sun. At least they have a very superficial seeing. The sun illuminates only the eye of the man, but shines into the eye and the heart of the child."[28]

The desired point of view is one which allows nature unhindered, uninterrupted access to the eye, thence to the heart. Because for Emerson this meant capitulation to a superior source of virtue. "Man is fallen; nature is erect"[29] and "all things are moral."[30] It follows we must not try and impose our will on nature but rather "suffer nature to intrance us"[31] for our own good. Man's fall is not into knowledge of evil—but into consciousness: for Emerson, as Yeats noted, has no "vision of evil" and maintains, rather incredibly, that what we call evil would disappear if we acquired a new way of looking at things: "the evils of the world are such only to the evil eye." How such evil finds its way into an intrinsically benign and moral universe is not clear—but the extremity of Emerson's position is. To be conscious is the curse, for to be conscious is to be alienated from our original home or womb (and Emerson often uses words like "cradle" and "nestle" and "embosomed" to describe the proper quasi-infantile relationship with nature), it is to have lost the comfort of our primary ties. The unselfconsciousness of animals is enviable. "The squirrel hoards nuts and the bee gathers honey, without knowing what they do, and they are thus provided for without selfishness or disgrace."[32] Man's dilemma is based solely on his consciousness. "Man owns the dignity of the life which throbs around him, in chemistry, and tree, and animal, and in the involuntary functions of his own body; yet he is balked when he tries to fling himself into this enchanted circle, where all is done without degradation."[33] Only the *involuntary* actions of man have any dignity: we hear nothing of "the dignity of judgment" in James's phrase, nothing of the enlightened will, of considered intent, of the disciplined pursuit of noble ends. Consciousness is seen only as an inhibitor—for what Emerson really wants is to get back into the enchanted circle, to regain what he calls "the forfeit paradise."

> And so, perchance, in Adam's race,
> Of Eden's bower some dream-like trace
> Survived the Flight and swam the Flood,
> And wakes the wish in the youngest blood
> To tread the forfeit Paradise,
> And feed once more the exile's eyes:[34]

And he makes the point as strongly in prose: "Infancy is the perpetual Messiah, which comes into the arms of fallen men, and pleads with them to return to paradise."[35] Not a change of heart but a change of eye, a new mode of access into nature, is the burden of Emerson's lay sermons. As exemplars he cites "children, babes, and even brutes" because "their mind being whole, their eye is as yet unconquered; and when we look in their faces we are disconcerted."[36] Man's eye has been conquered—that was the fall: man has been "clapped into jail by his consciousness."[37] This is why the child sees the sun properly and the adult does not. "Infancy, youth, receptive, aspiring, with religious eye looking upward, counts itself nothing and abandons itself to the instruction flowing from all sides."[38] This is the child's genius: the openness to sensations, the visual abandon he is capable of. We are at our best when we too can "gaze like children."[39] "It is very unhappy, but too late to be helped, the discovery we have made that we exist. That discovery is called the Fall of Man. Ever afterwards we suspect our instruments. . . . Once we lived in what we saw; now the rapaciousness of this new power, which threatens to absorb all things, engages us."[40] "We suspect our instruments"—Emerson diagnoses a crisis of vision: we see, but we are not sure what we see and how correct is our seeing. There is perhaps something greedy and predatory about the conscious eye, which scans the panorama of creation with utilitarian intention, every glance of which is an act of visual spoliation. But the eye which seeks passively and humbly for true connection and orientation lacks confidence. However the child and the animal still seem to live in what they see with no subject-object dichotomy to haunt them, with none of the sense of severance which assaults the conscious eye. If the adult eye is glazed and dull and blind to the lessons of nature, still the naive eye—idiot, Indian, infant—seems to pay the most profitable kind of attention to things, to enjoy a lost intimacy with the world, to have the freshest, clearest perceptions. Thus Emerson seems to have seen the problem and located the salvation.

Whether or not Emerson felt he had any medical and anthropological evidence for his description of the naive eye of the child and native is not important: for ultimately he was using the notion as a metaphor. His conception of the naive eye is not scientific so much as religious. It was a prelude to worship rather than a preparation for action. It is in this light that such curious passages as the following should be read:

> The child with his sweet pranks, the fool of his senses, commanded by every sight and sound, without any power to compare and rank his sensations, abandoned to a whistle or a painted chip, to a lead dragoon or a ginger-bread dog, *individualising everything, generalising nothing,* delighted with every new thing, lies down at night overpowered by the fatigue which this day of continual pretty madness has incurred. *But nature has answered her purpose with the curly dimpled lunatic.* . . . This glitter, this opaline lustre plays around the top of every toy to his eye to insure his fidelity, and he is deceived to his good. *We are made alive and kept alive by the same arts.*[41] [my italics]

It is the intellectual (not the mystical) generalization, so detrimental to a proper habit of awe, which Emerson is writing against; it is a new sort of naive wondering individualizing he is anxious to inculcate. And although he indulgently calls the child a "dimpled lunatic" he elsewhere talks more seriously of "the wisdom of children."[42] Although he sometimes asserts a superior mode of vision which sees through all particulars to the Over-Soul, although he sometimes warns against the rapt attention to detail with which he credited the child, the savage and the animal; nevertheless he often returns to the superiority of the naive eye precisely because of the generous attentive wonder it displays in front of nature's multiple particulars.

Perhaps the child was ultimately Emerson's image for his own best intentions. "The first questions are always to be asked, and the wisest doctor is gravelled by the inquisitiveness of the child."[43] Adult maturity is no real maturity since we have lost the right approach to nature, the knack of correct penetration: in fact we no longer ask the right questions. The child in his unencrusted innocence does. There is a dangerous form of extremism here: Emerson's rejection of the past includes not only a denial of the accumulated wisdom of the race but also the lessons of experience. The inquiry ideally should commence afresh each day. Nothing accrues, everything is always to be asked: such is the extreme implication of the Emersonian stance. And certainly since his time the habit of renewed wonder, the ever-novel interrogation of experience has become a recurring theme in American literature, a temperamental predisposition and a literary strategy. Naivety has become an important form of wisdom.

> If we cannot make voluntary and conscious steps in the admirable
> science of universals, let us see the parts wisely, and infer the genius
> of nature from the best particulars with a becoming charity.[44]
>
> (Emerson)

I have already suggested that although Emerson's vision alternated between detail and generalization, the "mud pies" and the "celestial
influences," the overall effect of his work is to secure a new respect for
close vision. What I want to point out in this section is how Emerson, despite
his own preference for "the admirable science of universals," focused unusual and exciting attention on "the best particulars." More remarkably he
often equated the best particulars with low and commonplace objects and
continually suggested that the need for "a language of facts"[45] could best
be answered by turning to the vernacular. These emphases alone make him
a major figure in American literature and they merit special attention here.
Only rarely does Emerson give the impression that it might be disconcerting
if one could not make the pieces of the mosaic add up to one flowing, binding picture. We just have some hints. "But all is sour if seen as experience.
Details are melancholy; the plan is seemly and noble."[46] Having lost all
sense of the "seemly and noble" plan Henry Adams, for one, found the remaining heaps of particulars not only sour and melancholy but terrifying.
Emerson, to whom mystical generalizations came all too easily, could tie up
the world in a sentence. "Our globe seen by God is a transparent law, not a
mass of facts."[47] Facts on their own were indeed "heavy, prosaic" and
"dull strange despised things": but Emerson maintained that simply by
wondering at them man would find "that the day of facts is a rock of dia-
monds; that a fact is an epiphany of God."[48] With such experience open to
him Emerson could well afford to stress the value of a close regard for
facts.

If you believe that the universe is *basically* such a perfect continuous
whole then certain things follow. For a start every detail will be equally significant. "A leaf, a drop, a crystal, a moment of time, is related to the
whole, and partakes of the perfection of the whole. Each particle is a microcosm, and faithfully renders the likeness of the world."[49] "There is no fact
in nature which does not carry the whole sense of nature."[50] "The world
globes itself in a drop of dew. The microscope cannot find the animalcule
which is less perfect for being little."[51]

Now the interesting aspect of this belief that "the universe is represented in every one of its particles"[52] is that it can easily lead, not to the
mystical generalization, but to an extreme of particularization, a devoted
preoccupation with the minutiae of existence. It can encourage a prose devoted to ensnaring the crystalline fragments of momentary experience.

Emerson works against his own intentions here by giving a tremendous prestige to the smallest details of the material world: his mystical enthusiasm is, as it were, diffused among all the details he sees. There is no hierarchy of value or significance operative: *all* details are worthy of the most reverent attention because all are equally perfect and equally meaningful. If Thoreau, as Emerson said, was "equally interested in every natural fact,"[53] then he was only putting into practice an Emersonian prescription. The implications of this attitude are worth pondering. If every fact is equally interesting where does one find a criteria of exclusion, a principle of abridgement without which art cannot start to be art for it cannot leave off being nature? Emerson is endorsing an eye which refuses to distinguish and classify, which denies priorities of importance and significance, which refuses to admit of any sort of difference in import and value. From one point of view one could call this the egalitarian eye: an eye which affirms the equality of all facts. All facts are born equal and have an equal claim on man's attention. Yet in most art there is what we might call an aristocratic tendency: a claimed prerogative to exercise a lordly right of selection, omission, evaluation, and rearrangement. The aristocratic eye tyrannizes its facts: the egalitarian eye is tyrannized by them. This is not to say that the egalitarian or naive eye cannot discover things to which the aristocratic eye remains blind: it can, for it has that humility which makes new insights possible. It needed the naive eye as described by Emerson and adopted by Thoreau and Whitman, for America to be seen at all in its own right. But it is worth pointing out at this stage that there are distinct problems of organization and evaluation inherent in Emerson's concept of vision. What is completely absent is any sense of a scale of relative complexity, any feeling that small clusters of selected facts can yield a restricted amount of wisdom, any notion of a gradual increase of intelligence, any awareness of various modes of classification, any reference to the accumulating density of experience. There is the leaf—and there are the hidden laws of the universe: and nothing in between. Certainly not society, the notable omission in Emerson. For Emerson is a man talking metaphysics with his eye glued to the microscope, and plenty of American writers have taken their turn at the microscope after Emerson and his disciple Thoreau. This notion of Emerson's had far-reaching repercussions. For if the meaning of the world is to be found in a drop of dew, then the meaning of a given situation may be contained in the contingent objects which surround the participants. The lesson could be drawn from Emerson's thought that if the writer looks after the details the significances will look after themselves. A writer might construe his task to be a scrupulous itemizing of particulars, from the smallest to the largest with no accompanying distribution of significance, no perspective with its recession of priorities, no "comparison and ranking of sensations." Indeed he gives a clear warrant for such an attitude. Thus: "the truth-speaker may dismiss all solicitude as to the proportion and congruency of the aggregate of his thoughts, so long as he is a faithful reporter of particular impressions."[54] This means that a work of art depends for its form on the individual notation; no larger unit of meaning need be constructed. As he very revealingly wrote—"ask the fact for the form":[55] an attitude far removed from that which relies on the form to assign meaning to the fact. Although Emerson talked of the importance of the "Intellect Constructive," the major emphasis of his work falls on the "Intellect Receptive."[56]

Emerson's belief that the part contained the whole—by implication, or in shorthand as it were—leads quite naturally to his mystique of facts. We remember his instructions to "see the miraculous in the common": he goes on to arraign our blindness to the worth and significance of small everyday facts. "To the wise, therefore, a fact is true poetry, and the most beautiful of fables."[57] Facts contain their own story if we will simply look at them afresh. "Pleads for itself the fact"[58] he says in one of his poems and he means just that: things will "sing themselves"[59] if we learn to listen in the right way. Again we note that the prescribed attitude is passive. We do not impose a meaning on facts, rather we try and make "facts yield their secret sense."[60] "Every moment instructs and every object; for wisdom is infused into every form."[61] Genius, then, will consist of "the habit of fronting the fact";[62] the intellect is ravished "by coming nearer to the fact."[63]

Emerson's emphasis was most important for American writers of the time: because among other things he was continually dragging eyes back to the worth and status of American facts. He scorned artists who could only discern beauty through the conventions of the old "sublime." "They reject life as prosaic, and create a death which they call poetic."[64] Emerson was constantly canvassing for an artistic acceptance of prosaic everyday life. It is the instinct of genius, he affirmed,

> to find beauty and holiness in new and necessary facts, in the field and road-side, in the shop and mill. Proceeding from a religious heart it will raise to a divine use the railroad, the insurance office, the joint-stock company; our law, our primary assemblies, our commerce, the galvanic battery, the electric jar, the prism, and the chemist's retort; in which we seek now only an economical use. . . . The boat at St. Petersburg which plies along the Lena by magnetism, needs little to make it sublime.[65]

We can hear prophetic echoes of Whitman's enthusiastic listing of things here. It may sound naive to us but at the time this opinion of Emerson's rendered American literature a real service: his influence helped to make available whole areas of contemporary American life which had hitherto been considered all but ineligible for serious treatment. It was Emerson's insistence on "the worth of the vulgar" which made Whitman's work possible. He himself chooses the simplest of objects as carriers of sublime revelations. His prose often seems to create a still-life of separately attended-to particulars. It conveys a sense of the radiance of things seen. Emerson succeeded in vivifying the "common, the familiar, the low": [66] he dignified the details of "the earnest experience of the common day."[67] He invokes a new respect for contingent, mundane particulars.

But in order to see details properly man has to separate one thing from another. So although Emerson believes that there are no walls or separating barriers in the flowing tide of nature he yet talks of "the cool disengaged air of natural objects"[68] and affirms that "things are not huddled and lumped, but sundered and individual."[69] Emerson the mystic talked on and on about the fluid inter-relatedness of all things, the transparency of nature to the ONE: but the Emerson whose influence is most marked in American literature was the man who asserted that "the virtue of art lies in detachment, in sequestering one object from the embarrassing variety,"[70] who approved "the power to fix the momentary eminency of an object."[71] And if it be asked what connection this particular virtue has with the naive eye we should recall that Emerson said: "To the young mind everything is individual, stands by itself."[72] The naive eye, as he depicted it, was likely above all others to be alert to the unique significance of the isolated random details of the material world.

In encouraging a new way of "seeing" Emerson also made some comments on "saying," on "the language of facts" which we must now examine. First, the indictment: "The corruption of man is followed by the corruption of language . . . new imagery ceases to be created, and old words are perverted to stand for things which are not; a paper currency is employed, when there is no bullion in the vaults. . . . But wise men pierce this rotten diction and fasten words again to visible things."[73] Secondly, the precedent from which we should learn. "Children and savages use only nouns or names of things, which they convert into verbs, and apply to analogous acts."[74] As well as the child and the savage, Emerson cites the "strong-natured farmer or backwoodsman"[75] as exemplifying the proper use of language. This equating of the child, the savage, and the vernacular type is questionable if a serious attempt to analyse speech-habits is being offered. But they occur more as exemplars in a sermon. Emerson wants to communicate the notion of some sort of verbal intimacy with the stuff of nature, a state in which words and things are at their closest. We should see like children: we should also speak like children and vernacular types, or at least with the simple, specifying concreteness that Emerson imputes to them.

Just as Emerson wanted the eye to concentrate on concrete facts, so he wishes language to be full of concrete factualness, and for the same reasons: a new or renewed intimacy with these facts affords us our quickest means of contact with the unifying sublime presence which runs through all things. So the concentration is always on the simplest forms of speech, on the speech which arises from physical involvement with nature rather than the subtle refined concepts used by those who meditate on life through the mind's eye. "Life lies behind us as the quarry from whence we get tiles and copestones for the masonry of to-day. This is the way to learn grammar. Colleges and books only copy the language which the field and work-yard made."[76]

An important by-product of this contention of Emerson's is his complete rejection of the classification of facts, things, and words into "high" and "low," a classification based on the dualism of spirit and body which was then still a major influence on New England thought. "The vocabulary of an omniscient man would embrace words and images excluded from polite conversation. What would be base, or even obscene, to the obscene, becomes illustrious, spoken in a new connection of thought."[77] The effect of this enlightened passage is to offer a card of eligibility to a whole range of experience and vocabulary which had hitherto been considered inherently unfit for literature.

More central to Emerson's theory of language is his assertion that "It does not need that a poem should be long. Every word was once a poem," and the related idea that "bare lists of words are found suggestive to an imaginative and excited mind."[78] Every word was once a poem because every word was once a thing, or at least a "brilliant picture" of a thing. ("Language is fossil poetry"[79] wrote Emerson, thus anticipating Fenellosa's notion of language as a pyramid with an apex of generality and a base composed of "stunned" things.) Since every thing equally displays or hints at the divine plan of the universe, a list of words becomes a list of revelations, each noted fact an encountered epiphany. The influence of this belief on Emerson's own style can be discerned. His style, most characteristically, is composed of an effortless shifting from the suggestive list of facts and things to what he revealingly calls "casual"[80] abstraction and generalization. In his own words: "There is the bucket of cold water from the spring, the wood-fire to which the chilled traveller rushes for safety—and there is the sublime moral of autumn and noon."[81] The philosophy is revealed in the style: he ascends direct from "a crystal" to the "Universal Spirit."[82] Clusters of unrelated facts occur continually, embedded in his discursive sentences, pegging them to the ground. Examples can be proliferated. "There is nothing but is related to us, nothing that does not interest us— kingdom, college, tree, horse, or iron shoe—the roots of all things are in man."[83] His prose asserts but never analyses these relationships. We could recall the famous passage on the "worth of the vulgar" which employs a similar method of assembling "things," but things left separate and static: "The meal in the firkin; the milk in the pan; the ballad in the street; the news of the boat; the glance of the eye; the form and gait of the body";[84] —details which reveal not any one man's world but God's world. Such passages in Emerson serve as the springboards for his sublime leaps: and obviously even as he is enumerating these "things," telling his beads of facts as we might say, they seem to reveal universal laws to him. As in Whitman, they "sing" to him. The more successful passages in Emerson are weighed down with concrete facts, laced with particulars which alert the mental eye. What has gone from his writing is almost all purposive complexity of syntax: his style is extremely paratactic and his sentences often start with an unintroduced enumeration of things, things held up for our beholding in the belief that they will "plead for themselves." One final example must suffice:

> The fall of snowflakes in a still air, preserving to each crystal its perfect form; the blowing of sleet over a wide sheet of water, and over plains; the waving rye field; the mimic waving of acres of houstonia, whose innumerable florets whiten and ripple before the eye; the reflections of trees and flowers in glassy lakes; the musical, steaming, odorous south wind, which converts all trees to wind-harps; the crackling and spurting of hemlock in the flames, or of pine logs, which yield glory to the walls and faces in the sitting-room—these are the music and pictures of the most ancient religion.[85]

This is writing of considerable visual sensitivity but which has no sense whatever of the relation and inter-relation of things and things, things and people, people and other people. It is a prose that stops before society and the problems of human behaviour start. His idea that "bare lists of words are suggestive" is crucial here. They are suggestive if the words are what he thought words should be—concrete facts, pictures of things—but even so such bare lists help us not at all in the problems of living among those facts and things. Emerson's prose feels its way over the surfaces and round the contours of parts of the empirical world but has no means of discussing the problems of action and interruption in that world. By way of meaning he can only produce the mystical generalization, but as faith in such generalizations has diminished it is the former aspect of his prose, the respect for details, which seems to have had most influence in American literature.

Of the duality of his own vision he writes very clearly. "We are amphibious creatures, weaponed for two elements, having two sets of faculties, the particular and the catholic. We adjust our instruments for general observation, and sweep the heavens as easily as we pick out a single figure in the terrestrial landscape."[86] Emerson found it easy to "sweep the heavens" but subsequent writers have found it less so. The heavens have changed for one thing—or rather man's relationship with them has. They now seem to mock, whereas to Emerson they seemed to smile on, the "casual" all-explaining generalization. But there remains the "faculty" for particulars, and the ability to isolate "single figures in the terrestrial landscape" and this faculty has perhaps been cultivated as the other faculty has increasingly come under suspicion—though it has by no means disappeared. Not surprisingly Emerson admired Plato above all others, and in his essay on him he manages to tell us a good deal about himself. This is Emerson's Plato: "If he made transcendental distinctions, he fortified himself by drawing all his illustrations from sources disdained by orators and polite conversers; from mares and puppies; from pitchers and soup-ladles; from cooks and criers; the shops of potters, horse-doctors, butchers and fishmongers."[87] Plato, that is, obeyed Emerson and "embraced the common, explored and sat at the feet of the familiar, the low." Perhaps the most revealing thing that Emerson says about Plato is this: "Plato keeps the two vases, one of ether and one of pigment, at his side, and invariably uses both."[88] The pigment of low concrete facts and the ether of mystical generalization—they are both to be found in Emerson. And it is worth repeating that for him peculiar prestige attaches itself to the "low" in language and in facts and in people. "The poor and the low have their way of expressing the last facts of philosophy as well as you."[89] As well as, and by veiled implication, perhaps better. There is actually a preference for those minds which "have not been subdued by the drill of school education."[90] "Do you think the porter and the cook have no anecdotes, no experiences, no wonders for you? Everybody knows as much as the savant. The walls of crude minds are scrawled over with facts, with thoughts."[91] This is an attitude which could endorse the vernacular as a literary mode; which could encourage the belief in the superior wisdom of the backwoodsman, the rural inhabitant, the person living outside any urban-civilized field of force. It is difficult to assess the influence of one writer. Emerson is perhaps as much symptom as cause. The point is that certain novel attitudes and predilections which recur in many American writers seem to emerge articulated in Emerson's work for the first time. Some of these might be summed up as follows: the emphasis on "seeing" things freshly; the prescription for the innocent non-generalizing eye; the concomitant preference for simple people and simple speech, whether that of the uneducated labourer, the savage or the child; the exhortation to accept *all* facts, the vulgar trivia of the world, as being potential harbingers of meaning; the celebration of the details of the concrete world and the (more than intended, perhaps) prestige accorded to the particularizing faculty, that faculty which develops the closest relationships between man and the natural world. "We penetrate bodily this incredible beauty; we dip our hands in this painted element; our eyes are bathed in these lights and forms."[92] Mysticism, yes: but a mysticism which encouraged a scrupulous yet wondering rediscovery of material appearances, which attached maximum importance to a new intimacy with the basic undistorted "pigment" of "this painted element," the world. In encouraging men to "wonder at the usual" Emerson bestowed perhaps his greatest benefit on American literature.

[1] Henry Nash Smith, "Emerson's Problem of Vocation", *New England Quarterly,* vol. XII (March–December 1939).

[2] For more sympathetic treatment of Emerson's handling of the problem of pain and evil see "The House of Pain" by Newton Arvin *(Hudson Review,* vol. XII, No. 1, Spring 1959) and "Emerson's Tragic Sense" by Stephen Whicher *(American Scholar,* vol. XXII, Summer 1953).

[3] Ralph Waldo Emerson, *Complete Works* (Houghton Mifflin, Boston and New York, 1903), vol. XII, p. 10.

[4] Ralph Waldo Emerson, *Journals,* in *Complete Works,* VIII, p. 550.

[5] *Works,* vol. I, pp. 73–74.

[6] *Ibid.* vol. II, p. 147.

[7] *Ibid.* vol. I, p. 3.

[8] *Ibid.* vol. I, p. 4.

[9] *Ibid.* vol. III, p. 92.

[10] *Ibid.* vol. I, pp. 127–128.

[11] *Ibid.* vol. I, p. 330.

[12] *Ibid.* vol. II, p. 269.

[13] *Journals,* X, p. 238.

[14] Sherman Paul, *Emerson's Angle of Vision* (Harvard University Press, 1952), p. 73.

[15] *Journals,* V, pp. 310–311.

[16] Paul, *Emerson's Angle of Vision,* p. 75.

[17] A. G. McGiffert (ed.), *Young Emerson Speaks* (Houghton Mifflin, Boston, 1938), p. 48.

[18] Quoted by Leo Marx in his edition of Thoreau's *Excursions* (Corinth Books, New York, 1962), p. xiii.

[19] *Works,* vol. III, p. 59.

[20] *Ibid.* vol. III, p. 236.

[21] *Ibid.* vol. I, p. 63.

[22] *Ibid.* vol. IX, p. 181.

[23] *Ibid.* vol. II, p. 354.

[24] *Ibid.* vol. III, p. 285.

[25] *Ibid.* vol. I, p. 74.

[26] *Ibid.* vol. I, p. 10.

[27] Quoted by F. O. Matthiessen, *The American Renaissance* (Oxford, 1941), p. 62.

[28] *Works,* vol. I, p. 8.

[29] *Ibid.* vol. III, p. 178.

[30] *Ibid.* vol. I, p. 40.

[31] *Ibid.* vol. III, p. 170.

[32] *Ibid.* vol. I, p. 338.

[33] *Ibid.* vol. I, p. 339.

[34] *Ibid.* vol. IX, p. 166.

[35] *Ibid.* vol. I, p. 139.

[36] *Ibid.* vol. II, p. 48.

[37] *Ibid.* vol. II, p. 49.

[38] *Ibid.* vol. II, p. 319.

[39] *Ibid.* vol. II, p. 329.

[40] *Ibid.* vol. III, pp. 75–76.

[41] *Ibid.* vol. III, pp. 185–186.

[42] *Ibid.* vol. I, p. 73.

[43] *Ibid.* vol. II, p. 325.

[44] *Ibid.* vol. III, p. 244.

[45] *Ibid.* vol. II, p. 335.

[46] *Ibid.* vol. II, p. 171.

[47] *Ibid.* vol. II, p. 302.

[48] Quoted by F. O. Matthiessen in *The American Renaissance,* p. 58.

49 *Works,* vol. I, p. 43.
50 *Ibid.* vol. III, p. 17.
51 *Ibid.* vol. II, p. 101.
52 *Ibid.* vol. II, p. 101.
53 *Ibid.* vol. X, p. 474.
54 Quoted by Feidelson, Jr, in *Symbolism and American Literature,* p. 150.
55 Quoted by Norman Foerster in "Emerson on the Organic Principle in Art", *PMLA,* XLI (1926).
56 *Works,* vol. II, p. 334.
57 *Ibid. vol.* I, p. 75.
58 *Ibid.* vol. III, p. 88.
59 *Ibid.* vol. I, p. 82.
60 *Ibid.* vol. I, p. 9.
61 *Ibid.* vol. III, p. 196.
62 *Ibid.* vol. III, p. 92.
63 *Ibid.* vol. III, p. 28.
64 *Ibid.* vol. II, p. 367.
65 *Ibid.* vol. II, p. 369.
66 *Ibid.* vol. I, pp. 111–112.
67 *Ibid.* vol. II, p. 290.
68 *Ibid.* vol. III, p. 183.

69 *Ibid.* vol. I, p. 38.
70 *Ibid.* vol. II, p. 354.
71 *Ibid.* vol. II, p. 355.
72 *Ibid.* vol. I, p. 85.
73 *Ibid.* vol. I, pp. 29–30.
74 *Ibid.* vol. I, p. 26.
75 *Ibid.* vol. I, p. 31.
76 *Ibid.* vol. I, p. 98.
77 *Ibid.* vol. III, p. 17.
78 *Ibid.* vol. III, pp. 17–18.
79 *Ibid.* vol. III, p. 22.
80 *Ibid.* vol. III, p. 237.
81 *Ibid.* vol. III, p. 171.
82 *Ibid.* vol. I, pp. 43–44.
83 *Ibid.* vol. II, p. 17.
84 *Ibid.* vol. I, pp. 111–112.
85 *Ibid.* vol. III, p. 172.
86 *Ibid.* vol. III, p. 229.
87 *Ibid.* vol. IV, p. 55.
88 *Ibid.* vol. IV, p. 56.
89 *Ibid.* vol. II, p. 315.
90 *Ibid.* vol. II, p. 330.
91 *Ibid.* vol. II, p. 330.
92 *Ibid.* vol. III, p. 173.

HENRY DAVID THOREAU
****

A discriminating contemporary estimate of Thoreau by his Concord neighbor Ralph Waldo Emerson is the "Biographical Sketch"
in Thoreau's *Excursions in Field and Forest* (Boston, 1863, and included in most subsequent editions). The best biography is still
Henry S. Salt's *The Life of Henry David Thoreau* (London, 1890),
though Walter S. Harding's *The Days of Henry Thoreau* (New
York, 1966) is better filled with detail, and Joseph Wood Krutch's
Thoreau (New York, 1949) is a mature and sensible appraisal of
the man and his writing. Book-length critical estimates include
Mark Van Doren's *Thoreau: A Critical Study* (Boston, 1916),
George F. Whicher's *Walden Revisited* (Chicago, 1945), Reginald
L. Cook's *A Passage to Walden* (Boston, 1949), J. L. Shanley's
The Making of Walden (Chicago, 1957), Sherman Paul's *The
Shores of America: Thoreau's Inward Exploration* (Urbana, Ill.,
1958), and Charles R. Anderson, *The Magic Circle of Walden*
(New York, 1968). Among discriminating critical essays are
Robert Louis Stevenson's in *Familiar Studies of Men and Books*

(London, 1891), Paul Elmer More's "A Hermit's Notes on Walden," *Atlantic Monthly,* CLXXVII (November 1946), pp. 137–146, and William Bysshe Stein's *"Walden:* The Wisdom of the Centaur," *ELH,* XXV (September 1958), pp. 194–215. Other fine examples are collected in *Thoreau: A Collection of Critical Essays,* edited by Sherman Paul (Englewood Cliffs, N.J., 1962), *Thoreau: A Century of Criticism* (Dallas, Tex., 1954) and *The Thoreau Centennial* (Albany, N.Y., 1964), both edited by Walter Harding, *Thoreau in Our Season* (Amherst, Mass., 1966), edited by John H. Hicks, and *The Recognition of Henry David Thoreau* (Ann Arbor, Mich., 1969), edited by Wendell Glick.

THOREAU

F. O. Matthiessen

****

"True, there are architects so called in this country," wrote Thoreau as he began the account of how he had built his cabin, "and I have heard of one at least possessed with the idea of making architectural ornaments have a core of truth, a necessity, and hence a beauty, as if it were a revelation to him. All very well from his point of view, but only a little better than the common dilettantism. A sentimental reformer in architecture, he began at the cornice, not at the foundation." This passage in *Walden* derives from a circumstance recorded in his journal for January 1852. Emerson had shown him with enthusiasm a letter he had just received from Greenough,[1] and

From F. O. Matthiessen, *American Renaissance: Art and Expression in the Age of Emerson and Whitman* (New York: Oxford University Press, 1941).

[1] Though several short letters from Greenough are to be found among the Emerson papers, this one has not yet come to light. It may have been the same one from which Emerson quoted in *English Traits:* "Here is my theory of structure: A scientific arrangement of spaces and forms to functions and to site; an emphasis of features proportioned to their *gradated* importance in function; color and ornament to be decided and arranged and varied by strictly organic laws, having a distinct reason for each decision; the entire and immediate banishment of all make-shift and make-believe."

Thoreau's one glimpse of the sculptor's theories drew out these hard remarks. In their context in *Walden* he is making his sharpest argument against the division of labor, which reduces not merely the tailor but the preacher and the merchant and the farmer to "the ninth part of a man." (A note in the manuscript added: "That remark applies universally to the condition of men to-day.") He was so opposed to any complicating of life that did not correspond to a real need that he declared that no house should be painted except with the color of its builder's own blood and sweat. (This expression in his journal was softened in *Walden* to "Better paint your house your own complexion.") His dislike of ornament finally carried him to the length of protesting against a nation's trying to commemorate itself by any architecture instead of by its powers of thought: "How much more admirable the Bhagvat-Geeta than all the ruins of the East!"

It was too bad that Thoreau's prickly reaction against anything proposed by Emerson—an attitude that, following his first discipleship, seems to have grown habitual—should have kept him from appreciating that in Greenough he had a natural ally whose maturer thought could have guided his own. In fancied disagreement with the sculptor's theories, he said that the only true architectural beauty "has gradually grown from within outward, out of the necessities and character of the indweller." Yet he was simply repeating, in looser, less technical language, one of Greenough's cardinal assumptions. And the radicalism that led Thoreau to declare that the most interesting dwellings in this country were commonly the most unpretending, the logger's hut and the cottages of the poor, found a fuller voice in Greenough's conviction that the genuine taste of the day would become "enamored of the old, bald, neutral-toned Yankee farmhouse which seems to belong to the ground whereon it stands, as the caterpillar to the leaf that feeds him."

Wherever Thoreau turned for fresh confirmation of his belief that true beauty reveals necessity, he saw that "Nature is a greater and more perfect art," and that there is a similarity between her operations and man's even in the details and trifles. He held, like Emerson, that "man's art has wisely imitated those forms into which all matter is most inclined to run, as foliage and fruit." But Thoreau studied more examples in detail than Emerson did. Any glance from his door could provide him with fresh evidence. The sumach and pine and hickory that surrounded his cabin reminded him of the most graceful sculptural forms. The tracery of frostwork suggested the intricate refinements of design; and when he wanted his basic lesson in Coleridge's distinction between mechanic and organic form, all he had to do was to mould a handful of earth and to note that however separately interesting its particles might be, their relation was one of mere lifeless juxtaposition. In marked contrast was the shape of even "the simplest and most lumpish fungus," and the reasons for its fascination crowded upon him: "it is so obviously organic and related to ourselves. . . . It is the expression of an idea; growth according to a law; matter not dormant, not raw, but inspired, appropriated by spirit." With so many principles to be gleaned from the humblest growth, no wonder he held it "monstrous when one cares but little about trees but much about Corinthian columns."

When he tried to apply these principles to creation in literature, he sometimes was content with saying that "true art is but the expression of our love of nature." But he often pushed to a rigorous extreme not merely the supremacy of nature over art and of content over form, but also that of the artist's life over his work. He developed his own version of Milton's view that the heroic poem could be written only by the man who had lived a heroic life. As Thoreau put it, "Nothing goes by luck in composition. . . . The best you can write will be the best that you are." His distrust of "the *belles lettres* and the *beaux arts* and their professors" sprang from his desire to break down all artificial divisions between art and living. He often confronted the problem that "it is not easy to write in a journal what interests us at any time, because to write it is not what interests us."[2] His only solution for this dilemma was, as he said in a letter to one of his followers: "As for style of writing, if one has anything to say, it drops from him simply and directly, as a stone falls to the ground." He came to the same point when he praised the style of John Brown: "The *art* of composition is as simple as the discharge of a bullet from a rifle, and its masterpieces imply an infinitely greater force behind them. This unlettered man's speaking and writing are standard English. Some words and phrases deemed vulgarisms and Americanisms before, he has made standard American." Again Thoreau was much closer than he knew to Greenough, who had insisted that the style indicated by our mechanics was miscalled economical and cheap. On the contrary, Greenough said, "It is the dearest of styles. . . . Its simplicity is not the simplicity of emptiness or of poverty, its simplicity is that of justness, I had almost said, of justice."

When Thoreau said, "Give me simple, cheap, and homely themes," he had no notion that their execution would prove easy. Even when he declared that the real poem is what the poet himself has become, he added that "our whole life is taxed for the least thing well done." In adopting the tenet that poetry consists in knowing the quality of a thing, he had realized by his early thirties that such knowledge could be arrived at only through

---

[2] Or as he phrased it in an awkward couplet in the *Week:*

> My life has been the poem I would have writ,
> But I could not both live and utter it.

the slowest unconscious process, for "at first blush a man is not capable of reporting truth; he must be drenched and saturated with it first. What was *enthusiasm* in the young man must become *temperament* in the mature man." We might compare this with Lawrence's realization that "we have to know ourselves pretty thoroughly before we can break through the automatism of ideals and conventions. . . . Only through fine delicate knowledge can we recognize and release our impulses." Only in seasoned maturity, to shift back to Thoreau's imagery, will the poet's truth exhale as naturally from him as "the odor of the muskrat from the coat of the trapper."

He often spoke of the organic style in an equally characteristic image —of its being a slow growth, unfolding under the care of the poet's patient hands. The degree to which his own practice lived up to that metaphor is also the degree to which his craftsmanship goes beyond Emerson's. He accepted the older man's view that genius is the abundance of health, but was less intermittent in his demand that talent must go with genius. To be sure, he hardly ever discusses specific forms. He apparently took it for granted that the artist's intuition will shape what is proper for it, and, in the course of objecting to some of Carlyle's extravagances, said little more than that the great writer works not by introducing new forms but by reinvigorating old ones. However, in his perception that this renewal comes through the fresh handling of words, he generally sensed a more integral connection between the words and the thought than Emerson did. That was why he regarded translations as an impossibility, and held that the classics could be read only after a training as rigorous "as the athletes underwent." Moreover, he made another discrimination, essentially foreign to Emerson, between the spoken and the written word. He held that "what is called eloquence in the forum is commonly found to be rhetoric in the study," that however much we may admire the orator's power, the style that lives beyond the emotion of the moment demands a much more exacting composition. When Thoreau said of the poet, almost in Frost's words, that "the tone and pitch of his voice is the main thing," he knew that "a perfect expression requires a particular rhythm or measure for which no other can be substituted." Such knowledge—the product, as we have seen, of his own sensitive organization —was his firmest defense against the formlessness that beset his desire to speak in harmony with nature. If it seldom rescued his immature verse—almost the type instance of mechanic form in its imitation of the surface tricks of the metaphysicals—it brought both precision and timbre to the movement of his ripened prose.

Only by the accumulation of such slight threads as those spun out in the last paragraph can we finally distinguish between Thoreau's and Emerson's understanding of the organic style. In Emerson's record of one of the early conversations between them (1838), it was Thoreau who was complaining that "if the man took too much pains with the expression, he was not any longer the Idea himself." Emerson agreed, but pointed out "that this was the tragedy of Art that the artist was at the expense of the man." However, as the years advanced, it was the younger writer who was to accept this inevitable fact. Observing, two decades later, that farmer Tarbell had at last got his barn built, he knew that the artist could make his structure only through an equally "steady struggle, with alternate failure and success." He must learn both endurance and detachment, for his work consists in performing *"post-mortem* examinations of himself before he is dead." Or, in a different figure, he must have "the cold skill" to quarry and carve a statue out of his own feelings. This subordination of himself to the work to be done reminds us, even in its phrasing, of what Eliot has valued in Hawthorne: "the firmness, the true coldness, the hard coldness of the genuine artist."

NEW ENGLAND LANDSCAPES

"Concord woods were more to me than my library, or Emerson even. They were more to him than they were to me, and still more to Thoreau than to either of us. Take the forest and skies from their pages, and they, E. and T., have faded and fallen clean out of their pictures."

—ALCOTT's *Journal* (1851)

One reason why both Emerson and Thoreau thought instinctively of art as "a natural fruit," was that they had chosen visible nature for so much of their subject matter. To be sure, they both insisted that their interest in this was subordinate to their concern with man. Nevertheless, what drew man out in Concord, what constituted a major resource unknown to cities, was the beauty of his surroundings. One way, therefore, of distinguishing between Emerson's and Thoreau's handling of the organic style is by appraising the differing qualities of their landscapes.[3]

William James, who also loved New England landscapes, singled out as among Emerson's best things the opening of his second essay on "Nature": "There are days which occur in this climate, at almost any season of the year, wherein the world reaches its perfection." These halcyons may be looked for with most assurance in that pure October weather called Indian summer, for then "the day, immeasurably long, sleeps over the broad hills

[3] Both Emerson and Thoreau were treated in great detail by Norman Foerster, *Nature in American Literature* (1923).

and warm wide fields," then "everything that has life gives signs of satisfaction, and the cattle that lie on the ground seem to have great and tranquil thoughts." This buoyant tone bears out the fact that if "the two most obvious characteristics of Nature are loveliness and power," as Whitehead has suggested, the former was all that Emerson generally saw. This is curious, in view of his environment, for even though he was not hemmed in by the savage energies of the jungle, "red in tooth and claw," nevertheless two centuries of New England had provided enough lessons of the hardihood essential to wrest a living from the bare recalcitrant elements. However, by Emerson's time the struggle had relaxed in the self-subsisting villages that "whitened the land." His own assurance could lead him into such blind generalizations as this in "Prudence," which Melville marked: "The terrors of the storm are chiefly confined to the parlor and the cabin. The drover, the sailor, buffets it all day, and his health renews itself at as vigorous a pulse under the sleet, as under the sun of June." "To one who has weathered Cape Horn as a common sailor," said Melville, "what stuff all this is." His experience had taught him that primitive brutality was not gone out of the world—not out of nature, and not out of man, as he knew man in America: a conviction that actuated his bitter attack on transcendentalism in *Pierre*.

That Emerson was not wholly negligent of nature's power can be seen in his early (1838) detailed analysis of the task confronting any American who would record her. Notwithstanding his joy in the English poets, he felt that they had conversed with the mere surface and show, that whenever he went into the forest he would find all as new and undescribed as "the honking of the wild geese flying by night." Debating, three years later, whether he ought not call his first collection *Forest Essays,* he seized upon what was still the significant feature of the American landscape. For Harriet Martineau had recently reported that in her travels throughout the country she was never out of sight of the woods except when on the prairies of Illinois. Emerson had tried to describe his mixed sensation at seeing the day break in Concord—of pain at feeling himself in "an alien world," a world not yet subdued by thought, and of exultation as his soul broke down its narrow walls and ranged out to the very horizon. He came to the source of his sensation when he wrote:

> The noonday darkness of the American forest, the deep, echoing, aboriginal woods, where the living columns of the oak and fir tower up from the ruins of the trees of the last millennium; where, from year to year, the eagle and the crow see no intruder; the pines, bearded with savage moss, yet touched with grace by the violets at their feet . . . where the traveller, amid the repulsive plants that are native in the swamp, thinks with pleasing terror of the distant

town; this beauty,—haggard and desert beauty, which the sun and
the moon, the snow and the rain, repaint and vary, has never been
recorded by art . . . .

In view of this desire to catch nature's very features, we are surprised
at Emerson's early hostility towards Wordsworth. At his first discussion of
him (1826), Emerson was bothered by his "being too much a *poet*," and
could not read his "mystic and unmeaning verses without feeling that if he
had cultivated poetry less, and learning and society more, he would have
gained more favor at the hands of the Muses"—an objection that you could
readily imagine to have been written against the later Emerson by a survivor
from the eighteenth century. Two years later he was still put off by Wordsworth's "trying to distil the essence of poetry from poetic things. . . . He
mauls the moon and the waters and the bulrushes, as his main business." He
had a low opinion of *The Excursion* since it was wanting in fact, in coarse
and tangible details, and was merely "metaphysical and evanescent." Such
strictures are the sharpest reminder of how much inherited rationalism
Emerson had to throw away before he could begin to feel (1831) that
Wordsworth had written lines "that are like outward nature, so fresh, so
simple, so durable," or could come to his final recognition (1840) that, in
spite of the poet's many glaring lapses in talent, his genius was "the exceptional fact of the period," since he had done "as much as any living man to
restore sanity to cultivated society."
    Even then he would still have felt that no Englishman could speak to
him adequately of the different nature he knew, not trim hedgerows but a
great sloven continent, "nature sleeping, overgrowing, almost conscious, too
much by half for man in the picture, and so giving a certain *tristesse,* like
the rank vegetation of swamps and forests seen at night"—for such remained one of his dominant images. But its sadness was only infrequently
uppermost. In some lines that he wrote soon after his arrival in Naples
(1833), he said that

> Not many men see beauty in the fogs
> Of close, low pinewoods in a river town.

But for him, as he looked back across the ocean, there was no happier vision than that of a morning walk by a moist roadside where

> Peep the blue violets out of the black loam.

Ten years earlier the stiff abstractness of his poem, "Good-bye, proud
world! I'm going home," had been relieved by the details that drew him to

the country—the blackbird, the pines and the evening star. He liked to call himself "the bantling of a country Muse," and when he came to write "Self-Reliance" he was still certain that "My book should smell of pines and resound with the hum of insects." The year before writing *Nature* he had played with the idea of composing a book of the seasons, which "should contain the natural history of the woods around my shifting camp for every month in the year"—a partial description of what was fulfilled by *Walden*. In 1837, only a few months before the first mention in his journal of Thoreau, he said that "the American artist who would carve a wood-god, and who was familiar with the forest in Maine where . . . huge mosses depending from the trees and mass of timber give a savage and haggard [again those adjectives] strength to the grove, would produce a very different statue from the sculptor who only knew a European woodland—the tasteful Greek, for example."

Yet when Emerson came to carve his own, even Alcott had to say that his Nature, "caught, it is true, from our own woods," was "never American, nor New English, which were better, but some fancied realm, some Atlantides of this Columbia, very clearly discernible to him but not by us." As Alcott conceived it, Emerson "was forbidden pure companionship with Nature" because "he dwelt rather in an intellectual grove." Emerson himself declared (1849) that the characteristic of the Greek age was that "men deified Nature"; of the Christian, that Nature was looked upon as evil and that the soul craved a heaven above it; of the modern age, that men have returned again to Nature, "but now the tendency is to marry mind to Nature, and to put Nature under the mind." The conclusion of scholarship, in J. W. Beach's *The Concept of Nature in Nineteenth-Century English Poetry* (1936), reinforces Alcott's perception by finding that "Emerson almost invariably views nature all too blandly through the eyes of the 'mind'. . . . Almost never does it occur to him that the mind may have something to learn from nature, from the world which it finds given to it from without."

Emerson phrased the relationship in two lines in "Woodnotes":

So waved the pine-tree through my thought
And fanned the dreams it never brought.

The nature to which he gave utterance is far more etherealized than Wordsworth's since it has so little of the freshening that was produced by Wordsworth's delicate but full trust in the knowledge that came from his senses. Emerson approached nearest to such trust when he confessed that, although the realm of nature remained strictly subordinate to the ideal, he had no hostility towards it, but rather a child's love for its "gypsy attraction." In such moments of shy fondness he achieved the lyric grace of his "Gardener," who,

> True Brahmin, in the morning meadows wet,
> Expound[s] the Vedas of the violet.

The single blossom against the soil is again the apt symbol for his kind of beauty, as were the petals of the rhodora in the black waters of the pool. From these fragile details his eye always moved off to the horizon, since he believed that in its distant line "man beholds somewhat as beautiful as his own nature."

It is no wonder then that many of his landscapes were composed not out of tangible materials but from the evanescent light of reflections. He liked to recount his excursions with Henry, how "with one stroke of the paddle I leave the village politics and personalities, yes, and the world of villages and personalities, behind, and pass into a delicate realm of sunset and moonlight, too bright almost for spotted man to enter without novitiate and probation. We penetrate bodily this incredible beauty; we dip our hands in this painted element; our eyes are bathed in these lights and forms." Or, again, with Ellery: "My eye rested on the charming play of light on the water which he was striking with his paddle. I fancied I had never seen such color, such transparency, such eddies; it was the hue of Rhine wines, it was jasper and verd-antique, topaz and chalcedony, it was gold and green and chestnut and hazel in bewitching succession. . . ."[4]

---

[4] It seems worth notice in passing that Hawthorne also described such an excursion with Channing. Although his language is more stiffly Latinate and unable to register Emerson's vibrancy, he arrives at a conception of beauty to which Emerson could have subscribed: "The river sleeps along its course and dreams of the sky and of the clustering foliage, amid which fall showers of broken sunlight, imparting specks of vivid cheerfulness, in contrast with the quiet depth of the prevailing tint. Of all this scene, the slumbering river has a dream picture in its bosom. Which, after all, was the most real—the picture, or the original?—the objects palpable to our grosser senses, or their apotheosis in the stream beneath? Surely the disembodied images stand in closer relation to the soul." Notwithstanding such a transcendent flight, Hawthorne proceeds to a conclusion very different from the thoughts of liberation that Emerson rejoiced in: "And yet how sweet, as we floated homeward adown the golden river at sunset,—how sweet was it to return within the system of human society, not as to a dungeon and a chain, but as to a stately edifice, whence we could go forth at will into statelier simplicity!" As he saw the Old Manse from the river, he thought "how gently did its gray, homely aspect rebuke the speculative extravagances of the day! It had grown sacred in connection with the artificial life against which we inveighed; it had been a home for many years in spite of all." And reflecting that it was his home too, he "prayed that the upper influences might long protect the institutions that had grown out of the heart of mankind."

When Thoreau came to describe the course of his boat on the river, the impression is quite different, as a passage near the outset of the *Week,* a sample of his level style, can show:

> Late in the afternoon we passed a man on the shore fishing with a long birch pole, its silvery bark left on, and a dog at his side, rowing so near as to agitate his cork with our oars, and drive away luck for a season; and when we had rowed a mile as straight as an arrow, with our faces turned towards him, and the bubbles in our wake still visible on the tranquil surface, there stood the fisher still with his dog, like statues under the other side of the heavens, the only objects to relieve the eye in the extended meadow; and there would he stand abiding his luck, till he took his way home through the fields at evening with his fish. Thus, by one bait or another, Nature allures inhabitants into all her recesses.

Unlike Emerson's series of ejaculations, the aim of Thoreau's passage is not just to suggest the diffused radiance that stimulated him, but to present by minute notations the record of a whole scene. Although the perceived details are the slightest—the silvery bark on the pole, the bubbles on the tranquil surface—their exactness carries you down that particular unswerving mile, and gives you the illusion of sharing in the lapse of space and time during which the fisherman was still standing still on the bank with his dog. The quality of Thoreau's landscapes depends on his belief that "man identifies himself with earth or the material." Yet he also remained clear that "we are not wholly involved in Nature," and, in the awareness of his partial detachment, felt that he associated with it as a soul with its body. Although he often contrasted nature's innocence and serenity with perturbable man, in *The Maine Woods,* at least, he declared that "we have not seen pure Nature, unless we have seen her thus vast and drear and inhuman, though in the midst of cities. Nature was here something savage and awful, though beautiful." It was "Matter, vast, terrific," not man's familiar Mother Earth but the realm "of Necessity and Fate."

Here Thoreau was most akin to the tradition of the pioneer settlers, who had regarded the lonely wilderness with awe that could mount to terror. But it was not in his temperament to dwell on the diabolic power of the unsubdued dark wastes; his more characteristic mood is that of the Sunday morning worshipper of Pan. He repeatedly asserted that "in literature it is only the wild that attracts us." On that ground he felt that the English poets had "not seen the west side of any mountain," that they had missed the sterner primeval aspects, that Wordsworth was "too tame for the Chippeway." And despite his pleasure in Gilpin's *Forest Scenery,* Thoreau decided that the limitations of its mild picturesqueness came from looking too much at nature with the eye of the artist instead of in the more normal way of the hunter or woodchopper. In saying, "as Cowley loved a garden, so I a forest," he implied just the relation that he wanted and that he developed in *Walden:* "I found in myself, and still find, an instinct toward a higher, or, as it is named, spiritual life, as do most men, and another toward a primitive rank and savage one, and I reverence them both." He could describe this second instinct with a dash of humor when he said he might learn some wisdom from the woodchuck, since "his ancestors have lived here longer than mine"; or when he delivered the jeremiad of the huckleberry picker over the fact that "the wild fruits of the earth" disappear before the encroachments of civilization; or when he veered for a moment into thinking of Concord as an effete and emasculated region with its nobler animals exterminated, and thanked God for New Hampshire "everlasting and unfallen." He spoke from his heart when he said that he had no greater satisfaction in America than when he reflected that what William Bradford saw he still could see, since "aboriginal Nature" had not changed one iota. And one night at Chesuncook, listening to his guide talk to the other Indians, he felt that he had come as near to primitive man as any of the discoverers ever did.

He left at his death eleven manuscript notebooks, running to over half a million words, in which he had recorded what he had learned of the Indians, their customs and lore, and their enduring struggle with the elements. He believed it the duty of the poet to report the residual effects that this race had made on the life of his own white generation. He felt an untold debt to the example of their discipline as he trained himself to comparable alertness of eye and ear. When Emerson said that his friend had "turned a face of bronze to expectations," he symbolized the fact that the stoic strain in his behavior was owing far more to his veneration of the red men than to any study of Zeno. Certainly the lessons he had learned from them contributed to the firm reality that distinguishes his portrayal of nature. And they had helped him discover that beneath the bright surfaces of the civilized mind, "the savage in man is never quite eradicated."[5]

[5] Although repelled by transcendentalism and by what he considered Thoreau's eccentricities, Parkman made a kindred response to the forest as the great feature of the American landscape. He said that at sixteen he had become "enamored of the woods." "Before the end of the sophomore year my various schemes had crystallized into a plan of writing the story of what was then known as the 'Old French War,' that is, the war that ended in the conquest of Canada, for here, as it seemed to me, the forest drama was more stirring and the forest stage more thronged with appropriate actors than in any other passage of our history. It was not till some years later that I enlarged the plan to include the whole course of the American conflict between France and England, or, in other words, the history of the American forest; for this was the light in which I regarded it. My theme fascinated me, and I was haunted with wilderness images day and night." Out of his lifelong devotion to that theme sprang the most imaginative work of history that we have yet had in America.

In contrasting Thoreau with Emerson, Alcott felt that the former revealed secrets of nature "older than fields and gardens," that "he seems alone, of all the men I have known, to be a native New Englander." Yet he could not help regretting at times that Thoreau was so earthbound, and wished that he might come out of the woods to the orchards, and so be pastoral instead of wild. It is doubtful whether most readers now sense in Thoreau more than a whiff of wildness. He wanted to bring into his writing "muck from the meadows"; but what he really managed to bring finds an apter image in the delicate fragrance of the ferns or perhaps the ranker odor of the pines. His instinct towards the higher life was so inordinately encouraged by his contemporaries that it was only by the sturdiest action that he held fast to the soil. He described his most fertile process while saying why he went to the woods: "Let us settle ourselves, and work and wedge our feet downward through the mud and slush of opinion, and prejudice, and tradition, and delusion, and appearance, that alluvion which covers the globe, through Paris and London, through New York and Boston and Concord, through Church and State, through poetry and philosophy and religion, till we come to a hard bottom and rocks in place, which we can call *reality,* and say, This is, and no mistake."

This positive dredging beat reminds us again of his awareness of the physical basis of rhythm. It can remind us also of what Lawrence felt, that "the promised land, if it be anywhere, lies away beneath our feet. No more prancing upwards. No more uplift." Lawrence's discovery was quickened by watching and almost identifying himself with the downward thrust into the earth of the feet of Indian dancers. But Thoreau's knowledge was owing less directly to the Indians than to his re-creation for himself of the conditions of primitive life. He approximated Lawrence's words when he said that in good writing, "the poem is drawn out from under the feet of the poet, his whole weight has rested on this ground." Emerson, by contrast, wanted to "walk upon the ground, but not to sink." What Thoreau's language gained from his closer contact can be read in his evocation of a river walk, where every phrase is expressive of acute sensation: "Now your feet expand on a smooth sandy bottom, now contract timidly on pebbles, now slump in genial fatty mud, amid the pads."

But as you think again of the prolonged sensuous and rhythmical experience that Lawrence was able to make out of his response to the New Mexican corn dance, or of Hemingway's account of fishing on Big Two-Hearted River, you realize that Thoreau's product was ordinarily somewhat less full-bodied. When he said, "Heaven is under our feet as well as over our heads," he was speaking of the luminous clarity of the pond. A characteristic example to put beside Emerson's "Snow-Storm" is the poem "Smoke":

Light-winged Smoke, Icarian bird,
Melting thy pinions in thy upward flight,
Lark without song, and messenger of dawn,
Circling above the hamlets as thy nest;
Or else, departing dream, and shadowy form
Of midnight vision, gathering up thy skirts;
By night star-veiling, and by day
Darkening the light and blotting out the sun;
Go thou my incense upward from this hearth,
And ask the gods to pardon this clear flame.

The delicacy of the wraith-like movement finds its articulation in the succession of predominantly high-pitched vowels in the opening two lines. The "Icarian bird," a neat image for the melting away of the smoke in the bright morning sky, may then lead into too many fanciful conceits, but any tendency to vagueness is checked by the accurate epithet, "star-veiling." With that the contrast between the "shadowy form" and the rays of light, latent from the start, flowers exquisitely and prepares the way for the final statement, which makes the poem no mere descriptive exercise but Thoreau's declaration of his ever fresh renewal of purpose with the kindling of his fire in the morning. The "clear flame" of his spirit is so distinct and firm that it needs his plea for pardon to keep him from verging on *hubris* as he confidently contrasts his life with a world which is obscure and desperate in its confusion. That full contrast, to be sure, emerges only through the poem's context in *Walden,* but enough of the human situation is implied in the verses themselves to let them serve as a rounded, if minute, instance of Coleridge's distinction between imitation and mere copying. Coleridge held that the artist must not try to make a surface reproduction of nature's details, but "must imitate that which is within the thing . . . for so only can he hope to produce any work truly natural in the object and truly human in the effect." That combination has been created in this poem, since the reader's pleasure does not spring from the specific recordings, however accurate, but from the imperceptible interfusion with these of the author's own knowledge and feeling, and of his skill in evolving an appropriate form.

WALDEN: CRAFTSMANSHIP VS. TECHNIQUE

"You can't read any genuine history—as that of Herodotus or the Venerable Bede—without perceiving that our interest depends not on the subject but on the man,—on the manner in which he treats the subject and the importance he gives it. A feeble writer . . . must have what he thinks a great theme, which we are already interested

in through the accounts of others, but a genius—a Shakespeare, for
instance—would make the history of his parish more interesting
than another's history of the world."
                                        —THOREAU's *Journal* (March 1861)

It is apparent, in view of this last distinction of Coleridge's, that the
real test of whether Thoreau mastered organic form can hardly be made on
the basis of accounting for the differences in body and flavor between his
portrayal of the natural world and Emerson's, revelatory as these differences are. Nor can it be made by considering one of the rare occasions
when his verse was redeemed by virtue of his discipline in translating from
the Greek Anthology. Nor is it enough to reckon with the excellence of individual passages of prose, since the frequent charge is that whereas Emerson
was master of the sentence, Thoreau was master of the paragraph, but that
he was unable to go farther and attain "the highest or structural achievements of form in a whole book." The only adequate way of answering that
is by considering the structure of *Walden* as a whole, by asking to what extent it meets Coleridge's demand of shaping, "as it develops, itself from
within."

On one level *Walden* is the record of a personal experience, yet even in
making that remark we are aware that this book does not go rightfully into
the category of *Two Years Before the Mast* or *The Oregon Trail*. Why it
presents a richer accumulation than either of those vigorous pieces of contemporary history is explained by its process of composition. Although Thoreau said that the bulk of its pages were written during his two years of sojourn by the pond (1845–47), it was not ready for publication until seven
years later, and ultimately included a distillation from his journals over the
whole period from 1838. A similar process had helped to transform his
week's boat trip with his brother from a private to a symbolical event, since
the record was bathed in memory for a decade (1839–49) before it found
its final shape in words. But the flow of the *Week* is as leisurely and discursive as the bends in the Concord river, and the casual pouring in of miscel-
laneous poems and essays that Thoreau had previously printed in *The Dial*
tends to obscure the cyclical movement. Yet each day advances from dawn
to the varied sounds of night, and Thoreau uses an effective device for putting a period to the whole by the shift of the final morning from lazy August
to the first sharp forebodings of transforming frost.

The sequence of *Walden* is arranged a good deal more subtly, perhaps
because its subject constituted a more central symbol for Thoreau's accruing
knowledge of life. He remarked on how the pond itself was one of the earliest scenes in his recollection, dating from the occasion when he had been
brought out there one day when he was four, and how thereafter "that wood-

land vision for a long time made the drapery of my dreams." By 1841 he had already announced, "I want to go soon and live away by the pond," and when pressed by friends about what he would do when he got there, he had asked in turn if it would not be employment enough "to watch the progress of the seasons"? In that same year he had said: "I think I could write a poem to be called 'Concord.' For argument I should have the River, the Woods, the Ponds, the Hills, the Fields, the Swamps and Meadows, the Streets and Buildings, and the Villagers." In his completed "poem" these last elements had receded into the background. What had come squarely to the fore, and made the opening chapter by far the longest of all, was the desire to record an experiment in "Economy" as an antidote to the "lives of quiet desperation" that he saw the mass of men leading. This essay on how he solved his basic needs of food and shelter might stand by itself, but also carries naturally forward to the more poignant condensation of the same theme in "Where I lived, and What I lived for," which reaches its conclusion in the passage on wedging down to reality.

At this point the skill with which Thoreau evolved his composition begins to come into play. On the one hand, the treatment of his material might simply have followed the chronological outline; on the other, it might have drifted into being loosely topical. At first glance it may appear that the latter is what happened, that there is no real cogency in the order of the chapters. That would have been Lowell's complaint, that Thoreau "had no artistic power such as controls a great work to the serene balance of completeness."[6] But so far as the opposite can be proved by the effective arrangement of his entire material, the firmness with which Thoreau binds his successive links is worth examining. The student and observer that he has settled himself to be at the end of his second chapter leads easily into his discussion of "reading," but that in turn gives way to his concern with the more fundamental language, which all things speak, in the chapter on "Sounds." Then, after he has passed from the tantivy of wild pigeons to the whistle of the locomotive, he reflects that once the cars have gone by and

[6] The don of Harvard was not entirely blind to the man of Concord. Even in his notorious essay on *Walden* in *My Study Windows* he perceived that Thoreau "had caught his English at its living source, among the poets and prose-writers of its best days," and compared him with Donne and Browne. When Lowell tried to dismiss Thoreau as a crank, he was really bothered, as Henry Canby has pointed out, by Thoreau's attack upon his own ideals of genteel living. How different from Emerson's is Lowell's tone when he says that while Thoreau "studied with respectful attention the minks and woodchucks, his neighbors, he looked with utter contempt on the august drama of destiny of which his country was the scene, and on which the curtain had already risen." As Mr. Canby has added: "By destiny, Lowell clearly means the 'manifest destiny' of the exploitation of the West, whose more sordid and unfortunate aspects Thoreau had prophesied two generations before their time of realization."

the restless world with them, he is more alone than ever. That starts the transition to the chapter on "Solitude," in which the source of his joy is to live by himself in the midst of nature with his senses unimpaired. The natural contrast is made in the next chapter on "Visitors," which he opens by saying how he believes he loves society as much as most, and is ready enough to fasten himself "like a bloodsucker for the time to any full-blooded man" who comes his way. But after he has talked enthusiastically about the French woodchopper, and other welcome friends from the village, he remembers "restless committed men," the self-styled reformers who felt it their duty to give him advice. At that he breaks away with "Meanwhile my beans . . . were impatient to be hoed"; and that opening carries him back to the earlier transition to the chapter on "Sounds": "I did not read books the first summer; I hoed beans."

The effect of that repetition is to remind the reader of the time sequence that is knitting together all these chapters after the building of the cabin in the spring. From "The Bean Field" as the sphere of his main occupation, he moves on, in "The Village," to his strolls for gossip, which, "taken in homeopathic doses, was really as refreshing in its way as the rustle of leaves and the peeping of frogs." Whether designedly or not, this chapter is the shortest in the book, and yields to rambles even farther away from the community than Walden, to "The Ponds" and to fishing beyond "Baker Farm." As he was returning through the woods with his catch, and glimpsed in the near dark a woodchuck stealing across his path, then came the moment when he "felt a strange thrill of savage delight, and was strongly tempted to seize and devour him raw." And in the flash of his realization of his double instinct towards the spiritual and the wild, he has the starting point for the next two contrasting chapters, "Higher Laws" and "Brute Neighbors," in considering both of which he follows his rule of going far enough to please his imagination.

From here on the structure becomes cyclical, his poem of the seasons or myth of the year. The accounts of his varied excursions have brought him to the day when he felt that he could no longer warm himself by the embers of the sun, which "summer, like a departed hunter, had left." Consequently he set about finishing his cabin by building a chimney, and called that act "House-Warming." There follows a solid block of winter in the three chapters, "Winter Visitors," "Winter Animals," and "The Pond in Winter," that order suggesting the way in which the radius of his experience contracted then more and more to his immediate surroundings. However, the last pages on the pond deal with the cutting of the ice, and end with that sudden extraordinary expansion of his thought which annihilates space and time.

The last movement is the advance to "Spring." The activity of the ice company in opening its large tracts has hastened the break-up of the rest of the pond; and, listening to its booming, he recalls that one attraction that brought him to the woods was the opportunity and leisure to watch his renewal of the world. He has long felt in his observations that a day is an epitome of a year, and now he knows that a year is likewise symbolical of a life; and so, in presenting his experience by the pond, he foreshortens and condenses the twenty-six months to the interval from the beginning of one summer to the next. In the melting season he feels more than ever the mood of expanding promise, and he catches the reader up into this rich forward course by one of his most successful kinesthetic images, which serves to round out his cycle: "And so the seasons went rolling on into summer, as one rambles into higher and higher grass." To that he adds only the bare statement of when he left the woods, and a "Conclusion," which explains that he did so for as good a reason as he had gone there. He had other lives to live, and he knew now that he could find for himself "a solid bottom everywhere." That discovery gave him his final serene assurance that "There is more day to dawn," and consequently he was not to be disturbed by the "confused *tintinnabulum*" that sometimes reached his midday repose. He recognized it for the noise of his contemporaries.

The construction of the book involved deliberate rearrangement of material. For instance, a single afternoon's return to the pond in the fall of 1852 was capable of furnishing details that were woven into half a dozen passages of the finished work, two of them separated by seventy pages. Nevertheless, since no invention was demanded, since all the material was a *donnée* of Thoreau's memory, my assertion that *Walden* does not belong with the simple records of experience may require more establishing. The chief clue to how it was transformed into something else lies in Thoreau's extension of his remark that he did not believe himself to be "wholly involved in Nature." He went on to say that in being aware of himself as a human entity, he was "sensible of a certain doubleness" that made him both participant and spectator in any event. This ability to stand "as remote from myself as from another" is the indispensable attribute of the dramatist. Thoreau makes you share in the excitement of his private scenes, for example, by the kind of generalized significance he can give to his purchase and demolishment of an old shanty for its boards:

> I was informed treacherously by a young Patrick that neighbor
> Seeley, an Irishman, in the intervals of the carting, transferred the
> still tolerable, straight, and drivable nails, staples, and spikes to his
> pocket, and then stood when I came back to pass the time of day,
> and look freshly up, unconcerned, with spring thoughts, at the

devastation; there being a dearth of work, as he said. He was there to represent spectatordom, and help make this seemingly insignificant event one with the removal of the gods of Troy.

The demands he made of great books are significant of his own intentions: "They have no cause of their own to plead, but while they enlighten and sustain the reader his common sense will not refuse them." Propaganda is not the source of the inner freedom they offer to the reader, for their relation to life is more inclusive than argument; or, as Thoreau described it, they are at once "intimate" and "universal." He aimed unerringly to reconcile these two extremes in his own writing. His experience had been fundamental in that it had sprung from his determination to start from obedience to the rudimentary needs of a man who wanted to be free. Greenough had seen how, in that sense, "Obedience is worship," for by discerning and following the functional patterns of daily behavior, you could discover the proportions of beauty that would express and complete them. It was Thoreau's conviction that by reducing life to its primitive conditions, he had come to the roots from which healthy art must flower, whether in Thessaly or Concord. It was not just a figure of speech when he said that "Olympus is but the outside of the earth everywhere." The light touch of his detachment allows the comparison of his small things with great, and throughout the book enables him to possess the universe at home.

As a result *Walden* has spoken to men of widely differing convictions, who have in common only the intensity of their devotion to life. It became a bible for many of the leaders of the British labor movement after Morris. When the sound of a little fountain in a shop window in Fleet Street made him think suddenly of lake water, Yeats remembered also his boyhood enthusiasm for Thoreau. He did not leave London then and go and live on Innisfree. But out of his loneliness in the foreign city he did write the first of his poems that met with a wide response, and "The Lake Isle"—despite its Pre-Raphaelite flavor—was reminiscent of *Walden* even to "the small cabin" Yeats built and the "bean rows" he planted in his imagination. *Walden* was also one of our books that bulked largest for Tolstoy when he addressed his brief message to America (1901) and urged us to rediscover the greatness of our writers of the fifties: "And I should like to ask the American people why they do not pay more attention to these voices (hardly to be replaced by those of financial and industrial millionaires, or successful generals and admirals), and continue the good work in which they made such hopeful progress." In 1904 Proust wrote to the Comtesse de Noailles: "Lisez . . . les pages admirables de *Walden*. Il me semble qu'on les lise en soi-même tant elles sortent du fond de notre expérience intime."

In his full utilization of his immediate resources Thoreau was the kind of native craftsman whom Greenough recognized as the harbinger of power for our arts. Craftsmanship in this sense involves the mastery of traditional modes and skills; it has been thought of more often in connection with Indian baskets or Yankee tankards and hearth-tools than with the so-called fine arts. In fact, until fairly lately, despite Greenough's pioneering, it has hardly been consistently thought of in relation to American products of any kind. The march of our experience has been so dominantly expansive, from one rapid disequilibrium to the next, that we have neglected to see what Constance Rourke, among others, has now pointed out so effectively: that notwithstanding the inevitable restlessness of our long era of pioneering, at many stages within that process the strong counter-effort of the settlers was for communal security and permanence. From such islands of realization and fulfilment within the onrushing torrent have come the objects, the order and balance of which now, when we most need them, we can recognize as among the most valuable possessions of our continent. The conspicuous manifestation of these qualities, as Greenough already knew, has been in architecture as the most social of forms, whether in the clipper, or on the New England green, or in the Shaker communities. But the artifacts of the cabinet maker, the potter and the founder, or whatever other utensils have been shaped patiently and devotedly for common service, are likewise a testimony of what Miss Rourke has called our classic art, recognizing that this term "has nothing to do with grandeur, that it cannot be copied or imported, but is the outgrowth of a special mode of life and feeling."

Thoreau's deep obligation to such traditional ways has been obscured by our thinking of him only as the extreme protestant. It is now clear that his revolt was bound up with a determination to do all he could to prevent the dignity of common labor from being degraded by the idle tastes of the rich. When he objected that "the mason who finishes the cornice of the palace returns at night perchance to a hut not so good as a wigwam," he showed the identity of his social and aesthetic foundations. Although he did not use Greenough's terms, he was always requiring a functional relationship. What he responded to as beauty was the application of trained skill to the exigencies of existence. He made no arbitrary separation between arts, and admired the Indian's woodcraft or the farmer's thorough care in building a barn on the same grounds that he admired the workmanship of Homer.[7] The depth to which his ideals for fitness and beauty in writing

[7] Emerson also said, "I like a man who likes to see a fine barn as well as a good tragedy." And Whitman added, as his reaction to the union of work and culture, "I know that pleasure filters in and oozes out of me at the opera, but I know too that subtly and unaccountably my mind is sweet and odorous within while I clean up my boots and grease the pair that I reserve for stormy weather."

were shaped, half unconsciously, by the modes of productive labor with which he was surrounded, or, in fact, by the work of his own hands in carpentry or pencil-making or gardening, can be read in his instinctive analogies. He knew that the only discipline for Channing's "sublimo-slipshod style" would be to try to carve some truths as roundly and solidly as a stonecutter. He knew it was no good to write, "unless you feel strong in the knees." Or—a more unexpected example to find in him—he believed he had learned an important lesson in design from the fidelity with which the operative in the textile-factory had woven his piece of cloth.

The structural wholeness of *Walden* makes it stand as the firmest product in our literature of such life-giving analogies between the processes of art and daily work. Moreover, Thoreau's very lack of invention brings him closer to the essential attributes of craftsmanship, if by that term we mean the strict, even spare, almost impersonal "revelation of the object," in contrast to the "elaborated skill," the combinations of more variegated resources that we describe as technique. This contrast of terms is still Miss Rourke's, in distinguishing between kinds of painting, but it can serve equally to demonstrate why Thoreau's book possesses such solidity in contrast, say, with *Hiawatha* or *Evangeline*. Longfellow was much the more obviously gifted in his available range of forms and subject matters. But his graceful derivations from his models—the versification and gentle tone of Goethe's *Hermann und Dorothea* for *Evangeline,* or the metre of the *Kalevala* for *Hiawatha*—were not brought into fusion with his native themes.[8] Any indigenous strength was lessened by the reader's always being conscious of the metrical dexterity as an ornamental exercise. It is certainly not to be argued that technical proficiency must result in such dilutions, but merely that, as Greenough saw, it was very hard for American artists of that day, who had no developed tradition of their own, not to be thus swamped by their contact with European influences. Their very aspiration for higher standards of art than those with which they were surrounded tended to make them think of form as a decorative refinement which could be imported.

The particular value of the organic principle for a provincial society thus comes into full relief. Thoreau's literal acceptance of Emerson's proposition that vital form "is only discovered and executed by the artist, not arbitrarily composed by him," impelled him to minute inspection of his own existence and of the intuitions that rose from it. Although this involved the

---

[8] And as F. L. Pattee has said of *Hiawatha,* in *The Feminine Fifties* (1940): "The only really Indian thing about the poem is the Indian summer haze that softens all its outlines, but even this atmosphere is Indian only in name: it was borrowed from German romantic poets."

restriction of his art to parochial limits, to the portrayal of man in terms only of the immediate nature that drew him out, his study of this interaction also brought him to fundamental human patterns unsuspected by Longfellow. Thoreau demonstrated what Emerson had merely observed, that the function of the artist in society is always to renew the primitive experience of the race, that he "still goes back for materials and begins again on the most advanced stage." Thoreau's scent for wildness ferreted beneath the merely conscious levels of cultivated man. It served him, in several pages of notes about a debauched muskrat hunter (1859), to uncover and unite once more the chief sources for his own art. He had found himself heartened by the seemingly inexhaustible vitality of this battered character, "not despairing of life, but keeping the same rank and savage hold on it that his predecessors have for so many generations, while so many are sick and despairing." Thoreau went on, therefore, half-playfully to speculate what it was that made this man become excited, indeed inspired by the January freshet in the meadows:

> There are poets of all kinds and degrees, little known to each other. The Lake School is not the only or the principal one. They love various things. Some love beauty, and some love rum. Some go to Rome, and some go a-fishing, and are sent to the house of correction once a month . . . I meet these gods of the river and woods with sparkling faces (like Apollo's) late from the house of correction once a month. . . . I meet these gods of the river and woods with sparkling faces (like Apollo's) late from the house of correction, it may be carrying whatever mystic and forbidden bottles of representatives of heathen gods, when I can see natural living ones by an infinitely superior artist, without perspective tube? If you read the Rig Veda, oldest of books, as it were, describing a very primitive people and condition of things, you hear in their prayers of a still older, more primitive and aboriginal race in their midst and round about, warring on them and seizing their flocks and herds, infesting their pastures. Thus is it in another sense in all communities, and hence the prisons and police.

The meandering course of Thoreau's reflections here should not obscure his full discovery that the uneradicated wildness of man is the anarchical basis both of all that is most dangerous and most valuable in him. That he could dig down to the roots of primitive poetry without going a mile from Concord accounts for his ability to create "a true Homeric or Paphlagonian man" in the likeness of the French woodchopper. It also helps account for the fact that by following to its uncompromising conclusion his belief that great art can grow from the center of the simplest life, he was able to be universal. He had understood that in the act of expression a man's whole being, and his natural and social background as well, function organically together. He had mastered a definition of art akin to what Maritain has extracted from scholasticism: *Recta ratio factibilium,* the right ordering of the thing to be made, the right revelation of the material.

NATHANIEL HAWTHORNE

****

Henry James's *Hawthorne* (London, 1879) is valuable because it seems to inform as much about its writer as about its subject; Newton Arvin's excellent *Hawthorne* (New York, 1929) is livened by psychological insights; but Randall Stewart's *Nathaniel Hawthorne: A Biography* (New Haven, Conn., 1948) seems most accurately to reveal to most readers Hawthorne's life and literary aims. Contemporary notices of importance include Edgar Allan Poe's reviews of *Twice-Told Tales* in *Graham's Magazine* (1842), best available in *Poe: Selected Prose and Poetry,* edited by W. H. Auden (New York, 1950), and Herman Melville's "Hawthorne and His Mosses" in the *Literary World* (1850), best available in *Herman Melville: Representative Selections,* edited by Willard Thorp (New York, 1938). D. H. Lawrence's chapter on Hawthorne in *Studies in Classic American Literature* (New York, 1923) is teasingly provocative, as is Austin Warren's prim essay in *Rage for Order* (Chicago, 1948). For me, the most useful critical studies have been Leland Schubert's analytical *Hawthorne, the Artist* (Chapel

Hill, N.C., 1944), Mark Van Doren's sympathetic *Hawthorne* (New York, 1949), Millicent Bell's *Hawthorne's View of the Artist* (Albany, N.Y., 1962), and especially Richard Harter Fogle's *Hawthorne's Fiction: The Light and the Dark* (Norman, Oklahoma 1952; revised 1964), from which I present two important chapters here. The reader who is serious about meanings will enjoy H. H. Waggoner's *Hawthorne: A Critical Study* (Cambridge, Mass., 1955) and R. R. Male's *Hawthorne, Tragic Vision* (Austin, Tex., 1957); one who enjoys watching critical imagination at work will like Rudolph Von Abele's *The Death of an Artist* (The Hague, 1955) and Frederick C. Crewes's Freudian *The Sins of the Fathers* (New York, 1966). Briefer evaluations of note are Walter Blair's "Color, Light and Shadow in Hawthorne's Fiction," *New England Quarterly,* XV (March 1942), pp. 74–94, Philip Rahv's "The Dark Lady of Salem," *Partisan Review,* VIII (September–October 1941), and Lionel Trilling's "Hawthorne in Our Time," *Beyond Culture* (New York, 1965).

HAWTHORNE'S FICTION:
THE LIGHT AND THE DARK

Richard Harter Fogle

****

Hawthorne is a great writer in absolute terms, and many men have written well about him. Yet modern critics, led astray by mistaken notions about realism and by fallacies about inevitable progress, are still a little condescending. Most general readers, among them Somerset Maugham, find him naïve and old-fashioned. Given their perspective, both critics and readers are honestly reporting what they see; but the perspective itself is out of focus. A character in Mr. Marquand's recent *Point of No Return* comments sardonically upon those people who consider *The House of the Seven Gables* a good story for children. It is a fact that generations of high-school students have been reared on the book with no very favorable results. Because of premature exposure to it, I contracted a dislike for gentle Phoebe Pyncheon which was surpassed only by my distaste for Lucie Manette in Dickens's *Tale of Two Cities,* a lady who ranks among the great emetics of

English literature. Doubtless most readers remember Hawthorne from an experience like mine, which also includes memories of "A Rill from the Town Pump" (interpreted as a temperance lecture), as it appeared in my eighth-grade reader.

Hawthorne's writing is misleading in its simplicity, which is genuine enough but tempts us to overlook what lies beneath. In the end, simplicity is one of his genuine charms—combined with something else. The essence of Hawthorne is, in fact, distilled from the opposing elements of simplicity and complexity. This essence is a clear liquid, with no apparent cloudiness. Hawthorne, together with Henry James, perhaps, is the only American novelist who has been able to see life whole without, in Thackeray's words, "roaring ai, ai, as loud as Prometheus," like Melville, Wolfe, and Faulkner; droning interminably an account of its details, like Dreiser; or falling into a thin, shrill irony, the batlike twittering of souls in Hades, like all the sad young men. Hawthorne's tone is equable, "not harsh nor grating, but with ample power to chasten and subdue." He is a unique and wonderful combination of light and darkness.

The light in Hawthorne is clarity of design. He has a classic balance; his language is exquisitely lucid. He gives one the sense of an invulnerable dignity and centrality; he is impenetrably self-possessed. He holds his characters to the highest standards, for he literally brings them to judgment at the bar of eternity as immortal souls. The "dark" in Hawthorne, that blackness which Herman Melville applauded in him, is his tragic complexity. His clarity is intermingled with subtlety, his statement interfused with symbolism, his affirmation enriched with ambiguity. The whole which results is captivating. In attack he is mild but deadly. His blow is so delicately delivered that a man would have to turn his head in order to realize that he had just lost it. "The Custom House" essay, for example, which rather oddly precedes *The Scarlet Letter,* seems at first sight merely agreeable. Look closer, however, and the effect is devastating. These gently humorous character portraits are murderous, not from malice or heat, but from judgment and icy cold. Hawthorne is not indignant; he is merely certain of his grounds. And his certainty is that of one whose father was called "the sternest man who ever walked a deck."

He is so entirely unsentimental that he does not need, as we sometimes do, to avoid sentimentality. He combines sympathy with a classic aloofness, participation with cool observation. "My father," said Julian Hawthorne, "was two men, one sympathetic and intuitional, the other critical and logical; together they formed a combination which could not be thrown off its feet." Thus Hawthorne's writing has a tone of exquisite gravity, harmonized strangely with a pervasive irony and humor. In the use of irony he is a lighter, more sensitive Fielding, with depths besides which Fielding could not plumb. In the matter of irony Hawthorne's antecedents in the eighteenth-century novel might well be re-examined.

Corresponding to the clarity and the complexity of Hawthorne are his "philosophy" and the crosscurrents which modify its course. For the best understanding one should always attend to the thought of the author. But one grasps that author wholly only by observing his characters, his settings, the patterns of his diction, the trends of his imagery, the concrete mechanics of telling a story. What one has grasped is admittedly not easy to describe, however—therefore the advantage of seizing upon the writer's thought, which can be systematically abstracted.

The philosophy of Hawthorne is a broadly Christian scheme which contains heaven, earth, and hell. Whether heaven and hell are realities or only subjective states of mind is one of Hawthorne's crucial ambiguities. I do not call him a Christian humanist, as do some excellent critics, for it seems to me that heaven and hell *are* real to him and play too large a part in his fiction to be relegated to the background. In his mixed macrocosm, man is a microcosm also mixed. Man's chief temptation is to forget his limits and complexities, to think himself all good, or to think himself all bad. Either way he falls into spiritual isolation and pride. He needs a proper mixture of the earthly and the ideal—with a touch of the flame to temper it. Thus Aylmer, the scientist-hero of "The Birthmark," violates the covenant of humankind when he tries to eradicate the only blemish of his beautiful wife, a tiny mark on her cheek. He succeeds, but kills her in the process. The birthmark, which is shaped like a hand, is her grip upon earthly existence. She dies to the sound of the laughter of Aminadab, Aylmer's assistant, a kind of earth-fiend. Even the pit has its claims, which must not be slighted. The conclusion epitomizes Hawthorne's thinking: ". . . had Aylmer reached a profounder wisdom, he need not thus have flung away the happiness which would have woven his mortal life of the selfsame texture with the celestial. The momentary circumstance was too strong for him; he failed to look beyond the shadowy scope of time, and living once for all in eternity, to find the perfect future in the present." There is a time for everything, and an eternity. Aylmer should have waited.

But the system does not make the story. The tale of "The Minister's Black Veil" will illustrate the difference between an abstract and a literary meaning. The minister dons the veil as an emblem of secret sin, of which all men are presumably guilty. Elizabeth, his betrothed, implores him to discard it. The minister has found a dreadful truth, while Elizabeth may have discovered a greater—that men are evil *and also* good. The meaning lies not in either but in both. So Hawthorne condemns his strange seekers, his Aylmers, his Ethan Brands, but he makes them noble. His reconciliation is not finally in logic, for he accepts the mystery of existence. His reconciliation is the acceptance itself, realized in balance, structure, and tone.

Hawthorne still suffers from our prejudice against allegory. This prejudice comes partly from a false theory of realism, a legacy of the late nineteenth century, and partly from a misconception of what allegory is. We assume that allegory subordinates everything to a predetermined conclusion: that allegory, in short, is a dishonest counterfeit of literary value. But the great allegories, *The Faerie Queene* and *The Pilgrim's Progress,* possess the literary virtues. And Hawthorne, whose subjects are moral and psychological problems, feels for these problems a passion which transfigures them. All we can ask of a writer is that he treat his material honestly, without unduly simplifying: that he keep faith with his own imagination. T. S. Eliot has said that good religious poetry teaches us not a doctrine but how it feels to believe it; and so it should be with allegory.

Allegory is organic to Hawthorne, an innate quality of his vision. It is his disposition to find spiritual meaning in all things natural and human. This faculty is an inheritance from the Puritans, who saw in everything God's will. To this inheritance was added a gift from nineteenth-century Romanticism, which endowed the natural world with meaning by seeing it as life. In Hawthorne allegory is inseparable from moral complexity and aesthetic design, qualities to be enjoyed in themselves. So, in his "Endicott and the Red Cross" the focus of meaning and the focus of setting are one, and the conclusion takes on an increased value from the subtlety of its preparation. The scene, the village green of seventeenth-century Salem, radiates outward from a center, to return upon it once more. The center is Endicott, the iron Puritan, in whose breastplate, significantly, the scene is mirrored. Endicott is the temporal, active power, the central ethos and intelligence of the story. The Puritan meeting-house, the spiritual power, is "the central object in the mirrored picture."

On the church porch is nailed the head of a wolf, "a token of the perils of the wilderness." Close by is the whipping-post; at the corners of the meeting-house stand the pillory and the stocks. Various evildoers are suffering punishment: an Episcopalian, a royalist, a Wanton Gospeller who has given unsanctioned interpretations of Holy Writ, and a woman with her tongue in a cleft stick who has spoken against the elders of the church. There is also "a young woman, with no mean share of beauty," who is condemned to wear upon her breast a scarlet *A*. In the background are armored men, for Endicott is drilling his trainbands.

The Reverend Roger Williams appears—as he might well have done—bearing news of the English crown's intention to send a royal governor to rule the New England colonies. Endicott, in a symbolic gesture of rebellion, rips the cross from the flag of St. George, which flies over the scene.

> With a cry of triumph the people gave their sanction to one of the boldest exploits which our history records. And forever honored be the name of Endicott! We look back through the mist of ages, and recognize in the rending of the Red Cross from New England's banner the first omen of that deliverance which our fathers consummated after the bones of the stern Puritans had lain more than a century in the dust.

The story is beautifully compact; it contains an entire era of American history in a single scene and action. The allegorical economy of its dramatis personae is merged with firmly symmetrical composition. The abstract meaning is compressed into one flashing concrete image. The "moral" or summary has considerably more than its surface value, and should be read in the light of the whole story. Before his decisive action Endicott had addressed the crowd, asking rhetorically for what purpose the Puritans fled to the New England wilderness:

> "Was it not for liberty to worship God according to our conscience?"
>
> "Call you this liberty of conscience?" interrupted a voice on the steps of the meeting-house.
>
> It was the Wanton Gospeller. A sad and quiet smile flitted across the mild visage of Roger Williams.

Thus the meaning of Endicott's gesture remains, but deeper and richer for the moral complexity of its context.

Even so allegorical a figure as Chillingworth, the villain of *The Scarlet Letter,* has his complexities. Hawthorne keeps before our eyes his humanity as well as his evil. So intricate, indeed, are Hawthorne's complications that he has sometimes been accused of indecision. All profound studies of spiritual problems, however, eventually run against a blank wall. Do we know the ultimate destiny of James's Isabel Archer? It is a tribute to *The Portrait of a Lady* that the question so much as occurs to us. What do we decide about Conrad's *Lord Jim?* What is the meaning of Jim's one act of cowardice? The whole book tries to tell us, and at the end we are left with the action still unexplained. There is a point where a writer must stop for fear of saying more than his imagination has authorized. The killing of the model is the central action of *The Marble Faun;* yet Donatello kills almost involuntarily, and Miriam, who has incited to murder, is honestly unaware that she has done so. Hawthorne nevertheless holds both to strict account.

This ambiguity in Hawthorne was noticed early but was not fully understood. Contemporary reviews of *The Marble Faun* objected to its vagueness. To friendlier critics Hawthorne's ambiguity was a chiaroscuro effect which deepened the tints of his picture. John Lothrop Motley wrote, "I like those shadowy, weird, fantastic, Hawthornesque shapes flitting through the golden gloom, which is the atmosphere of the book." In his prefaces Hawthorne himself speaks chiefly of this quality of picturesqueness. He says of *The House of the Seven Gables:*

> It is a legend prolonging itself, from an epoch now gray in the distance, down into our own broad daylight, and bringing along with it some of its legendary mist, which the reader, according to his pleasure, may either disregard, or allow it to float almost imperceptibly about the characters and events for the sake of a picturesque effect.

This type of ambiguity is a way of introducing the marvelous without offending against probability. It has a deeper purpose, as well—to convey in legend or superstition a moral or psychological truth. In the story of the Pyncheons the whisper of tradition is truer than history; the legend of Maule's Curse has weighty meaning concealed in it. ". . . ancient superstitions," says Hawthorne, "after being steeped in human hearts and embodied in human breath, and passing from lip to ear in manifold repetition, through a series of generations, become imbued with an effect of homely truth."

Yvor Winters and F. O. Matthiessen have illuminated Hawthorne's ambiguity, which Winters calls "the formula of alternative possibilities," and Matthiessen "the device of multiple choice." It is not, however, a device; it is a pervasive quality of mind. It can be an evasion, and it is sometimes no more than a mannerism. But as a whole it embodies Hawthorne's deepest insights. It outlines the pure form of truth by dissolving irrelevancies; this is its positive function. Negatively, it marks the limit of eyeshot, beyond which is shadow. Thus Hawthorne's effects of light—his shadows, his mirror images, his masquerades—all examine the relationships of appearance and reality. Hawthorne's ambiguity involves both light and darkness. As light it is the means of seeing through opacities; as darkness it is the difficulty of seeing.

Hawthorne's simplest ambiguity is a playful mystification. In retelling the Greek myths in *A Wonder-Book* and *Tanglewood Tales* he uses ambiguity to introduce the Olympian gods. Mortals continually have glimpses of the supernatural. In "The Miraculous Pitcher" old Baucis and Philemon entertain Jove and Mercury, who are disguised as casual wayfarers. The old couple see miracles without being able to believe their eyes, and Hawthorne also pretends to be skeptical. Thus Mercury's caduceus is ostensibly an optical illusion:

> Two snakes, carved in the wood, were represented as twining themselves about the staff, and were so very skilfully executed that old Philemon (whose eyes, you know, were getting rather dim) almost thought them alive, and that he could see them wriggling and twisting.

(This same staff is used more seriously in "Young Goodman Brown" and *The Blithedale Romance,* in both of which it indicates the presence of evil.) This ambiguity is proper to the childen's tale; as with fairy stories, what is required is not real belief, but a temporary suspension of disbelief. Yet even here there is a hint of truth before eyes too blind to see it.

The issues are more serious in such legends of New England as "The Gray Champion" and the "Legends of the Province House" in the volume of *Twice-Told Tales.* In these stories the ambiguity underlines the significance by dissolving irrelevant actuality in the mists of the past and leaving only an ideal history. Ambiguity invests the events with the rich pathos and patina of time and counterpoints unreality against truth. In "The Gray Champion" the hero's background is shadowed, the better to project his image in the foreground. In "Howe's Masquerade" disguise reveals identity; the procession of royal governors is a masquerade, but there is nothing false about its meaning. The ambiguity of the "Legends" is a vision of the Past in the light of the Present, a picture in a frame of distance.

Hawthorne uses ambiguity structurally to create suspense and retard conclusions, especially in tales where the primary emphasis would otherwise be too clear. "The Celestial Railroad," an ironic nineteenth-century *Pilgrim's Progress*, is an example of this usage. Hawthorne's railroad is scheduled to the Celestial City, but its real destination is Hell. By disguising the way to Perdition as the road to Heaven, he takes the reader into his confidence by a sustained ironic reversal of values and curbs impatience for the end by supplying attractions on the way. "The Celestial Railroad," however, is closer to abstract allegory than Hawthorne generally gets. More fundamental is the tragic ambiguity which threatens the bases of accepted values, as in "Young Goodman Brown," where the final interpretation is in genuine doubt. Hawthorne judges relentlessly, yet with sympathy, and his ambiguity always leaves room for a different verdict. He preserves the sanctity and independence of his characters by allowing them at bottom an inviolable individuality.

In their recently published *Theory of Literature,* Rene Wellek and Austin Warren define the symbol as "an object which refers to another object but which demands attention also in its own right, as a presentation." The symbol must be interesting in itself, not merely as it points to something else. This crucial requirement, which divides *mere* allegory from literature, Hawthorne fulfills. The minister's black veil is truly a veil, as well as an emblem of secret sin. The brook of *The Scarlet Letter* has water in it, though it symbolizes life and time. The fountain in Rappaccini's garden is an object of art in addition to being an image of eternity. Hawthorne's symbols have the clarity of allegory, with the complexity and density of life. They are rarely obscure, but they will abide the test of long use without wearing out. Since they are generally accompanied by an explanation, it is natural to pass by them quickly—too quickly.

The rosebush before the prison in Chapter I of *The Scarlet Letter* is an instance of this misleading simplicity. It stands, says Hawthorne, "in token that the deep heart of nature can pity and forgive." The rose is pitying nature, as the prison is pitiless man. The rose is also, however, Hester Prynne, a red rose against the gray Puritan background; and therefore it is the scarlet letter, the natural passion which the prison exists to quell. Beside the fortress-like prison the rose seems pitiably frail, but it is strong with the power of natural vitality.

Hawthorne's symbols are broadly traditional, drawn from the main stream of Western thought. In his pages are the red cavern of the heart and the gray cavern of isolation; the wild forest and the winding path of error (from Spenser); the fountain and the sea of eternity, and the river of time; the Garden of Eden, with Adam and Eve and the serpent; the flames of hell, strangely mingled with the forge fire of Vulcan's smithy, and the bright blaze of the hearth; the devil's stigmata, and the sunlight of holiness. Created as they are of old materials, these symbols are yet fresh from Hawthorne's imagination. He invests them with a new vitality and suggestiveness.

THE SCARLET LETTER

Interpretations of *The Scarlet Letter* have been almost startlingly various. This is not surprising, for Hawthorne has himself pointed the way to a wide range of speculations. The concluding words of *The Scarlet Letter,* however, summarily dismiss the more cheerful readings, of which there are a number. In describing the heraldic device on the common tombstone of Hester and Dimmesdale, they describe "our now concluded legend; so sombre is it, and relieved only by one ever-glowing point of light gloomier than the shadow:—

'ON A FIELD, SABLE, THE LETTER A, GULES.' "

These words alone, in my opinion, are sufficient evidence for disproving the notion that *The Scarlet Letter* is "about" Hester Prynne the advanced feminist, or that the story can be satisfactorily summarized either by the moral which Hawthorne attaches to Dimmesdale, " 'Show freely to the world, if not your worst, yet some trait whereby the worst may be inferred!' " or by the doctrine of *felix culpa,* "the fortunate fall," that out of sin and evil comes good and that Hester is educated and refined by her wrongdoing. The sentiment is too darkly tragic to be appropriate to any of these conclusions, though Hawthorne at one place and another in *The Scarlet Letter* has suggested the possibility of all of them. The true conclusion of *The Scarlet Letter* is an unresolved contradiction—unresolved not from indecision or lack of thought but from honesty of imagination. Hawthorne gives the only answer that his formulation of the terms permits. If we consider that the problem of *The Scarlet Letter* is primarily the problem of Hester Prynne, the verdict is at best suspension of judgment after full examination of the evidence. And, as we know, Hester emerges from trial in better condition than her codefendants Dimmesdale and Chillingworth.

This is the contradiction, and a very widely representative contradiction it is: the sin of *The Scarlet Letter* is a symbol of the original sin, by which no man is untouched. All mortals commit the sin in one form or another, which is perhaps the meaning of "your worst" in the exhortation occasioned by the death of Dimmesdale. Hester, having sinned, makes the best possible recovery; and the crime itself is of all crimes the most excusable, coming of passionate love and having "a consecration of its own." Yet the sin remains real and inescapable, and she spends her life in retribution, the death of her lover Dimmesdale having finally taught her that this is the only way. This is the dilemma: human beings by their natures must fall into error—and yet it would be better if they did not.

The letter, an "ever-glowing point of light," is gloomier than the shadow of its background. The shadow, the "Field, Sable," is roughly the atmosphere of Puritanism, the "Letter A, Gules" the atmosphere of the sin. These are at odds, and no absolute superiority is granted to either. The Puritan doctors are no fit judges of a woman's heart; nor, on the other hand, is Hester to be absolved. The letter is glowing, positive, vital, the product of genuine passion, while the sable may certainly be taken as the negation of everything alive. Yet the letter is gloomier.

These shades are both of hell, and there is no hue of heaven in *The Scarlet Letter* which really offsets them. Sunlight is the nearest approach to it, and its sway is too fleeting to have any great effect. In the forest scene of chapters XVI–XIX sunshine, "as with a sudden smile of heaven," bursts over Hester and Dimmesdale, but this is merely a momentary relief. The hope which accompanies it is short-lived, delusory, and dangerous. A more steadfast light, "The sun, but little past its meridian," shines down upon Dimmesdale as he stands on the scaffold to confess his guilt. This is triumph, indeed, but little to counterbalance the continual power of the "bale fire" and "lurid gleam" of the letter. Hope and regeneration are sometimes symbolized in Hawthorne by the celestial colors of dawn, transfigured by light: blues, greens, and golds. In "Ethan Brand" the tender hues of the twilight sky are overpowered by night and the red and black of Brand's Unpardonable Sin, but they are revivified by the atmosphere of dawn. So the storm in *The House of the Seven Gables,* which accompanies the crisis and blows itself out with the death of Judge Pyncheon, gives way to a world made new and bathed in morning sunshine. There is no such scene in *The Scarlet Letter.*

The problem of *The Scarlet Letter* can be solved only by introducing the supernatural level of heaven, the sphere of absolute knowledge and justice and—hesitantly—of complete fulfillment. This may seem to be another paradox, and perhaps a disappointing one. Without doubt *The Scarlet Letter* pushes *towards* the limit of moral judgment, suggesting many possible conclusions. It is even relentless in its search in the depths of its characters. There is yet, however, a point beyond which Hawthorne will not go; ultimate solutions are not appropriate in the merely human world. His sympathy with Hester and Dimmesdale is clear enough, but he allows them only to escape the irrevocable spiritual ruin which befalls Chillingworth. Figuratively his good wishes pursue them beyond life, but he does not presume himself to absolve them. Even in the carefully staged scene of Dimmesdale's death, where every impulse of both author and reader demands complete forgiveness, Hawthorne refuses to grant it. With his "bright dying eyes" Dimmesdale looks into eternity, but nothing he sees there permits him to comfort Hester. To her questions, " 'Shall we not meet again? . . . Shall we not spend our immortal life together?' " he can answer only, " 'The law we broke!—the sin here so awfully revealed!—let these alone be in thy thoughts! I fear! I fear!' " A grim and unflinching conclusion, considering everything. Dimmesdale is not of course Hawthorne, but the very preservation of dramatic propriety at this crucial point is significant.

There are four states of being in Hawthorne: one subhuman, two human, and one superhuman. The first is Nature, which comes to our attention in *The Scarlet Letter* twice. It appears first in the opening chapter, in the wild rosebush which stands outside the blackbrowed Puritan jail, and whose blossoms

> might be imagined to offer their fragrance and fragile beauty to
> the prisoner as he went in, and to the condemned criminal as

he came forth to his doom, in token that the deep heart of Nature could pity and be kind to him.

The second entrance of Nature comes in the forest scene, where it sympathizes with the forlorn lovers and gives them hope. "Such was the sympathy of Nature—that wild, heathen Nature of the forest, never subjugated by human law, nor illuminated by higher truth. . . ." The sentence epitomizes both the virtues of Nature and its inadequacy.   In itself good, Nature is not a sufficient support for human beings.

The human levels are represented by Hawthorne's distinction between Heart and Head. The heart is closer to nature, the head to the supernatural. The heart may err by lapsing into nature, which means, since it has not the innocence of nature, into corruption. The danger of the head lies in the opposite direction. It aspires to be superhuman, and is likely to dehumanize itself in the attempt by violating the human limit. Dimmesdale, despite his considerable intellect, is predominantly a heart character, and it is through the heart that sin has assailed him, in a burst of passion which overpowered both religion and reason. The demoniac Chillingworth is of the head, a cold experimenter and thinker. It is fully representative of Hawthorne's general emphasis that Chillingworth's spiritual ruin is complete. Hester Prynne is a combination of head and heart, with a preponderance of head. Her original sin is of passion, but its consequences expose her to the danger of absolute mental isolation. The centrifugal urge of the intellect is counteracted in her by her duty to her daughter Pearl, the product of the sin, and by her latent love for Dimmesdale. Pearl herself is a creature of nature, most at home in the wild forest: ". . . the mother-forest, and these wild things which it nourished, all recognized a kindred wildness in the human child." She is made human by Dimmesdale's confession and death: "The great scene of grief, in which the wild infant bore a part, had developed all her sympathies. . . ."

The fourth level, the superhuman or heavenly, will perhaps merely be confused by elaborate definition. It is the sphere of absolute insight, justice, and mercy. Few of Hawthorne's tales and romances can be adequately considered without taking it into account. As Mark Van Doren has recently emphasized, it is well to remember Hawthorne's belief in immortality. It is because of the very presence of the superhuman in Hawthorne's thinking that the destinies of his chief characters are finally veiled in ambiguity. He respects them as he would have respected any real person by refusing to pass the last judgment, by leaving a residue of mysterious individuality untouched. The whole truth is not for a fellow human to declare.

These four states are not mutually exclusive. Without the touch of nature human life would be too bleak. The Puritans of *The Scarlet Letter* are deficient in nature, and they are consequently dour and overrighteous. Something of the part that nature might play in the best human life is suggested in the early chapters of *The Marble Faun,* particularly through the character Donatello. The defects of either Heart or Head in a state of isolation have already been mentioned. And without some infusion of superhuman meaning into the spheres of the human, life would be worse than bestial. Perhaps only one important character in all of Hawthorne's works finds it possible to dispense completely with heaven—Westervelt, of *The Blithedale Romance*—and he is essentially diabolic. In some respects the highest and the lowest of these levels are most closely akin, as if their relationship were as points of a circle. The innocence of nature is like the innocence of heaven. It is at times, when compared to the human, like the Garden before the serpent, like heaven free of the taint of evil. Like infancy, however, nature is a stage which man must pass through, whereas his destination is heaven. The juxtaposition of highest and lowest nevertheless involves difficulties, when perfect goodness seems equivalent to mere deprivation and virtue seems less a matter of choosing than of being untempted.

The intensity of *The Scarlet Letter,* at which Hawthorne himself was dismayed, comes from concentration, selection, and dramatic irony. The concentration upon the central theme is unremitting. The tension is lessened only once, in the scene in the forest, and then only delusively, since the hope of freedom which brings it about is quickly shown to be false and even sinful. The characters play out their tragic action against a background in itself oppressive—the somber atmosphere of Puritanism. Hawthorne calls the progression of the story "the darkening close of a tale of human frailty and sorrow." Dark to begin with, it grows steadily deeper in gloom. The method is almost unprecedentedly selective. Almost every image has a symbolic function; no scene is superfluous. One would perhaps at times welcome a loosening of the structure, a moment of wandering from the path. The weedy grassplot in front of the prison; the distorting reflection of Hester in a breastplate, where the Scarlet Letter appears gigantic; the tapestry of David and Bathsheba on the wall of the minister's chamber; the little brook in the forest; the slight malformation of Chillingworth's shoulder; the ceremonial procession on election day—in every instance more is meant than meets the eye.

The intensity of *The Scarlet Letter* comes in part from a sustained and rigorous dramatic irony, or irony of situation. This irony arises naturally from the theme of "secret sin," or concealment. "Show freely of your worst," says Hawthorne; the action of *The Scarlet Letter* arises from the failure of Dimmesdale and Chillingworth to do so. The minister hides his sin, and Chillingworth hides his identity. This concealment affords a constant drama. There is the irony of Chapter III, "The Recognition," in which Chillingworth's ignorance is suddenly and blindingly reversed. Separated from his wife by many vicissitudes, he comes upon her as she is dramatically exposed to public infamy. From his instantaneous decision, symbolized by the lifting of his finger to his lips to hide his tie to her, he precipitates the further irony of his sustained hypocrisy.

In the same chapter Hester is confronted with her fellow-adulterer, who is publicly called upon to persuade her as her spiritual guide to reveal his identity. Under the circumstances the situation is highly charged, and his words have a double meaning—one to the onlookers, another far different to Hester and the speaker himself. " 'If thou feelest it to be for thy soul's peace, and that thy earthly punishment will therefore be made more effectual to salvation, I charge thee to speak out the name of thy fellow-sinner and fellow-sufferer!' "

From this scene onward Chillingworth, by living a lie, arouses a constant irony, which is also an ambiguity. With a slight shift in emphasis all his actions can be given a very different interpretation. Seen purely from without, it would be possible to regard him as completely blameless. Hester expresses this ambiguity in Chapter IV, after he has ministered to her sick baby, the product of her faithlessness, with tenderness and skill. " 'Thy acts are like mercy,' said Hester, bewildered and appalled. 'But thy words interpret thee as a terror!' " Masquerading as a physician, he becomes to Dimmesdale a kind of attendant fiend, racking the minister's soul with constant anguish. Yet outwardly he has done him nothing but good. " 'What evil have I done the man?' asked Roger Chillingworth again. 'I tell thee, Hester Prynne, the richest fee that ever physician earned from monarch could not have bought such care as I have wasted on this miserable priest!' " Even when he closes the way to escape by proposing to take passage on the same ship with the fleeing lovers, it is possible to consider the action merely friendly. His endeavor at the end to hold Dimmesdale back from the saving scaffold is from one point of view reasonable and friendlike, although he is a devil struggling to snatch back an escaping soul. " 'All shall be well! Do not blacken your fame, and perish in dishonor! I can yet save you! Would you bring infamy on your sacred profession?' " Only when Dimmesdale has successfully resisted does Chillingworth openly reveal his purposes. With the physician the culminating irony is that in seeking to damn Dimmesdale he has himself fallen into damnation. As he says in a moment of terrible self-knowledge, " 'A mortal man, with once a human heart, has become a fiend for his especial torment!' " The effect is of an Aristotelian reversal, where a conscious and deep-laid purpose brings about totally unforeseen and opposite results. Chillingworth's relations with Dimmesdale have the persistent fascination of an almost absolute knowledge and power working their will with a helpless victim, a fascination which is heightened by the minister's awareness of an evil close beside him which he cannot place. "All this was accomplished with a subtlety so perfect that the minister, though he had constantly a dim perception of some evil influence watching over him, could never gain a knowledge of its actual nature." It is a classic situation wrought out to its fullest potentialities, in which the reader cannot help sharing the perverse pleasure of the villain.

From the victim's point of view the irony is still deeper, perhaps because we can participate still more fully in his response to it. Dimmesdale, a "remorseful hypocrite," is forced to live a perpetual lie in public. His own considerable talents for self-torture are supplemented by the situation as well as by the devoted efforts of Chillingworth. His knowledge is an agony. His conviction of sin is in exact relationship to the reverence in which his parishioners hold him. He grows pale and meager—it is the asceticism of a saint on earth; his effectiveness as a minister grows with his despair; he confesses the truth in his sermons, but transforms it "into the veriest falsehood" by the generality of his avowal and merely increases the adoration of his flock; every effort deepens his plight, since he will not—until the end—make the effort of complete self-revelation. His great election-day sermon prevails through anguish of heart; to his listeners divinely inspired, its power comes from its undertone of suffering, "the complaint of a human heart, sorrow-laden, perchance guilty, telling its secret, whether of guilt or sorrow, to the great heart of mankind. . . ." While Chillingworth at last reveals himself fully, Dimmesdale's secret is too great to be wholly laid bare. His utmost efforts are still partially misunderstood, and "highly respectable witnesses" interpret his death as a culminating act of holiness and humility.

Along with this steady irony of situation there is the omnipresent irony of the hidden meaning. The author and the reader know what the characters do not. Hawthorne consistently pretends that the coincidence of the action or the image with its significance is merely fortuitous, not planned, lest the effect be spoiled by overinsistence. In other words, he attempts to combine the sufficiently probable with the maximum of arrangement. Thus the waxing and waning of sunlight in the forest scene symbolize the emotions of Hester and Dimmesdale, but we accept this coincidence most easily if we can receive it as chance. Hawthorne's own almost amused awareness of his problem helps us to do so. Yet despite the element of play and the deliberate self-deception demanded, the total effect is one of intensity. Hawthorne is performing a difficult feat with sustained virtuosity in reconciling a constant stress between naturally divergent qualities.

The character of Pearl illuminates this point. Pearl is pure symbol, the living emblem of the sin, a human embodiment of the Scarlet Letter. Her mission is to keep Hester's adultery always before her eyes, to prevent her from attempting to escape its moral consequences. Pearl's childish questions are fiendishly apt; in speech and in action she never strays from the control of her symbolic function; her dress and her looks are related to the letter. When Hester casts the letter away in the forest, Pearl forces her to reassume it by flying into an uncontrollable rage. Yet despite the undeviating arrangement of every circumstance which surrounds her, no single action of hers is ever incredible or inconsistent with the conceivable actions of any child under the same conditions. Given the central improbability of her undeviating purposiveness, she is as lifelike as the brilliantly drawn children of Richard Hughes's *The Innocent Voyage.*

These qualities of concentration, selectivity, and irony, which are responsible for the intensity of *The Scarlet Letter,* tend at their extreme toward excessive regularity and a sense of over-manipulation, although irony is also a counteragent against them. This tendency toward regularity is balanced by Hawthorne's use of ambiguity. The distancing of the story in the past has the effect of ambiguity. Hawthorne so employs the element of time as to warn us that he cannot guarantee the literal truth of his narrative and at the same time to suggest that the essential truth is the clearer; as facts shade off into the background, meaning is left in the foreground unshadowed and disencumbered. The years, he pretends, have winnowed his material, leaving only what is enduring. Tradition and superstitition, while he disclaims belief in them, have a way of pointing to truth.

Thus the imagery of hell-fire which occurs throughout *The Scarlet Letter* is dramatically proper to the Puritan background and is attributed to the influence of superstitious legend. It works as relief from more serious concerns and still functions as a symbol of psychological and religious truth. In Chapter III, as Hester is returned from the scaffold to the prison, "It was whispered, by those who peered after her, that the scarlet letter threw a lurid gleam along the dark passage-way of the interior." The imagery of the letter may be summarized by quoting a later passage:

> The vulgar, who, in those dreary old times, were always contributing a grotesque horror to what interested their imaginations, had a story about the scarlet letter which we might readily work up into a terrific legend. They averred, that the symbol was not mere scarlet cloth, tinged in an earthly dye-pot, but was red-hot with infernal fire, and could be seen glowing all alight, whenever Hester Pyrnne walked abroad in the nighttime. And we must needs say, it seared Hester's bosom so deeply, that perhaps there was more truth in the rumor than our modern incredulity may be inclined to admit.

The lightness of Hawthorne's tone lends relief and variety, while it nevertheless reveals the function of the superstitition. "The vulgar," "dreary old times," "grotesque horror," "work up into a terrific legend"—his scorn is so heavily accented that it discounts itself and satirizes the "modern incredulity" of his affected attitude. The playful extravagance of "red-hot with infernal fire" has the same effect. And the apparent begrudging of the concession in the final sentence—"And we must needs say"—lends weight to a truth so reluctantly admitted.

Puritan demonology is in general use with the same effect. It has the pathos and simplicity of an old wives' tale and yet contains a deep subterranean power which reaches into daylight from the dark caverns of the mind. The Black Man of the unhallowed forest—a useful counterbalance to any too-optimistic picture of nature—and the witchwoman Mistress Hibbins are cases in point. The latter is a concrete example of the mingled elements of the superstitious legend. Matter-of-factly, she is a Puritan lady of high rank, whose ominous reputation is accounted for by bad temper combined with insanity. As a witch, she is a figure from a child's storybook, an object of delighted fear and mockery. Yet her fanciful extravagance covers a real malignity, and because of it she has an insight into the secret of the letter. With one stroke she lays bare the disease in Dimmesdale, as one who sees evil alone but sees it with unmatched acuteness: " 'When the Black Man sees one of his own servants, signed and sealed, so shy of owning to the bond as is the Reverend Mr. Dimmesdale, he hath a way of ordering matters so that the mark shall be disclosed to the eyes of all the world.' "

This use of the past merges into a deep-seated ambiguity of moral meaning. Moral complexity and freedom of speculation, like the lighter ambiguity of literal fact, temper the almost excessive unity and symmetry of *The Scarlet Letter* and avoid a directed verdict. In my opinion the judgment of Hawthorne upon his characters is entirely clear, although deliberately limited in its jurisdiction. But he permits the possibility of other interpretations to appear, so that the consistent clarity of his own emphasis is disguised. Let us take for example the consideration of the heroine in Chapter XIII, "Another View of Hester." After seven years of disgrace, Hester has won the unwilling respect of her fellow-townsmen by her good works and respectability of conduct. From one point of view she is clearly their moral superior: she has met rigorous cruelty with kindness, arrogance with humility. Furthermore, living as she has in enforced isolation has greatly developed her mind. In her breadth of intellectual speculation she has freed herself from any dependence upon the laws of Puritan society. "She cast away the fragments of a broken chain." She pays outward obedience to a system which has no further power upon her spirit. Under other conditions, Hawthorne suggests, she might at this juncture have become another Anne Hutchinson, the foundress of a religious sect, or a great early feminist. The author's conclusions about these possibilities, however, are specifically stated: "The scarlet letter had not done its office." Hester is wounded and led astray, not improved, by her situation. Hawthorne permits his reader, if he wishes, to take his character from his control, to say that Hester Prynne is a great woman unhappily born before her time, or that she is a good woman wronged by her fellow men. But Hawthorne is less confident.

In the multiple interpretations which constitute the moral ambiguities of *The Scarlet Letter* there is no clear distinction of true and false, but there *is* a difference between superficial and profound. In instances where interpretation of observed fact fuses with interpretation of moral meaning, conclusions are generally relative to those who make them. After Dimmesdale's climactic death scene

> Most of the spectators testified to having seen, on the breast of the unhappy minister, a SCARLET LETTER—the very semblance of that worn by Hester Prynne—imprinted in the flesh. As regarded its origin, there were various explanations, all of which must necessarily have been conjectural. Some affirmed that the Reverend Mr. Dimmesdale, on the very day when Hester Pyrnne first wore her ignominious badge, had begun a course of penance,—which he afterwards, in so many futile methods, followed out,—by inflicting a hideous torture on himself. Others contended that the stigma had not been produced until a long time subsequent, when old Roger Chillingworth, being a potent necromancer, had caused it to appear, through the agency of magic and poisonous drugs. Others, again,— and those best able to appreciate the minister's peculiar sensibility, and the wonderful operation of his spirit upon the body,—whispered their belief, that the awful symbol was the effect of the ever-active tooth of remorse, gnawing from the inmost heart outwardly, and at last manifesting Heaven's dreadful judgment by the visible presence of the letter.

Most singular is the fact that some spectators have seen no letter at all.

The presence of so many possibilities hints strongly that the whole truth is not to be found in any single choice, but Hawthorne's own preference is clearly indicated by "those best able to appreciate."

In a different case all interpretations are equally false, or at least equally erring. In Chapter XII, "The Minister's Vigil," a meteor flashes across the sky, which to the morbid eye of Dimmesdale takes the form of a gigantic *A*. This vision is attributed to the disordered mental state of the minister, though we cannot accept even this disclaimer with complete simplicity. This being the night of Governor Winthrop's death, one good old Puritan interprets the portent as *A* for Angel—an observation which has the effect of giving objective support to Dimmesdale's vision.

There is also the ambivalence of the Puritans. It is easy to pass them by too quickly. One's first impression is doubtless, as Hawthorne says elsewhere, of a set of "dismal wretches," but they are more than this. The Puritan code is arrogant, inflexible, overrighteous; and it is remarked of their magistrates and priests that "out of the whole human family, it would not have been easy to select the same number of wise and virtuous persons, who should be less capable of sitting in judgment on an erring woman's heart. . . ." Nevertheless, after finishing *The Scarlet Letter* one might well ask what merely human society would be better. With all its rigors, the ordeal of Hester upon the scaffold is invested with awe by the real seriousness and simplicity of the onlookers. Hawthorne compares the Puritan attitude, and certainly not unfavorably, to "the heartlessness of another social state, which would find only a theme for jest in an exhibition like the present." And it is counted as a virtue that the chief men of the town attend the spectacle without loss of dignity. Without question they take upon themselves more of the judgment of the soul than is fitting for men to assume, but this fault is palliated by their complete sincerity. They are "a people amongst whom religion and law were almost identical, and in whose character both were so thoroughly interfused, that the mildest and the severest acts of public discipline were alike made venerable and awful." By any ideal standard they are greatly lacking, but among erring humans they are, after all, creditable.

Furthermore, the vigor of Hawthorne's abuse of them is not to be taken at face value. They are grim, grisly, stern-browed and unkindly visaged; amid the gaiety of election day "for the space of a single holiday, they appeared scarcely more grave than most other communities at a period of general affliction." In this statement the tone of good-humored mockery is unmistakable. Hawthorne's attacks have something of the quality of a family joke; their roughness comes from thorough and even affectionate understanding. As his excellent critic and son-in-law G. P. Lathrop long ago pointed out, Hawthorne is talking of his own people and in hitting at them is quite conscious that he hits himself.

Finally, the pervasive influence of Hawthorne's style modifies the rigorous and purposeful direction of the action and the accompanying symmetrical ironies. The style is urbane, relaxed, and reposeful and is rarely without some touch of amiable and unaccented humor. This quality varies, of course, with the situation. Hester exposed on the scaffold and Dimmesdale wracked by Chillingworth are not fit subjects for humor. Yet Hawthorne always preserves a measure of distance, even at his most sympathetic. The effect of Hawthorne's prose comes partly from generality, in itself a factor in maintaining distance, as if the author at his most searching chose always to preserve a certain reticence, to keep to what is broadly representative and conceal the personal and particular. Even the most anguished emotion is clothed with decency and measure, and the most painful situations are softened by decorum.

HERMAN MELVILLE

****

Of the numerous studies of Melville, many students find most helpful William Ellery Sedgwick's *Herman Melville: The Tragedy of Mind* (Cambridge, Mass., 1944). Other especially stimulating treatments of his writing include Newton Arvin's *Herman Melville* (New York, 1950; reprinted 1957), Warner Berthoff's *The Example of Melville* (Princeton, N.J., 1962), Richard Chase's *Herman Melville* (New York, 1948), Edgar H. Dryden's *Melville's Thematics of Form: The Great Art of Telling the Truth* (Baltimore, Md., 1968), H. Bruce Franklin's *The Wake of the Gods: Melville's Mythology* (Stanford, Calif., 1963), and Lawrance Thompson's *Melville's Quarrel with God* (Princeton, N.J., 1953). Also useful are Willard Thorp's thoughtful introduction to *Herman Melville: Representative Selections* (New York, 1938), and Leon Howard's meticulous biography, *Herman Melville* (Berkeley, Calif., 1951), the details of which are taken from a day-by-day recording of Melville's life in Jay Leyda's *The Melville Log* (New York, 1951). Some of the better single essays on Melville have been collected by

Hershel Parker in *The Recognition of Herman Melville: Selected Criticism Since 1846* (Ann Arbor, Mich., 1967), and, on his best known novel, by Tyrus Hillway and Luther S. Mansfield in *Moby-Dick: Centennial Essays* (Dallas, Tex., 1953). James E. Miller's carefully devised *A Reader's Guide to Herman Melville* (New York, 1962) is often found useful. C. L. R. James's *Mariners, Renegades, and Castaways* (New York, 1953) presents "The Story of Herman Melville and the World We Live In."

MOBY-DICK: WORK OF ART

Walter E. Bezanson

****

Among those who still read books there are few who do not know at
least the outward adventure of Ishmael, the young whaleman: how he
signed with his South Seas friend, Queequeg, to go aboard the fated *Pequod;* what happened when Captain Ahab enchanted his crew into hunting
down the White Whale "on both sides of land, and over all sides of earth,
till he spouts black blood and rolls fin out"; and how the "god-bullied hull"
of the *Pequod* at last went down before the battering brow of Moby Dick,
who smashed in the ship, sending them all to drown—"O Christ! to think
of the green navies and the green-skulled crews!"—all, that is, but Ishmael,
who lived to tell the tale. Some readers, looking beyond the simpler narrative, take *Moby-Dick* as *vade mecum,* in our peculiarly bedeviled times
searching out what its ethical imperatives may be. Still other readers help to
multiply its influence through scholarship and art; for in addition to shaking

From Moby-Dick, *Centennial Essays,* edited by Tyrus Hillway and Luther S.
Mansfield (Dallas, Tex., 1953). Reprinted by permission of the author and the
Southern Methodist University Press.

down a white snowstorm of books, essays, and commentaries, *Moby-Dick* has inspired fine poems by Hart Crane and W. H. Auden, illustrations by Rockwell Kent and Boardman Robinson, paintings by Gil Wilson, a concerto by Ghedini, several radio dramas, two old-time films of flickering merit (who could forget the anguished, silent groaning of John Barrymore?); and from time to time good artists and directors are tempted to produce a *Moby-Dick* opera, a *Moby-Dick* ballet, and a good (if the temptations could be resisted) *Moby-Dick* movie. Then, too, readers of *Moby-Dick* are almost inevitably drawn to reading something about Melville himself: his memorable Pacific adventures, his immersion in the rich world of books and ideas, his complex spiritual and psychological history, and the nearly unique decline and recovery of his subsequent reputation.

All these matters have their attractions, and will continue to have them. Yet underlying them all is at once a simpler and a more complex attraction—the fact that the book is a work of art, and that it is a work of art of a most unusual sort. Curiously enough, it is precisely here that our reading and scholarship have been least adequate. Interest in *Moby-Dick* as direct narrative, as moral analogue, as modern source, and as spiritual autobiography has far outrun commentary on it as a work of art. A proper criticism of so complex a book will be a long time in the making and will need immense attention from many kinds of critics. In the meantime I am struck by the need just now for contributions toward a relatively impersonal criticism directed at the book itself. The surrounding areas—such as *Moby-Dick* and Melville, *Moby-Dick* and the times in which it was made—are significant just because the book is a work of art. To ask what the book means is to ask what it is about, and to ask what it is about is in turn to ask how art works in the case at hand.

My remarks are therefore in this direction. Beginning with a look at the materials out of which *Moby-Dick* is created, we shall explore the means of activation and some of the forms that contain and define them. The three roadmarks we shall follow are *matter, dynamic,* and *structure.*

I

By *matter* I mean here the subject (or subject matter) in the gross sense. *Moby-Dick* has as its gross subject not Indian fighting or railroad building but whaling.

Any book about mid-nineteenth-century American whaling must in some fashion or other deal with certain phenomena, artifacts, and processes. There they are, and they must be used or the book is not about whaling. A rough inventory of data would include at least the following areas:

NATURAL WORLDS: *The seas and oceans,* covering three-fifths of the globe: on the surface—tides, currents, winds, and weather; under the surface—countless forms of life of extreme diversity. Marine animals of the order *Cetacea,* ranging from small dolphins and porpoises to whales, the largest form of life in earth history (up to 125 tons). The Sperm Whale *(Physeter Macrocephalus)*: one of the larger varieties (up to 75–85 feet), wrapped in a fat blanket (blubber) like other whales but unique in carrying a pool of pure spermaceti oil (up to 500 gallons) in his great square head; protects himself with rows of ivory teeth and the slap of his tail (20 feet across), or dives to the sea bottom; known to attack great objects which threaten him.

HISTORICAL WORLD: *Man,* a prolific, social, land animal constantly in search of animal, mineral, and vegetable resources for survival and use. *Seventeenth century:* discovering the use of whale products, especially the oil for lighting, man begins to bring to bear on the pursuit of whales the technologies developed in transportation and war. *Nineteenth century:* the United States, a newly created and powerfully expanding democracy in the early stages of capitalism, builds a whaling fleet of over seven hundred vessels and commits itself to a sea frontier that girdles the globe. New Bedford, Nantucket, and Sag Harbor become the world centers for the pursuit of sperm whales.

ARTIFACTS: *The whale-ship:* a wooden vessel, length about 105 feet, beam about 28 feet; three vertical masts (foremast, mainmast, mizzenmast), each with four horizontal yards (crosspieces); rigged to the yards more than thirty separate sails, each named for identification. *Nautical equipment:* windlass, capstan, chocks, pins, block and tackle, pumps; lines for handling sails, anchors, cargo. *Navigation equipment:* chronometer, quadrant, compass, charts, log and line, wheel or tiller; for finding location and keeping on course. *Spaces:* below decks two levels of compartments, including forecastle bunkroom for the crew and cabins aft for the captain and mates; storage quarters for food, water, whaling gear, casks, shooks (staves and barrel heads); sail and chain lockers, blubber room, holds for the cargo. *Pursuit equipment:* whaleboats of cedar planking, length 25 feet; plank seats for five oarsmen, platforms bow and stern for harpooner and boatsteerer, five pair of oars, steering oar, harpoons, lances, waif poles (for signal flags), line tubs, assorted gear. *Processing equipment:* try-works (deck furnaces), kettles, forks, spades, mincing knives, etc.

TECHNIQUES: innumerable skills demanded by all artifacts, especially ship and boat handling, maintenance, attack, butchering.

SOCIAL ORGANIZATION: *In the background:* Yankee owners who furnish capital and artifacts for voyages, to whom the products of voyages are returnable for sale at a profit. *In the foreground:* a ship's company of about thirty-five men brought aboard under individual contracts giving each a percentage of the profits (lay) according to his skill with men or artifacts. *The hierarchy,* in descending order of authority: absentee owners; captain, three mates, three harpooners, boat crews, blacksmith, cooper, cook, cabin boy. *Politics:* manhandling.

OBJECT OF VOYAGE: in three or four years' time to sight, chase, kill, and process into oil as many whales as possible, returning to port safely with a profitable cargo.

These are the given elements of whaling as a major industry in nineteenth-century America. They may be thought of as simply existing in nature and experience; we have been thinking of them independent of communication, though they are necessarily written down here. In art, however, communication is the heart of the matter; and the subject of whaling, it chances, offers good historical instances of some planes on which the communication problem may be conceived.

Looking back into nineteenth-century Anglo-American history, we find at least four different levels of communication on whaling. The first was that of the typical whaling logbook. A whaleman's log was a record kept for the owners by the mates or captain; it consisted of daily entries giving the ship's position, weather, landfalls, ships sighted or hailed, whales taken and their size (expressed in barrels of oil), crew desertions, injuries, deaths, etc. What any of this felt like or meant, except in terms of navigation and trade, was purposely excluded. The whaler's log was meant to be an abstraction of group experience in terms of pragmatic ends.

A second level was that of the standard histories. The aim here was the compilation of reliable data on the natural history of the whale (as part of the zoölogical record) or on the happenings in the fishery (as a contribution to economic history). Classic examples of the histories that had wide circulation in the second quarter of the nineteenth century include Thomas Beale's *Natural History of the Sperm Whale* (1835, 1839), Frederick Bennett's *A Whaling Voyage Round the Globe, from the Year 1833 to 1836* (1840), and William Scoresby's *An Account of the Arctic Regions with a History and Description of the Northern Whale Fishery* (1820). Empirical knowledge set the aims and limits for such books as these, too; their meaning and function were conditioned by the rise of the life sciences and of inductive historiography.

A third level of communication was the simple transcription of generalized personal experience. Americans who had never been whaling were interested to know something of the representative experiences of the seventeen thousand men engaged in the American fisheries in the 1840s. So came the reports of scenes and adventures, of duties and dangers, in books like J. Ross Browne's *Etchings of a Whaling Cruise* (1846) and the Reverend Henry Cheever's *The Whale and His Captors; or the Whaleman's Adventures and the Whale's Biography* . . . (1849). Such books were records of outward experience to whose general validity any ex-whaleman could testify. They were the journalism of the whaling industry, written by the Lowell Thomases and John Gunthers of the day (or perhaps one should say *Jonah* Gunthers, as no doubt he would have called his book *Inside the Whale*).

A generous distance beyond these logbooks, histories, and personal narratives lies the problem of fiction. When Melville was composing *Moby-Dick* in 1850 and 1851 he did not hesitate to make quite shameless use of all the books just named, as well as others, in the preparation of his own. Reading for facts and events, for recall and extension, he took on an enormous cargo of whaling matter. But facts are not fiction. In *Moby-Dick* the inert matter of whaling has been subjected to the purposes of art through a dynamic and a structure.

II

By the term "dynamic" I mean the action of forces on bodies at rest. The whaling matter in *Moby-Dick* is in no sense at rest, excepting as here or there occurs a failure in effect. For the most part the stuff and data of whaling are complexly subject to the action of a force which can be defined and illustrated. So too is the whole narrative base of the book, which is something far more than a record of what anyone aboard the *Pequod* would agree had happened. There is a dynamic operating on both matter and narrative which distinguishes *Moby-Dick* from logs, journals, and histories.

One of two forces, or their combination, is commonly assumed to provide the dynamic of *Moby-Dick*. The first, of course, is Captain Ahab, the dark protagonist, the maimed king of the quarter-deck whose monomania flows out through the ship until it drowns his men—mind and (finally) body. That he is the dominant "character" and the source of "action" seems obvious. The reader's image of him is a lasting one. Is Ahab the dynamic?

The alternative force, it is commonly assumed, is Moby Dick himself, that particular white "spouting fish with a horizontal tail" about whom legend and murmured lore have woven enchantments, so that he looms a massive phantom in the restless dreams of the *Pequod's* captain and crew. His name gives the novel its title. He is prime antagonist of the tale. Is Moby Dick the dynamic?

Both these interpretations have their uses, especially when taken together in a subject-predicate relation. But there is a third point of view from which neither Ahab nor the White Whale is the central dynamic, and I find it both compelling and rewarding, once recognized. This story, this fiction, is not so much about Ahab or the White Whale as it is about Ishmael, and I propose that it is he who is the real center of meaning and the defining force of the novel.

The point becomes clearer when one realizes that in *Moby-Dick* there are two Ishmaels, not one. The first Ishmael is the enfolding sensibility of the novel, the hand that writes the tale, the imagination through which all matters of the book pass. He is the narrator. But who then is the other Ishmael? The second Ishmael is not the narrator, not the informing presence, but is the young man of whom, among others, narrator Ishmael tells us in his story. He is simply one of the characters in the novel, though to be sure a major one whose significance is possibly next to Ahab's. This is forecastle Ishmael or the younger Ishmael of "some years ago." There is no question here of dual personality or *alter ego,* such as really exists, for instance, in Poe's "William Wilson" or Conrad's "The Secret Sharer." Narrator Ishamel is merely young Ishmael grown older. He is the man who has already experienced all that we watch forecastle Ishmael going through as the story is told.

The distinction can be rendered visual by imagining, for a moment, a film version of the novel. As the screen lights up and the music drops to an obbligato we look on the face of narrator Ishmael (a most marvelous face, I should judge), and the magic intonation begins:

> Call me Ishmael. Some years ago—never mind how long precisely—having little or no money in my purse, and nothing particular to interest me on shore, I thought I would sail about a little and see the watery part of the world. It is a way I have of driving off the spleen, and regulating the circulation. Whenever I find myself . . . .

And as the cadenced voice goes on, the face of the Ishmael who has a tale to tell fades out, the music takes up a brisk piping air, and whom should we see tripping along the cobbled streets of New Bedford, carpetbag in hand, but forecastle Ishmael. It is a cold winter's night, and this lonely young man is in search of lodgings. For very soon now he plans to go a-whaling.

Meanwhile we hear the voice, always the magic voice, not of the boy we watch with our eyes, but of one who long since went aboard the *Pequod,* was buried in the sea and resurrected from it. This voice recounts the coming adventures of young Ishmael as a story already fully experienced. Experienced, but not fully understood; for as he explicitly says: "It was the whiteness of the whale that above all things appalled me. But how can I hope to explain myself here; and yet, in some dim, random way, explain myself I must, else all these chapters might be naught." So we are reminded by shifts of tense from time to time that while forecastle Ishmael is busy hunting whales narrator Ishmael is sifting memory and imagination in search of the many meanings of the dark adventure he has experienced. So deeply are we under the spell of the narrator's voice that when at last the final incantation begins—" 'And I only am escaped alone to tell thee'. . . . The drama's done. . . ."—then at last, as forecastle Ishmael floats out of the *Pequod's* vortex, saved, we look again on the face of Ishmael narrator. And we realize that for many hours he has been sitting there and has never once moved, except at the lips; sitting in profound reverie, yet talking, trying to explain "in some dim, random way" what happened, for "explain myself I must."

The distinction between the function of the two Ishmaels is clear. Yet is would be a mistake to separate them too far in temperament. Certainly young Ishmael is no common sailor thoughtlessly enacting whatever the fates throw his way. He is a pondering young man of strong imagination and complex temperament; he will, as it were, become the narrator in due time. But right now he is aboard the *Pequod* doing his whaleman's work and trying to survive the spell of Ahab's power. The narrator, having survived, is at his desk trying to explain himself to himself and to whoever will listen. The primary use of the distinction is to bring the narrator forward as the essential sensibility in terms of which all characters and events of the fiction are conceived and evaluated. The story is his. What, then, are some of his primary commitments of mind and imagination as he shapes his story through one hundred and thirty-five chapters?

As a lover of laughter and hilarity, Ishmael delights in the incongruities. Of whales, for instance: whales spout steam because they think so much; they have no nose, but don't really need one—there are no violets in the sea; they are very healthy, and this is because they get so much exercise and are always out of doors, though rarely in the fresh air; and they like to breakfast on "sailor tarts, that is whaleboats full of mariners." Ishmael has too a deep belly laugh for the crudities and obscenities that mark the life of animal man, making much more than is proper of some talk about gentlemen harpooning ladies, relishing a Rabelaisian remark about "head winds" versus "winds from astern," and penning a memorable canonization of a rarely discussed part of the anatomy in "The Cassock." But as a purveyor of the "genial, desperado philosophy," his most characteristic humor is that of the hyena laugh: he begins his tale with a mock confession of suicidal impulses; he sends young Ishmael running to his bunk after his first encounter with a whale to make out his will; he reports that some sailors are so neat that they wouldn't think of drowning "without first washing their faces"; and he delights in Queequeg's solemn decision, when he seems mortally ill, whereby the good savage suddenly "recalled a little duty ashore, which he was leaving undone; and therefore. . . changed his mind about dying." Beneath Ishmael's mask of hypochondria is the healthy grimace of a man who stands braced to accept "the universal thump" and to call out: "Who ain't a slave?" To Ishmael "a good laugh is a mighty good thing, and rather too scarce a good thing; the more's the pity."

As narrator Ishmael betrays a passion for all faraway places and things, "Patagonian sights and sounds," imagined cities, fabled heroes, the sepulchers of kings. His rich imagination is stirred by all that is secret, mysterious, and undecipherable in the great riddles of mankind. He both cherishes and mocks the great systems of the philosophers, the operations of "chance, free will, and necessity," the great religions and heresies of the past. His fascination with ancient lore and wisdom runs from Adam to Zoroaster; to help him tell his tale he marshals the great mythic figures of past centuries and all black-letter commentaries thereon.

His temperament is complex. If one of its facets, that of the "Sub-Sub-Librarian," has an antiquarian glint, another glows with the love of action. Each cry from the masthead alerts him from dreamy speculations to the zest of the hunt. Every lowering away starts his blood pounding. He is a superb narrator of the frenzied strivings of the boat crew as they press in for the kill, chanting their terror and competence as they enter "the charmed, churned circle" of eternity. When the death-deed is done, when the whirl slowly widens, he takes up the song of dismemberment. For the weapons of the chase, the red tools of slaughter, the facts of procedure, he has an insatiable curiosity. Cutting in, trying out, stowing down—the whole butcher-slab routine of processing the dead whale he endows with ritual certainty, transforming dirty jobs into acts of ceremonial dignity. Ishmael's voice translates the laughter and wild deeds of the bloody crew into the ordered rites of primitive tribal priests.

Narrator Ishmael has an instinct for the morally and psychologically intricate. He presses close in after the intertwinings of good and evil, tracks down the baffling crisscross of events and ideas, ponders their ambiguities and inversions. He is keen for a paradox and quick to see polarities—so keen in fact that the whole experience seems a double vision of what is at once noble and vile, of all that is lovely and appalling. This two-fold sensitivity marks his probings into the life-images of those he has known—whether in his grand-scale exposition of the "ungodly, god-like man, Captain Ahab" or in the compassionate recollection of little Pip, for a time lost overboard in the "heartless immensity" of the sea, and gone divinely mad from it. Whether noting that Queequeg's tomahawk-pipe "both brained his foes and soothed his soul" or contemplating "the interlinked terrors and wonders of God," he turns the coin both ways. He makes it a crisis of the first order that young Ishmael, both a brooder and a good companion, was drawn with the rest of the crew by the dark magnetic pull of the captain's monomania, wavering between allegiance to that uncommon king—Ahab— and to "the kingly commons"—the crew. Only the traumatic revulsion on the night of "The Try-Works" saved young Ishmael—"a strange (and ever since inexplicable) thing" which the narrator now explains symbolically: "Give not thyself up, then, to fire, lest it invert thee, deaden thee; as for the time it did me."

Above all one notes the narrator's inexhaustible sense of wonder. Wonder at the wide Pacific world, with its eternal undulations; wonder at the creatures of the deep; wonder at man—dreamer, doer, doubter. To him in retrospect the whale has become a mighty analogue of the world, of man, of God. He is in awe before the whale: its massive bulk, tiny eyes, great mouth, white teeth; its narrow throat and cavernous belly; the spout; the hump; the massed buttress of its domed head; the incomparable power and magic of its fanning, delicate tail. It is wonder that lies at the center of Ishmael's scale of articulation, and the gamut runs out either way toward fear and worship.

Enough of evocation. Every reader of *Moby-Dick* can and will want to enlarge and subtilize the multiple attributes of Ishmael. The prime experience for the reader is the narrator's unfolding sensibility. With it we have an energy center acting outward on the inert matter of nature and experience, releasing its possiblities for art. Whereas forecastle Ishmael drops in and out of the narrative with such abandon that at times a reader wonders if he has fallen overboard, the Ishmael voice is there every moment from the genesis of the fiction in "Call me Ishmael" to the final revelation of the "Epilogue" when "The drama's done." It is the narrator who creates the microcosm and sets the terms of discourse.

But this Ishmael is only Melville under another name, is he not? My suggestion is that we resist any one-to-one equation of Melville and Ishmael. Even the "Melville-Ishmael" phrase, which one encounters in critical discussions, though presumably granting a distinction between autobiography and fiction, would seem to be only a more insistent confusion of the point at stake unless the phrase is defined to mean either Melville or Ishmael, not both. For in the process of composition, even when the artist knowingly begins with his own experience, there are crucial interventions between the act that was experience and the re-enactment that is art—intrusions of time, of intention, and especially of form, to name only a few. Which parts of Ishmael's experience and sensibility coincide with Melville's own physical and psychological history and in just what ways is a question which is initially only tangential to discussion of *Moby-Dick* as a completed work of art.

III

But what of structure? That there is a dynamic excitation in *Moby-Dick* sympathetic readers have not denied. Is the effect of Ishmael's energy, then, simply to fling the matter in all directions, bombarding the reader with the accelerated particles of his own high-speed imagination? Is Ishmael's search for "some dim, random way" to explain himself not merely a characterization of the complexity of his task but also a confession of his inadequacy to find form? The questions are crucial, for although readers will presumably go on reading *Moby-Dick* whichever way they are answered, the critical reader will not be encouraged to keep coming back unless he can "see" and "feel" the tension of controlling forces.

To an extraordinary extent Ishmael's revelation of sensibility is controlled by rhetoric. Throughout the tale linguistic versatility and subtle rhythmic patterns exploit sound and sense with high calculation. Almost at random one chooses a sentence: "And ever, as the white moon shows her affrighted face from the steep gullies in the blackness overhead, aghast Jonah sees the rearing bowsprit pointing high upward, but soon beat downward again towards the tormented deep." It is a successful if traditional piece of incantation with its rising and falling movements manipulated to bring a striking force on the qualitative word "aghast." Its mood is typically Gothic-romantic (pictorial equivalents would be certain passages from Poe or the sea-paintings of Ryder), but structurally its allegiance is to the spacious prose of the seventeenth century. Although the passage is from Father Mapple's sermon, it is in no way unrepresentative; there are scores of sentences throughout *Moby-Dick* of equal or greater rhetorical interest.

Of the narrative's several levels of rhetoric the simplest is a relatively straightforward *expository* style characteristic of many passages scattered through the cetological accounts. But it is significant that such passages are rarely sustained, and serve chiefly as transitions between more complex levels of expression. Thus a series of expository sentences in the central paragraph of the chapter on "Cutting In" comes to this point: "This done, a broad, semicircular line is cut round the hole, the hook is inserted, and the main body of the crew striking up a wild chorus, now commence heaving in one dense crowd at the windlass." Whether it cannot or will not, Ishmael's sensibility does not endure for long so bare a diction: "When instantly, the entire ship careens over on her side; every bolt in her starts like the nailheads of an old house in frosty weather; she trembles, quivers, and nods her frighted mastheads to the sky." The tension is maintained through a following sentence, strict exposition returns in the next, and the paragraph concludes with an emotionally and grammatically complex sentence which begins with exposition, rises to a powerful image of whale flesh hoisted aloft where "the prodigious blood-dripping mass sways to and fro as if let down from the sky," and concludes with a jest about getting one's ears boxed unless he dodges the swing of the bloody mess. Even in the rhetorically duller chapters of exposition it is a rare paragraph over which heat lightning does not flicker.

A second level of rhetoric, the *poetic,* is well exemplified in Ahab's soliloquy after the great scene on the quarter-deck. As Matthiessen has shown, such a passage can easily be set as blank verse:

> I leave a white and turbid wake;
> Pale waters, paler cheeks, where'er I sail.
> The envious billows sidelong swell to whelm
> My track; let them; but first I pass.

Because the rhythms here play over an abstract metrical pattern, as in poetry, they are evenly controlled—too evenly perhaps for prose, and the tone seems "literary."

Quite different in effect is a third level of rhetoric, the *idiomatic.* Like the poet it occurs rather rarely in a pure form, but we have an instance in Stubb's rousing exordium to his crew:

> "Pull, pull, my fine hearts-alive; pull, my children; pull, my little ones . . . Why don't you break your backbones, my boys? . . . Easy, easy; don't be in a hurry—don't be in a hurry. Why don't you snap your oars, you rascals? Bite something, you dogs! . . ."

Here the beat of oars takes the place of the metronomic meter and allows more freedom. The passage is a kind of rowing song and hence is exceptional; yet it is related in tone and rhythm to numerous pieces of dialogue and sailor talk, especially to the consistently excellent idiom of both Stubb and young Ishmael.

One might venture a fourth level of rhetoric, the *composite,* simply to assure the inclusion of the narrator's prose at its very best. The composite is a magnificent blending of the expository, the poetic, the idiomatic, and whatever other elements tend to escape these crude categories:

> The Nantucketer, he alone resides and riots on the sea; he alone, in Bible language, goes down to it in ships; to and fro plough-

ing it as his own special plantation. *There* is his home; *there* lies his business, which a Noah's flood would not interrupt, though it overwhelmed all the millions in China. He lives on the sea, as prairie cocks in the prairie; he hides among the waves, he climbs them as chamois hunters climb the Alps. For years he knows not the land; so that when he comes to it at last, it smells like another world, more strangely than the moon would to an Earthsman. With the landless gull, that at sunset folds her wings and is rocked to sleep between billows; so at nightfall, the Nantucketer, out of sight of land, furls his sails, and lays him to his rest, while under his very pillow rush herds of walruses and whales.

The passage is a great one, blending high and low with a relaxed assurance; after shaking free from the literary constrictions of the opening lines, it comes grandly home. And how does it relate to event and character? Ishmael's memory of the arrival at Nantucket, a mere incident in the movement of the plot, is to Ishmael now an imaginative experience of high order; and this we must know if we are to know about Ishmael. The whole chapter, "Nantucket," is a prose poem in the barbaric jocular vein, and it is as valuable a part of the documentation of Ishmael's experience as are the great "scenes." It is less extraneous to the meaning of the book than are many of the more average passages about Captain Ahab. The same could be said for other great passages of rhetoric, such as the marvelous hymn to spiritual democracy midway in "Knights and Squires." The first level of structure in *Moby-Dick* is the interplay of pressure and control through extraordinarily high rhetorical effects.

Beneath the rhetoric, penetrating through it, and in a sense rising above it, is a play of symbolic forms which keeps the rhetoric from dropping into exercise or running off in pyrotechnics. The persistent tendency in *Moby-Dick* is for facts, events, and images to become symbols. Ahab makes the most outright pronouncement of the doctrine of correspondences on which such a tendency depends, and to which almost all characters in the book are committed: "O Nature, and O soul of man! how far beyond all utterance are your linked analogies! not the smallest atom stirs or lives on matter, but has its cunning duplicate in mind." No less sensitive to symbolic values than Ahab is the young Ishmael in the forecastle. It is he who unfolds moral analogues from the mat-making, from the monkey-rope, from squeezing the case. He resembles Ahab in his talent for taking situations "strongly and metaphysically."

So on down the roster of the crew, where symbols and superstitions blend. Can there be any doubt that it is above all the enfolding imagination of the narrator which sets and defines the symbolic mode that pervades the entire book? From the richly emblematic theme of "meditation and water" in the opening chapter, to the final bursting of the "black bubble" of the sea which releases young Ishmael, the narrator sets the symbolic as the primary mode of self-examination and communication. He is predisposed to see events, however incidental, as "the sign and symbol" of something larger. To Ishmael "some certain significance lurks in all things, else all things are little worth, and the round world itself but an empty cipher. . . ."

Most commonly the symbols begin with a generative object: a waif-pole, a coin, a compass needle, a right-whale's head. The symbolic events begin with a chance incident: the dropping of his speaking trumpet by the Captain of the *Goney* (the nameless future), finding ambergris in a blasted whale (unexpected sweetness at the core of corruption), the chasing of the *Pequod* by Malay pirates (the pursuer pursued). Both give the tale solidity, for the objects and events are objects and events before they become meanings. But all the symbols do not rise out of tangible referents. We have to take into account also the narrator's love for "a furious trope" which often far exceeds the simple metaphorical function of comparison; the thing to which analogy is made—a pyramid, an elephant, a Leyden jar, a bird, a mythic figure—may itself enter the circle of symbolic values through recurrent reference. Thus the imagery brings scope to the limited range of symbols available on board the *Pequod*. Whereas the object-symbols in a sense carry the "plot," elucidating the experience of young Ishmael, Ahab, the mates and crew (as well as serving the narrator), the image-symbols chiefly reveal the psyche of the narrator through images of procreation and animality, mechanization and monomania, enchantment and entombment.

Though simpler objects, events, or images may connote primarily some one thing, as a shark means rapacious evil, most symbols which Ishmael develops in his narration express a complex of meanings which cannot easily be reduced to paraphrase and are not finally statable in other than their own terms. So it is with the *Pequod* herself and the ships she passes, with the root metaphors of earth, air, fire, and water which proliferate so subtly; and so it is with the most dynamic word-image-symbol of the tale: "white" (or "whiteness"). Their meanings are not single but multiple; not precisely equatable but ambiguous; not more often reinforcing than contradictory. The symbolism in *Moby-Dick* is not static but is in motion; it is in process of creation for both narrator and reader. Value works back and forth: being extracted from objects, it descends into the consciousness; spiraling up from the consciousness, it envelops objects.

Symbolism is so marked a characteristic of the narrator's microcosm that it is possible to phrase Ahab's tragedy not only in moral, social, and psychological terms, but in "structural" terms as well. Clearly Ahab accepts the symbolic as a source of cognition and of ethics. It was a symbolic vision that brought him on his quest, as no one senses with stronger discomfort than Starbuck, who stands alone in his sturdy, limited world of facts and settled faith. Yet the tragedy of Ahab is not his great gift for symbolic perception, but his abandonment of it. Ahab increasingly reduces all pluralities to the singular. His unilateral reading of events and things becomes a narrow translation in the imperative mood. Unlike young Ishmael, who is his equal in sensitivity but his inferior in will and authority, Ahab walls off his receptiveness to the complexities of experience, replacing "could be" or "might be" with "must." His destruction follows when he substitutes an allegorical fixation for the world of symbolic potentialities.

Ishmael's predilection for keying his narrative in the symbolic mode suggests another aspect of structure. *Moby-Dick* lies close to the world of dreams. We find the narrator recalling at length a remembered dream of his childhood. Stubb attempts a long dream-analysis to Flask after he has been kicked by Ahab. It is not strange, then, that young Ishmael's moment of greatest crisis, the night of the try-works when he is at the helm, should be of a traumatic order. More subtly, numerous incidents of the narrative are bathed in a dream aura: the trancelike idyll of young Ishmael at the masthead, the hallucinatory vision of the spirit spout, the incredible appearance on board of the devil himself accompanied by "five dusky phantoms," and many others. The narrator's whole effort to communicate the timeless, spaceless concept of "The Whiteness of the Whale" is an act of dream analysis. "Whether it was a reality or a dream, I never could entirely settle," says the narrator of his childhood dream; and so it was with much of what occurred aboard the *Pequod*. Ishmael's tale is to be listened to in terms of a tradition that runs from Revelation to *Finnegan's Wake*. Dream sense is an important mood in *Moby-Dick;* and dream form, to the extent there is such a verbal form, is an incipient structural device of the book. At regular intervals the narrator, in his intense effort to explain himself, resorts to a brief passage in which there is a flashing concentration of symbols that hold for a moment and then disappear. It is a night device for rendering daytime experience, and in *Moby-Dick* it happens again and again.

Any rigorous definition of structure must lead us on to consider the nature and relation of the constituent parts. Since the tale is divided into "parts" by the narrator himself (135 chapters, plus prefatory materials and "Epilogue"), one cannot escape considering the extent to which individual chapters themselves are structural units. We shall have to pass over such chapters, probably the largest group, as are devoted to the movement of narrative or to character analysis; the form here falls in a general way within the customary patterns of novelistic structure. Two chapter forms, however, are sufficiently non-novelistic to invite comment, the first of these being the dramatic. The term "dramatic" is here used in a technical, not qualitative sense, and refers to such devices of the playwright's script as italicized stage directions, set speeches with the speaker named in capitals, straight soliloquies, and dialogue without commentary. More than a tenth of the chapters are in this sense dramatic, some ten having strictly dramatic form without narrative intrusion, and another half-dozen or so using some script devices along with the narrative. The most successful of the strict-form group is certainly "Midnight, Forecastle," a ballet-like scene which superbly objectifies the crew in drunken exaltation over the quest. But the two greatest are in the second group. "The Quarter-Deck," Ishmael's curtain-raising treatment of the quest theme, is a triumph of unified structure, conceived with extreme firmness and precision of detail. The powerful dramatic structure of the chapter—prologue, antiphonal choral address, formal individual debate, and group ceremonial—is a superb invention on free-traditional lines, unhampered by stage techniques yet profiting from them. The other great dramatic scene, a counterpart to "The Quarter-Deck" both thematically and structurally, is the massive Ahab-and-his-crew scene late in the book, "The Candles." The chapter is not so firmly conceived as its forerunner; and this, rather than its subject matter, is what brings it dangerously close to seeming overwrought and a bit out of hand. The key to the structure here lies in the narrator's word "tableau," a dramatic device of considerable currency in nineteenth-century America. As the primary symbols of fire and whiteness melt hotly into each other for the first time, we see a series of memorable tableaux lit by storm lightning and corposant flames between "intervals of profound darkness." The piece is a series of blinding kaleidoscopic flashes which reveal the alarmed mates, the primitives in their full demonic strength, Ahab in a fury of ritual power. The "enchanted" crew, which near this same quarter-deck had made its jubilant pledge, now hangs from the rigging "like a knot of numbed wasps"; and when Ahab brandishes his burning harpoon among them (an unstated completion of the image), "the mariners did run from him in a terror of dismay." The two chapters, "The Quarter-Deck" and "The Candles," are twin centers of gravity in ordering the structure of the Ahab theme. The two fields of force are possibility and necessity, and Ahab's shift is from initial ecstasy to final frenetic compulsiveness.

A second unusual element of chapter structure in *Moby-Dick* grows out of the sermon form. Most famously there is Father Mapple's sermon (chapter ix), a piece of sustained eloquence in the idiomatic-composite style. From his *text* in Jonah the old sailor-preacher moves at once to two *doctrines* (the Christian pattern of sin and repentance, and the hardness of obeying God); enters a highly imaginative narrative *explication* of the Biblical story; comes next to *applications* and *uses* (that the congregation shall take Jonah as "a model for repentance" and the preacher shall "preach the Truth to the face of Falsehood"); and concludes with an *exhortation* (the very subtly constructed incantation on the double-themed coda of Woe and Delight). Somewhat buried away in another chapter, "Stubb's Supper," is the shorter sermon in which Fleece, the Negro cook, one night preaches to the sharks in a seriocomic vein. As he peers over the *Pequod's* side with his lantern at the murderous feasting down below, Fleece addresses his "congregation" first as "Fellow-critters," then as "Belubed fellow-critters," and finally as "Cussed fellow-critters," the final imprecation sharpening Fleece's ominous doctrine that "all angel is not'ing more dan de shark well goberned." The structural pattern, especially in its repetitive address, is clearly derived from the folk tradition of the Negro sermon.

These are not the only two "sermons" in *Moby-Dick*. Although the free essay tradition from Montaigne to Hazlitt provides a more comfortable prototype for the more loosely ordered speculative chapters, most of these have a prophetic or protestant vein that pulls them over toward the sermon tradition. Again and again throughout the narrative a chapter comes to its climax in a final paragraph of moral exhortation (Mapple) or imprecation (Fleece). Nor should we forget that young Ishmael's crisp moral analogues (above) start with symbols and end as parables. It is especially interesting to note that some of the cetological chapters can be analyzed in terms of sermon structure. In "The Line," for instance, the narrator takes hemp for his text, makes a full-scale explication of its history and uses, gives admonitions on its subtleties and dangers, and concludes with a full-scale application of the doctrine that "All men live enveloped in whale-lines." In "The Blanket" the text is whale blubber; and preacher Ishmael comes inevitably to the doctrine of internal temperatures, raising it to a high exhortation (Mapple) and then cutting it down with three lines of wry counterstatement (Fleece). Nor is it hard to identify text, inferences, uses, doctrine, and admonition in the brief "sermon" the narrator preaches over the peeled white body of a whale in "The Funeral." The technique lies midway between the Protestant sermon of the nineteenth century and the tradition of the digressive-antiquarian essay.

Coming to the problem of the mutual relation of the chapters in *Moby-Dick,* we can observe several tendencies, of which *chapter sequences* is one. The simplest sequence is likely to be one of narrative progression, as in "The Chapel," "The Pulpit," and "The Sermon," or in the powerful concluding sequence on "The Chase": "First Day," "Second Day," "Third Day." Or we get chapter sequences of theme, as in the three chapters on whale paintings. Or again sequences of structural similarity: the five chapters beginning with "The Quarter-Deck" all use dramatic techniques, as do the four beginning with "The Candles." More typical than strict sequences, however, are the *chapter clusters* in which two or three (or five or six) chapters are linked by themes or root images, other chapters intervening. For example, chapters xlii, li, lii, and lix make a loose cluster that begins with "The Whiteness of the Whale" and carries through the white apparitions in "The Spirit-Spout," "The Albatross," and "Squid." Similarly, later in the narrative, fine imagery becomes dominant, breaking out in young Ishmael's fire-dream ("The Try-Works") and running intermittently until the holocaust of Ahab's defiance ("The Candles"). In addition to sequences and clusters there are also widely separated *balancing chapters,* either of opposites ("Loomings" and the "Epilogue") or of similars ("The Quarter-Deck" and "The Candles"); here the problem is infinitely complex, for the balancing units shift according to the standard of comparison: theme, event, root image, structure, and so forth. Two points can be made in tentative summary of this complex aspect of structure: there are definable relations between any given chapter and some other chapter or chapters; and these relations tend to be multiple and shifting. Like the symbols, the chapters are "in process."

Looking beyond chapter units and their interrelations we find the most obvious larger structural effect in the narrative line of the book, such as it is, which records the preparations for going on board, leaving port, encountering adventures, and meeting some final consequence. Along this simple linear form of The Voyage occur two sets of events: the whale killings and the ship meetings. The question is whether either of these event groups performs more for the structure than the simple functions of marking the passage of time and adding "interest." Of the whale pursuits and killings some ten or more are sufficiently rendered to become events. They begin when the narrative is already two-fifths told and end with the final lowerings for Moby Dick during which the killers are themselves killed. The first lowering and the three-day chase are thus events which enclose all the whaling action of the novel as well as what Howard Vincent has aptly called "the cetological center," and the main point I wish to make about the pursuits is that in each case a killing provokes either a chapter sequence or a chapter cluster of cetological lore growing out of the circumstances of the particular killing. The killings in themselves, except for the first and last, are not so much narrative events as structural occasions for ordering the whaling essays and sermons. Their minimized role is proof enough, if any were needed, that Ishmael's tale is not primarily a series of whaling adventures.

Much more significant structurally than the killings is the important series of ship meetings also occurring along the time line of the voyage. The nine gams of the *Pequod* are important in several ways, of which three might concern us here. First of all, even a glance at the numbers of the chapters in which the gams occur shows a clear pattern: the first two are close together; the central group are well spaced (separated by an average of twelve chapters, with not very wide divergences); the last two are close together. The spatial pattern looks like this:

1 2   3   4   5   6   7   8 9

This somewhat mechanical pattern is a stiffening element in the structure of the book, a kind of counterforce, structurally, to the organic relationship of parts we have been observing. The gams are bones to the book's flesh. Secondly, their sequence is meaningful in terms of the Ahab theme. The line of Ahab's response from ship to ship is a psychograph of his monomania showing the rising curve of his passion and diagraming his moral hostility. The points on the graph mark off the furiously increasing distance between Ahab and the world of men. And thirdly, their individual meanings are a part of the Ishmael theme. Each ship is a scroll which the narrator unrolls and reads, like a prophet called to a king's court. They provide what Auden calls "types of the relation of human individuals and societies in the tragic mystery of existence," though his superbly incisive reading of each type is perhaps too narrowly theological and does scant justice to either the tone of the episodes (are not the *Jungfrau* and *Rosebud* accounts hilariously comic and ironic?) or their rich amplitude of meanings. The ships the *Pequod* passes may be taken as a group of metaphysical parables, a series of biblical analogues, a masque of the situations confronting man, a pageant of the humors within men, a parade of the nations, and so forth, *as well as* concrete and symbolic ways of thinking about the White Whale. Any single systematic treatment of all of the ships does violence to some of them. The gams are symbolic, not allegorical.

It is time in fact to admit that our explorations of structure suggest elaborate interrelations of the parts but do not lead to an overreaching formal pattern. For the reader predisposed to feel that "form" means "classical form," with a controlling geometric structure, *Moby-Dick* is and will remain an aesthetically unsatisfying experience. One needs only to compare it with *The Scarlet Letter,* published a year and a half earlier, to see how nonclassical it is. If this is the sort of standard by which one tries to judge *Moby-Dick,* he will end by dismissing it as one of the more notable miscarriages in the history of literary lying-in. But surely there is no one right form the novel must take—not the one used by Hawthorne, not even the form, one might wryly add, perfected by James. For Hawthorne the structural frame of reference was neoclassical; for Melville it was romantic.

To go from *The Scarlet Letter* to *Moby-Dick* is to move from the Newtonian world-as-machine to the Darwinian world-as-organism. In the older cosmology the key concepts had been law, balance, harmony, reason;

in the newer, they became origin, process, development, growth. Concurrently biological images arose to take the place of the older mechanical analogies: growing plants and life forms now symbolized cosmic ultimates better than a watch or the slow-turning rods and gears of an eighteenth-century orrery. It is enough for our purposes to note that the man who gave scientific validity to the organic world view concluded the key chapter of his great book, *The Origin of Species,* with an extended image of "the great Tree of Life . . . with its ever branching and beautiful ramifications." It was a crucial simile that exploited not the tree but the tree's growth.

Of course the poets had been there first. Coleridge had long since made his famous definition of organic form in literature. The roots of his theory had traveled under the sea to the continent of Emerson, Thoreau, and Whitman (as Matthiessen brilliantly showed in *American Renaissance),* where they burst into native forms in the minds of a few men haunted simultaneously by the implications of the American wilderness, by the quest for spiritual reality, and by the search for new literary forms. *Moby-Dick* is like Emerson's *Essays* and *Poems,* like *Walden,* like *Leaves of Grass,* in its structural principles. In the literature of the nineteenth century it is the single most ambitious projection of the concept of organic form.

Recharting our explorations we can see now where we have been. The matter of *Moby-Dick* is the organic land-sea world where life forms move mysteriously among the elements. The dynamic of the book is the organic mind-world of Ishmael whose sensibility rhythmically agitates the flux of experience. The controlling structure of the book is an organic complex of rhetoric, symbols, and interfused units. There is no over-reaching formal pattern of literary art on which *Moby-Dick* is a variation. To compare it with the structure of the Elizabethan play, or the classical epic, or the modern novel is to set up useful analogies rather than congruous models. It is a free form that fuses as best it can innumerable devices from many literary traditions, including contemporary modes of native expression. In the last analysis, if one must have a prototype, here is an intensively heightened rendition of the logs, journals, and histories of the Anglo-American whaling tradition.

Organic form is not a particular form but a structural principle. In *Moby-Dick* this principle would seem to be a peculiar quality of making and unmaking itself as it goes. The method of the book is unceasingly genetic, conveying the effect of a restless series of morphic-amorphic movements. Ishmael's narrative is always in process and in all but the most literal sense remains unfinished. For the good reader the experience of *Moby-Dick* is a participation in the act of creation. Find a key word or metaphor, start to pick it as you would a wild flower, and you will find yourself ripping up the whole forest floor. Rhetoric grows into symbolism and symbolism into structure; then all falls away and begins over again.

Ishmael's way of explaining himself in the long run is not either "dim" or "random." He was committed to the organic method with all its possibilities and risks. As he says at the beginning of one chapter: "There are some enterprises in which a careful disorderliness is the true method." And at the beginning of another chapter we have an explicit image whose full force as a comment on method needs to be recognized: "Out of the trunk, the branches grow; out of them, the twigs. So, in productive subjects, grow the chapters."

IV

From our considerations of *Moby-Dick* a few simple, debatable propositions emerge. More accurately they are, I suppose, the assumptions which underlie what has been said. The first is that *nature,* ultimately, is chaos. Whatever order it has in the mind of God, its meaning is apparent to man only through some more or less systematic ordering of what seems to be there. The second is that *experience* is already one remove from nature; filtered through a sensibility, nature begins to show patterns qualified by the temperament and the culture of the observer. And the third is that *art,* which is twice removed from nature, is a major means for transforming experience into patterns that are meaningful and communicable. As in part it is the function of religion to shape experience for belief and conduct, and of science to organize nature for use and prediction, so it is the business of art to form man's experience of nature for communication. In art the way a thing is said is what is being said. To the maker the form is completion; to the receiver it is possibility. Art is an enabling act for mankind without which life may easily become meager, isolated; with it the mind can be cleared and the spirit refreshed; through it memory and desire are rewoven.

The great thing about fiction, which is simply the telling of a story in written words, is that it is fiction. That it is "made up" is not its weakness but, as with all art, its greatest strength. In the successful work of fiction certain kinds of possibilities, attitudes, people, acts, situations, necessities, for the first and last time exist. They exist only through form. So it is with *Moby-Dick*—Ishmael's vast symbolic prose-poem in a free organic form. From *olim erat* to *finis* is all the space and time there is.

WALT WHITMAN

****

Whitman's life and personal peculiarities have been variously interpreted, probably with best balanced judgment in Gay Wilson Allen's *The Solitary Singer* (New York, 1955). Frederick Schyberg's *Walt Whitman* (New York, 1951) and Roger Asselineau's *The Evolution of Walt Whitman* (Cambridge, Mass., 1960) contain interesting psychological interpretations of Whitman's life, but also, especially the latter, excellent criticism of his writing; his social thought is examined in Newton Arvin's *Whitman* (New York, 1938). Richard Chase's *Walt Whitman Reconsidered* (New York, 1955) speaks freshly and with original insight of Whitman as a comic. The symposium *Leaves of Grass One Hundred Years After,* edited by Milton Hindus (New York, 1955), contains interpretations by William Carlos Williams, Leslie A. Fiedler, and Kenneth Burke. *The Presence of Walt Whitman,* edited by R. W. B. Lewis (New York, 1962), includes essays by Stephen E. Whicher, Paul Fussell, and James Wright. *Whitman: A Collection of Critical Essays,* edited by Roy Harvey Pearce (Englewood Cliffs, N. J., 1962), is notable for contributions by Perry Miller, Richard Chase, and Josephine Miles. Some readers find James E. Miller helpful in *A Critical Guide to "Leaves of Grass"* (Chicago, 1957); others find him more arbitrary than they would wish. Also helpful may be Richard P. Adams, "Whitman: A Brief Evaluation," *Tennessee Studies in English,* V (1955), pp. 111–149, Leslie A. Fiedler's introduction to *Whitman* (New York, 1957), Paul Lauter, "Walt Whitman: Lover and Comrade," *American Imago,* XVI (Winter 1959), pp. 407–435, and James E. Miller's introduction to *Walt Whitman: Complete Poetry and Prose* (Boston, 1958). Almost everyone admires George Santayana's "Walt Whitman: The Poetry of Barbarism," in *Interpretations of Poetry and Religion* (New York, 1900), F. O. Matthiessen's penetrating observations in *American Renaissance* (New York, 1941), and Mark Van Doren's "Walt Whitman, Stranger," in *The Private Reader* (New York, 1942).

WALT WHITMAN:
HE HAD HIS NERVE

Randall Jarrell

****

Whitman, Dickinson, and Melville seem to me the best poets of the 19th Century here in America. Melville's poetry has been grotesquely underestimated, but of course it is only in the last four or five years that it has been much read; in the long run, in spite of the awkwardness and amateurishness of so much of it, it will surely be thought well of. (In the short run it will probably be thought entirely too well of. Melville is a great poet only in the prose of *Moby Dick.*) Dickinson's poetry has been thoroughly read, and well though undifferentiatingly loved—after a few decades or centuries almost everybody will be able to see through Dickinson to her poems. But something odd has happened to the living changing part of Whitman's reputation: nowadays it is people who are not particularly interested in poetry, people who say that they read a poem for what it says, not for how it says it,

who admire Whitman most. Whitman is often written about, either approvingly or disapprovingly, as if he were the Thomas Wolfe of 19th Century
democracy, the hero of a de Mille movie about Walt Whitman. (People
even talk about a war in which Walt Whitman and Henry James chose up
sides, to begin with, and in which you and I will go on fighting till the day
we die.) All this sort of thing, and all the bad poetry that there of course is
in Whitman—for any poet has written enough bad poetry to scare away anybody—has helped to scare away from Whitman most "serious readers of
modern poetry." They do not talk of his poems, as a rule, with any real lik-
ing or knowledge. Serious readers, people who are ashamed of not knowing
all Hopkins by heart, are not at all ashamed to say, "I don't really know
Whitman very well." This may harm Whitman in your eyes, they know, but
that is a chance that poets have to take. Yet "their" Hopkins, that good
critic and great poet, wrote about Whitman, after seeing five or six of his
poems in a newspaper review: "I may as well say what I should not otherwise have said, that I always knew in my heart Walt Whitman's mind to be
more like my own than any other man's living. As he is a very great scoun-
drel this is not a very pleasant confession." And Henry James, the leader of
"their" side in that awful imaginary war of which I spoke, once read Whitman to Edith Wharton (much as Mozart used to imitate, on the piano, the
organ) with such power and solemnity that both sat shaken and silent; it
was after this reading that James expressed his regret at Whitman's "too extensive acquaintance with the foreign languages." Almost all the most "original and advanced" poets and critics and readers of the last part of the 19th
Century thought Whitman as original and advanced as themselves, in manner as well as in matter. Can Whitman really be a sort of Thomas Wolfe or
Carl Sandburg or Robinson Jeffers or Henry Miller—or a sort of Balzac of
poetry, whose every part is crude but whose whole is somehow good? He is
not, nor could he be; a poem, like Pope's spider, "lives along the line," and
all the dead lines in the world will not make one live poem. As Blake says,
"all sublimity is founded on minute discrimination," and it is in these "minute particulars" of Blake's that any poem has its primary existence.

To show Whitman for what he is one does not need to praise or explain or argue, one needs simply to quote. He himself said, "I and mine do
not convince by arguments, similes, rhymes,/We convince by our presence."
Even a few of his phrases are enough to show us that Whitman was no
sweeping rhetorician, but a poet of the greatest and oddest delicacy and
originality and sensitivity, so far as words are concerned. This is, after all,
the poet who said, "Blind loving wrestling touch, sheath'd hooded sharp-
tooth'd touch"; who said, "Smartly attired, countenance smiling, form up-
right, death under the breast-bones, hell under the skull-bones"; who said,
"Agonies are one of my changes of garments"; who saw grass as the "flag of

my disposition," saw "the sharp-peak'd farmhouse, with its scallop'd scum and slender shoots from the gutters," heard a plane's "wild ascending lisp," and saw and heard how the amputation "what is removed drops horribly in a pail." This is the poet for whom the sea was "howler and scooper of storms," reaching out to us with "crooked inviting fingers"; who went "leaping chasms with a pike-pointed staff, clinging to topples of brittle and blue"; who, a runaway slave, saw how "my gore dribs, thinn'd with the ooze of my skin"; who went "lithographing Kronos . . . buying drafts of Osiris"; who stared out at the "little plentiful mannikins skipping around in collars and tail'd coats, / I am aware who they are, (they are positively not worms or fleas)." For he is, at his best, beautifully witty: he says gravely, "I find I incorporate gneiss, coals, long-threaded moss, fruits, grain, esculent roots, / And am stucco'd with quadrupeds and birds all over"; and of these quadrupeds and birds "not one is respectable or unhappy over the whole earth." He calls advice: "Unscrew the locks from the doors! Unscrew the doors from their jambs!" He publishes the results of research: "Having pried through the strata, analyz'd to a hair, counsel'd with doctors and calculated close, / I find no sweeter fat than sticks to my own bones." Everybody remembers how he told the Muse to "cross out please those immensely overpaid accounts, / That matter of Troy and Achilles' wrath, and Aeneas', Odysseus' wanderings," but his account of the arrival of the "illustrious emigré" here in the New World is even better: "Bluff'd not a bit by drainpipe, gasometer, artificial fertilizers, / Smiling and pleas'd with palpable intent to stay, / She's here, install'd amid the kitchenware." Or he sees, like another Breughel, "the mechanic's wife with the babe at her nipple interceding for every person born, / Three scythes at harvest whizzing in a row from three lusty angels with shirts bagg'd out at their waists, / The snag-toothed hostler with red hair redeeming sins past and to come"—the passage has enough wit not only (in Johnson's phrase) to keep it sweet, but enough to make it believable. He says:

> I project my hat, sit shame-faced, and beg.
> Enough! Enough! Enough!
> Somehow I have been stunn'd. Stand back!
> Give me a little time beyond my cuff'd head, slumbers, dreams,
>   gaping,
> I discover myself on the verge of a usual mistake.

There is in such changes of tone as these the essence of wit. And Whitman is even more far-fetched than he is witty; he can say about Doubters, in the most improbable and explosive of juxtapositions: "I know every one of you, I know the sea of torment, doubt, despair and unbelief. / How the flukes splash! How they contort rapid as lightning, with splashes and spouts of blood!" Who else would have said about God: "As the hugging and loving bed-fellow sleeps at my side through the night, and withdraws at the break of day with stealthy tread, / Leaving me baskets cover'd with white towels, swelling the house with their plenty"?—the Psalmist himself, his cup running over, would have looked at Whitman with dazzled eyes. (Whitman was persuaded by friends to hide the fact that it was God he was talking about.) He says, "Flaunt of the sunshine I need not your bask—lie over!" This unusual employment of verbs is usual enough in participle-loving Whitman, who also asks you to "look in my face while I snuff the sidle of evening," or tells you, "I effuse my flesh in eddies, and drift it in lacy jags." Here are some typical beginnings of poems: "City of orgies, walks, and joys. . . . Not heaving from my ribb'd breast only. . . . O take my hand Walt Whitman! Such gliding wonders! Such sights and sounds! Such join'd unended links. . . ." He says to the objects of the world, "You have waited, you always wait, you dumb, beautiful ministers"; sees "the sun and stars that float in the open air, / The apple-shaped earth"; says, "O suns— O grass of graves— O perpetual transfers and promotions, / If you do not say anything how can I say anything?" Not many poets have written better, in queerer and more convincing and more individual language, about the world's *gliding wonders:* the phrase seems particularly right for Whitman. He speaks of those "circling rivers the breath," of the "savage old mother incessantly crying, / To the boy's soul's questions sullenly timing, some drown'd secret hissing"— ends a poem, once, "We have voided all but freedom and our own joy." How can one quote enough? If the reader thinks that all this is like Thomas Wolfe he *is* Thomas Wolfe; nothing else could explain it. Poetry like this is as far as possible from the work of any ordinary rhetorician, whose phrases cascade over us like suds of the oldest and most-advertised detergent.

The interesting thing about Whitman's worst language (for, just as few poets have ever written better, few poets have ever written worse) is how unusually absurd, how really ingeniously bad, such language is. I will quote none of the most famous examples; but even a line like *O culpable! I acknowledge. I exposé* is not anything that you and I could do—only a man with the most extraordinary feel for language, or none whatsoever, could have cooked up Whitman's worst messes. For instance: what other man in all the history of this planet would have said, "I am a habitan of Vienna"? (One has an immediate vision of him as a sort of French-Canadian half-breed to whom the Viennese are offering, with trepidation, through the bars of a zoological garden, little mounds of whipped cream.) And *enclaircise*— why, it's as bad as *explicate!* We are right to resent his having made up his own horrors, instead of sticking to the ones that we ourselves employ. But when Whitman says, "I dote on myself, there is that lot of me and all so luscious," we should realize that we are not the only ones who are amused. And the queerly bad and the merely queer and the queerly good will often change into one another without warning: "Hefts of the moving world, at innocent gambols silently rising, freshly exuding, / Scooting obliquely high and low"—not good, but *queer!*—suddenly becomes, "Something I cannot see puts up libidinous prongs, / Seas of bright juice suffuse heaven," and it is sunrise.

But it is not in individual lines and phrases, but in passages of some length, that Whitman is at his best. In the following quotation Whitman has something difficult to express, something that there are many formulas, all bad, for expressing; he expresses it with complete success, in language of the most dazzling originality:

> The orchestra whirls me wider than Uranus flies,
> It wrenches such ardors from me I did not know I
>   possess'd them,
> It sails me, I dab with bare feet, they are lick'd by the
>   indolent waves,
> I am cut by bitter and angry hail, I lose my breath,
> Steep'd amid honey'd morphine, my windpipe throttled in
>   fakes of death,
> At length let up again to feel the puzzle of puzzles,
> And that we call Being.

One hardly knows what to point at—everything works. But *wrenches* and *did not know I possess'd them;* the incredible *it sails me, I dab with bare feet; lick'd by the indolent; steep'd amid honey'd morphine; my windpipe throttled in fakes of death*—no wonder Crane admired Whitman! This originality, as absolute in its way as that of Berlioz' orchestration, is often at Whitman's command:

> I am a dance—play up there! the fit is whirling me fast!
>
> I am the ever-laughing—it is new moon and twilight,
> I see the hiding of douceurs, I see nimble ghosts whichever way
>   I look,
> Cache and cache again deep in the ground and sea, and where
>   it is neither ground nor sea.
>
> Well do they do their jobs those journeymen divine,
> Only from me can they hide nothing, and would not if they could,
> I reckon I am their boss and they make me a pet besides,
> And surround me and lead me and run ahead when I walk,

> To lift their sunning covers to signify me with stretch'd arms,
> and resume the way;
>
> Onward we move, a gay gang of blackguards! with mirth-
> shouting music and wild-flapping pennants of joy!

If you did not believe Hopkins' remark about Whitman, that *gay gang of blackguards* ought to shake you. Whitman shares Hopkins' passion for "dappled" effects, but he slides in and out of them with ambigious swiftness. And he has at his command a language of the calmest and most prosaic reality, one that seems to do no more than present:

> The little one sleeps in its cradle.
> I lift the guaze and look a long time, and silently brush away
> flies with my hand.
>
> The youngster and the red-faced girl turn aside up the bushy hill,
> I peeringly view them from the top.
>
> The suicide sprawls on the bloody floor of the bedroom.
> I witness the corpse with its dabbled hair, I note where the
> pistol has fallen.

It is like magic: that is, something has been done to us without our knowing how it was done; but if we look at the lines again we see the *gauze, silently, youngster, red-faced, bushy, peeringly, dabbled*—not that this is all we see. "Present! present!" said James; these are presented, put down side by side to form a little "view of life," from the cradle to the last bloody floor of the bedroom. Very often the things presented form nothing but a list:

> The pure contralto sings in the organ loft,
> The carpenter dresses his plank, the tongue of his foreplane
> whistles its wild ascending lisp,
> The married and unmarried children ride home to their
> Thanksgiving dinner,
> The pilot seizes the king-pin, he heaves down with a strong arm,
> The mate stands braced in the whale-boat, lance and harpoon
> are ready,
> The duck-shooter walks by silent and cautious stretches,
> The deacons are ordained with cross'd hands at the altar,
> The spinning-girl retreats and advances to the hum of the
> big wheel,
> The farmer stops by the bars as he walks on a First-day loafe
> and looks at the oats and rye.
> The lunatic is carried at last to the asylum a confirm'd case,
> (He will never sleep any more as he did in the cot in
> his mother's bed-room;)

The jour printer with gray-head and gaunt jaws works at his case,
He turns his quid of tobacco while his eyes blur with the
      manuscript,
The malform'd limbs are tied to the surgeon's table,
What is removed drops horribly in a pail. . . .

It is only a list—but what a list! And how delicately, in what different ways
—likeness and opposition and continuation and climax and anticlimax—the
transitions are managed, whenever Whitman wants to manage them. Notice
them in the next quotation, another "mere list":

The bride unrumples her white dress, the minute-hand of the
      clock moves slowly,
The opium-eater reclines with rigid head and just-open'd lips,
The prostitute draggles her shawl, her bonnet bobs on her
      tipsy and pimpled neck. . . .

The first line is joined to the third by *unrumples* and *draggles, white dress*
and *shawl;* the second to the third by *rigid head, bobs, tipsy, neck;* the first
to the second by *slowly, just-open'd,* and the slowing-down of time in both
states. And occasionally one of these lists is metamorphosed into something
we have no name for; the man who would call the next quotation a mere list
—anybody will feel this—would boil his babies up for soap:

Ever the hard unsunk ground,
Ever the eaters and drinkers, ever the upward and downward sun,
Ever myself and my neighbors, refreshing, wicked, real,
Ever the old inexplicable query, ever that thorned thumb,
      that breath of itches and thirsts,
Ever the vexer's hoot! hoot! till we find where the sly one hides
      and bring him forth,
Ever the sobbing liquid of life,
Ever the bandage under the chin, ever the trestles of death.

Sometimes Whitman will take what would generally be considered an
unpromising subject (in this case, a woman peeping at men in bathing
naked) and treat it with such tenderness and subtlety and understanding
that we are ashamed of ourselves for having thought it unpromising, and
murmur that Chekhov himself couldn't have treated it better:

Twenty-eight young men bathe by the shore,
Twenty-eight young men and all so friendly,
Twenty-eight years of womanly life and all so lonesome.

She owns the fine house by the rise of the bank,
She hides handsome and richly drest aft the blinds of the window.

Which of the young men does she like the best?
Ah the homeliest of them is beautiful to her.

Where are you off to, lady? for I see you,
You splash in the water there, yet stay stock still in your room.

Dancing and laughing along the beach came the twenty-ninth
     bather,
The rest did not see her, but she saw them and loved them.

The beards of the young men glistened with wet, it ran
     from their long hair,
Little streams pass'd all over their bodies.

An unseen hand also pass'd over their bodies,
It descended tremblingly from their temples and ribs.

The young men float on their backs, their white bellies bulge
     to the sun, they do not ask who seizes fast to them,
They do not know who puffs and declines with pendant and
     bending arch,
They do not know whom they souse with spray.

And in the same poem (that "Song of Myself" in which one finds half
his best work) the writer can say of a sea-fight:

Stretched and still lies the midnight,
Two great hulls motionless on the breast of the darkness,
Our vessel riddled and slowly sinking, preparations to pass
     to the one we have conquer'd,
The captain on the quarter-deck coldly giving his orders
     through a countenance white as a sheet,
Near by the corpse of the child that serv'd in the cabin,
The dead face of an old salt with long white hair and
     carefully curl'd whiskers,
The flames spite of all that can be done flickering aloft and below,
The husky voices of the two or three officers yet fit for duty,
Formless stacks of bodies and bodies by themselves, dabs
     of flesh upon the masts and spars,
Cut of cordage, dangle of rigging, slight shock of the
     soothe of waves,
Black and impassive guns, litter of powder-parcels, strong scent,
A few large stars overhead, silent and mournful shining,
Delicate snuffs of sea-breeze, smells of sedgy grass and fields by
     the shore, death-messages given in charge to survivors,

The hiss of the surgeon's knife, the gnawing teeth of his saw,
Wheeze, cluck, swash of falling blood, short wild scream,
    and long, dull, tapering groan,
These so, these irretrievable.

There are faults in this passage, and they *do not matter:* the serious truth, the complete realization of these last lines make us remember that few poets have shown more of the tears of things, and the joy of things, and of the reality beneath either tears or joy. Even Whitman's most general or political statements often are good: everybody knows his "When liberty goes out of a place it is not the first to go, nor the second or third to go, / It waits for all the rest to go, it is the last"; these sentences about the United States just before the Civil War may be less familiar:

Are those really Congressmen? are those the great Judges?
    is that the President?
Then I will sleep awhile yet, for I see that these States sleep,
    for reasons;
(With gathering murk, with muttering thunder and lambent
    shoots we all duly awake,
South, North, East, West, inland and seaboard, we will
    surely awake.)

How well, with what firmness and dignity and command, Whitman does such passages! And Whitman's doubts that he has done them or anything else well—ah, there is nothing he does better:

The best I had done seemed to me blank and suspicious,
My great thoughts as I supposed them, were they not in
    reality meagre?
I am he who knew what it was to be evil,
I too knitted the old knot of contrariety . . .
Saw many I loved in the street or ferry-boat or public assembly,
    yet never told them a word,
Lived the same life with the rest, the same old laughing,
    gnawing, sleeping,
Played the part that still looks back on the actor and actress,
The same old role, the role that is what we make it . . .

Whitman says once that the "look of the bay mare shames silliness out of me." This is true—sometimes it is true; but more often the silliness and affectation and cant and exaggeration are there shamelessly, the Old Adam that was in Whitman from the beginning and the awful new one that he created to keep it company. But as he says, "I know perfectly well my own egotism, / Know my omnivorous lines and must not write any less." He says over and over that there are in him good and bad, wise and foolish, anything at all and its antonym, and he is telling the truth; there is in him almost everything in the world, so that one responds to him, willingly or unwillingly, almost as one does to the world, that world which makes the hairs of one's flesh stand up, which seems both evil beyond any rejection and wonderful beyond any acceptance. We cannot help seeing that there is something absurd about any judgment we make of its whole—for there is no "point of view" at which we can stand to make the judgment, and the moral categories that mean most to us seem no more to apply to its whole than our spatial or temporal or causal categories seem to apply to its beginning or its end. (But we need no arguments to make our judgments seem absurd—we feel their absurdity without argument.) In some like sense Whitman is a world, a waste with, here and there, systems blazing at random out of the darkness. Only an innocent and rigidly methodical mind will reject it for this disorganization, particularly since there are in it, here and there, little systems as beautifully and astonishingly organized as the rings and satellites of Saturn:

> I understand the large hearts of heroes,
> The courage of present times and all times,
> How the skipper saw the crowded and rudderless wreck of the
>   steam-ship, and Death chasing it up and down the storm,
> How he knuckled tight and gave not back an inch, and was
>   faithful of days and faithful of nights,
> And chalked in large letters on a board, Be of good cheer,
>   we will not desert you;
> How he follow'd with them and tack'd with them three days
>   and would not give it up,
> How he saved the drifting company at last,
> How the lank loose-gown'd women looked when boated
>   from the side of their prepared graves,
> How the silent old-faced infants and the lifted sick, and the
>   sharp-lipp'd unshaved men;
> All this I swallow, it tastes good, I like it well, it becomes mine,
> I am the man, I suffered, I was there.

In the last lines of this quotation Whitman has reached—as great writers always reach—a point at which criticism seems not only unnecessary but absurd: these lines are so good that even admiration feels like insolence, and one is ashamed of anything that one can find to say about them. How anyone can dismiss or accept patronizingly the man who wrote them, I do not understand.

The enormous and apparent advantage of form, of omission and selection, of the highest degree of organization, are accompanied by important disadvantages—and there are far greater works than *Leaves of Grass* to make us realize this. But if we compare Whitman with that very beautiful poet Alfred Tennyson, the most skillful of all Whitman's contemporaries, we are at once aware of how limiting Tennyson's forms have been, of how much Tennyson has had to leave out, even in those discursive poems where he is trying to put everything in. Whitman's poems *represent* his world and himself much more satisfactorily than Tennyson's do his. In the past a few poets have both formed and represented, each in the highest degree; but in modern times what controlling, organizing, selecting poet has created a world with as much in it as Whitman's, a world that so plainly *is* the world? Of all modern poets he has, quantitatively speaking, "the most comprehensive soul"—and, qualitatively, a most comprehensive and comprehending one, with charities and concessions and qualifications that are rare in any time.

"Do I contradict myself? Very well then I contradict myself," wrote Whitman, as everybody remembers, and this is not naïve, or something he got from Emerson, or a complacent pose. When you organize one of the contradictory elements out of your work of art, you are getting rid not just of it, but of the contradiction of which it was a part; and it is the contradictions in works of art which make them able to represent to us—as logical and methodical generalizations cannot—our world and our selves, which are also full of contradictions. In Whitman we do not get the controlled, compressed, seemingly concordant contradictions of the great lyric poets, of a poem like, say, Hardy's *During Wind and Rain;* Whitman's contradictions are sometimes announced openly, but are more often scattered at random throughout the poems. For instance: Whitman specializes in ways of saying that there is in some sense (a very Hegelian one, generally) no evil—he says a hundred times that evil is not Real; but he also specializes in making lists of the evil of the world, lists of an unarguable reality. After his minister has recounted "the rounded catalogue divine complete," Whitman comes home and puts down what has been left out: "the countless (nineteen-twentieths) low and evil, crude and savage . . . the barren soil, the evil men, the slag and hideous rot." He ends another such catalogue with the plain unexcusing "All these—all meanness and agony without end I sitting look out upon, / See, hear, and am silent." Whitman offered himself to everybody, and said brilliantly and at length what a good thing he was offering:

> Sure as the most certain sure, plumb in the uprights,
>   well entretied, braced in the beams,
> Stout as a horse, affectionate, haughty, electrical
> I and this mystery here we stand.

Just for oddness, characteristicalness, differentness, what more could you ask in a letter of recommendation? (Whitman sounds as if he were recommending a house—haunted, but what foundations!) But after a few pages he is oddly different:

> Apart from the pulling and hauling stands what I am,
> Stands amused, complacent, compassionating, idle, unitary,
> Looks down, is erect, or bends an arm on an impalpable
>   certain rest
> Looking with side curved head curious what will come next,
> Both in and out of the game and watching and wondering at it.

Tamburlaine is already beginning to sound like Hamlet: the employer feels uneasily, *Why, I might as well hire myself.* . . . And, a few pages later, Whitman puts down in ordinary-sized type, in the middle of the page, this warning to any *new person drawn toward me:*

> Do you think I am trusty and faithful?
> Do you see no further than this façade, this smooth
>   and tolerant manner of me?
> Do you suppose yourself advancing on real ground
>   toward a real heroic man?
> Have you no thought O dreamer that it may be all maya,
>   illusion?

Having wonderful dreams, telling wonderful lies, was a temptation Whitman could never resist; but telling the truth was a temptation he could never resist, either. When you buy him you know what you are buying. And only an innocent and solemn and systematic mind will condemn him for his contradictions: Whitman's catalogues of evils represent realities, and his denials of their reality represent other realities, of feeling and intuition and desire. If he is faithless to logic, to Reality As It Is—whatever that is—he is faithful to the feel of things, to reality as it seems; this is all that a poet has to be faithful to, and philosophers even have been known to leave logic and Reality for it.

Whitman is more coordinate and parallel than anybody, is *the* poet of parallel present participles, of twenty verbs joined by a single subject: all this helps to give his work its feeling of raw hypnotic reality, of being that world which also streams over us joined only by *ands,* until we supply the subordinating conjunctions; and since as children we see the *ands* and not the *becauses,* this method helps to give Whitman some of the freshness of childhood. How inexhaustibly *interesting* the world is in Whitman! Arnold all his life kept wishing that we could see the world "with a plainness as near, as flashing" as that with which Moses and Rebekah and the Argonauts saw it. He asked with elegiac nostalgia, "Who can see the green earth any more / As she was by the sources of Time?"—and all the time there was somebody alive who saw it so, as plain and near and flashing, and with a kind of calm, pastoral, biblical dignity and elegance as well, sometimes. The *thereness* and *suchness* of the world are incarnate in Whitman as they are in few other writers.

They might have put on his tombstone WALT WHITMAN: HE HAD HIS NERVE. He is the rashest, the most inexplicable and unlikely—the most impossible, one wants to say—of poets. He somehow *is* in a class by himself, so that one compares him with other poets about as readily as one compares *Alice* with other books. (Even his free verse has a completely different effect from anybody else's.) Who would think of comparing him with Tennyson or Browning or Arnold or Baudelaire?—it is Homer, or the sagas, or something far away and long ago, that comes to one's mind only to be dismissed; for sometimes Whitman *is* epic, just as *Moby Dick* is, and it surprises us to be able to use truthfully this word that we have misused so many times. Whitman *is* grand, and elevated, and comprehensive, and real with an astonishing reality, and many other things—the critic points at his qualities in despair and wonder, all method failing, and simply calls them by their names. And the range of these qualities is the most extraordinary thing of all. We can surely say about him, "He was a man, take him for all in all. I shall not look upon his like again"—and wish that people had seen this and not tried to be his like: one Whitman is miracle enough, and when he comes again it will be the end of the world.

I have said so little about Whitman's faults because they are so plain: baby critics who have barely learned to complain of the lack of ambiguity in *Peter Rabbit* can tell you all that is wrong with *Leaves of Grass*. But a good many of my readers must have felt that it is ridiculous to write an essay about the obvious fact that Whitman is a great poet. It is ridiculous—just as, in 1851, it would have been ridiculous for anyone to write an essay about the obvious fact that Pope was no "classic of our prose" but a great poet. Critics have to spend half their time reiterating whatever ridiculously obvious things their age or the critics of their age have found it necessary to forget: they say despairingly, at parties, that Wordsworth is a great poet, and *won't* bore you, and tell Mr. Leavis that Milton is a great poet whose deposition *hasn't* been accomplished with astonishing ease by a few words from Eliot and Pound. . . . There is something essentially ridiculous about critics, anyway: what is good is good without our saying so, and beneath all our majesty we know this.

Let me finish by mentioning another quality of Whitman's—a quality, delightful to me, that I have said nothing of. If some day a tourist notices, among the ruins of New York City, a copy of *Leaves of Grass,* and stops and picks it up and reads some lines in it, she will be able to say to herself: "How very American! If he and his country had not existed, it would have been impossible to imagine them."

EMILY DICKINSON

****

More has been written about Emily Dickinson as the eccentric recluse of Amherst than about her poetry. A biography which also includes sensible literary interpretation is Thomas H. Johnson's *Emily Dickinson: An Interpretive Biography* (Cambridge, Mass., 1955), while Theodora Ward's *The Capsule of the Mind* (Cambridge, Mass., 1961) and William Robert Sherwood's *Circumference and Circumstance: Stages in the Life and Art of Emily Dickinson* (New York, 1968) speak perceptively of the poet's personality as revealed in her writings. Useful brief studies include Henry W. Wells's *Introduction to Emily Dickinson* (Chicago, 1957) and John B. Pickard's *Emily Dickinson: An Introduction and Interpretation* (New York, 1967). Richard Chase's *Emily Dickinson* (New York, 1951) and Clark Griffith's *The Long Shadow* (Princeton, N. J., 1964) stress tragic strains in Dickinson's poetry; Albert J. Gelpi's *Emily Dickinson: The Mind of the Poet* (Cambridge, Mass., 1965), from which this essay is extracted, seems to me to view it more completely. Students examine her poetry in Charles R. Anderson's

Emily Dickinson's Poetry: Stairway of Surprise (New York, 1960);
poets talk of it in Archibald MacLeish, Louise Bogan, and Richard
Wilbur's *Emily Dickinson: Three Views* (Amherst, Mass., 1960).
Important critical essays include R. P. Blackmur's "Emily Dickinson," *Southern Review,* III (Autumn 1937), pp. 325–347, Northrop
Frye's "Emily Dickinson," *Major Writers of America* (New York,
1962), F. O. Matthiessen's "The Problem of a Private Poet,"
Kenyon Review, VII (Autumn 1945), pp. 584–597, Allen Tate's
often reprinted "New England Culture and Emily Dickinson,"
Symposium, III (April 1932), pp. 206–226, Austin Warren's carefully sympathetic "Emily Dickinson," *Sewanee Review,* LXV
(1957), pp. 565–586, and Yvor Winters's acerbic "Emily Dickinson
and the Limits of Judgment," *Maule's Curse* (Norfolk, Va., 1938).

SEEING NEW ENGLANDLY:
FROM EDWARDS TO EMERSON
TO DICKINSON

Alfred J. Gelpi

****

Beneath Emily Dickinson's little jokes about being a "Pagan" there lay an honest recognition, but beneath her allusion, just a few years before her

133

death, to her "Puritan Spirit,"[1] there lay a recognition equally honest. No commentary on Emily Dickinson can avoid the observation that despite her restlessness she was very much of New England. The crucial question asks precisely in what respects hers was a Puritan spirit in the larger evolution of the American character.

I

The Puritan's "vision" of himself and the cosmos[2] was formulated into theological tenets the truth of which rested not on scriptural authority alone but on the individual's sense of things. To the Puritan, God was the self-existent Being who devised the magnificent harmony of Creation and sustained it in contingent existence while He reigned above in incomprehensible sovereignty. But God's plan had been ruined by man's original sin, through which he lost grace. The loss of grace, that projection of the divine whose indwelling presence united man and nature and God, left man in solitary need and ushered in death, pain, depravity—the consequences of man's descent to a merely natural existence. Blind and impotent, crippled in mind and will, he stood in cringing dependence before an unseen and now angry Jehovah, who could elect to strike him with thunderbolts or to confer through Christ's mediation the grace which, all-undeserved, would span the gaping separation, raise man's faculties, and restore him to unity with his God and his world. The Scriptures were God's words to man, through which he could understand the truth of his plight and the nature of his regeneration. Man's duty was to ponder and elucidate God's message and to carry out His Commandments. Hence the single-minded concern of Puritan divines with applying man's reason to God's revelation; and the unrelenting labor to erect a vast theological system on which fallen man could rely and within which he could think and act.

Needless to say, at its best Puritanism amounted to more than an arid rationalism or an abject surrender to formulae. Within the theological structure, the obligation of the individual man strained his stamina to the uttermost. He had to confront the universe starkly and answer within the privacy of his heart all the basic questions: Who am I? What is my relation to the not-me? How must I live in the certitude of death? Have I grounds for hope or not? In this confrontation the noblest Puritans neither winced nor succumbed. On the contrary, within their theology they lived as individuals fully and passionately; universal religious truth and individual human experience were working not at cross-purposes but toward concentricity. One has only to turn to Bradford's *Of Plimmoth Plantation* or Winthrop's "Journal" or Nathaniel Ward or Samuel Sewell or the verse of poets as different as Anne Bradstreet and Edward Taylor to realize with what vigor and passion the Puritan could commit himself, mind and heart and soul, to life. Most splendidly, there is the fierce brightness of Jonathan Edwards, illuminating both worlds. He resolved "to live with all my might, while I do live," and so to strive for heaven "with all the power, might, vigour, and vehemence, yes violence I am capable of." He asserted the importance of the passions and the holiness of religious affections. He loved his wife and God's radiant world, while rejoicing all the more in the "Divine and Supernatural Light."

Only seventy-five years after Edwards' death it seemed to Emerson that the body of doctrine had become a corpse, devoid of feeling or response, stiffened by rigor mortis. What could a living person do but inter the dead? But then he was left to confront the cosmos without even the authority of the Scriptures or the protective framework of established truth. Moreover, Emerson started from a different philosophical viewpoint from Edwards: Emerson's epistemology was not based on Locke's inductive method but on the intuitive perception of the post-Kantian transcendentalists; his metaphysic found German idealism and Oriental mysticism more congenial than Christian dualism.

Nevertheless, Edwards' and Emerson's formulations bespeak continuity as well as change. Like a good New Englander, Emerson also began with a double awareness of things: there was, or seemed to be, Nature and Soul, matter and spirit, not-me and me, Understanding and Reason. There was an "inevitable dualism," and the purpose of life was to resolve the opposition —not in some hypothetical future but here and now. He could admit the appalling impingements and limitations which constituted "Fate"; he could concede that "there is a crack in every thing that God has made"; he could see the world as fragmented and out of joint. But for Emerson the remedy was right at hand. The Fall was an illusion; nor was man helpless and debased, except by choice. Man was the vessel of divinity and need only release his energies; he was "a god in ruins," and could be a god in fact, like Jesus Christ. Man's Fall was only his first realization of himself as an existence apparently distinct, but the process of living was the opening out of one's self to discover "an occult relation" with all other things. In moments of most expansive perception the divine energy flowing from "me" became one again with the divine energy surging from the "not-me." At such times "I am nothing; I see all; the currents of the Universal Being circulate through me; I am part or parcel of God." Each and all, matter and spirit are One.

What had happened over the years[3] was that the masterful synthesis which Edwards represented—that glowing fusion of intellectual and emotional character, that precarious poising of delight in this world against commitment to the next, that careful balance between individual and church—had been split asunder, and the Puritan mind, unable to repair the damage, would not be whole again. Thus, however similar are the axiomatic assumptions of Edwards' "vision" and the "vision" of Emerson, they could hardly have projected more dissimilar views of man's situation. Both men would agree that the individual loses himself in the highest knowledge only through a supra-logical spiritual power which manifests itself in a movement of the affections. Edwards would call that power grace; and Emerson, Reason. Edwards would place its source in God, and Emerson would place it in man. Finally, Edwards would support even the perceptions of grace with a rational system and with a community, while Emerson would leave the self reliant only on intuitive "Reason" and the responsive heart. For Emerson, Reason made each man "full of grace," and instituted a new scheme of "redemption" (though Emerson would not have invoked the theological terms he had so conspicuously shed). Man was god; hence he saved himself; and then earth was heaven. For Edwards heaven was the transcendence of earth; for Emerson it was the fulfillment of earth.

From the beginning there had been in Protestantism the impulse to push the notion of private conscience to its final extreme—namely, unquestioned reliance on individual revelation. In America there had been the related heresies of Anne Hutchinson and Roger Williams and the Friends, and there had been Cotton Mather's concept of "a particular faith" and Solomon Stoddard's awed respect for the unfathomable workings of grace in the individual. For a long time the orthodox had been effective in restraining the tendency to fix on the "inner light" by controlling it within themselves and by driving the heretics out. Ironically, both Edwards and Emerson became, for their respectable contemporaries, irrational enthusiasts. However, while the conservative "Arminians" had successfully stamped out the fires that spread from Edwards' Northampton, their Unitarian grandchildren pitted themselves in a losing effort against the hotheads from Concord. Indeed, the momentum of the rebellious young Turks succeeded in routing a debilitated theological Protestantism and establishing the primacy of personal, innate, and now "secular" vision. Thereby the drama of "salvation," or rather fulfillment, was located in the individual consciousness—a word whose connotations are very different from those of the word "soul." The final step in the transition was the recognition of the poet as the priest and saint and representative man of the new "religion" (he "stands among partial men for the complete man"), and the recognition of the creative imagination as man's divine faculty.

For the Puritans, "a religious heart inevitably translated itself into the formulae of theology; to them the conception of private experience was real, but not of private expression—wherein they differed from modern poets."[4] Although Edwards might have disagreed, Allen Tate has argued that the best poetry is written when the control of the intellectual and religious order of an age is breaking down.[5] Then, says Mr. Tate, the poet—who knows the elements of this order as part of his heritage without being able any longer to accept them unquestioningly—is forced to examine that heritage in terms of his own experience. The shattering of the tradition frees yet directs the energies of the imagination, and the result is magnificent poetry. If Mr. Tate is correct, Emily Dickinson came at the auspicious moment and to precisely the right place. Nurtured in the conservative Connecticut Valley, she not only came to distrust its theology but was personally incapable of logical, not to say theological, thought. System and argument, like the austere New England winter, were too hard and frigid for her, but now, at the crucial period of thaw, she came upon the warm, swelling, swirling notions of the Romantic poet-prophets. In Margaret Fuller's energetic words from the manifesto of the first issue of *The Dial,* Emily Dickinson was merely responding to

> the strong current of thought and feeling, which, for a few years past, has led many sincere persons in New England to make new demands on literature, and to reprobate that rigor of our conventions of religion and education, which is turning us to stone, which renounces hope, which looks only backward, which . . . holds nothing so much in horror as new views and the dreams of youth.[6]

2

The testimony of Emily Fowler Ford, one of Emily Dickinson's closest girlhood friends, indicates that as early as the mid-1840s, before the poet had met Benjamin Newton or Henry Vaughan Emmons, the two girls were reading Byron, Lowell, Emerson, Motherwell, and Margaret Fuller's translation of *Günerode,* and Emily Dickinson was particularly "steeped" in Emerson's *Essays.*[7]

In 1847 a series of lectures on the history of literature delivered at Amherst College by a man named John Lord was reported to be scandalously "pantheistic" and "transcendental." When Professor William Tyler, a neighbor and friend of the Dickinsons, wrote scornfully of the tone of the proceedings, his correspondent replied: "I picture to myself all the grave Prof's of Am. assembled at a transcendental poetical lecture, and I am taken in a very humorous state of mind to say the least . . . Miss Emily should not be absent." Of course, this may not have been our Miss Emily, but the possibility is too intriguing not to mention, especially since Emily would almost certainly have heard the substance of the lectures, even if she herself were not there.[8]

Among Emily's Amherst friends Leonard Humphrey was interested in Wordsworth and Carlyle, and George Gould delivered a prize speech during Commencement Week, 1848, on "Carlyle's 'Dream of Jean Richter.' " Emily's acquaintance with Dr. Josiah G. Holland dates from the early fifties; and Holland, like Higginson later, was a genteel liberal who was interested in "Women in Literature" and had written an article on the subject for the *Springfield Republican.* He stood for a personal "creedless, churchless, ministerless Christianity," and hailed Emerson's thought as "a chain of brilliant ideas strung as thickly as Wethersfield onions when packed for export." In 1881 Emily warmly recalled to Mrs. Holland that when she had first heard her husband pray, she had thought that she felt "a different God" who was a friend.[9]

Emily gave some idea of Emerson's influence upon her own thought in her comments on the *Poems, Representative Men,* and the Holmes biography, and in several allusions to his "immortal" poems.[10] Emerson spoke in Amherst in 1855 on "A Plea for the Scholar," in 1857 on "The Beautiful in Rural Life," in 1879 on "Superlative or Mental Temperance," and led off a course of lectures in 1865 with "Social Aims." That he met with small crowds and little enthusiasm, even as late as his lecture of 1879 (by which time he was something of a national monument), indicates the extent to which Emily's interest outran that of her Amherst neighbors. Although there is no evidence that she attended any of these lectures, she must have listened from a distance, and after the 1857 visit, when Emerson stayed at the house next door with Austin and Sue, she wrote breathlessly to her sister-in-law: "It must have been as if he had come from where dreams are born!" In her last years she copied out several scraps of Emerson's verse. This was a special tribute, for she rarely copied the words of other poets, even her favorites; and the attribution to Emerson of the anonymously published "Success" (the only poem of hers to appear in print outside of a newspaper during her lifetime) must have amused and delighted her.[11] She wrote of the severe shock which Emerson's death dealt her in April 1882. Since the Reverend Wadsworth had died just a few weeks before, death had struck down within a single month the men who symbolized and supported the two sides of her divided spirit.

For Emily Dickinson's indebtedness to Thoreau we have fewer hard facts to point to than in the case of Emerson, but circumstantial evidence intimates a great deal (though the influence here was somewhat later and so less directly formative than that of Emerson). The Dickinson library copies of *Letters to Various Persons* and *A Week on the Concord and Merrimack* and the two copies of *Walden* are dated from the middle sixties, but she might have read any of them earlier. Besides, she must have read the essays which appeared in the pages of the *Atlantic* during 1862: "Walking," "Autumnal Tints," "Wild Apples," and others. And her remark to Sue and Austin on a seaside vacation in 1865—"Was the Sea cordial? Kiss him for Thoreau"—shows that she knew the recently issued *Cape Cod*. Her writing is filled with scattered remarks which suggest Thoreau's influence: " 'My Country, 'tis of Thee,' has always meant the Woods—to me—'Sweet Land of Liberty,' I trust is your own—"; "The fire-bells are oftener now, almost, than the church-bells. Thoreau would wonder which did the most harm." There is, too, the charming anecdote of the lady who, having been "recently introduced in the family by marriage," was brought for the first time to Edward Dickinson's house to meet her new relatives. When by chance she "quoted some sentence from Thoreau's writings, Miss Dickinson, recognizing it, hastened to press her hand as she said, 'From this time we are acquainted;' and this was the beginning of a friendship that lasted till the death of the poetess."[12] Emily must have felt a deep kinship with Thoreau for a passing reference to provoke so spontaneous and wholehearted a response to a stranger.

As for other Transcendentalists, she read some of Theodore Parker and later O. B. Frothingham's biography of Parker; and she knew enough about William Ellery Channing to use a verse of his as the basis for a poem of her own (P 1234, III.858). But since specific information is so meager, the full extent of her knowledge of what was going on in Concord can best be suggested through her own words. Curiously enough it is the conclusion of a comic valentine which indicates how clearly she had absorbed, as early as 1850, the essential features of Transcendentalism—the optimism, the emphasis on experimentation and originality, the sense of social purpose, the metaphysical and mystical speculations, the pulse of rhythm and imagery:

> But the world is sleeping in ignorance and error, sir, and we must be crowing cocks, and singing larks, and a rising sun to awake her; or else we'll pull society up to the roots, and plant it in a different place. We'll build Alms-houses, and transcendental State prisons, and scaffolds – we will blow out the sun, and the moon, and encourage invention. Alpha shall kiss Omega – we will ride up the hill of glory – Hallelujah, all hail! [13]

The shock of Transcendentalism had been registered on the American consciousness even as far as Amherst; Brook Farm and *The Dial* were experiments now defunct, but they were events of such import that henceforth

New England could not think without taking into account what they had stood for. In *The Blithedale Romance* (1852) Hawthorne would tell of Hollingsworth's schemes for penal reform; in *Walden* (1854) Thoreau would "brag as lustily as chanticleer in the morning . . . if only to wake my neighbors up," for "only that day dawns to which we are awake. There is more day to dawn. The sun is but a morning-star." Emily Dickinson's words of 1850 had already caught much of the imagery and fanfare.

3

The early letters of Emily's correspondence record the development of her imagination and her growing sense of poetic mission. From the first she welcomed the opportunity for "improving" a situation. In her earliest extant letter, written in 1842 when she was twelve, she told Austin of sleeping alone and imagining deliciously dire perils, then went on to describe Austin's hens which "will be so large that you cannot perceive them with the naked Eye when you get home," and narrated the theft of an egg by "a skonk . . . or else a hen In the shape of a skonk and I dont know which."[14] These capricious childhood fantasies are not remarkable in themselves, except to indicate the play of fancy which she was soon to apply to increasingly serious purpose.

At about the time when she was discovering some of the new writers, she indulgently warned Abiah Root about the enchainment of the free spirit; and after loosing a flutter of metaphors on another occasion she paused to intone to her professing friend in sly mockery:

> Now my dear friend, let me tell you that these last thoughts are fictions – vain imaginations to lead astray foolish young women. They are flowers of speech, they both *make,* and *tell* deliberate falsehoods, avoid them as the snake . . . Honestly tho', a snake bite is a serious matter, and there can't be too much said, or done about it . . . *I* love those little green ones that slide around by your shoes in the grass – and make it rustle with your elbows – they are rather my favorites on the whole, but I wouldn't influence *you* for the world![15]

With a wave of the hand she had charmed the venomous serpent into a harmless grass snake, which was, after all, her favorite sort of reptile. The nimble feat of verbal prestidigitation was to admit the sins of fancy and then absolve them through the fancy's ingenuity.

In April 1850 (the year Emily received Emerson's *Poems* from Benjamin Newton) she wrote Jane Humphrey a long letter which, underneath all the inarticulate confusion, bespoke a special sense of dedication. The importance of the passage to the emergence of the poet—it may even be roughly analogous to the moment of consecration in Wordsworth's *Prelude*—merits its quotation in full:

> I would whisper to you in the evening of many, and curious things – and by the lamps eternal read your thoughts and response in your face, and find out what you thought about me, and what I have done, and am doing . . . I have dared to do strange things – bold things, and have asked no advice from any – I have heeded beautiful tempters, yet do not think I am wrong . . . Oh Jennie, it would relieve me to . . . confess what *you only* shall know, an experience bitter, and sweet, but the sweet did so beguile me – and life has had an aim, and the world has been too precious for your poor – and striving sister! The winter was all one dream, and the spring has not yet waked me, I would *always* sleep, and dream, and it never should turn to morning, so long as night is so blessed. What do you weave from all these threads . . . I hope belief is not wicked, and assurance, and perfect trust – . . . do you dream from all this what I mean? Nobody *thinks* of the joy, nobody *guesses* it, to all appearance old things are engrossing, and new ones are not revealed, but there *now* is nothing old, things are budding, and springing, and singing, and you rather think you are in a green grove, and it's branches that go, and come.[16]

Twice she asks the momentous question: what do you make of all this? Momentous indeed was the implication of the painful transition to a sweet new life and a renewed world. Perhaps it was a dream, as it seemed at first, but then the dream of joyous vision was better than hopeless reality. Excitement, mingled with reticence, blurred the point in a whirl of words, but even in her most intimate moments she would refer only obliquely to that "attitude toward the Universe, so precisely my own," for which she had relinquished the Christian "Vision of John at Patmos."[17]

Now she was bold enough to appropriate to herself the title of poet. In 1851 she spoke of "the fancy that we are the only poets, and everyone else is *prose*." A few months later, while the rest of the family was at church, she conducted her own service for Sue in her heart and only regretted the lack of things "which I may poetize" for "this sweet Sabbath of our's." In 1853 she good-naturedly chided Austin, her "Brother Pegasus," for writing verses, because as a poet in her own right she was reluctant to share the laurels with him. To the Hollands she identified herself with the village poet in Longfellow's *Kavanagh*. A sermon (given by Professor E. A. Park of the Andover Theological Seminary) on "the importance of Aesthetic in connection with Religious and Moral Culture" brought this exclamation: "I never heard anything like it, and dont expect to again. . . . ." By 1854 Sue's persistence about her sister-in-law's unregenerate state pressed too hard, but in her wounded reply Emily would not compromise her new calling: "Sue— you can go or stay—There is but one alternative . . . I have lived by this. It is the lingering emblem of the Heaven I once dreamed. . . ."[18] If in Sue's eyes she had abandoned Christ for Satan, it was too bad; her decision was unalterable, and, as if to emphasize her new role, she finished the letter with a poem. Most frequently now her signature read "Emilie," which some critics have taken as the mask of the child-poet (in the Blake-Words-worth-Emerson tradition) but which might just as well be read as the sign of the new poet enjoying the embellishment of verbal curlicues.

During the fifties the letters began to mention and display a concern for style.[19] The struggle for stylistic effects grew out of the necessity to make a language adequate to the more ambitious descriptions of nature that she was attempting. They are often keenly perceived and crisply phrased, and even the exuberant excesses are interesting as a novice's explorations of the resources of her medium. To Sue in Maryland she mused: the moon "looks like a fairy tonight, sailing around the sky in a little silver gondola with stars for gondoliers. I asked her to let me ride a little while ago—and told her I would *get out* when she got as far as Baltimore, but she only smiled to herself and went sailing on." The autumn countryside which she dispatched to the city-bound Austin is more finely realized:

> I have tried to delay the frosts, I have coaxed the fading flowers, I thought I *could* detain a few of the crimson leaves until you had smiled upon them, but their companions call them and they cannot stay away – you will find the blue hills, Austin, with the autumnal shadows silently sleeping on them, and there will be a glory lingering round the day, so you'll know autumn has been here, and the *setting sun* will tell you . . . . The earth looks like some poor old lady who by dint of pains has bloomed e'en till *now,* yet in a forgetful moment a few silver hairs from out her cap come stealing, and she tucks them back so hastily and thinks nobody *sees.*

At the end of this message to her Brother Pegasus she set down (unobtrusively as rhymed prose) the first serious poem sent in a letter. In 1852 we find this imagistic scene: "The shy little birds would say chirrup, chirrup, in the tall cherry trees, and if our dresses rustled, hop frightened away; and there used to be some farmer cutting down a tree in the woods, and you and I, sitting there, could hear his sharp ax ring." In 1856 her cousin John Graves received a prose lyric whose landscape and logic are now completely imaginative: "Ah John—*Gone?* Then I lift the lid to my box of Phantoms, and lay another in, unto the Resurrection—Then will I gather in *Paradise,* the blossoms fallen here, and on the shores of the sea of Light, seek my missing sands."[20]

By 1858, after some years of apprenticeship, she felt sufficiently sure of her sight and insight and of her technique to begin recopying verses and preserving them in bound packets. The letters and the rapidly expanding body of poems displayed increasing control of theme, image, and diction. Under the stress of emotional crisis she composed more than five hundred poems in 1862 and 1863. Nor were they all written to relieve the pressure of pain; there is in the nature poetry a deepening wonder at the awesome beauty of the world. The verse of these years includes nature poems, poems of states of feeling, poems about poetry and the poet, poems about love, death, and immortality—in short, all the major patterns of theme and imagery. By the early sixties the design of Emily Dickinson's art was set; the rest of her poetic life was an elaboration and a perfection.

4

The critic can cull the poems and letters for a catalogue of transcendental "doctrines" which the poet had, for the moment at any rate, espoused. If Emerson referred to the world as "a divine dream, from which we may presently awake," Dickinson said: "Reality is a dream from which but a portion of mankind have yet waked . . ." If Emerson urged self-knowledge and self-reliance, Dickinson exhorted her poetic persona:

> Soto! Explore thyself!
> Therein thyself shalt find
> The "Undiscovered Continent" –
> No Settler had the Mind.   (P 832, II.631)*

And:

> Lad of Athens, faithful be
> To Thyself,
> And Mystery –
> All the rest is Perjury –   (P 1768, III.1183)

If Emerson perceived the correspondence which made the world the emblematic "web of God," Dickinson saw things as "trembling Emblems" and

* Reprinted by permission of Houghton Mifflin Co. from *Emily Dickinson Face to Face* by Martha Dickinson Bianchi (Boston, 1932).

felt the movements of an unseen Weaver. If Emerson's position rested on the divine faculty of Intuition, Dickinson claimed "Glee intuitive" as "the gift of God."[21]

Anyone who has given Emerson and Dickinson a thorough reading can indulge in the game of finding more cases in point, but such analogies could be misleading if they are insisted upon too rigidly, because the words of a lyric poet like Emily Dickinson express not philosophic generalizations but the measure of a particular moment. On the other hand, the critic cannot resign himself to an aimless chronological reading of almost 1800 lyrics. He must try to perceive in the shifting record of successive moments the salient recurrences, relations, and patterns without reducing the poet's mind to an abstraction. And so we must watch Emily approach Emerson by a dark and circuitous path.

Wherever Emily Dickinson's mental processes may have led, they began with an intolerable sense of emptiness which drove her to project as concrete evidence of her incompleteness the loss of childhood, father, mother, lover. She could list childhood and the dead among the "Things that never can come back"; she could even enumerate the things lost with childhood. But in all honesty she had to add: "But is that all I have lost— memory drapes her Lips."[22] These losses—genuine and heartfelt—were at least definable and hence bearable, but what seemed excruciating was the fact that almost the first act of the mind was an awareness of isolation. Edwards would have attributed this knowledge to original sin, and Emerson to the separation of the object from the Oversoul. But Emily Dickinson's was a characteristically personal response: all she knew was that she had to manage somehow from day to day, eating and sleeping and speaking and acting in the hollowness of the void:

> A loss of something ever felt I –
> The first that I could recollect
> Bereft I was – of what I knew not   (P 959, II.694)

The poem does not specify what was lost; all she could say was that she was bereft of something in and of herself, something so private that it belonged to her as an individual and would make her, as she was not now, a whole person.

> I cannot buy it – 'tis not sold –
> There is no other in the World –
> Mine was the only one   (P 840, II.635)

Before anything—faith, love, happiness—were possible, before she could give or take or act, the unknown factor had somehow to be found:

If I could find it Anywhere
I would not mind the journey there
Though it took all my store   (P 840, II.636)

So hers was a quest through an interior waste land, trackless and guideless, without even the name of the missing treasure. She could call it what she would—friend, lover, mother, father, "Golden Fleece," God—but these names could never contain the dark immensity of "Missing All." Life began with "Missing All"; and its trek through time seemed a dreary repetition of losses, of missing in turn each of the things most dear, until "Parting is all we know of heaven,/ And all we need of hell." In this private hell the lonely mourner "walked among the children."[23]

Even Satan, however, soon found that hell had its own compensations —the stimulus to yearn and struggle and resist. And in her own way Emily Dickinson came to draw sustenance from the substance of her sorrow. "I always try to think in any disappointment that had I been gratified, it had been sadder still, and I weave from such suppositions, *at times,* considerable consolation; consolation upside down as I am pleased to call it." "Consolation upside down" gave way sometimes to a brighter possibility: "To miss you, Sue, is power"; "Possession—has a sweeter chink/ Upon a Miser's Bar." Nor was she seeking solace in futile paradox; she was stating, flatly and deliberately, her recognition of the only grounds on which life without delusion was possible: "The stimulus of Loss makes most Possession mean."[24]

How could loss be power beyond possession? Because loss made us desire, made us project an object for our desire, made us strain urgently toward it. What we lacked we wanted, and if we lacked all, we wanted all. Fulfillment was static, like eternity; but desire was a process, and was therefore the prerequisite and condition of human life. At times, even, desire found response; for a moment we glimpsed what we wanted to see, grasped what we wanted to hold. Afterward, these fleeting moments of fulfillment provided the stimulus for the continuation of the process. Although we know that possession "is past the instant/ We achieve the Joy," we can accept life for the memory of past moments, the ecstasy of the present, the anticipation of the future:

Satisfaction – is the Agent
Of Satiety –
Want – a quiet Comissary
For Infinity.   (P 1036, II. 735)

In other words, man's littleness was, in a strange way, the condition for his greatness, and his limitations pointed him toward infinity. Edwards would have regarded this thesis as untenable, and Emerson would have found it morbid. There is something peculiarly modern about it. Nietzsche defined the tragic sense as the assertion of the will to live in the face of death and the inexhaustible joy which that assertion releases. Yeats wrote in his autobiography, "We begin to live when we have conceived of life as tragedy." In his version of *Women of Trachis* Ezra Pound had the dying and thwarted Herakles exclaim: "what/ SPLENDOUR, IT ALL COHERES." In *The Myth of Sisyphus* Albert Camus rejects suicide and chooses life despite its absurdity. Emily Dickinson, who spoke of "Confident Despair," would have understood these expressions of tragic joy. It was knowledge of "This brief Tragedy of Flesh" that made life precious; it was acceptance of loss and defeat that made an unexpected moment of vision into "that bright tragic thing."[25]

For this reason "Life never loses it's startlingness, however assailed," or—to state the idea in personal terms—"Who never lost, are unprepared / A Coronet to find!"[26] The crown's shining and full circle did descend on us, if only in momentary glory, and life was not only possible but beautiful as long as there were times when the void was filled with abundance. In "Burnt Norton" T. S. Eliot restated the moment for a waste-land century, but it is very much the same event:

> Dry the pool, dry concrete, brown edged,
> And the pool was filled with water out of sunlight,
> And the lotos rose, quietly, quietly,
> The surface glittered out of heart of light, . . .
> Then a cloud passed, and the pool was empty.*

If many of the Romantic prophets did not share her experience of darkness, they confirmed and defined for her the experience of overwhelming brightness. At its most sublime intensity, the momentary incandescence consumed the categories of human Understanding and held all in its illumination. In Emerson's words, with the movements of Reason, "there is the incoming or the receding of God: that is all we can affirm; and we can show neither how nor why." In Dickinson's image the manifestation was "a Blossom of the Brain," "the Spirit fructified." The cessation of such epiphanies would be "the Funeral of God," for each of these sublime moments was indeed "a cordial interview / With God"—not, she told her nephew Ned, the unseen Jehovah in epaulettes but another Eleusinian Deity who revealed Himself in an overpowering efflux of life. Heaven vested itself for each man,

---

* T. S. Eliot, "Burnt Norton," in *Four Quartets* (New York: Harcourt Brace Jovanovich, Inc., 1943), p. 4.

and for the sake of those incarnations one could endure the residue of life and "entertain Despair."[27] For Thoreau they had the same vitalizing function:

> Within the circuit of this plodding life,
> There enter moments of an azure hue,
> Untarnished fair as is the violet
> . . . .
> So by God's cheap economy made rich
> To go upon my winter's task again.[28]

So vital was the illumination that Emily tried time and again to make stubborn words render some sense of the glory: it was God's intrusion through which He was known and through which He confounded "Time's possibility"; it was "Eternity—obtained—in Time"; it was "Reversed Divinity," which, falling like a thunderbolt, transfixed mortality "in a moment of Deathlessness."[29] The quatrain below suggests metrically the moment's uncertain approach which reaches climactic force in the last leaping phrase:

> 'Tis this – invites – appalls – endows –
> Flits – glimmers – proves – dissolves –
> Returns – suggests – convicts – enchants –
> Then – flings in Paradise –   (P 673, II.520)

For most of the Romantics, however transcendental, Nature served as intermediary between self and Deity, as the meeting place of the new "religion." Among Emily Dickinson's earliest poems there is a splendid evocation of a very special summer's day (P 122, I.88), and many such poems followed over the years. At the beginning of her correspondence with Higginson, when she was trying to make him understand her "vision," she spoke in one letter alone of the "noiseless noise in the Orchard," of the stopping of breath "in the core of the Woods," of the sight of the chestnut tree that made the skies blossom for her, and finally of the wood visited by Angels. During her childhood her religious elders had forbidden her to enter the woods because of the venomous snake and the poisonous flowers (remember her warning to Abiah Root about the snake and the flowers of the imagination), but on later investigation despite their warnings she had found in Nature only an angelic visitation.[30]

Nature was precious because it was the material medium through which God or the Life Spirit touched man and through which man touched Him or It. Several poems invent images for the indefinable fusion of matter and spirit:

'Tis Compound Vision –
Light – enabling Light –
The Finite – furnished
With the Infinite –
Convex – and Concave Witness –
Back – toward Time –
And forward –
Toward the God of Him –   (P 906, II.666)

Elsewhere she wrote that the ear could not hear without the "Vital Word" that "came all the way from Life to me," nor could the eye see without divine light. During these visitations dust and Deity, time and eternity, were one, like Eliot's moment neither in time nor out of time, neither flesh nor fleshless.[31]

Man was by no means impotent in the process. Did not his openness, his striving for self-transcendence, indicate something in himself that answered to Spirit? Light, she said, enabled Light; for God to show Himself, we must be able to see. In these supreme moments our cringing souls, covert in the void, did emerge, did in turn show ourselves, did move and expand, so that we ourselves became microscopic incarnations, like "Holy Ghosts in Cages."[32] For the soul exists only in the body, and the body acts only under the soul's impulsion. Or, in poetic imagery:

The Music in the Violin
Does not emerge alone
But Arm in Arm with Touch, yet Touch
Alone – is not a Tune –
The Spirit lurks within the Flesh
Like Tides within the Sea
That make the Water live, estranged
What would the Either be?   (P 1576, III.1086)

Nevertheless, like all occurrences in the material order, these "sumptuous moments" went as inexplicably as they came: "Not of detention is Fruition," or, as Frost was to say, "Nothing gold can stay."[33] Despite his ebullient optimism, even Emerson had to admit that in the present state of things Reason's grasp was only momentary: "Like a bird which alights nowhere, but hops perpetually from bough to bough, is the Power which abides in no man and no woman, but for a moment speaks from this one, and for another moment from that one." Emily Dickinson endeavored mightily to accept joy's brevity as part of the process which impelled life to further inspiration. In the following poem the verses, seesawing back and forth in syntax and sound, suggest the oscillation from loss to recovery, from resonant correspondence back to hollow isolation:

Image of Light, Adieu –
Thanks for the interview –
So long – so short –
Preceptor of the whole –
Coeval Cardinal –
Impart – Depart –   (P 1556, III.1072)

In the whole span of the New England tradition, from Bradford and
Winthrop and Edwards to Emerson and Dickinson and later to Eliot and
Frost, individual experience finally focused and rested upon the pivotal moments of revelation and insight—the moments of divine manifestation and
human vision. This union—however insecure—in which the individual lost
himself in totality is the sole end of that Augustinian strain of piety which
Perry Miller saw as the bright heart of Puritanism. "Without it individual
life was a burden; with it living became richness and joy." But while Chris-
tians see regeneration as the moment of grace, "other people have found
other names for the experience: to lovers it is love, to mystics it is ecstasy,
to poets inspiration."[34] Edwards called men to the "Great Awakening";
Emerson smiled in the calm assurance of Reason's ever-expanding sway;
and in *Four Quartets* Eliot—that Puritan misplaced in the Midwest, who
moved through Boston back to orthodoxy in the Church that his forebears
had abandoned—composed a masterful meditation on "the still point of the
turning world." But Emily Dickinson, somewhat after Emerson and before
Eliot, could not arrive at the peace and assurance that they found at the
ends of divergent paths. In the face of conflicting evidences her problem,
like Frost's, was "what to make of a diminished thing," and her response,
like his, was "to get now and then elated." For a poet she was; and, in some
senses of the words, a lover and a mystic as well. What remains, therefore,
is to see what she made of and with her fitful vision.

5

If transcendence comes only to individuals and only in time and space,
these moments of personal revelation must be made to shape the totality of
meaning and of experience. The conquering of time through time of which
Eliot spoke was possible only if the instant's revelation-vision was fixed in a
world of flux, drawing time and space into perspective around itself and defining the design of faith. The center of light projects the encircling design
on all things, and sustains the design through time and perhaps (who
knows?) through eternity. If Christian theology no longer provided viable
terms to formulate the design, the new "religion" would have to create a
new vision; if the discarding of heaven left only earth as the arena of experience, the poet-priest would have to refashion the perception of the here and
now.

In "New Views of Christianity, Society, and the Church,"[35] Orestes Brownson insisted that he was beginning the process of redefinition within the existing ecclesiastical organization, but the force of his thought carried him and others far beyond. He defined the religious dilemma of the nineteenth century in terms of the interaction of Materialism and Spiritualism. In the intensity of its genesis Christianity had fused the two modes of thinking and living into a dynamic unity. The Middle Ages had erred in an inordinate Spiritualism which scourged the flesh, fanatically blinded to its inherent goodness and beauty. The Protestant reaction swung wrongheadedly to Materialism, so that the only spiritual elements in religion since the Reformation were clinging vestiges of the medieval Church. Now that these had gradually fallen away, the last and supreme expression of Protestant Materialism was the Unitarians' gross and bloated complacency. Christianity could survive, Brownson concluded, only with a resurgence of the primal energy which would again join both orders—matter and spirit, nature and heaven, body and soul—into an organic whole.

In "A Discourse of Matters Pertaining to Religion,"[36] Theodore Parker invoked the same dialectic with slightly different labels and pushed the argument further—in fact, out of the Christian context. According to Parker, Naturalism made a substantial distinction between creation and Creator; it envisioned man in Nature, with God "but *transiently* present and active" at the moment of creation, "not *immanently* present and active" from instant to instant. Without God's immanence man could know only naturally through his human intellect; and the Naturalist train of argument soon propelled man into "the Doubt of Hume, the Selfishness of Paley, the coarse materialism of Hobbes," and the rationalism of the Deists and the Unitarians. Supernaturalism also conceived creation as separate from God but insisted that man could know only through God's special intervention and express commands; and this train of argument soon debased man into the superstition of miracles, sacraments, churches, heaven, and hell. However, Parker's argument ran, there was a third approach—Spiritualism, or the Natural-Religious View—which superseded both these partial and divisive views; it eliminated the materiality of the one and the necromancy of the other. Its great synthesis recognized the "connection between God and the soul, as between light and the eye, sound and the ear, food and the palate, truth and the intellect, beauty and the imagination." The authority of the Natural-Religious View, therefore, rested on the "religious consciousness" of "free and conscious men," and its revelation was the perception of the glorious coherence of all things in the immanent Godhead.

Thoreau eliminated the clumsy labels and abstractions of Brownson and Parker to catch the smack and sting of the concrete experience: "I see, smell, taste, hear, feel, that everlasting Something to which we are allied, at once our maker, our abode, our destiny, our very Selves . . ."; "I explore, too, with pleasure, the sources of the myriad sounds which crowd the summer noon, and which seem the very grain and stuff of which eternity is made." His celebration of "a natural Sabbath" was the prayer "for no higher heaven than the pure senses can furnish, a *purely* sensuous life." For "may we not *see* God? . . . Is not Nature, rightly read, that of which she is commonly taken to be the symbol merely? . . . What is it, then, to educate but to develop these divine germs called the senses?" When the senses operated freely, heaven took place all around us, and multiplicity blended into the one divine articulation of Nature.

There was in Emily Dickinson a similar inclination of mind and heart. Whether or not she derived it from reading Brownson and Parker and Thoreau, her response to her own religious dilemma had much in common with theirs. In a letter to the Hollands she had expressed her love of " 'time and sense'—and fading things, and things that do *not* fade."[37] It was hard to love time and sense, unless she could somehow transmute fading things into unfading permanence. She could sometimes hope for, sometimes believe in, heaven, and then she accepted earth as a preparation for immortality.[38] But so uncertain a trust was no basis for a life's experience.

The stirrings of a new trust are suggested in these lines:

> The worthlessness of Earthly things
> The Ditty* is that Nature Sings –
> And then – enforces their delight
> Till Synods** are inordinate –   (P 1373, III. 947)

>   * Alternate word: Sermon   ** Alternate phrase: Zion is

Viewed rightly, the crumbling impermanence of things was lost in the incandescence which illuminated them as it consumed them to ashes. Overpowered by splendor, "I'm half tempted to take my seat in that Paradise of which the good man writes, and begin forever and ever *now,* so wondrous does it seem." Since her vision of nature lay beyond and above the temptation to heaven, she could claim to be luckier than God Himself: "If God had been here this summer, and seen the things that *I* have seen—I guess that He would think His Paradise superfluous." Often Heaven seemed "a fictitious Country": merely a name for "what I cannot reach," a designation for the furthest extension of experience to an unknown but intuited absolute. Eternity, therefore, was here, not there, if one were but worthy of the vision, and the vision of Heaven below came to replace that of "Papa above." Though "the time to live is frugal," it is sufficient, for "each of us has the skill of life." That is, since each "gives or takes heaven in corporeal person," we can see Nature as Heaven and Heaven in Nature simply by being true to our best selves.[39]

Weighing earth against a doubtful "Heaven to come," she summed up her choice with Yankee shrewdness in an aphorism that reads like Franklin pronouncing through Emerson: "A Savior in a Nut, is sweeter to the grasp than ponderous Prospectives." In the same vein she adapted another folk adage, using Poor Richard's pragmatism to ponder the choice between the temporal world and celestial eternity*:

> I cannot help esteem
>
> The "Bird within the Hand"
> Superior to the one
> The "Bush" may yield me
> Or may not
> Too late to choose again.   (P 1012, II.726)

As a matter of fact, the old terms of distinction might audaciously be reversed: "To be human is more than to be divine, for when Christ was divine, he was uncontented till he had been human."[40] So she would not be the proud wren who vainly sought "a home too high" but rather the lark who

>   is not ashamed
> To build upon the ground
> Her modest house –
>
> Yet who of all the throng
> Dancing around the sun
> Does so rejoice?   (P 143, I.102–103)

The assumption underlying her moments of exultation was not so much that earth as earth was superior to heaven but that earth was heaven, that indeed as Emerson and Thoreau had said, "The 'Supernatural,' was only the Natural, disclosed."[41] In the following poem the structure dramatically conveys the meaning. The statement of the first line—concise, declara-

---

* Cf. Frost's maxim, "Earth is still our fate" *(In the Clearing,* New York: Holt, Rinehart and Winston, 1962, p. 52), or the famous lines from "Birches":
>   May no fate wilfully misunderstand me
>   And half grant what I wish and snatch me away
>   Not to return. Earth's the right place for love:
>   I don't know where it's likely to go better.
(From *Complete Poems of Robert Frost.* Copyright 1916, 1921, 1923 by Holt, Rinehart and Winston, Inc. Copyright 1942, 1944, 1945 by Robert Frost. Reprinted by permission of Holt, Rinehart and Winston, Inc.).

tive—stands out from the subsequent verses, grammatically tangled and blurred by the recurrence of negatives:

> The Fact that Earth is Heaven – *
> Whether Heaven is Heaven or not
> If not an Affidavit
> Of that specific Spot
> Not only must confirm us
> That it is not for us
> But that it would affront us
> To dwell in such a place –   (P 1408, III.977)

"The Fact that Earth is Heaven"; in other poems "Universe" and "Firmament" and "Deity" become interchangeable alternatives. In her favorite metaphor of house and home—suggesting, as always, that odd Dickinson combination of coziness and awe—she called Nature a haunted house, a mystic house, God's house[42]: the lost Father in Heaven found in His neighborhood lodgings.

The vision of the earth-heaven conferred, at least for those moments, a total acceptance of the natural order of time and process. "Time," cried Emily, "why Time was all I wanted!"[43] With the great Romantic poets she celebrated the mysterious and vital process of growth in which self realized itself in cosmic unity.[44] Time was preferable to eternity, "for the one is still, but the other moves." Immortality was an "ablative estate" which carried us from the dynamic drama of experience, and death's encroachment, which alone kept life from being perfect (that is, from being eternity), nonetheless provided the pressure which made life the more intensely experienced, the more frugally felt. The process—for Dickinson as for Wordsworth, Shelley, Keats, Emerson, and Thoreau—made the world "Fairer though Fading." Besides, the individual process contained and revealed the pattern: to Thoreau's "The revolution of the seasons—is a great and steady flow," Emily added: "Changelessness is Nature's change."[45] So with the acceptance of change and death, the circle of the seasons could become for each of us the unwinding disclosure of heaven. Matter and Spirit, concrete and universal, are the same:

> "Nature" is what we see –
> The Hill – the Afternoon –

* Similarly, but much more skeptically, the only God that Frost will admit is the principle of matter penetrated by thought: the "God of the machine," the spirit working "in substantiation" in "the mixture mechanic" (*In the Clearing,* New York: Holt, Rinehart and Winston, Inc. 1962, pp. 49, 57, 58).

> Squirrel – Eclipse – the Bumble bee –
> Nay – Nature is Heaven –
> Nature is what we hear –
> The Bobolink – the Sea –
> Thunder – the Cricket –
> Nay – Nature is Harmony –   (P 668, II.515)

The force which swept through the world, animating matter into heaven, is sometimes symbolized in the spontaneous harmony of bird-song, but more often in the breath of the wind.[46] Emerson spoke of "the currents of the Universal Being," and Thoreau wrote, "In enthusiasm we undulate to the divine spiritus—as the lake to the wind." In Emily Dickinson's world, too, the wind was the Spiritus Sanctus, unseen but felt in all its operations: "The Wind didn't come from the Orchard—today— / Further than that—"; or, "A Murmur in the Trees—to note— / Not loud enough—for Wind—"; or:

> Exhiliration is the Breeze
> That lifts us from the Ground
> And leaves us in another place
> Whose statement is not found –   (P 1118, II.786)

The culmination of the wind's sweep is a sudden and momentary breathlessness: "When Winds take Forests in their Paws— / The Universe—is still." Suspended in stillness, we open eyes and heart, and we see and know. The event was thus double: outward and inward, revelation and vision, "The Capsule of the Wind / The Capsule of the Mind."[47]

Those climactic capsule moments are most often symbolized in "Lightning—and the Sun—" In Emerson's phrase, revelation traveled "like a thunderbolt to the centre," and repeatedly in Dickinson poems[48] the lightning, striking to the center with light so bright as to be borne for only a flashing second, illuminated all the landscape for her stunned and reeling consciousness. Sometimes she softened the remembrance of the impact by domesticating the lightning image to "yellow feet" or "electric Mocassin" or "a yellow Fork / From Tables in the sky," but she had felt, in ravished awe, the slamming, blinding force. Thunder-stricken like Ahab, but shaken to life and not to death, she saw things "Not yet suspected—but for Flash / And Click—and Suddenness"; and so she "would not exchange the Bolt / For all the rest of Life." Considered in their fullness, these spots of time seemed "torrid Noons,"[49] and noon became a major image for their concentric radiance:[50]

You'll know it – as you know 'tis Noon –
By Glory –
As you do the Sun –
By Glory –   (P 420, I.326)

Even when Emily Dickinson tried to conjure up a conception of heaven as it was or would be, she could imagine only the natural order extended through time and space. "Forever—is composed of Nows": "not a different time," but a perfected time, an Arcadian Golden Age where "Sun constructs perpetual Noon," where "perfect Seasons wait," where "Consciousness—is Noon."[51]

A Nature be
Where Saints, and our plain going Neighbor
Keep May!   (P 977, II.706)

On the other hand the peerless moments revealed earth as Eden before the Fall—Nature perfected to Paradise. If heaven is Arcadia, Eden is heaven. An early poem tells a charming parable about a lost, frost-bitten Puritan flower (a floral variant of the image of herself as a little girl locked out in the cold) who found an unfallen Eden aglow with summer:[52]

As if some little Arctic flower
Upon the polar hem –
Went wandering down the Latitudes
Until it puzzled came
To continents of summer –
To firmaments of sun –
To strange, bright crowds of flowers –
And birds, of foreign tongue!
I say, As if this little flower
To Eden, wandered in –
What then? Why nothing,
Only, your inference therefrom!   (P 180, I.132)

One inference is that under the thrust of that "bright" strain of the Romantic spirit of which Wordsworth and Scott are good examples in England, and Bryant, Emerson, and Whitman in America, Emily Dickinson was able to break open the dark inner void to a shining world outside in which, paradoxically, she could both lose and fulfill herself. We dwell in Eden every day, she said, would we but open our eyes, for "Paradise is of the option," is "always eligible." "Not—'Revelation'—'tis—that waits, / But our unfurnished eyes." To the poet's eyes " 'Eden' a'nt so lonesome / As New England used to be!"[53]

Once again it is very easy to underestimate the complexity of Emily Dickinson's mind by fastening too exclusively on one aspect of it. Although her rhetorical question "With the Kingdom of Heaven on his knee, could Mr Emerson hesitate?" is a transcendentalist assertion, Mr. Emerson himself spoke in statements, not questions; and he would have shied away from the Christian connotation of "Kingdom of Heaven" and preferred an allusion to Hamatreya or Brahma or the Kingdom of Pan ("the patient Pan," "the eternal Pan"). Although Emily's prayer "In the name of the Bee— / And of the Butterfly— / And of the Breeze—Amen!" suggests the immanent Deity of Parker's Natural-Religious view, it is expressed in a parody of the Christian formula whose playfulness is utterly serious. Emily recognized the complicated motive: when we have lost something precious, we hasten to compensate by fashioning its image elsewhere, perhaps within ourselves, perhaps in Nature.[54]

> And a Suspicion, like a Finger
> Touches my Forehead now and then
> That I am looking oppositely
> For the site of the Kingdom of Heaven –   (P 959, II.695)

Emily Dickinson could not say as wholeheartedly as Frost's protagonist in *A Masque of Mercy* (whose mother "was left over from the Brook Farm venture"): "I say I'd rather be lost in the woods / Than found in church."

Unsatisfied by Emerson's pagan paradise, she had to invest the new-found Eden through image and metaphor with the import of the Christian faith which she had rejected. So she came to speak of creative energy as an inexplicable force much like Edwards' "indwelling vital principle" of grace —in fact, precisely a "Conversion of the Mind / Like Sanctifying in the Soul." Christening by water in the country church was superseded by a new baptism, in which the poet freely gave herself to the call of a full natural existence.[55] Thereafter natural ecstasy corresponded to God's grace, and even the impermanence of ecstasy was transformed into the renunciation which was a sign of justification and election. The only commandment was to "Consider the Lilies" each ordained day, for Nature was the sacrament unto sanctification and spring the miracle of redemption and resurrection.[56] The process of "sacramental" experience constituted, in Thoreauvian terms, the "natural Sabbath" of heaven at home:

> Some keep the Sabbath going to Church –
> I keep it, staying at Home –
>
> . . . .
>
> So instead of getting to Heaven, at last –
> I'm going, all along.   (P 324, I.254–255)

Here again Emily Dickinson circles back to her point of departure. If she had her Sabbath in Nature, it was still in some sense a Sabbath, as it was not for Thoreau. Moreover, at the same time that the poems constructed a new Sabbath in a romantic Eden, the term "old-fashioned" began to take on warm and comfortable associations. She often claimed to be old-fashioned; she dressed and looked old-fashioned; with another turn of the fancy she could even dress Eden up in New England garb: "Eden is that old-fashioned House"; in fact, "Nature is 'old-fashioned,' perhaps a Puritan."[57] She could not resolve the paradox (or was it a contradiction?) logically or intellectually. Its origin, if not its resolution, lay in her emotional character. By yoking together two sets of associations she attempted to reconcile metaphorically her divided consciousness.

In reality, of course, a mutable earth could not really be heaven—if there were such a place. In the imagery of the poems noon declines into twilight and dawn only follows night. She might say, "That a pansy is transitive, is its only pang. This, precluding that, is indeed divine"; but she knew that the pang was real and fatal. In the grip of ecstasy she might accept the life-process, but still she was left with the compulsion to escape a "rotatory" life and the "ceaseless flight of the seasons."[58] The transforming experience was the momentous interview—the *"separated* hour . . . more pure and true than *ordinary* hours," the "supreme italic" that punctuated life's course.[59] But, suspended between italics, she could only relive earlier bliss in memory or anticipate bliss to come:

> Looking back is best that is left
> Or if it be – before –
> Retrospection is Prospect's half,
> Sometimes, almost more.   (P 995, II.720)

Unable to rest, Emily Dickinson cast herself before and after. Prospect and retrospect became major themes in her poetry:[60] in the desperate race with time they enabled her to keep in sight the emblazoned signposts that marked the journey; they solaced her in the empty stretches that intervened.

Emily Dickinson hoped that she had discarded the Calvinist God for another Deity who was friend instead of foe, but she found that her relation to Him was in many respects unchanged. He remained the unknown Jove-Jehovah, hurling lightning-bolts and leaving a stricken "little girl" to make what she could of the experience. If He lent no abiding stay, she would have to provide of herself, and turn once again to her own creative resources. Poetry had to do more than "pile like Thunder to it's close / Then crumble grand away."[61] She would have to make its image catch and keep the blinding flash.

Emerson had already ponderously pronounced in the verses which preface the essay on "Art":

> 'Tis the privilege of Art
> Thus to play its cheerful part,
> Man in earth to acclimate
> And bend the exile to his fate,
> And, moulded of one element
> With the days and firmament,
> Teach him on these stairs to climb
> And live on even terms with Time;
> Whilst upper life and slender rill
> Of human life doth overfill.

Emily Dickinson also came, though less sanguinely, to conceive of art as the mediator between time and eternity. Isolating certain things from the flux, "We hasten to adorn" and use them, in order to construct marmoreal art; thereby "We—temples build"[62]—not public temples but private shrines for the meeting of spirit and Spiritus. As an artist she made permanent the momentary acts of consciousness despite time's inexorable wheel. She might say that she lived in an Eden of unfading seasons and perpetual noon, but such a world existed only in her saying it—that is, only in the transcendent ordering of art. Over the last century and a half, poets have come to rely increasingly on this redeeming and immortalizing function of art: Wordsworth recollected and recorded in tranquillity, and Keats aspired to the nightingale's song and the moving stillness of the urn.

Faced with the increasing difficulty of coming to terms with personal experience within the safety of received religion, Emily Dickinson like many modern poets affirmed her supreme (and religious) dedication to comprehending her experience through the intense concentration of artistic expression. For Yeats the choice between religion and art was the "perfection of the life" or the perfection "of the work." In "Vacillation" he wrote:

> I – though heart might find relief
> Did I become a Christian man and choose for my belief
> What seems most welcome in the tomb – play a predestined part.
> Homer is my example and his unchristened heart.*

For Yeats the part was not a rejection of heaven but a commitment to transmuting time's torments into "the artifice of eternity." For her own reasons

* Reprinted with permission of The Macmillan Co. from *Collected Poems* by William Butler Yeats (New York, 1956), p. 247. Copyright by The Macmillan Co., renewed 1961 by Bertha Georgie Yeats.

Emily Dickinson rejected the comforts of Christianity and felt compelled to choose instead the life of the conscious artist. Only in conscious experience —if anywhere—could she find herself; and only in the perfection of art—if anywhere—would she escape the temporal wheel on which self turned. Born in Congregational Amherst half a century before Yeats, she could not transport herself to Byzantium any more easily than to Emerson's Eden. Still she lived for her own poetry and said to herself and to her neighbors: "Who has not found the Heaven—below— / Will fail of it above—"[63]

6

In the history of the New England spirit Emily Dickinson occupies a pivotal place. Puritan orthodoxy had reached its culmination as a religious and social order in the mid-seventeenth century and a century later had found its most magnificent exponent in Jonathan Edwards, after the order itself had begun to pull apart. By the 1850s Emerson had reinvigorated the New England spirit, but only by isolating certain aspects of Edwards' thought and combining and infusing them with the vitality of Transcendentalism. Nevertheless, by so doing Emerson brought about a further disintegration of the great Puritan synthesis, a separation of the heart from the head, just as Benajmin Franklin, Charles Chauncy, and Andrewes Norton represented a separation of the head from the heart. For all his Calvinism —or rather precisely because of his acceptance of Calvinism with his mind and heart—Edwards was a more complete person than any of these men.

Emily Dickinson points to the end of the tradition not because she represents, as Emerson does, a splintering off of part of that tradition, but because she embodies in her life and poetry the painful divisions that sundered the New England mind. Emerson was essentially a serene soul, as she was essentially a tormented one. He could be happy because out of selected fragments he had made a shining new faith—shorn now of sin and dogma and devils. To reliance on the intuitive vision of the man-god in a sinless Eden he gave thumping assent with all the eloquent enthusiasm of the poet-preacher. But as Emily Dickinson realized—along with Hawthorne and Melville—he had had to close his mind and heart to much of the complex reality in order to achieve this serenity.

There is no indication that Emily Dickinson was acquainted with the writings of Jonathan Edwards; but from the remarks she made he was associated in her mind with the faith of the fathers.[64] Since what remained of New England Protestantism seemed to her intellectually preposterous and emotionally spurious, she heeded Emerson's call to the poet's rather than the Christian's vocation. With Wordsworth and Emerson and Whitman, she sought to find herself by losing herself, to lose herself by opening "an original relation to the universe." For dazzling moments she and the world were transfigured into divinity, but the difficulty lay in holding the transfiguration in a sustaining vision. In a late poem she weighed "Orpheus' Sermon" against the preacher's, or Emerson's sermon against Edwards', and aligned herself again with Emerson and the "warbling teller."[65] Nevertheless, her unshakable conception of reality and awareness of the human condition were derived not so much from Emerson as from the "old-fashioned" Puritans:

> Paradise is that old mansion
> Many owned before –
> Occupied by each an instant
> Then reversed the Door –
> Bliss is frugal of her Leases
> Adam taught her Thrift
> Bankrupt once through his excesses –   (P 1119, II.787)

These seven lines of an unfinished poem rehearse all the major elements of the Puritan "vision": the initial harmony of the universe; man's violation of that harmony and his consequent alienation; the possibility of reunion and its fulfillment in visionary instants; the backruptcy of life without vision.

In Dickinson's poetry there is a determined rigor of sight and mind which is largely lacking in Emerson: a flinty honesty which would spare her nothing, which wished (in Thoreau's words) "to live deliberately, to front only the essential facts of life," to know the abyss as well as the empyrean. There is a complexity of sensibility that brings us back to Bradford, Taylor, and Edwards and is found among the Transcendentalists perhaps only at times in Thoreau. Yet in Emily Dickinson this double consciousness finds resolution neither in Emerson's and Thoreau's belief in heaven here nor in Edwards' faith in heaven hereafter. The complexity of her mind is not the complexity of harmony but that of dissonance. Her peculiar burden was to be a Romantic poet with a Calvinist's sense of things; to know transitory ecstasy in a world tragically fallen and doomed. Her poems display a range and variety of emotional experience which far surpass that of Edwards, Emerson, Thoreau, or Whitman, but the work of all these men has a wholeness, a consistency, and finally a repose which hers lacks. She could be possessed only by the experience of the immediate moment, and so her art expressed itself in short lyrics each of which incarnated a moment. As a result her poetry emerged not in a consistent and overmastering design but in an intricate pattern of individual and contrasting fragments.

In Emily Dickinson the opposing tendencies that divided the New England mind met at cross-purposes, and after her the tendencies were to diverge again. One line of development would lead to T. S. Eliot, who was able in mid-twentieth century to hold timeless moments amid the stretching wastes of time by subsuming them both again in the Christian vision. For Eliot, perfection of the life and perfection of the work converged once more to a single center; mind and heart and art moved with one purpose; his beginning and his end were the Alpha and the Omega. That he could pursue his purpose, however, only away from his native shores signalized, in the one direction, the all-but-final collapse of the New England tradition. Of those who stayed at home, Robinson Jeffers' Calvinist sensibility could find root only in the brute beauty of the wilderness on the opposite coast. Of those who stayed in New England, Robert Frost exemplifies in many respects another line of development that proceeded from Emily Dickinson. In Frost's poetry—"Bereft," for example—man is alone in an indifferent universe without Edwards' grace or Emerson's Reason or Jeffers' pantheism; he sees "neither out far nor in deep"; from nature (no longer with a capital N) he receives either no response, as in "The Most of It," or at best an indecipherable hint that might be something or nothing, as in "For Once, Then, Something." In a chaos without objective absolutes Frost draws his materials from experience and imposes his own order in "the figure a poem makes"; perfection of the work provides "a momentary stay against confusion."[66] Robert Lowell, the most distinguished of the younger New England poets, would readily agree: obsessed by a dead tradition and a shattered world, he sought refuge in Catholicism for a time; now he sifts the pieces through his mind, constructing blazing cries of loss and failure.

In the long list of those who saw "New Englandly," Emily Dickinson occupied a critical position. She came after the fatal cleavage that split the Puritan mind between 1740 and 1840, and in her, for the last time, the dislocated elements came together to struggle for articulation, if not for readjustment, before they diverged, by Henry Adams' law of acceleration, to dissipate their last energies. The astonishing and characteristic thing about Emily Dickinson is that at the crosspoint of the X she could have written both these quatrains about earth and heaven:

In thy long Paradise of Light
No moment will there be
When I shall long for Earthly Play
And mortal Company –   (P 1145, II.803)

God is indeed a jealous God –
He cannot bear to see
That we had rather not with Him
But with each other play.   (P 1719, III.1159)

[1] L II 620; L III 866, 798.
[2] See Perry Miller, *The New England Mind: The Seventeenth Century* (Cambridge, Mass., 1954), pp. 7–8, 10–34.
[3] See Perry Miller, "From Edwards to Emerson," in *Errand into the Wilderness* (Cambridge, Mass., 1956), pp. 184–203.
[4] Perry Miller, *The New England Mind: From Colony to Province* (Cambridge, Mass., 1953), p. 69.
[5] See Allen Tate, "Emily Dickinson," in *Reactionary Essays on Poetry and Ideas* (New York, 1936), pp. 3–26.
[6] *Margaret Fuller: American Romantic,* ed. Perry Miller (New York, 1963), p. 58.
[7] See George Frisbie Whicher, *This Was a Poet: A Critical Biography of Emily Dickinson* (New York, 1939), pp. 190ff.
[8] *Ibid.,* p. 190.
[9] *Ibid.,* pp. 39–40; Leyda I 150, 296, 331, 356; L III 713.
[10] Cf. L II 539; L III 756, 775, 856, 882.
[11] Leyda I 334, 351–352, 102, 309–310; L III 913, 928; *Home,* p. 572; L II 626, 627.
[12] L II 455, 586; L III 692; Leyda II 141.
[13] L I 92.
[14] L I 3.
[15] L I 13, 88.
[16] L I 95.
[17] L III 751.
[18] L I 144, 181; L II 327–328; L I 235, 264; *Home,* p. 319; L I 272, 305–306.
[19] See L I 117, 296.
[20] L I 143, 148–149, 196; L II 330.
[21] L III 911; L II 315, 594, 560.
[22] L III 714, 928–929.
[23] P985 II 711; P1732 III 1166; P959 II 695.
[24] L I 167; L II 489; P1093 II 770.
[25] P552 II 401; P664 II 511; P1660 III 1133.
[26] L III 750–751; P73 I 58.
[27] P945 II 687; P844 II 637; L III 880; P964 II 536.
[28] "Natural History of Massachusetts," in *Excursions* (Boston, 1893), pp. 127–128.
[29] P1462 III 1010; P349 I 279; P800 II 605; P1090 II 769.
[30] L II 415.
[31] P1039 II 736.
[32] P184 I 134.
[33] P1315 III 911; in addition, cf. P319 I 243–244; P1125 II 790; P1382 III 952.
[34] Perry Miller, *The New England Mind: The Seventeenth Century,* p. 25.
[35] Orestes A. Brownson, "New Views of Christianity, Society, and the Church" in *The Transcendentalists,* ed. Perry Miller (Cambridge, Mass., 1950), pp. 115–123.
[36] Theodore Parker, "A Discourse of Matters Pertaining to Religion" in *The Transcendentalists,* pp. 316–324.
[37] L II 329.
[38] Cf., for example, P63 I 48; P65 I 50–51; P428 I 331–332; P977 II 706; P1024 II 730–731; P1043 II 738; P1228 III 854.
[39] L II 329; P562 II 430; P239 I 172; P1684 III 1144; L II 579, 504.
[40] P1012 II 726; L II 593, 592.
[41] L II 424. For other comments on earth and heaven, see P418 I 325; P575 II 439; P1544 III 1065; L II 478, 550, 553, 594–595; L III 928.
[42] P766 II 582; P783 II 591; L II 554; P1077 II 762; L II 333.
[43] Leyda II 414. For other poems on nature as process, see P386 I 305; P1114 II 783; P1154 II 808; P1267 III 882; P1369 III 945; P1669 III 1137; P1756 III 1178; P1762 III 1181.
[44] See, for example, P1067 II 751; P1142 II 801; P1349 III 932; P1422 III 986–987; P1434 III 994; P1741 III 1171.

[45] L II 490; P1741 III 1171; P938 II 682; L III 848.

[46] For poems on wind, see P315 I 238; P316 I 239–240; P416 I 323–324; P513 II 394–395; P516 II 396–397; P774 II 586–587; P945 II 687; P998 II 721; P1118 II 786–787; P1271 III 884; P1397 III 967; P1418 III 984; P1530 III 1055; P1656 III 1131.

[47] P316 I 239; P416 I 323; P315 I 238; P1397 III 967; P998 II 721.

[48] For poems on lightning, see P362 I 288; P393 I 309; P420 I 326; P480 I 368; P630 II 485; P824 II 624–625; P925 II 675; P974 II 704; P1129 II 792; P1173 II 819; P1247 III 866; P1468 III 1017; P1475 III 1021; P1581 III 1089; P1593 III 1098; P1660 III 1133.

[49] P974 II 704; P1581 III 1089.

[50] For poems referring to noon, see P63 I 48; P112 I 82; P197 I 216–217; P512 II 393–394; P575 II 439; P579 II 443; P638 II 490; P646 II 497; P673 II 520; P882 II 653; P916 II 671; P930 II 678; P931 II 679; P978 II 706; P1023 II 730; P1056 II 745; P1233 III 858; P1581 III 1089.

[51] P624 II 480; P1056 II 745. For other poems referring to Eden or earth-heaven, see P24 I 24–25; P148 I 106; P374 I 298; P756 II 575–576; P839 II 635; L III 928.

[52] P180 I 132. See also P249 I 179; P385 I 304–305; P503 II 386; P1657 III 1131–1132.

[53] P1657 III 1131–1132; L II 454, 254, 508; P215 I 151.

[54] L II 482; P18 I 21; P1209 III 841.

[55] L III 683; P508 II 389–390; P473 I 363.

[56] For references to grace in the poems, see P343 I 274; P359 I 286; P472 I 362; P569 II 434–435; P743 II 566; P744 II 586–587; P968 II 700–701; P1313 III 910. For references to revelation, see L II 424; P694 II 535–536. For references to renunciation, justification, and election, see P313 I 236–237; P322 I 249–250; P343 I 274–275; P528 II 405; P569 II 434; P745 II 568; P751 II 572. For references to Sacrament and miracles, see L I 207; L III 825; P74 I 59–60; P130 I 92–93; P495 II 379; P646 II 497; P1297 III 900. For other poems referring to Sacrament, see P383 I 303; P535 II 412; P751 II 572; P812 II 613; P1651 III 1129.

[57] P1157 III 1131–1132; L III 699. See also P70 I 56; P788 II 594–595; P973 II 704; Leyda II 114, 377.

[58] L II 539; L I 37; L II 504. See also L I 16, 66; L II 323, 354; P1178 III 822; P1437 III 995–996; P1530 III 1055; P1682 III 1143–1144; P1764 III 1182.

[59] L I 130; P1498 III 1034; L III 843. For other poems referring to a momentous interview, whether with God, lover, or friend, see P247 I 177–178; P293 I 211–212; P296 I 215–216; P322 I 249–250; P410 I 319; P663 II 510–511; P768 II 583; P800 II 605; P902 II 663.

[60] For poems about prospect and retrospect, see P379 I 300; P867 II 646; P1196 III 833; P1227 III 853–854; P1271 III 884; P1353 III 943; P1416 III 982–983; P1498 III 1034; P1742 III 1171; L II 452; L III 922.

[61] L II 474; P1247 III 866.

[32] P1585 III 1092; P1209 III 841; P488 I 372–373.

[63] P1544 III 1065.

[64] Emily Dickinson mentioned Edwards only twice: L I 121; P1522 III 1049.

[65] P1545 III 1065–1066.

[66] *The Complete Poems of Robert Frost* (New York, 1949), p. vi.

HENRY JAMES

****

The writings of Henry James sometimes seem smothered under the weight of commentary heaped upon them. Leon Edel has
published four volumes (New York, 1953–1963) of what seems
now likely to be a five-volume biography. The most trustworthy
introductory guides, however, remain Joseph Warren Beach's *The
Method of Henry James* (New York, 1918; reprinted, 1954) and
Frederick W. Dupee's perceptive and unpretentious *Henry James*
(New York, 1952). Eighteen of James's own critical prefaces to
the twenty-six volume New York Edition of his writings were
brought together by R. P. Blackmur as *The Art of the Novel*
(New York, 1934; reprinted, 1948). James's *Notebooks* (Cam-
bridge, Mass., 1947) is edited by F. O. Matthiessen and Kenneth B.
Murdock; his *Autobiography* (New York, 1956), by Frederick W.
Dupee. Many find provocative Quentin Anderson's *The American
Henry James* (New Brunswick, N. J., 1956), Jacques Barzun's
"James the Melodramist," *Kenyon Review*, V (Autumn 1943),
pp. 508–521, R. P. Blackmur's "The Loose and Baggy Monsters

of Henry James," *The Lion and the Honeycomb* (New York, 1955), André Gide's "Henry James," *Yale Review,* XIX (March 1930), pp. 641–643, F. R. Leavis's "The Appreciation of Henry James," *Scrutiny,* XIV (Spring 1947), pp. 229–237, F. O. Matthiessen's authoritative *Henry James, The Major Phase* (London and New York, 1944), Philip Rahv's often reprinted "Attitudes to Henry James," *New Republic,* CVIII (February 15, 1943), pp. 220–224, and his "Heiress to All the Ages," *Partisan Review,* X (May–June 1943), pp. 227–247. Richard Poirier has written of *The Comic Sense of Henry James* in the early novels (New York, 1960), and Frederick C. Crews of *The Tragedy of Manners* in the later novels (New Haven, Conn., 1957). Frederick W. Dupee collected many of the better critical essays in *The Question of Henry James* (New York, 1945), and Oscar Cargill has put together an orderly review of commentary in *The Novels of Henry James* (New York, 1961).

HENRY JAMES AND
THE MORALITY OF FICTION

Robert J. Reilly

✶✶

I

If the notion of height is a natural metaphor, always implying superiority of some kind, then it is a metaphor singularly appropriate to the true Jamesian—or Jacobite, in Geismar's acid phrase. For the Jamesian, the work of James is really above and beyond most other fiction; it is a high palace of art which he enters with genuine reverence, by virtue of those qualities which James himself required of the ideal critic—perception at the pitch of passion, insight that is only once removed from the original creative act. In James's work the Jamesian perceives the quintessence of conscious art; he learns to delight in the process of total artistic consciousness presenting, or projecting, vessels of consciousness nearly as full as its own. And

From *American Literature*, XXIX (March, 1967), pp. 1–30. Reprinted by permission of the author and the Duke University Press.

after Bach, who can descend to Strauss, or even Wagner? For the Jamesian, only James is really satisfactory—other fiction seems fumbling and accidental, or easy and obvious, or simply gross. The Jamesian nearly always speaks from heights; it is impossible for him not to judge by Jamesian standards, because in order to become a Jamesian he has had to ascend to these standards.

Below, they argue still, long after Frank Moore Colby said it all so well, that James's people have no bodies, that they are unattached consciousness casting no shadows. But that complaint has no more force for a Jamesian than for a Platonist. The Jamesian has long since discovered that the only means he has of defending Hemingway or Lawrence is to hope that they have dimly tried to construct James's dramas of consciousness but have only rarely been equal to it, have darkly scuffled about in the vestibule of physical reality until by accident or luck they have strayed inside and seen for a moment the altar of human consciousness. The Jamesian does not care that James's people have no bodies, or at most bodies like gold to airy thinness beat, for he long ago learned from James that to deal with the body is to retreat from truth, or from the only reality that matters. The singularity of man, for the Jamesian, is man's consciousness, not his body. If dogs and sheep wrote novels, they would deal with physical reality. But if anything is recorded in the book of human life it is the actions of human consciousness, the sunlight of the human mind, not the refractions and shadows that the mind casts through the body—these James and the Jamesians leave for history and the lower forms of imitative literature.

Nor is the Jamesian ruffled by the other ancient rebukes: that James's people are hypersensitive, almost extrasensitive, alert to mental tones and pitches beyond normal human perception, like dogs hearing an apparently silent whistle; that they speak an impossible language never heard on land or sea; that their passions consist in their intricate analyses of each other, and their detumescences in psychological discovery. Against all these, and more, the Jamesian has sealed his mind; for him these are phantom issues; the only real issue is the premise from which they proceed. That premise is simply that the norm for judging fiction is established by combining many of the characteristic aims and techniques of the great body of twentieth-century realistic fiction: the newspaper realism of Dreiser's details, the panoramic social view of Dos Passos's trilogy, the celebration of physical sex in Lawrence, the calculated formlessness in the stream of consciousness of Joyce and Faulkner, the mindless violence in Hemingway. If one adds to these the general twentieth-century preoccupation with mental freaks, neurotics, and endless surrogates of formal religion, one has what might be called the normative twentieth-century novel. Set next to it, James's work seems of another world, for James has not Dreiser's realism, nor Dos Passos's social conscience, nor Lawrence's overt sexuality, nor Joyce's and Faulkner's free flow of the unconscious, nor Hemingway's violence. But for the Jamesian the norm is James. It is not James who fails to do what these others do, but they who fail to do what James does. James is orthodox; they are heretical. And if James is the norm, then Dreiser's realism is dreary and insignificant, and Dos Passos has strayed into social history, and Lawrence has elevated a body function into a religion, and Joyce and Faulkner have let the formlessness of their material dictate their aesthetic order, and Hemingway has written boys' books. For the Jamesian they all fall short: some are windy and intrusive pessimists, some are word-drunk, some are lost in the secondary and easily pictured reality of the body, and none has sufficiently felt "the torment of form."

But there is at least one ghost that the Jamesian adept has not laid, one question that hauntingly recurs like Peter Quint's white face outside the windows at Bly. That is the question of the moral character, or direction, of James's work; whether or not the work can be said to subscribe to a moral viewpoint, even in the most general way; and, if so, whether this moral viewpoint is traditional or wholly personal to James. The question is a peculiarly tormenting one for the Jamesian; however he answers it, he seems for the first time vulnerable to the assaults of the crowd.

The first inclination of the avowed Jamesian when faced with the moral question of James's fiction is to stand aloof, to treat the whole issue ironically, as James himself did in "The Art of Fiction"—to reduce the question to absurdity by means of analogy: "Will you not define your terms and explain how (a novel being a picture) a picture can be either moral or immoral?"[1] But to answer thus is to leave James open to the accusation of *fin de siècle* aestheticism, to seem to lodge him uncomfortably with Whistler and Wilde, a grouping that the anti-Jamesians would cherish only a little less than an admission of James's homosexuality. Worse, the Jamesian knows how wrong such a grouping is. Though in his passion for technique James often spoke as if that were his whole concern, the Jamesian knows that this was not James's moral indifference but his singlemindedness. His prefaces and notebooks are as full of technical data as a painter's notebook or a cabinetmaker's—comments on the looseness of the first-person point of view, the importance of foreshortening, the desirability of an intense perceiver as protagonist. They are largely the records of a craftsman's successes and failures, and if they do not often deal with the large questions of life, neither do Da Vinci's sketchbooks. On the other hand, if the Jamesian as-

---

[1] *The Future of the Novel*, ed. Leon Edel (New York, 1956), p. 24.

serts what is for him very apparent, that there is a positive moral quality in James's work but that it is not easily described, not fixed to any traditional dogmatic religion, then James seems liable to another indictment: that he was cynically using morality because, consummate artist that he was, he found moral decisions dramatic and difficult to "do." From this point of view his morality is unspecifiable because it is relatively unimportant; any vague kind of religion would do, as for a writer who is concerned to dramatize a soldier's cowardice under fire any kind of war will do. According to this indictment, all the famous Jamesian "renunciations"—Isabel Archer's, Fleda Vetch's, Lambert Strether's—occur because they are interesting psychological or spiritual processes, not because what produced them is important. The moral motivation behind them is in fact irrelevant, or at best nominal; if one could conceive of any other cause bringing them about, then that would have done as well. The branches are dramatic; the roots are not. But the Jamesian knows truth from opinion, and he knows that James was anything but a cynical manipulator of religion, that James's attitude toward traditional religion is at least partly revealed in that magnificant scene in *The Ambassadors* in which Strether watches Mme. de Vionnet praying in Notre Dame and comes very close to envying her faith, before he steps back into his role of the Jamesian gentleman visiting a monument.

Perhaps it would give aid and comfort to the Jamesians to remind them that this problem is not peculiar to James, that the question of an author's moral attitudes seems naturally to arise in every case where the author's reputation is almost wholly "aesthetic" or "artistic," when an author invariably appears in every book of literary history but only rarely in a book dealing with intellectual history or philosophic attitudes, for the very good reason that there is not in his work any identifiable moral code or set of attitudes that can be extracted, abstracted, and discussed. No one is puzzled by the moral qualities of Hemingway's fiction, for example, because the Hemingway "code" or "world view" is relatively easy to abstract; one can discuss it as he can that of Milton or Camus or Zola, because in all these cases the moral or religious pattern seems not so much an organic part of the work as a paradigm which the work fills out and gives body to. But with Shakespeare, Conrad, and James the moral patterns, the figures in the carpets, are much harder to trace and are only partly detachable; and this is certainly in part because the textures of the carpets are so rich, the writers are so manifestly great artists in command of their mediums. Thus it happens with writers like Shakespeare and James that the question sooner or later arises: what are their moral views? what is the moral direction of their work? And because they are clearly the master workers, it is natural that the questions ultimately shift from the moral direction of their specific work to the moral possibilities of the mediums themselves, and the questions become general and speculative: is drama moral? is fiction moral? It is one of the marks of the great artist that he forces attention to the form in which he works as if, like Homer, he had invented his medium and had left his shaping impression everywhere through it.

It is these related problems of the morality of James's fiction in particular and the morality of fiction in general that I wish to deal with here, though warily and tentatively, as befits one scaling lofty peaks in rarefied air. But as a prologue to the problems, it may be wise to point out, if not clear away, some of the thickets of difficulty which surround them.

First, there is the obvious fact that in dealing with an artist's moral views one has two bodies of evidence. He has what the artist has himself said about morality, outside the art works—unless, like Shakespeare, he has said nothing at all that we know of. And he has the moral view, or attitudes, to be found in the art work itself. It is not self-evident that these views will coincide, though we usually assume they do. But as you cannot argue with any assurance from the moral views in *Lear* to the personal moral views of Shakespeare himself, so you cannot argue the reverse of the process—that what James said discursively about morality is automatically reproduced in aesthetic form in his fiction. And clearly, the more dramatic and objective the art work is—Shakespeare's plays, James's late novels—the more difficult it is to assign to its author any moral view or views advocated by a character in the work. It was this impenetrable dramatic quality of Shakespeare's work that so distressed Johnson: Shakespeare had so faithfully held the mirror up to life that though he reflected all the elements of a moral system, he nowhere ordered them into a system. But in some of the commentaries on James's morality this distinction between primary and secondary evidence is ignored, and it is assumed that what James said in his letters, for example, is clear and ample evidence of a certain moral view to be found in his work. It is true that the letters contain many moral formulations and also many unforgettable comments on the human condition. That they throw light on James's fiction is indisputable; but they are not a substitute for the fiction; more important, they are not reductions of the fiction. Even supposing that James was perfectly accurate in his self-analysis, that he did have "the imagination of disaster" and did see life as "ferocious and sinister,"[2] the question remains still: do the phrases describe James's imagination or James's work? Further, as an unreconstructed New Critic might have it, are the letters (and the prefaces and the notebooks) necessary for

<hr />

[2] *Letters to A. C. Benson and Auguste Monod,* ed. E. F. Benson (London, 1930), p. 35.

us to appreciate the qualities of the fiction? What is objectively "there" in the fiction if we do not properly see it until the letters point it out? Did we see the depicted life in *The Golden Bowl* as ferocious and sinister before we read James's fine phrase? Do the letters (and prefaces and notebooks) sharpen our perceptions or introduce us to qualities we have not seen before? If, as James insisted, a novel consists of what is dramatized, what is represented, what is pictured—then what is outside the picture is irrelevant, does not formally exist. The old joke about *The Waste Land* was that the structure is in the footnotes, and the implied principle is relevant to James's work; for if we judge it by his own standards—holding that fiction is representational, not discursive—then what is not dramatized has no bearing. The meaning of the picture is in the picture or nowhere.[3]

Another way of suggesting secondary evidence in such a way as to make it seem primary evidence from the fiction itself is to dwell on the temperaments of James's father and brother William and to imply that James shared these temperaments. Thus Graham Greene makes much of the father's and brother's encounters with evil—the "vastations" which both seem to have undergone—and then notes too that Henry's sister Alice had strong suicidal tendencies. The inference that Greene draws from these facts is that James, too, had this sixth sense for evil, that his imagination was "clouded by the Pit."[4] He goes on to argue that James's awareness of evil was so intense and so Puritanical that one thinks he might be talking about Jonathan Edwards. But if we may use secondary evidence to comment on secondary evidence, one would suppose that if James had this almost Calvinistic sense of evil, his brother William would have noticed it. But the letters show that William had no more sympathy with Henry's work—and no more understanding of it—than Wells had. The recent emphasis on James's awareness of evil in the world is perhaps an attempt to make him seem contemporary, as we have made Melville, Hawthorne, and Emily Dickinson seem to be contemporary with Camus and Wallace Stevens. We currently value the literature of negation and try to extend our present norms backward in time whenever we can. This is an understandable procedure; any intellectual view "rectifies" the whole of literature, so long as the view is accepted—as Eliot pointed out years ago. But earlier readers of James were not necessar-

---

[3] Of the form of *The Awkward Age,* James wrote that it was a "form all dramatic and scenic—of presented episodes, architecturally combined and each making a piece of the building; with no going behind, no *telling about* the figures save by their own appearance and action and with explanations reduced to the explanation of everything by all other things *in* the picture" (*The Letters of Henry James,* ed. Percy Lubbock, New York, 1920, I, p. 333).

[4] "Henry James: The Private Universe," *The Lost Childhood* (New York, 1952), p. 26.

ily blind to the existence of evil in his work, as some contemporary critics seem to assume. It is rather that the earlier judgments of his work were more purely literary than our own. As Colby noted, James could deal with any kind of horrors that he chose to and his books could still be left open in the nursery, because his style was "his sufficient fig leaf."[5] But recent critics, with intense dedication, have brushed form aside to get at meanings that for earlier readers existed only in a dim way behind what they saw as an indeterminate veil of words.

One of the more interesting oddities of James criticism is the way James himself has so often pointed the way for his interpreters, somewhat in the manner by which a fox will lead hounds over ground he knows. If one reads James's preface to one of his novels and then turns to the critical commentary on the novel, he has a distinct sense that the commentary exists within a framework that has been "given"—like the innumerable medieval commentaries on the "given" *Sentences* of Peter Lombard. This practice goes back at least as far as Percy Lubbock's *The Craft of Fiction,* which analyzes fictional techniques in wholly Jamesian terms, and continues to its absolute *reductio* in a recent book on James in which the writer makes an incredible attempt to imitate the Jamesian style, like a demented sparrow trying to hover on imaginary eagle wings.[6] Even the omissions in James criticism are interesting in this respect. One must search hard to find any serious comment on *Washington Square,* which James did not include in the New York Edition and so did not comment on formally. Yet, if one can avoid James's judgment by exclusion and look at the book on its merits, one finds that it is clearly not inferior to *The Spoils of Poynton,* for example, and is in addition one of the wittiest of James's stories. And in the matter of the novelist's moral views, or the moral qualities of his fiction, most of the critics approach the problem in ways that James himself sketched out, and they state in James's terms moral issues in the fiction which James himself introduced in his backward-looking prefaces. Fleda Vetch is a case in point. To one who had not read James's preface her moral behavior would surely seem bizarre, would seem in fact almost a classic of moral hyperscrupulousness. As a moral agent, if she does not belong with the neurotics in Faulkner or Tennessee Williams or with Strindberg's Miss Julie, she surely

[5] "In Darkest James," *Imaginary Obligations* (New York, 1905), p. 321.

[6] Robert Marks, *James's Later Novels* (New York, 1960). Thus: "The ambition of this book is the imputation to him, with an equanimity of confidence, of some ideas—both of life and form—cherished as convictions, those of which his novels and stories are dramatizations and embodiments, supreme ideas and recurrent techniques of his thought that constitute an underlying point of view sharp and bright by which his work all hangs together, which impart to it a unity, a character, a tone, and from which it derives its final value" (pp. 10–11).

belongs with the ritualistic moralists of love in the court of Marie de Champagne. But James indicated in his preface that she had "character" and that he took her conscience seriously, and thus this view echoes through the commentaries.

The next difficulty is one which James's fiction shares with other psychological fiction and perhaps with all fiction that assumes a certain degree of free will in its characters, all fiction that is not professedly "naturalistic" or deterministic. Any discussion of the moral elements of James's work has to touch on what we call the "moral acts" or "moral choices" of his characters: Isabel Archer's decision to return to her husband, Strether's decision to return to America, Newman's decision to renounce vengeance on the Bellegarde family. James himself, characteristically, has led the discussion of many of these moral choices and has evaluated them from what might be called the orthodox or conventional point of view—as if Isabel Archer's choice, for example, is a perfectly "free" choice for which she is to be commended or censured. But if you examine her decision—or Strether's or Newman's—you find that in every case the moral choice is in accordance with, and really seems to proceed from, the temperament or "humor" of the character. In other words, the more closely you examine the decision, the less it seems to be a perfectly free moral choice and the more it seems to be an automatic or determined one. And the more you know about a given character—the more fully and delicately he is analyzed by the author—the less likely it becomes that you can ever accept his decisions as free in any real sense. It may be put as an inverse ratio: the greater the psychological knowledge we have of a character, the less the illusion of free choice, and total knowledge absolutely precludes this illusion. If this is so, then the process of psychological analysis in fiction is self-destructive—so long, that is, as the writer wishes to maintain the illusion of his people's free will; the ultimate aim, the presentation of character "in the round" or "in depth," if it is ever wholly successful, presents not a living being but an automaton. Perhaps, then, the only kind of fiction that can give us totally believable moral agents is non-analytical fiction in which the characters are depicted entirely from the outside, where we have no knowledge of the working of the character's consciousness, fiction that approximates the wholly dramatic quality of the stage play.

And in this respect literature, as Johnson said, may appeal to life for justification. The difficulty in ascribing praise or blame in life varies according to how well we know the person whose acts we are judging. The perfect stranger is the easiest to judge, and is proved most easily a villain; but even a little knowledge leads to leniency. And we hardly ever pass a strictly moral judgment on one of our own acts because we know so well the complexities of the situation—our own strains and stresses, the shaping influence of time and place, and so on. Of people we know, we say that they acted "characteristically," implying that their acts were predictable, as proceeding from their temperaments. But for "predictable" we almost have to read "unfree," for if the decision accords with the temperament, then it seems nearly automatic, unless we assume that all of us are choosing all the time, deciding every minute to be what we are. That is a *reductio* of a well-known existential tenet, and it is simply impossible that it should be true in practice. What all this means is that the closer James, or any other psychological novelist, comes to imitating life, or existential human reality, the more nearly impossible it becomes for him to depict a real moral choice; for, assuming the possibility of moral choice, it is apparently either incredibly more complex or incredibly more simple than we generally assume it to be. And in either case one can no more isolate it in fiction than he can in real life. If this is so, most of the elements in the fiction that we use as evidence of James's moral opinions are irrelevant. In the same way, let us hope, most of the elements in life on which we base our moral judgments, and on which others base their moral judgments of us, are also irrelevant. Judge not, say the Scriptures, that ye be not judged, meaning presumably that we are all hopelessly wicked or that all judgments are partial and thus wrong.

It is hypothetically possible that the difficulty I have been describing here is one of which James himself was unaware; in that case we should have in the fiction the portrayal of acts which James himself saw as free but which we (on reflection) cannot recognize as such, and if this were true then the fiction would still hold up as evidence of James's moral views. But I believe it is a mistake to underestimate the sophistication of James's mind, or to assume there were many problems related to his art of which he was ignorant. If we consider his passion for process as such, for causality as such, for action and reaction in the realm of human behavior, we should be very surprised if we found that at a certain point in his study of this process he had simply abandoned it, as if he had gone carefully up a tortuous staircase only to leap out a fifth-story window. The possibility surely occurred to him that in dealing with process he might well be dealing *only* with process, with endless or circular causality. We make much of some of James's remarks about his characters, about his ability to see them as "real," but this capacity does not cancel out the possibility that in some way or other, or at least intermittently, he also saw them as determined. "What will she *do?*" he asked concerning Isabel Archer as he went about setting up her character, and we are inclined to see this curiosity as charmingly ingenuous. But of course the answer is that she will do what James will make her do once he has decided for himself what kind of person she is; his curiosity cannot be from total but only partial ignorance. His curiosity, in the beginning stages of his composition of the novel, can only apply to the specific circumstances under which this "set" character will "issue into action" (in A. C. Bradley's fine phrase). Or if her character is not wholly settled on an a priori basis, if James himself kept discovering (or making up) new aspects of her character as he went along, the fact still remains that she acts characteristically; that is, it does not matter whether James created her instantaneously (as it were) or by a kind of creative evolution: she is still what she is. "What will she do?" She will do what a train will do once it has been set on rails that have already been built. In a word, she will become—at least for James, and for the reader too, if James's analysis is successful—predictable. All experience is against free will, as Johnson once commented, and all belief is for it. To give James his intellectual due and in order not to sell him short, I think we must assume that at best he wrote "as if" free will were present in human affairs but without much positive reason for thinking so; and while such an attitude perhaps does not weaken his art, it surely makes the art unreliable evidence in a discussion of James's moral views. If James did not take this view, or something like it, if he did not suspect at least occasionally that analysis of human behavior seems to lead always to the whirligig of determinism, then that famous passage in *The Ambassadors* seems wholly cryptic—that remarkable scene that James himself called the core of the book, in which Strether advises Little Bilham: " 'Live all you can; it's a mistake not to.' " Then, having urged Little Bilham toward a choice, Strether adds:

> "What one loses one loses; make no mistake about that. The affair—I mean the affair of life—couldn't, no doubt, have been different for me; for it's at the best a tin mould, either fluted and embossed, with ornamental excrescences, or else smooth and dreadfully plain, into which, a helpless jelly, one's consciousness is poured—so that one 'takes' the form, as the great cook says, and is more or less compactly held by it; one lives, in fine, as one can. Still, one has the illusion of freedom; therefore don't be, like me, without the memory of that illusion."[7]

I do not argue that Strether's view is necessarily James's, only that Strether could not have said it if James had not first thought it. Scott Fitzgerald once remarked that "the test of a first-rate intelligence is the ability to hold two opposed ideas in the mind at the same time, and still retain the ability to function."[8] He might well have been describing the accumulated wisdom of

---

[7] *The Ambassadors,* New York Edition, I, pp. 217–218.
[8] *The Crack-Up,* ed. Edmund Wilson (New York, 1956), p. 69.

the race on the subject of responsibility in human behavior, the double view of human existence that sees human acts in life, and human acts in art, as only provisionally understandable and as ultimately ambiguous. I do not think we can fairly deny James this perception.

Finally, in respect to this matter, it has been noted by critics that James typically relieves his characters of financial needs—Isabel Archer is the most obvious case—and the assumption is that he does this in order to set them free from the partly determining force of poverty and the limited horizons of the very poor. But this assumption also underestimates James if it implies that James thought he was thus setting his people "free." He may have been freeing them of a particular factor in mental life because, for any of a number of reasons, he did not want to deal with it except in rare cases such as those of Hyacinth Robinson and Kate Croy. But it is absurd to believe that because James's people are "comfortably fixed" they live in a moral vacuum; if one siphons away one potentially determining factor in life, another rushes in to take its place; life, in fact, abhors a moral vacuum. To remove potentially determining factors is to remove the atmosphere from the earth; man acts amid existential stresses—interior and exterior forces so strong and so apparent that the Naturalist believes them overwhelming—and these stresses comprise the elements of human choice, in fact the very conditions of choice. An absolutely unconditioned human act is inconceivable, like a poem without the conditioning factor of language. James may have wanted to exchange one set of conditions for another because he found one more interesting or more complex than the other; but, with his passion for analysis, he surely was not trying to uproot his people from existential reality, for if he did he would have nothing to analyze. We sometimes speak of James's characters as if they were solipsists, or as if James thought they were; but even the subtlest of their mental processes has "reality" as its object; it is the action-reaction of a sensitive being who has been "put in relation" with something outside himself. James, for all his distrust of the pessimistic pattern that the Naturalists "projected" onto human life, was always aware of the vital tension between human consciousness and the outer world. So little did he want to isolate his people from the world that, like a transcendentalist, he more than once remarked on the fact of consciousness as a web, as a homogeneous tissue in which inner and outer reality shaded into each other in blendings so subtle that one could hardly specify boundaries.

II

There have been notable attempts both to state and to resolve the specific problem of the morality of James's fiction, attempts sufficient in quality and number to emphasize its importance and persistency as a critical issue for some half a century. Joseph Warren Beach was among the first to note one of the phenomena already mentioned, that James's characters are rarely affected by ethical or religious orthodoxies. Beach argued that the characters' moral sense was not separable from their aesthetic sense and that this integrity of consciousness placed James in the transcendental moral tradition of Emerson, Thoreau, and Hawthorne.[9] David Daiches held that there is a progression in James's work, that early work such as *Roderick Hudson* contains "specific"[10] and "overt"[11] morality but that in the late novels the morality does not exist "apart from their totality of meaning, apart from the 'felt life' the author presents through the novel."[12] Yvor Winters credited James with a belief in a peculiarly American moral sense, a moral outlook that was a product of the centuries-long discipline of the Roman, Anglo-Catholic, and Calvinist churches, a moral sense finally destroyed by Emerson's "anti-moral"[13] philosophy and by the immoralities of "the new financial aristocracy which had arisen after the Civil War. . . ."[14] C. B. Cox found elements of Stoicism in James's religious views.[15] F. O. Matthiessen argued for a "religion of consciousness"[16] in James's work and held that James placed his characters on a scale of good and evil that is based on their "awareness,"[17] the stage of sensitivity to which their consciousness has advanced. John H. Raleigh also posited a religion of consciousness in James's characters but on grounds that James's philosophical assumptions were derived from the British empirical tradition of Locke. "The consciousness most sensitive to impressions is liable to be the most moral. So in James there is an equation between the esthetic and the moral sense, and the individual who most appreciates the beauty of a Renaissance painting is also the most moral."[18] Quentin Anderson traced the moral structure of James's later work to James's use of his father's Swedenborgian religious views and argued that the work of the "major

[9] *The Method of Henry James* (New Haven, 1918), pp. 141–144.

[10] "Sensibility and Technique (Preface to a Critique)," *Kenyon Review*, V, p. 577 (1943).

[11] *Ibid.*, p. 576.

[12] *Ibid.*, pp. 576–577.

[13] *In Defense of Reason* (New York, 1947), p. 306.

[14] *Ibid.*

[15] "Henry James and Stoicism," *Essays and Studies*, N.S. (London, 1955), VIII, pp. 76–88.

[16] *Henry James: The Major Phase* (New York, 1944), p. 131.

[17] *Ibid.*, p. 146.

[18] "Henry James: The Poetics of Empiricism," *PMLA*, LXVI, III (March, 1951).

phase" is in fact a single "divine novel"[19] based on the father's religious convictions. Dorothea Krook held that James's world view is not to be attributed to any single source but was formed by "the ambient air of nineteenth-century speculation, whose main current was the preoccupation with the phenomenon of self-consciousness."[20]

Considering these critical commentaries I believe two things are evident: *(a)* all are interesting in themselves, and *(b)* none of them wholly explains the moral phenomenon of James's work. If it is possible to have such a thing as an unhelpful truth, what might be called a non-operative truth, then Beach's view is such a truth, and so is that of Daiches. To the reader who finds himself afoot "in darkest James" (Colby's phrase) it is not very useful to be told that James's people act as they do because, in effect, they have a "unified sensibility," whether that unity be described as transcendental or not. Nor is it very useful even to the advanced reader of James to be told that the moral quality of James's fiction is not separable from the "totality of meaning" of the work. Though we may agree with Aristotle that we know things in their causes, we must also say that there are different spheres of causality and that a metaphysical cause throws little light on a question of psychology or morality. Beach and Daiches explain without satisfying. Strether's rejection of the good life remains just as cryptic, or maddening, as if Beach and Daiches had not spoken. The crudest kind of dismissal of Strether as a bloodless neurotic is really more satisfactory, in the sense that it at least is on the same level of causality as the act itself. It may be wrong, but it is relevent.

As to Winter's assertion of an American moral sense, it serves well enough as a kind of working description of only part of James's work, and it is logically indefensible if taken as explanation. It is true that some of James's Americans act as if their moral nature were different from that of some of James's Europeans—Christopher Newman, Daisy Miller, Strether, Isabel Archer, for example. But that is really a matter of contrast for dramatic purposes. Set next to the general moral corruption of the Bellegarde family, Newman's morality seems bright and refreshing and wholly different from theirs. But the two members of the Bellegarde family with whom Newman has the closet relations—Claire (who rejects his love in order to become a nun) and her brother Valentin (who, while on his death bed, apologizes for his family's corruption)—act according to moral beliefs quite as distinct as those of Newman. In fact, what the contrast really shows, and what many of the Jamesian American-European contrasts show, is the rela-

[19] *The American Henry James* (New Brunswick, N. J., 1957), p. 349.
[20] *The Ordeal of Consciousness in Henry James* (Cambridge, England, 1962), p. 411.

tively ingenuous American moral view versus the relatively complex European moral view. But that is no argument for the moral sense being peculiarly American but rather for the moral sense being universal. In fact, when we look over the great range of James's people, we find that if it is the moral sense that makes people moral, then all James's people have it but not under the same conditions of life. And Winters's whole thesis about the moral sense—whatever its limited usefulness as description—can hardly be more than a mental construct parading as a historical phenomenon. If the moral sense is viewed as a product of ages of Roman Catholic and Anglo-Catholic thought, then how can it be peculiar to America, where this thought came only so recently? If an infusion of American Puritanism modified it, then that seems only another way of saying that the original sense remained unmodified—but of course remained. But even if Winters's ingenious intellectual history were truer than it is, it would still have little to say about the basic problem of the morality of James's fiction. Because Winters was working on an irrelevant level of causality, like Beach and Daiches he seems to be saying that James's people act as they do because they are what they are.

Cox has surely hit on one of the most important aspects of James's protagonists—what he calls their "rigid self-control and consistent moral behaviour"[21]—for nothing can be more clear than that they act according to a code which, if not personal, is at least never revealed. But rigid self-control and consistent moral behavior are not peculiar to Stoicism and are in fact distinguishing characteristics of any religion that holds to an ethical system. If James, as Cox believes, rejected the Stoic notion of *apatheia,* or the determination not to feel, then it seems clear that James rejected Stoicism itself, since it is *apatheia* that is the core of Stoicism. And since it is evident that James's people do feel, and feel profoundly, about a great many things, then if there are self-control and consistent moral behavior in the fiction they come from a different source.

The notion of a "religion of consciousness," as advocated by Matthiessen and Raleigh, perhaps comes closest to saving the Jamesian appearances. It accords with what most readers feel in the fiction, and it has the added advantage of according with James's comments outside the fiction. There can be no doubt that James in some way graded his characters according to their degrees of consciousness. I say "in some way" because it is not immediately evident that the gradation is as simple as Raleigh's comments would suggest—that the person of the most advanced consciousness, most likely to appreciate a Renaissance painting, is likely to be the most moral. One

---

[21] Cox, p. 77.

thinks of Gilbert Osmond, Madame Merle, John Marsh, Charlotte Stant—
all belong to the class that James called his "supersubtle fry," yet all are
presumably evil in one way or another. Matthiessen makes the matter less
simple, and thus probably closer to truth: the character having the refined
Jamesian consciousness sees the greatest number of moral possibilities.
And yet, if one turns from speculation and examines the work itself, the one
thing that strikes the reader is the essential similarity of mind among all the
important Jamesian characters, the fact that James hardly ever dealt with
characters who had not advanced to this refinement of consciousness. In the
Jamesian world there are people we see as good and those we see as evil,
but a little reflection suggests that the difference between them is not to be
found in levels of consciousness but where the difference is always said by
moralists to reside—in the will. Where all people are nearly equally advanced in self-consciousness the moral differences among them cannot derive from this self-consciousness. Matthiessen's argument would be much
stronger if he could point to cases of obvious evil in James and say, in effect, "This man is evil because he is lumpish and unrefined, because he has
not advanced to Strether's level of self-consciousness." But this is impossible
to do. If Newman is the moral hero of *The American* it is not because his
consciousness is more refined than that of the Bellegarde family; it is obviously *less* refined, less analytical, less articulate. Christina Light is as conscious an agent as any of James's protagonists, yet she is clearly in the rank
of those ranged against the Jamesian heroes. And what is true of her is also
true of Madame Merle, the greedy publisher in *The Aspern Papers,* Mrs.
Gereth in *The Spoils of Poynton,* the aesthetic novelist in "The Author of
'Beltraffio,' " and many others. It is not really that James's villains are relatively unconscious but rather that James deals primarily with characters
whom we assume to be "good." Most of the intricate Jamesian analysis is
devoted to his protagonists, whom we identify with, and whom we assume
to be heroes. This is so generally the case that when we are treated to the
examination of a consciousness set against the protagonist we are likely to
mistake it for something else—who has not been in sympathy with Merton
Densher of *The Wings of the Dove* or with the prince in *The Golden Bowl?*
Most of James's evil characters are not necessarily unconscious, only unana-
lyzed. Moreover, it is not always indisputably true that the refined consciousnesses that James presents us with are necessarily to be taken as heroes;
they may in some cases be merely interesting protagonists. James himself may have thought of his protagonists as heroes, and thus have led the
way in our critical estimates of them, but there really is no reason to assume
that we have to admire Maggie Verver or Fleda Vetch, or even Strether or
Isabel Archer, any more than we feel forced to admire the intricately ana-

lyzed people in Durrell's quartet or in Faulkner. If we allow ourselves this freedom with James, if we pay him the deserved compliment of accepting his people as dramatic presentations, as we do for contemporary novelists in general, then we are relieved of the necessity (surely a burdensome one) of thinking of Fleda Vetch as a moral heroine or of Charlotte Stant as a moral monster. We are free to be impatient with Strether, sympathetic to Mme. de Vionnet, suspicious of Maggie Verver, infinitely bored with Milly Theale; we are free, in short, to form opinions of these people as if they were real, as if life itself rather than James had thrust them at us. It is the compliment we pay to Shakespeare, almost the highest one we can pay to an imitative writer, and James himself could have asked for no more. But if we pay this compliment we abandon the conventional distinctions between heroes and villains, and with them the real basis for Matthiessen's argument for a religion of consciousness.

Quentin Anderson's provocative thesis, that James's later work is a subtle allegorizing of his father's Swedenborgian religious views, has not been generally accepted, though one critic has called it "an exciting work of interpretive criticism and scholarship."[22] Anderson argued that much of the later Jamesian imagery is really to be read as a use of Swedenborgian "emblems"—the House of Life, the Tree of Life, the Portrait, the bowl or the "great containing vessel"[23]—and that these emblems are "rigidly determined by an intention which must be called allegorical."[24] The most basic objection to this glossing of James's images is that what Anderson sees as emblems are really only the "literary currency of the day,"[25] or, as Leon Edel has called them, no more than a "verbal inheritance"[26] from the elder James. And it is Edel who has said what seems to be the last word on the subject, not by leveling a specific objection but by asserting a general and far-reaching truth about James's work as a whole. Any allegorical reading of James's work that places him alongside Dante (as Anderson's reading does) ignores the profound truth that James was above all things a novelist, that he proudly represented himself as such, and that his work "is rooted not in the *Divine Comedy* of Dante but in the *Human Comedy* of Balzac."[27]

[22] Unsigned review of Anderson's book in *Modern Fiction Studies,* III, p. 181 (Summer, 1957).

[23] Anderson, p. 347.

[24] *Ibid.,* p. 350.

[25] *Modern Fiction Studies,* p. 182.

[26] Review of Anderson's book, *American Literature,* XXIX, p. 494 (January, 1958).

[27] *Ibid.,* p. 495.

Now these critical commentaries we have been examining range from the assignment of causes at one end of the scale, through what may be called working descriptions, to allegorical interpretation, and finally to very broad general statement, as in Dorothea Krook's comment that James was preoccupied with the phenomenon of self-consciousness. Matthiessen's argument, whether wholly right or not, is probably most successful in the sense that it makes the reader feel more "at home" with James, though the argument suffers, as most of the others do, from the attempt to present a single moral pattern and then fit all of James's people into it. But what the reader —and perhaps even the Jamesian—needs in order to be comfortable with James is to feel that the moral world that James presents is not unique. It is even possible that one of the great laws of art is that analogy is more helpful than exegesis; analysis of a new and novel work of art is not as useful as comparison, for it is only by comparison, or analogy, that the seeming uniqueness of the art work is accommodated. A reader innocent of most contemporary fiction might be bowled over by *The Catcher in the Rye,* and might then discover by exegesis something of the cause of his reaction. But the more general meaning of the book, the significance of its form, everything that makes Holden Caulfield so pitifully symbolic of the current phase of the human condition—all this the reader comprehends from analogy, from reading books comparable to Salinger's, from seeing into the minds of other adolescent searchers such as Holly Golightly and Ike McCaslin and Frankie (F Jasmine) Addams. And so it is with the phenomenon of James's morality; the reader can be made comfortable with it, not so much by having it explained, as by seeing it reproduced elsewhere. It is the odd blandness, the opacity, of James's moral dramas that puzzle the reader, that he can in fact hardly describe. It is James's seeming acceptance of the moral postures of his protagonists without comment (as Beach noted) as if all of them were of equal value—Strether's, and Fleda Vetch's, and Maggie Verver's; it is this apparent equalitarianism of moral views that puts the reader off, that raises the question whether James was not, like Jefferson, tolerant to the point of indifference, treating all moral views impartially because he saw them as all equally wrong. It is this apparently all-accepting quality of James's moral outlook that remains enigmatic unless there is an analogue for it.

That analogue, I believe, is to be found precisely in the concluding chapter of his brother William's *Varieties of Religious Experience.* I do not argue that Henry was a pragmatist; his famous remark that he was amazed to discover to what extent he had been a pragmatist all his life may or may not have been ironic and in any case is only secondary evidence. Nor do I argue that William's work is a source in any direct way. I argue simply that to know William's religious cast of mind—as he reveals it at the end of his survey of the variety and quality of religious feelings and experiences—is the best practical way of coming to some kind of accommodation with the moral qualities of Henry's fiction.

William's "conclusion" is a marvel of deism in the original sense of that term, as we apply it, for example, to the work of Lord Herbert of Cherbury. Like Herbert's work, William's is a wholly sympathetic attempt to find the least common denominator of all religions—not, as with Paine and Voltaire and later agnostics like Ingersoll, in order to ridicule all religions on the grounds of their essential similarity but in order to save them on that same basis. Nothing could be more amiable, more understanding, more tolerant than William's discussion of "the religious life."[28] Such life, William holds, is based on the belief that the visible world is made significant by the more spiritual world of which it is a part, that man's proper end is "union or harmonious relation" (p. 485) with that spiritual world, that communion with that world produces psychological and material effects in the visible world—"work is really done" (p. 485). Psychologically, religion gives man "zest," which "adds itself like a gift to life" and which "takes the form either of lyrical enchantment or of appeal to earnestness and heroism" (p. 485); religion gives "an assurance of safety and a temper of peace" and, toward others, "a preponderance of loving affections" (p. 486).

Within this framework of common beliefs marked by common characteristics there is room for endless variety of individual religious acceptance. Not all men will have "identical religious elements" (p. 487); in fact, "no two of us have identical difficulties, nor should we be expected to work out identical solutions" (p. 487). Each of us has his "peculiar angle of observation" from which he perceives "a certain sphere of fact and trouble, which each must deal with in a unique manner" (p. 487). And this pluralism, or multiplicity of religious acceptances, is as it should be, because it brings about human awareness of the multiplicity of the qualities of "the divine" (p. 487). "The divine can mean no single quality, it must mean a group of qualities, by being champions of which in alternation, different men may all find worthy missions. Each attitude being a syllable in human nature's total message, it takes the whole of us to spell the meaning out completely" (p. 487). Thus, "for each man to stay in his own experience . . . and for others to tolerate him there, is surely best" (p. 488).

For William, the most important thing about these individual and perhaps unique experiences is that they are real; they are facts of consciousness. And facts of consciousness have more verifiable reality than objects as

---

[28] *The Varieties of Religious Experience* (New York, 1923), p. 485. The following several page references to this book are indicated in parentheses in the text.

such, than things "outside" human consciousness. Such outer objects are "ideal pictures of something whose existence we do not wholly possess" (p. 499)—they share their reality with our experience of them. Thus "things in themselves" constitute no more than "a mere abstract element of experience" (p. 499); they are not "full facts" (p. 499) until they are registered on a human consciousness which has "an attitude towards the object *plus* the sense of a self to whom the attitude belongs" (p. 499). Not things, but things as felt, are what constitute reality. It is as if when an "abstract element" became registered on a human consciousness it was raised, not exactly from potency to act, but from a lower act to a higher; and this higher act, or existence, is what William calls reality. In other words, what is "subjective"—not the phenomenon but the *felt* phenomenon—is what is real. This subjective reality is, of course, susceptible of gradation, but for William the gradations do not seem important, as (let us say) the gradations of bliss in heaven do not seem important when that bliss is set against "non-bliss" or earthly life.

Now it is in human consciousness, in this reality-maker, that the religious experiences exist; it is in the human consciousness that religious experiences, like all other phenomena, are made real. It follows that all subjective religious experiences have value in the sense that they are real, for "as soon as we deal with private and personal phenomena as such, we deal with realities in the completest sense of the term" (p. 498). Thus we may say that, for William, whatever registers on human consciousness is wholly real, and what is wholly real is "good," in the sense of having significance, in the sense of *being* and having connections with other realities—for "a full fact . . . is of the *kind* to which all realities whatsoever must belong; the motor currents of the world run through the like of it; it is on the line connecting real events with real events" (p. 499).

Religious feelings, then, are real and do real work. And it is religious feelings and the conduct they lead to which form, for William, the indispensable element of the religious life. These feelings and conduct are common to all religions—"the feelings . . . and the conduct . . . are almost always the same, for Stoic, Christian, and Buddhist saints are practically indistinguishable in their lives" (p. 504). It is in the theories, the intellectual superstructures that men erect on these common feelings, that men differ. These theories William calls "additional beliefs" or "over-beliefs" (p. 504) or even "individualistic excrescences" (p. 503), and they are secondary to the essence of religious life. Dogmas, creeds, ideas, symbols "are not to be regarded as organs with an indispensable function, necessary at all times for religious life to go on" (p. 504). The "faith-state" brought about by the religious feelings "may hold a very minimum of intellectual content. . . . It may be a mere vague enthusiasm, half spiritual, half vital, a courage, and a feeling that great and wondrous things are in the air" (p. 505). When the faith-state is associated with a creed (even a creed of minimal intellectual content), then there occurs the phenomenon we call "religion," which profoundly affects the "action and endurance" (p. 506) of men. William quotes Professor Leuba:

> "The truth of the matter can be put in this way: *God is not known, he is not understood; he is used*—sometimes as meat-purveyor, sometimes as moral support, sometimes as friend, sometimes as an object of love. If he proves himself useful, the religious consciousness asks no more than that. Does God really exist? How does he exist? What is he? are so many irrelevant questions. Not God, but life, more life, a larger, richer, more satisfying life is . . . the end of religion. The love of life, at any and every level of development, is the religious impulse." (pp. 506–507)

Such is William's view of what we might call operative religion, and it is at once evident that it is open to many of the same objections that Henry's work has had to bear. The "religious life," for example, is wholly subjective; we all have our own peculiar "angles of vision"; we all "use" God in our own way, according to our needs and our capacities. But most important, behind William's commentary lies a belief almost too obvious to be seen: the religious life is a way to the source of psychic power, a means of producing "work," a cause of energy which literally moves its recipients to action. As a force, and of itself, it is unknowable except in its effects; but those effects are enormously significant in the sense that they are real phenomena—and for "real" we must read "valid." A "faith-state" is a valid phenomenon, a part of the interconnected world of other real phenomena. And if it is real, and thus valid, it requires no justification or defense; it simply is, and the only thing that one can put against it for comparison is not other real phenomena but only the nothingness of non-being. William's view is not one of cynical tolerance of all religious points of view but rather an almost exuberant glee in their infinite variety, a profoundly religious conviction that "the divine" is not exhausted in any one view, nor even perverted in any one view. What can be seen in an infinite number of ways is infinite; the sun that is capable of infinite refractions is an infinite sun. William is not a philosopher of the Negative Way but of the Positive: all views of God are true views, all angles of vision are accurate. Or more precisely, all views of God are true so far as they remain primary and largely a matter of feeling; perversion begins when one begins to add "over-beliefs" or "additional beliefs" or "individual excrescences" to the elemental faith-state—when (by analogy) the church fathers began to erect a church on the "primitive Christianity" of the apostles. If we were trying to put a name to William's religious views, I believe we should be driven to the term I have already mentioned in connection with him—deism, but (again) deism in its original sense before it became associated with political radicalism. Tolerant though he is of all religious "over-beliefs," William's sympathy is clearly with "natural religion," not the religion of visible forms but the religious affections of the inner life. The very effort itself to discover the least common denominator of all formal religions must indicate a dissatisfaction with those religions. Dogma, Chesterton once remarked, is merely articulate religion. True religion, William might have replied, is really inarticulate dogma.

A moral universe in which all individual religious feelings are equally valid; a sense of the divine mind revealing itself endlessly in these peculiar religious feelings; a distrust in the hardening forms that conventional religions assume; a delight in the infinite variety of religious affections in their inchoate state—it really seems we might as easily be talking of Henry as of William. If there is one thing that is clear about Henry's protagonists it is that their moral attitudes are personal, deeply felt, and "real" in the sense of producing real work done. And Henry's interest in—even sympathy with—these peculiar attitudes is legendary. The kind of moral world that William arrived at inductively, Henry created out of his "moral consciousness"[29]—a world in which no moral act is uninteresting, or untypical, or unimportant. Henry's fiction, in fact, might well serve as a series of *exempla* for the last chapter of William's book: Henry's people all perceive "a certain sphere of fact and trouble, which each must deal with in a unique manner," and each of Henry's people stays "in his own experience." The religious cast of mind that William and Henry share simply rejects the notion of typicality, of fidelity to a norm. A moral agent, for both brothers, is always *sui generis,* as the theologians tell us that every angel is a species. Both brothers show this profound respect for singularity, for the always fascinating individual case. They have the psychologist's love of endless particularity. If the case seems aberrant, seems to deviate from the norm—as with Fleda Vetch, perhaps—that is only because all norms are provisional. In the long run it will be seen that what human nature is capable of is the only true definition of human nature—existence precedes essence, as Sartre might say; every moral attitude is "a syllable in human nature's total message." Strether's rejection is perhaps one such syllable, uttered from the depths of his being, beneath the predictable over-beliefs of churches like Mme. de Vionnet's, uttered from down deep (as Emily Dickinson said) where the meanings are.

[29] *The Letters of Henry James,* ed. Lubbock, I, p. 115.

What we miss in Henry's fiction is not morality but the "over-beliefs" that we generally associate with morality. Henry's religion, as Eliot said, is marked by an "indifference to religious dogma" but an "exceptional awareness of spiritual reality."[30] Henry's tolerance of formal religious structure is just as real as his brother's, but his true sympathies are just as obviously with the "free" religious elements that make up the individual human mind. If we see Henry's famous "rejections" in his brother's terms, then perhaps what are often thought of as their weaknesses becomes virtues. Fleda Vetch's hyperconscientiousness, Strether's amiable withdrawal, Catherine Sloper's prescinding from all vital life are valid precisely because they do not proceed from a fixed moral code but from unique moral beings. By contrast, those Jamesian people who remain even loosely within an orthodox moral framework seem shallow and predictable—Mme. de Vionnet, who maintains her nominal Catholic marriage; or the prince in *The Golden Bowl;* or Christina Light. The typical Jamesian protagonist is an Emersonian individual who exists in an unintellectualized faith-state that will lead him to unique moral action. He is not in touch with law but with the divine.

> Creeds and schools in abeyance,
> Retiring back awhile sufficed at what they are, but never forgotten,
> I harbor for good or bad, I permit to speak at every hazard,
> Nature without check with original energy.

Whitman's lines are an apt description of Henry's protagonists: as William described them and Henry dramatized them, they are moral originals.

III

There remains, finally, the large question of which the specific morality of James's fiction is a part. It is the ancient question of the moral possibilities of fiction itself, or of imitative art in general, the question that James posed so ironically: How can a novel, since it is a picture, be either moral or immoral? It is almost the oldest question in art, and no critic has been able to evade it successfully. Against the maligners of fiction, or drama, or epic poetry—no matter what the era—the defender of these forms has had to argue for their moral goodness, if only because the accusers have always fixed on the obvious moral harm that "stories" can do. The accusers—Plato, Gosson, the compilers of the Index Librorum Prohibitorum, any local master of revels—have always had a clear-cut case drawn from the common sense of the world. Certain depictions of life inflame the passions, present

---

[30] Matthiessen, p. 145.

vice and depravity as attractive, and in general allow the reader to see the conventional social and moral laws as antiquated or impractical or even absurd. It follows from this (the accusers always assume) that the reader is either forced into, or strongly tempted toward, immoral or anti-social behavior, or at the least that he has endangered the foundation of his moral life. This consequence is not strictly demonstrable, of course, but it is rarely challenged. Instead, the defenders of art—Aristotle, Sidney, Coleridge— have generally asserted that art (or "great art" at least) is somehow edifying, is somehow a force for moral good. They have had to assert this because the alternative is unthinkable. For if great art is not *utile* as well as *dulce,* if it does not sweetly teach in some way or other, then great art is in the long run only a game, only a kind of superior pastime, only accidentally different from tennis or bridge. But of course it is just as difficult to show how great art enhances practical morality as it is to show that some art causes practical immorality. Neither side can really make the deductive leap from the general assumption to the particular case; the nature of the problem will allow no such happy precision.

The defenders of drama and fiction and epic poetry have always advanced the thesis that these forms "imitate" or "represent" life and that this imitation or representation needs little or no justification. The history of literary theory shows the greatest possible variety of opinion about what this imitation consists of. Aristotle is perhaps at one end of the spectrum, arguing for a kind of ritualized and stylized reproduction of life; at the other end are the advocates of absolutely literal "realism" whose stock in trade is the strongest possible illusion of reality—Farrell, O'Hara, the makers of contemporary movies; and between these extremes are innumerable positions —the varying kinds of representation to be found in Shakespeare, O'Neill, Proust, Joyce, and Albee. It is this variety of opinion that cripples the defenders of imitative art in any kind of polemical situation. They are forced to fight with blunted weapons, for they have no univocal terms. There is not one of the words or phrases ordinarily used in a discussion of the problem that is not ambiguous. Imitation, representation, mimesis, reproduction, holding the mirror up to life, illusion of reality, objective and subjective reality—even the term life—none of these lends itself to sharp practical discussion, and no one (as Chesterton said) ever went into battle shouting a distinction in terms.

But perhaps it would not darken counsel to suggest that not all the moral implications of mimesis have been sufficiently drawn out. Any argument for imitative art assumes that the imitation—whether "literal" or "ritualistic" or "symbolic"—imitates the "essence" of life, if not all the accidents, that art re-creates the qualities of life that make life what it is. It follows that if "essential life" contains any moral elements, serious imitative art will reproduce these elements. That is, if life is essentially homiletic, imitative art will also be homiletic. If life is morally bland, has no reference to morality, then imitative art will be bland and will have no reference to morality. But surely it is the essence of life that it is a texture of "real" occurrences which we all accept no matter what our philosophical or religious affiliations. A man may be a Platonist or Buddhist and not "believe" in the reality presented to his consciousness through his senses, but that does not prevent him from dying, nor does it prevent his mourning the deaths of his loved ones and friends. A man may not believe in linear or sequential time, but that does not prevent his growing old. A man may be a solipsist, but that does not prevent his being run over by a bus. A man accepts this reality existentially, as his lungs accept air, though his philosophy may explain it away. This reality of sequential time, of change and growth, of bodies occupying space, may or may not be the ultimate reality; it may even be a universal delusion; but however we think of it, even if only as a kind of tentative reality, it is the reality which is relevant to man's moral life. A man deals morally with these realities or he does not deal morally at all. He loves or lusts or hates always with time's winged chariot at his back, knowing that the object of his passion will change and eventually disappear from human perception, as his passion and even he himself will change and disappear. If he inflicts mental pain on another, or betrays another, or wishes another well, he does these things not as one disembodied consciousness to another, but as a consciousness associated with a body in a time and place to another consciousness similarly defined. It is in the context of time and place and body that we are good or evil—

> Love's mysteries in souls do grow,
> But yet the body is his book.[31]

As soon as we think of our existential self in any way abstracted from this world of common experience—as in death, or in mystical experience, or in severe psychosis, or even in dreams—we assume automatically that the self no longer exists in the moral sphere. Our union with common human experience is the "subtle knot"[32] that makes us moral man.

We may say, then, that life has relevance to morality in the profoundly significant sense that it provides the context in which we perform our moral acts; it provides the real "things as such" among which we must trace our

---

[31] Donne, "The Ecstacy."
[32] *Ibid.*

moral paths. And it follows that if imitative art reproduces the essential quality of life, then it too provides these real things—the sense of time passing, the immanence of death, the transcience of human relationships, the certainty of anguish to come. If it is true that a man must be conscious of his acts before they can be said to be either moral or immoral—if, in Matthiessen's phrase about James's protagonists, we must be aware of moral possibilities—then we may say that imitative art performs the same function that life itself does. They both provide, not morality, but the conditions of morality; they provide the realities of which we must be aware if we are to act as moral agents. Moreover, if imitative art is a kind of "second life," or reminder of life, it may act as a corrective of, or substitute for, life so far as morality is concerned. It is often possible to ignore life, at least for a while —to act as if time does not pass and as if death were not immanent; in fact it is this state of contrived ignorance that most of us struggle to maintain. It is, of course, only a temporary state, because life, through a death or a failure, sooner or later shocks us back to the reality of things. But in the meantime, to the extent that we live a kind of vegetable existence, we can hardly be said to be moral agents at all. We live in a kind of non-moral fog; the sharp outlines of the great realities of life lose their distinction, as skyscrapers lose their form and magnitude in mist. It is at times like these, when life itself is in abeyance, that imitative art can restore true vision, can bring back the awareness of things as they are that is the condition of the moral life. With a precision that life itself has only intermittently, a scene from a novel can raise us from moral potency to moral act, can nourish our moral life with the sunlight and rain of reality, so that we become again "intense perceivers" of life, have again the heightened awareness of things as such that makes us capable of meaningful choice. If we have allowed ourselves to forget the prison that sheer physical lust places us in, and if life leaves us for a while to our fancy of lust in prospect, a scene from James brings us back. Merton Densher, after seducing Kate Croy, finds himself on the dreadful treadmill of mental repetition of the act:

> The door had but to open for him to be with it again and for it to be all there; so intensely there that . . . no other act was possible to him than the renewed act, almost the hallucination, of intimacy. Wherever he looked or sat or stood, to whatever aspect he gave for the instant the advantage, it was in view as nothing of the moment, nothing begotten of time or of chance could be, or ever would; it was in view as, when the curtain has risen, the play on the stage is in view, night after night, for the fiddlers.[33]

[33] *The Wings of the Dove,* New York Edition, II, pp. 236–237.

Seeing Densher's portion of reality, we are brought back to our own; and surely this notion of imitative art as memento of reality is somehow at the bottom of every argument, classical or modern, for the edifying influence of mimesis. And perhaps James was aware of this when he made the famous comment that the "moral" sense of the work of art is wholly dependent "on the amount of felt life concerned in producing it." Fiction is no more moral than life, but no less either. The substantial connection between life and imitative art is that neither is the cause of either goodness or wickedness but that both present to man the essential condition of morality. It is a relationship ironic enough to have met with James's approval.

MARK TWAIN

****

Many writers about Mark Twain have been very serious men, and this has not always seemed appropriate. Walter Blair, however, maintains admirable perspective in presenting Mark Twain's literary backgrounds in *Native American Humor* (New York, 1937) and his methods of composition in *Mark Twain and Huck Finn* (Berkeley, Calif., 1960). Everything on Mark Twain by Mr. Blair is read with respect, as is Delancey Ferguson's *Mark Twain: Man and Legend* (New York, 1943) and James M. Cox's *Mark Twain: The Fate of Humor* (Princeton, N. J., 1967). Justin Kaplan's deservedly popular *Mr. Clemens and Mark Twain* (New York, 1966) is more consistently true to the spirit than to details of Mark Twain's life. Some have found Henry Nash Smith's *Mark Twain: The Development of a Writer* (Cambridge, Mass., 1962) a useful introduction; others have liked my briefer *Mark Twain* (Minneapolis, Minn., 1960). The quarrel about Mark Twain's integrity, begun with Van Wyck Brooks's *The Ordeal of Mark Twain* (New York, 1920), and angrily answered by Bernard De Voto's *Mark Twain's America*

(New York, 1932), is summarized in my *Mark Twain's Wound* (New York, 1962). Stimulating essays include Richard Altick's "Mark Twain's Despair," *South Atlantic Quarterly,* XXXIV (October 1935), pp. 359–367, Edgar M. Branch's "The Two Providences," *College English,* XI (January 1950), pp. 188–195, Leslie Fiedler's "Come Back to the Raft Ag'in Huck Honey," *Partisan Review,* XV (June 1948), pp. 664–671, and John L. Gerber's "Mark Twain's Use of the Comic Pose," *PMLA,* LXXVII (June 1962), pp. 297–304. Almost everyone reads what Ernest Hemingway says of Mark Twain in *The Green Hills of Africa* (New York, 1935), what T. S. Eliot says in his introduction to *The Adventures of Huckleberry Finn* (New York, 1950), and Lionel Trilling's comments in *The Liberal Imagination* (New York, 1950). Some find interesting the debate between Lauriat Lane and William Van O'Connor in *College English,* XVII (October 1955), pp. 1–10, over whether Huckleberry Finn is or is not a great novel. Other critical essays are available in Albert L. Scott's *Mark Twain: Selected Criticism* (Dallas, Tex., 1955).

SOUTHWESTERN VERNACULAR

James M. Cox

****

Huckleberry Finn is the book in which Mark Twain discovered the fullest possibilities of his humor. Later in his career he was to try what he thought were more ambitious projects, but never again was his humor to embody so rich a range of experience, never again was it able to hold so many contradictions in suspension. That is why *Huckleberry Finn* stands not only chronologically but critically at the center of Mark Twain's career, and why any study of Mark Twain is irrevocably anchored to it. Without it, Mark Twain would be in the position of Nathaniel Hawthorne without *The Scarlet Letter,* Herman Melville without *Moby Dick,* or Henry Thoreau without *Walden.* From the time it was published, sensitive critics were able to see its power. Andrew Lang, for example, recognized it as the masterpiece

From "Southwestern Vernacular," in James M. Cox, *Mark Twain: The Fate of Humor* (copyright © 1966 by Princeton University Press), pp. 156–184. Reprinted by permission of Princeton University Press.

which Americans were overlooking in their lofty search for the Great American Novel.[1] To be sure, the book *was* overlooked, but not to the extent that one can indulge in sentimental regret about the wrong done to its author. The commercial success it had in its own time, coupled with the intelligent response fairly lavished on it in our own, more than compensate for any neglect it may have suffered. In the face of its almost universal acceptance, a defense of *Huckleberry Finn* can be little more than a sentimental posture. The attitudes of acceptance fall essentially into two categories: those which try to discover meaning in the book and those which insist that it is a humorous book. Critics who pursue the meaning, the myth, the sociology, or even the structure of the book, usually fail to explore its humor. Their typical reaction is likely to be, "Of course the book is humorous, but behind the humor there is a serious world," and they proceed to search for this seriousness. Critics who insist upon the humor fare even worse, for they seem never to say anything *about* the humor. Instead, they strike negative postures, resisting meaning by proclaiming that the book is simply and marvelously a humorous narrative of a boy's adventure. The humor to which they proudly point is left untouched, presumably on the ground that it is too delicate to touch. Their standard locution becomes "Despite the pompous attempts to read grand interpretations into *Huckleberry Finn,* the book remains indefinable in its simplicity and beauty," or some equivalent evasion.

Both attitudes describe part of the reality of the book; neither begins to define it. For quite clearly the book does powerfully touch upon "serious" themes, yet just as clearly it remains a humorous narrative. Its being humorous does not mean that it has no sad moments or violent actions, but rather than all the sadness and killing and morality are contained within a humorous point of view. Thus, although *Huckleberry Finn* contains much more serious matter than *Tom Sawyer,* it is just as certainly the much more humorous book. The critic's task is to define the form of that humor, to approach its sources and its power, and to recognize its possibilities and necessities. Such an approach should accomplish, or at least begin to accomplish, three things. It should give us a better understanding of *Huckleberry Finn*—both in relation to its creator and its narrator—than we have hitherto had; it should throw genuine light on the problem of the ending of the

---

[1] Lang's brief article on the book—published in *Illustrated News of the World* (February 14, 1891), p. 222—is masterly in critical sensibility and perception. It is reprinted in *Mark Twain: Selected Criticism,* ed. Arthur L. Scott (Dallas, Tex., 1955), pp. 36–40. For an account of the reception of *Huckleberry Finn,* see Arthur L. Vogelback, "The Publication and Reception of *Huckleberry Finn* in America," *American Literature,* XI (November, 1939), pp. 260–272.

novel; and, most important, it should bring us closer to a recognition of Mark Twain's humor.

The first—and, one wants to say, the most important—fact about *Huckleberry Finn* is that Mark Twain began it the summer after he completed *Tom Sawyer* and considered it a continuation of the earlier book, which in many ways it is. He had thought of elaborating Huck's experiences at the Widow Douglas' in the last chapter of *Tom Sawyer,* but—as he wrote to Howells—something told him that he had reached the end of the story, and he restrained his impulse to extend himself.[2] When he did begin the book in the summer of 1876, he wrote four hundred manuscript pages of it. He told Howells that he did, and there is no reason to believe that he did not. According to De Voto and Walter Blair, both of whom have struggled manfully to establish a chronology of composition, Mark Twain's first impulse took him to the point in the novel where the raft is overrun by the steamboat.

Then almost as quickly as he had begun the book, he stopped, saying in his well-known letter to Howells that he liked it only tolerably well and might pigeonhole or burn the manuscript. According to De Voto, who studied the manuscript and typescripts, Mark Twain did not return to *Huckleberry Finn* for seven long years, until, upon returning from his Mississippi trip in 1883, he mounted the buoyant stream of composition which carried the book to completion. But Walter Blair, beginning from Paine's statement in the *Biography* that Mark Twain worked alternately on *The Prince and the Pauper* and *Huckleberry Finn* during the summer of 1880, has painstakingly gathered evidence showing that Mark Twain *did* work on the book during those seven years.[3]

If Blair is right, and there are excellent reasons for believing that he is, then *Huckleberry Finn* is not only "our" book of all those years; it was Mark Twain's book too. It was the defining act for him, and of all his novels it took him longest to complete. If he went out of his way to leave the impression that his relation to his masterpiece was perfunctory rather than profound, leaving such an impression was precisely the necessity of the humorist. He could not project himself as the seriously laboring craftsman any more than he could write a long preface to *Huckleberry Finn* in the manner of Henry James. This does not mean that Mark Twain worked long and laboriously plotting and planning his masterpiece. In all probability he did

[2] *Mark Twain-Howells Letters,* I, 113.

[3] Blair's argument ("When Was *Huckleberry Finn* Written," *American Literature,* XXX [March, 1958], pp. 1–25) is a lucid account and gives a fine summary of De Voto's contentions.

not; but it is absurd to lecture Mark Twain, as many critics have done, for failing to take his genius seriously—as if he could![4] What becomes evident to anyone considering the years *Huckleberry Finn* was in the process of being born is that it emerged slowly and at great cost.

The cost is to be measured in all the literary failures which lay between the beginning and ending of *Huckleberry Finn*. There were three book-length efforts—*A Tramp Abroad, The Prince and the Pauper,* and *Life on the Mississippi*—not to mention the countless short stories, sketches and literary projects which have value only for whatever obscure light they throw on Mark Twain's masterpiece. In every instance, the failure is for one of two reasons—either Mark Twain wrote reflexively, which is to say he simply exercised his art, or he took himself seriously. He either sold himself or betrayed himself, or—and this was the usual case—did both. When he sold himself, he became merely Mark Twain acting his role, doing what was expected of him. When he betrayed himself, as in *The Prince and the Pauper,* he betrayed his genius by trying to be serious—which is to say that he put truth, virtue, and morality before pleasure.

The two modes of failure are not contradictory but complementary, one begetting the other. For the more Mark Twain dropped back into his act, the more he needed to do something noble, to show somehow that he was a serious writer. The burlesque routine is fairly clear, for it is no more than a repetition of the perspective which was discovered in *The Innocents Abroad.* But the "serious" Mark Twain, who emerges in *The Prince and the Pauper* plays two roles. On the one hand he is satiric, disclosing a growing indignation at the world's injustice. This is the bitter Mark Twain who ultimately came to make sad jokes about the damned human race. On the other hand, he becomes respectable and literary—the genteel Mark Twain. Instead of being contradictory, these two roles reinforce each other. The satiric Mark Twain who flays the world's abuses is actually the respectable Mark Twain trying to please members of a cultured audience who approved the right causes.

This serious and satiric Mark Twain is increasingly evident in *A Tramp Abroad, The Prince and the Pauper,* and *Life on the Mississippi.* In all three books, beyond the growing tendency to criticize, there is a marked emergence of outrage at monarchy, class, caste, and slavery—an outrage related to all the "serious" issues in *Huckleberry Finn.* But the language of *Huckleberry Finn* was the form of humor which contained the serious issues

---

[4] Van Wyck Brooks beautifully set the style for those who assume a readiness to lecture Mark Twain. It is as if Mark Twain in typical bad-boy fashion had played truant to his art and put himself in line to be disciplined by a generation of serious critics.

Mark Twain saw between 1878 and 1884. Yet this language was more than a way of containing such issues—it was a way of seeing them. To recognize this is to be reminded how much Mark Twain, who seems such a writer of experience, was a writer of style. Just as his pseudonym had both required humor and made it possible, the language of *Huckleberry Finn* both caused and required experience. The experience that the language made Mark Twain need was precisely that which would arouse the emotions of indignation, pathos, and guilt—which the language of Huck Finn would in turn control and convert into humor.

Probably the best way to see this necessity at work is to examine *Life on the Mississippi,* the record of Mark Twain's return to the river in 1882, twenty-two years after he left it to join the Confederate Army. To make up his travel book, Mark Twain simply used "Old Times on the Mississippi" as the first part of the book—the part devoted to an account of the flush times of the river's great steamboating epoch. He then laboriously expounded his own record of his return trip, which constitutes the last two-thirds of the book. It is finally impossible to tell how much the emergent *Huckleberry Finn* affected the vision and substance of the travel book, and how much the travel book provided the raw material of *Huckleberry Finn.*

Certainly much material of *Life on the Mississippi* is either directly or subtly woven into *Huckleberry Finn.* There is Mark Twain's memory of the two Englishmen who came to Hannibal, "got themselves up in royal finery," and did *Richard III, Othello,* and *Hamlet* to a group of gawking villagers. Then there are the two drummers who sell oleomargarine and synthetic cottonseed oil respectively; there is the burglar Williams, who writes the fradulent conversion letter as a means of exploiting the charity of a hundred gullible congregations; there is the undertaker who considers himself to be a member of the "dead surest business in Christendom"; there is Mr. Manchester, the false spiritualist. All of these confidence men bear striking resemblance to the King and Duke. Then, too, there is the chapter on ornate funeral preparations which is quite obviously assimilated into the Peter Wilks episode. There is also the fine description of the House Beautiful which reads like a conventionalized version of Huck's description of the Grangerford home. Finally, there is Mark Twain's obsession with Sir Walter Scott's influence on Southern Culture which finds its way into several of Huck's observations of manners and morals of the "quality," and is also tallied in the name of the steamboat Huck and Jim board in order to have an adventure. Obviously the content of *Life on the Mississippi,* written during the late summer and fall of 1882, has much to do with the magnificent writing drive which carried Mark Twain through the latter stages of *Huckleberry Finn* during the summer of 1883.

But there are aspects of Mark Twain's trip down the river which reveal that he may have been instinctively *acting out* the novel which lay half-finished and waiting behind him. For example, Mark Twain's attempt to travel down the river incognito recalls Huck's voyage—a voyage begun six years before Mark Twain, in company with Major Pond, boarded the packet *Ajax* for a rather breezy trip to New Orleans. Most revealing, however, is the character of Brown, the pilot of the *Pennsylvania* who sarcastically lashes the cub pilot. Clearly modeled upon Pap, Brown resembles that derelict even more than does John Canty, the other representation of the evil father.

The dominating figure of Brown actually constitutes the transition between "Old Times on the Mississippi" and *Life on the Mississippi*. Since the last *Atlantic* sketch stopped abruptly with no hint of what became of the fledgling initiate, it was necessary for Mark Twain to invent a concluding episode in order to incorporate "Old Times" with *Life on the Mississippi*. The tyrant pilot Brown, who speaks in the tone if not the very accents of Pap, is the chief figure of that episode. Brown had appeared in "Old Times," but there he played the role of the victim of total recall, something like the figure in "My Grandfather's Ram" who could not forget anything. In the new episode, however, he becomes a ruthless brute who takes pleasure in humiliating his cub.

After a siege of Brown's sarcasm, the cub rebels. The incident rousing him to action is Brown's physical assault upon his younger brother, Henry, also on the *Pennsylvania*. Springing to the defense of his brother, the cub Mark Twain commits the crime of crimes—he attacks, and thrashes, the pilot with a handy stool. The Captain, being apprised of the situation, instead of hanging the mutinous cub, secretly congratulates him for his pluck. And when Brown demands that the insubordinate cub be taken off the boat, the Captain blithely says that if anyone goes it will be Brown himself. Mark Twain describes his elation: "During the brief remainder of the trip I knew how an emancipated slave feels, for I was an emancipated slave myself."[5] But the incident culminates in tragedy. Unable to work with Brown, Mark Twain transfers to the *A. T. Lacey,* just before the *Pennsylvania* leaves New Orleans for St. Louis. He arrives at Memphis on his new vessel in time to see his beloved brother die—a victim of an explosion on the *Pennsylvania*. Thus the episode of Mark Twain's piloting which had been executed as a masterpiece of humor in the *Atlantic* sketches ends in *Life on the Mississippi* on a note of utmost pathos.

If Brown is no longer the old Brown, the cub in this new episode is no longer the apprentice Mark Twain of "Old Times on the Mississippi." Far

[5] *Writings,* IX, 176.

from being the mock-ignorant apprentice, he is the Boy of Pluck bravely fighting the tyrant and applauded for his derring-do by the Benevolent Protector himself. The death of Henry Clemens constitutes the theatrically sad ending of the little melodrama. In this essentially Victorian theatrical, Bixby the mock tyrant is replaced by Brown the villain; and Mark Twain, the mock innocent cub, becomes the sensitive, injured boy bearing the blows which Brown mercilessly inflicts.

This story not only marks the transition from "Old Times on the Mississippi" to the travel book *Life on the Mississippi;* it defines the change from the essential humor of the earlier work to the essential pathos of *Life on the Mississippi.* In this new structure, "Old Times on the Mississippi" becomes merely one of the stages in the irrecoverable past of the great river. And the "present" trip of 1883, from St. Louis to New Orleans, becomes a chronical of the changes which have all but blotted out the landscape of Mark Twain's remote past. In his downward journey to New Orleans, Mark Twain, the apostle of progress, sees the false pasts which the society has erected to defend itself from the ruins of time; at the same moment, he laments the lost glory of the steamboating epoch. From the irony of recognizing the false pasts and the nostalgia for the lost past which characterize the down-river journey, Mark Twain moves back up-river toward his Hannibal home, recalling along the way episodes from his childhood. These memories which Mark Twain indulges are, like the story of Henry, essentially guilt fantasies cast in the form of nostalgic recollections and boyhood adventures. Although there is an element of play in Mark Twain even at his most nostalgic, there is a strong presence of the sensitive author recounting the guilt, injury, and fear of his bygone youth as he tells of burning the jail house and killing the prisoner, of diving into the river and touching the hand of his drowned companion, and of lying in terror while the thunder storms raged in the night.

All of these experiences are essentially false in a way that the tall tales of Mark Twain are not false. The tall tale, as told in *Roughing It,* is true in that it is the only lie in a world of lies which reveals itself to be a lie. But these experiences are not tall tales of Mark Twain; they are the fantasy life of Samuel Clemens which remained to be converted into the *fiction* of *Huckleberry Finn.* Although interesting as biography, they are essentially conventional.

The most genuine truth in *Life on the Mississippi* is to be found, characteristically, in the one authentic tall tale in the volume—the tale of the birth of "Mark Twain," which Mark Twain tells for the first time. That tale, as it is told, identifies "Mark Twain" as having emerged from an essentially guilty act. Samuel Clemens had gratuitously parodied old Captain Isaiah

Sellers and had adopted the old gentleman's pseudonym of "Mark Twain" years later—half-humorously in order to carry on the tradition of Sellers' incredible memory, half-guiltily to pay off the debt incurred by the wound the parody had inflicted. Here is the tall tale told in the grand manner, for it exposes Mark Twain as the figure who, like old Captain Sellers, has a memory which invariably *enlarges* upon fact. Mark Twain concludes his account by emphasizing how the old man had been hurt by the burlesque, and how he had tried to make up for the wound he had dealt.

> Captain Sellers did me the honor to profoundly detest me from that day forth. When I say he did me the honor, I am not using empty words. It was a very real honor to be in the thoughts of so great a man as Captain Sellers, and I had wit enough to appreciate it and be proud of it. It was a distinction to be loved by such a man; but it was a much greater distinction to be hated by him, because he loved scores of people; but he didn't sit up nights to hate anybody but me.
>
> He never printed another paragraph while he lived, and he never signed "Mark Twain" to anything. At the time the telegraph brought me the news of his death, I was on the Pacific coast. I was a fresh, new journalist, and needed a *nom de guerre;* so I confiscated the ancient mariner's discarded one, and have done my best to make it remain what it was in his hands—a sign and symbol and warrant that whatever is found in its company may be gambled on as being the petrified truth. How I've succeeded, it would not be modest in me to say.[6]

Here is an exquisite bit of self-definition. The tale, so far as the most serious Mark Twain scholars have been able to discover, cannot be corroborated from the life of Samuel Clemens. But then why should it be? For Mark Twain, even as he insists upon his extreme veracity, actually arouses comic doubt about the entire episode. All this, of course, is the ancient strategy of Mark Twain's tall tale. What is new for Mark Twain is the substance of the tale. As he defines himself almost on the eve of making the great endeavor which was to complete *Huckleberry Finn,* "Mark Twain" is at once a name and an act. As a name it has to do with the most ancient memory of The Great Mississippi—a memory containing an ancient yet personal past in which possibilities existed on a grander scale than in the dwarfed present. As an act, the name is an attempt to make reparation for a personal injury inflicted as a result of a literary burlesque. The act is a *making up* in both

[6] *Ibid.,* pp. 402–403.

senses of the phrase. It is an invention or tall tale; at the same time, it is an effort to make amends for the humiliation suffered by the old Captain.

In "Old Times on the Mississippi," Mark Twain had converted his own humiliations into humor. The climactic scene of the sketches came when Mark Twain humorously reconstructed the public humiliation to which Bixby had exposed him. But in *Life on the Mississippi,* Mark Twain identifies himself as having been born not out of humiliation inflicted upon him, but out of humiliation he had inflicted upon another. In other words, to the sense of shame, Mark Twain had added, or was adding, a sense of guilt. Whereas he had converted the shame into the series of humorous humiliations of "Old Times on the Mississippi," the guilt, which he had gone almost out of his way to experience from 1876 until 1883, had been indulged rather than converted. It had manifested itself either in the form of indignation—as in *The Prince and the Pauper* and portions of *A Tramp Abroad*—or in the emergence of the nostalgia and sentimental guilt fantasies of *Life on the Mississippi.*[7] The book which was assimilating, and finally converting into humor the guilt, indignation, and nostalgia—those aspects we want to call the darker side of Mark Twain's genius—was *Huckleberry Finn.* Growing through the years between *Tom Sawyer* and *Life on the Mississippi,* it was the book which was extending Mark Twain's humor into all that "serious" territory both discovered and required by the style of *Huckleberry Finn.*

To say that in *Huckleberry Finn* Mark Twain extended his humor into serious territory is not to say that his humor became serious, but that larger areas of seriousness came under the dominion of his humor. If the turning of serious issues into the form of humor was the substantial inversion of the book, the formal inversion lay in transforming dialect into vernacular, which is to say making it the vehicle of vision. In terms of literary history, *Huckleberry Finn* marks the full emergence of an American language, and although Mark Twain did not accomplish the process alone, he *realized* the tradition which he inherited. The "Southwest" humorists—Hooper, Long-

[7] Kenneth Lynn (*Mark Twain and Southwestern Humor,* p. 203) perceptively observes that the coming revolt against the conservative opinions of his friends could be heard in the humor of "The Facts Concerning the Recent Carnival of Crime in Connecticut," a sketch Mark Twain read to the Monday Evening Club of Hartford on January 24, 1876. This sketch, interestingly enough, depicted Mark Twain killing his conscience after being haunted and taunted by it beyond endurance. Having accomplished the murder, he has a carnival of crime. Though the sketch does disclose possible revolt, its strong fantasy element provides ample protection and forecasts the relatively safe exercises into fantasy Mark Twain was to make much later in his career.

street, Harris, and Thorpe; the comic journalists—Artemus Ward, Petroleum V. Nasby, Josh Billings, and John Phoenix; and the local colorists—Harriet Beecher Stowe, Bret Harte, Mary E. Wilkins Freeman, and Sarah Orne Jewett—had all used dialect. Yet in the humor of the old Southwest and in the literary achievements of the local colorists, the dialect was framed by a literary language which invariably condescended to it. The comic journalists, though they dropped the literary frame to appear as "characters," reduced dialect to a comic image. If the Southwest humorists tended to brutalize dialect characters and local colorists to sentimentalize them, the comic journalists, by reducing themselves to dialect, sought to give pungency and quaintness to conventional thought.

But something altogether different happens in *Huckleberry Finn*. The language is neither imprisioned in a frame nor distorted into a caricature; rather, it becomes a way of casting character and experience at the same time. This combination is the fine economy of Huckleberry Finn's style. Thus when Huck declares at the outset that he, not Mark Twain, will write this book, the language at one and the same time defines character and action.

> You don't know about me without you have read a book by the name *The Adventures of Tom Sawyer;* but that ain't no matter. That book was made by Mr. Mark Twain, and he told the truth, mainly. There was things which he stretched, but mainly he told the truth. That is nothing. I never see anybody but lied one time or another, without it was Aunt Polly, or the Widow, or maybe Mary. Aunt Polly—Tom's Aunt Polly, she is—and Mary, and the Widow Douglas is all told about in that book, which is mostly a true book, with some stretchers, as I said before.[8]

Nothing more seems to be going on here than in previous uses of dialect. But by allowing Huck's vernacular merely to *imply* the literary form, Mark Twain was reorganizing the entire value system of language, for all values had to be transmitted directly or indirectly through Huck's vernacular. In turning the narration over to Huck, Mark Twain abandoned the explicit norms and risked making his vernacular force the reader to supply the implied norms. The vernacular he developed created the means of control within the reader's mind, chiefly in three ways. First of all, Huck's incorrect language implied standard, correct, literary English. Second, Huck's status as a child invited an indulgence from the reader. Finally, Huck's action in time and place—freeing a slave in the Old South before the Civil War—in-

[8] *Writings,* XIII, 1.

sured moral approval from the reader. Though he is being a bad boy in his own time, he is being a good boy in the reader's imagination.

All these controls, which are really *conventions,* exist outside the novel. They are just what the style of the novel is *not;* for the style is the inversion which implies the conventions yet remains their opposite. And this style is Mark Twain's revolution in language, his rebellion in form; and it marks the emergence of the American language to which both Hemingway and Faulkner allude when they say that Mark Twain was the first American writer, the writer from whom they descend.[9]

The freeing of the vernacular from the conventions is the larger historical fact of form which provides an index to the action of the novel. For this vernacular language, which implies respectable language, is not only the form of the book; it is at one and the same time the character of Huckleberry Finn. To talk about the revolt of the one should be to talk about the revolt of the other. I say *should,* because Huck's revolt seems on the face of things a genuinely tame performance. He is involved in a subversive project which has the reader's complete approval—the freeing of a slave in the Old South, a world which, by virtue of the Civil War, has been declared morally reprehensible because of the slavery it condoned. Huck's rebellion is therefore being negotiated in a society which the reader's conscience indicts as morally wrong and which history has declared legally wrong. Moreover, Huck is a boy, a relatively harmless figure who drifts helplessly into his rebellion, making his subversion not only an act which the reader can approve but can indulge. His badness is inverted into goodness.

All this seems obvious, yet many readers never cease to celebrate the pluck of Huck's rebellion, when if this were all there was to it we would have nothing but the blandest sentimental action. What, after all, was courageous about writing in Hartford twenty years after the Civil War—or what is courageous about reading in a post-Civil War world—a book about a boy who was helping a slave to freedom? Such an act would be roughly equivalent to writing a novel in our time about a boy in Hitler's Germany helping a Jew to the border. Not that a great novel could not emerge from either of these subjects. In the case of *Huckleberry Finn* one did. Yet the boldness of the book—its exploration and discovery—does not reside in so tame a representation, but in the utilization of the action to gain the reader's assent to make the voyage downstream.

[9] Hemingway's words were: "All modern American literature comes from one book by Mark Twain called *Huckleberry Finn* . . . it's the best book we've had. All American writing comes from that. There was nothing before. There has been nothing as good since" (*Green Hills of Africa* [New York, 1935], p. 22).

This built-in approval, stemming from Huck's initial "moral" advantage and from his being a boy—and thus evocative of the indulgent nostalgia Mark Twain had learned to exploit in *Tom Sawyer*—is what I take to be the "moral sentiment" of the book. But this moral sentiment is not the action of the book any more than the implicit conventional language is the style of the book. Rather, Huck's action is the inversion of the sentiment.

The humor of the book rides upon and at the same time requires this crucial inversion. For the more Huck berates himself for doing "bad" things, the more the reader approves him for doing "good" ones. Thus what for Huck is his worst action—refusing to turn Jim in to Miss Watson—is for the reader his best. When Huck says "All right, then, I'll *go* to hell," the reader is sure he is going to heaven. If this ironic relationship should ever break down, Huck's whole stature would be threatened. If Huck ever begins to think he is doing a good thing by helping Jim, he will become a good boy like Sid—one knowingly engaged in virtuous action; or a bad boy like Tom —one who can seem to go against society because he really knows that he is doing right. Clear though all this should be, the moral sentiment implied by the style inexorably arouses a wish that Huck have some recognition of his achievement.

It is just this wish which the ending of the novel frustrates; and since the wish is so pervasively exploited by the action of the novel, it is no wonder that the ending has been not a small problem. Of course, defenses of the ending can be made and have been made, but the point remains that they are defenses. No matter how adroit the critic, he begins from a position of special pleading, as if he were trying to convince himself that in an acknowledged masterpiece there could not really be such a wanton collapse. Even the most sympathetic critics of Mark Twain find the wiser path is to regret the closing ten chapters. Thus, Ernest Hemingway, after observing that modern American literature stemmed from *Huckleberry Finn,* went on to say, "If you read it you must stop where the Nigger Jim is stolen from the boys. That is the real end. The rest is just cheating."[10] Philip Young, following Hemingway, has gone so far as to declare that the beginning as well as the end could well be omitted without substantially taking away from the book.[11] So passionate an admirer of the book as Bernard De Voto acknowledged that Mark Twain lost his purpose at the end and drifted into "inharmonious burlesque":

> A few pages earlier he had written the scene in which many readers have found his highest reach. . . . And now, without any

[10] *Ibid.*
[11] Philip Young, *Ernest Hemingway* (New York, 1952), p. 196.

awareness that he was muddying the waters of great fiction, he plunges into a trivial extravaganza on a theme he had exhausted years before. In the whole history of the English novel there is no more abrupt or more chilling descent.[12]

Probably the most formidable attack ever made on the ending of the book is found in Leo Marx's extremely interesting essay, "Mr. Eliot, Mr. Trilling, and Huckleberry Finn." Exposing Trilling's and Eliot's rather perfunctory and evasive approvals of the ending, Marx presents a rigorous analysis of Mark Twain's failure in the closing chapters of his masterpiece. Mark Twain failed, Marx believes, because he refused the responsibilities which went with the vision of the journey. For the journey was, according to Marx, the Quest—the great voyage toward freedom which Huck and Jim had so precariously made. But in the last ten chapters, Marx feels that Mark Twain simply turns the book over to the high jinks of Tom Sawyer, while Huck shrinkingly assumes the stature of a little straight man, observing the burlesque antics of his companion, but apparently unmoved by them. The cause of this slump on Mark Twain's part, Marx concludes, is simply that the journey, the Quest, *cannot* succeed. The drifting river has taken Huck and Jim ever deeper into slavery, and Mark Twain, unable to resolve the paradox of this reality which defeats his wish, simply evades the entire issue by shifting to burlesque.[13]

Persuasive through this argument is, Mark Twain's form rules out the possibilities which Marx insists on. Since Huck's entire identity is based upon an inverted order of values just as his style is based upon "incorrect" usage, he cannot have any recognition of his own virtue. Failure to acknowledge this necessity causes Marx to see the journey as a quest, whereas it simply is not at any time a quest. A quest is a positive journey, implying an effort, a struggle to reach a goal. But Huck is escaping. His journey is primarily a negation, a flight *from* tyranny, not a flight toward freedom.

In fact, Huck's central mode of being is that of escape and evasion. He forgets much more than he remembers; he lies, steals, and in general participates in as many confidence tricks as the King and the Duke. But the two cardinal facts—that he is a boy and is involved in helping a runaway slave —serve endlessly to sustain the reader's approval. It is precisely this approval which, putting the reader's moral censor to sleep, provides the central good humor pervading the incongruities, absurdities, and cruelties through which the narrative beautifully makes its way. The vernacular in-

---

[12] Bernard De Voto, *Mark Twain at Work* (Cambridge, Mass., 1942), p. 92.

[13] Leo Marx, "Mr. Eliot, Mr. Trilling, and Huckleberry Finn," *American Scholar*, XXIII (Autumn, 1953), pp. 423–439.

version, which so surely evokes the feeling of approval and indulgence, is narratively embodied in the very drift of the great river on which the raft miraculously rides.[14]

To be sure, at the fateful moment when Huck determines to set Jim free, he finds himself in open rebellion against Negro slavery. But he comes reluctantly, not gloriously, forward; even as he makes his famous declaration to go to hell, he is looking for a way out. He is certainly not a rebel; he is in a tight place and does the *easiest* thing. The role of Abolitionist is not comfortable nor comforting to him and in turning over to Tom Sawyer the entire unpleasant business of freeing Jim, Huck is surely not acting out of but remarkably *in* character.

Marx's inversion of Huck's escape into a quest drives him to the position of saying that Mark Twain could not "acknowledge the truth his novel contained" and thus evaded the central moral responsibilities of his vision. Yet for Marx the "truth" amounts to nothing more than Huck's perceiving that Negro slavery is wrong and involving himself in a quest for *political* freedom. In saying that the ending of the book discloses a failure of nerve and a retreat to the genteel tradition, it seems to me that Marx is completely turned around. Surely the genteel Bostonians would have applauded the moral sentiment of antislavery and political freedom which the novel entertains. They would have welcomed the quest rather than the escape. Yet if Marx is wrong, what is there to say about the ending?

To begin with, the ending is, to use Huck's term, uncomfortable. The problem is to define the source of this discomfort. Without question, there is a change when Tom Sawyer reappears. The narrative movement changes from one of adventure to burlesque—a burlesque which, in place of Huck's sincere but helpless involvement in freeing a real slave, puts Tom Sawyer's relatively cruel yet successful lark of freeing a slave already free. It is not Mark Twain's failure to distinguish between the two actions which jeopardizes his book; rather, it is his ironic exposure of Tom's action which threatens the humor of the book and produces the inharmonious burlesque De Voto regrets. Tom appears in such an unfortunate light in the closing pages that many readers of *Huckleberry Finn* can never again read *Tom Sawyer* without in one way or another holding Tom responsible for motives he had not had in the earlier book.

---

[14] The perfect integration between this drift and the river's motion is in part responsible for the beautiful economy with which Mark Twain treats the river. Far from needing to provide extensive descriptions and facts about the river as he did in *Life on the Mississippi*, he was able to render the river enormously real with economy of means. The reason: the fugitive boy and the river are made one through Huck's language.

Tom's play seems unpardonable because he already knows that Jim is free. Yet this knowledge—which Tom withholds from Huck—finally clears up for Huck the mystery of Tom's behavior toward him. Upon at last discovering the knowledge Tom has withheld from him, Huck, who has been troubled by Tom's "badness," at last understands why his respectable companion has been able to commit such a crime. His only remaining problem is to find out why Tom spent so much effort "setting a free nigger free." This, too, is cleared up when Tom explains to the long-suffering Aunt Sally that he made his elaborate and vexing arrangements purely for "adventure."

Tom's adventures are a unique cruelty in a book which depicts so much cruelty. All the other cruelties are committed for some "reason"—for honor, money, or power. But Tom's cruelty has a purity all its own—it is done solely for the sake of adventure. After facing Tom's long play, it is possible to see Huck's famous remark about the King and the Duke in a larger perspective. "Human beings can be awful cruel to each other," Huck had said upon seeing the scoundrels ridden out of town on a rail. This statement not only points backward to the episodes with the King and the Duke, but serves as a gateway leading from the King and the Duke's departure to Tom Sawyer's performance. For Tom's pure play runs directly counter to a wish the journey has generated. That is the frustration of the ending—the inversion. Having felt Huck's slow discovery of Jim's humanity, the reader perforce deplores Tom's casual ignorance and unawareness.

Yet the judgment which the last ten chapters render upon Tom is surely the judgment rendered upon the moral sentiment on which the book has ridden. If the reader sees in Tom's performance a rather shabby and safe bit of play, he is seeing no more than the exposure of the approval with which he watched Huck operate. For if Tom is rather contemptibly setting a free slave free, what after all is the reader doing, who begins the book after the *fact* of the Civil War? This is the "joke" of the book—the moment when, in outrageous burlesque, it attacks the sentiment which its style has at once evoked and exploited. To see that Tom is doing at the ending what we have been doing throughout the book is essential to understanding what the book has meant to us. For when Tom proclaims to the assembled throng who have witnessed his performance that Jim "is as free as any cretur that walks this earth," he is an exposed embodiment of the complacent moral sentiment on which the reader has relied throughout the book. And to the extent the reader has indulged the complacency he will be disturbed by the ending.

To be frustrated by the ending is to begin to discover the meaning of this journey, which evokes so much indulgence and moral approval that the censor is put to sleep. Beneath the sleeping censor, the real rebellion of

Huckleberry Finn is enacted. For there must be a real rebellion—a rebellion which cannot so easily be afforded—else Mark Twain is guilty of a failure far greater than the ending. If the "incorrect" vernacular of *Huckleberry Finn* is to be more than décor, it must enact an equally "incorrect" vision. Otherwise, the style becomes merely a way of saying rather than a way of being. It is not simply the "poetry" or "beauty" or "rhythm" of Huck's vernacular which makes his language work, but the presence of a commensurate vernacular vision. The reason that imitators of *Huckleberry Finn* fail —the reason that Mark Twain himself later failed—is that they lack the vision to match their style, and thus their language is merely décor. One has but to read Edgar Lee Masters' *Mitch Miller*—which is a "modern" attempt to show what the childhood of Huck and Tom was really like—to know how sentimental such language can be unless it is sustained by a genuinely radical vision. Even Sherwood Anderson's "I Want to Know Why," in many ways the finest example of vernacular vision directly derivative from *Huckleberry Finn,* falls far short of Mark Twain, because its end, though finely climactic, is unfortunately sentimental. The young boy's anguished appeal upon discovering the Jockey with the whore is, after all, just the same old truth we knew all the time.

What then *is* the rebellion of *Huckleberry Finn?* What is it but an attack upon the conscience? The conscience, after all is said and done, is the real tyrant in the book. It is the relentless force which pursues Huckleberry Finn; it is the tyrant from which he seeks freedom. And it is not only the social conscience which threatens Huck, but *any* conscience. The social conscience, represented in the book by the slaveholding society of the Old South, is easily seen and exposed. It is the false conscience. But what of the true conscience which the reader wishes to project upon Huck and which Huck himself is at last on the threshold of accepting? It, too, is finally false. Although the book plays upon the notion that all conscience is finally social, it does not stand on that line; for the action is not defining the conscience so much as rejecting it. Whether the conscience is "lower" social conscience or the "higher" inner conscience, it remains the tyrant which drives its victims into the absurd corners from which they cannot escape. Thus on the one hand, there is the "law" or "right" of slavery from which Jim is trying to escape and against which Huck finds himself in helpless rebellion. But there are then the "inner" codes which appear as equally absurd distortions. There is Pap's belief in freedom; there is the code of the feud which the Grangerfords and Shepherdsons hold to; there is the "honor" of Colonel Sherburn; and finally there is the "principle" of Tom Sawyer who rises proudly to the defense of Jim because he "is as free as any cretur that walks this earth." In every case the conscience, whether it comes from society or from some apparent inner realm, is an agent of aggression—aggression against the self or against another. Either the means or the excuse by which pain is inflicted, the conscience is both law and duty, erasing the possibility of choice and thereby constraining its victims to a necessary and irrevocable course of action.

From the "Southern" conscience, Huck first attempts to flee. But even in flight from it, borne southward on the great river, his "Northern" conscience begins to awaken. This is the apparently internal conscience—the Civil War he finds himself engaged in on the raft as it glides deeper and deeper into the territory of slavery, not of freedom. Our moral sentiment approves his flight from his Southern conscience, but with the approval comes the hope that he will discover his Northern conscience. But it is just here that Huck will not accept the invitation. For chapter after chapter he remains the fugitive—in flight from the old conscience and evading the development of a new one.

And the reason he evades it is clear—the conscience is *uncomfortable*. Indeed, comfort and satisfaction are the value terms in *Huckleberry Finn*. Freedom for Huck is not realized in terms of political liberty but in terms of pleasure. Thus his famous pronouncement about life on the raft: "Other places do seem so cramped and smothery, but a raft don't. You feel mighty free and easy and comfortable on a raft."[15] And later, when the King and the Duke threaten to break the peace, Huck determines not to take a stand against them, observing, "What you want above all things, on a raft, is for everybody to be satisfied, and feel right and kind toward the others."[16] In almost every instance Huck projects the good life in terms of ease, satisfaction, comfort. A satirist would see it in terms of justice; a moralist would have it as a place of righteousness. But a humorist envisions it as a place of good feeling, where no pain or discomfort can enter. This is why Huck does not see clothes, which figure so prominently as the garments of civilization, as veils to hide the body, or as the false dress whereby a fiction of status is maintained. This would be the satiric vision. As far as Huck is concerned, clothes and civilization itself are undesirable because they are essentially *uncomfortable*. "But I reckon I got to light out for the territory," he says as he departs, "because Aunt Sally she's going to adopt me and sivilize me, and I can't stand it."[17] When Huck says he "can't stand it," he is literally

[15] *Writings*, XIII, 162. The conscience, on the other hand, is the source of discomfort. As Huck says, ". . . it don't make no difference whether you do right or wrong, a person's conscience ain't got no sense, and just goes for him *anyway*. If I had a yeller dog that didn't know no more than a person's conscience does I would pison him" (*Writings*, XIII, 321).

[16] *Ibid.*, p. 174.

[17] *Ibid.*, p. 405.

referring to the cramped discomfort of submitting to the clothes and quarters of civilization. To be sure, the phrase suggests a vastly wider range of significances, but significances that are inexorably rooted in a logic of feeling, comfort, and bodily satisfaction. The significances are *our* discoveries, which are at once made possible by and anchored to the concrete image of the raft, the boy, and the Negro. The good feeling, comfort, and ease dominating this journey which makes its way through a society of meanness, cowardice, and cruelty are perfectly embodied by the raft adrift upon the river.

This logic of pleasure at the heart of the book must also be at the heart of any "positive" value we may wish to ascribe to the experience of reading it. Most criticism of *Huckleberry Finn,* however, retreats from the pleasure principle toward the relative safety of "moral issues" and the imperatives of the Northern conscience. This flight is made because of the uncomfortable feeling relating to Huck's "evasion," his "escape," and finally his "rejection" of civilization. What Huck is rejecting is, of course, the conscience—which Mark Twain was later to rail at under the name of the "Moral Sense." The conscience, the trap of adult civilization which lies in wait for Huck throughout the novel, is what he is at such pains to evade. It is his successful evasion which we as readers cannot finally face. The reader who rejects the paradox usually does so on the grounds that the book is "just" a humorous book. The one who detects and is disturbed by it is more likely to follow William Van O'Connor's pronouncements about the "dangers" of innocence and the "failure" of moral vision. A weakness in Huck—pontificates O'Connor in his attempt to prove that the book is *not* a great American novel—is that he does not "acknowledge the virtues of civilization and live, as one must, inside it."[18] Huck does acknowledge the virtues, of course, and upbraids himself for being uncomfortable with them.

But far from relying upon such cozy affirmations as O'Connor longs for, the book moves *down* the river into the deeper repressions of slavery, enacting at every moment a conversion of morality into pleasure. Extending the range of humor through the ills, the agonies, and the cruelties of civilization, it shows how much the conscience—whether Northern or Southern—is the negative force leading to acts of violence upon the self or upon another. Huck's "escape" is of course an escape from violence, a rejection of cruelty —his instinct is neither to give nor to receive pain if he can avoid it.

The prime danger to his identity comes at the moment he chooses the developing inner or Northern conscience. This moment, when Huck says "All right, then, I'll *go* to hell," is characteristically the moment we fatally

[18] William Van O'Connor, "Why *Huckleberry Finn* Is Not The Great American Novel," *College English,* XVII (October, 1955), p. 8.

approve, and approve *morally*. But it is with equal fatality the moment at which Huck's identity is most precariously threatened. In the very act of choosing to go to hell he has surrendered to the notion of a *principle* of right and wrong. He has forsaken the world of pleasure to make a moral choice. Precisely here is where Huck is about to negate himself—where, with an act of positive virtue, he actually commits himself to play the role of Tom Sawyer which he *has* to assume in the closing section of the book. To commit oneself to the idea, the *morality* of freeing Jim, is to become Tom Sawyer. Here again is the irony of the book, and the ending, far from evading the consequences of Huck's act of rebellion, realizes those consequences.

Mark Twain's real problem—his real dilemma—was not at all his inability to "face" the issues of slavery; certainly it was not a fear of the society or a failure of moral and political courage which brought Mark Twain to the tight place where Huck had to decide forever and ever. Rather, it was the necessities of his humorous form. For in order to achieve expression of the deep wish which *Huckleberry Finn* embodies—the wish for freedom from any conscience—Mark Twain had to intensify the moral sentiment. The moment there is any real moral doubt about Huck's action, the wish will be threatened. Yet when Huck makes his moral affirmation, he fatally negates the wish for freedom from the conscience; for if his affirmation frees him from the Southern conscience, it binds him to his Northern conscience. No longer an outcast, he can be welcomed into the society to play the role of Tom Sawyer, which is precisely what happens. When he submits to Tom's role, we are the ones who become uncomfortable. The entire burlesque ending is a revenge upon the moral sentiment which, though it shielded the humor, ultimately threatened Huck's identity.

This is the larger reality of the ending—what we may call the necessity of the form. That it was a cost which the form exacted no one would deny. But to call it a failure, a piece of moral cowardice, is to miss the true rebellion of the book, for the disturbance of the ending is nothing less than our and Mark Twain's recognition of the full meaning of *Huckleberry Finn*. If the reader is pushed to the limits of his humor, Mark Twain had reached the limits of his—he had seen through to the end. The disillusion begins not when Tom returns to the stage, but when Huck says "All right, then, I'll *go* to hell"—when our applause and approval reach their zenith. At that moment, which anyone would agree is Mark Twain's highest achievement, Huck has internalized the image of Jim; and that image, whose reality he has enjoyed during the fatal drift downstream, becomes the scourge which shames him out of his evasion. The whole process is disclosed in the lyric utterance leading to his decision. Having written the note to Miss Watson telling where Jim is, Huck feels cleansed and at last able to pray:

But I didn't do it straight off, but laid the paper down and set there thinking—thinking how good it was all this happened so, and how near I come to being lost and going to hell. And went on thinking. And got to thinking over our trip down the river; and I see Jim before me all the time: in the day and in the night-time, sometimes moonlight, sometimes storms, and we a-floating along, talking and singing and laughing. But somehow I couldn't seem to strike no places to harden me against him, but only the other kind. I'd see him standing my watch on top of his'n, 'stead of calling me, so I could go on sleeping; and see him how glad he was when I come back out of the fog; and when I come to him again in the swamp, up there where the feud was; and such-like times; and would always call me honey, and pet me, and do everything he could think of for me, and how good he always was; and at last I struck the time I saved him by telling the men we had smallpox aboard, and he was so grateful, and said I was the best friend old Jim ever had in the world, and the *only* one he's got now; and then I happened to look around and see that paper.

It was a close place.[19]

This lyrical rehearsal of the journey is also the journey's end. And the decision which ends it is cast in the positive locution of Tom Sawyer, not in Huck's essentially negative vernacular.[20] When Huck says he will go to hell, in five minutes of reading time he is there. For in this novel, which constantly plays against superstitious hereafters, there is no fire-and-brimstone hell but only civilization—which is precisely where Huck finds himself as a consequence of his own determination.

This dilemma and disillusion are what Mark Twain would not shrink from, but carried through, though it cost him almost everything—which is saying it cost him his good humor. In the burlesque chapters, he understandably though precariously turned upon his invention, upon his reader, and upon himself. Yet even here he did not entirely abandon the pleasure principle, but left his "serious" readers pleased with themselves instead of the book, their moral complacency ruffled by nothing more than comfortable indignation at the evasions of humor.

[19] *Writings,* XIII, 296–297. Although Huck's language constantly describes his feelings and thoughts, they are so directly wedded to external action and dependent on it that he seems to have no independent "thought." This passage is the only extended narrative of such an inner life. Once the decision is made, he hardly reflects upon his past. If he remembers, he keeps it to himself.

[20] Huck's most characteristic errors of grammar are, significantly enough, his constant use of the double negative and his persistent confusion of verb tense.

As for Mark Twain, he had seen through to the end, and it almost killed him. He never would have so good a humor again. His despair, having set in at the moment of Huckleberry Finn's affirmation, never really let up. The only way he could survive was to try to swallow the joke which became more and more sour the rest of his embattled way. Having seen the limits of his humor, he turned upon them and railed at the conscience and the need for self-approval, the twin human characteristics which seemed to make the human race utterly ridiculous and damned.

And what of Huck? As Nick Carraway said of Gatsby, he came out all right. He went to the territory because he was true to himself and to his creator. He didn't go there to lead civilization either, but to play outside it. Refusing to grow up and tell the lie of the conscience, he left behind him a novel for all time. It was truly a novel of reconstruction. First, it had brought into fiction not the Old South but an entirely new one which the Northern conscience could welcome back into the Union. And in the process of its humor, it reconstructed the psyche, following the pleasure principle as far as it would go to discover in the southern reaches of the Great River the tyranny of the conscience which keeps the adult in chains and makes his pleasure the enactment of greater and greater cruelty. He had not reached childhood's end, but had disclosed the lie of the adult world. In his last moment he said, "so there ain't nothing more to write about, and I am rotten glad of it, because if I'd 'a'knowed what a trouble it was to make a book I wouldn't 'a'tackled it, and ain't a-going to no more." We of course constantly lecture Mark Twain about having turned away from his true vein of ore. The fact is, however, that he could not turn away but kept trying to do just what we want of him. He kept trying to call Huck back to tell another story. But Huck, though he came docilely, could never tell the truth. He had told all the truth he had to tell in one glorious lie.

WILLIAM DEAN HOWELLS

****

Because he is remembered as a "reticent realist," Howells is not often sought after today. Lionel Trilling, however, in this essay, makes plain how difficult was the path which Howells in dogged honesty attempted to follow. Howells's life is most completely set forth by Edwin H. Cady, in two volumes, *The Road to Realism, The Early Years, 1837–1885* and *The Realist at War, The Mature Years, 1885–1920* (Syracuse, N.Y., 1956 and 1958); an authoritative but briefer account is Clara M. and Rudolf Kirk's *William Dean Howells* (New York, 1962). Critical examination of his intention and achievement include George C. Carrington, Jr.'s *The Immense Complex Drama: The World and Art of the Howells Novel* (Columbus, Ohio, 1966), Everett Carter's *Howells and the Age of Realism* (Philadelphia, Pa., 1954), William M. Gibson's *William Dean Howells* (Minneapolis, Minn., 1967), and William McMurray's *The Literary Realism of William Dean Howells* (Carbondale, Ill., 1967). Shorter studies of aspects of his thought and writing include A. W. Amacher, "The Genteel Primitivist and the

Semi-Tragic Octoroon," *New England Quarterly,* XXIX (June 1956), pp. 216–227; George J. Becker, "William Dean Howells: The Awakening of Conscience," *College English,* XIX (April 1957), pp. 283–291; William F. Ekstrom, "The Equalitarian Principle in the Fiction of William Dean Howells," *American Literature,* XXIV (March 1952), pp. 40–50; Thomas W. Ford, "Howells and the American Negro," *Texas Studies in Literature and Language,* V (Winter 1964), pp. 530–537; Edd Winfield Parks, "Howells and the Gentle Reader," *South Atlantic Quarterly,* L (April 1951), pp. 239–247; and William Wasserstrom, "William Dean Howells: The Indelible Stain," *New England Quarterly,* XXXII (December 1959), pp. 486–495. Collections of essays have been gathered by Edwin H. Cady and David L. Frazier in *The War of the Critics over William Dean Howells* (Evanston, Ill., 1962) and Kenneth E. Eble in *Howells: A Century of Criticism* (Dallas, Tex., 1962).

WILLIAM DEAN HOWELLS AND THE ROOTS OF MODERN TASTE

Lionel Trilling

****

1

Every now and then in the past few years we have heard that we might soon expect a revival of interest in the work of William Dean Howells. And certainly, if this rumor were substantiated, there would be a notable propriety in the event. In the last two decades Henry James has become established as a great magnetic figure in our higher culture. In the same period Mark Twain has become as it were newly established—not indeed, like James, as a source and object of intellectual energy, but at least as a permanent focus of our admiring interest, as the representative of a mode of the American mind and temperament which we are happy to acknowledge. To say that Henry James and Mark Twain are opposite poles of our national character would be excessive, yet it is clear that they do suggest tendencies which are very far apart, so that there is always refreshment and enlightenment in thinking of them together. And when we do think of them together, diverse as they are, indifferent to each other as they mostly were, deeply suspicious of each other as they were whenever they became aware of each other, we naturally have in mind the man who stood between them as the affectionate friend of both, the happy admirer of their disparate powers, who saw so early the fullness of their virtues which we now take for granted. It would make a pleasant symmetry if we could know that William Dean Howells has become the object of renewed admiration, that he is being regarded, like his two great friends, as a large, significant figure in our literature.

But the rumor of the revival is surely false. A certaiin number of people, but a very small number, do nowadays feel that they might find pleasure in Howells, their expectation being based, no doubt, on an analogy with the pleasure that is being found in Trollope. And the analogy is fair enough. Howells produced in the free Trollopian way, and with the same happy yielding of the rigorous artistic conscience in favor of the careless flow of life; and now and then, even in our exigent age, we are willing to find respite from the strict demands of conscious art, especially if we can do so without a great loss of other sanctions and integrities. Howells, it is thought, can give us the pleasures of our generic image of the Victorian novel. He was a man of principle without being a man of heroic moral intensity, and we expect of him that he will involve us in the enjoyment of moral activity through the medium of a lively awareness of manners, that he will delight us by touching on high matters in the natural course of gossip.

This is a very attractive expectation and Howells does not really disappoint it. He is not Trollope's equal, but at his best he is in his own right a very engaging novelist. Whether or not he deserves a stronger adjective than this may for the moment be left open to question, but engaging he undoubtedly is. And yet I think that he cannot now engage us, that we cannot expect a revival of interest in him—his stock is probably quite as high in the market as it will go. The excellent omnibus volume of Howells which Professor Commager recently brought out was piously reviewed but it was not bought. And when, in a course of lectures on American literature, I imagined that it might be useful to my students to have a notion of the cultural and social situation which Howells described, and therefore spent a considerable time talking about his books, I received the first anonymous letter I have ever had from a student—it warned me that the lapse of taste shown by my excessive interest in a dull writer was causing a scandal in the cafeterias.

As a historical figure, Howells must of course always make a strong claim upon our attention. His boyhood and youth, to which he so often returned in memory in his pleasant autobiographical books, were spent in circumstances of which everyone must be aware who wishes to understand the course of American culture. Howells's induction into the intellectual life gives us one of the points from which we can measure what has happened to the humanistic idea in the modern world. If we want to know what was the estate of literature a hundred years ago, if we want to be made aware of how the nineteenth century, for all its development of science and technology, was still essentially a humanistic period, we have only to take Howells's account of the intellectual life of the Ohio towns in which he lived—the lively concern with the more dramatic aspects of European politics, the circulation of the great English reviews, the fond knowledge of the English and American literature of the century, the adoration of Shakespeare, the general, if naïve, respect for learning. It was certainly not elaborate, this culture of little towns that were almost of the frontier, and we must not exaggerate the extent to which its most highly developed parts were shared, yet it *was* pervasive and its assumptions were general enough to support Howells in his literary commitment. In a log cabin he read to the bottom of that famous barrel of books, he struggled to learn four or five languages, he determined on a life of literature, and his community respected his enterprise and encouraged him in it. And it is worth observing that, as he himself says, he devoted himself to a literary career not so much out of disinterested love for literature as out of the sense that literature was an institutional activity by which he might make something of himself in the worldly way.

Howells's historical interest for us continues through all his developing career. His famous pilgrimage to New England, his round of visits to the great literary figures of Massachusetts, is a *locus classicus* of our literary history. It culminated, as everyone remembers, in that famous little dinner which Lowell gave for him at the Parker House; it was the first dinner that Howells had ever seen that was served in courses, in what was then called the Russian style, and it reached its significant climax when Holmes turned to Lowell and said, "Well, James, this is the apostolic succession, this is the laying on of hands." Much has been made of this story, and indeed much must be made of it, for although Holmes probably intended no more than an irony-lightened kindliness to a very young man, his remark was previsionary, and the visit of Howells does mark a succession and an era, the beginning of an American literature where before, as Howells said, there had been only a New England literature. Then Howells's uprooting himself from Boston to settle in New York in 1888 marks, as Alfred Kazin observes, the shifting of the concentrations of literary capital from the one city to the other. And when, as old age came on and Howells was no longer a commanding figure with the New York publishers, when he suffered with characteristic mild fortitude the pain of having his work refused by a new generation of editors, the culture of the American nineteenth century had at last come to its very end.

Howells's historical importance is further confirmed by the position he attained in the institutional life of American letters. Not long after Howells died, H. D. Mencken, who had been at pains to make Howells's name a byword of evasive gentility, wrote to regret his death, because, as he said, with irony enough but also with some seriousness, there was now no American writer who could serve as the representative of American letters, no figure who, by reason of age, length of service, bulk of work, and public respect, could stand as a literary patriarch. And since Mencken wrote, no such figure has arisen. Howells was indeed patriarchal as he grew older, large and most fatherly, and if he exercised his paternity only in the mild, puzzled American way, still he was the head of the family and he took his responsibility seriously. He asserted the dignity of the worker in literature at the same time that he defined the writer's place as being economically and socially with the manual worker rather than with the business man. He was receptive to the new and the strange; his defense of Emily Dickinson, for example, does him great credit. His personal and cultural timidity about sexual matters made him speak harshly of writers more daring in such things than himself, yet he fought effectively for the acceptance of contemporary European literature, and he was tireless in helping even those of the young men who did not share his reticences. Edmund Wilson once defined the literary character of Stephen Crane by differentiating him from "the comfortable family men of whom Howells was chief," yet Crane was in Howells's debt, as were Boyesen, Hamlin Garland, Norris, and Herrick.

He was not a man of great moral intensity, but he was stubborn. His comportment in the Haymarket affair marks, I think, the beginning of our life of the problem of what came to be called the writers "integrity," and his novel *A Hazard of New Fortunes* is probably the first treatment of the theme which became almost obsessive in our fiction in the Thirties, the intellectual's risking his class position by opposing the prejudices of his class. Some years ago, it seemed appropriate for almost any academic writer on American literature to condescend to Howells's social views as being, in comparison with the tradition of revolutionary Marxism, all too "mild," and quite foolish in their mildness, another manifestation of his "genteel" quality. The fact is that Howells's sense of the anomalies and injustices of an expanding capitalism was very clear and strong. What is more, it was very *personal;* it became a part, and a bitter part, of his temperament. In his criticism of American life, he was not like Henry Adams or Henry James, who thought of America in reference to their own grand ambitions. Howells's ambitiousness reached its peak in youth and then compromised itself, or democratized itself, so that in much of his work he is only the journeyman, a craftsman quite without the artist's expectably aristocratic notions, and in his life, although he was a child of light and a son of the covenant, he also kept up his connection with the Philistines—he was, we remember, the original of James's Strether; and when such a man complains about America, we do not say that his case is special, we do not discount and resist what he says, we listen and are convinced. His literary criticism still has force and point because it is so doggedly partisan with a certain kind of literature and because it always had a social end in view.

It is of course in his novels that Howells is at his best as a social witness, and he can be very good indeed. The reader who wants to test for himself what were in actual fact Howells's powers of social insight, which have for long been slighted in most accounts of them, might best read *A Modern Instance,* and he would do well to read it alongside so perceptive a work of modern sociology as David Riesman's *The Lonely Crowd,* for the two books address themselves to the same situation, a change in the American character, a debilitation of the American psychic tone, the diminution of moral tension. Nothing could be more telling than Howells's description of the religious mood of the seventies and eighties, the movement from the last vestiges of faith to a genteel plausibility, the displacement of doctrine and moral strenuousness by a concern with "social adjustment" and the amelioration of boredom. And the chief figure of the novel, Bartley Hubbard, is worthy to stand with Dickens's Bradley Headstone, or James's Basil Ransom and Paul Muniment, or Flaubert's Sénécal, or Dostoevski's Smerdyakov and Shigalov, as one of a class of fictional characters who foretell a large social actuality of the future. Howells has caught in Hubbard the quintessence of the average sensual man as the most sanguine of us have come to fear our culture breeds him, a man somewhat gifted—and how right a touch that Hubbard should be a writer of sorts, how deep in our democratic culture is the need to claim some special undeveloped gift of intellect or art!—a man trading upon sincerity and half-truth; vain yet self-doubting; aggressive yet self-pitying; self-indulgent yet with starts of conscience; friendly and helpful yet not loyal; impelled to the tender relationships yet wishing above all to live to himself and by himself, essentially resenting all human ties. In the seventy years since *A Modern Instance* appeared, no American novelist has equaled Howells in the accuracy and cogency of his observation, nor in the seriousness with which he took the social and moral facts that forced themselves on his unhappy consciousness.

Yet if we praise Howells only as a man who is historically interesting, or if we praise him only as an observer who testifies truthfully about the American social fact of his time, we may be dealing as generously and as piously with his memory as the nature of his achievement permits, but we cannot be happy over having added to the number of American writers who must be praised thus circumspectly if they are to be praised at all. We have all too many American writers who live for us only because they can be so neatly "placed," whose life in literature consists of their being influences or precursors, or of being symbols of intellectual tendencies, which is to say that their life is not really in literature at all but in the history of culture.

Perhaps this is the fate to which we must abandon Howells. The comparison that is made between him and Trollope, while it suggests something of his quality, also proposes his limitations, which are considerable. As an American, and for reasons that Henry James made clear, he did not have Trollope's social advantages, he did not have at his disposal that thickness of the English scene and of the English character which were of such inestimable value to the English novelists as a standing invitation to energy, gusto, and happy excess. Nor did he have Trollope's assumption of a society essentially settled despite the changes that might be appearing; his consciousness of the past could not be of sufficient weight to balance the pull of the future, and so his present could never be as solid as Trollope's. "Life here," as he said, "is still for the future—it is a land of Emersons—and I like a little present moment in mine." He never got as much present moment as the novelist presumably needs, and his novels are likely to seem to most readers to be of the past because nothing in America is quite so dead as an American future of a few decades back, unless it be an American personage of the same time.

And yet it is still possible that Howells deserves something better than a place in the mere background of American literature. It is clear enough that he is not of a kind with Hawthorne, Melville, James, and Whitman; nor of a kind with Emerson and Thoreau; nor with Poe; nor with Mark Twain at his best. But neither is he of a kind with H. B. Fuller and Robert Herrick, whose names are usually mentioned with his as being in a line of descent from him. If Howells is experienced not as he exists in the textbooks, but as he really is on his own page, we have to see that there is something indomitable about him; at least while we are reading him he does not consent to being consigned to the half-life of the background of literature. For one thing, his wit and humor save him. Much must be granted to the man who created the wealthy, guilty, hypersensitive Clara Kingsbury, called her "a large blonde mass of suffering," and conceived that she might say to poor Marcia Hubbard, "Why, my child, you're a Roman matron!" and come away in agony that Marcia would think she meant her nose. And the man is not easily done with who at eighty-three, in the year of his death, wrote that strange "realistic" idyl, *The Vacation of the Kelwyns,* with its paraphernalia of gypsies and dancing bears and its infinitely touching impulse to speak out against the negation and repression of emotion, its passionate wish to speak out for the benign relaxation of the will, for goodness and gentleness, for "life," for the reservation of moral judgment, for the charm of the mysterious, precarious little flame that lies at the heart of the commonplace. No one since Schiller has treated the genre of the idyl with the seriousness it deserves, yet even without a standard of criticism the contemporary reader will, I think, reach beyond the quaintness of the book to a sense of its profundity, or at least of its near approach to profundity. It will put him in mind of the early novels of E. M. Forster, and he will even be drawn to think of *The Tempest,* with which it shares the theme of the need for general pardon and the irony of the brave new world: Howells, setting his story in the year of the centennial of the Declaration of Independence, is explicit in his belief that the brave newness of the world is all behind his young lovers.

When we praise Howells's social observation, we must see that it is of a precision and subtlety which carry it beyond sociology to literature. It is literature and not sociology to understand with Howells's innocent clarity the relationship of the American social classes, to know that a lady from Cambridge and the farmer's wife with whom she boards will have a natural antagonism which will be expressed in the great cultural issue of whether the breakfast steak should be fried or broiled. Again, when we have said all that there is to say about Howells's theory of character, have taken full account of its intentional lack of glory, we must see that in its reasoned neutrality, in its insistence on the virtual equality in any person of the good and the bad, or of the interesting and the dull, there is a kind of love, perhaps not so much of persons as of persons in society, of the social idea. At the heart of Herrick there is deadness and even a kind of malice. At the heart of Fuller there is a sort of moral inertness. But at the heart of Howells there is a loving wonder at the fact that persons of the most mediocre sort somehow manage to make a society.

I don't mean by this to define the whole quality and virtue of Howells but only to offer enough in his defense to make his case at least doubtful, because I want to ask the question, How much is our present friendly indifference to him of his making and how much is it of ours? It is a question which cannot be fully answered at this time but only in some later generation that is as remote from our assumptions as from Howells's, yet it is worth attempting for what small self-knowledge the effort might bring.

2

Henry James's essay on Howells is well known, and in that essay there are three statements which by implication define the ground of our present indifference to Howells. They have the advantage for our inquiry of appearing in the friendliest possible context, and they are intended not as judgments, certainly not as adverse judgments, but only as descriptions.

This is the first statement: "He is animated by a love of the common, the immediate, the familiar, and the vulgar elements of life, and holds that in proportion as we move into the rare and strange we become vague and arbitrary; that truth of representation, in a word, can be achieved only so long as it is in our power to test and measure it."

Here is the second statement: "He hates a 'story', and (this private feat is not impossible) has probably made up his mind very definitely as to what the pestilent thing consists of. Mr. Howells hates an artificial fable, a denouement that is pressed into service; he likes things to occur as in life, where the manner of a great many of them is not to occur at all."

And here is the third: "If American life is on the whole, as I make no doubt whatever, more innocent than that of any other country, nowhere is the fact more patent than in Mr. Howells's novels, which exhibit so constant a study of the actual and so small a perception of evil."

It will be immediately clear from these three statements how far from our modern taste Howells is likely to be. I have said they are objective statements, that they are descriptions and not judgments, yet we can hear in them some ambiguity of tone—some ambiguity of tone must inevitably be there, for James is defining not only his friend's work but, by inversion, his own. And almost in the degree that we admire James and defend his artistic practice, we are committed to resist Howells. But I think we must have the grace to see that in resisting Howells, in rejecting him, we are resisting and rejecting something more than a literary talent or temperament or method. There is in Howells, as I have tried to suggest, an odd kind of muted, stubborn passion which we have to take account of, and respect, and recognize for what it is, the sign of a commitment, of an involvement in very great matters—we are required to see that in making our judgment of him we are involved in considerations of way of life, of quality of being.

His passion and its meaning become apparent whenever he speaks of the commonplace, which was the almost obsessive object of his literary faith. "The commonplace? Commonplace? The commonplace is just that light, impalpable, aerial essence which [the novelists] have never got into their confounded books yet. The novelist who could interpret the common feelings of commonplace people would have the answer to 'the riddle of the painful earth' on his tongue." We might go so far as to grant that the passion of this utterance has a kind of intellectual illumination in it which commands our respect, but we in our time cannot truly respond to it. We are lovers of what James calls the rare and strange, and in our literature we are not responsive to the common, the immediate, the familiar, and the vulgar elements in life.

Or at least we have a most complicated relation to these elements. In our poetic language we do want something that has affinity with the common, the immediate, the familiar, and the vulgar. And we want a certain aspect or degree of these elements in all our literature—we want them in their extremity, especially the common and vulgar. We find an interest in being threatened by them; we like them represented in their extremity to serve as a sort of outer limit of the possibility of our daily lives, as a kind of mundane hell. They figure for us in this way in *Ulysses,* in *The Waste Land,* in Kafka's novels and stories, even in Yeats, and they account, I believe, for the interest of comfortable middle-class readers in James Farrell's *Studs Lonigan.* In short, we consent to the commonplace as it verges upon and becomes the rare and strange. The commonplace of extreme poverty or ultimate boredom may even come to imply the demonic and be valued for that —let life be sufficiently depressing and sufficiently boring in its commonplaceness and we shall have been licensed to give up quiet desperation and to become desperately fierce. We are attracted by the idea of human life in, as it were, putrefaction, in stewing corruption—we sense the force gathering in the fermentation. But of course Howells's kind of commonness suggests nothing of this. The objection that many readers made to his early work was that it was drab and depressing, the point of comparison being fiction of plot and melodramatic incident, what Howells called the "romantic." But after a time the objection was to his tame gentility, the comparison being then with Zola. Howells admired Zola enormously and fought for his recognition, but he eventually thought that Zola failed in realism and surrendered to "romanticism." He meant that the matter of Zola's realism would lead his readers away from the facts of their middle-class lives. For Howells the center of reality was the family life of the middle class.

The feeling for the family with which Howells's theory of the commonplace was bound up was very strong in him, and Mr. Wilson is accurate when he makes it definitive of Howells's quality. His family piety seems to have amounted almost to a superstitiousness, for as such we must interpret his having said to Mark Twain, "I would rather see and talk with you than with any other man in the world," and then feeling it necessary to add, "outside my own family." His sorrows were family sorrows; after his marriage the direction of his life was given chiefly by the family necessities. All this, we may well feel, is excessive, and very likely it accounts for the insufficiency of personality, of self, in Howells that makes the chief trouble in our relation with him. He is too much the *pius Aeneas* without having Aeneas's sad saving grace of being the sire of an enormous destiny. Yet this must not lead us to lessen the credit we give to Howells for being the only nineteenth-century American writer of large reputation who deals directly and immediately with the family.

I do not know whether or not anyone has remarked the peculiar power the idea of the family has in literature—perhaps it has never been worth anyone's while to remark what is so simple and obvious, so easily to be observed from the time of the Greek epics and of the Greek drama down through the course of European literature. Even today, when our sense of family has become much attenuated, the familial theme shows its power in our most notable literature, in Joyce, in Proust, in Faulkner, in Kafka. But our present sense of the family is of the family in dissolution, and although of course the point of any family story has always been a threatened or an actual dissolution, this was once thought to be calamity where with us it is the natural course of things. We are sure that the nineteenth-century family was an elaborate hoax and against nature. It is true that almost every second-rate novel will represent one of its good characters expressing the hope of a quiet home and charming and satisfying children; it is true that the family is at the center of the essential mythology of our social and economic life, the good and sufficient reason for accumulation and expenditure, and that the maintenance of the family in peace is the study of our psychological science, yet in our literature the family serves as but an ideality, a rather wistful symbol of peace, order, and continuity; it does not exist in anything like actuality.

This may explain our feeling of indifference to the realism of the commonplace. But our attitude toward the family must be understood in a very large context, as but one aspect of our attitude to the idea of *the conditioned,* of the material circumstances in which spirit exists. From one point of view, no people has ever had so intense an idea of the relationship of spirit to its material circumstances as we in America now have. Our very preoccupation with *things,* as Mary McCarthy once observed, is really a way of dealing with the life of spirit in the world of matter—our possessions, although they have reference to status and comfort, have a larger reference to the future of our souls, to energy and the sense of cleanliness and fitness and health; our materialism cannot be represented as the Roman *luxus* has been represented—its style is not meant to imply ease and rest and self-indulgence but rather an ideal of alertness and readiness of spirit. And this sense of the conditioned is carried out in our elaborate theories of child-rearing, and the extravagent store we set by education; and in our theories of morality and its relation to social circumstance.

Yet it is to be seen that those conditions to which we do respond are the ones which we ourselves make, or over which we have control, which is to say conditions as they are virtually spirit, as they deny the idea of *the conditioned*. Somewhere in our mental constitution is the demand for life as pure spirit.

The idea of unconditioned spirit is of course a very old one, but we are probably the first people to think of it as a realizable possibility and to make that possibility part of our secret assumption. It is this that explains the phenomenon of our growing disenchantment with the whole idea of the political life, the feeling that although we are willing, nay eager, to live in society, for we all piously know that man fulfills himself in society, yet we do not willingly consent to live in a particular society of the present, marked as it is bound to be by a particular economic system, by disorderly struggles for influence, by mere approximations and downright failures. Our aesthetic sense—I mean our deep comprehensive aesthetic sense, really our metaphysics—which is satisfied by the performance of a Bendix washing machine, is revolted by such a politically conditioned society. The wide disrepute into which capitalistic society has fallen all over the world is justified by the failures and injustices of capitalism; but if we want to understand the assumptions about politics of the world today, we have to consider the readiness of people to condemn the failures and injustices of that society as compared with their reluctance to condemn the failures and injustices of Communist society. The comparison will give us the measure of the modern preference for the unconditioned—to the modern more-or-less thinking man, Communist society is likely to seem a close approximation to the unconditioned, to spirit making its own terms.

The dislike of the conditioned is in part what makes so many of us dissatisfied with our class situation, and guilty about it, and unwilling to believe that it has any reality, or that what reality it may have is a possible basis of moral or spiritual prestige, the moral or spiritual prestige which is the most valuable thing in the world to those of us who think a little. By extension, we are very little satisfied with the idea of family life—for us it is part of the inadequate bourgeois reality. Not that we don't live good-naturedly enough with our families, but when we do, we know that we are "family men," by definition cut off from the true realities of the spirit. This, I venture to suppose, is why the family is excluded from American literature of any pretensions. Although not all families are thus excluded—for example, the family of Faulkner's *As I Lay Dying* is very happily welcomed. And on every account it should be, but probably one reason for our eager acceptance of it is that we find in that family's extremity of suffering a respite from the commonplace of the conditioned as we know it in our families, we actually find in it an intimation of liberty—when conditions become extreme enough there is sometimes a sense of deep relief, as if the conditioned had now been left quite behind, as if spirit were freed when the confining comforts and the oppressive assurances of civil life are destroyed.

But Howells was committed totally and without question to civil life, and when he wrote an essay called "Problems of Existence in Fiction," although he did include among the existential matters that the novelist might treat such grim, ultimate things as a lingering hopeless illness, it is but one item among such others as the family budget, nagging wives, daughters who want to marry fools, and the difficulties of deciding whom to invite to dinner.

In extenuation of Howells we remember that this is all the matter of Jane Austen, the high reverberations of whose touch upon the commonplace we have habituated ourselves to hear. But Howells does not permit us to defend him with the comparison; he is profligate in his dealings with the ordinary, and in *A Hazard of New Fortunes* he does not think twice about devoting the first six chapters to an account of the hero's search for an apartment. I have heard that someone has written to explicate the place of these chapters in the total scheme of the novel, and in perfect ignorance of this essay I hazard the guess that its intention is to rescue Howells from the appearance of an excess of literalness and ordinariness, and that, in the carrying out of this intention, Basil March's fruitless ringing of janitors' bells is shown to be a modern instance of the age-old theme of The Quest, or an analogue of the Twelve Tribes in the Wilderness, or of the flight into Egypt, or a symbol of the homelessness of the intellectual. But it is really just a house-hunt. Of course any house-hunt will inevitably produce lost and unhappy feelings, even a sense of cosmic alienation—so much in our dull daily lives really does make a significant part of man's tragic career on earth, which is what Howells meant by his passionate sentence about the charm and power of the commonplace. But when we yield to our contemporary impulse to enlarge all experience, to involve it as soon as possible in history, myth, and the oneness of spirit—an impulse with which, I ought to say, I have considerable sympathy—we are in danger of making experience merely typical, formal, and *representative,* and thus of losing one term of the dialectic that goes on between spirit and the conditioned, which is, I suppose, what we mean when we speak of man's tragic fate. We lose, that is to say, the actuality of the conditioned, the literality of matter, the peculiar authenticity and authority of the merely denotative.[1] To lose this is to lose not a material fact but a spiritual one for it is a fact of spirit that it must

---

[1] Students have a trick of speaking of money in Dostoevski's novels as "symbolic," as if no one ever needed, or spent, or gambled, or squandered the stuff—and as if to think of it as an actuality were subliterary.

exist in a world which requires it to engage in so dispiriting an occupation as hunting for a house. The knowledge of the antagonism between spirit and the conditioned—it is Donne's, it is Pascal's, it is Tolstoi's—may in litera- ture be a cause of great delight because it is so rare and difficult; beside it the knowledge of pure spirit is comparatively easy.

3

To James's first statement about Howells, his second is clearly a corol- lary—"He hates a 'story' . . . [he] hates an artificial fable." We cannot nowadays be sure that all of our reading public loves a story in the way James did. Quite simple readers can be counted on to love a story, but there is a large, consciously intelligent middle part of our reading public that is in- clined to suspect a story, in James's sense, as being a little dishonest. How- ever, where theory of a certain complexity prevails, the implications of story, and even of "artificial fable," are nowadays easily understood. In these uplands of taste we comprehend that artificial devices, such as manip- ulated plot, are a way not of escaping from reality but of representing it, and we speak with vivacity of "imaginary gardens with real toads in them." Indeed, we have come to believe that the toad is the less real when the gar- den is also real. Our metaphysical habits lead us to feel the deficiency of what we call literal reality and to prefer what we call essential reality. To be sure, when we speak of literal reality, we are aware that there is really no such thing—that everything that is *perceived* is in some sense *conceived*, or created; it is controlled by intention and indicates intention; and so on. Nev- ertheless, bound as we are by society and convention, as well as by certain necessities of the mind, there still is a thing that we persist in calling "literal reality," and we recognize in works of art a greater or less approximation to it. Having admitted the existence of literal reality, we give it a low status in our judgment of art. Naturalism, which is the form of art that makes its ef- fects by the accumulation of the details of literal reality, is now in poor re- pute among us. We dismiss it as an analogue of an outmoded science and look to contemporary science to give authority to our preference for the ab- stract and conceptual; or we look to music to justify our impatience with the representational; and we derive a kind of political satisfaction from our taste, remembering that reactionary governments hate what we admire.

Our metaphysical and aesthetic prejudices even conspire to make us believe that our children have chiefly an "essential" sense of reality. We characterize the whole bent of their minds by their flights of fancy and by the extremity of distortion in their school paintings, preferring to forget that if they are in some degree and on some occasions essential realists, they are also passionately pedantic literalists—as they must be when their whole souls are so directed toward accommodation and control. The vogue of the "educational" toy with its merely essential representation is an adult vogue; the two-year-old wants the miniature Chevrolet with as many precise details as possible; it is not the gay chintz ball designed for the infant eye and grasp that delights him but rather the apple or the orange—its function, its use, its being valued by the family, give him his pleasure; and as he grows older his pedantry of literalism will increase, and he will scorn the adult world for the metaphysical vagaries of its absurd conduct—until he himself is seduced by them.

Now we must admit that Howells's extravagance of literalism, his down-right, declared hatred of a story, was on the whole not very intelligent. He said of Zola that "the imperfection of his realism began with the perfection of his form." That is, just where Zola appeals to us, just where he disregards his own syllabus of the experimental novel to introduce dramatic extravagance, he is disappointing to Howells. And Howells, in his character of programmatic literalist, spoke disrespectfully of Scott (one of the founders of realism), of Dickens, and of Balzac, saying that the truth was not in them; and he went so far as to express impatience with the romancing of George Eliot, despite the clear affinity his realism has with hers. It is difficult to know what he made of his adored Jane Austen. Clearly it never occurred to him, as he sought to learn from her, that some of her finest effects are due to her carefully contrived stories. We, of course, find it natural to say that the perfection of her realism begins with the perfection of her form.

It is perhaps an expression of our desire for unconditioned spirit that we have of late years been so preoccupied with artifice and form. We feel that the shape which the mind gives to what the mind observes is more ideally characteristic of the mind than is the act of observation. Possibly it is, and if the last decades of criticism have insisted rather too much that this is so,[2] it is possible that a view of our historical situation might lead us to justify the overemphasis, for in the historical perspective we perceive such a depressing plethora of matter and so little form. Form suggests a principle of control—I can quite understand that group of my students who have become excited over their discovery of the old animosity which Ezra Pound and William Carlos Williams bear to the iamb, and have come to feel that could they but break the iambic shackles, the whole of modern culture could find a true expression.

---

[2] Who can imagine any of our critics saying with Ruskin that "No good work whatever can be perfect, and the demand for perfection is always a sign of a misunderstanding of the ends of art"; and ". . . No great man ever stops working till he has reached his point of failure . . ."?

The value of form must never be denigrated. But by a perversity of our minds, just as the commitment to a particular matter of literature is likely to be conceived in terms of hostility to form, so the devotion to the power of form is likely to be conceived in terms of hostility to matter, to matter in its sheer literalness, in its stubborn denotativeness. The claims of form to pre-eminence over matter always have a certain advantage because of the feeling to which I have just referred, that the mind's power of shaping is more characteristic of mind than its power of observation. Certainly the power of shaping is more intimately connected with what Plato called the "spirited" part of man, with the will, while observation may be thought of as springing from the merely "vegetative" part. The eye, it cannot choose but see, we cannot bid the ear be still; things impress themselves upon us against or with our will. But the plastic stress of spirit is of the will in the sense that it strives against resistance, against the stubbornness of what Shelley called the dull, dense world—it compels "all new successions to the forms they wear."

But Shelley's description of the act of creation suggests that the plastic will cannot possibly exercise itself without the recalcitrance of stupid literal matter. When we consider what is going on in painting at this moment, we perceive what may happen in an art when it frees itself entirely from the objective. No doubt the defense of the legitimacy of nonobjective art which is made by referring to the right of music to be unindentured to an objective reality is as convincing as it ever was. Yet do we not have the unhappy sense that sterility is overtaking the painters, that by totally freeing themselves from the objective reality which they believed extraneous to their art, they have provided the plastic will with no resisting object, or none except itself as expressed by other painters, and are therefore beginning to express themselves in mere competitive ingenuity? It is no accident of the *Zeitgeist* that the classic painting of our time is Cubism. The Cubists, bold as they were, accepted the conditioned, and kept in touch with a world of literality. And this is the opinion of one of the greatest of the Cubists, Juan Gris. "Those who believe in abstract painting," he wrote in a letter of 1919, "are like weavers who think they can produce material with only one set of threads and forget that there has to be another set to hold these together. Where there is no attempt at plasticity how can you control representational liberties? And where there is no concern for reality how can you limit and unite plastic liberties?"

What is true of the Cubists is also true of the great classic writers of our time—the sense of *things* is stronger in them than in their expositors. They grew in naturalism, in literalism, and they in their way insist on it as much as Flaubert, or the Goncourts, or Zola. The impulse of succeeding writers to build on Joyce is pretty sure to be frustrated, for it is all too likely to be an attempt to build on Joyce's notions of form, which have force only in relation to Joyce's superb sense of literal fact, his solid simple awareness that in the work of art some things are merely denotative and do not connote more than appears, that they are *data* and must be permitted to exist as data.

4

The last of James's statements about Howells concerns his indifference to evil. For us today this constitutes a very severe indictment. We are all aware of evil; we began to be aware of it in certain quasi-religious senses a couple of decades or so ago; and as time passed we learned a great deal about the physical, political actuality of evil, saw it expressed in the political life in a kind of gratuitous devilishness which has always been in the world but which never before in Western Europe had been organized and, as it were, rationalized. A proper sense of evil is surely an attribute of a great writer, and nowadays we have been drawn to make it almost a touchstone of greatness, drawn to do so in part by our revived religious feelings or nostalgia for religious feelings, but of course also in part by our desire that literature should be in accord with reality as we now know it.

Our responsiveness to the idea of evil is legitimate enough, yet we ought to be aware that the management of the sense of evil is not an easy thing. Be careful, Nietzsche said, when you fight dragons, lest you become a dragon yourself. There is always the danger, when we have insisted upon the fact of evil with a certain intensity, that we will go on to cherish the virtue of our insistance, and then the very fact we insist upon. I would make a distinction between the relation to evil of the creator of the literary work and that of the reader, believing that the active confrontation of the fact of evil is likelier to be healthy than is the passive confrontation—there is something suspect in making evil the object of, as it were, aesthetic contemplation. But not even the creator is nowadays immune from all danger. Consider that the awareness of evil is held by us to confer a certain kind of spiritual status and prestige upon the person who exercises it, a status and prestige which are often quite out of proportion to his general spiritual gifts. Our time has a very quick sensitivity to what the sociologists call *charisma,* which, in the socio-political context, is the quality of power and leadership that seems to derive from a direct connection with great supernal forces, with godhead. This power we respond to when we find it in our literature in the form of alliances with the dark gods of sexuality, or the huge inscrutability of nature, or the church, or history; presumably we want it for ourselves. This is what accounts in our theory of literature for our preference for the hidden and ambiguous, for our demand for "tension" and "tragedy."

And evil has for us its own *charisma.* Hannah Arendt, in *The Origins of Totalitarianism,* speaking of the modern disintegration, remarks that with us today "to yield to the mere process of disintegration has become an irresistible temptation, not only because it has assumed the spurious grandeur of 'historical necessity' but also because everything outside it has begun to appear lifeless, bloodless, meaningless, and unreal." Disintegration itself fascinates us because it is a power. Evil has always fascinated men, not only because it is opposed to good but also because it is, in its own right, a power.

Lifeless, bloodless, meaningless, and *unreal*—without stopping to estimate just how much life, blood, meaning, and reality Howells actually has, we must observe that the modern reader who judges him to have little is not exactly in a position to be objective, that he is likely to deal with Howells under the aspect of a universal judgment by which it is concluded that very little in our life has life, blood, meaning, and reality.

The sentence in which Howells invites American novelists to concern themselves with the "more smiling aspects" of life as being the "more American" is well known and has done much harm to his reputation. In fairness to Howells, we ought to be aware that the sentence may not be quite so dreadful as it generally supposed. For one thing, it is rather ambiguous—when Howells says "we invite," it is not clear whether "we" is the editorial pronoun referring to himself or is meant to stand for the American people: the phrase, that is, may be read as simply descriptive of a disposition of American culture. And even if we take the sentence in its worst construction, we ought to recall that it appears in an essay on Dostoevski in which Howells urges the reading of Dostoevski; that when he speaks of the more smiling aspects of life as being the more American it is in the course of a comparison of America with the Russia of Dostoevski; that he is careful to remark that America is not exempt from the sorrows of the natural course of life, only from those which are peculiar to the poverty and oppression of Dostoevski's land; and that he says he is not sure that America is in every way the gainer by being so thoroughly in material luck, so rich in the smiling aspects. But let us leave all extenuation aside and take the sentence only as it has established itself in the legendary way, as the clear sign of Howells' blindness to evil, his ignorance of the very essence of reality. Taken so, it perhaps cannot be thought a very wise statement, but our interpretation of it, the vehemence with which we are likely to press its meaning, tells us, I think, more about ourselves than about Howells. It raises the question of why we believe, as we do believe, that evil is of the very essence of reality.

The management of the sense of evil, I have said, is not easy. The sense of evil is properly managed only when it is not allowed to be preponderant over the sense of self. The reason Shakespeare holds his place in our imagination is that in him the sense of evil and the sense of self are in so delicate and continuous a reciprocation. And the ground of Keats's greatness, I have come to feel, is that precarious reciprocation of self and evil, similar to Shakespeare's. He maintained this reciprocation in a more conscious and explicit way than Shakespeare found necessary. He called to his aid in the affirmation of self against the knowledge of evil his intense imagination of pleasure—of pleasure of all kinds, the simplest and most primitive, such as eating and drinking, as well as the highest. He boldly put pleasure, even contentment, at the center of his theory of poetry, and at one point in the development of his theory he spoke of poetry as being most itself when it tells "heart-easing things." It is just for this reason that some readers denigrate him; they quite miss the intensity of his sense of reality, for where they make a duality of the principle of pleasure and the principle of reality, Keats made a unity—for him pleasure was a reality; it was, as Wordsworth had taught him, the grand principle of life, of mind, and of self. And it was this commitment to pleasure that made it possible for him to write the greatest exposition of the meaning of tragedy in our literature.

When we are so eager to say how wrong Howells was to invite the novelist to deal with the smiling aspects of life, we have to ask ourselves whether our quick antagonism to this mild recognition of pleasure does not imply an impatience with the self, a degree of yielding to what Hannah Arendt calls the irresistible temptation of disintegration, of identification by submission to the grandeur of historical necessity which is so much more powerful than the self. It is possible that our easily expressed contempt for the smiling aspects and our covert impulse to yield to the historical process are a way of acquiring charisma. It is that peculiar charisma which has always been inherent in death. It was neither a genteel novelist nor a romantic poet who most recently defended the necessity of the smiling aspects and the heart-easing things—Dr. Bruno Bettelheim was first known in this country for his study, made at first hand, of the psychology of the inmates of the German concentration camps. Dr. Bettelheim recently found occasion to remark that "a fight for the very survival of civilized mankind is actually a fight to restore man to a sensitivity toward the joys of life. Only in this way can man be liberated and the survival of civilized mankind be assured. Maybe a time has come in which our main efforts need no longer be directed toward modifying the pleasure principle. [Dr. Bettelheim is speaking of the practice of psychoanalysis.] Maybe it is time we became concerned with restoring pleasure gratification to its dominant role in the reality principle; maybe this society needs less a modification of the pleasure principle by reality, and more assertion of the pleasure principle against an overpowering pleasure-denying reality." It cannot be said of Howells's smiling aspects that they represent a very intense kind of pleasure; yet for most men they will at least serve, in Keats's phrase, to bind us to the earth, to prevent our being seduced by the godhead of disintegration.

5

"Your really beautiful time will come," wrote Henry James to Howells on the occasion of his seventy-fifth birthday—what James characteristically meant was the time when the critical intelligence would begin to render Howells its tribute. The really beautiful time has come to James, but it has not yet come to Howells, and probably it will be a very long time coming. We are not easy with the quiet men, the civil personalities—the very word *civil*, except as applied to disobedience or disorders, is uncomfortable in our ears. "Art inhabits temperate regions," said André Gide in 1940. Well, not always; but if the statement is perhaps a little inaccurate in the range of its generality, we can understand what led Gide to make it, for he goes on: "And doubtless the greatest harm this war is doing to culture is to create a profusion of extreme passions which, by a sort of inflation, brings about a devaluation of all moderate sentiments." And the devaluation of the moderate sentiments brings a concomitant devaluation of the extreme passions: "The dying anguish of Roland or the distress of a Lear stripped of power moves us by its exceptional quality but loses its special eloquence when reproduced simultaneously in several thousand copies." The extreme has become the commonplace of our day. This is not a situation which can be legislated or criticized out of existence, but while it endures we are not in a position to make a proper judgment of Howells, a man of moderate sentiments. It is a disqualification that we cannot regard with complacency, for if Gide is right, it implies that we are in a fair way of being disqualified from making any literary judgments at all.

STEPHEN CRANE

****

Probably the most satisfactory critical study of Crane is Daniel G. Hoffman's *The Poetry of Stephen Crane* (New York, 1957), though poet John Berryman's *Stephen Crane* (New York, 1950) contains occasional brilliant insights, and Robert W. Stallman's *Stephen Crane: A Biography* (New York, 1968) is rich in detail. Except for Eric Solomon's *Stephen Crane: From Parody to Realism* (Cambridge, Mass., 1966) and for perceptive remarks in such general books as Warner Berthoff's *The Ferment of Realism* (New York, 1965), Charles Feidelson's *Symbolism and American Literature* (Chicago, 1953), Leslie A. Fiedler's *Love and Death in the American Novel* (New York, 1960), and Maxwell Geismar's *Rebels and Ancestors* (Boston, 1953), most writings about Crane are reminiscent, concerned with textual or biographical detail, or excessively repetitious about symbolism in *The Red Badge of Courage* or colorful impressionism in *Maggie* and *The Monster*. It may be some measure of Crane's stature that, although there is a *Stephen Crane Newsletter* which circulates among his admirers, no completely satisfying criticism of his writings has yet appeared. Theodore Dreiser speaks well of him in "The Great American Novel," *American Spectator,* I (December 1932), pp. 1–2, as does Hamlin Garland in *Roadside Meetings* (New York, 1930) and Ford Maddox Ford in *Thus to Revisit* (London, 1921) and *Portraits from Life* (Boston, 1937). The beginnings of a minor battle on how Crane should, or might, be read are found in Philip Rehv's "Fiction and the Criticism of Fiction," *Kenyon Review,* XVIII (Spring 1956), pp. 276–299, and Robert W. Stallman's reply, "Fiction and Its Critics," in the same periodical one year later.

OUTSTRIPPING THE EVENT

Larzer Ziff

****

Unlike Richard Harding Davis, Stephen Crane accepted fraternities as a part of undergraduate life and swiftly joined Delta Upsilon after entering Lafayette College in September 1890. As a tough talker with nicotine-stained fingers and a reputation as a pool-player and baseball catcher, he should not have objected to hazing as Davis had done, and most likely he didn't in principle. But the sophomores who burst into his room one fall night to subject him to the customary harassments were stopped short by the sight of tough Stevie, green with fear, standing in his nightgown in a corner of the room, a revolver dangling from his limp hand.[1] They left. The degree of his opposition was ludicrous.

Stephen Crane's expectations had a way of outstripping the event. The youngest of the fourteen children of a minister, he knew that his behavior would be observed a little more closely in whatever New Jersey town the family was then living than that of the butcher's boy. He knew also that legend would have him be either Little Lord Fauntleroy or the wildest kid in town. His athletic accomplishments, his constant cigarette, and his persistent inquiries into the life from which his ministerial upbringing ostensibly excluded him were his youthful answers to society. He sought out the notoriety which he assumed would come to the misbehaving preacher's kid with a vehemence that was ridiculously extravegant in view of the nonchalance with which he and other such children were really regarded. Before his community could impose its standards upon him, before his mother, widowed when he was nine, could impose her Methodism on him, before his friends could explain the terms on which the gang played, Stephen Crane had developed a set of responses that anticipated the reality. These responses were formed in great part from the shreds and patches of the conventions being imposed upon him: his anti-Methodism assumed gods, angels, and sinful men; his rejection of the boys' world led to his studious proficiency at baseball and his rigor in captaining the corps at his military preparatory school. But these were strengthened and increasingly shaped by an inner consciousness that told him that whatever was accepted was suspect; that there was an inside story behind every public history.

At Lafayette such convictions built hazing into a monstrous outrage, and he got the revolver out when he heard footsteps in the hall. He transferred at the end of the term to Syracuse, a school founded by his mother's late uncle, Jesse Truesdell Peck, Bishop of the Methodist Church, uncertain yet as to whether it was college or Lafayette that he found unbearable, and within the year learned that it was college. He played the smart aleck in class, refusing to take the things in books seriously because, he implied, he knew better. His habitual distrust of the arrangements and explanations by which society perpetuated itself attracted him, rather, to his brother Townley's newsgathering agency, and in the spring of 1891 he left formal education for journalism. After a brief period of working for Townley, he made his way into the New York newspapers, where he was unpopular with the other reporters, who thought that his aloofness was an arty pose. The defensive Crane might well have armed himself with such a pose, but he was by nature set apart anyway because, unlike his fellows, he thought of the real story, the big scoop, not as a piece of news which was going to come to him from outside but as fiction he would produce from within. He was too impatient to wait upon daily happenings to provide him with his materials. His response to them was preparing before they actually occurred. Events were a test of his consciousness, not its instructor.

In July 1891 Hamlin Garland lectured in Avon-by-the-Sea on "The Local Novel," and Stephen Crane, the nineteen-year-old New York *Tribune* correspondent, came up to him afterward to borrow his notes. The sallow and laconic youth did not impress Garland, but the report he wrote of the lecture did, and Garland befriended Crane during his stay at Avon. The acquaintanceship lasted after Crane was fired from the *Tribune* for sarcastically representing a labor parade he had covered as a procession of slaves marching behind the chariots of their monopolistic conquerors, and drifted away from Avon into Bohemian New York. There a variety of newspaper jobs and friendship with a group of art students who, like him, were leading a hand-to-mouth existence on East Twenty-third Street kept Crane slightly above subsistence level. At Syracuse he had begun work on *Maggie,* the story of a New York girl of the streets, before he had had much, if any, opportunity to explore the slums of New York or learn of the actual experiences of a prostitute. He completed the book in the city and, on money borrowed from his brother, had it published in 1893. Nobody bought it, but Crane sent a copy to Garland, who vigorously sought him out and, struck by his paleness and thinness, fed him. Soon after, Garland delivered him to Howells, who, immensely impressed by *Maggie,* administered encouragement and his customary sound advice. Crane was grateful but far quicker to follow leads the older men gave him as to possible publishers for his stories or jobs writing newspaper sketches than suggestions they gave him as to materials or techniques he might employ. Both men hailed him as a brilliant recruit to realism, one who exposed social injustice, and at their urging he joined a breadline, slept in a flophouse, and reported on these incidents. But his mind was elsewhere.

Garland found this out in March 1893, when Crane, shabby as usual, turned up for a meal. Cutting through his guest's apparent nonchalance, Garland demanded to see the papers with which, with a studied unostentatiousness, Crane had crammed the side pockets of his seedy gray ulster. "Upon unrolling the manuscript," Garland wrote, "I found it to be a sheaf of poems written in blue ink upon single sheets of legal cap paper, each poem without blot or correction, almost without punctuation, all beautifully legible, exact and orderly in arrangement."[2] He read the neat hand quickly and with increasing excitement. The verses appeared to be compressed little capsules of symbolic meaning, but, once read, they expanded into all corners of the consciousness. Garland asked if Crane had more, and he answered that he had four or five, pointing to his temple, "up here, all in a little row."[3] He sat down and wrote one off in finished form; they were, he said, on tap and he could draw them off complete. Howells had read some of Emily Dickinson's poems to Crane, and these somewhat resembled hers. Garland thought they also were like the French translations of Japanese poetry then popular among the more rarefied aesthetes.

On another day the bulge in the seedy pocket turned out to be a tale of the Civil War, which, however, stopped abruptly. Garland read what there was and, now convinced that he was talking to nothing less than a full-fledged genius, asked, "Where's the rest of it?" "In hock," Crane told him, to his typist,[4] and Garland sent him off with $15 to redeem the remainder of *The Red Badge of Courage* from captivity. You're going to be rich and famous, he kept telling Crane. His prediction required no great soothsaying powers: the manuscript he had seen took possession of its reader with a swiftness and a confidence unlike anything then being written. Crane did not dispute his coming fame and glory but offered to sell his prospects for $23 in ready cash: "If I had some money to buy a new suit of clothes I'd feel my grip tighten on the future."[5]

On January 6, 1896, *The New York Times,* under the headline STEPHEN CRANE'S TRIUMPH, carried a story by its London man, Harold Frederic, on how that literary capital was ringing in praise of *The Red Badge.* This echoed the acclaim which had begun with the syndicated newspaper appearance of the novel, in abridged form, in 1894, and had become a roar after October 1895, when Appleton's published it in book form. On the strength of Crane's spreading fame, Copeland and Day in 1895 published his little poems in a volume titled *Black Riders,* and that same year the Bacheller Syndicate, which had first printed *The Red Badge,* sent him on a Western trip and on an abortive filibustering expedition to Cuba, which ended in shipwreck.

By January 1896 Crane, though not yet twenty-five years old, was famous enough to be assured of employment by Pulitzer or Hearst as a star reporter. Then he began reaping the crop of malice he had confidently expected when, as an unknown youngster, he had sown the seeds of naughty behavior. If his life with the art students on East Twenty-third Street now gave rise to fallacious stories of his alcoholism and dope addiction, he was not surprised; indeed, he may have felt some gratification. A neophyte reporter caught up with him one night in New York, where Crane had stopped off after the shipwreck of his filibustering expedition, en route to the Greek War, and where he seemed to be lurking about the perimeter of night life. The cub tried to draw out his idol about his literary career with no success. But when he mentioned that he too was a minister's son, Crane immediately came to life and greeted him as a brother in a very special fraternity. "Have you ever observed," asked Crane, "how the envious laity exult when we are overtaken by misfortune?"[6] And then, the cigarette in his lips marking time to the words, he added, "This is the point of view: The bartender's boy falls from the Waldorf roof. The minister's son falls from a park bench. They both hit the earth with the same velocity, mutilated beyond recognition."[7]

Crane was so convinced of this that his life had been led in anticipation of extreme reactions; he was determined to make good his belief if he had to climb to the roof of the Waldorf to be seen falling off the park bench. When he made enemies of the New York police by defending Dora Clark from their harrying, even though she was a known prostitute, he was acting on his sense of the way society would behave, a sense which he had projected into *Maggie* three years earlier without benefit of queanly associates. When rumor seized upon his gallant efforts on Dora Clark's behalf and concocted legends about his sexual life, he walked unerringly into an actual though less publicized liaison with the madam of a house of assignation, Cora Taylor. He would outstrip the event.

In the copy of *Maggie* which he had presented to Garland in 1893, Crane wrote:

> It is inevitable that you be greatly shocked by this book but continue, please, with all possible courage to the end. For it tries to show that environment is a tremendous thing in the world and frequently shapes lives regardless. If one proves that theory one makes room in Heaven for all sorts of souls (notably an occasional street girl) who are not confidently expected to be there by many excellent people.
>
> It is probable that the reader of this small thing may consider the Author to be a bad man, but, obviously, this is of small consequence to
>
> THE AUTHOR[8]

Before Garland read the book, the twenty-one-year-old author had been telling him what his reaction should be—"shock"—and how this might lead him to feel that the author was a bad man. The inscription reveals that in *Maggie* Crane was attempting to impose his personality on imagined material rather than to organize documentary material into a fiction. For the young author burning to be recognized, *Maggie* had less of an objective existence apart from himself than is ordinarily seen in the relation between novelists and their works. The objective content laid claim to in the inscription, that "environment is a tremendous thing," is qualified by the subjective expectation that "many excellent people" will have their confident beliefs overturned by it. Crane was, in *Maggie,* calling attention to himself, to a reality projected by his will rather than to one observed and ordered.

The shock received by the few early readers of the work, however, was probably no different from the one received today by those unfamiliar with the work of Stephen Crane, and it did not stem from fancying any wickedness in the author. It came, rather, from encountering an imagination so powerful that it could sweep customary fictional devices aside, replacing them with a series of compressed scenes set forth in a style that was somewhat mannered, to be sure, but was nevertheless amazingly effective in its reliance on the simple sentence, vividly put, to carry its meaning.

Here was no recruit to Howells' realism. The world projected by Crane has no topographical or temporal existence. To be sure, the tale opens in Rum Alley and never strays far from it, and Rum Alley is in the slums of New York. But the sense of Rum Alley's being a specific—even if symbolic —piece of a total social structure, like, say, Dickens's Tom-All-Alone's, is missing. Instead we are plunged into selected details of urban squalor and human viciousness, unrelieved by specific addresses, commonplace activities, or basic communicative speech. Crane's characters, gabbling on in a lingo which is, like their setting, chosen only for being extreme, communicate not at all when they talk to one another. There is no literal level of social reality. With regard to the setting, for instance, the reader realizes that there simply isn't enough furniture and crockery available in a habitation like that of the Johnsons to yield the supply necessary for the crunching destruction which is as fixed a feature of that place as the breaking waves are of a beach scene. While *Maggie* is not an allegory, it is a vision of what typically happens rather than a report of what actually happens. The wilderness equivalent of the world of *Maggie* would be a landscape in which all mountains are towering, all streams are rushing, all birds are singing, and all flowers are blooming.

To some extent, the extremes of this world are the inevitable result of the fact that the writer is making it all up. What Hesketh Pearson says of Oscar Wilde's *Lord Arthur Savile's Crime* may easily be applied to Crane's *Maggie:* "His picture of low life . . . has the unreal melodramatic quality one might expect from a youth who is making the most of his first contact with things beyond his normal experience."[9] But the work is the beneficiary as well as the victim of the youth's imagination, and Crane's was powerful. The grotesque setting, though it achieves only uneasy coherence with the social theme, is of a piece with the rest of *Maggie* viewed as a subjective projection that finds its center in the psyches of the characters, chiefly Maggie and Jimmie. The longings of these dumb creatures are represented as images rather than as ideas. Jimmie stood at street corners, "dreaming blood-red dreams"; he "menaced mankind at the intersections of streets."[10] Maggie's "dim thoughts were often searching for far away lands where the little hills sing together in the morning."[11] Not only does Crane emphasize in this way the irrational, non-verbal sources of their behavior, but he gains his impression through using particular kinds of images. In the brief quotations, for instance, Jimmie in his furious outlook is not dangerous because he over-leaps the mark; instead of threatening anybody in particular, his mute wrath is drained off into a generalized menacing of "mankind." Maggie's wistfulness, similarly, does not carry any specific pathos, since it is directed past things presumably within her ken toward a biblical image of joy, ideal and unattainable.

These images are typical of the ruthless irony dealt out by the young Crane. He has, as it were, no middle distance. On one hand, his inarticulate characters exist in a vortex of maiming incidents. On the other hand, they are not measured in terms of what they could be under realistically improved conditions, that is, what they could be if they had more money or if they lived in Scarsdale rather than Rum Alley. Instead, their condition is contrasted with hints of romantic, chivalric, or biblical ideals which never had a real embodiment. What Maggie is is the result not of the action of her environment on a plastic personality, but rather of the reaction of that environment to the proposals made to it by her pretensions and her longings. She, not the environment, is the first mover. Jimmie and the other characters also have pretensions and fears which underlie their behavior and which are imperfectly realized in it rather than being significantly shaped by it. In this kind of world the flaws in the setting that result from the author's lack of experience are not damaging, because the setting is an appropriate symbolic extension of inner chaos; it is of a piece with the characters who inhabit it.

Maggie, however, cannot be read as a consistently subjective performance, although its strengths lie in this area. The youthful Crane was also drawn to the objective view that society has crushing effects on the individual, and the result is that *Maggie,* brief as it is, is an uneven performance. Its undeniable power, though, comes from his not hesitating to brush aside social reality in favor of his vision of what is really happening and from his freeing himself from any concern with the actual or with conscious reflection and relying upon his inner consciousness as the source of his creation. Crane was mining himself, as his inscription to Garland showed when he calls attention to that self and its fancied relation to society far more than he does to a detached work of fiction.

Copeland and Day, the firm that brought out *Black Riders,* published chiefly literature of an esoteric kind,[12] so that its imprint added to the reader's expectation of something novel and strange from Crane. When *The Red Badge* brought him into prominence, the earlier poems, whose brevity made them eminently quotable, were parodied widely. Their aphoristic, unrhymed, and unorthodox conciseness seemed of a piece with the iconoclastic literary efforts generally labeled *fin de siècle.*

Black Riders, like *Maggie,* represents a response to the world prepared before the world had actually put its proposition, but the poems are more coherent in their presentation of a view of life.[13] The irony which was tone in *Maggie,* and was based on the contrast of images of a cosmic nature with the lives of lowly irrational beings, now becomes subject matter. In most of the poems there is a creature and there is the cosmos, with nothing intervening either to give a sense of proportion and power to man or to shield him from the direct thrust of his God. The world is a rudderless ship before stupid winds, and God is silent in response to the spirit that seeks Him, until the spirit announces that there must, then, be no God. At this remark a swift hand, a sword from the sky, strikes him dead.

One poem in *Black Riders* reads:

A youth in apparel that glittered
Went to walk in a grim forest.
There he met an assissin
Attired all in garb of old days;
He, scowling through the thickets,
And dagger poised quivering,
Rushed upon the youth.
"Sir," said this latter,
"I am enchanted, believe me,
"To die, thus,
"In this medieval fashion,
"According to the best legends;
"Ah, what joy!"
Then took the wound smiling,
And died, content.[14]

The glittering youth of the poem is one of Crane's few satisfied characters. The ridiculously unserviceable ideals by which he has been raised and the unrealistic conventions he applies to life have in this case not, after all, proved false. He has his romantic adventure. The episode, to be sure, leads to his death, but he comes to that death satisfied that life is working out according to the pattern he imagined for it.

The poem, of course, can also be saying that anybody committed to false romantic notions is fit only to die, but no other Crane characters are allowed to enjoy an incident which proceeds "according to the best legends." The most notable example of one who wishes to enjoy such an indicent is Henry Fleming in *The Red Badge of Courage,* and his failure to find war romantic is representative of an important strain in that novel: *The Red Badge,* whatever else it does, debunks.

Maggie and *Black Riders* are Stephen Crane's self-conscious challenge to the genteel religious and ethical pieties that governed his home and dominated the communities in which he was raised. *The Red Badge* is his challenge to the culture of those communities. The folklore built on romantic memories of the Civil War was Shakespeare and the *Iliad* for the American village, giving its inhabitants a sense of identity and of shared achievement, and strengthening their confidence in the future of the American people. The war had proved that it was Union forever. The minister's son, with his habitual distrust of the pieties and with no experience whatsoever of war, but with the puerile notion that it was really a different sort of football game, nevertheless projected himself into that event, determined to write a war story. His inexperience, however, gave even him pause, and he consulted the *Century Magazine's* series, "Battles and Leaders of the Civil War," from which he gained a sense of the details of the Battle of Chancellorsville to serve as a frame for his tale. But he did not go to the books for an impression of what war was like; this was what, to him, was dramatically lacking in the accounts. He would supply this from his imagination.

Although proper names are occasionally used in *The Red Badge,* most prominently at the very beginning and the very end, the tale proceeds, in the main, through the use of epithets—"the youth," "the loud soldier," "the tattered soldier," etc.; thus, even as he deliberately works against a traditional view of the war, Crane (probably unconsciously but still reflecting the original reasons) is using an obsolete fictional device. The eighteenth-century novel and the English drama which preceded it would have used as proper names "Master Youthful," "Mister Loudly," and "Sir Tattery," the names being not only characteristics but indicative of a generalized view of mankind. This tradition is, in turn, related to the earlier one of allegory. Although *The Red Badge,* like *Maggie,* is far from being allegorical, it builds on the trappings of allegory that can be noted in *Maggie.* The landscape, though presented in detail, is now entirely without name; topographically we can be anywhere, so far as Crane identifies places. Although the elapsed time may clearly be traced, the sense of the specific period of the narrative, as opposed to that before and after, is missing. We know that this is the Civil War, we know, on that basis, that we are somewhere in the United States between the years 1861 and 1865; otherwise, within those limits, this can be anywhere, any time, and, the use of epithets for names adds, anybody.

The way in which Crane uses this generalized sense to heighten the specificity of what happens in his tale indicates the growth of his genius in the two years since *Maggie.* Except for his much-debated concluding paragraphs, he is no longer concerned with an environment which has an objective reality apart from his character's consciousness. After the opening view of the army, we close in on Henry and remain with him throughout, so that the test of credibility is placed squarely where it should be, on Crane's ability to inhabit in imagination the inner consciousness of another.

That there is no world apart from Henry Fleming is made clear by Crane throughout, and most dramatically in Henry's conflicting views of nature. He sees it as kind or cruel, depending upon the state of his own feelings. While nature, to be sure, goes its way, sometimes in parallel to what he feels, but mostly in rude contradiction, and is therefore established by Crane as having a definite independent existence; nevertheless, what are constantly kept in focus are Henry's projections and adjustments. If nature is, indeed, separate, that separateness has no meaning except as ironic commentary on the inner workings of the youth.

As Crane had clarified his context since *Maggie,* so he had clarified his view of man. In *Maggie,* Jimmie and his fellow toughs are characterized as "kings, to a certain extent, over the men of untarnished clothes, because these latter dreaded, perhaps, to be either killed or laughed at."[15] As *Maggie* developed, however, it was not entirely clear that there was an order of men exempted from fear and pretension. Now, in *The Red Badge,* these are the all but exclusive sources of behavior. Henry's fear and his pretensions are like scales on a beam, and what happens is a series of tippings of these scales too far in one direction or in another, so that he is compelled to win his way back to a balance again. As John Berryman has pointed out,[16] the pretension fits Henry for irony, not sarcasm, so long as it is balanced by the pathos evoked by his fear. Should his fear gain dominance over his strutting pretension (as it does over the Swede in "The Blue Hotel"), then he is doomed. In following Henry, we follow a pretentious braggart whose fears in combat silence him, but who in the returning inflow of pretension is again operative, ridiculously so in view of his earlier fears, until fear again mounts up and moves the balance.

Before the steady creative vision of Stephen Crane, the causal framework of traditional ethics evaporates, and the youth acts from impulses starker than words. His thoughts are pathetic rationalizations after the fact, never reflections that lead to decisions and deeds. When he talks he utters banalities, and in so doing indirectly reveals his anxious self. That self thrusts its identity forth directly in the uncontrolled gestures produced under violent stress. Therefore, war is the ideal setting for an examination of man, since it provides the tumult which forces out direct expression. Man is the same under more tranquil conditions, but placidity affords him greater opportunity to mask his nature with irrelevant sentiments.

If coherent thought has so little part in the actions of man, then the traditional literary syntax must be replaced by a new one. The major triumph of *The Red Badge of Courage* is Crane's perfection of a stylistic equivalent for the behavior he wishes to present. In a traditional English paragraph the very syntax and diction weave a web of connections, of causes and consequences. But Crane, viewing man as an uneasy juggler of fears and pretensions who acts as they compel him, no longer uses this syntax. The complex sentence with its independent clause and one or more dependent clauses, in the main, gives way to separate images independently and equally represented. Taken together, they may form a pattern, as the dots of the pointillist taken together form colors and shapes which do not inhere in the particular dot, but the creator puts down only the dots and leaves the generalizations to the observer. One who was actually in the war would afterward in memory attempt to impose some coherence on his experience. But Crane, who wasn't, and who projected himself through sheer imaginative force into the midst of the turmoil, recorded the independent details.[17]

So distrustful is Crane of the intercession of reason between the observation and its impression upon the reader that he even refuses to make mental corrections, like those for distance, which are all but automatic: "Once he saw a tiny battery go dashing along the line of the horizon," he tells us of Henry. "The tiny riders were beating the tiny horses."[18] On the other hand, the immediate is inseparable from the coloring given it by the emotions of the human being in its midst. It is therefore frequently represented in images, because they dominate the literal event. So, when the youth sees a brigade enter a wood, and then, awaiting the event, sees the brigade emerge again, we read, "The brigade was jaunty and seemed to point a proud thumb at the yelling wood."[19]

The Red Badge of Courage is a tour de force requiring the constant adroit presence of its creator, and though there are slips—especially with regard to the irony, which sometimes turns rusty when Crane puts into Henry's mind a vocabulary not fittingly his, in order to mock at his pretensions —its success is overwhelming. It is a tour de force because, brief as the novel is, without the presence of its author at every point life would not go on. The setting, the action, and the style suit one another startlingly, but their brilliant coherence is the result of the power and consistency of the imagination which projected them. *The Red Badge* is like a dream which impresses one as being truer than daily events, but which requires the dreaming mind and which, unlike daily events, never develops a life of its own apart from the dreamer.

Just as Crane's view precluded traditional syntactic organization, it also precluded plotting, which is, after all, a controlling causal framework. Henry is scared but curious at the outset; in his first trivial engagement his confidence grows and his pretensions dominate him; in the next engagement the fears win and his pretensions evaporate, so that he flees; in his flight he receives his red badge, and with it his pretensions build up to a point where they again dominate and he can rejoin the community of the camp; and then in another engagement they remain on top of his fears so that he acts heroically. Does this mean that his character has developed? Well, yes. He has now learned to control a certain degree of fear, and if he is reasonably lucky he will not soon be put into a situation in which the fear will be so amplified that the compensatory swagger he now possesses will be inadequate to check its total seizure of him. The novel closes with a renewed use of proper names omitted since the opening scene, and a return to the same uninformed gossip of the ranks which began the novel. Again somebody says they are going to cross the river and come in behind them. This emphasizes the sense that what has happened is a fragment of what happens time and again; not a complete tale but a chunk which contains in it a picture of the ceaseless vibration that preceded it and will follow it.

At the very close Crane makes Henry's newly acquired cockiness so great that it becomes ambiguous when we remember his shortcomings and his rationalizations: "He had been to touch the great death and found that, after all, it was but the great death." The concluding paragraphs are self-consciously lofty, invoking a vocabulary that strongly contrasts with the banalities just uttered by the tramping soldiers: "He came from hot plowshares to prospects of clover tranquillity, and it was as if hot plowshares were not."[20] Pretension is on the rise again, and, to the extent that the soldiers did indeed act bravely in their last action, it takes a higher flight. In Crane's world, this is character development. Possessed now of such a confidence, Henry Fleming will not again flee, as he once did, "like a rabbit." But he may, of course, at some future date, flee like a lion.

Stephen Crane took the nineties by storm. At a time when writers were lending a half-willing support to the anthropomorphism of twilight notions, he burst forth young, yet fully grown, seemingly owing no allegiance to any tradition. He cut through the problems of American society by dealing with men's nerve ends and with the pathetically pompous idealizations through which they attempt to give their messages importance. Crane darted below and he soared above the daily events of his day, the communal problems and the manners of Americans. He did not evade them; he simply refused to acknowledge them as part of his vision of the world. But this vision, which had been formed without reference to seeming actuality, while it had the strength of untrammeled clarity, was also terminal. Once the seer has set forth his vision, what can he add unless he turns his attention to the commonplace life around him and attempts now to order that according to his view; unless he allows the world to inform and shape his vision as he had at first tried to inform and shape the world? *The Red Badge* was a tour de force also because it was unrepeatable. Once it was finished, there was nowhere for its author to go. Crane's productions up to 1895 seemed to be all but assembled within him; after a period of gestation he produced them. After 1895 he could only go on repeating himself unless he grew through observation of manners, through reflection, and through periods of rest when gestation could take place.

Life did not present him with those opportunities, and he was incapable of making them. The fame and notoriety which rushed in upon him had sent him off to the West and to Mexico, to Florida and to shipwreck, to Greece and to war. In escape from notoriety and in pursuit of the tranquillity necessary for the gestation that would produce a second phase of his work, he settled in 1897, at the age of twenty-six, in England. To his home there came a host of parasites to bask in his fame and subsist at his expense. The financial demands of his way of life were so great that he was unable to afford the time to digest his experiences or to learn from his newly acquired friends: Joseph Conrad, who had nothing but tranquillity as he strove to write and be recognized, and Henry James, who, now at Lamb House, was holding himself steadily to his art. Rather, Crane heeded the counsels of Harold Frederic, *New York Times* correspondent and practical novelist of the Howells school, who urged Crane to an immediate mining of his experiences, not of his imagination, which required refreshment. Thus he produced *Active Service* (1899), a novel about a journalist in love who risks his life during the Greek war, and abandoned stories like "The Monster," in which he was attempting to transmute his boyhood memories into art. In 1896 he had written *The Third Violet,* which much too facilely drew upon his experiences with the art students on East Twenty-third Street, and *Active Service* only compounded the flaws of this work.

Frederic's advice was well intended. He wished to save his friend from the taint of artiness which he fancied he would catch from such as James, and at the same time, through his practical knowledge of the market, help him to understand the point at which his experience and realistic literature intersected. But realism of the Frederic and Howells sort was alien to Crane, and his material when forced into this frame resembled a hollow imitation of Richard Harding Davis. An occasional story after *The Red Badge* indicated that the young man's failing was not in his genius but in the circumstances which pressed him into hasty production. "The Open Boat," "The Monster," "The Bride Comes to Yellow Sky," and "The Blue Hotel" all showed that he was capable of growth. As *The Red Badge* first sounded a note of distrust of rationalizing after the event, a note consistently to be echoed in style and content by Hemingway, so "The Open Boat" introduced another theme which was to dominate the imagination of the writers of the twenties: the positive values to be found in a company of unpretentious men going about their tasks efficiently and with respect for one another. But there was no time to allow the themes to grow. Just as Crane had, to the age of twenty-five, outstripped the event and offered himself in place of it, now events, the adventures he had been sent on by syndicates and newspapers, were, in his writings, replacing Crane himself.

So mercilessly did extraneous demands beat in upon Crane in England that when the Spanish-American War broke out he gratefully ran to it, not this time to gain experience of war, but rather to enlist; his English tranquillity had turned to chaos, and he hoped submitting to another chaos might afford him relief. Conrad saw the destructiveness of Crane's ambition but, unable to check him, mortgaged his unfinished work in order to lend Crane the necessary funds for his trip to America. The United States Navy, however, detected the tuberculosis that would within a few years kill Crane, and declared him physically unfit for service. He turned again to reporting and hurried off to the fighting as correspondent for Pulitzer's *World*. That he was there determined to regain his control over events was made clear by his behavior. He courted death in order not to become the victim of life. In a long, dirty white raincoat, Crane made a good target for snipers, and he strode about the battle lines, disregarding orders to get down. Richard Harding Davis finally found the way to get him to cover. He shouted, "You're not impressing anyone by doing that, Crane."[21] Immediately the white raincoat collapsed, and Crane came crawling over to the men in cover. He would not be taken for a show-off.

Davis, his golden luck ever with him, was the best correspondent in the war, but Davis himself claimed that Crane was, because he knew that Crane was the best writer there. Still, he was mystified by Crane's dark behavings. In admiration of *The Red Badge* he had adapted certain of Crane's mannerisms to his breezier ends; shocked by Crane's liaison with Cora Taylor, he had nevertheless stuck to his code of fair play and had beaten a man who publicly insinuated that Crane's illness was syphilis.

Thanks to such mothering as Davis's, the war did not kill Crane; nor did the tuberculosis that was fast growing on him. At war's end, still in need of a resting place, Crane disappeared into an underground existence in Havana. He ignored Cora's frantic inquiries—to which she was driven partly by love and partly by pressure from creditors—in an attempt either to discover his death or to gain sufficient time for his powers to recover control of experience. But Cora's anxiety and publicity about his disappearance broke through to him, and reluctantly he headed north. After dallying in New York, where he enjoyed the companionship of James Huneker and Albert Pinkham Ryder and indulged himself in dreams of buying a ranch in Texas, he surrendered to life and returned in 1899 to his costly manor house in Sussex, Brede Place.

Seriously ill, Crane plunged back into trying to meet his debts, seeing *Active Service* through the press and beginning work on a historical romance, *The O'Ruddy,* an admitted potboiler with which he hoped to make enough money to provide himself with the respite he desperately needed. In the time spared him from this labor he drove himself to produce poems, impressions of the Spanish-American War, and a series of tales, *Whilomville Stories* (1900), which revealed the direction he would have taken if events had given him the opportunity. In these stories, based on his childhood experiences, he now began to apply his vision to the manners of the American village. The stories were savage, too savage, but they showed the durability of his genius.

His body, however, was not durable, and in the spring of 1900, five months before his twenty-ninth birthday, still running to catch up with an opportunity to rest, Stephen Crane died of tuberculosis.

In the year before his death Crane wrote a letter which might have been addressed to his father had he been alive, but which instead was addressed to the Reverend Charles J. Little, who had been his professor of history at Syracuse and was now president of the Garret Bible Institute. Talking about his activities at Brede Place in the third person, Crane said, "He often tells about his fireside the tale of the man who exhorted him— somewhat without accurate knowledge in regard to crime—but with some kindliness and interest—indeed almost affection—that the lad has almost made it a part of his creed of conduct."[22] He let Little know, if the minister did not already know it, that his erstwhile student was now a widely published and successful author. Stephen Crane, picking up the pieces once again in England, was still sufficiently rebellious to patronize his elders, but, more important, he was now sufficiently mature to acknowledge his connection with the kindly Methodist tradition of his family and to send feelers back along the line of his inheritance. He was ready in his art, if not in his actual presence, to return home, as the *Whilomville Stories* also showed.

Crane's Civil War novel had not been concerned with man as a social animal, but his sketches of the Spanish-American War carried a new tone of communal identity. He wrote of the regular army at San Juan:

> I feel that things were often sublime. But they were *differently* sublime. They were not of our shallow and preposterous fictions. They stood out in a simple, majestic commonplace. It was the behaviour of men. In one way, each man was just pegging along at the heels of the man before him, who was pegging along at the heels of still another man, who was pegging along at the heels of still another man who—It was that in the flat and obvious way. In another way it was pageantry, the pageantry of the accomplishment of naked duty. One cannot speak of it—the spectacle of the common man serenely doing his work, his appointed work. It is the one thing in the universe which makes one fling expression to the winds and be satisfied to simply feel.[23]

A human community was challenging his attention, but he had yet to work out a way of talking about it and not falsifying it, as he had worked out a way, earlier, of giving the feeling of battle without falsifying the immediacy.

Until then he would rely upon "one cannot speak of it"; expression had to be flung to the winds.

Or he experimented with pathos, as in his account of the wounded troops debarking at Hampton Roads, shamefacedly passing the verandas of the resort hotels where well-dressed women, shocked at their wasted bodies, sobbed as they shuffled by:

> Most of them seemed to be suffering from something which was like stage-fright during the ordeal of this chance but supremely eloquent reception. No sense of excellence—that was it. Evidently they were willing to leave the clacking to all those natural-born major-generals who after the war talked enough to make a great fall in the price of that commodity all over the world.
>
> The episode was closed. And you can depend upon it that I have told you nothing at all, nothing at all, nothing at all.[24]

Richard Harding Davis talked incessantly about what Crane said one could not speak of, and his undaunted heroes stood jauntily amidst admiring smiles rather than stumbling shamefacedly past women in tears. His note rang false. Crane, having condemned the glorification of battle in *The Red Badge,* was attempting the more difficult task of recognizing human values without cheapening them with talk. He differed from Bierce in seeing war as a magnifying glass through which human behavior could be minutely examined rather than as a metaphor of life in general; for Crane the human condition was not one of constant hopelessness. To this extent he shared with Davis a sense of something splendid. In his later sketches he began to move toward the notion that the something splendid was an intensification of the human community rather than what Davis presented it as being, mere deeds of derring-do.

Crane's art, though it shocked some, as he intended it to, nevertheless won the respect of his society and gave him the fame that at first he willingly turned to notoriety. That notoriety, however, made him a marketable commodity and lured him to let our mortgages on his future to so great an extent that the last four years of his life were a furious and futile pursuit to meet his obligations so that his exhausted imagination could again draw breath. Hamlin Garland, throbbing with social sympathies as the decade began, had by its close succumbed to the limitations placed on his imaginative powers by his Midwestern environment and had turned into a hack writer. Crane, on the other hand, at the start of the nineties had a high disregard for collective social action but at their end was hopelessly seeking a respite that would allow him now to turn to the society with which he had been in constant combat and incorporate it into his art. He went down before he had fought his way free to the prospects of "clover tranquillity" that swam before Henry Fleming at the close of *The Red Badge of Courage.* For Crane the nineties had meant only hot plowshares, and he died before the scar could heal.

[1] Unless otherwise noted, details of Crane's life are taken from Edwin H. Cady, *Stephen Crane* (New York, 1962). Thomas Beer's *Stephen Crane* (New York, 1923) was a consistent source of pleasures and suggestions, but not of facts.

[2] Hamlin Garland, *Roadside Meetings* (New York, 1930), p. 193.

[3] Ibid., p. 194.

[4] Ibid., p. 197.

[5] Ibid., p. 199.

[6] Robert H. Davis, "Introduction," *The Work of Stephen Crane* (New York, 1925), vol. II, p. xv.

[7] Ibid., pp. xv–xvi.

[8] Cady, op. cit., p. 108.

[9] Hesketh Pearson, *The Life of Oscar Wilde* (London, 1954), p. 133.

[10] Stephen Crane, *The Red Badge of Courage and Other Writings,* ed. by Richard Chase (Boston, 1960), p. 12.

[11] Ibid., p. 18.

[12] Amy Lowell, "Introduction," *The Work,* vol. VI, p. ix.

[13] A most useful study is: Daniel G. Hoffman, *The Poetry of Stephen Crane* (New York, 1957).

[14] Crane, *The Work,* vol. VI, p. 59.

[15] Crane, *Red Badge and Other Writings,* p. 12.

[16] John Berryman, *Stephen Crane* (New York, 1950).

[17] For suggestions on Crane's style I am indebted to an unpublished essay by Lee E. Siegel, "Impressionism and Irony in *The Red Badge of Courage.*"

[18] Crane, *Red Badge and Other Writings,* p. 147.

[19] Ibid., p. 219.

[20] Ibid., pp. 230–231.

[21] Cady, op. cit., p. 64.

[22] Stephen Crane, *Letters,* ed. by Robert Stallman and Lillian Gilkes (New York, 1960), p. 209.

[23] Crane, *The Work,* vol. IX, p. 238.

[24] Ibid., p. 258.

THEODORE DREISER

****

Dreiser's life story has often been told, by himself and by friends and admirers. Most complete is W. A. Swanberg's *Dreiser* (New York, 1965); focused more directly on Dreiser as a writer are F. O. Matthiessen's *Theodore Dreiser* (New York, 1951) and Ellen Moer's *Two Dreisers* (New York, 1969). Critics who have found fault with Dreiser include Stuart Sherman in "The Naturalism of Theodore Dreiser," *On Contemporary Literature* (New York, 1917) and Lionel Trilling in "Dreiser and the Liberal Mind," *The Liberal Imagination* (New York, 1950). He is stoutly championed by H. L. Mencken in *A Book of Prefaces* (New York, 1917), by Vernon L. Parrington in *The Beginnings of Critical Realism in America* (New York, 1930), and by James T. Farrell in *The League of Frightened Philistines* (New York, 1945), and in *Literature and Morality* (New York, 1947). Clifton Fadiman writes of "Dreiser and the American Dream," *Nation,* CXXV (October 19, 1932), pp. 364–365; Maxwell Geismar in "Theodore Dreiser: The Double Soul," *Rebels and Ancestors* (Boston, 1963), finds him both artist and social critic, as does Robert E. Spiller in "The Alchemy of Literature," *The Third Dimension* (New York, 1965) and in his *The Cycle of American Literature* (New York, 1965). Charles Child Walcutt has meticulously detailed Dreiser's literary method in *American Literary Naturalism: A Divided Stream* (Minneapolis, Minn., 1956). Many of the more perceptive critical essays on Dreiser and his writing have been collected by Alfred Kazin and Charles Shapiro in *The Stature of Theodore Dreiser* (Bloomington, Ind., 1955).

THEODORE DREISER:
HIS EDUCATION AND OURS

Alfred Kazin

****

The fortunes of literature can reverse the fortunes of life. The luxury that nourished Edith Wharton and gave her the opportunities of a gentle-woman cheated her as a novelist. It kept her from what was crucial to the world in which she lived; seeking its manners, she missed its passion. Theo-dore Dreiser had no such handicap to overcome. From the first he was so oppressed by suffering, by the spectacle of men struggling aimlessly and alone in society, that he was prepared to understand the very society that re-jected him. The cruelty and squalor of the life to which he was born sug-gested the theme of existence; the pattern of American life was identified as the figure of destiny. It was life, it was immemorial, it was as palpable as hunger or the caprice of God. And Dreiser accepted it as the common vic-tim of life accepts it, because he knows no other, because this one summons all his resources.

Winter, Dreiser wrote in his autobiography, had always given him a physical sense of suffering. "Any form of distress—a wretched, down-at-heels neighborhood, a poor farm, an asylum, a jail, or an individual or group of individuals anywhere that seemed to be lacking in the means of subsistence or to be devoid of the normal comforts of life—was sufficient to set up in me thoughts and emotions which had a close kinship to actual and severe physical pain." He grew up in the friendly Indiana country of the eighties, in the very "Valley of Democracy" to be rhapsodized by Booth Tarkington and Meredith Nicholson; but he never shared its legendary happiness. His father, a crippled mill superintendent who was unable to provide for the family of fifteen, was a rigidly devout Catholic. The family separated periodically, the father going to Chicago to pick up work, the mother and younger children living in one small town after another. The bugaboo of social disapproval and scandal followed them insistently; at one time the mother kept a boardinghouse and a sister furnished the village gossips with a first-rate scandal. The family poverty was such that the town prostitute, his brother Paul's mistress, once sent them food and clothes, and even arranged for their removal to another city.

Dreiser grew up hating the shabby and threadbare rationale of the poor as only their sensitive sons learn to hate it; he hated his father and pitied his mother because she seemed so ineffectual in the face of disaster. The shining success in the family was his brother Paul, who became a popular vaudeville artist and composer. It was a painful, brooding boyhood, whose livid scars were to go into the first chapters of *An American Tragedy;* a boyhood touched by the lonely joys of wallowing in Ouida and *Tom Jones,* but seared by the perennial separations of the family and its grim and helpless decline. There was stamped upon Dreiser from the first a sense of the necessity, the brutal and clumsy dispensation of fate, that imposed itself upon the weak. He hated something nameless, for nothing in his education had prepared him to select events and causes; he hated the paraphernalia of fate—ill luck, the shadowy and inscrutable pattern of things that ground effort into the dust. He did not rebel against it as one who knows what the evil is and how it may be destroyed; he was so overpowered by suffering that he came to see in it a universal principle.

As Dreiser wandered disconsolately through the nineties, a reporter and magazine writer in New York and Chicago, St. Louis and Pittsburgh and Toledo, he began to read the pronouncements of nineteenth-century mechanism in Darwin and Spencer, in Tyndall and Huxley. They gave him not a new insight but the authority to uphold what he had long suspected. They taught him to call a human life a "chemism," but they did not teach him the chemical nature of life; they suggested that man was an "underling," a particle of protoplasm on a minor planet whirling aimlessly in the solar system, which for such a mind as Dreiser's was an excellent way of calling man what Dreiser had from his earliest days known man to be—a poor blind fool. The survival of the fittest was not a lesson in biology to be gathered in Darwin; it was the spectacle of the nineties as Dreiser watched and brooded over it in the great industrial cities that had within the memory of a single generation transformed the American landscape. For whatever the middle-class environment of his boyhood had given him, it was not laissez-faire theology. Capitalism had denied the young Dreiser its prizes, but it had not blinded him to its deceptions. All about him in the convulsive nineties, with their railroad strikes and Populist riots, Dreiser saw American society expanding as if to burst, wealth rising like mercury in the glass, the bitter shambles of revolt, the fight for power. While Robert Herrick was peering anxiously through his academic window and Edith Wharton was tasting the pleasures of Rome and Paris, while David Graham Phillips was reporting the stale scandals of New York high society for Pulitzer and Frank Norris was eagerly devouring the history of California for *The Octopus,* Dreiser was walking the streets of Chicago, the dynamic, symbolic city which contained all that was aggressive and intoxicating in the new frontier world that lived for the mad pace of bull markets and the orgiastic joys of accumulation. He was not of that world, but he understood it. Who could resist the yearning to get rich, to scatter champagne, to live in lobster palaces, to sport the gaudy clothes of the new rich? It was easy enough for those who had made a religion of their desire; it was easier still for a poor young writer who had been so hurt by poverty and the poor that the call of power was the call of life.

What Dreiser learned from that world was that men on different levels of belief and custom were bound together in a single community of desire. It was not the plunder that excited him, the cheating and lying, the ruthlessness and the pious excuses; it was the obsession with the material. A subtler mind, or a less ambitious one, might have cackled in derision; but Dreiser was swept away by the sheer intensity of the passion for accumulation. In *The Titan* he was to introduce a staggering procession of Chicago buccaneers on 'change with the same frowning, slow, heavy earnestness with which Abraham might have presented his flocks to God. He was fascinated by the spectacular career of Charles T. Yerkes, the most dazzling financier of his day, whose reckless energy and demoniac thirst for money spelled the highest ambition of his culture. Power had become not an instrument but a way of life. The self-conscious tycoons sat a little insecurely before their gold plate, their huge and obvious pictures, giggled perhaps in rare moments at their ostentatious and overdressed wives; but to Dreiser they represented the common soul's most passionate hopes made flesh. The symbols of power had become monumental, stocks and bonds blown feverishly into imitation French châteaux, the luxury of yachts, and conquerors' trips to Europe.

These evidences of success were something Dreiser could neither approve nor disapprove. Secretly, perhaps, he may have admired them for taking the American dream out of the literary testaments and crowning it with a silk hat; but what caught him was the human impulse that stole through the worst show of greed and gave it as natural and simple a character as local pride or family affection. As he wrote the story of Frank Algernon Cowperwood (Yerkes himself) in *The Financier* and *The Titan,* his plan was to build by tireless research and monumental detail a record of the industrial-commercial ethic. Though both novels were published at the height of the Progressive agitation, they have nothing in common with the superficial distaste that ruled David Graham Phillips's books, or with the sensitive homilies of Robert Herrick's. For the muckraking novel of the Theodore Roosevelt era assumed as its first premise that the society it excoriated was a passing condition; the novelists of the period based their values either on the traditional individualism and amenity of an agricultural and small owner's way of life (which was the ideal of the Progressive movement), or on the ideal society of Socialism, as did London and Sinclair. Dreiser would neither tinker with that society nor reject it. It was the only society he knew, the only society he had been allowed to understand; it was rooted in the same rock with poverty and mischance, strength and valor; it was life in which, as he wrote, "nothing is proved, all is permitted."

It was this very acceptance that gave him his strength. Since he could conceive of no other society, he lavished his whole spirit upon the spectacle of the present. Where the other novelists of his time saw the evils of capitalism in terms of political or economic causation, Dreiser saw only the hand of fate. Necessity was the sovereign principle. "We suffer for our temperaments, which we did not make," he once wrote, "and for our weaknesses and lacks, which are no part of our willing or doing." There was in nature "no such thing as the right to do, the right not to do." The strong went forward as their instinct compelled them to; the weak either perished or bore life as best they could. Courage was one man's fortune and weakness another man's incapacity.

In a lesser novelist this very dependence upon fate as a central idea might have been disastrous; it would have displayed not an all-encompassing intensity but mere ignorance. Dreiser rose to the top on the strength of it. He raised Cowperwood-Yerkes to the level of destiny, where another might have debased him below the level of society. Cowperwood becomes another Tamburlane; and as one remembers not the cities that Tamburlane sacked, but the character that drove him to conquest and the Oriental world that made that character possible, so one sees Cowperwood as the highest expression of the acquisitive society in which he rules so commandingly. His very spirit may seem repulsive; his ostentation, his multitudinous adulteries, his diabolism, his Gothic pile in Philadelphia and Renaissance palace in New York, merely a display of animalism. But we do not indict him for his ruthlessness and cunning; we despise his rivals because they envy him the very brutality with which he destroys them. When Cowperwood slackens (it cannot be said that he ever fails), it is not because his jungle world has proved too much for him, but because it is not enough. He has exhausted it by despoiling it, as he has exhausted his wives, his partners, his friends, and the sycophantic ingenuity of the architects to the rich. One remembers that poignant episode in which Cowperwood confesses to Stephanie Platow that his hunger for life increases with age but that men have begun to judge him at their own value. He must accept less from life because he has surged beyond its traditional limitations.

It was by a curious irony that Dreiser's early career became the battleground of naturalism in America. He stumbled into the naturalist novel as he has stumbled through life. It is doubtful that he would have become a novelist if the fight for realism in American letters had not been won before he arrived on the scene; but when he did, he assumed as a matter of course that a tragic novel so indifferent to conventional shibboleths as *Sister Carrie* was possible. Frank Norris became a naturalist out of his admiration for Zola; Stephen Crane, because the ferocious pessimism of naturalism suited his temperament exactly. Naturalism was Dreiser's instinctive response to life; it linked him with the great primitive novelists of the modern era, like Hamsun and Gorki, who found in the boundless freedom and unparalleled range of naturalism the only approximation of a life that is essentially brutal and disorderly. For naturalism has always been divided between those who know its drab environment from personal experience, to whom writing is always a form of autobiographical discourse, and those who employ it as a literary idea. The French naturalists, and even their early disciples in America, found in its clinical method, its climate of disillusion, their best answer to romantic emotion and the romantic ideal. Naturalism was the classicism of the nineteenth century. Flaubert, Zola, Stephen Crane, and Frank Norris were all suckled in the romantic tradition; they turned to naturalism to disown romantic expansiveness, lavishness of color, and the inherent belief that man is capable of molding his own destiny. To a Flaubert and a Stephen Crane the design became all; it was the mark of fatality in human life rather than life as a seamless web of imponderable forces that interested them. Much as Pope proclaimed in *An Essay on Man* that

> In human works, though laboured on with pain,
> A thousand movements scarce one purpose gain . . .
>
> So Man, who here seems principal alone,
> Perhaps acts second to some sphere unknown,

so the classic naturalists furnished case histories of suffering to describe the precise conditions under which, as a citizen of the urban industrial world, modern man plans his life, fumbles in the void and dies.

What Dreiser gave to the cause of American naturalism was a unique contribution. By exploding in the face of the Genteel Tradition, *Sister Carrie* made possible a new frankness in the American novel. It performed its function in literary history by giving the "new" morality of the nineties the example of solid expression; but it liberated that morality quite undeliberately. The young Dreiser, as John Chamberlain has put it, "had not been accepted by Puritan-commercial folk; therefore he was not loaded down in childhood with hampering theories of the correct way in which to live and act and write." The same formless apprenticeship and labored self-education which kept him from the stakes of modern society shielded him from its restrictions. He had no desire to shock; he was not perhaps even conscious that he would shock the few people who read *Sister Carrie* in 1900 with consternation. It would never have occurred to Dreiser that in writing the story of Hurstwood's decline he was sapping the foundations of the genteel. With his flash, his loud talk and fine linen, his rings and his animal intelligence, Hurstwood was such a man as Dreiser had seen over and over again in Chicago. The sleek and high-powered man of affairs automatically became Dreiser's favorite hero. To tell his story was to match reality; and the grossness and poignance of that reality Dreiser has known better than any other novelist of our time.

Dreiser's craftsmanship has never been copied, as innumerable writers have copied from Stephen Crane or even from Jack London. There has been nothing one could copy. With his proverbial slovenliness, the barbarisms and incongruities whose notoriety has preceded him into history, the bad grammar, the breathless and painful clutching at words, the vocabulary dotted with "trig" and "artistic" that may sound like a salesman's effort to impress, the outrageous solecisms that give his novels the flavor of sand, he has seemed the unique example of a writer who remains great despite himself. It is by now an established part of our folklore that Theodore Dreiser lacks everything except genius. Those who have celebrated him most still blush a little for him; he has become as much a symbol of a certain fundamental rawness in American life as Spanish villas on Main Street, and Billy Sunday.

Yet by grudging complete homage to him, Americans have innocently revealed the nature of the genius that has moved them. As one thinks of his career, with its painful preparation for literature and its removal from any literary tradition, it seems remarkable not that he has been recognized slowly and dimly, but that he has been recognized at all. It is because he has spoken for Americans with an emotion equivalent to their own emotion, in a speech as broken and blindly searching as common speech, that we have responded to him with the dawning realization that he is stronger than all the others of his time, and at the same time more poignant; greater than the world he has described, but as significant as the people in it. To have accepted America as he has accepted it, to immerse oneself in something one can neither escape nor relinquish, to yield to what has been true and to yearn over what has seemed inexorable, has been Dreiser's fate and the secret of his victory.

An artist creates form out of what he needs; the function compels the form. Dreiser has been one of the great folk writers, as Homer, the author of *Piers Plowman,* and Whitman were folk writers—the spirits of simplicity who raise local man as they have known him to world citizenship because their love for him is their knowledge of him. "It was wonderful to discover America," Dreiser repeated once after another, "but it would have been more wonderful to lose it." No other writer has shared that bitterness, for no other has affirmed so doggedly that life as America has symbolized it is what life really is. He has had what only Whitman in all the history of the American imagination had before him—the desire to give voice to the Manifest Destiny of the spirit, to preserve and to fulfill the bitter patriotism of loving what one knows. All the rest have been appendages to fate.

T. S. ELIOT

****

The quality of the writings about Eliot seems to me superior
to that of writings about any other American writer. F. O. Matthiessen's *The Achievement of T. S. Eliot* (New York, 1935; revised
1947; expanded 1948 by C. L. Barber) is a model of honest and
perceptive literary criticism. Edmund Wilson in *Axel's Castle* (New
York, 1931), F. R. Leavis in *New Bearings in English Poetry*
(London, 1932), R. P. Blackmur in *The Double Agent* (New York,
1935) and *The Expense of Greatness* (New York, 1940), Cleanth
Brooks in *Modern Poetry and the Tradition* (Chapel Hill, N.C.,
1939), Hugh Kenner's *The Invisible Poet: T. S. Eliot* (New York,
1959), and J. Hillis Miller's chapter on Eliot in *Poets of Reality*
(Cambridge, Mass., 1965), provide commentaries which rank cer-
tainly among the best of this century. Elizabeth Drew's *T. S. Eliot:
The Design of His Poetry* (New York, 1949) and Helen Gardiner's
The Art of T. S. Eliot (London, 1949) are reliable guides to Eliot's
verse, as is George Williamson's useful but more pedestrian *A
Reader's Guide to T. S. Eliot* (New York, 1953). Eliot as literary

critic is examined and found to some degree wanting by Delmore Schwartz in "The Literary Dictatorship of T. S. Eliot," *Partisan Review,* XVI (February 1949), pp. 119–137, by F. R. Leavis who was doubtful of "T. S. Eliot's Stature as Critic," *Commentary,* XXVI (October 1958), pp. 399–410, by Stanley Edgar Hyman in *The Armed Vision* (New York, 1948), and most heatedly by Karl Shapiro in "The Death of Literary Judgment," *In Defense of Ignorance* (New York, 1960). Excellent collections of critical essays have been gathered by Hugh Kenner in *T. S. Eliot: A Collection of Critical Essays* (Englewood Cliffs, N. J., 1962), by Allen Tate in a commemorative issue of the *Sewanee Review* in January 1966, and by Jay Martin in *Twentieth Century Interpretations of The Waste Land* (Englewood Cliffs, N. J., 1968).

T. S. ELIOT'S MAGIC LANTERN

Leonard Unger

****

I

"I perceived that I myself had always been a New Englander in the South West [meaning St. Louis, Missouri], and a South Westerner in New England." This comment of T. S. Eliot's, referring to his childhood and youth in the United States, was published in 1928—a year after he had become an English subject and had entered the Church of England. About thirty years later, in an interview conducted in New York, he affirmed that his poetry belongs in the tradition of American literature: "I'd say that my poetry has obviously more in common with my distinguished contemporaries in America, than with anything written in my generation in England.

From Leonard Unger, *T. S. Eliot: Movements and Patterns,* University of Minnesota Press, Minneapolis. © Copyright 1956, 1961, 1969, University of Minnesota. Excerpts from the poetry of T. S. Eliot are reprinted from his volume COLLECTED POEMS 1909–1962 by permission of Harcourt, Brace Jovanovich Inc. Copyright, 1936, by Harcourt Brace Jovanovich, Inc.; Copyright © 1943, 1963, 1964 by T. S. Eliot. Also reprinted by permission of Faber and Faber Ltd.

That I'm sure of." To the question whether there was "a connection with the American past," he answered: "Yes, but I couldn't put it any more definitely than that, you see. It wouldn't be what it is, and I imagine it wouldn't be so good; putting it as modestly as I can, it wouldn't be what it is if I'd been born in England, and it wouldn't be what it is if I'd stayed in America. It's a combination of things. But in its sources, in its emotional springs, it comes from America."*

The poet's parents were both descended from old New England families. His paternal grandfather had come to St. Louis from Harvard Divinity School to establish the city's first Unitarian church and then to found and preside over Washington University. His father, Henry Ware Eliot, became president of a local industry, the Hydraulic Press Brick Company of St. Louis. His mother, Charlotte Chauncey Stearns, was the author of a long poem on the life of Savonarola and an extended biography of her father-in-law. Thomas Stearns Eliot, the youngest of seven children, was born September 26, 1888. In his own words, the Eliot family in St. Louis "guarded jealously its connexions with New England."

After attending the Smith Academy in St. Louis, Eliot completed his preparation for college at the Milton Academy in Massachusetts and then entered Harvard in the fall of 1906, where he pursued philosophy as his major field of study. As an undergraduate he edited and contributed poems to the *Harvard Advocate*. He completed the college course in three years and then continued to study philosophy in the Graduate School, with an interruption for one year's study (1910–11) at the Sorbonne. In 1914 he returned to Europe, studying first in Germany and then, after the outbreak of the war, at Oxford. Although he completed a doctoral dissertation on the philosophy of F. H. Bradley, he never returned to Harvard for formal acceptance of the degree. After marrying Miss Vivienne Haigh Haigh-Wood in 1915, Eliot was employed briefly as a teacher of various subjects at a boy's school near London, and after that at Lloyds Bank. A physical condition prevented him from entering the United States Navy in 1918. From 1917 to 1919 he was assistant editor of the *Egoist,* and for that period and the years immediately following, besides writing poetry, he supported himself by writing for magazines and periodicals reviews and essays, some of which have since become famous. Eliot's personal literary relations led him into the publishing business—eventually to become a director of Faber and Faber. He became editor of the *Criterion* at its outset in 1922, a quarterly review which played an important part in literary developments for the period of its duration. (It ceased publication, by Eliot's decision, at the ap-

---

* The interview from which this and other statements are quoted was conducted by Donald Hall and appears in the *Paris Review,* Number 21 (Spring–Summer 1959).

proach of World War II.) After an absence of eighteen years, he returned to the United States in order to give the Charles Eliot Norton lectures at Harvard in 1932–33. He made increasingly frequent visits to his native country, lecturing and giving readings at various institutions, and accepting official awards of honor. The British Order of Merit and the Nobel Prize for Literature were awarded to him in 1948, and other distinctions of international eminence followed. In 1947 his first wife died, after prolonged illness and residence in a nursing home. In January of 1957 he married Miss Valerie Fletcher, who had been his private secretary.

It would be too crudely simple to regard the divided regional identity of Eliot's youth as the cause of qualities which have characterized his thought and work. But this early dual identity does prefigure and illustrate a large and inclusive pattern. Eliot was both Westerner and New Englander, but not wholly one or the other. So with his migration to England and Englishness. In his early literary criticism, the prose of the twenties and thirties, there are sometimes tones and gestures which out-English the English as only a foreigner, and perhaps only an American, could do. In religion he became a "Catholic" and an apologist for Catholicism, but he was not a Roman Catholic. His criticism urged a program of the classical, the traditional, and the impersonal, while he was producing a poetry which is poignantly romantic, strikingly modernist, and intensely personal. When others protested that there was a marked contradiction between his theory and his practice, Eliot explained: "In one's prose reflexions one may be legitimately occupied with ideals, whereas in the writing of verse one can only deal with actuality." And yet, in the later stages of his career Eliot frequently referred to the intimate relation between his prose—especially the discussions of specific poets—and his own poetry. Of that kind of criticism —which he has called "workshop criticism"—he said that it has been an attempt "to defend the kind of poetry he is writing, or to formulate the kind he wants to write," and again, that "its merits and its limitations can be fully appreciated only when it is considered in relation to the poetry I have written myself."

Eliot's boyhood enthusiasms for poetry were commonplace enough, and yet they also prefigure his own development. At the age of fourteen he was deeply impressed and excited by the *Rubáiyát,* and then by Byron and Swinburne—for all the differences, a body of poetry marked by melancholy, cynicism, and cleverness. But it was at about the age of nineteen, while he was a junior at Harvard University, that an event took place which was to be of the greatest importance to Eliot as a poet—and to the course of English poetry in the twentieth century. The event was his discovery of *The Symbolist Movement in Literature,* a book on the French symbolist writers of the nineteenth century by the English critic Arthur Symons. Eliot was eventually to be influenced, in a general way, by several of the French poets, from Baudelaire to Mallarmé, but it was Jules Laforgue, discovered through Symons' book, who was to have by far the greatest effect. Eliot's acknowledgement of this is well known: "The form in which I began to write, in 1908 or 1909, was directly drawn from the study of Laforgue together with the later Elizabethan drama; and I do not know anyone who started from exactly that point." Insofar as Eliot started from an *exact point,* it was exclusively and emphatically the poetry of Laforgue. The later Elizabethan dramatists had a less immediate and less intense effect, and their influence is not positively apparent until "Gerontion," which was written about ten years after the initial encounter with Laforgue. The early poems published in the *Harvard Advocate* during 1909–10 read like translations or adaptations from Laforgue. "Conversation Galante," included in *Prufrock and Other Observations,* still has a highly imitative quality and serves very well to illustrate the first stages of influence. The poem is obviously modeled on "Autre Complainte de Lord Pierrot," which is quoted entire by Symons. These two stanzas are enough to show the closeness between the two poems:

> Et si ce cri lui part: "Dieu de Dieu que je t'aime!"
> —"Dieu reconnaîtra les siens." Ou piquée au vif:
> —"Mes claviers ont du cœur, tu sera mon seul thème."
> Moi: "Tout est relatif."
> * * *
> And I then: "Someone frames upon the keys
> That exquisite nocturne, with which we explain
> The night and moonshine; music which we seize
> To body forth our own vacuity."
> She then: "Does this refer to me?"
> "Oh no, it is I who am inane."

If we consider these two poems, Laforgue's and Eliot's, and then recall Eliot's "Portrait of a Lady," it is easy to see how that poem, too, is another *conversation galante,* a dialogue between a man and a woman in which at once too much and too little is being communicated. In like manner, the *Harvard Advocate* poem called "Spleen" may be seen as a rudimentary form of "The Love Song of J. Alfred Prufrock." This early poem records the distraction and dejection produced by the "procession . . . of Sunday faces," by the social routines of the day and the sordid aspects of an urban alley, and then ends with a personification of "Life" as a balding and graying man, fastidiously attired and mannered, waiting with self-conscious correctness as a social caller upon the "Absolute." But "Prufrock" is also related to the "Portrait" and "Conversation Galante." The poem opens with the promise "To lead you to an overwhelming question . . ." and this question is not so much an interrogation as a problem—the problem of communication between a man and a woman.

> And would it have been worth it, after all,
> After the cups, the marmalade, the tea,
>
> . . . .
>
> To have squeezed the universe into a ball
> To roll it toward some overwhelming question,
> To say: "I am Lazarus, come from the dead,
> Come back to tell you all, I shall tell you all"—
> If one, settling a pillow by her head
> > Should say: "That is not what I meant at all.
> > That is not it, at all."

This theme of the failure of communication, of a positive relationship, between a man and a woman is found again in the other early poems "Hysteria" and "La Figlia che Piange," and it is indeed a major theme of the whole body of Eliot's work. It appears early in *The Waste Land* with the image of the "hyacinth girl."

> —Yet when we came back, late, from the Hyacinth garden,
> Your arms full, and your hair wet, I could not
> Speak, and my eyes failed, I was neither
> Living nor dead, and I knew nothing,
> Looking into the heart of light, the silence.

This theme is developed by various means throughout Eliot's poetry and plays. It becomes related to other emerging themes, especially to religious meanings—for example, in the symbolic imagery of the "rose-garden" which appears in the works *Ash Wednesday, Four Quartets, The Family Reunion,* and *The Confidential Clerk.*

II

One of the most familiar aspects of Eliot's poetry is its complex echoing of multiple sources. In the early poems, those of the "Prufrock" period, this aspect is not yet very marked, but it is nonetheless already present in some degree. The title "Portrait of a Lady" immediately suggests Henry James, and there is indeed much about this poetry which is Jamesian. For one thing, the theme of the man-woman relationship frustrated or imperfectly realized is a common one in James's fiction. Commentators have noticed particularly a similarity of situations in Eliot's poem and the short novel called *The Beast in the Jungle*—in which the protagonist becomes poignantly and devastatingly aware of a woman's love for him only after she has died. Besides this specific similarity, there is a general Jamesian atmosphere which pervades the early poems. The man and woman of the "Portrait," Prufrock himself, "The readers of the *Boston Evening Transcript,*" Aunt Helen, Cousin Nancy, the foreign Mr. Appollinax and his American hosts, all are Jamesian personae. Eliot, like James, presents a world of genteel society, as it is seen from within, but seen also with critical penetration, with a consciousness that is deliberately and intensely self-consciousness. Both writers, in their ultimate meanings, show a liberation from the genteel standard of decorum, while the style and manner which have familiarly attended the decorum not only remain, but have become more complicated and strange. After the period of the early poems, the Jamesian qualitites, like the Laforguean, are not abandoned but are assimilated and survive in the later stages of development. The opening strophe of *The Waste Land,* with its vision of a cosmopolitan society, ends on a Jamesian note: "I read, much of the night, and go south in the winter." The Jamesian quality emerges with great clarity in all the plays on contemporary subjects. They are all set in James-like genteel worlds. Such dramatic intensity as they have resides, as in so much of James's fiction, in crises of sensibility and awareness. Significantly enough, a specific Jamesian note is strongly sounded at the opening of the earliest of these plays. In the very first minute of *The Family Reunion* Ivy echoes *The Waste Land* with rather heavy emphasis:

> I have always told Amy she should go south in the winter.
> Were I in Amy's position, I would go south in the winter.
> . . . .
> I would go south in the winter, if I could afford it . . .

In the same scene, only a few minutes later, Agatha is commenting on Harry's return to his parental home, and she speaks the phrase "it will not be a very *jolly* corner," thus invoking Henry James, who had written a story called "The Jolly Corner," also about a man's homecoming and his search for an earlier identity.

While the theme of estrangement between man and woman is, so to speak, an ultimate subject throughout much of Eliot's work, it also signifies the larger theme of the individual's isolation, his estrangement from other people and from the world. There are intimations of this larger theme even in "Portrait of a Lady," where the young man's twice-mentioned "self-possession" means not only his poise but, in the Eliotic context, his isolation, his inability to give himself to or to possess others. In "Prufrock" the theme of isolation is pervasive and represented in various ways, from the "patient etherised upon a table," at the beginning, to the mermaids, at the end, who will not "sing to me"—but especially in the well-known lines

> I should have been a pair of ragged claws
> Scuttling across the floors of silent seas.

In a sense, all of Eliot's works in verse are variations on the theme of isolation. *The Waste Land* presents a procession of characters locked within themselves. The subject emerges into definition toward the end of the poem.

> We think of the key, each in his prison
> Thinking of the key, each confirms a prison . . .

When we turn to the plays, we find characters either accepting isolation or struggling to escape from it. In *Murder in the Cathedral,* the saint, Thomas, is by definition set apart from ordinary humanity. Harry, toward the end of *The Family Reunion,* says, "Where does one go from a world of insanity?"—and the implication of his subsequent and final statement is that he goes the way of the saint and the martyr. This is the way, too, that Celia Coplestone goes in *The Cocktail Party,* while the estranged Edward and Lavinia Chamberlayne are reconciled, not to love, or even to understanding, but merely to mutual toleration, making "the best of a bad job." The theme of isolation is in focus throughout the play, and with especial clarity in such words as these of Celia to the psychiatrist, Sir Henry Harcourt-Reilly:

> No . . . it isn't that I *want* to be alone,
> But that everyone's alone—or so it seems to me.
> They make noises, and think that they are talking
>   to each other;
> They make faces, and think they understand each other.
> And I'm sure that they don't.

Unlike the earlier plays, *The Confidential Clerk* contains no suggestion of the martyred saint, but nonetheless the central character, Colby Simpkins, like Harry and Celia before him, goes his own way. Finally indifferent as to who are his earthly parents, he turns to religion, first to be a church organist, and probably in time an Anglican clergyman. *The Cocktail Party* and *The Confidential Clerk* are each in turn, and with increasing measure, departures from the extreme and intense isolation represented in *The Family Reunion.* In *The Cocktail Party* marriage is regarded as a way of life, though cheerless, yet necessary and acceptable, "the common routine." *The Confidential Clerk* offers a brighter perspective on marriage and on the possibilities of mutual sympathy and understanding among human beings.

Then, with *The Elder Statesman,* there is the most marked departure of all from the theme of isolation. Lord Claverton, invalided and retired statesman and business executive of hollow success, has been a failure as friend, lover, husband, and father. His frustrations and anxieties are dramatized by the return of the man and woman whom in his youth he had abused. But his daughter Monica and her fiancé Charles encourage him to explain his problems, and in explaining he confesses all the pretenses and deceptions of his life, while they listen with an understanding and sympathy which restore him to himself and thus release him from his isolation. He discovers not only the love which Monica and Charles have for him, but also the love which they have for each other. In *The Elder Statesman,* Eliot has for the first time depicted with ardency and exaltation real and normal relations between a man and a woman. Toward the very end of the play, Charles tells Monica that he loves her "to the limits of speech, and beyond." And she replies that she has loved him "from the beginning of the world," that this love which has brought them together "was always there," before either of them was born. As compared with Eliot's other plays, there is no apparent religious dimension in *The Elder Statesman*—except for the intimations of these words of Monica. The play as a whole is an affirmation of human relations, a drama of escape from isolation within the limits of those relations.

It has been said of some writers that they write as if no one has ever written before. Of Eliot it is the reverse which is true—and true with a special significance, so that one cannot speak of his *sources* in the usual scholarly fashion. The point is that Eliot has been in a respect his own scholar, having brought to his work not only the influence of his sources but what might more aptly be called an awareness of his predecessors. This is true in a variety of ways. For example, the theme of isolation is so obviously universal and so readily available that a writer might very well pursue it without any awareness of particular antecedents or analogues. But for Eliot there is such an awareness. This is indicated by the footnote which Eliot fixed to the "key-prison" passage of *The Waste Land.* The footnote refers us to *Appearance and Reality,* a work by the British philosopher F. H. Bradley, and quotes as follows from that work: "My external sensations are no less private to myself than are my thoughts or my feelings. In either case my experience falls within my own circle, a circle closed on the outside; and, with all its elements alike, every sphere is opaque to the others which surround it. . . . In brief, regarded as an existence which appears in a soul, the whole world for each is peculiar and private to that soul." Eliot's deep interest in this idealist philosopher is indicated by his Harvard doctoral thesis (1916), "Experience and the Objects of Knowledge in the Philosophy of F. H. Bradley," and by a few other pieces, one of which is included in his *Selected Essays*. The Bradleyan element in Eliot's thought emerges as an echo of the circle image in one of the choruses of *The Family Reunion*.

> But the circle of our understanding
> Is a very restricted area.
> Except for a limited number
> of strictly practical purposes
> We do not know what we are doing;
> And even, when you think of it,
> We do not know much about thinking.
> What is happening outside of the circle?
> And what is the meaning of happening?

Eliot has defined his position by vividly portraying the world from which he is isolated and alienated. This practice is consistent with the Bradleyan philosophy. The individual mood, the quality of consciousness, the private feeling, is continuous with, in a sense identical with, the seemingly objective material that has provoked it. A person's identity is defined by his world, and to escape one is as difficult as to escape the other. This concept is implied in that early poem "Spleen," where a "waste land" is already beginning to emerge, where an environment of people and things is a "dull conspiracy" against which depression is "unable to rally." Prufrock's escape to the beautiful and the ideal from the ugly and the real, his reverie of the mermaids, is only momentarily sustained, "Till human voices wake us, and we drown."

Characteristically, the moments of beauty in Eliot's work are meager and brief and are obviously calculated to serve as a contrasting emphasis on the opposite, as in *The Waste Land:*

> . . . the nightingale
> Filled all the desert with inviolable voice
> And she cried, and still the world pursues,
> "Jug Jug" to dirty ears.

Up through *The Waste Land* Eliot's poetry is richly furnished with images of the sordid, the disgusting, and the depressing, and with personalities of similar quality. In the poems of the "Prufrock" group (1917) there are the one-night cheap hotels and sawdust restaurants, the vacant lots, faint stale smells of beer, a thousand furnished rooms and the yellow soles of feet, the dead geraniums, the broken spring in a factory yard, all the old nocturnal smells, the basement kitchens, and the damp souls of housemaids. In the poems of the "Gerontion" group (1920), there are "Rocks, moss, stone-crop, iron, merds," and such obnoxious persons as Bleistein, Sweeney, and Grishkin. *The Waste Land* (1922) and *The Hollow Men* (1925) are titles indicating clearly enough the grounds of alienation. *The Waste Land* is a grand consummation of the themes, techniques, and styles that Eliot had been developing, and *The Hollow Men* is at once an epilogue to that development and a prologue to a new stage in the career.

The new stage is marked by the difference between the titles *The Hollow Men* and *Ash Wednesday* (1930), and by Eliot's entry into the Church of England in 1927. But the new stage is not, of course, a sudden and abrupt change. Its emergence may be seen, especially in retrospect, in the prose—even as early as 1917, the date of "Tradition and the Individual Talent," which is relevant both by its title and its general argument—and the emergence may be seen in the poetry as well. The continuity of Eliot's poetry is, indeed, most impressive, already indicated here in some measure, and will be further considered. For the moment, it is appropriate to observe that *The Waste Land* and *The Hollow Men* have in retrospect been considered more Christian than they originally appeared to be. The way in which theme and imagery of *The Waste Land* blend and merge into those of *Ash Wednesday* is illustrated by these passages from *The Hollow Men:*

> This is the dead land
> This is the cactus land
> Here the stone images
> Are raised, here they receive
> The supplication of a dead man's hand
> Under the twinkle of a fading star.
>   *   *   *
> Sightless, unless
> The eyes reappear
> As the perpetual star
> Multifoliate rose
> Of death's twilight kingdom
> The hope only
> Of empty men.

The rocks that are red in *The Waste Land* reappear in *Ash Wednesday* as cool and blue. In the one poem there is the lament "Amongst the rocks one cannot stop or think," while the other poem moves toward conclusion with the prayer

> Teach us to care and not to care
> Teach us to sit still
> Even among these rocks.

Eliot's deliberate echoing of the earlier poem in the later one signifies that the difference in position is produced by a development rather than a departure or a break. While the position of isolation and alienation from the world is the foremost theme of the poetry up through *The Waste Land,* the same position, but with respect to God, is the theme of *Ash Wednesday.* Thus the first position, considered as a problem, has not been resolved. It has, rather, been incorporated into the second position and thus reinterpreted and re-evaluated. If one does not love the world, one is already well prepared for making an effort to love God. Isolation and alienation from the world become a stage in the discipline of religious purgation, an ideal to be further pursued. With Eliot's profession of Christian belief, this is the meaning which has been found in the lines concluding *The Waste Land:*

> Shall I at least set my lands in order?
> London Bridge is falling down falling down
>   falling down
> *Poi s'ascose nel foco che gli affina* . . .

III

The idea of isolation, of the impossibility of communication and understanding, has a direct bearing on Eliot's style, his mode of composition, and the structure of his poems, for the thematic problem is not only that of communication between one person and another but, finally, that of articulation itself. Prufrock, toward the end of his monologue, declares,

> It is impossible to say just what I mean!
> But as if a magic lantern threw the nerves in
>   patterns on a screen . . .

This statement has a multiplicity of implications which are appropriate to Eliot's work, both the poetry and the criticism. The statement is Prufrock's, and it is also Eliot's, spoken through the mask of Prufrock. We may consider first its relevance to the poem in which it occurs. A familiar complaint about Eliot's early poetry, including "Prufrock," was that it was difficult, obscure, and so on—that it did not clearly and directly say what it means. And indeed, it does not. Instead, like the magic lantern, it throws "the nerves in patterns on a screen." The poem "Prufrock" is like a series of slides. Each slide is an isolated, fragmentary image, producing its own effect, including suggestions of some larger action or situation of which it is but an arrested moment. For example, "Prufrock" proceeds from the half-deserted streets at evening, to the women coming and going, to the yellow fog, to Prufrock descending the stair, and so on, to the mermaids at the end of the poem. Each part of the poem, each fragment, remains fragmentary even within its given context—a series of larger wholes is suggested, and yet the series of suggestions is itself a kind of whole. It is the poem. It is Prufrock. He has gone nowhere and done nothing. He has conducted an "interior monologue," as the critics have said, and he is the monologue. All the scenery of the poem, indoor and outdoor, is finally the psychological landscape of Prufrock himself. The streets, rooms, people, and fancies of the poem all register on Prufrock's consciousness, and thus they are his consciousness, the man himself. Prufrock the man, his self-awareness, his state of feeling—each is equal to the other, and to his *meaning*. In order to say *just what* he means, he must render the essential man himself, he must throw, as it were ("But as if"), the nerves in patterns on a screen. But so to project the *real* nerves, the feelings in all their fullness which are the man himself, is impossible. It is the incommunicable secret of the mystics, and the ideal of romantic lovers. It is also the myth of romantic poets, from Byron and Shelley to Whitman, and since then. And it is distinctive of Eliot's modernness, of his modern romanticism, that he knows that it is a myth, while still recognizing the impulse (which is not the same as the desire) to pursue it.

Emerging from these considerations of "Prufrock" are generalizations which are applicable to all of Eliot's poetry. The characteristic poem, whether "Prufrock" or other, is analogous to the series of slides, highly selective and suggestive. And like "Prufrock," the poem contains a statement acknowledging this aspect of the poem and of its structure. (In this regard Eliot is more conservative than the French symbolist poets who served him as model and authority for this mode of composition.) "Preludes" is a series of four sketches of urban scenes in winter, followed by an explicatory comment:

> I am moved by fancies that are curled
> Around these images, and cling:
> The notion of some infinitely gentle
> Infinitely suffering thing.

"These images" constitute the main body of the poem. The poet has tried to guide the reader toward the "meaning" of the poem by mentioning the "fancies" which attend the images, and then by illustrating with a particular "notion." There are still other fancies or notions in the conclusion to the poem.

> Wipe your hands across your mouth and laugh;
> The worlds revolve like ancient women
> Gathering fuel in vacant lots.

The final image picks up thematically from the first scene the image of "newspapers from vacant lots." The poem thus ends on the note of the fragmentary, which is in various senses the subject of the poem.

In the earlier stages of Eliot's development "Prufrock," "Gerontion," and *The Waste Land* are obviously the major landmarks. Each of these poems in turn deepens, expands, and complicates features of the preceding poem, and among such features are the theme of alienation, the fragmentary quality of the parts, and finally the acknowledgment of these within the poem. While Prufrock exclaims that it is impossible to say just what he means, Gerontion announces that he has lost all the faculties of perception:

> I have lost my sight, smell, hearing, taste and touch:
> How should I use them for your closer contact?

And Gerontion concludes with a statement which is a characterization of the monologue he has delivered:

>   Tenants of the house,
> Thoughts of a dry brain in a dry season.

At the opening of the poem he calls himself "A dull head among windy spaces," and thus at the opening and close of the poem there are justifications, and hence admissions, of the nature of the poem—of its lack of conventional continuity and coherence. It is the critics who have described "Prufrock" as an "interior monologue," but it was Eliot himself who indicated the peculiarly private relevance of "Gerontion": "Thoughts of a dry brain."

As for *The Waste Land,* only a few reminders serve well to evoke the central themes and general qualities of that work. "A heap of broken images"; "I could not / Speak"; "Is there nothing in your head?"; "I can connect / Nothing with nothing"; "We think of the key, each in his prison." And then finally, at the end of the poem, among the collection of quoted fragments, there is the statement "These fragments I have shored against my ruins." The fragments are, of course, the amalgam of quotations in which the statement is imbedded. But the statement may also be taken as a reference to the entire poem, for the whole of *The Waste Land* is in a respect an amalgam of quotations, of fragments. At the opening there are the snatches of conversation, and then the poem is under way, with the addition of fragment to fragment, selected parts of a variety of sources mingled together and flowing into each other, the sources being life itself past and present as well as writings, until all the broken images are assembled into the heap which is the poem itself, the completed mixture of memory and desire. The series of fragments at the end compresses and intensifies the technique, the mode of expression, which has operated throughout the poem. In this respect, the very technique of the poem, especially as symbolized by the conclusion, is significant of the poet's meaning—or of part of his meaning—which is his despair of ever succeeding in fully articulating his meaning. If the poet's own voice finally fails him, he can at least intimate that much, confirm his prison, by withdrawing almost altogether, while the poem dies away with the echo of other voices, and thus reaches a termination which is, appropriately, not altogether a conclusion. It is impossible for the poet to say *just* what he means, and yet he manages to say that much. And to say that much, to say it effectively, to make the claim persuasively, is after all a kind of consummation. If he could have entirely articulated his meaning, then it would no longer have been the meaning with which he was concerned.

There are external facts related to these subjects of the fragmentary and the problem of articulation. It is well known, for example, that the form in which *The Waste Land* was published was the result of Ezra Pound's extensive editing of Eliot's manuscript. We do not know precisely and fully what changes Pound made, for the original manuscript seems to be irretrievably lost. But we know quite a bit, from surviving correspondence between Pound and Eliot and from Eliot's testimony. Pound persuaded Eliot not to use as epigraph a quotation from Conrad's *Heart of Darkness,* not to use "Gerontion" as a prelude to *The Waste Land,* to retain the section called "Death by Water" (which is Eliot's translation of his own French verses in "Dans le Restaurant"), and to accept excisions which reduced the poem to about half its original length. Eliot's decision to accept Pound's recommendations is, of course, part of his own creative responsibility and achievement, but it also forcibly illustrates the essential fragmentariness of Eliot's work. *The Waste Land* could survive, and with benefit, the amputation of fragments because it was and is essentially an arrangement of fragments. But it is no more so than the poetry that had been written earlier and the poetry that was to follow. Both *The Hollow Men* and *Ash Wednesday* began as short individual poems published independently in periodicals, and the pieces were later fitted together and other sections added to make the completed longer poems. This piecemeal mode of composition is emphasized by the fact that some of the short poems written during the same period and having similar themes, style, and imagery are excluded from *The Hollow Men* and in the collected editions preserved among the "Minor Poems." There is a nice implication here—that "minor" pieces, when assembled under an inclusive title and according to some thematic and cumulative principle, produce a "major" and more formidable whole. The relationship between whole and parts is again suggested by the "Ariel Poems," first published between 1927 and 1930 (except for "The Cultivation of Christmas Trees," 1954), the same period during which *Ash Wednesday* was taking shape. The earlier "Ariel Poems" are closely related in structure, style, and meaning to those poems which eventually became sections of *Ash Wednesday*. It is conceivable that some of the "Ariel Poems" might have been built into larger wholes and the earliest sections of *Ash Wednesday* left as separate poems. As it is, the "Ariel Poems" make a kind of series of appendixes to *Ash Wednesday*.

Turning from the external to the internal, we find in *The Hollow Men* and *Ash Wednesday* the same features already noted in earlier work. In *The Hollow Men* the themes of the fragmentary and the inarticulate are represented by both the form and the content of the statements. Throughout the poem the themes are symbolized by a wealth of images, and especially notable are "broken glass," "broken column," "broken stone," and "broken jaw." At the opening of the poem the voices of the hollow men "Are quiet and meaningless," and toward the end their speech is broken into stammered fragments of the Lord's Prayer. The first and last passages of the final section are inane and sinister parodies of a children's game song. Similar elements are present in *Ash Wednesday*. The poem begins with the translated quotation from Cavalcanti, and this is immediately broken into fragments, thus suggesting, among other things, the speaker's struggle to find expression:

> Because I do not hope to turn again
> Because I do not hope
> Because I do not hope to turn . . .

Exactly the same passage, but with "Because" changed to "Although," opens the final section of the poem. Section II is centrally concerned with fragmentation as symbolized by the scattered bones which sing, "We are glad to be scattered, we did little good to each other." As for the problem of articulation, it is the "unspoken word" which is the central concern of section V:

> Where shall the word be found, where will the word
> Resound? Not here, there is not enough silence
> Not on the sea or on the islands, not
> On the mainland, in the desert or the rain land . . .

The final words of the poem are "Suffer me not to be separated / And let my cry come unto Thee." These statements are fragments quoted from Catholic ritual—and they clearly convey both of the familiar and related themes: isolation (which is also fragmentation) and spiritual communion (which is also articulation).

In the collected editions of Eliot's poetry, placed between "Ariel Poems" and "Minor Poems," there is a section called "Unfinished Poems." This is comprised of *Sweeney Agonistes* and "Coriolan." The two parts of *Sweeney Agonistes* are "Fragment of a Prologue" and "Fragment of an Agon," and they first appeared in 1926 and 1927 respectively. Arranged together, they are described by Eliot in a subtitle as "Fragments of an Aristophanic Melodrama." But *Sweeney Agonistes* is not actually an "unfinished" work. Each part and the two parts together are deliberate ironical parodies of surviving fragments of classical texts, and thus the fragmentariness is a justifiable aspect of the finished product. The device of parodying (classical) fragments provided Eliot with an opportunity for experimental exercises in the use of dramatic verse and thus also in the use of rhythms borrowed from the conventions of the music hall and of colloquial speech. Another aspect of the fragmentariness is the deliberate continuity with, or reiteration of, elements from his earlier work—meaning, of course, that Sweeney had first appeared in the quatrians of *Poems* (1920) and then again briefly in *The Waste Land*. In the satirically trite and empty speech which makes up so much of the dialogue in these pieces, the subject of articulation, of communication, is plainly implicit, and it is finally explicit in the lines spoken by Sweeney toward the end of the second "Fragment":

> I gotta use words when I talk to you
> But if you understand or if you dont
> That's nothing to me and nothing to you . . .

The fragmentariness of *Sweeney Agonistes* is a structural device, but also, as in earlier works, it is related to subject and meaning. "Coriolan," on the other hand, is appropriately described as "unfinished." Its two sections, "Triumphal March" and "Difficulties of a Statesman," appeared respectively in 1931 and 1932. The work was apparently motivated by the political pressures of the time. Eliot's description of "Coriolan" as unfinished is meaningful in a number of ways. It obviously signifies that a suite of sections constituting a larger and self-contained work was intended. Eliot clearly abandoned the project at an early date, for in *Collected Poems 1909–1935* the work is already classified as unfinished. And "Coriolan" does have a quality of incompleteness in greater measure than is characteristic of Eliot's work. There is, for example, more "completeness," more clarity of effect, a more decided achievement of tone, in any section of *The Waste Land* or *The Hollow Men* or *Ash Wednesday*. Perhaps Eliot was aware of this measure of failure in deciding to abandon the project and then to classify it as unfinished. It was, in fact, uncharacteristic of Eliot to have projected a poem on so large a scale, and the failure of the project is therefore significant. When questioned by an interviewer, Eliot clearly acknowledged what was otherwise implicit in his practice. To the question whether *Ash Wednesday* had begun as separate poems, he answered: "Yes, like *The Hollow Men,* it originated out of separate poems. . . . Then gradually I came to see it as a sequence. That's one way in which my mind does seem to have worked throughout the years poetically—doing things separately and then seeing the possibility of fusing them together, altering them, and making a kind of whole of them."

A *kind* of whole—that is an apt and significant description. That kind of whole is nowhere more obvious than in what appears to be Eliot's final major performance in nondramatic verse, the *Four Quartets.* He has informed us that the first of these, *Burnt Norton,* grew out of passages deleted from his play *Murder in the Cathedral.* The *Four Quartets* was hardly conceived as "a kind of whole" at the time of the composition of *Burnt Norton.* That poem, eventually to be the first Quartet, appeared in 1935, and the next Quartet, *East Coker,* not until 1940. Thus the *Four Quartets* had an unpremeditated beginning in the salvaging of fragments removed from the play. *Burnt Norton* itself becomes a "kind of fragment" in retrospect from the other Quartets. In the years immediately following its appearance it received relatively little attention, while the *Four Quartets* was soon, and then often, praised as Eliot's supreme achievement. By itself, *Burnt Norton* revealed themes and elements of structure familiar enough against the background of earlier work. Like *The Waste Land,* it is divided into five sections. It has affinities of meaning and style with *Ash Wednesday* and *Murder in the Cathedral,* and also with the play *The Family Reunion,* which came later (1939). But in serving as the model for the other three quartets, it derived a clarity of structure and patterning of themes which could not otherwise be claimed for it. To extend the musical metaphor of the inclusive title, it is the variations which locate and define the theme. And it is that title which announces most succinctly the quasi-wholeness and the quasi-fragmentariness which are characteristic of Eliot's work. The title *Four Quartets* allows for the separate unity of each of the Quartets, and at the same time makes each a part of the larger whole.

While this ambivalence of parts and wholes is a structural convenience of which Eliot had always availed himself, it operates with special purpose in *Four Quartets.* A central subject of the work is the relation of the individual consciousness and identity to the passage of time—and time is meaningful in the work not only as a consideration and a grounds of discourse, but also in respect to the history of the composition of *Four Quartets,* to its having been written over a period of time. During this period of time there were changes in the poet's attitudes. According to *Burnt Norton,* "To be conscious is not to be in time." Escape from time into consciousness is achieved in the transcendent ecstasy symbolized by "the moment in the rose-garden," so that all other time, unless it is a means to this end, is meaningless:

> Ridiculous the waste sad time
> Stretching before and after.

The later Quartets, on the other hand, are less subjective and are increasingly concerned with reconciling the temporal and the timeless—as toward the end of *The Dry Salvages:*

> . . . And right action is freedom
> From the past and future also.
> For most of us, this is the aim
> Never here to be realised;
> Who are only undefeated
> Because we have gone on trying . . .

Four Quarters is (or are) essentially meditative and reflective poetry, but the mode of composition over a period of time, the fresh attack in each Quartet on the same themes, the willingness to acknowledge and define changes in attitude—these give a dramatic quality to the reflections. The changes wrought by time are thus not only a general subject of the work, they are particularized and dramatized meaning, and in being such they are also a lineament of the form. The poet's awareness of this fact is among the reflections he makes in the poetry. In *East Coker* there is the plaintive observation that "every attempt / Is a wholly new start," and in *The Dry Salvages* the problem is expressed again, this time as a broader, less subjectively personal preoccupation:

> . . . time is no healer: the patient is no longer here.
> · · · · · · · · · · · · · · · · · · ·
> You are not the same people who left that station
> Or who will arrive at any terminus . . .

Each of the Quartets and then all of them together have a greater conventional unity than Eliot's previous nondramatic poetry. Whereas so much of the earlier work is a direct representation of the fragmentariness of experience, *Four Quartets* is a deliberate and sustained discourse on that subject, and it ends with a serene vision of that wholeness which lies beyond the reach of time:

And all shall be well and
All manner of thing shall be well
When the tongues of flame are in-folded
Into the crowned knot of fire
And the fire and the rose are one.

As in earlier work, the problem of articulation is among the interrelated themes of *Four Quartets*. In *Ash Wednesday* blame was placed upon the external world for this problem:

. . . there is not enough silence
. . . .
The right time and the right place are not here . . .

The same complaint is made in the early Quartets, as in the final section of *Burnt Norton:*

. . . Words strain,
Crack and sometimes break, under the burden,
Under the tension, slip, slide, perish,
Decay with imprecision, will not stay in place,
Will not stay still. Shrieking voices
Scolding, mocking, or merely chattering,
Always assail them.

In *East Coker* the poet complains of "the intolerable wrestle / With words and meanings." If it is impossible to say just what he means, this is because his meanings have changed with the passage of time.

Because one has only learnt to get the better of words
For the thing one no longer has to say, or the
    way in which
One is no longer disposed to say it.

Blame is still put upon the external world, for the struggle must be made, he says,

. . . now, under conditions
That seem unpropitious.

In the final Quartet, *Little Gidding,* there is greater candor, greater objectivity, an acknowledgment of his own achievement, but still a note of alienation, as the poet sees his work (so long a dominant and determining influence) recede with the passage of time into the perspective of literary history:

> . . . Last season's fruit is eaten
> And the fullfed beast shall kick the empty pail.
> For last year's words belong to last year's language
> And next year's words await another voice.

In the last section of *Little Gidding* there is a final statement on the subject, a statement which combines a celebration of the possible with an acceptance of the inevitable.

> . . . And every phrase
> And sentence that is right (where every word is
>   at home,
> Taking its place to support the others,
> The word neither diffident nor ostentatious,
> An easy commerce of the old and the new,
> The common word extract without vulgarity,
> The formal word precise but not pedantic,
> The complete consort dancing together)
> Every phrase and every sentence is an end and
>   a beginning,
> Every poem an epitaph.

As already noted, the isolation of the individual is a theme of Eliot's plays, and closely related to it is the problem of articulation and mutual understanding. In *The Cocktail Party,* two ways of life are set in contrast, the way of the saint and the way of ordinary experience. While it is allowed that "Both ways are necessary," that a choice must be made of one or the other, and that the ordinary way is not inferior, it is nonetheless presented unattractively. Husband and wife, representing the ordinary way, are described as

> Two people who know they do not understand each other,
> Breeding children whom they do not understand
> And who will never understand them.

If in *The Cocktail Party* there is an affirmation of the ordinary way, this affirmation includes the attitude of being resigned to isolation. With *The Confidential Clerk,* however, the polarities of absolute isolation and absolute understanding are resolved by the acceptance of intermediate possibilities, of partial understanding. Colby Simpkins, the young confidential clerk, speaks of the limitations of mutual understanding not as a negative aspect of human relations but as a ground for mutual respect:

> I meant, there's no end to understanding a person.
> All one can do is to understand them better,
> To keep up with them; so that as the other changes
> You can understand the change as soon as it happens,
> Though you couldn't have predicted it.

The Confidential Clerk ends on the theme of understanding between husband and wife and between parents and children. The aging couple, Sir Claude and Lady Elizabeth, have finally achieved a measure of understanding with each other. When she says, "Claude, we've got to try to understand our children," her illegitimate son (who is engaged to his illegitimate daughter) says, "And we should like to understand *you.*" *The Elder Statesman* similarly finds dramatic resolution in the understanding achieved between the generations, between the father on the one hand and the daughter and her fiancé on the other. Toward the end of the play the familiar problem of articulation arises between the lovers, when Charles tells Monica that he loves her beyond "the limits of speech," and that the lover, despite the inadequacy of words, must still struggle for them as the asthmatic struggles for breath. Not the measure of communication achieved, but the will and effort to communicate receive the emphasis here.

In the dedicatory verses to his wife at the opening of the published volume of *The Elder Statesman,* Eliot returns yet again to the matter of words and meanings. In this poem he speaks of himself and his wife as "lovers" who share each other's thoughts "without need of speech" and who "babble . . . without need of meaning." The dedication ends with the statement that some of the words of the play have a special meaning "For you and me only." These lines document the extreme change in attitude that has taken place since Eliot first recorded Prufrock's lament that he could linger among the sea-girls of his restrained erotic fantasies only "Till human voices wake us, and we drown." In these lines to his wife he celebrates a mutual understanding which requires no articulation and a speech which does not strain toward meaning. In the final lines there is again the matter of words and meanings, and of isolation, but it is an isolation which is shared—"For you and me only"—and thus it is also communion—but still, in a sense, isolation. Hence, Eliot has changed his attitude without departing from his theme. "A Dedication to My Wife," with some interesting revisions, is included in *Collected Poems 1909–1962.*

IV

In his criticism Eliot has said a number of times that the entire output of certain writers constitutes a single work, that there is a meaningful inter-relationship of compositions, and that individual pieces are endowed with meaning by other pieces and by the whole context of a writer's work. Like so many of Eliot's generalizations, this is particularly applicable to his own poetry. If there is a fragmentary aspect to much of his work, there is also a continuity and wholeness. As we have already seen, a frequent practice of Eliot's was "doing things separately" and then "making a kind of whole of them," so that the fragmentary quality of the work is finally operative in the unity of the whole. The recurrent themes of time, alienation, isolation, and articulation obviously contribute to the continuity. And so does a steadily developing pattern of interrelated images, symbols, and themes. There is for example, the underwater imagery of the poems of the "Prufrock" group:

> I should have been a pair of ragged claws
> Scuttling across the floors of silent seas.
> * * *
> We have lingered in the chambers of the sea
> By sea-girls wreathed with seaweed red and brown
> Till human voices wake us, and we drown.
> * * *
> The memory throws up high and dry
> A crowd of twisted things;
> A twisted branch upon the beach . . .
> * * *
> The brown waves of fog toss up to me
> Twisted faces from the bottom of the street . . .
> * * *
> His laughter was submarine and profound
> Like the old man of the sea's
> Hidden under coral islands
> Where worried bodies of drowned men drift
>   down in the green silence,
> Dropping from fingers of surf.

Comparable images, of water and underwater, of rain and river and sea, continue to appear throughout the poetry, reflecting and echoing each other with cumulative effect. There is a similar development of flower and garden imagery, from beginning to end, and extending into the plays. The "hyacinth girl" of *The Waste Land* is related to the "smell of hyacinths" in "Portrait of a Lady," to the girl, "her arms full of flowers," in "La Figlia che Piange," and to the little girl ("Elle était toute mouillée, je lui ai donné des primevères") of "Dans le Restaurant." The rose-garden dialogue of Harry and Agatha in *The Family Reunion* remains enigmatic unless related to this garden imagery in Eliot's poetry, and especially to the symbolic rose-gardens of *Ash Wednesday* and *Burnt Norton*. Each garden passage, whether early or late, gains in clarity and scope of meaning when in relation to the others. At the outset of *The Confidential Clerk,* when Eggerson speaks of Colby—

> He's expressed such an interest in my garden
> That I think he ought to have window boxes.
> Some day he'll want a garden of his own.

—the informed reader is alerted to the spiritual and religious intimations of the ecstatic childhood experience in the rose-garden, variously represented elsewhere in Eliot's poetry. In addition to such meaningful recurrence of symbolic imagery, there is at times a merging of one kind of imagery with another, as in these lines from "Marina":

> Whispers and small laughter between leaves and hurrying feet
> Under sleep, where all the waters meet.

Here the garden imagery and the water imagery are related to each other, and related also to that deeper realm of consciousness in which such associations occur. Two patterns of imagery, each already intricate and extensive, have been joined to produce a pattern that is still larger and more intricate.

In the continuity of Eliot's poetry, there is not only an accumulation of meaning but an alteration of meaning, a retroactive effect of later elements upon earlier. For example, the lines quoted from "Marina" have a relevance to the final lines of "Prufrock." Marina is the girl, the daughter, in Shakespeare's *Pericles,* and, as her name indicates, a "sea-girl." There are, thus, in both passages the details of underwater, of sleep, and of the sea-girls. Considered alone, the sexual fantasy of the earlier passage is expressive of Prufrock's isolation and alienation—"Till human voices wake us, and we drown." But when considered in relation to "Marina" and to the entire pattern of the rose-garden imagery, Prufrock's erotic daydream becomes an intimation of what is presented in later poems as spiritual vision. The mermaids of Prufrock's self-indulgent reverie are an antecedent type of the female figure who is later to represent spiritual guidance—such as the "Lady" in *Ash Wednesday,* who is "spirit of the fountain, spirit of the garden . . . spirit of the river, spirit of the sea."

Another example of retroactive effect is Eliot's use of ideas found in the mystical work of St. John of the Cross, *The Dark Night of the Soul.* The Spanish mystic outlines a course of spiritual discipline leading to purgation and spiritual rebirth. The initial condition requisite for entering this discipline is described by St. John as of a negative nature, a state of inertia of sense and of spirit, the purpose being ultimately to eliminate the sensual and to bring the spiritual under control. This condition is one of isolation, alienation, bleakness, emptiness, dryness. St. John's system is summarized in *Burnt Norton* and *East Coker,* in each case in the final passage of section III—with particular clarity in *Burnt Norton:*

> Internal darkness, deprivation
> And destitution of all property,
> Desiccation of the world of sense,
> Evacuation of the world of fancy,
> Inoperancy of the world of spirit . . .

It is this system of spiritual discipline which provides the underlying scheme of *Ash Wednesday* and which is the clue to the meaning of that poem. The renunciation and impotency of section I, the dry and scattered bones of section II, seem to be a reiteration of the bleaker themes of *The Waste Land* and *The Hollow Men*—but with a difference. In *Ash Wednesday* there is an acceptance of the plight, and the bones sing, "We are glad to be scattered." The wasted and hollow condition, unrelieved in the earlier poems, is in *Ash Wednesday* a preparation for "strength beyond hope and despair" (section III). Hence the ambiguous prayer, in the first and last sections, "Teach us to care and not to care." In *Ash Wednesday* Eliot maintains the themes of the earlier poetry, but in relating them to St. John's system of spiritual discipline, the themes are reinterpreted and re-evaluated. Thus, from the perspective of *Ash Wednesday* and the *Four Quartets,* the earlier poetry takes on a meaning which it did not previously have. Once we have followed Eliot in relating his themes to St. John's system, the relevance extends to all expressions of the theme. The statement in "Gerontion," "I have lost my sight, smell, hearing, taste and touch," becomes an anticipation of "Desiccation of the world of sense." This is not to say that the earlier apparent meanings of "Gerontion," *The Waste Land,* and *The Hollow Men* are canceled out by the later poems, any more than one Quartet cancels another, or the later plays the earlier plays and poems. While each work remains itself, it takes on an additional aspect, a qualification of meaning, in the larger context. Eliot's observation, in "Tradition and the Individual Talent," about literature in general, that "the past [is] altered by the present as much as the present is directed by the past," is precisely applicable to his own career as a poet.

In discussing Eliot's poetry, we have, inevitably, considered some of the ways in which the poetry and the criticism are related to each other. This intricate and extensive subject has received the attention of numerous critics, including Eliot himself in recent years. But a few more illustrations of the relation will be appropriate and will serve as a further documentation of the emphases here pursued. It is particularly some of the more famous essays which lend themselves to this purpose. For example, in "The Metaphysical Poets" (1921) we find ideas which are applicable to Eliot's poetry, such as the following familiar passage: "We can only say that it appears likely that poets in our civilization, as it exists at present, must be *difficult*. Our civilization comprehends great variety and complexity, and this variety and complexity, playing upon a refined sensibility, must produce various and complex results. The poet must become more and more comprehensive, more allusive, more indirect, in order to force, to dislocate if necessary, language into his meaning." This belongs to the period of *The Waste Land,* and it is clearly enough an argument for such poetry. At the same time, one may see in this argument a recurring theme of Eliot's verse: the poet's struggle to state his meaning and the obstacles he faces in the contemporary world. Eliot offers the metaphysical poets as a precedent for this forcing and dislocating of language. But such deliberate struggle seems hardly to accord with the "direct sensuous apprehension of thought" and the ability to "feel their thought as immediately as the odour of a rose" which Eliot approvingly attributes to the metaphysical poets. These *direct* and *immediate* abilities of the metaphysical poets are, of course, functions of that "unified sensibility" which Eliot claimed for them. But when he speaks of them as being "engaged in the task of trying to find the verbal equivalent for states of mind and feeling," the poets would appear to be in pursuit of something rather than already in possession of it. Eliot's theory of the sensibilities—"unified" and "dissociated"—which has had such tremendous influence, crumbles into confusion with his later (1931) remark that a "deep fissure" was already evident in Donne's sensibility. Whatever inconsistencies and changes may have been in the critic's theories, it is clear that the poet's sustained preoccupation has been with "the verbal equivalent for states of mind and feeling."

This idea is repeated in the criticism in various ways and at various times throughout Eliot's career. Even the famous "objective correlative" defined in "Hamlet and His Problems" (1919) has this meaning: "The only way of expressing emotion in the form of art is by finding an 'objective correlative'; in other words, a set of objects, a situation, a chain of events which shall be the formula of that *particular* emotion; such that when the external facts, which must terminate in sensory experience, are given, the emotion is immediately evoked." Although the statement is more involved, the essential meaning is the same—the poet seeks to say exactly what he means, to find "the verbal equivalent for states of mind and feeling." Eliot's purpose in defining the objective correlative was to indicate what he considered to be a failing in Shakespeare's play: "Hamlet (the man) is dominated by an emotion which is inexpressible, because it is in *excess* of the facts as they appear. . . . We must simply admit that here Shakespeare tackled a problem which proved too much for him." It is not necessary to agree with this view of *Hamlet* in order to find it impressive—indeed, fascinating. For here again Eliot is concerned with the poet's struggle to express and evoke his meaning in all its fullness. The comment on *Hamlet* is especially interesting when compared with remarks Eliot was to make, so many years later, in the *Paris Review* interview:

> "I think that in the early poems it was a question of not being able to—of having more to say than one knew how to say, and having something one wanted to put into words and rhythm which one didn't have the command of words and rhythm to put in a way immediately apprehensible.
>
> "That type of obscurity comes when the poet is still at the stage of learning how to use language. You have to say the thing the difficult way. The only alternative is not saying it at all, at that stage. By the time of *The Four Quartets,* I couldn't have written in the style of *The Waste Land.* In *The Waste Land,* I wasn't even bothering whether I understood what I was saying."

These remarks forcefully suggest that in the essay on *Hamlet* Eliot was characteristically preoccupied with his own problems as poet. Nor is it, again, necessary to agree with the remarks in order to find them valuable and meaningful. If Eliot's earlier meanings exceeded his ability to express them, then the inability was actually an essential part of the meanings—and the meanings were expressed, after all! For we have seen that so much of Eliot's meaning, so much of the "state of mind" evoked by his poetry, is the state of isolation, of the ineffable and inarticulate. It is impossible to conceive of Eliot's earlier meanings as having any measure of fullness without the intimations of the ineffable. We have seen how much this theme contributes to the continuity and the larger meaning of his work. Although Eliot contrasted the *Four Quartets* with *The Waste Land,* it is well to recall that in *East Coker* he said:

. . . one has only learnt to get the better of words
For the thing one no longer has to say, or the way in which
One is no longer disposed to say it.

Other comments made by the author of *The Waste Land* on his own poem serve to illustrate various aspects of his behavior as a critic. In "Thoughts after Lambeth" (1931) he said: ". . . when I wrote a poem called *The Waste Land* some of the more approving critics said that I had expressed the 'disillusionment of a generation,' which is nonsense. I may have expressed for them their own illusion of being disillusioned, but that did not form part of my intention." This passage has been a favorite target of Eliot's detractors, but it has also been cited justly enough by more objective critics in calling attention to the haughty posturing which at times marred his pronouncements. Eliot himself was eventually to acknowledge a distaste for the pontifical tone which occasionally appears in his earlier prose. But to return to *The Waste Land*—when the interviewer observed that "more recent critics, writing after your later poetry, found *The Waste Land* Christian," Eliot answered, "No, it wasn't part of my conscious intention." We may surmise that Eliot had his own poetry in mind when in 1951 he was discussing the poetry of Virgil. He said then that while a poet may think that he has given expression to a "private experience" but "without giving himself away," his readers may find his lines expressing "their own secret feelings . . . the exultation or despair of a generation."

Much of Eliot's later criticism and comment is concerned with readjusting his position, with recording an achieved capacity for tolerance and a catholicity of taste, and with diluting or eliminating the asperity with which he had treated various figures and issues. The essays on Tennyson, Milton, Goethe, and Kipling present such readjustments and reconsiderations. In both the prose and the poetry, Eliot has shown an increasing tendency to talk candidly about himself, and with less fear of "giving himself away." It must have been as clear to Eliot as to his readers that Harry, the protagonist of *The Family Reunion,* in his complacent suffering and arrogant isolation, was a recognizable "objective correlative" for the author—since in "Poetry and Drama" (1950), Eliot said of Harry that "my hero now strikes me as an insufferable prig." It should not be necessary to quibble about what and how much the author intended to give away in these few words. But it is well worth pondering, along with the harsh judgment of Harry, Eliot's equally sound opinion (stated in the interview) that *"The Family Reunion* is still the best of my plays in the way of poetry."

Eliot has been less concerned to publicize a readjustment of position on political and social questions than on matters of literary criticism. He has been comparatively reticent on those political pronouncements which, in the light of later history, have appeared to be in accord with Fascist programs and practices. It may at least be said for him that he was not alone in failing to envisage the brutality to which the Nazis would extend the "corrective" doctrines of the reactionary position. Closely related to some of the quasi-Fascistic pronouncements made by Eliot is the question of anti-Semitism. The distasteful portrayal of Jews in "Gerontion" and in some of the quatrains of *Poems* (1920)—

> But this or such was Bleistein's way:
>   A saggy bending of the knees
> And elbows with the palms turned out,
>   Chicago Semite Viennese.

—may be considered as literary grotesqueries comparable to the portraits of Sweeney and Grishkin. But the evidence of the prose is another matter. In *After Strange Gods* (1933), discussing the virtues of a regional culture and homogeneous community, he said: ". . . reasons of race and religion combine to make any large number of free-thinking Jews undesirable. . . . And a spirit of excessive tolerance is to be deprecated." The contrived allusion to Karl Marx (in 1935) as a "Jewish economist" was again an amazing lapse in dignity. Merely to assert that he was not, or is not, anti-Semitic is an insufficient reckoning with such indiscretions. But it is a well-established habit of Eliot's readers and critics to discover meanings by relating seemingly remote details from various parts of his writings. It may therefore be no excessive tolerance to apply to Eliot's earlier deprecations the splendid and moving lines, in *Little Gidding,* with which the "familiar compound ghost" describes "the gifts reserved for age":

> . . . the conscious importance of rage
>   At human folly, and the laceration
>   Of laughter at what ceases to amuse.
> And last, the rending pain of re-enactment
>   Of all that you have done, and been; the shame
>   Of motives late revealed, and the awareness
> Of things ill done and done to others' harm
>   Which once you took for exercise of virtue.
>   Then fools' approval stings, and honour stains.

In 1955 Eliot said of Wordsworth, "his name marks an epoch," and it is even more true of Eliot himself. But this has already been said in various ways by various writers with various intentions. Indeed, so much has been said about the poet, dramatist, critic of literature and culture, that any effort to add a further comment can hardly escape repeititions of the familiar. And so, to end briefly with an appropriate summation and illustration of his achievement as poet and critic, it may be most fitting to follow in the convention of quoting the man himself: ". . . the best contemporary poetry can give us a feeling of excitement and a sense of fulfilment different from any sentiment aroused by even very much greater poetry of a past age." If "next year's words await another voice," it is to be hoped that the voice will be not only different from Eliot's, but equal to it in giving us excitement and fulfillment.

ROBERT FROST

****

Among the more interesting essays on Frost are two by Randall Jarrell, "The Other Frost" and "To the Laodiceans," both in *Poetry and the Age* (New York, 1953), which present the poet, not simply as a writer of bucolic verse, but as a delver into what is dark, serious, and sorrowful in human existence. When Lionel Trilling called Frost a "terrifying poet" ("A Speech on Robert Frost," *Partisan Review*, XXVI, Summer 1959, pp. 445–452), many voices were raised in protest (see M. L. Rosenthal, "The Robert Frost Controversy," *Nation*, CLXXXVIII, June 20, 1959, pp. 559–561), but since then Frost has been remembered as more than just a folksy man. The person of the poet can best be seen in Sidney Cox's *A Swinging of Birches: A Portrait of Robert Frost* (New York, 1957) and Reginald Cook's *The Dimensions of Robert Frost* (New York, 1958), but especially in Lawrance Thompson's *Robert Frost: The Early Years, 1874–1915* (New York, 1966) and *Robert Frost: The Years of Triumph, 1915–1938* (New York, 1970), the first volumes of an "authorized" biography. Thompson's brief critical volume, *Fire and Ice: The Art and Thought of Robert Frost* (New York, 1942), provides a basic introduction to the poet's themes and methods. Among those critical of Frost are R. P. Blackmur, "The Instincts of a Bard," *Nation,* CXLIV (June 24, 1936), p. 819, Malcolm Cowley, "Frost: A Dissenting Opinion," *New Republic* CXI (September 11 and 18, 1944), pp. 312–313, 345–347, and Yvor Winters, "Robert Frost: or, the Spiritual Drifter as Poet," *Sewanee Review,* LVI (August 1948), pp. 564–596. Other essays, mostly favorable, have been gathered by Richard Thornton in *Recognition of Robert Frost* (New York, 1937), by Robert A. Grunberg and James G. Hepburn in *Robert Frost: An Introduction* (New York, 1961), and by James M. Cox in *Robert Frost: A Collection of Critical Essays* (New York, 1962). It is difficult not to agree with F. O. Matthiessen when he says in *The Oxford Book of American Verse* (New York, 1950), "When the history of American poetry in our time comes to be written, its central figures will probably be Frost and Eliot."

ROBERT FROST'S
THEORY OF POETRY

Lawrance Thompson

✳✳✳

A poem begins with a lump in the throat; a home-sickness or a love-sickness. It is a reaching-out toward expression; an effort to find fulfilment. A complete poem is one where an emotion has found its thought and the thought has found the words. . . . My definition of poetry (if I were forced to give one) would be this: words that have become deeds.[1]

—Robert Frost

In a literary age made nervous by the tugging conflicts of factions, Robert Frost has been able to win the admiration and respect of opposed

[1] Robert Frost's definitions of poetry, printed on the dust jacket of *West-Running Brook* (New York: Holt, Rinehart and Winston, Inc., 1929).

individuals even while he has stoutly refused to take sides in the controversies. Almost miraculously he has moved about in the conflagration unscathed—like one of those figures in the fiery furnace. A glance at his sojourn among poets will reveal the paradox of his friendships. Before the turn of the century his early verse was praised by Richard Hovey; before the first World War, he had earned and returned the warm affections of such English poets as Edward Thomas, W. W. Gibson, and Lascelles Abercrombie. In 1913 that American renegade in London, Ezra Pound, had sent to his countrymen an enthusiastic review of *North of Boston*—and Harriet Monroe printed it in *Poetry*. Returning home, Frost found that he had been praised warmly in an early issue of the *New Republic* by Amy Lowell, leader of the free-verse Imagists. More understandably, Edwin Arlington Robinson sent a letter of rich priase in 1917. Poets so diverse in method as Ransom, MacLeish, and Hillyer revealed their obligation to Frost's poetry in their early work. And in 1936 an English edition of his *Selected Poems* was issued with introductory essays by a curious foursome: W. H. Auden, C. Day Lewis, Paul Engle, and Edwin Muri. The secret of Frost's wide appeal seems to have been that his poetry, from the beginning, caught fresh vitality without recourse to the fads and limitations of modern experimental techniques.

The problem of the experimentalists was to determine how free poetry should be if it were to escape the threadbare conventionalism of an outworn tradition. Naturally the emphasis was on new forms, in this declaration of poetic independence, for freedom of the poet's material has always existed, together with certain abiding limitations of the poet's method. Frost carried on his own distinct experiments, emphasizing speech rhythms and "the sound of sense." He has called attention to "those dramatic tones of voice which had hitherto constituted the better half of poetry." In Frost's theory of poetry, the self-imposed restrictions of meter in form and of coherence in content stand not halfway down the scale of grace. He has made many casual references to the general quality of those limitations which work to the advantage, not to the disadvantage, of new and lively poetry.

The restrictions of the experimentalists, ironically seeking liberation, have amused Frost. With pleasant banter he has teased his contemporaries by jesting about their desperate "quest for new ways to be new." Behold the fantastic variety of restrictions in their freedom, he said: "Poetry, for example, was tried without punctuation. It was tried without capital letters. It was tried without any image but those to the eye. . . . It was tried without content under the trade name of poesie pure. It was tried without phrase, epigram, coherence, logic and consistency. It was tried without ability. . . . It was tried premature like the delicacy of unborn calf in Asia. It was tried without feeling or sentiment like murder for small pay in the underworld. These many things was it tried without, and what had we left? Still something."[2]

There were other kinds of restrictions which amused Frost, such as those of overemphasis. Perhaps poetry could be used to purge the world of wickedness and bring heaven down to earth in the form of an international brotherhood. This was a shift of emphasis from one type of pure poetry to another type of pure poetry! Frost offered his own anecdote for comment:

> "I had it from one of the youngest lately: 'Whereas we once thought literature should be without content, we now know it should be charged full of propaganda.' Wrong twice, I told him. Wrong twice and of theory prepense. But he returned to his position after a moment out for reassembly: 'Surely art can be considered good only as it prompts to action.' How soon? I asked him. But there is danger of undue levity in teasing the young. . . . We must be very tender of our dreamers. They may seem like picketers, or members of the committee on rules, for the moment. We shan't mind what they seem, if only they produce real poems." [3]

The restrictions which Frost accepts in his theory of poetry save him from the dangers of two extremes: nothing of content (pure art) and nothing except content (pure preaching). He is also unsympathetic with those who think they may set up as goals of perfection the expression of thought or emotion in the form of abstractions: sound merely for the sake of sound, or inner agitation which becomes wildness with nothing important enough to be wild about. The danger of this last experiment, he says, is that "we bring up as aberrationists, giving way to undirected associations and kicking ourselves from one chance suggestion to another in all directions as of a hot afternoon in the life of a grasshopper."[4] So much for those who have imitated that beauty of free association in thought or emotion which the impressionistic Symbolists established as a fad in poetry. Furthermore, Frost hates to see poets use their medium as a vehicle for shrieking frustration and disgust. Grievances he would willingly restrict to prose, so that poetry might concentrate on griefs, on "woes, woes immedicable"; might be permitted to go its way in tears.

[2] Robert Frost's introduction to Edwin Arlington Robinson's posthumous *King Jasper* (Toronto: The Macmillan Company, 1935).

[3] "Education by Poetry: A Meditative Monologue," given by Robert Frost at Amherst College; published in the *Amherst Graduates' Quarterly*, XX, No. 2 (February 1931), 75–85.

[4] Frost, "The Figure a Poem Makes."

These, then, are some of the restrictions which Frost considers to be of false value in poetry, popular as they may have been among the straining experimentalists. But this process of paring away at the nonessentials does not bring us in to any kernel, any simple answer which Frost has as to the nature of poetry. To him the mystery, the wonder, the virtue, the magic of poetry is its heterogeneity of elements somehow blended to a single autonomous unit. The problem of the poet is to achieve this integration, this fusion. The difficulty of calling on a poet to explain is that we call on him to reverse the process and resort to deliberate analysis, disintegration, diffusion. Such a task, repugnant to Frost and to many poets, is left to the analysis of the critics. But the gulf between integration and analysis is one which criticism has never succeeded in bridging, nor is there much hope that even our specialized scientific approaches through the terms of psychology, philology, and metaphysics will bridge the gulf. Fortunately, the hints and observations thrown off by the poets themselves help us to reach across the gulf until the distance is at least reduced.

FORM

Refusing to arrange his observations into any kind of systematic theory, Frost has mentioned several specifics and factors which seem to him important. Rejecting the hard and fast boundaries of definition as too dangerous, he has indicated certain elastic principles which seem not only sensible and salutary but also deeply rooted in the experience of poets in any age. Cautiously, he begins by finding the initial impetus of the poet to rise out of intensely perceived experiences which are given expression because of the hunger, the need for expression, in the Emersonian sense of the word. But he qualifies his use of the word "expression" with some care. How dangerous it might be to suppose that the response to the desire for expression should inevitably produce an artistic utterance. There have been some inartistic screams in modern poetry. But to "gape in agony," he says, and to write "huge gobs of raw sincerity bellowing with pain" are obviously kinds of expression which, be they ever so heartfelt, are too formless to be considered as anything other than mere expression. They lack shape.

Form, then, may be said to be the most important characteristic which Frost finds essential to poetry in any age. But the spread of meaning in that very elastic word must be suggested before such a simple statement is understood. For example, we may start with the great variety of stanzaic forms and then break any of them down to the rich formal relationships of rhyme to rhyme, of line to line, of sentence to sentence, of words which talk back and forth to each other in the poem. When we recall that another characteristic of form is balance and equilibrium, or controlled unbalance, we open up entirely new vistas. Furthermore, form in poetry is modulated also by the relation, the balance, of emotion and emotion, of thought and thought, of emotion and thought, of the image and the metaphor, of the specific and the general, of the trivial and the significant, of the transient and the permanent. All these facets appear to Frost as related aspects of that terse but by no means simple word "form."

To give form in poetry is also to employ that intricate method of conveying organization, shapeliness, fitness, to the matter or substance of context of meaning of the poem. Before meaning finds its place in a poem it must become subordinated to its proper balance with structure. And Frost goes further to assert quite bluntly that another requirement of peotry is that this formal fusion of distinct elements shall achieve the personal idiom of the poet's expression without sacrificing that happy correspondence which must exist between his own experience and the experience of those who come after to read or hear the poem.

Such fundamentals are even more complicated than they seem to be. But it is the duty of the lover of poetry to perceive at least the outer aspects of these fundamentals. And those who have tried to explain have sought different ways of getting at the problem. For example, it may be appreciated that modern critics have with good reason rejected the conventional division of poetry into two simple components: form and content. A peculiar interrelationship is disregarded in such arbitrary separation. Out of the fusion grows a quality which is neither form nor content, but somehow a by-product of the fusion. John Crowe Ransom has described this extra quality as "texture" and is willing to call the fusion which produces it "structure." But this new combination of terms helps only slightly to increase our awareness of the complexity in a good poem. For example, none will claim that meaning or content or context has disappeared because it has become integrated as structure. To the contrary, the process should have increased our acuteness in perceiving the overtones of meaning enriched by the position of meaning in the structure of the poem. Now it happens that many modern poets and critics are willing to assume that meaning, having undergone a peculiar metamorphosis in a poem, is no longer meaning; that it has been translated into something rich and strange. Granted, Frost says, that it has been enriched; still it is meaning. And he is willing to go so far as to say that meaning is the ingredient best able to save poetry from effeteness. He finds variety in poetry more closely allied to many-sidedness of content than to the many-sidedness of form, difficult as it may be to extricate the one from the other in a poem. To me, the odds seem to favor neither the one nor the other. And I believe that Frost's own poetry is at its best when the two elements have become so completely reconciled that they are happily joined in a holy marriage and defy any attempted separation.

THE POETIC IMPULSE

But how does this complicated relationship first begin to take shape? Frost has told us something of his own personal experience as it concerns the genesis, the working out of a poem. Again and again he has said that there is a striking analogy between the course of a true poem and of a true love. Each begins as an impulse, a disturbing excitement to which the individual surrenders himself. "No one can really hold that the ecstasy should be static and stand still in one place. It begins in delight, it inclines to the impulse, it assumes direction with the first line laid down, it runs a course of lucky events, and ends in a clarification of life—not necessarily a great clarification, such as sects and cults are founded on, but in a momentary stay against confusion. It has denouement. It has an outcome that though unforeseen was predestined from the first image of the original mood—and indeed from the very mood. . . . It finds its own name as it goes and discovers the best waiting for it in some final phrase at once wise and sad—the happy-sad blend of the drinking song."[5]

In this aspect of the poet's intent, Frost implies that he finds himself impelled forward as if by faith, so that the poem is somehow believed into existence. "The beauty, the something, the little charm of the thing to be, is more felt than known." As for the source of that initial impetus, he finds it growing out of a flash of recognition; a fresh perception. But there is another kind of recognition which might be called a correlation. Somehow it amounts to a new awareness of self. The present moment serves as a fulminating agent which fires experience lost in the dark of memory and causes that experience to burst into flame. This accident, producing an emotional intensity, might be described as an act which projects the past into the future. Frost has his own striking analogy:

"For me the initial delight is in the surprise of remembering something I didn't know I knew. I am in a place, in a situation, as if I had materialized from a cloud or risen out of the ground. There is a glad recognition of the long lost and the rest follows. Step by step the wonder of unexpected supply keeps growing. The impressions most useful to my purpose seem always those I was unaware of and so made no note of at the time when taken, and the conclusion is come to that like giants we are always hurling experience ahead of us to pave the future with against the day when we may want to strike a line of purpose across it for somewhere."[6]

This kind of inspiration is in no way related to what Wordsworth had in mind when he referred to "emotion recollected in tranquillity." It is more closely related to the recognition-scene, so long a source of surprise and

[5] *Ibid.*
[6] *Ibid.*

emotional tension in dramatic narratives. In a peculiar sense, the poet's fresh recognition creates an emotional crisis. He is impelled to find release from that crisis—and the resolution of it is the poem.

Frost implies that there are two kinds of recognition which he has experienced as one part of the poetic impulse; two different ways in which this sense of interplay between the past and the present is first motivated and finally resolved in the form of a poem. The first way occurs when some experience in the present inspires an emotional recognition that is more a matter of sense impression than of clear mental perception. The emotional tension —the lump in the throat—which is established through such a recognition, impels the poet into the physical act of recording in poetry the details of the immediate moment; the details of that immediate experience which happens to the poet in the physical world, or which is happened upon by the poet in the nonphysical world of his own reverie. Uncertain as to the precise nature of this sudden meeting between past experience and present experience, the poet ventures into the recording of the moment, the capturing of the incident. He proceeds with this recording as an act of faith, without foreseeing the outcome. And as this emotional tension finds its gradual resolution in the poem, the emotion finds its thought. In other words, the mental recognition of meaning in this emotional experience gradually asserts itself on a new plane of metaphorical reference. It may find its expression in a stated simile or it may find its expression merely through that which is implied or suggested.

This first kind of recognition which Frost suggests, as a part of his poetic impulse, may be demonstrated by examining a single poem. The more easily understood the poem may be, the better are the chances of making it serve as an illustration here. For that reason I choose the graceful and familiar "Stopping by Woods on a Snowy Evening." In fair warning, I must confess that I do not know the story as to how Robert Frost happened to write this poem. But my guess, even if it should prove wrong in specific details, may still have validity as a general illustration of that process which I am trying to clarify. The poem is a dramatic lyric which breaks into the middle of an incident, so that there is a drama-in-miniature revealed with setting and lighting and actors and properties complete. At the beginning, the reader finds the curtain going up on a little action which approaches the climax of an experience, real or imagined; that is, an experience which happened to the poet or one which came to the mind of the poet as possible. A rural traveler is the actor whose brief soliloquy describes the circumstances under which he has stopped his horse-drawn sleigh to enjoy, in spite of cold and loneliness, the strange beauty of white snowflakes falling against a background of dark trees. There are many reasons why he should not stop; common-sense reasons which seem to occur even to the traveler's little horse.

But the spell of the moment is so strong that the traveler is reluctant to leave, regardless of the winter night and the cold storm. He is impelled to move on by the realization of duties and distances; those "promises" which he must keep and the "miles to go" before he completes his journey. Thus the poem ends, and the images which crowd the statements are direct and unmistakable. Where, in such lines, does the emotional tension resolve itself into the mental focus of a metaphor? If this simple little poem is to be considered as one in which the resolution suggests two planes of reference, the reader must be made aware of words and images which face two ways at once. Considered from the viewpoint of the poetic impulse, it is quite probable that the poet, impelled emotionally to record this real or imagined experience, did not immediately see in it any metaphorical correspondence between the sight of the moment and the insight of the past-in-the-present. Yet a correspondence appears with dramatic clarity in the final stanza. The reader is aware of more than one possible meaning for such words as "promises" and "miles" and "sleep." And it is probable that the poet also came upon these words with a conscious perception and recognition of a rational focus which grew out of this moment first felt vaguely and emotionally in the form of an inner tension. Almost with a sense of surprise the poet may have found a second plane of reference which gave deeper importance to the little incident which became the poem. But Frost's characteristic reticence and shyness, a part of his New England heritage, led him to be satisfied with those three words which suggest, without explanation or elaboration, the rationally perceived focus of this correspondence.

Each reader has no difficulty in making an elaboration from this implied metaphor. In the poem, the specific incident has completely displaced the general analogy. If a reader is satisfied to settle for the specific as satisfactory in itself, there is nothing to hinder him from so doing. On the other hand, if he wishes to continue with the extensions of the metaphor, there is nothing to hinder him from that added pleasure. The most obvious correspondence would suggest the analogy between the specific experience of the rural traveler and the general experience of any individual whose life is so frequently described as a journey; a journey including pleasures and hardships, duties and distances. In the light of such analogies, the other images offer correspondences which are valid. There is even a slightly tragic implication suggested by "the coldest evening of the year." Yet within this bitter cold occurs an elementary revelation of beauty which lays claim on us as existing nowhere else. Regardless of the dark and cold, we are prone to tarry quite irrationally because of this paradoxically somber excitement and recompense. The reluctance to leave becomes an expression of the endless hunger for holding and making permanent a dark moment of pleasurable discovery in a transient experience. But we are impelled forward and away by other and inevitable commitments. There are the "promises" which we have made to ourselves and to others, or which others have made for us. And there are the "miles" we must travel through other kinds of experience before we yield to that final and inevitable commitment: sleep in death.

I am well aware that this kind of metaphorical extension is distasteful to some, and is frequently branded by others as impressionistic nonsense. I am equally sure that any poet who uses metaphors with the deliberate purpose of suggesting more than is stated offers his readers, through the very nature of his method, the freedom to read the poem on as many different planes of reference as may be discovered. The only restriction is that such induced correspondences must not be made if they invalidate the initial relationship of the specifics to each other. The rules of the game are as old as poetry. Children derive much pleasure from playing with those square boxes of different sizes which may be put together, one inside another, until they are contained within a single block. They may be treated without imagination as a single block, but the pleasure begins when they are telescoped outward. In a restricted sense, the pleasure derived from opening up a metaphor may be compared to the pleasure derived from opening up that single block which has so many proportionate identities hidden within it.

I have said that Frost implies a second kind of recognition which he has experienced in the poetic impulse. The second occurs when the emotional pleasure is derived from the sudden mental perception of a thought which comes into sharp focus through the discovery and recognition of a particularly apt correspondence or analogy. The difference between these two approaches to the writing of a poem should be clear. The first begins as an emotional response which gradually finds its resolution in a thought metaphorically expressed; the second begins with the perception of the metaphor, and the rational focus is so pleasurable in its sudden discovery that it produces an emotional afterglow. The first leads the poet to venture into the writing of the poem as an act of faith, without foreseeing the outcome; the second leads the poet to give shape and weight to a rational correspondence which has been perceived clearly before he begins the writing of the poem. Nevertheless, Frost is fond of handling each of these by letting the specific displace the general until the analogy is implied or stated as a kind of climax to the poem.

In selecting an illustration for this second process, I again venture a guess. For reasons which may become clear before I finish, I am willing to suppose that one poem written in this second manner is that entitled "For Once, Then, Something." Here also is a dramatic lyric, with its single actor unfolding, through his brief monologue, a setting which builds directly to a climactic moment. At the beginning, there is an implied reference to other actors who may be considered collectively as the antagonists. Before we go

further, let us imagine the manner in which the poet's thoughts may have
led him to recognize in the action of this moment the apt incident or metaphor which brought a sense of pleasurable response and emotional tension.
Those who have examined Frost's poetry with care are familiar with his increasing fondness for metaphors which make use (or fun) of concepts and
problems in systematic philosophy. His own middle-ground position permits
him to control an ingrained skepticism in such a manner as to deal playfully
with the extremes of affirmation and denial. He has frequently suggested
that he is particularly wary of hydra-headed Platonic idealism and of all
those glorious risks taken by any who boldly arrive at transcendental definitions. Pleasantly scornful of those who assume too much as to the extent
and validity of human knowledge, Frost tells us, he has often shared the
longing which inspires philosophers to project their systems beyond the
realms of the known and the knowable. He has never grown tired in his own
cautious search for truth, yet he has never been tempted to believe that absolute truth could be defined satisfactorily even by the most profound philosophic systems. As he says in his poem entitled "Neither Out Far Nor In
Deep," we all will continue forever to watch and hope, "wherever the truth
may be." In *A Witness Tree,* he sums up the persistent attempt to resolve
the inscrutable, thus:

> We dance round in a ring and suppose,
> But the Secret sits in the middle and knows.

"For Once, Then, Something" is the record of an incident which pleased
Frost, apparently, as a happy analogy which might serve to state the paradox between his own watchfulness and his own skepticism. Obviously, the
poem is so nicely constructed that the reader may enjoy it on a single plane
of reference, without any concern for the epistemological implications. But
my supposition is that Frost's experience happened to bring the analogy into
sharp focus with his lifelong accumulation of prejudices concerning the extent and validity of knowledge; that he deliberately prepared the incident for
interpretation on an epistemological plan of reference, by using one word
which is so obviously placed that it stands out like a sore thumb. Here is the
poem, complete:

> Others taunt me with having knelt at well-curbs
> Always wrong to the light, so never seeing
> Deeper down in the well than where the water
> Gives me back in a shining surface picture
> Me myself in the summer heaven godlike
> Looking out of a wreath of fern and cloud puffs.

Once, when trying with chin against a well-curb,
I discerned, as I thought, beyond the picture,
Through the picture, a something white, uncertain,
Something more of the depths—and then I lost it.
Water came to rebuke the too clear water.
One drop fell from a fern, and lo, a ripple
Shook whatever it was lay there at bottom,
Blurred it, blotted it out. What was that whiteness?
Truth? A pebble of quartz? For once, then, something.

As soon as that naked word "Truth?" asserts itself with whimiscal and teasing boldness at the beginning of the final line, the reader is made aware of a new kind of game. One may enjoy trying to examine the bottom of a well through water, but only a poet would look there for truth. So the reader turns back to the beginning of the poem to examine the images and phrases in the light of that single word. Do the images corroborate the implication of such a brazen hint? The first line immediately becomes an oblique reference to the long-standing quarrel between the speaker as a skeptical relativist and his antagonists as believing absolutists. Next we come to the nature of the taunt: the speaker has been ridiculed as an egocentric who can do no better than perceive the absolute being as the reflection of his own not-too-pathetic human image. Then a further correspondence is suggested between the specific search below the surface of the well-water and the general search below the surface of human experience for some meaning which will satisfy human yearnings for certainty. Having perceived this general connotation, the reader finds an easy addition in the description of the speaker who is also taunted by his more idealistic, possibly religious, friends because he has hindered his own search by taking his position "always wrong to the light" —and suddenly the religious extensions of the word "light" fall naturally into the pattern of this second plane. Once, however, the poet humorously suggests that his endeavor seemed to permit a passing glimpse of something. Perhaps he had caught sight of the hidden mystery itself. But too soon the spell was broken by a seemingly deliberate accident and a rebuke. It seemed as though there might be some intelligence which intended that this human being and others should never have more than a glimpse.

Thus the incident of the traveler in the snowy woods and of the spectator peering down into a well are two examples which help to explain Frost's remarks concerning his own experience in analyzing that mysterious process which has to do with the poetic impulse. Wordsworth took pleasure in turning from the present to find an emotional excitement and inspiration in happy memories of the past. Paradoxically, Wordsworth's pursuit of ultimate reality in the impulses from a vernal wood became a form of escape from the unpleasantness of the momentary and transient actuality. Frost's method is diametrically opposed. He takes pleasure in ignoring the ultimate reality of the philosophic and religious absolute; takes pleasure even in turning his back on the past, until a momentary experience is illuminated with richer value by that which his past experience accidentally brings to the present. And Frost's quest of the present moment as the greatest reality becomes a pursuit in the Emersonian sense; it becomes implicit with newly perceived aspects of an evident design in the universe. Always, the past cuts across the present moment to reveal and illuminate the moment by transforming it into a metaphor which has for him beauty and meaning. It may be valuable to reconsider his own statement here:

"For me the initial delight is in the surprise of remembering something I didn't know I knew. I am in a place, in a situation, as if I had materialized from a cloud or risen out of the ground. There is a glad recognition of the long lost and the rest follows. Step by step the wonder of unexpected supply keeps growing. The impressions most useful to my purpose seem always those I was unaware of and so made no note at the time when taken, and the conclusion is come to that like giants we are always hurling experience ahead of us to pave the future with against the day when we may want to strike a line of purpose across it for somewhere."

But in the process of that resolution from the moment of poetic impulse to the final completion of the poem, there arises the persistent need for cunning and artistry. Frost does not imply that the poem writes itself. The poet must establish a careful balance between the personal intimacy of the experience and the separation of the experience through statement which gains perspective without loss of intensity. The thoughtful statement of the relationship between the present experience and the remembered experience balances the emotion. Equilibrium is truly a large part of what is meant by artistry. "Keeping the thing in motion," Frost has said, "is sometimes like walking a rolling barrel." Again he feels it analogous to riding an untamed horse: "The great pleasure in writing poetry is in having been carried off. It is as if you stood astride of the subject that lay on the ground, and they cut the cord, and the subject gets up under you and you ride it. You adjust yourself to the motion of the thing itself. That is the poem."[7]

Accidentally, a poet may lose one kind of equilibrium, fall off, and continue his journey to the end of the poem in a truly pedestrian fashion. Then the critical reader becomes painfully aware of the accident and is able to point out the place: "This is where he fell off." To Frost this loss of balance was a part of what Poe meant when he said that there was no such

---

[7] "The Poet's Next of Kin in a College," a talk given by Robert Frost at Princeton University on October 26, 1937; published in *Biblia*, IX, No. 1 (February 1938).

thing as a long poem; that he could show any reader of a long poem where the rider fell, and how far he limped before he again managed to climb astride his Pegasus.

There is a pertinent paradox in the poet's craving for the intimacy of experience which gives insight and, at the same time, his longing for separation which permits objectivity and perspective. As a part of the poet's preparation, Frost has often hinted at this problem. The dark woods seem to become a symbol of that withdrawal from life for the sake of clarification. The first poem in his first book, "Into My Own," sang the yearning for lostness in "dark trees" that "stretched away unto the edge of doom," because such lostness would lead to self-discovery. One might not do violence to "Birches" by discovering in the final passage a reflection of the poetic hunger for withdrawal which might permit swift and exciting return, with grace and without effort, to a new sense of life:

> I'd like to get away from earth awhile
>
> . . . .
> And climb black branches up a snow-white trunk
> *Toward* heaven, till the tree could bear no more,
> But dipped its top and set me down again.
> That would be good both going and coming back.

In the response to poetic materials and poetic insight the deliberate and conscious craftsmanship must be combined with a sense of surrender to the material which has been possessed. "You adjust yourself to the motion of the thing itself." The muscular assertiveness of the will defeats its own purpose. The poet as rider finds his curious animal to be tender-mouthed. Or it might be said that the poem which succeeds has the casual grace of the dancer completely responsive to the rhythm of the music and concerned only with an almost reflexive expression of the emotion thus inspired. The shrewdness of the poet is to remain true to the mood and true to the material at the same time. We may not like Plato's metaphor of the perfect image concealed in the untouched block of marble. But in the nature of poetic response to a moment and situation in time and space, the poet is responsible in a strange way to elements which he may distort only at the peril of destruction and loss. I find a happy analogy, regardless of the original intent, tucked away at the heart of Frost's poem, "The Ax-Helve":

> He showed me that the lines of a good helve
> Were native to the grain before the knife
> Expressed them, and its curves were no false curves
> Put on it from without. And there its strength lay. . . .

So the perfection of the poem arises out of the poet's pleasure in discovering words, images, metaphors, phrases, "native to the grain" of the emotion, the thought, the situation.

There is a peculiar satisfaction which Frost finds from the ultimate resolution, release, or completion of a poem. Out of the chaotic confusion of daily impressions and thoughts the poet captures a moment with his words and achieves a kind of crystallization which gives to his chaotic raw materials not only shape but weight. And this metamorphosis creates that sense of stability which Frost refers to when he speaks of "a momentary stay against confusion." His poem "West-running Brook," which furnished the title for his fifth book, is built around an elaborate metaphor which has a particularly happy connotation if one interprets it in the light of the poet's intent. The metaphor is built around the image of one wave which rides forever above a sunken rock: permanence in transience. "The stream of everything that runs away" is able to create the illusion, but only the illusion, of "not gaining but not losing" because of the black water "flung backward on itself in one white wave." It suggests to the poet the analogy of existence:

> And it is time, strength, tone, light, life and love—
> And even substance lapsing unsubstantial;
> The universal cataract of death
> That spends to nothingness—and unresisted,
> Save by some strange resistance in itself,
> Not just a swerving, but a throwing back,
> As if regret were in it and were sacred.
> It has this throwing backward on itself
> So that the fall of most of it is always
> Raising a little, sending up a little.

We may go on to play the age-old game of analogies and say that the poet's hunger for creating a sense of stability and of crystallization from the flux of things has in it a sacred regret of its own—and a sense of triumph in his accomplishment, for this very reason. From the viewpoint of the artist, Frost hints that we all know that sense of comfort and pleasure because it is also derived even from the most humble achievement of form in our lives.

MEANING

If we may return a bit, Frost's image of experience hurled into the future, as if by intuitive foreknowledge of the eventual need, is very closely related in spirit to Emerson's theory of poetry. The flash of recognition is a happy response to that union of impressions present and past. But the gradual elaboration of the thing felt with delight leads naturally to a statement of the larger understanding, the half-sad, half-happy wisdom of the conclusion. In quite a different context of associations, Emerson once spoke of the way in which the thoughts of the present gave to the thoughts of the past a new arrangement in the mind of the perceptive individual, so that the utterance was fresh. He continued: "It came into him life; it went out from him truth. It came to him short-lived actions; it went out from him immortal thoughts. It came to him business; it went from him poetry. It was dead fact; now, it is quick thought. It can stand, and it can go. It now endures, it now flies, it now inspires. Precisely in proportion to the depth of the mind from which it issued, so high does it soar, so long does it sing."

We may recognize a further relationship between the theories of Emerson and Frost. One speaks of dead fact becoming quick thought; the other speaks of a "clarification of life" which grows out of poetry. We are back to the problem of meaning, and of its importance to the poem. Is meaning in a poem a means to an end or is it an end in itself? Each would say that there is no pat answer to such a question. There are several different planes of thought on which the question may be considered. On the first plane, each would say that beauty is its own excuse for being; that the delight is the goal. On a higher plane, there is a new by-product analogous to that which is created when the material merges with the shape the poem gives it. There is a difference between making poetry a means to an end and in finding, at the conclusion of a poem, that something more than pleasurable emotion has been created. I am convinced that both Frost and Emerson have sometimes confused these differences in their own poems, but I am sure that in theory their awareness of the difference is demonstrable. On this higher plane of reference, there is a pleasure which arises from a deeper understanding. Let the poem start and finish ever so playfully; it will touch and illuminate experience. Robinson put it thus:

> The games we play
> To fill the frittered minutes of a day
> Good glasses are to read the spirit through

The little game, the poem, is in no sense a picture of life as it actually exists. It is not a key to the poet's philosophy of life. It is more closely akin to a momentary glimpse which is at once a distillation and an elaboration of a moment. Yet somehow in the preservation of that transience the poet touches on the permanent. Relationships are the essence of metaphor and of poetry to Frost. And Emerson calls the poet "the Sayer" not only because he is namer of beauty but also because he is "a perceiver and dear lover of the harmonies that are in the soul and in matter—and specially of the correspondences between these and those."

The first concern of the poet is with that substance which he wishes to express. And he must have enough drive in an emotional sense to encompass and relate the parts. If he is able to possess his material with an intensity which gives artistic validity to the material, he may then take pleasure in the shapeliness of the poem, the autonomousness of the creation. In that shapeliness is its excuse for being. But this does not inhibit either artist or reader from finding another kind of pleasure in the meaning.

Because a poem subordinates meaning to its proper balance in structure, one is not able to test the validity of a poem's morality by the standards either of religious creeds or of scientific fact. What may be true for a poem may be false when tested by the average rules of good conduct. For example, Eliot's ironic poem "The Hollow Men" may outlast all his other poems. It is an excellent poetic epitome of pessimism and disillusionment. As such, it has its own validity, its own truth, its own morality, even though its meaning is plainly opposed to the idealism of Christian morality or to the facts of human nobility and heroism in the face of a tragic world. Quite obviously a poem is able to succeed and have its entity without recourse to these standards. Yet, because the material of poetry is so deeply rooted in life and living, that material inevitably relates itself to, and is colored by, the larger affirmations of human morality. And it would seem to be one characteristic of lasting poetry in any language, in any age, to reaffirm in its independent fashion the various aspects of strength in human courage, human love, human aspiration. Because fear, hatred, despair, and negation are equally aspects of human experience, these also demand their place as materials for poetry.

It is the poet's virtue to develop that insight and wisdom which enable him to recognize and represent the apparent conflict between the constructive and destructive elements, the good and the bad, in nature and in human experience. Those elements, so inextricably related to each other, furnished the basis for dramatic conflict in Greek tragedy. Again, the all-inclusiveness of Shakespeare's insight, with its recognition of the good in the bad, the bad in the good, and triumph of constructive forces only at great cost and waste of good, tallies with our own experience after more than three hundred years, and helps to give his poetry permanence. Obviously, the possession of insight and wisdom in perceiving these spiritual relationships is not enough to create poetry; but it seems to be one of the essentials of lasting poetry. And at the risk of being called didactic in his affirmations, Robert Frost has subscribed to such a general rule, such a limitation if you wish, in the writing of his poetry.

It has been said that "in the high artist, ethics and aesthetics are one." How true—and how dangerous. The test is a familiar one: does the artist handle his ethical and moral observations in such a way as to make them implicit? If he does not, he has failed in a very serious way. Robert Frost's poetry frequently takes that risk, and does not always succeed in keeping the thoughts implicit. When the ethical or the moral content becomes explicit, it threatens to destroy the artistic structure, which may not be strong enough to contain it. Such an accident does not invalidate the ideas or concepts, but it does invalidate the position of these ideas or concepts in a poetic frame. No matter how noble or profound the thought, it fails to justify the shortcomings of intended artistry. There have been few poets who could set out bluntly, like Milton, "to justify the ways of God to man"—and proceed to subordinate, or to keep implicit within the structure of the poem, such an overpowering goal. Most of the Puritans were more bold than talented in their attempts to prove that art is concerned with directing the individual to apprehension; that art is therefore a means to knowledge and truth. It would seem to me that any aesthetic theory which begins by reducing art to a means is doomed to failure; but the double handicap of Puritan theory was that the end, in their eyes, was redemption from human depravity. And such an end was so important to them that the intended balance was often sacrificed almost eagerly!

Robert Frost's poetic theory, quite at odds with Puritan aesthetics, is nevertheless colored by his Yankee heritage of Puritan teaching. His own belief in poetry as "a clarification of life" seems to have close relation to the ideas of that other New England individualist who was not ashamed to find certain virtues in Puritan concepts provided they could be inspired with flexible vitality. Emerson said that the poet's creative power was derived from his passionate craving to express the existence of harmonies and correspondences which are discovered between the present and the past, the seen and the unseen, the material and the spiritual. And Frost's personal description of his poetic intent seems closely related to this explicit statement from Emerson:

"For it is not metres, but a metre-making argument that makes a poem —a thought so passionate and alive that like the spirit of a plant or an animal it has an architecture of its own, and adorns nature with a new thing. The thought and the form are equal in the order of time, but in the order of genesis the thought is prior to the form. The poet has a new thought; he has a whole new experience to unfold; he will tell us how it is with him, and all men will be the richer in his fortune."

But there are nice differences between the Puritan desire to redeem the individual from his human depravity, the Emersonian desire to interpret "harmonies" as proofs of human divinity, and the Frostian desire to make poetry "a clarification of life." The Puritan argument is as debatable as the Emersonian argument. Frost prefers to leave to prose those questions suitable for debate; he finds poetry at its best when its statements and observations touch realms of spiritual values where there is no room for argument: sorrow, aspiration, loneliness, love. Songs are built around everlastingly perceived values which are true for us all. It is not the poet's function to argue that "in Adam's fall we sinned all" or that in Christ's death we were all saved. There are still a few of us who consider these as subjects for controversy. And Frost points out that we don't join together in singing an argument. But in human nature there are certain enduring qualities and everlasting truths which permit us to join in hymns of joy or threnodies of sorrow. Let a poem be written on these themes and it will last, says Frost, for "it will forever keep its freshness as a petal keeps its fragrance." So he has generally avoided venturing into poetic argument. Poetry deals with a meaning and truth which may clarify the mingled goodness and badness of life without growing too optimistic over the existence of the one or too pessimistic over the existence of the other. And these overtones of significance, implicit in the poem, are permissible as subject matter for connotation on that higher plane of poetry. This is Frost's answer to those who ask how poetry can become a "clarification of life" without making meaning an end in itself.

THE POEM AND THE READER

We are now in a better position to consider that aspect of a poem which faces outward to find response from the reader. The poet's aim and purpose represents one plane of the poem; but when he has achieved release from the need which prompted his utterance, the test of the poem has just begun. For the poem, "Twice blest," faces not only toward the poet and his intent but also toward the reader and the understanding which the reader brings to it. And the difference between these two planes of reference is obviously the difference between the poet's experience and that artfully limited expression of the poet's experience which is projected in the content of the poem so that it may be shared by the reader. Thus the content must risk the danger of being further restricted by the reader's experience and perceptivity. These determine the degree to which the poem's inherent merit and meaning may be appreciated. Thus considered, the poem is something more than a mere expression of release for the poet; its function is not fulfilled as an autonomous unit if it has merely satisifed the poet. For the poem must be able to establish a basic correspondence between writer and reader. If it fails to contain statement intelligible at least to the intelligent, and intelligible to the degree that there is a common ground in experience for general agreement as to its denotation, then it does not succeed as a poem, no matter how certain the poet may be that his intent is stated. A good example of such failure is Eliot's most famous poem, "The Waste Land," and Eliot acknowledged its failure on this score when he felt obliged to supplement it with his erudite and esoteric footnotes. Such a solution of the problem through the trappings of explanation invalidates the required autonomy of the poem and delivers it immediately into the arms of the snobbish or the academic readers who may keep it limping about on flimsy crutches of praise and elucidation. The simple fact remains: the poem, as such, fails to satisfy the initial requirement of autonomy, regardless of its curiously ingenious pastiche craftsmanship.

But the reader's recognition of correspondence between himself and the poet in that denotation which is essential to autonomy may readily be seen to constitute only the first step in appreciation. It might be called the foundation on which are built higher levels of perception. For it is the nature of poetry to convey or suggest moods and meanings apart from the explicit and recognized meanings. And this difference between that suggested and that stated is the difference between connotation and denotation. Although connotation may be made in several different ways, Robert Frost has concentrated in theory and practice on his two particular favorites: on the tone or sound of words themselves or in their relation to each other— and on the symbolic meaning of words and phrases. To him these seem to be the basic elements in the poetry of any age and remain today the most fecund of the "old ways to be new." The first of these he has elaborated as "the sound of sense," as opposed to the more limited poetic theory concerning the musical sounds. To Frost . . . this phrase of his tends to deprecate the *merely* musical: the sensuously titillating, at one extreme, or the spiritually moving, at the other extreme. And it will be seen that his theory of "the sound of sense" is quietly antipathetic to that particular attitude toward sound in poetry which was the preoccupation of Poe or to Lanier's theory of musical notation in verse.

The connotation of words and phrases in their double meaning is, of course, related to the age-old poetic use of comparisons, implied or stated. But Frost has developed his theory of the metaphor in a manner peculiar to his poetry. And this development will also be considered at length in a subsequent chapter.

It is essential to remember that these different aspects of poetry which have been considered separately in this analysis of Frost's theory are completely merged in the artistic expression so that they become inseparable parts of the whole. On consideration, the reader may be conscious of the manner in which the content of the poem faces inward toward the poet's experience and outward toward the experience of the reader. And our enjoyment may be heightened by the hints at experiences greater than those which find their way into the poem. This is part of the charm of poetry. But no reader is fair to the poem if he insists on crowding the poet with questions as to what is "back of it." Frost is willing to laugh at anyone "who stands at the end of a poem ready in waiting to catch you by both hands with enthusiasm and drag you off your balance over the last punctuation mark into more than you meant to say." His answer is always ready: "If I had wanted you to know, I should have told you in the poem."

F. SCOTT FITZGERALD

****

The short, unhappy life of F. Scott Fitzgerald can best be studied from Arthur Mizener's *The Far Side of Paradise* (Boston, 1951; revised, 1965), supplemented by Sheila Graham's autobiographical *Beloved Infidel* (New York, 1958), Nancy Milford's revelatory biography of Fitzgerald's wife, in *Zelda* (New York, 1970), and Budd Schulberg's fictionized *The Disenchanted* (New York, 1950). Reminiscent accounts by expatriate friends include Morley Callaghan's *That Summer in Paris* (New York, 1964), Ernest Hemingway's *A Moveable Feast* (New York, 1964), and John Dos Passos's *The Best Times* (New York, 1966). The most persuasive critical volumes are James E. Miller, Jr.'s *F. Scott Fitzgerald: His Art and Technique* (New York, 1964) and Milton Hindus's *F. Scott Fitzgerald: An Introduction and Interpretation* (New York, 1968). Essays have been collected by Alfred Kazin in *F. Scott Fitzgerald: The Man and His Work* (Cleveland, Ohio, 1951), by Arthur Mizener in *F. Scott Fitzgerald: A Collection of Critical Essays* (Englewood Cliffs, N.J., 1963), and by Ernest

323

Lockridge in *Twentieth Century Interpretations of The Great Gatsby* (Englewood Cliffs, N.J., 1968). Noteworthy essays include Maxwell Geismar's "F. Scott Fitzgerald: Orestes at the Ritz," *The Last of the Provincials* (Boston, 1943), Charles Weir, Jr.'s "An Invite with Gilded Edges," *Virginia Quarterly Review,* XX (April 1944), pp. 100–113, William Troy's "Scott Fitzgerald: The Anatomy of Failure," *Accent,* VI (August 1945), pp. 56–60, John W. Aldridge's "Fitzgerald: The Horror and the Vision of Paradise," in *After the Lost Generation* (New York, 1951), Richard Chase's brief but brilliant commentary in *The American Novel and Its Tradition* (New York, 1957), and W. M. Frohock's chapter on Fitzgerald in *Strangers to This Ground* (Dallas, Tex., 1961). Wright Morris in this essay speaks as one novelist of another.

THE FUNCTION OF NOSTALGIA

Wright Morris

****

"Can't repeat the past?" he cried incredulously. "Why of course you can."
　　　　　　　　　　　　　　　　　　　　—Jay Gatsby

The "subject" of Wolfe, Hemingway, and Faulkner, however various the backgrounds, however contrasting the styles, pushed to its extremity, is nostalgia. But it was left to F. Scott Fitzgerald, the playboy, to carry this subject to its logical conclusion. In fictional terms this is achieved in *The Great Gatsby*. In personal terms it is achieved in *The Crack-up*.

Thomas Wolfe's nostalgia, his cry of *"Lost, lost, lost—"* was a cliché he neither transformed nor examined, but Fitzgerald made of it a form of consciousness. Nostalgia, quite simply, is *all* there is. In plumbing this sentiment to its depths, rather than merely using or abusing it, Fitzgerald dropped to the deep, dead-end center of the American mind. He let his line out deeper than Hemingway and Twain, deeper than the Mississippi and the Big Two-Hearted River, down to that sunken island that once mythically flowered for Dutch sailors' eyes.

That was where the dream began, he tells us, that still pandered to men in whispers: that was where man held his breath in the presence of this brave new world. It was Fitzgerald, dreaming of paradise, who was compelled to an aesthetic contemplation that made of nostalgia, that snare and delusion, a work of art.

> Through all he said, even through his appalling sentimentality, I was reminded of something—an elusive rhythm, a fragment of lost words, that I had heard somewhere a long time ago. For a moment a phrase tried to take shape in my mouth and my lips parted like a dumb man's, as though there was more struggling upon them than a wisp of startled air. But they made no sound and what I had almost remembered was uncommunicable, forever.

That elusive rhythm, that fragment of lost words, that ghostly rumble among the drums are now, thanks to Fitzgerald, a part of our inheritance. Those who were never there will now be there, in a sense more compelling than those who were there, since they will face it, and grasp it, in the lucid form of Fitzgerald's craft. Like Gatsby, he, too, believed in the green light, in the orgiastic future that recedes before us, leading by a strange circumambulation back into the past, back to those dark fields of the republic where the Big Two-Hearted River flows into the Mississippi, and the Mississippi flows, like time, into the territory ahead. Time and the river flow backward, ceaselessly, into the mythic past. Imperceptibly, the function of nostalgia reduces the ability to function.

The power and sources of nostalgia lie beyond the scalpel. Nostalgia sings in the blood, and with age it grows thicker, and when all other things fail it joins men in a singular brotherhood. Wherever they live in the present, or hope to live in the future, it is in the past that you will truly find them. In the past one is safely out of time but not out of mind.

Nostalgia is a limbo land, leading nowhere, where the artist can graze like a horse put to pasture, feeding on such clover of the past as whets the appetite. The persuasive charm of Fitzgerald is that this clover, which he cups in both hands, is almost chokingly sweet. We dip our faces into the past as into the corridor of that train, homeward bound at Christmas, the air scented with luggage, coonskin coats, and girls with snow melting in their hair. But it has a greater virtue still. It is inexhaustible. It is the artist—not the vein of nostalgia—that gives out or cracks up.

As a man steps from the wings of his own imagination to face the music, the catcall facts of life, Fitzgerald stepped forward in the *The Crack-up* to face the audience. It is a *performance*. He knows the crowd is openly snickering at him. For this curtain call, however, which nobody asked for, an apologetic *apologia pro vita sua,* he has reserved the few lines, implicit but unspoken, in his books. Self-revelation as revealing as this, many found contemptible. Not that he had cracked up—that was common-place—but that in cracking up he had owned up to it. Nor would that have really mattered if, in owning up, he hadn't owned anything. But Fitzgerald *knew*. That was the hell of it. He was the first of his generation to know that life was *absurd*.

It is fitting that Fitzgerald, the aesthete of nostalgia, of the escape clause without question, should be the first American to formulate his own philosophy of the absurd. But nostalgia, carried to its conclusion, leads no-where else. Had he been of the temperament of Albert Camus, he might have been the first to dramatize the idea that the only serious question is sui-cide. Fitzgerald sensed that. In admitting to the concept that life is absurd he confronted the one idea totally alien to American life.

Therein lies the to-be or the not-to-be, the question of suicide. He goes on to tell us, in a further installment, why he had lost the ability to function. He had become *identified* with the objects of his horror and his compassion. He was in the shadow of the hallucinative world that destroyed Van Gogh. He points out that when Wordsworth came to the conclusion that "there had passed away a glory from the earth," he was not compelled to pass away with it, nor did Keats, dying of consumption, ever give up his dream of being among the great poets.

Fitzgerald had been able, for many years, to hold certain opposing ideas in his mind, but when he had lost the ability to *function* he had cracked up. The myth of Sisyphus became his personal myth. While he had the resources, he was able to function in spite of the futility of the situation, but when he had overdrawn these resources, he cracked up. He lay at the bottom of the incline, the rock on top of him.

Some time before World War II made it fashionable, Fitzgerald had discovered the philosophy of the absurd. Different from the philosophers themselves, he lived and died of it. He had come, alone and prematurely, on a fact that was not yet fashionable: he had come on the experience rather than the cliché. The absurd, for Fitzgerald, was truly absurd, though noth-ing is ever *truly* absurd if enough clever people seem to believe in it.

The Crack-up is a report from the limbo of the All-American mind. At the point where these two opposing dreams cross, the dreamer cracks up. Such crack-ups are now common, the Nervous Breakdown now joins the All-American in a fraternity that goes deeper than his gold lodge pin. But only Fitzgerald, twenty years ago, was both sufficiently aware and sufficiently honest to look through this crack into the limbo of the mind and report what he saw.

Those deformed souls in Dante's hell, the Diviners, each so strangely twisted between the chin and the chest that they had to come backward, since seeing forward was denied them, symbolize the schizoid state of the American mind. In this confusion of dreams it is the orgiastic future that engages our daytime talents and energy, but the dark fields of the past is where we take refuge at night. The genius and progressive drive of a culture that is both the reproach and the marvel of the world is crossed with a prevailing tendency to withdraw from the world and retire into the past.

The ability of most Americans to *function*—as artists, citizens, or men of business—resides in their capacity to indulge in one of these conflicting dreams at a time; to be all for the future, that is, or all for the past. Sometimes the rhythm is that of an alternating current, the past and the present playing musical chairs, but when they meet in the mind at the same moment, that mind is apt to lose its ability to function. It cracks up.

No more curious or revealing statement than *The Crack-up* exists in our literature. After such knowledge Rimbaud wrote *A Season in Hell,* then stopped writing, and Dostoevski gave us his *Notes from Underground.* The author of *Gatsby,* reduced to "clowning it" in the pages of *Esquire,* had to strike a "tone" that would permit him to commit hari-kiri in public. It is this tone, plus the setting of *Esquire,* that gave the statement its curious reputation. The sober-minded need not take it "seriously." What Fitzgerald *knew* can be discounted because of *where* and *how* he said it. Most readers found, as Fitzgerald had predicted, such self-revelation contemptible, and dismissed the testimony of *The Crack-up* as an ill-bred example of self-pity. It is the *giving up,* rather than the cracking up, that we find inadmissible.

The author of *The Great Gatsby,* stripped of his luck and his illusions, neither had the guts to keep it to himself nor the talent to forge new ones. In this complaint there is some justice. It is an indictment, however indirect, of the limbo of Nostalgia. But where others merely lost themselves, Fitzgerald knew where he was lost. He knew what they did not know—that from this maze there was no way out. It was neither fatigue nor the aimless wandering, but the paralysis of will that grew out of the knowledge that the past was dead, and that the present had no future. The Good, that is, in the last analysis, might not prevail. It led him to a conclusion not unlike that reached by Twain in *What is Man?*

> So what? This is what I think now: that the natural state of the sentient adult is a qualified unhappiness.

Does it seem a tame monster—after the sense of horror—to be frightened by? Qualified unhappiness, if we examine it, is the opposite of *un*qualified happiness. It is the opposite, that is, of Jay Gatsby, of the Goethe-Byron-Shaw medley of Fitzgerald, of J. P. Morgan and Beauclerk, and St. Francis of Assisi, of all those giants who were now relegated, as Fitzgerald tells us, to the junk heap—the same junk heap where we will find the shoulder pads worn for one day on Princeton football field, and that overseas cap never worn overseas.

It seems a little hard to believe—hard in the sense that we would rather not believe it—but Master Hemingway, whose nostalgia is carefully de-mothed before he wears it, bears witness to those things in *Death in the Afternoon.* Speaking of the Good Old Days, those times when men were men and bulls were tremendous, he sums up the past, the mythic past, in these words:

> Things change very much and instead of great athletes only children play on the high-school teams now . . . they are all children without honor, skill or virtue, much the same as these children who now play football, a feeble game it has become, on the high-school team and nothing like the great, mature, sophisticated athletes in canvas elbowed jerseys, smelling vinegary from sweated shoulder pads, carrying leather head guards, their moleskins clotted with mud, that walked on leather-cleated shoes that printed in the earth along beside the sidewalk in the dusk, a long time ago.

The irony of this passage neutralizes the charge of sentiment that it carries. Hemingway mocks it: Fitzgerald admits to its crippling effects. It seems manly to mock; it seems unmanly to acknowledge the effects. Sure, we felt that way long ago, but certainly we are not suffering from it *now.* It is this knowledge, knowledge that we *are* suffering, that deprives Fitzgerald, in spite of his power, of the manly persuasion the reader derives from Hemingway. It is classically summarized in Fitzgerald's observation that "the rich are different from us," and Hemingway's characteristic rejoinder, "Sure, they've got more money."

That kind of answer, that kind of simplification, understandably pleases the athlete in each of us, grown old, who feels that he has put such childish things behind him, and is not dying of them. Fitzgerald knew otherwise. Not only Tom Buchanan, but every American, in his fashion, went through life with invisible goal posts on his shoulders, torn from the green sod on an afternoon of never-to-be-forgotten triumph.

But was this unqualified happiness? It takes some doing; it takes the total recall of what the *ambiance* of such a dream is like, one wherein the towers of Princeton, the Triangle Club, the football shoulder pads, and the overseas cap are all transmuted by the dreamer into pure gold. On the night the world changed, Fitzgerald tells us, he hunted down the specter of womanhood and put the final touch to the adolescent season in hell. On just the other side, a mere year or two later, was paradise.

It was not the vein that played out in Fitzgerald—since nostalgia is inexhaustible—but when he knew *where* he was, when he grasped the situation, he stopped mining it. In this sense, as in many others, he reminds us of James. As a man he continued to indulge in it, but as an artist he knew it was finished. He did not know, however, that art can sometimes begin where life stops. He was too profoundly and incurably committed to life itself.

"I have not at last become a writer only," he said, but he had been suckled too long on the sweet pap of life, and the incomparable milk of wonder, to be more than a writer in name only, resigned to that fact.

> . . . just as the laughing stoicism which has enabled the American negro to endure the intolerable conditions of his existence—so in my case there is a price to pay. I do not any longer like the postman, nor the grocer, nor the editor, nor the cousin's husband, and he in turn will come to dislike me, so that life will never be very pleasant again, and the sign *Cave Canem* is hung permanently just above my door.

Knowing better as an artist could not salvage him as a man. The depths of nostalgia, the slough of its despair, offered him no key to the facts of the absurd. They merely became absurd in their turn, like everything else. Having drawn on the resources he no longer possessed, and having mortgaged his remains, body and soul, he did what his countrymen now do by the thousands—he cracked up. He was different in the sense that he knew what had happened—and owned up to it.

Both *The Great Gatsby* and *Tender Is the Night* are full of personal revelation and prophecy. It is why they have such haunting immediacy when read today. The issues are still alive in anyone who is still alive. The cost of consciousness, like the expense of greatness, sometimes defies accounting, but we can see it more clearly in the life of Fitzgerald than in his works. In the life it *showed*. He was not a subtle craftsman on that plane. He was one of the lost, the truly lost; his flight established the classic itinerary, including that final ironic genuflection on the bright tan prayer rug of the Riviera.

If we reflect that Fitzgerald, while writing *Gatsby,* might have been one of the playboys in *The Sun Also Rises*—one of them, not merely with them, observing—his achievement is almost miraculous. The special charm of *Gatsby,* its durable charm, is that of recollection in tranquillity. The enchantment itself seems to come from the distance the narrator stands from the experience. The book has a serene, almost elegiac air; there is nothing frenetic or feverish about it, and the fires of spring, no longer burning, have filled the air with the scent of leaf smoke. The dark fields of the republic are bathed in a moonlit, nostalgic haze.

Fitzgerald was not yet thirty, but he was aware how well he had written. But the *meaning* of the book, its haunting tonal range, opening out into the past and portending the future, went considerably beyond both intentions and performance, into prophecy. This lucid moment of balance, when he was both fully engaged with living, yet aesthetically detached, may account for the higher level of performance than he achieved in *Tender Is the Night*. The later book is wiser, consciously wiser; the sun that had been rising is now setting, and Dick Diver is plainly stigmatized with the author's sense of his own predicament. But both books, however different in conception, close in such a manner that they blend together. The final scenes have a fugue-like harmony—an invocation in the one, a requiem in the other, to the brooding fertile god of nostalgia, dearer than life *in* life, and, at the moment of parting, sweeter than death.

Where else, we might ask, in the literature of the world has the landscape of nostalgia, created by the author, served as the refuge for both the author and his characters? Dick Diver, having had his enchantment, having listened to the dream that pandered in whispers, and having been compelled to an aesthetic contemplation he has finally come to understand, returns to the dream of West Egg, knowing the green light will be missing from Daisy's dock, knowing that the future now stands behind him, with its tail in its mouth.

So he drifts from Buffalo to Batavia, from Geneva, New York, to Hornell, where that dream of a girl, Nicole, finally lost track of him. But Fitzgerald was too honest, now, to kill him off, or to let him die He also knew too much to let the reader see him alive. So he deposited him in that limbo where there is neither a past nor a future, the world of nostalgia where he was an aimless drifter himself. Up ahead, but not too far ahead now, faint but persistent as the music from Gatsby's parties, the blinking marsh lights of *The Crack-up* were all that shimmered in the dark fields of the republic.

My own happiness in the past often approached such an ecstacy that I could not share it even with the person dearest to me but had to walk away in the quiet streets and lanes with only fragments of it to distill into little lines in books. . . .

What sort of happiness was this? *Un*qualified happiness, of course. The kind Gatsby had the moment he kissed Daisy, seeing, at the same moment, out of the corner of his eye that the blocks in the sidewalk seemed to form a ladder to the stars. At that moment the incomparable milk of wonder over-flowed his cup of happiness, and Fitzgerald was able to distill it into more than a few little lines. In *Gatsby* this gift of hope is made flesh, and the promise is still one that Americans live by.

But the quiet streets and lanes of nostalgia soon turn upon themselves, a labyrinth without an exit, both a public madness and a private ecstacy. The strings of reminiscence tangle on themselves, they spin a choking web around the hero, and he must either surrender himself, without a struggle, or risk cracking up. Fitzgerald ran the risk. He did not, with Wolfe's adolescent bellow, try to empty the house of its ghosts by shouting, nor did he, like Faulkner, generate his escape with an impotent rage. He simply faced it. But he faced it too late. Having dispensed with his resources, he cracked up. The artist in him, as self-aware as Henry James, went on plying its hand, sharpening all the old pencils, but the man within him had died of nostalgia. The sign of *Cave Canem* that hung above his door meant exactly what it said.

ERNEST HEMINGWAY

****

Hemingway is said not to have liked the explanation of his writings provided by Philip Young in *Ernest Hemingway* (New York, 1952; revised, 1956), from which an important chapter is printed here; he preferred Carlos Baker's less psychologically probing *Ernest Hemingway: The Writer as Artist* (New York, 1952), and, after Hemingway's death, Baker was encouraged to write a complete "authorized" biography, *Ernest Hemingway: A Life Story* (New York, 1969). Lilian Ross's *Portrait of Hemingway* (New York, 1961), A. E. Hotchner's *Papa Hemingway: A Personal Memoir* (New York, 1966), and Hemingway's own autobiographical *A Moveable Feast* (New York, 1964) tell more of the man than of his writings. Among the better essays on Hemingway are John Peale Bishop's "The Missing All," *Virginia Quarterly Review*, XIII (Winter 1937), pp. 107–121, Malcolm Cowley's "A Portrait of Mr. Papa," *Life*, XXVI (January 14, 1948), pp. 86–101, W. H. Frohock's "Ernest Hemingway: Violence and Discipline," *Southwest Review*, XXXII (Winter and Spring 1947), pp.

89–97, 184–193, and Edmund Wilson's "Ernest Hemingway: Bourbon Gauge of Morality," *Atlantic Monthly,* CLXIII (July 1939), pp. 36–46. These and other essays have been collected by John K.M. McCaffery in *Ernest Hemingway: The Man and His Work* (Cleveland, Ohio, 1950); still others will be found in Robert F. Weeks's *Hemingway: A Collection of Critical Essays* (Englewood Cliffs, N.J., 1962). Also of interest are Edwin Fussell's "Hemingway and Mark Twain," *Southwest Review,* XIV (Summer 1954), pp. 199–206, Wyndham Lewis's "The Dumb Ox," *American Review,* VI (June 1964), pp. 289–312, Gertrude Stein's "Ernest Hemingway and the Post-War Decade," *Atlantic Monthly,* CLII (August 1933), pp. 197–208, and Ray B. West's "Ernest Hemingway: The Failure of Sensibility," *Sewanee Review,* LIII (Winter 1949), pp. 120–135.

THE HERO AND THE CODE

Philip Young

****

I did not care what it was all about. All I wanted to know was how to live in it.

THE SUN ALSO RISES

" 'AYEE!' suddenly screamed the lieutenant," in a story of Hemingway's called "A Natural History of the Dead."

> "You have blinded me! You have blinded me!"
> "Hold him tight," said the doctor. "He is in much pain. Hold him very tight."

As doctors are not always available, and are often of little use, holding tight against pain is an exercise which was to become important to the Heming-

From *Ernest Hemingway: A Reconsideration,* by Philip Young. Copyright © 1966 by Philip Young. The Pennsylvania State University Press, 1966.

way hero. Considerably broadened and elaborated, the effort to hold tight developed into what is known as the Hemingway "code." But the hero is still only a sketch, and before one is in the best position to understand the code, there are some more stories in Hemingway's "first forty-nine"—in addition to the Nick ones—which fill out the main body of that man a good deal. These are "I"-stories, written in the first person. None of them contains anything that basically conflicts with the outline already given of Adams; several of them do deepen, broaden, and clarify the pattern that has been working itself out. We have already seen one of these, for the "Author's Introduction" to *In Our Time* appears in Hemingway's collected stories as "On the Quai at Smyrna." This was the sketch in which appear the women who will not give up their dead babies, and, among other things, the mules with broken forelegs drowning in the shallow water—pictures hard for the author to get rid of, apparently, since he uses them twice again in *Death in the Afternoon.* This brief piece was already significant as a forecast, because "I got so I dreamed about things," which is of course what was to happen to Nick.

That this "I" *is* Nick becomes perfectly apparent in the war story called "Now I Lay Me" which appeared in *Men without Women.* Here the "I" says he cannot sleep unless he has a light, as Nick could not in "A Way You'll Never Be," and although still in uniform he is not in the fighting, as before. If there is any doubt that this is Nick it disappears when, remembering his parents as he tries to occupy himself on a sleepless night, he hears his father call him by that name.

The story itself presents the picture of the man who cannot sleep "for thinking," and Nick tells of the many ways he has of occupying his mind harmlessly on these bad nights, the principal one of which is to reconstruct trout streams he has fished. In terms which clearly identify this part of the story with the trip to "Big Two-Hearted River," Hemingway tells how he pictures this fishing. And thus we suspect again that we were right when we saw that fishing trip as conducted against a background of escape and terror, that it was taken as a device to keep Nick from going crazy, for that is its clearly stated function here. The swamp he could not enter is present again, too, this time it is a place where he runs out of bait and has to cut up one of the trout he caught, to use pieces of it to catch other trout with. This, like the wounded hyena in *Green Hills of Africa* which eats its own intestines, is a cannibalism which Hemingway does not approve: the swamp is a "bad place" again.

Then Nick remembers scenes from his childhood (in which the doctor's wife comes off poorly again) and he tries to pray for his parents. However, when he is very badly off he fails at this. Then he has a conversation with an Italo-American named John; we learn that Nick has been wounded twice and that he is now a lieutenant. John decides that it is "worry" that keeps Nick awake all night: "You ought to get married, Signor Tenente. Then you wouldn't worry." Signor Tenente suspects that the problem is not so simple and he ends thinking somewhat wryly of John: "He was very certain about marriage and knew it would fix up everything."

"In Another Country," also from *Men without Women,* is another first-person-Nick story. It is moving as a story, and is interesting for the way in which it points two directions in the development of the hero. Looking backward, it deals with his physical recuperation in Milan from the second of what have now become two separate woundings. The story has to do with a fellow patient in a hospital, a wounded major whose young wife has just died suddenly. The major gives the hero the reverse of the advice he got from John above: "A man must not marry. . . . If he is to lose everything, he should not place himself in a position to lose that." Nick is still unwell, but—and here the story points forward—for once Hemingway is not concerned so much with Nick alone. It is the major's pain that the story is about; the hero's wounds have been established, and there are now two casualties. This points to *The Sun Also Rises,* where a whole "lost generation" is wounded as Jake (Nick) is wounded, and even to *A Farewell to Arms* where Catherine Barkley is, just as Brett Ashley was in the former novel, a woman completely unsettled by the fact that she had a former lover die in the war under terrible circumstances. The pattern thus is broadening for a while, and what was the history of Nick becomes—loosely speaking—the history of a war generation. This story presents, too, the same picture of Milan to be found in *A Farewell to Arms—In Einem Andern Land* was the title for the German edition of that novel. Unless one knows the origin of this title its point is lost. In the story it is a brutal allusion to the major's bereavement, and in the novel it was—in the German—an even more terrible commentary. Catherine Barkley, everyone remembers, had an idyllic and very moving love affair with Lt. Henry in the novel; they lived together in Italy and in Switzerland, out of wedlock, until she died in childbirth. The allusion is to Marlowe's *Jew of Malta:*

> Thou hast committed—
> Fornication: but that was in another country,
> And, besides, the wench is dead.

Another new development turns up in a story from the same *Men without Women* called "An Alpine Idyll." The tale is again told in the first person and returns, very likely, to the skiing trip Nick was on in "Cross Country Snow." Again the story is utterly without a "point" if not seen in the context of the other stories. Nick and a friend named John are drinking before dinner in a Swiss inn and they hear the tale of a Swiss peasant whose wife (whom he loved) had died some months before. The peasant kept her body in his woodshed all winter, waiting for the earth to thaw before digging her grave. Every night he cut wood in this shed, and

> "When I started to use the big wood she was stiff and I put her up against the wall. Her mouth was open and when I came into the shed at night to cut up the big wood, I hung the lantern from it."

This is the pattern of "The Killers" again, and again the rest of the story —and its focus—centers on the responses of the listeners. A change in these responses is the point: Nick is hardening a little. When the story is over he is silent. John says, "How about eating?" Nick says, "You order," and talks on for a moment with the innkeeper about the peasant. Where his reaction to the incident in "The Killers" was a horrified inability even "to think about it," and a desire to get completely out of that town, he is now not so sensitive. John repeats impatiently, "Say . . . how about eating?" Nick replies, "All right," and the story ends. A shell is growing over the wound to protect it a little; by 1940 the defense will be nearly impenetrable.

The "I" of these stories is Nick Adams; it is also possible to see correspondences between Nick Adams and Ernest Hemingway, the man who for a long time after his wounding in Italy in 1917 could not sleep with the light out. A glance at the briefest paragraph biographies which exist of the author would convince most people of this; the last of the Nick stories, "Fathers and Sons" from *Winner Take Nothing,* is itself convincing enough. This story, with its title presumably from Turgenev, presents to us a relatively placid thirty-eight-year-old Nick, who is driving in a car with his son. Nick is thinking about his father, the doctor (who is described precisely as photographs represent Dr. Hemingway), and specifically he is thinking about the man's death. (Hemingway's father died suddenly in 1928.) This death is very troubling to Nick; it was violent and unpleasant, and "he could not write about it yet, although he would." We now get our first real insight into how Hemingway writes, and why—among other reasons—he is a writer:

> Nick had loved him very much and for a long time. Now, knowing how it had all been, even remembering the earliest times before things had gone badly was not good remembering.

Here then is another instance of violence that is "not good remembering" —"the handsome job the undertaker had done on his father's face had not blurred in his mind." Such scars are permanent, and if time will not take the

soreness from them, writing "fiction" will, and it is the only way, apparently, he can purge himself of the image that bothers him. Literature,
thought to be in some way cathartic for its audience, becomes here supreme
catharsis for its creator:

> If he wrote it he could get rid of it. He had gotten rid of many
> things by writing them. But it was still too early for that.

Readers had to wait until *For Whom the Bell Tolls* (where Robert Jordan is
to explain carefully and at length what is the matter here) for it to be no
longer too early for Hemingway to get rid of this unpleasant piece of his
past, but his method is already apparent: the things which have happened to
Nick which are "not good remembering" he has been writing away in his
stories. That he has had some success with this treatment is suggested by the
composure which—most of the time—the hero as Jordan is able to maintain.

In the "Fathers and Sons" story the author plays subtly with the complexities of the relationships between generations—Nick's relationship to his
father and to his son. Just as the doctor taught his son to hunt so Nick is
teaching his; and just as the doctor was not much help with other problems,
Nick cannot communicate either. Nick remembers what he learned from an
Indian girl named Trudy—a reasonable change from the "Prudie" of "Ten
Indians," which would have inappropriate connotations now:

> "You think we make a baby?"
> "I don't think so," he said.
> "Make plenty baby what the hell."

But when Nick's son wants to know what the Ojibway Indians were like
Nick can only tell him "It's hard to say." ("Could you say she did first what
no one has ever done better?") Also the boy causes trouble by wanting to
visit his grandfather's grave, a place he has never been. This is precisely
what Nick does not want to think about, but his son is insistent and the
story ends with the father giving in: "I can see we'll have to go." There is
the merest suggestion of defeat in this; Nick is failing as his father had
failed, and the present must acknowledge the past.

It is pretty clear, then, that Nick Adams has much in common with Ernest Hemingway. This is not to say that he "is" Hemingway. He is, rather, a
projection of certain kinds of problems Hemingway is deeply concerned to
write about, and write out. Nick is a special kind of mask.

But there are masks which do not disguise or conceal very much, and
some of them, like the theatrical masks of ancient Greece, actually serve to

identify character and even to reveal it. These are odd distortions indeed in that they are really clarifications. By selection among the possibilities of personality, and by emphasis of some few of its features, they expose as well as hide, disclose as well as cover. Nick Adams is such a mask, for while he presents to the world a face that is not exactly Hemingway's, he also projects chiefly that one set of problems, revolving around the wound, that is the best aid in our recognition of Hemingway. Thus Nick is a simplification, and to that extent a distortion, of the actual complex personality, but is also a kind of revelation.

In much the same way, the adventures which Hemingway has related are not always wholly and strictly autobiographical, for literature does not work with life in quite that way. But investigation shows that actually many of the stories about Nick are very literal translations of some of the most important events in Hemingway's own life, and that remarkably little has been changed in the telling. Indeed it would be hard to think of even an "autobiographical writer" (like Thomas Wolfe, for instance) who has given a more exact account of his own experience and of his own personality in the guise of prose fiction.

Obviously something was needed to bind the wounds these experiences had made in that personality, and for that reason there is another "I" in the Hemingway short stories, a minor figure who is a kind of spectator or reporter. This man is not Hemingway, is not the hero, and is not even a center of interest. Instead he observes a man, not the hero either, who in importance rates second only to the hero himself. This man changes form—his profession and even his nationality—much more than the hero ever will, but he is still a consistent character in that he always introduces and exemplifies a theme in the author's work that has rightly been made a good deal of. This is the Hemingway "code"—a "grace under pressure." It is made of the controls of honor and courage which in a life of tension and pain make a man a man and distinguish him from the people who follow random impulses, let down their hair, and are generally messy, perhaps cowardly, and without inviolable rules for how to live holding tight.

This code is very important because the "code hero," as he might be called, presents a solution to the problems of Nick Adams, of the true "Hemingway hero," and for Hemingway it is about the only solution. He finds this code operating among various sporting figures, and he has written several short stories the intention of which is to formulate the basic principles of the code by illustrating it in action. These stories deal as is logical for a man broken from respectability, with such persons of disrepute as a fixed prizefighter and a crooked gambler who, since they have the code, are admired by the man who created them.

As Hemingway once put it, "There is honor among pickpockets and honor among whores. It is simply that the standards differ." What Hemingway is thinking of becomes most clear in a story like "Fifty Grand," which presents this honor-and-courage-among-thieves concept in pristine form. Here, as in some other stories, the reportorial "I" is part of the retinue which surrounds a prizefighter named Jack. This welterweight (who has passed his prime, knows he is going to lose his championship, does not want to fight any more, is lonesome for his wife and daughters, and needs money) bets fifty thousand dollars on his opponent. But he has been double-crossed by some gamblers who were party to this arrangement, and in the fight, as he is well on his way to successful defeat, he is viciously fouled by his opponent. If he succumbs to the low blow, which has him in the most intense and debilitating pain, he will win the fight on the basis of the obvious misdeed of the challenger. This would be to lose fifty thousand dollars and to go back on his part in the swindle; it would be dishonorable. And so he denies he has been fouled, makes the supreme effort, and sticks it out until he has fouled the challenger into writhing submission. Thus he loses the fight, wins his bet, establishes his courage and maintains his honor.

Here is the reverse of the wealthy homosexual fighter in "Mother of a Queen" (who lets the bones of his mother be thrown into the public bone heap, and will not take offense when "I" insults him in every manner he can think of). This, Hemingway seems to be saying flatly in "Fifty Grand," is life and the way to live in it. These are the conditions of life, which is a highly compromising affair, and a man can be a man only by making a deal with it, and then sticking to his bargain if it kills him.

But it is a mistake to think of this man as the "Hemingway hero"; he is rather an illustration of qualities which are essential to that legend. It is a mistake because it confuses and blurs the clear picture Hemingway has been presenting. This is the same confusion that mistakes the hero, as practically all readers have done, for the outlaw Harry Morgan of *To Have and Have Not*. Actually, both this fighter and Morgan represent the man with the code, who is another man entirely. Sometimes the real hero talks like the code hero, but the distinction between them can always be made, and to consider this prizefighter, or Manuel ("The Undefeated" bullfighter), or the pirate Morgan as the Hemingway hero not only blurs and confuses what Hemingway makes fairly clear, but also and directly brings about a thoroughly erroneous misconception of that man. Too, it is to fail to see that actually Hemingway has, since 1924, been writing out the story of one man who is based on himself. The real hero is the protagonist who was up in Michigan, and was wounded while fighting as an American in the Italian army, who lived and wrote fiction in Paris; he is the generic Nick Adams.

All the proper parts fit this single story; the hero is—with each successive appearance—the sum of what has happened to him. And psychically it all happened to Hemingway, who was never a bullfighter (although he tried it), or a prizefighter (although he has tried that too), or a one-armed, two-daughtered smuggler of rum and Chinamen (which he has apparently never tried at all). The hero is a twentieth-century American, born, raised and hurt in the Middle West, who like all of us has been going through life with the marks his experiences have made on him. The outlaws and professional sportsmen who have appeared along the way have taught the man to try to live by a code, but they are not the man himself. What is more, the lessons have not always been of the sort the hero can immediately master.

This becomes clear in a story called "The Gambler, the Nun and the Radio" (1933), which presents in one place both the hero and the man who exemplifies the code, and presents them as two quite different people. The generic Nick is here called Mr. Frazer; he is having a "bad time" again, and he is also, once more, to be associated with the man who wrote the story. The man whom the hero admires and studies is this time an unlucky gambler.

In 1930 Hemingway was in an automobile accident with John Dos Passos in Montana and had his arm very badly broken. In *Green Hills of Africa* (1935) Hemingway is thinking of this pain when he writes that the most "horror" he can remember going through he experienced

> one time in a hospital with my right arm broken off short between the elbow and the shoulder . . . the points of the bone having cut up the flesh of the biceps until it finally rotted, swelled, burst, and sloughed off in pus. Alone with the pain in the night of the fifth week of not sleeping . . . .

This story, "The Gambler, the Nun and the Radio," transfers the injury to the leg, and tells again of that horror, and of life in the hospital. It introduces a gambler—honorable, according to the standards of his trade, and courageous—and a nun. Frazer, who is a writer, is having the bad time described just above, but, the author reminds us, this is not the first time for him: "His nerves went bad at the end of five weeks. . . . Mr. Frazer had been through this all before. The only thing which was new to him was the radio. . . . He was learning to listen to it without thinking." Clearly, this is our old friend Nick, and Montana (the location of the radio stations he hears signing off at night suggests this, as the songs he hears suggest 1930; Hemingway's own recuperation took place in a Billings hospital).

Part of the story (the radio part) has to do with the hero's insomnia, his bad nerves ("when the nurse goes out I cry an hour, two hours. It rests me . . .") and with his attempts to avoid thinking, which, as always, makes things worse. Alcohol ("the giant killer") and the radio are what keep him going; he plays the radio all night so quietly no one else can hear it. Lying there and concentrating on the sounds becomes another rite with which to keep off the "evil spirits"—the equivalent of fishing on the Big Two-Hearted, in actuality or retrospect. The sickness leads him as before to an extreme bitterness, and it is in this story that the nadir of Hemingway's pessimism is reached in the famous passage: "Religion is the opium of the people . . . and music . . . and sexual intercourse . . . and bread is the opium of the people."

This is one way to live in the world, but it is not a very good way. The nun, Sister Cecilia, represents an alternative: she believes she knows what the world is all about and she lives in it by her faith. Though quite charming, this faith seems also naïve to Frazer; it is Cayetano, the petty gambler, who has the code to live by. The Hemingway hero, although he greatly admires this code, is not able to live by it. He is too tortured, too thoughtful, too perplexed, for that; he cries at night—a grown man. This is incredibly "messy" of him, and messiness is above all things forbidden. The hero tries, but he cannot make it, and that is why the stories which most clearly present the code have a separate character to enact it. It is Cayetano (who is in much more pain—as the hero points out—than Mr. Frazer) who does not show a single sign of his suffering.

This Cayetano, a Mexican cardplayer, is brought into the hospital nearly dead, with two bullets in his stomach. A detective accompanies him and tries to get the dying man to name the one who shot him. The detective tries to convince the cardsharp: "It's all right to tell who shot you. . . . You don't have to act like a moving picture." This is just the point; he does. Frazer, acting as interpreter, obliges the detective by trying too: "One can, with honor, denounce one's assailant," he says. But he doesn't really believe it and is proud when Cayetano "won't talk." The Mexican suffers on alone at the hospital; his only visitors come to see him involuntarily, and are really partisan to the man who shot him. He suffers without a word of complaint and finally Frazer talks to him again, and learns he has been shot by a man who lost money to him in a crooked card game: the gambler will cheat at cards as Jack will throw a fight, but he will not take revenge on the man who nearly killed him for cheating, or even complain of it—as Jack would not back out of his agreement—and he insists, when he is praised for his courage, "it was nothing."

These distinctions between the hero and his tutor—the man whom the hero emulates, who has the code he would like to operate by, too—clarify and enrich a couple of Hemingway's later, best, and best-known stories, "The Short Happy Life of Francis Macomber," and "The Snows of Kilimanjaro." These long pieces are both clearly rituals—one a ceremonial triumph over fear, the other a rite in which a part of the self is destroyed. They present certain difficulties, however, because of new approaches the author takes to his material and his protagonists.

Hemingway distinguishes between "true" and "made up" stories. Both of these, though they make a great deal of use of autobiography, are of the latter type. These are personal stories, but they are not literal ones: in Africa in the thirties Hemingway did not die of an infection, nor was he chased by a lion and murdered by his wife. The protagonists are also "made up" in that in each of the stories the writer adopts a mask that is for once grotesque, incongruous and truly a distortion. Both Macomber and Harry (in "Kilimanjaro") exaggerate some of the hero's weaknesses, failings, shortcomings. Harry is a failure as a man and as a writer; Macomber is a coward. It is very much as if Hemingway were getting rid of things again, but here he has a new and hypercritical attitude toward his protagonists. These men are not wholly unfamiliar as leading players in Hemingway, but they are outside the pattern he has built up in that they are seen through a glass very darkly or, to put it more cogently, they are seen *in* a glass—as in a Coney Island funhouse—which mirrors into magnified prominence the growing paunch, the receding hairline, the sagging muscles.

"The Short Happy Life" is, among other things, a detailed description of the process of learning the code, and its value. Macomber, a coward, is seen in the story learning the code from Wilson, his professional hunting guide. He is presented as being very ignorant of this code at first, but he painfully learns it and he becomes a man in the process. Before that happens, however, it is apparent that Hemingway is using this plot of instruction in courage and honor to comment, as he has not done to this extent before, on many other things. The story is, for example, an analysis of the relationship between the sexes in America, and the relationship is in the nature of declared warfare.

D. H. Lawrence, in an essay on *The Scarlet Letter,* launches an assault on the American male who, he says, has lost his "ithyphallic authority" over the American woman who therefore dominates, and then destroys, what is left. "The Short Happy Life" develops and intensifies Lawrence's notion with enormous skill. Francis Macomber, when under the tutelage of the hunter Wilson, learns courage and honor and to embrace the code; he attains his manhood, which is not the same thing as losing his virginity or reaching his twenty-first birthday, as the characters point out. When he attains this manhood he regains the ithyphallic authority he had lost and his wife, now panicky herself in her new role, must destroy him literally. Before he became a man she had committed adultery almost in his presence, knowing him helpless to stop her. When he becomes a man, and she can no longer rule him in the Lawrencian sense, she sends a bullet to the base of his skull.

Obviously Macomber is something different from a grown Nick Adams. What he represents instead is an extreme projection of the hero's problem of fear, and the story about him delineates an imagined solution to that problem. Unlike Macomber, Hemingway has never "just shown himself, very publicly, to be a coward." When he wrote the story he had just very publicly and maliciously been *called* one by Gertrude Stein, and he retaliated in *Green Hills of Africa* by calling her a "bitch." But the facts of the matter seem to indicate that she had no more reason for calling him "yellow" than that she knew it was an insult which would hurt, for reasons to be examined later.

However, Macomber is not so extreme a projection that all contact with the hero and with Hemingway is lost. He is given Hemingway's age, his physical fitness and athleticism, and his expertness with big game and fish. Hemingway's own guide, "Pop," in *Green Hills of Africa,* looks very like Wilson, hunting guide of the story. In addition, the extraordinary "immediateness" with which the sensations of fear are felt by Macomber suggests the extent to which the author can feel for him. And fear, after all, was one of the hero's central problems.

In the course of this story Macomber completely disgraces himself in the presence of his wife and his hunting guide before he learns the code and gets their respect. He has already committed the unpardonable sin when the story opens: he ran away from a charging lion, and, as Wilson says, this is just not done—"no white ever bolts." Not only that, but he goes right on committing errors: he asks Wilson not to talk about his cowardice to other people, which for the professional hunter and possessor of the code's book of etiquette is "supposed to be bad form," and after Wilson insults him he spinelessly apologizes. In addition he cannot control his wife, who hounds him without mercy. He gets a chance to redeem himself when it comes time to track down another lion, which he has wounded badly, into the long grass where it is lying in wait for those who shot it. Again he completely fails. First he wants to send the inadequately armed African "boys" in after the animal; when Wilson refuses to be party to this type of slaughter he suggests they leave the beast hidden in the grass. He could not have stumbled on a more wretched violation: someone else might meet him unawares and be killed; even if this doesn't happen it is certain that the lion is in considerable pain and it is their responsibility to do for him what cannot be done for human beings. And then finally when they search out the lion Macomber bolts again, running wildly in panic. When the three hunters are reassembled in their car after Wilson has killed the charging, wounded animal, Margot Macomber celebrates the complete loss of her husband's authority by leaning in front of him and kissing Wilson on the mouth. That night Macomber wakes to discover that she is not in her cot in the tent with him. "He lay awake with that knowledge for two hours." This adultery does not go against Wilson's code, it is explained; as a matter of fact he "carried a double size cot on safari to accommodate any windfalls he might receive." The standards of the people who hired him were his standards: "They were his standards in all except the shooting."

It is these shooting standards which Macomber finally learns and which, although they eventually bring his death, make him, for a short happy lifetime, a man. Quite suddenly, when shooting a buffalo, he loses his fear. The lessons Wilson has been teaching him are now his own. A wounded buffalo gets away, as the lion did, and he can hardly wait to go in after the beast. In 1942 Hemingway, writing from his own experience an introduction to a collection of war stories, had this to say: "Cowardice . . . is almost always simply a lack of ability to suspend the functioning of the imagination." In "the Macomber affair" he explains it the same way:

> It had taken a strange chance of hunting, a sudden precipitation into action without opportunity for worrying beforehand, to bring this about with Macomber . . . .

Fear was "gone like an operation. Something else grew in its place . . . . Made him into a man."

Putting the bad things into words may rid one of them, but it is necessary for the earlier-initiated Wilson to make clear to the hero that the same principle applies to so good a thing as the transformation into manhood, which he has just undergone: "You're not supposed to mention it. . . . Doesn't do to talk too much about all this. Talk the whole thing away." Wilson, warming now to Macomber, also confides to him the "thing he had lived by"—a quotation from Shakespeare. The extent to which Hemingway is able to project himself even into this maladroit and cowardly Macomber is further brought out by these lines from Shakespeare. Hemingway revealed this, perhaps without realizing it, in 1942 in the introduction just cited, when he told how in the war, in 1917, *he* learned courage from a British officer (Wilson is very British) who gave him, Hemingway, the identical message Wilson here gives Macomber:

> "By my troth, I care not; a man can die but once; we owe God a death and let it go which way it will he that dies this year is quit for the next.

The climax of the story has come, and Macomber's wife, recognizing the hero's new life as a man, cannot tolerate a long denouement. When her husband goes in after the wounded buffalo she—ostensibly aiming for the beast in order to save Francis—kills him. Wilson prepares to exonerate her with explanatory photographs, and the story ends. Wilson is like the prizefighter Jack and the gambler Cayetano: he kills—as a profession—animals who have scarcely a chance of protecting themselves; he consorts with rich decadents and adopts their moral standards; he lives a lonely, compromised life. But out of this he builds the code he lives by; he has his courage and his honor: he would not "squeal" on his employer; he will not leave the animals he has pitilessly shot to suffer. He bristles with "won't do," "isn't done," "bad form," and "not supposed to." Macomber—not the hero, but like the heroes in this—admires the code and tries to attain to it. He makes the grade, but it costs him his life.

As the Macomber story dramatizes the casting off of fear, so "The Snows of Kilimanjaro" is a fictionalized purge, in this case of a whole set of guilty feelings. In this story Hemingway sourly depicts himself (there is no question of his identity here) as an abject failure, dying from an infected scratch five thousand miles from home. The story, interesting in many ways, is probably less tight and dramatic than the Macomber one, but it attempts different things. There is a conscious and explicit use of symbolism—which is unusual with Hemingway—and there is plenty of ammunition for the critics who have attacked the author for his preoccupation with death, for that preoccupation is at least ostensibly what the story is about.

There is no question that the protagonist Harry is the Hemingway hero. Harry is a writer, as was Nick, in "Fathers and Sons"; he has thought a great deal about death, as Hemingway has done; he thinks of his part in the war against the Austrians, whom Nick fought; he later went skiing with them, as Nick did; he tries to keep himself from thinking, as Nick tried; he had "sold vitality, in one form or another, all his life," which is a way of putting what Hemingway has done; Africa was "where he had been happiest," which the author says of himself in the *Green Hills;* and no one who had read that book, in which the second Mrs. Hemingway figures, could fail to suspect in Harry's wife a less flattering portrait of the same woman. Here, too, is again the man who had "seen the things that he could never think of and later still he had seen much worse." Harry is very autobiographically drawn: he thinks of that room in Paris (in which Verlaine once lived) where "he had written the start of all he was to do." He also identifies himself, to knowing readers of F. Scott Fitzgerald at least, by remembering "poor Julian" and his romantic awe of the rich. Julian had "started a story once that began, 'The rich are very different from you and me.' And someone had said to Julian, 'Yes, they have more money.' " The story was Fitzgerald's "Rich Boy," and it was Hemingway who made the joke.

There cannot be many writers who stick so rigorously to writing of themselves, and—in a way—*for* themselves, asking at the same time that an audience take an interest in what they are doing, and at the same time succeeding with a very large part of the reading public, as Hemingway has done. "The Snows of Kilimanjaro" is widely read, widely anthologized, widely interpreted, and Hollywood paid an all-time high for it. But despite the fact that several versions of what the story is about are meaningful, this is also a special and private thing: a statement by Hemingway of his aesthetic aims and beliefs, and an analysis of his past failures as a writer of prose fiction, as of 1936, a year that was crucial for him. It can be read quite legitimately as a more objective and generalized piece of prose—as, for instance, a story of a writer dying on a safari in Africa, reviewing his past and previewing his future. But for its author it was an exercise in personal and aesthetic hygiene.

Hemingway, in his curious, stubborn way, is a writer absolutely and wholeheartedly dedicated to his craft, and—as is the way of serious artists —he dreams of immortality for some of what he has done; he thinks, that is, of writing prose that will be so pure that it can never spoil, that will be permanent. In 1935, in *Green Hills of Africa,* a nonfiction work which supplies considerable background for "Kilimanjaro," he spoke of "how far prose can be carried if anyone is serious enough and has luck." As for luck, no man knows, but about his prose Hemingway has been serious enough— grimly, humorlessly serious—and in a book on writing and bullfighting he had announced that he himself was trying very hard to write prose "which would be as valid in a year or in ten years or, with luck and if you stated it purely enough, always."

But as ample evidence testifies, 1936 found Hemingway disgusted with himself. This story itself is eloquent. He had been chasing about Europe and Africa with the very rich (though they "were dull and they drank too much, or they played too much backgammon"), and drinking all the time himself ("so much that he blunted the edge of his perceptions"). Seven fallow years had elapsed since he had written a first-rate book, *A Farewell to Arms* ("and you made an attitude that you cared nothing for the work you used to do, now that you could no longer do it"). Two marriages, both discussed in the story, had ended badly; he felt he had been disgracing himself in *Esquire:* "He had destroyed his talent by not using it, by betrayals of himself and what he believed in, by drinking so much . . . by laziness, by sloth, and by snobbery, by pride and by prejudice. . . . It was a talent all right but instead of using it, he had traded on it." To make matters worse, "for years" death had "obsessed him": now in horror he sees the possibility that it could all end like this—on an idle safari, haggling with a woman. And very little stated purely enough to last always.

It is apparent that in 1936 Hemingway made a mighty resolve that he would not, like poor Julian, really be "wrecked," that he would achieve permanence despite everything he had done wrong. First it was necessary to inventory everything in the place, and to heave out everything that could not be used—to destroy it, indeed, to spit it away—before such a radical development as occurs in a book of the next year, *To Have and Have Not,* could be possible. "The Snows of Kilimanjaro" does precisely these things, in addition to describing the goal which is the reason for the stocktaking, and presenting the purge itself, and even to prophesying what the final outcome will be.

"The Snows" opens with an introductory paragraph whose symbols state the better part of the story's meaning:

> Kilimanjaro is a snow covered mountain 19,710 feet high, and is said to be the highest mountain in Africa. Its western summit is called the Masai "Ngàje Ngài," the House of God. Close to the western summit there is the dried and frozen carcass of a leopard. No one has explained what the leopard was seeking at that altitude.

This passage can seem enigmatic enough, and has been widely struggled with, but in this context its meaning emerges. It is Hemingway himself who "explains" what the leopard sought at that altitude: the House of God, immortality. The leopard did not quite make the summit, and in his mysterious attempt to reach it perished, but his carcass is dried and frozen: he died in the attempt to save his soul, as all who try it must, but frozen at that temperature and height the leopard is permanent. He can never spoil, and he presents a perfect contrast to Harry with a gangrened leg, who is very mortal, rotting fast away in the heat of the lowlands.

But Harry is a writer, and if a thing is said perfectly, if it is perfectly immaculate, if it is said "purely enough," it cannot spoil, it is frozen, and its author is immortal. At the end of the story Harry "dreams" of a plane which comes to rescue the writer, and after taking off with the pilot he sees, there, "unbelievably white in the sun . . . the square top of Kilimanjaro. And then he knew that there was where he was going." It is at this precise moment that Hemingway reorganizes his forces, and leaves the hero as failure for what he hopes will be greater things. Leaving it back under the mosquito bar with the woman who has come in some way to stand for all the things which corrupted it, he here sloughs off his contaminated skin— "somehow he had gotten his leg out and it hung down alongside the cot. The dressings had all come down and she could not look at it."

WILLIAM FAULKNER

****

Almost everyone agrees that Olga W. Vickery's *The Novels of William Faulkner* (Baton Rouge, La., 1959; revised 1964), Cleanth Brooks's *William Faulkner: The Yoknapatawpha County* (New Haven, Conn., 1963), and Michael Millgate's *The Achievement of William Faulkner* (New York, 1966) are among the most valuable guides to Faulkner's writing. Many readers find also indispensable Dorothy Tuck's *Handbook to Faulkner* (New York, 1964) for which I supplied what I hope is a useful introduction. George Marion O'Donnell's early and often reprinted "Faulkner's Mythology," *Kenyon Review,* I (Summer 1939), pp. 285–299, has been the source of important controversy, including Malcolm Cowley's essay printed here and Robert Penn Warren's important two-part critique of "Cowley's Faulkner," *New Republic,* LXV (August 12 and 16, 1946), pp. 176–180, 234–237. No satisfactory full-length biography of Faulkner has yet been published, though John Faulkner's *My Brother Bill* (New York, 1963) and brother Murry C. Faulkner's *The Faulkners of Mississippi* (Baton Rouge, La.

1967) are filled with interesting reminiscent anecdotes; complete biographical studies are being prepared, one by Joseph Blotner, the other by Carvel Collins; either should be worth careful attention. Some of the best writings about Faulkner have been collected by Frederick J. Hoffman and Olga W. Vickery in *William Faulkner: Three Decades of Criticism* (East Lansing, Mich., 1960) and by Robert Penn Warren in *Faulkner: A Collection of Critical Essays* (Englewood Cliffs, N.J., 1967), but there is more writing about him still to come, for Faulkner remains to many readers the most exciting writer of his generation.

INTRODUCTION TO . . . FAULKNER

Malcolm Cowley

✳✳✳

1

When the war was over—the other war—William Faulkner went back to Oxford, Mississippi. He had served in the Royal Air Force in 1918. Now he was home again and not at home, or at least not able to accept the postwar world. He was writing poems, most of them worthless, and dozens of immature but violent and effective stories, while at the same time he was brooding over his own situation and the decline of the South. Slowly the brooding thoughts arranged themselves into the whole interconnected pattern that would form the substance of his later novels.

This pattern, which almost all his critics have overlooked, was based on what he saw in Oxford or remembered from his childhood; on scraps of

From *The Portable Faulkner* edited by Malcolm Cowley. Copyright 1946 by The Viking Press, Inc. Reprinted by permission of The Viking Press, Inc. and Chatto and Windus Ltd.

family tradition (the Falkners, as they spelled the name, had played their part in the history of the state); on kitchen dialogues between the black cook and her amiable husband; on Saturday-afternoon gossip in Courthouse Square; on stories told by men in overalls squatting on their heels while they passed around a fruit jar full of white corn liquor; on all the sources familiar to a small-town Mississippi boy—but the whole of it was elaborated, transformed, given convulsive life by his emotions; until, by the simple intensity of feeling, the figures in it became a little more than human, became heroic or diabolical, became symbols of the old South, of war and reconstruction, of commerce and machinery destroying the standards of the past. There in Oxford, Faulkner performed a labor of imagination that has not been equaled in our time, and a double labor: first, to invent a Mississippi county that was like a mythical kingdom, but was complete and living in all its details; second, to make his story of Yoknapatawpha County stand as a parable or legend of all the Deep South.

For this double task, Faulkner was better equipped by talent and background than he was by schooling. He was born in New Albany, Mississippi, on September 25, 1897; he was the oldest of four brothers. The family soon moved to Oxford, where he attended the public school, but without being graduated from high school. For a year after the war, he was a student at the University of Mississippi, in Oxford, where veterans could then matriculate without a high-school diploma; but he neglected his classroom work and left without taking a degree. He had less of a formal education than any other good writer of his time, except Hart Crane—less even than Hemingway, who never went to college, but who learned to speak three foreign languages and studied writing in Paris from the best masters. Faulkner taught himself, largely, as he says, by "undirected and uncorrelated reading." Among the authors either mentioned or echoed in his early stories and poems are Keats, Balzac, Flaubert, Swinburne, Mallarmé, Wilde, Housman, Joyce, Eliot, Sherwood Anderson, and E. E. Cummings, with fainter suggestions of Hemingway (in a fishing scene), Dos Passos (in the spelling of compound words), and Scott Fitzgerald. The poems he wrote in those days were wholly derivative, but his prose from the beginning was a form of poetry; and in spite of the echoes it was always his own. He traveled less than any of his writing contemporaries. After a succession of odd jobs in Oxford, there was a brief period when he lived in New Orleans with Sherwood Anderson and met the literary crowd—he even satirized them in a very bad early novel, *Mosquitoes;* then he went to New York, where for a few unhappy months he clerked in a bookstore; in 1925 he took a long walking trip in Europe without settling on the Left Bank. Except for recent visits to Hollywood, the rest of his life has been spent in the town where he grew up, less than forty miles from his birthplace.

Although Oxford, Mississippi, is the seat of a university, it is even less of a literary center than was Salem, Massachusetts, during Hawthorne's early years as a writer; and Faulkner himself has shown an even greater dislike than Hawthorne for literary society. His novels are the books of a man who broods about literature but doesn't often discuss it with his friends; there is no ease about them, no feeling that they come from a background of taste refined by argument and of opinions held in common. They make me think of a passage from Henry James's little book on Hawthorne:

> The best things come, as a general thing, from the talents that are members of a group; every man works better when he has companions working in the same line, and yielding to the stimulus of suggestion, comparison, emulation. Great things of course have been done by solitary workers; but they have usually been done with double the pains they would have cost if they had been produced in more genial circumstances. The solitary worker loses the profit of example and discussion; he is apt to make awkward experiments; he is in the nature of the case more or less of an empiric. The empiric may, as I say, be treated by the world as an expert; but the drawbacks and discomforts of empiricism remain to him, and are in fact increased by the suspicion that is mingled with his gratitude, of a want in the public taste of a sense of the proportion of things.

Like Hawthorne, Faulkner is a solitary worker by choice, and he has done great things not only with double the pains to himself that they might have cost if produced in more genial circumstances, but sometimes also with double the pains to the reader. Two or three of his books as a whole and many of them in part are awkward experiments. All of them are full of over-blown words like "imponderable," "immortal," "immutable," and "immemorial" that he would have used, with more discretion, or not at all, if he had followed Hemingway's example and served an apprenticeship to an older writer. He is a most uncertain judge of his own work, and he has no reason to believe that the world's judgment of it is any more to be trusted; indeed, there is no American author who would be justified in feeling more suspicion of "a want in the public taste of a sense of the proportion of things." His early novels were overpraised, usually for the wrong reasons; his later and in many ways better novels have been obstinately condemned or simply neglected; and in 1945 all his seventeen books were out of print, with some of them unobtainable in the second-hand bookshops.

Even his warm admirers, of whom there are many—no author has a higher standing among his fellow novelists—have sometimes shown a rather vague idea of what he is trying to do; and Faulkner himself has never explained. He holds a curious attitude toward the public that appears to be lofty indifference (as in the one preface he wrote, for the Modern Library edition of *Sanctuary),* but really comes closer to being a mixture of skittery distrust and pure unconsciousness that the public exists. He doesn't furnish information or correct misstatements about himself (most of the biographical sketches that deal with him are full of preposterous errors). He doesn't care which way his name is spelled in the records, with or without the "u" —"Either way suits me," he said. Once he has finished a book, he is apparently not concerned with the question how it will be presented, to what sort of audience; and sometimes he doesn't bother to keep a private copy of it. He said in a letter, "I think I have written a lot and sent it off to print before I actually realized strangers might read it." Others might say that Faulkner, at least in those early days, was not so much composing stories for the public as telling them to himself—like a lonely child in his imaginary world, but also like a writer of genius.

2

Faulkner's mythical kingdom is a county in northern Mississippi, on the border between the sand hills covered with scrubby pine and the black earth of the river bottoms. Except for the storekeepers, mechanics, and professional men who live in Jefferson, the county seat, all the inhabitants are farmers or woodsmen. Except for a little lumber, their only product is baled cotton for the Memphis market. A few of them live in big plantation houses, the relics of another age, and more of them in substantial wooden farmhouses; but most of them are tenants, no better housed than slaves on good plantations before the Civil War. Yoknapatawpha County—"William Faulkner, sole owner and proprietor," as he inscribed on one of the maps he drew—has a population of 15,611 persons scattered over 2,400 square miles. It sometimes seems to me that every house or hovel has been described in one of Faulkner's novels; and that all the people of the imaginary county, black and white, townsmen, farmers, and housewives, have played their parts in one connected story.

He has so far written nine books wholly concerned with Yoknapatawpha County and its people, who also appear in parts of three others and in thirty or more uncollected stories. *Sartoris* was the first of the books to be published, in the spring of 1929; it is a romantic and partly unconvincing novel, but with many fine scenes in it, like the hero's visit to a family of independent pine-hill farmers; and it states most of the themes that the author would later develop at length. *The Sound and the Fury* was written before *Sartoris,* but wasn't published until six months later; it describes the fall of the Compson family, and it was the first of Faulkner's novels to be widely discussed. The books that followed, in the Yoknapatawpha series, are *As I Lay Dying* (1930), about the death and burial of Addie Bundren; *Sanctuary* (1931), always the most popular of his novels; *Light in August* (1932), in many ways the best; *Absalom, Absalom!* (1936) about Colonel Sutpen and his ambition to found a family; *The Unvanquished* (1938), a book of interrelated stories about the Sartoris dynasty; *The Wild Palms* (1939), half of which deals with a convict from back in the pine hills; *The Hamlet* (1940), a novel about the Snopes clan; and *Go Down, Moses* (1942), in which Faulkner's theme is the Negroes. There are also many Yoknapatawpha stories in *These Thirteen* (1931) and *Dr. Martino* (1934), besides other stories privately printed (like "Miss Zilphia Gant") or published in magazines and still to be collected or used as episodes in novels.

Just as Balzac, who seems to have inspired the series, divided his *Comédie Humaine* into "Scenes of Parisian Life," "Scenes of Provincial Life," "Scenes of Private Life," so Faulkner might divide his work into a number of cycles: one about the planters and their descendants, one about the townspeople of Jefferson, one about the poor whites, one about the Indians (consisting of stories already written but never brought together), and one about the Negroes. Or again, if he adopted a division by families, there would be the Compson-Sartoris saga, the still unfinished Snopes saga, the McCaslin saga, dealing with the white and black descendants of Carothers McCaslin, and the Ratliff-Bundren saga, devoted to the backwoods farmers of Frenchman's Bend. All the cycles or sagas are closely interconnected; it is as if each new book was a chord or segment of a total situation always existing in the author's mind. Sometimes a short story is the sequel to another earlier novel. For example, we read in *Sartoris* that Byron Snopes stole a packet of letters from Narcissa Benbow; and in "There Was a Queen," a story published five years later, we learn how Narcissa got the letters back again. Sometimes, on the other hand, a novel contains the sequel to a story; and we discover from an incidental reference in *The Sound and the Fury* that the Negro woman whose terror of death was described in "That Evening Sun" had later been murdered by her husband, who left her body in a ditch for the vultures. Sometimes an episode has a more complicated history. Thus, in the first chapter of *Sanctuary,* we hear about the Old Frenchman place, a ruined mansion near which the people of the neighborhood had been "digging with secret and sporadic optimism for gold which the builder was reputed to have buried somewhere about the place when Grant came through the country on his Vicksburg campaign." Later this digging for gold served as the subject of a story published in the *Saturday Evening Post:* "Lizards in Jamshyd's Courtyard." Still later the story was completely rewritten and became the last chapter of *The Hamlet.*

As one book leads into another, Faulkner sometimes falls into inconsistencies of detail. There is a sewing-machine agent named V. K. Suratt who appears in *Sartoris* and some of the later stories. By the time we reach *The Hamlet,* his name has changed to Ratliff, although his character remains the same (and his age, too, for all the twenty years that separate the backgrounds of the two novels). Henry Armstid is a likable figure in *As I Lay Dying* and *Light in August;* in *The Hamlet* he is mean and half-demented. His wife, whose character remains consistent, is called Lula in one book and Martha in another; in the third she is nameless. There is an Indian chief named Doom who appears in several stories; he starts as the father of Issetibeha and ends as his grandson. The mansion called Sutpen's Hundred was built of brick at the beginning of *Absalmon, Absalom!* but at the end of the novel it is all wood and inflammable except for the chimneys. But these errors are comparatively few and inconsequential, considering the scope of Faulkner's series; and I should judge that most of them are afterthoughts rather than oversights.

All his books in the Yoknapatawpha saga are part of the same living pattern. It is this pattern, and not the printed volumes in which part of it is recorded, that is Faulkner's real achievement. Its existence helps to explain one feature of his work: that each novel, each long or short story, seems to reveal more than it states explicitly and to have a subject bigger than itself. All the separate works are like blocks of marble from the same quarry: they show the veins and faults of the mother rock. Or else—to use a rather strained figure—they are like wooden planks that were cut not from a log, but from a still living tree. The planks are planed and chiseled into their final shapes, but the tree itself heals over the wound and continues to grow. Faulkner is incapable of telling the same story twice without adding new details. In the present volume I wanted to use part of *The Sound and the Fury,* the novel that deals with the fall of the Compson family. I thought that the last part of the book would be most effective as a separate episode, but still it depended too much on what had gone before. Faulkner offered to write a very brief introduction that would explain the relations of the characters. What he finally sent me is the much longer passage here printed as an appendix: a genealogy of the Compsons from their first arrival in this country. Whereas the novel is confined to a period of eighteen years ending in 1928, the genealogy goes back to the battle of Culloden in 1745, and forward to the year 1945, when Jason, last of the Compson males, has sold the family mansion, and Sister Caddy has last been heard of as the mistress of a German general. The novel that Faulkner wrote about the Compsons had long ago been given its final shape; but the pattern or body of legend behind the novel—and behind all his other books—was still developing.

Although the pattern is presented in terms of a single Mississippi county, it can be extended to the Deep South as a whole; and Faulkner always seems conscious of its wider application. He might have been thinking of his own novels when he described the ledgers in the commissary of the McCaslin plantation, in *Go Down, Moses*. They recorded, he said, "that slow trickle of molasses and meal and meat, of shoes and straw hats and overalls, of plowlines and collars and heelbolts and clevises, which returned each fall as cotton"—in a sense they were local and limited; but they were also "the continuation of that record which two hundred years had not been enough to complete and another hundred would not be enough to discharge; that chronicle which was a whole land in miniature, which multiplied and compounded was the entire South."

3

"Tell about the South," says Quentin Compson's roommate at Harvard, a Canadian named Shreve McCannon who is curious about the unknown region beyond the Ohio. "What's it like there?" he asks. "What do they do there? Why do they live there? Why do they live at all?" And Quentin, whose background is a little like that of Faulkner himself and who sometimes seems to speak for him—Quentin answers, "You can't understand it. You would have to be born there." Nevertheless, he tells a long and violent story that he regards as the essence of the Deep South, which is not so much a mere region as it is, in Quentin's mind, an incomplete and frustrated nation trying to relive its legendary past.

The story he tells—I am trying to summarize the plot of *Absalom, Absalom!*—is that of a mountain boy named Thomas Sutpen whose family drifted into the Virginia lowlands, where his father found odd jobs on a plantation. One day the father sent him with a message to the big house, but he was turned away at the door by a black man in livery. Puzzled and humiliated, the mountain boy was seized by the lifelong ambition to which he would afterward refer as "the design." He too would own a plantation with slaves and a liveried butler; he would build a mansion as big as any of those in the Tidewater; and he would have a son to inherit his wealth.

A dozen years later, Sutpen appeared in the frontier town of Jefferson, where he managed to obtain a hundred square miles of land from the Chickasaws. With the help of twenty wild Negroes from the jungle and a French architect, he set about building the largest house in northern Mississippi, using timbers from the forest and bricks that his Negroes molded and baked on the spot; it was as if his mansion, Sutpen's Hundred, had been literally torn from the soil. Only one man in Jefferson—he was Quentin's grandfather, General Compson—ever learned how and where Sutpen had acquired his slaves. He had shipped to Haiti from Virginia, worked as overseer on a sugar plantation and married the rich planter's daughter, who had borne him a son. Then, finding that his wife had Negro blood, he had simply put her away, with her child and her fortune, while keeping the twenty slaves as a sort of indemnity.

In Jefferson, Sutpen married again. This time his wife belonged to a pious family of the neighborhood, and she bore him two children, Henry and Judith. He became the biggest cotton planter in Yoknapatawpha County, and it seemed that his "design" had already been fulfilled. At this moment, however, Henry came home from the University of Mississippi with an older and worldlier new friend, Charles Bon, who was in reality Sutpen's son by his first marriage. Charles became engaged to Judith. Sutpen learned his identity and, without making a sign of recognition, ordered him from the house. Henry, who refused to believe that Charles was his half-brother, renounced his birthright and followed him to New Orleans. In 1861, all the male Sutpens went off to war, and all of them survived four years of fighting. Then, in the spring of 1865, Charles suddenly decided to marry Judith, even though he was certain by now that she was his half-sister. Henry rode beside him all the way back to Sutpen's Hundred, but tried to stop him at the gate, killed him when he insisted on going ahead with his plan, told Judith what he had done, and disappeared.

But Quentin's story of the Deep South does not end with the war. Colonel Sutpen came home, he says, to find his wife dead, his son a fugitive, his slaves dispersed (they had run away even before they were freed by the Union army), and most of his land about to be seized for debt. Still determined to carry out "the design," he did not even pause for breath before undertaking to restore his house and plantation to what they had been. The effort failed and Sutpen was reduced to keeping a crossroads store. Now in his sixties, he tried again to beget a son; but his wife's younger sister, Miss Rosa Coldfield, was outraged by his proposal ("Let's try it," he had said, "and if it's a boy we'll get married"); and later poor Milly Jones, with whom he had an affair, gave birth to a baby girl. At that Sutpen abandoned hope and provoked Milly's grandfather into killing him. Judith survived her father for a time, as did the half-caste son of Charles Bon by a New Orleans octoroon. After the death of these two by yellow fever, the great house was haunted rather than inhabited by an ancient mulatto woman, Sutpen's daughter by one of his slaves. The fugitive Henry Sutpen came home to die; the townspeople heard of his illness and sent an ambulance after him; but old Clytie thought they were arresting him for murder and set fire to Sutpen's Hundred. The only survival of the conflagration was Jim Bond, a half-witted creature who was Charles Bon's grandson.

"Now I want you to tell me just one thing more," Shreve McCannon says after hearing the story. "Why do you hate the South?"—"I don't hate it," Quentin says quickly, at once. "I dont hate it," he repeats, speaking for the author as well as himself. *I dont hate it,* he thinks, panting in the cold air, the iron New England dark; *I dont I dont hate it! I dont hate it!*

The reader cannot help wondering why this somber and, at moments, plainly incredible story had so seized upon Quentin's mind that he trembled with excitement when telling it and felt it revealed the essence of the Deep South. It seems to belong in the realm of Gothic romances, with Sutpen's Hundred taking the place of the haunted castle on the Rhine, with Colonel Sutpen as Faust and Charles Bon as Manfred. Then slowly it dawns on you that most of the characters and incidents have a double meaning; that besides their place in the story, they also serve as symbols or metaphors with a general application. Sutpen's great design, the land he stole from the Indians, the French architect who built his house with the help of wild Negroes from the jungle, the woman of mixed blood whom he married and disowned, the unacknowledged son who ruined him, the poor white whom he wronged and who killed him in anger, the final destruction of the mansion like the downfall of a social order: all these might belong to a tragic fable of Southern history. With a little cleverness, the whole novel might be explained as a connected and logical allegory, but this, I think, would be going far beyond the author's intention. First of all he was writing a story, and one that affected him deeply, but he was also brooding over a social situation. More or less unconsciously, the incidents in the story came to represent the forces and elements in the social situation, since the mind naturally works in terms of symbols and parallels. In Faulkner's case, this form of parallelism is not confined to *Absalom, Absalom!* It can be found in the whole fictional framework that he has been elaborating in novel after novel, until his work has become a myth or legend of the South.

I call it a legend because it is obviously no more intended as a historical account of the country south of the Ohio than *The Scarlet Letter* was intended as a history of Massachusetts or *Paradise Lost* as a factual description of the Fall. Briefly stated, the legend might run something like this: The Deep South was settled partly by aristocrats like the Sartoris clan and partly by new men like Colonel Sutpen. Both types of planters were determined to establish a lasting social order on the land they had seized from the Indians (that is, to leave sons behind them). They had the virtue of living single-mindedly by a fixed code; but there was also an inherent guilt in their "design," their way of life; it was slavery that put a curse on the land and brought about the Civil War. After the War was lost, partly as a result of their own mad heroism (for who else but men as brave as Jackson and Stuart could have frightened the Yankees into standing together and fighting back?) they tried to restore "the design" by other methods. But they no longer had the strength to achieve more than a partial success, even after they had freed their land from the carpetbaggers who followed the Northern armies. As time passed, moreover, the men of the old order found that they had Southern enemies too: they had to fight against a new exploiting class descended from the landless whites of slavery days. In this struggle between the clan of Sartoris and the unscrupulous tribe of Snopes, the Sartorises were defeated in advance by a traditional code that kept them from using the weapons of the enemy. As a price of victory, however, the Snopeses had to serve the mechanized civilization of the North, which was morally impotent in itself, but which, with the aid of its Southern retainers, ended by corrupting the Southern nation.

Faulkner's novels of contemporary Southern life continue the legend into a period that he regards as one of moral confusion and social decay. He is continually seeking in them for violent images to convey his sense of despair. *Sanctuary* is the most violent of all his novels; it is also the most popular and by no means the least important (in spite of Faulkner's comment that it was "a cheap idea . . . deliberately conceived to make money"). The story of Popeye and Temple Drake has more meaning than appears on a first hasty reading—the only reading that most of the critics have been willing to grant it. Popeye himself is one of several characters in Faulkner's novels who represent the mechanical civilization that has invaded and partly conquered the South. He is always described in mechanical terms: his eyes "looked like rubber knobs"; his face "just went awry, like the face of a wax doll set too near a hot fire and forgotten"; his tight suit and stiff hat were "all angles, like a modernistic lampshade"; and in general he had "that vicious depthless quality of stamped tin." Popeye was the son of a professional strikebreaker, from whom he had inherited syphilis, and the grandson of a pyromaniac. Like two other villains in Faulkner's novels, Joe Christmas and Januarius Jones, he had spent most of his childhood in an institution. He was the man "who made money and had nothing he could do with it, spend it for, since he knew that alcohol would kill him like poison, who had no friends and had never known a woman"—in other words, he was the compendium of all the hateful qualities that Faulkner assigns to finance capitalism. *Sanctuary* is not a connected allegory, as one critic explained it, but neither is it a mere accumulation of pointless horrors. It is an example of the Freudian method turned backward, being full of sexual nightmares that are in reality social symbols. It is somehow connected in the author's mind with what he regards as the rape and corruption of the South.

In all his novels dealing with the present, Faulkner makes it clear that the descendants of the old ruling caste have the wish but not the courage or the strength to prevent his new disaster. They are defeated by Popeye (like

Horace Benbow), or they run away from him (like Gowan Stevens, who had gone to school at Virginia and learned to drink like a gentleman, but not to fight for his principles), or they are robbed and replaced in their positions of influence by the Snopeses (like old Bayard Sartoris, the president of the bank), or they drug themselves with eloquence and alcohol (like Quentin Compson's father), or they retire into the illusion of being inviolable Southern ladies (like Mrs. Compson, who says, "It can't be simply to flout and hurt me. Whoever God is, He would not permit that. I'm a lady."), or they dwell so much on the past that they are incapable of facing the present (like Reverend Hightower of *Light in August),* or they run from danger to danger (like young Bayard Sartoris) frantically seeking their own destruction. Faulkner's novels are full of well-meaning and even admirable persons, not only the grandsons of the cotton aristocracy, but also pine-hill farmers and storekeepers and sewing-machine agents and Negro cooks and sharecroppers; but they are almost all of them defeated by circumstances and they carry with them a sense of their own doom.

They also carry, whether heroes or villains, a curious sense of submission to their fate. "There is not one of Faulkner's characters," says André Gide in his dialogue on "The New American Novelists," "who properly speaking, has a soul"; and I think he means that not one of them exercises the faculty of conscious choice between good and evil. They are haunted, obsessed, driven forward by some inner necessity. Like Miss Rosa Coldfield, in *Absalom, Absalom!* they exist in "that dream state in which you run without moving from a terror in which you cannot believe, toward a safety in which you have no faith." Or, like the slaves freed by General Sherman's army, in *The Unvanquished,* they blindly follow the roads toward any river, believing that it will be their Jordan:

> They were singing, walking along the road singing, not even looking to either side. The dust didn't even settle for two days, because all that night they still passed; we sat up listening to them, and the next morning every few yards along the road would be the old ones who couldn't keep up any more, sitting or lying down and even crawling along, calling to the others to help them; and the others—the young ones—not stopping, not even looking at them. "Going to Jordan," they told me. "Going to cross Jordan."

All Faulkner's characters, black and white, are a little like that. They dig for gold frenziedly after they have lost their hope of finding it (like Henry Armstid in *The Hamlet* and Lucas Beauchamp in *Go Down, Moses);* or they battle against and survive a Mississippi flood for the one privilege of returning to the state prison farm (like the tall convict in "Old Man"); or, a whole family together, they carry a body through flood and fire and corruption to bury it in the cemetery at Jefferson (like the Bundrens in *As I Lay Dying);* or they tramp the roads week after week in search of men who had promised but never intended to marry them (like Lena Grove, the pregnant woman of *Light in August);* or, pursued by a mob, they turn at the end to meet and accept death (like Joe Christmas in the same novel). Even when they seem to be guided by a conscious purpose, like Colonel Sutpen, it is not something they have chosen by an act of will, but something that has taken possession of them: Sutpen's great design was "not what he wanted to do but what he just had to do, had to do it whether he wanted to or not, because if he did not do it he knew that he could never live with himself for the rest of his life." In the same way, Faulkner himself writes not what he wants to, but what he just has to write whether he wants to or not.

4

He is not primarily a novelist: that is, his stories do not occur to him in book-length units of 70,000 to 150,000 words. Almost all his novels have some weakness in structure. Some of them combine two or more themes having little relation to each other, like *Light in August,* while others, like *The Hamlet,* tend to resolve themselves into a series of episodes resembling beads on a string. In *The Sound and the Fury,* which is superb as a whole, we can't be sure that the four sections of the novel are presented in the most effective order; at any rate, we can't fully understand and perhaps can't even read the first section until we have read the other three. *Absalom, Absalom!* though pitched in too high a key, is structurally the soundest of all the novels in the Yoknapatawpha series; but even here the author's attention shifts halfway through the book from the principal theme of Colonel Sutpen's ambition to the secondary theme of incest and miscegenation.

Faulkner is best and most nearly himself either in long stories like "The Bear," in *Go Down, Moses,* and "Old Man," which was published as half of *The Wild Palms,* and "Spotted Horses," which was first printed separately, then greatly expanded and fitted into the loose framework of *The Hamlet*—all three stories are included in this volume; or else in the Yoknapatawpha saga as a whole. That is, he is most effective in dealing with the total situation that is always present in his mind as a pattern of the South; or else in shorter units that can be conceived and written in a single burst of creative effort. It is by his best that we should judge him, like every other author; and Faulkner at his best—even sometimes at his worst—has a power, a richness of life, an intensity to be found in no other American novelist of our time. He has—once more I am quoting from Henry James's essay on Hawthorne—"the element of simple genius, the quality of imagination."

Moreover, he has a brooding love for the land where he was born and reared and where, unlike other writers of his generation, he has chosen to spend his life. It is ". . . this land, this South, for which God has done so much, with woods for game and streams for fish and deep rich soil for seed and lush springs to sprout it and long summers to mature it and serene falls to harvest it and short mild winters for men and animals." So far as Faulkner's country includes the Delta, it is also (in the words of old Ike Mc-Caslin)

> This land which man has deswamped and denuded and de-rivered in two generations so that white men can own plantations and commute every night to Memphis and black men own plantations and ride in jim crow cars to Chicago and live in millionaires' mansions on Lake Shore Drive, where white men rent farms and live like niggers and niggers crop on shares and live like animals, where cotton is planted and grows man-tall in the very cracks of the sidewalks, and usury and mortgage and bankruptcy and meas-ureless wealth, Chinese and African and Aryan and Jew, all breed and spawn together.

Here are the two sides of Faulkner's feeling for the South: on the one side, an admiring and possessive love; on the other, a compulsive fear lest what he loves should be destroyed by the ignorance of its native serfs and the greed of traders and absentee landlords.

No other American writer takes such delight in the weather. He speaks in various novels of "the hot still pine-winey silence of the August afternoon"; of "the moonless September dust, the trees along the road not rising soaring as trees should but squatting like huge fowl"; of "the tranquil sunset of October mazy with windless wood-smoke"; of the "slow drizzle of November rain just above the ice point"; of "those windless Mississippi December days which are a sort of Indian summer's Indian summer"; of January and February when there is "no movement anywhere save the low constant smoke . . . and no sound save the chopping of axes and the lonely whistle of the daily trains." Spring in Faulkner's country is a hurried season, "all coming at once, pell mell and disordered, fruit and bloom and leaf, pied meadow and blossoming wood and the long fields shearing dark out of winter's slumber, to the shearing plow." Summer is dust-choked and blazing, and it lasts far into what should be autumn. "That's the one trouble with this country," he says in *As I Lay Dying*. "Everything, weather, all, hangs on too long. Like our rivers, our land: opaque, slow, violent; shaping and creating the life of man in its implacable and brooding image."

And Faulkner loves these people created in the image of the land. After a second reading of his novels, you continue to be impressed by his villains, Popeye and Jason and Joe Christmas and Flem Snopes; but this time you find more place in your memory for other figures standing a little in the background yet presented by the author with quiet affection: old ladies like Miss Jenny DuPré, with their sharp-tongued benevolence; shrewd but kindly bargainers like Ratliff, the sewing-machine agent, and Will Varner, with his cotton gin and general store; long-suffering farm wives like Mrs. Henry Armstid (whether her name is Lula or Martha); and backwoods patriarchs like Pappy MacCullum, with his six middle-aged but unmarried sons named after the generals of Lee's army. You remember the big plantation houses that collapse in flames as if a whole civilization were dying, but you also remember men in patched and faded but quite clean overalls sitting on the gallery—here in the North we should call it the porch —of a crossroads store that is covered with posters advertising soft drinks and patent medicines; and you remember the stories they tell while chewing tobacco until the suption is out of it (everything in their world is reduced to anecdote, and every anecdote is based on character). You remember Quentin Compson not in his despairing moments, but riding with his father behind the dogs as they quarter a sedge-grown hillside after quail; and not listening to his father's story, but still knowing every word of it, because, as he thought to himself, "You have learned, absorbed it already without the medium of speech somehow from having been born and living beside it, with it, as children will and do: so that what your father was saying did not tell you anything so much as it struck, word by word, the resonant strings of remembering."

Faulkner's novels have the quality of being lived, absorbed, remembered rather than merely observed. And they have what is rare in the novels of our time, a warmth of family affection, brother for brother and sister, the father for his children—a love so warm and proud that it tries to shut out the rest of the world. Compared with that affection, married love is presented as something calculating, and illicit love as a consuming fire. And because the blood relationship is central in his novels, Faulkner finds it hard to create sympathetic characters between the ages of twenty and forty. He is better with children, Negro and white, and incomparably good with older people who preserve the standards that have come down to them "out of the old time, the old days."

In his later books, which have attracted so little attention that they seem to have gone unread, there is a quality not exactly new to Faulkner— it had appeared already in passages of *Sartoris* and *Sanctuary*—but now much stronger and no longer overshadowed by violence and horror. It is a sort of homely and sober-sided frontier humor that is seldom achieved in contemporary writing (except by Erskine Caldwell, another Southerner). The horse-trading episodes in *The Hamlet,* and especially the long story of the spotted ponies from Texas, might have been inspired by the Davy Crockett almanacs. "Old Man," the story of the convict who surmounted the greatest of all the Mississippi floods, might almost be a continuation of *Huckleberry Finn.* It is as if some older friend of Huck's had taken the raft and drifted on from Aunt Sally Phelps's farm into wilder adventures, described in a wilder style, among Chinese and Cajuns and bayous crawling with alligators. In a curious way, Faulkner combines two of the principal traditions in American letters: the tradition of psychological horror, often close to symbolism, that begins with Charles Brockden Brown, our first professional novelist, and extends through Poe, Melville, Henry James (in his later stories), Stephen Crane, and Hemingway; and the other tradition of frontier humor and realism, beginning with Augustus Longstreet's *Georgia Scenes* and having Mark Twain as its best example.

But the American author he most resembles is Hawthorne, for all their polar differences. They stand to each other as July to December, as heat to cold, as swamp to mountain, as the luxuriant to the meager but perfect, as planter to Puritan; and yet Hawthorne had much the same attitude toward New England that Faulkner has toward the South, together with a strong sense of regional particularity. The Civil War made Hawthorne feel that "the North and the South were two distinct nations in opinions and habits, and had better not try to live under the same institutions." In the Spring of 1861, he wrote to his Bowdoin classmate Horatio Bridge, "We were never one people and never really had a country."—"New England," he said a little later, "is quite as large a lump of earth as my heart can really take in." But it was more than a lump of earth for him; it was a lump of history and a permanent state of consciousness. Like Faulkner in the South, he applied himself to creating its moral fables and elaborating its legends, which existed, as it were, in his solitary heart. Pacing the hillside behind his house in Concord, he listened for a voice; you might say that he lay in wait for it, passively but expectantly, like a hunter behind a rock; then, when it had spoken, he transcribed its words—more slowly and carefully than Faulkner, it is true; with more form and less fire, but with the same essential fidelity. If the voice was silent, he had nothing to write. "I have an instinct that I had better keep quiet," he said in a letter to his publisher. "Perhaps I shall have a new spirit of vigor if I wait quietly for it; perhaps not." Faulkner is another author who has to wait for the spirit and the voice. Essentially he is not a novelist, in the sense of not being a writer who sets out to observe actions and characters, then fits them into the architectural framework of a story. For all the weakness of his own poems, he is an epic or bardic poet in prose, a creator of myths that he weaves together into a legend of the South.

HENRY MILLER

****

Henry Miller's name will not be found in the *Literary History of The United States,* for he has little established respectability. Most of the writings about him have appeared in foreign or avant-garde periodicals, and until recently even his better known books have not been available in this country. He may not be, as Karl Shapiro says in this essay, "The Greatest Living Author," nor is he simply "The *@&! - - 1 % \$ - D * * ! Genius" of whom Daniel Dixon wrote in *Pageant,* XIV (December 1958), pp. 81–87, nor is he "Bigotry's Whipping Boy," described by Harold Maine in the *Arizona Quarterly,* VII (August 1951), pp. 197–208: John Haverstick and William Barrett described him more accurately as "Henry Miller: Man in Quest of Life," *Saturday Review,* XL (August 3, 1957), pp. 8–10. No satisfactory biography has yet appeared, and perhaps one is not immediately necessary, for Miller himself writes without reserve and repetitively of his activities and experience. Early commentary on his writings is found in George Orwell's 1940 essay, "Inside the Whale," in *A Collection of Essays* (New

York, 1954) and in Anaïs Nin's preface to *The Tropic of Cancer* (New York, 1947). More recent and detailed studies are Annette Baxter Kar's *Henry Miller, Expatriate* (Pittsburgh, Pa., 1961), Kingsley Widmer's *Henry Miller* (New York, 1963), Kenneth B. Dick's *Henry Miller: Colossus of One* (Spittard, 1967), and William A. Gordon's *The Mind and Art of Henry Miller* (Baton Rouge, La., 1967). Ihab Habib Hassan has compared Miller with Samuel Beckett in *The Literature of Silence* (New York, 1968); Alfred Perlès has written affectionately of *My Friend, Henry Miller* (London, 1955) and collaborated with Lawrence Durrell in *Art and Outrage* (London, 1959). Charles Rembar in *The End of Obscenity* (New York, 1968) reviews Miller's conflicts with censors, and George Wickes has edited a volume on *Henry Miller and the Critics* (Carbondale, Ill., 1963), and his brief study, *Henry Miller* (Minneapolis, Minn., 1966) seems to me of essential importance, perhaps because he agrees with me that "Henry Miller is likely to outlast a great many writers who at the moment seem more important."

THE GREATEST LIVING AUTHOR

Karl Shapiro

****

I call Henry Miller the greatest living author because I think he is. I do not call him a poet because he has never written a poem; he even dislikes poetry, I think. But everything he has written is a poem in the best as well as in the broadest sense of the word. Secondly, I do not call him a writer, but an author. The writer is the fly in the ointment of modern letters; Miller has waged ceaseless war against writers. If one had to type him one might might call him a Wisdom writer, Wisdom literature being a type of literature which lies between literature and scripture; it is poetry only because it rises above literature and because it sometimes ends up in bibles. I wrote to the British poet and novelist Lawrence Durrell last year and said: Let's put together a bible of Miller's work. (I thought I was being original in calling it a bible.) Let's assemble a bible from his work, I said, and put one in every hotel room in America, after removing the Gideon Bibles and placing them in the laundry chutes. Durrell, however, had been working on this "bible" for years; I was a Johnny-come-lately. In fact, a group of writers all over the world have been working on it, and one version has now come out.

There was a commonplace reason why this volume was very much needed. The author's books have been almost impossible to obtain; the ones that were not banned were stolen from libraries everywhere. Even a copy of one of the nonbanned books was recently stolen from the mails en route to me. Whoever got it had better be a book lover, because it was a bibliography.

I will introduce Miller with a quotation from the *Tropic of Cancer:* "I sometimes ask myself how it happens that I attract nothing but crackbrained individuals, neurasthenics, neurotics, psychopaths—and Jews especially. There must be something in a healthy Gentile that excites the Jewish mind, like when he sees sour black bread." The "healthy Gentile" is a good sobriquet for Miller, who usually refers to himself as the Happy Rock, Caliban, "just a Brooklyn boy," "Someone who has gone off the gold standard of Literature" or—the name I like best—the Patagonian. What is a Patagonian? I don't know, but it is certainly something rare and *sui generis.* We can call Miller the greatest living Patagonian.

How is one to talk about Miller? There are authors one cannot write a book or even a good essay about. Arthur Rimbaud is one (and Miller's book on Rimbaud is one of the best books on Rimbaud ever written, although it is mostly about Henry Miller). D. H. Lawrence is another author one cannot encompass in a book "about" (Miller abandoned his book on Lawrence). And Miller himself is one of those Patagonian authors who just won't fit into a book. Every word he has ever written is autobiographical, but only in the way *Leaves of Grass* is autobiographical. There is not a word of "confession" in Miller. His amorous exploits are sometimes read as a kind of Brooklyn Casanova or male Fanny Hill, but there is probably not a word of exaggeration or boasting to speak of—or only as much as the occasion would call for. The reader can and cannot reconstruct the Life of Henry Miller from his books, for Miller never sticks to the subject any more than Lawrence does. The fact is that there isn't any subject and Miller is its poet. But a little information about him might help present him to those who need an introduction. For myself, I do not read him consecutively; I choose one of his books blindly and open it at random. I have just done this; for an example, I find: "Man is not at home in the universe, despite all the efforts of philosophers and metaphysicians to provide a soothing syrup. Thought is still a narcotic. The deepest question is *why.* And it is a forbidden one. The very asking is in the nature of cosmic sabotage. And the penalty is—the afflictions of Job." Not the greatest prose probably, but Miller is not a writer; Henry James is a writer. Miller is a talker, a street corner gabbler, a prophet, and a Patagonian.

What are the facts about Miller? I'm not sure how important they are. He was born in Brooklyn about 1890, of German ancestry, and in certain ways he is quite German. I have often thought that the Germans make the best Americans, though they certainly make the worst Germans. Miller understands the German in himself and in America. He compares Whitman and Goethe: "In Whitman the whole American scene comes to life, her past and her future, her birth and her death. Whatever there is of value in America Whitman has expressed, and there is nothing more to be said. The future belongs to the machine, to the robots. He was the Poet of the Body and the Soul, Whitman. The first and the last poet. He is almost undecipherable today, a monument covered with rude hieroglyphs, for which there is no key. . . . There is no equivalent in the languages of Europe for the spirit which he immortalized. Europe is saturated with art and her soil is full of dead bones and her museums are bursting with plundered treasures, but what Europe has never had is a free, healthy spirit, what you might call a MAN. Goethe was the nearest approach, but Goethe was a stuffed shirt, by comparison. Goethe was a respectable citizen, a pedant, a bore, a universal spirit, but stamped with the German trademark, with the double eagle. The serenity of Goethe, the calm, Olympian attitude, is nothing more than the drowsy stupor of a German bourgeois deity. Goethe is an end of something, Whitman is a beginning."

If anybody can decipher the Whitman key it is Miller. Miller is the twentieth-century reincarnation of Whitman. But to return to the "facts." The Brooklyn Boy went to a Brooklyn high school in a day when most high schools kept higher standards than most American universities today. He started at CCNY but quit almost immediately and went to work for a cement company ("Everlasting Cement"), then for a telegraph company, where he became the personnel manager in the biggest city in the world. The telegraph company is called the Cosmodemonic Telegraph Company in Miller's books, or in moments of gaiety the Cosmococcic Telegraph Company. One day while the vice-president was bawling him out he mentioned to Miller that he would like to see someone write a sort of Horatio Alger book about the messengers.

> I thought to myself [said Miller]—you poor old futzer, you, just wait until I get it off my chest. . . . I'll give you an Horatio Alger book. . . . My head was in a whirl to leave his office. I saw the army of men, women and children that had passed through my hands, saw them weeping, begging, beseeching, imploring, cursing, spitting, fuming, threatening. I saw the tracks they left on the highways, lying on the floor of freight trains, the parents in rags, the coal box empty, the sink running over, the walls sweating and between the cold beads of sweat the cockroaches running like mad; I saw them hobbling along like twisted gnomes or falling backwards

in the epileptic frenzy. . . . I saw the walls giving way and the pest pouring out like a winged fluid, and the men higher up with their iron-clad logic, waiting for it to blow over, waiting for everything to be patched up, waiting, waiting contentedly . . . saying that things were temporarily out of order. I saw the Horatio Alger hero, the dream of a sick America, mounting higher and higher, first messenger, then operator, then manager, then chief, then superintendent, then vice-president, then president, then trust magnate, then beer baron, then Lord of all the Americas, the money god, the god of gods, the clay of clay, nullity on high, zero with ninety-seven thousand decimals fore and aft. . . . I will give you Horatio Alger as he looks the day after the Apocalypse, when all the stink has cleared away.*

And he did. Miller's first book, *Tropic of Cancer,* was published in Paris in 1934 and was immediately famous and immediately banned in all English-speaking countries. It is the Horatio Alger story with a vengeance. Miller had walked out of the Cosmodemonic Telegraph Company one day without a word; ever after he lived on his wits. He had managed to get to Paris on ten dollars, where he lived more than a decade, not during the gay prosperous twenties but during the Great Depression. He starved, made friends by the score, mastered the French language and his own. It was not until the Second World War broke out that he returned to America to live at Big Sur, California. Among his best books several were banned: the two *Tropics (Tropic of Cancer,* 1934, and *Tropic of Capricorn,* 1939); *Black Spring,* 1936; and part of the trilogy *The Rosy Crucifixion* (including *Sexus, Plexus,* and *Nexus).*

Unfortunately for Miller he has been a man without honor in his own country and in his own language. When *Tropic of Cancer* was published he was even denied entrance into England, held over in custody by the port authorities and returned to France by the next boat. He made friends with his jailer and wrote a charming essay about him. But Miller has no sense of despair. At the beginning of *Tropic of Cancer* he writes: "I have no money, no resources, no hopes. I am the happiest man alive."

George Orwell was one of the few English critics who saw his worth, though *(mirabile dictu)* T. S. Eliot and even Ezra Pound complimented him. Pound in his usual ungracious manner gave the *Tropic of Cancer* to a friend who later became Miller's publisher, and said: Here is a dirty book worth reading. Pound even went so far as to try to enlist Miller in his eco-

*From *Tropic of Capricorn,* 1964 (Black Cat), by Henry Miller. Copyright © 1961 by Grove Press, Inc.

nomic system to save the world. Miller retaliated by writing a satire called *Money and How It Gets That Way,* dedicated to Ezra Pound. The acquaintanceship halted there, Miller's view of money being something like this (from *Tropic of Capricorn):* "To walk in money through the night crowd, protected by money, lulled by money, dulled by money, the crowd itself a money, the breath money, no least single object anywhere that is not money, money, money everywhere and still not enough, and then no money, or a little money or less money or more money, but money, always money, and if you have money or you don't have money it is the money that counts and money makes money, *but what makes money make money?"* Pound didn't care for that brand of economics.

But all the writers jostled each other to welcome Miller among the elect, for the moment at least: Eliot, Herbert Read, Aldous Huxley, John Dos Passos and among them some who really knew how good Miller was: William Carlos Williams, who called him the Dean, Lawrence Durrell, Paul Rosenfeld, Wallace Fowlie, Osbert Sitwell, Kenneth Patchen, many painters (Miller is a fanatical water colorist). But mostly he is beset by his neurasthenics and psychopaths, as any cosmodemonic poet must be. People of all sexes frequently turn up at Big Sur and announce that they want to join the Sex Cult. Miller gives them bus fare and a good dinner and sends them on their way.

Orwell has written one of the best essays on Miller, although he takes a sociological approach and tries to place Miller as a Depression writer or something of the sort. What astonished Orwell about Miller was the difference between his view and the existential bitterness of a novelist like Céline. Céline's *Voyage au bout de la Nuit* describes the meaninglessness of modern life and is thus a prototype of twentieth-century fiction. Orwell calls Céline's book a cry of unbearable disgust, a voice from the cesspool. And Orwell adds that the *Tropic of Cancer* is almost exactly the opposite! Such a thing as Miller's book "has become so unusual as to seem almost anomalous, [for] it is the book of a man who is happy." Miller also reached the bottom of the pit, as many writers do; but how, Orwell asks, could he have emerged unembittered, whole, laughing with joy? "Exactly the aspects of life that fill Céline with horror are the ones that appeal to him. So far from protesting, he is *accepting.* And the very word 'acceptance' calls up his real affinity, another American, Walt Whitman."

This is, indeed, the crux of the matter and it is unfortunate that Orwell cannot see past the socio-economic situation with Whitman and Miller. Nevertheless, this English critic recognizes Miller's mastery of his material and places him among the great writers of our age; more than that, he predicts that Miller will set the pace and attitude for the novelist of the future. This has not happened yet, but I agree that it must. Miller's influence today is primarily among poets; those poets who follow Whitman must necessarily follow Miller, even to the extent of giving up poetry in its formal sense and writing that personal apocalyptic prose which Miller does. It is the prose of the Bible of Hell that Blake talked about and Arthur Rimbaud wrote a chapter of.

What is this "acceptance" Orwell mentions in regard to Whitman and Henry Miller? On one level it is the poetry of cosmic consciousness, and on the most obvious level it is the poetry of the Romantic nineteenth century. Miller is unknown in this country because he represents the Continental rather than the English influence. He breaks with the English literary tradition just as many of the twentieth-century Americans do, because his ancestry is not British, and not American colonial. He does not read the favored British writers, Milton, Marlowe, Pope, Donne. He reads what his grandparents knew was in the air when Victorianism was the genius of British poetry. He grew up with books by Dostoevski, Knut Hamsun, Strindberg, Nietzsche (especially Nietzsche), Elie Faure, Spengler. Like a true poet he found his way to Rimbaud, Ramakrishna, Blavatsky, Huysmans, Count Keyserling, Prince Kropotkin, Lao-tse, Nostradamus, Petronius, Rabelais, Suzuki, Zen philosophy, Van Gogh. And in English he let himself be influenced not by the solid classics but by *Alice in Wonderland,* Chesterton's *St. Francis,* Conrad, Cooper, Emerson, Rider Haggard, G. A. Henty (the boy's historian—I remember being told when I was a boy that Henty had the facts all wrong), Joyce, Arthur Machen, Mencken, John Cowper Powys, Herbert Spencer's *Autobiography,* Thoreau on Civil Disobedience, Emma Goldman—the great anarchist (whom he met)—Whitman, of course, and perhaps above all that companion piece to *Leaves of Grass* called *Huckleberry Finn.* Hardly a Great Books list from the shores of Lake Michigan—almost a period list. Miller will introduce his readers to strange masterpieces like Doughty's *Arabia Deserta* or to the journal of Anaïs Nin which has never been published* but which he (and other writers) swears is one of the masterpieces of the twentieth century. I imagine that Miller has read as much as any man living but he does not have that religious solemnity about books which we are brought up in. Books, after all, are only mnemonic devices; and poets are always celebrating the burning of libraries. And as with libraries, so with monuments, and as with monuments, so with civilizations. But in Miller's case *(chez* Miller) there is no vindictiveness, no bitterness. Orwell was bothered when he met Miller because Miller didn't want to go to the Spanish Civil War and do battle on one side or the other. Miller is an anarchist of sorts, and he doesn't especially care which dog eats which dog. As it happens, the righteous Loyalists were eaten by the Communists and

*This journal is now published—ed.

the righteous Falangists were eaten by the Nazis over the most decadent hole in Europe; so Miller was right.

Lawrence Durrell has said that the *Tropic* books were healthy while Céline and D. H. Lawrence were sick. Lawrence never escaped his puritanism and it is his heroic try that makes us honor him. Céline is the typical European man of despair—why should he not despair, this Frenchman of the trenches of World War I? We are raising up a generation of young American Célines, I'm afraid, but Miller's generation still had Whitman before its eyes and was not running back to the potholes and ash heaps of Europe. Miller is as good an antiquarian as anybody; in the medieval towns of France he goes wild with happiness; and he has written one of the best "travel books" on Greece ever done (the critics are unanimous about the *Colossus of Maroussi*); but to worship the "tradition" is to him the sheerest absurdity. Like most Americans, he shares the view of the first Henry Ford that history is bunk. He cannot forgive his "Nordic" ancestors for the doctrines of righteousness and cleanliness. His people, he says, were painfully clean: "Never once had they opened the door which leads to the soul; never once did they dream of taking a blind leap into the dark. After dinner the dishes were promptly washed and put in the closet; after the paper was read it was neatly folded and laid on a shelf; after the clothes were washed they were ironed and folded and then tucked away in the drawers. Everything was for tomorrow, but tomorrow never came. The present was only a bridge and on this bridge they are still groaning, as the world groans, and not one idiot ever thinks of blowing up the bridge." As everyone knows, Cleanliness is the chief American industry. Miller is the most formidable anticleanliness poet since Walt Whitman, and his hatred of righteousness is also American, with the Americanism of Thoreau, Whitman, and Emma Goldman. Miller writes a good deal about cooking and wine drinking. Americans are the worst cooks in the world, outside of the British; and Americans are also great drunkards who know nothing about wine. The Germanic-American Miller reintroduces good food and decent wine into our literature. One of his funniest essays is about the American loaf of bread, the poisonous loaf of cleanliness wrapped in cellophane, the manufacture of which is a heavy industry like steel.

Orwell and other critics tend to regard Miller as a kind of hedonist and professional do-nothing. And morally, they tend to regard him as one of that illustrious line of Americans who undermine the foundations of traditional morals. Miller quotes Thoreau's statement, which might almost be the motto of the cosmic writer: "Most of what my neighbors call good, I am profoundly convinced is evil, and if I repent anything, it is my good conduct that I repent." One could hardly call Thoreau a criminal, yet he had his run-ins with the law, just as Miller has, and for the same reasons. The strain of anarchism and amorality is growing stronger in American literature, or that branch of it that I am talking about, and Miller is one of its chief carriers. It is not only Emma Goldman, Thoreau, Mark Twain, Whitman, and perhaps Salinger and Mailer, but that whole literature of Detachment from political hysteria and over-organization. I am influenced enough by these people and by Miller to tell my students, the poets at least, to cultivate an ignorance of contemporary political and military events because they do not matter. I tell them not to vote, to join nothing. I try to steer them toward their true leaders and visionaries, men almost unknown in the polite literary world, Reich for instance. Wilhelm Reich furthered a movement in Germany called "Work Democracy"; not machine politics, no politics at all, but democracy within one's immediate orbit; democracy at home. America is still the only country where social idealism and experimentation have elbow room; there are still communities that practice primitive Christianity, such as the Catholic anarchists; and just plain little homemade gardens of Eden such as Miller's cliff at Big Sur. The life he describes in *Big Sur and the Oranges of Hieronymus Bosch* is a far cry from the little fascist dreams of the New Classicists. And it is a far cry from the bitter isolationism of Robinson Jeffers or even of Lawrence. Morally I regard Miller as a holy man, as most of his adherents do—Gandhi with a penis.

Miller says in a little essay on Immorality and Morality: "What is moral and what is immoral? Nobody can ever answer this question satisfactorily. Not because morals ceaselessly evolve, but because the principle on which they depend is factitious. Morality is for slaves, for beings without spirit. And when I say spirit I mean the Holy Spirit." And he ends this little piece with a quotation from ancient Hindu scripture: Evil does not exist.

Whitman, Lawrence, Miller, and even Blake all have the reputation of being sex-obsessed, Miller especially. Whereas Whitman writes "copulation is no more rank to me than death is," Miller writes hundreds of pages describing in the minutest and clearest detail his exploits in bed. Every serious reader of erotica has remarked about Miller that he is probably the only author in history who writes about such things with complete ease and naturalness. Lawrence never quite rid himself of his puritanical salaciousness, nor Joyce; both had too much religion in their veins. It is funny to recollect that Lawrence thought *Ulysses* a smutty book and Joyce thought *Lady Chatterley* a smutty book. Both were right. But at least they *tried* to free themselves from literary morality. Miller's achievement is miraculous: he is screamingly funny without making fun of sex, the way Rabelais does. (Rabelais is, of course, magnificient; so is Boccaccio; but both write against the background of religion, like Joyce and Lawrence.) Miller is accurate and poetic in the highest degree; there is not a smirk anywhere in his writings. Miller undoubtedly profited from the mistakes of his predecessors; his aim was not to write about the erotic but to write the whole truth about the life he knew. This goal demanded the full vocabulary and iconography of sex, and it is possible that he is the first writer outside the Orient who has succeeded in writing as naturally about sex on a large scale as novelists ordinarily write about the dinner table or the battlefield. I think only an American could have performed this feat.

We are dealing with the serious question of banned books, burned books, and fear of books in general. America has the most liberal censorship laws in the West today, but we have done no more than make a start. I have always been amused by the famous decision of Judge Woolsey who lifted the ban on *Ulysses,* although it was certainly a fine thing to do and it is a landmark we can be proud of. Woolsey said various comical things, such as that he could not detect the "leer of the sensualist" in Joyce's book, and that therefore (the logic of it escapes me) it is not pornographic. In excusing the use of old Saxon words he noted that Joyce's "locale was Celtic and his season Spring." And, in order to push his decision through, Judge Woolsey stated that *Ulysses* "did not tend to excite sexual impulses or lustful thoughts," and he closed his argument with the elegant statement that although the book is "somewhat emetic, nowhere does it tend to be an aphrodisiac." Emetic means tending to produce vomiting and I doubt that Joyce savored that description of his masterpiece. The implication, of course, is that vomiting is good for you, and lustful thoughts not. Now everyone who has read *Ulysses* knows that the book is based largely on the lustful thoughts and acts of its characters and that Joyce spared no pains to represent these thoughts and deeds richly and smackingly. *Ulysses* is, since the Judge used the word, a pretty *good* aphrodisiac, partly because of Joyce's own religious tensions. Miller, on the other hand, is no aphrodisiac at all, because religious or so-called moral tension does not exist for him. When one of Miller's characters lusts, he lusts out loud and then proceeds to the business at hand. Joyce actually prevents himself from experiencing the beauty of sex or lust, while Miller is freed at the outset to deal with the overpowering mysteries and glories of love and copulation. Like other Millerites I claim that Miller is one of the few healthy Americans alive today; further, that the circulation of his books would do more to wipe out the obscenities of Broadway, Hollywood, and Madison Avenue than a full-scale social revolution.

Miller has furthered literature for all writers by ignoring the art forms, the novel, the poem, the drama, and by sticking to the autobiographical novel. He says in *The Books in My Life* (one of the available works), "The autobiographical novel, which Emerson predicted would grow in importance with time, has replaced the great confessions. It is not a mixture of truth and fiction, this genre of literature, but an expansion and deepening of truth. It is more authentic, more veridical, than the diary. It is not the flimsy truth of facts which the authors of these autobiographical novels offer but the truth of emotion, reflection and understanding, truth digested and assimilated. The being revealing himself does so on all levels simultaneously." Everything Miller has written is part of this great amorphous autobiographical novel and it must be read not entirely but in large chunks to make sense. Many of the individual works are whole in themselves, one dealing with his life in Paris, one with his life as a New Yorker, and there is, in fact, a definite span of years encompassed in the works. But the volumes of essays are also part of the story and there is no way to make a whole out of the parts. Miller is easy to quote if one quotes carefully; the danger is that one can find massive contradictions, unless there is some awareness of the underlying world and the cosmic attitudes of the author. These views are by no means unique, as they are the same as those of all those poets and mystics I referred to in a previous essay. What makes Miller unique is his time and place; he is the only American of our time who has given us a full-scale interpretation of modern America, other than the kind we find in the cultural journals, which, presuming an interest in letters and art, are really organs of social and political opinion.

Readers of Whitman recall that Whitman was blistering about the materialism of this country a century ago, and its departure from the ideals of the founding fathers. Miller is worse. Now it is a commonplace of modern poetry that the poet dissociates himself from life as it is lived by the average American today. Whitman and Miller heap abuse on the failure of the country to live up to its promise. Miller writes as a poet about the demonic hideousness of New York City, Chicago, the South, or he rhapsodizes when there is anything to be rapturous about. But it is not Art that he cares about; it is man, man's treatment of man in America and man's treatment of nature. What we get in Miller is not a sense of superiority but fury, even the fury of the prophet of doom.

Miller knows America from the bottom up and from coast to coast. In the same way he knows Paris as few Frenchmen do. But when Miller describes slums it is usually with the joyous eye of the artist, not with the self-righteous sneer of the social reformer. Here, too, one might describe his psychology as "Oriental" rather than modern. The cultural situation is a matter of complete indifference to him. Miller frequently immerses himself in such modern Indian mystics as Krishnamurti and Ramakrishna, but without any of the flapdoodle of the cultist. He is himself one of the foremost of the contemporary men of Detachment. His influence (like that of Lawrence) comes as much from his life as from his writings. Here it is better to quote. This is Myrtle Avenue in Brooklyn.

But I saw a street called Myrtle Avenue, which runs from Borough Hall to Fresh Pond Road, and down this street no saint ever walked (else it would have crumbled), down this street no miracle ever passed, nor any poet, nor any species of human genius, nor did any flower ever grow there, nor did the sun strike it squarely, nor did the rain ever wash it. For the genuine Inferno which I had to postpone for twenty years I give you Myrtle Avenue, one of the innumerable bridlepaths ridden by iron monsters which lead to the heart of America's emptiness. If you have only seen Essen or Manchester or Chicago or Levallois-Perret or Glasgow or Hoboken or Canarsie or Bayonne you have seen nothing of the magnificent emptiness of progress and enlightenment. Dear reader, you must see Myrtle Avenue before you die, if only to realize how far into the future Dante saw. You must believe me that on this street, neither in the houses which line it, nor the cobblestones which pave it, nor the elevated structure which cuts it atwain, neither in any creature that bears a name and lives thereon, neither in any animal, bird or insect passing through it to slaughter or already slaughtered, is there hope of "lubet," "sublimate" or "abominate." It is a street not of sorrow, for sorrow would be human and recognizable, but of sheer emptiness: it is emptier than the most extinct volcano, emptier than a vacuum, emptier than the word of God in the mouth of an unbeliever.*

This is a man describing his own neighborhood, but the street is a type that runs from the Atlantic to the Pacific, with variations:

The whole country is lawless, violent, explosive, demoniacal. It's in the air, in the climate, in the ultra-grandiose landscape, in the stone forests that are lying horizontal, in the torrential rivers that bite through the rock canyons, in the supranormal distances, the supernal arid wastes, the over-lush crops, the monstrous fruits, the mixture of quixotic bloods, the fatras of cults, sects, beliefs, the opposition of laws and languages, the contradictoriness of temperaments, needs, requirements. The continent is full of buried violence, of the bones of antediluvian monsters and of lost races of man, of mysteries which are wrapped in doom. The atmosphere is at times so electrical that the soul is summoned out of its body and runs amok. Like the rain everything comes in bucketsful—or not at all. The whole continent is a huge volcano whose crater is temporarily concealed by a moving panorama which is partly dream, partly

* From *Tropic of Capricorn*, 1964 (Black Cat), by Henry Miller. Copyright © 1964 by Grove Press, Inc.

fear, partly despair. From Alaska to Yucatan it's the same story. Nature dominates, Nature wins out. Everywhere the same fundamental urge to slay, to ravage, to plunder. Outwardly they seem like a fine, upstanding people—healthy, optimistic, courageous. Inwardly they are filled with worms. A tiny spark and they blow up.*

The passages on Times Square repeat and catalogue, like Whitman; they are a little too painful to read out of context. Here is a bit of Chicago; Miller is wandering in the Negro slums with a fellow visitor:

> We got into the car, rode a few blocks and got out to visit another shell crater. The street was deserted except for some chickens grubbing for food between the slats of a crumbling piazza. More vacant lots, more gutted houses; fire escapes clinging to the walls with their iron teeth, like drunken acrobats. A Sunday atmosphere here. Everything serene and peaceful. Like Louvain or Rheims between bombardments. Like Phoebus, Virginia, dreaming of bringing her steeds to water, or like modern Eleusis smothered by a wet sock. Then suddenly I saw it chalked up on the side of a house in letters ten feet high:
>
> GOOD NEWS! GOD IS LOVE!
>
> When I saw these words I got down on my knees in the open sewer which had been conveniently placed there for the purpose and I offered up a short prayer, a silent one, which must have registered as far as Mound City, Illinois, where the colored muskrats have built their igloos. It was time for a good stiff drink of cod-liver oil but as the varnish factories were all closed we had to repair to the abattoir and quaff a bucket of blood. Never has blood tasted so wonderful! It was like taking Vitamins A, B, C, D, E in quick succession and then chewing a stick of cold dynamite. Good news! Aye, wonderful news—for Chicago. I ordered the chauffeur to take us immediately to Mundelein so that I could bless the cardinal and all the real estate operations, but we only got as far as the Bahai Temple. . . .**

Or, again—in explanation:

> Oh, Henry, what beautiful golden teeth you have! exclaimed my four-year-old daughter the other morning on climbing into bed

* From *Tropic of Capricorn*, 1964 (Black Cat), by Henry Miller. Copyright © 1961 by Grove Press, Inc.

** Henry Miller, *Sunday After the War*. Copyright 1944 by Henry Miller. Reprinted by permission of New Directions Publishing Corporation.

with me. That's how I approach the works of my confreres. I see how beautiful are their golden teeth, not how ugly or artificial they are.

Combating the "system" is nonsense. There is only one aim in life and that is to live it. In America it has become impossible, except for a few lucky or wise people, to live one's own life; consequently the poets and artists tend to move to the fringes of society. Wherever there are individuals, says Miller (like Thoreau), there are new frontiers. The American way of life has become illusory; we lead the lives of prisoners while we boast about free speech, free press, and free religion, none of which we actually do enjoy in full. The price for security has become too great; abundance has become a travesty. The only thing for nonenslaved man to do is to move out to the edge, lose contact with the machines of organization which are as ubiquitous in this country as in Russia. "Instead of bucking your head against a stone wall, sit quietly with hands folded and wait for the walls to crumble. . . . Don't sit and *pray* that it will happen! Just sit and *watch* it happen!" These sayings the culture *littérateur* condemns as irresponsible. Miller follows through with the complete program of nonparticipation in our machine society, which is organized from the cradle to the grave. "Just as Gandhi successfully exploited the doctrine of nonresistance, these 'saints of the just' practiced nonrecognition—nonrecognition of sin, guilt, fear and disease . . . even death." Whitman also believed in nonrecognition of death. His view of death as part of life is one of the many reasons for his unpopularity in America, where death is considered a crime against society. "Why try to solve a problem? *Dissolve* it! [says Miller]. Fear not to be a coward, a traitor, a renegade. In this universe of ours there is room for all, perhaps even need for all. The sun does not inquire about rank and status before shedding its warmth; the cyclone levels the godly and the ungodly; the government takes your tax money even though it be tainted. Nor is the atom bomb a respecter of persons. Perhaps that is why the righteous are squirming so!"

All of this is about modern America and the high cost of security. Do we really have a high standard of living? Miller says not, as most poets do. If living means appreciation of life we have the lowest standard of living in the world, in spite of the fact that it costs more to live in America than in any country in the world. Miller says "the cost is not only in dollars and cents but in sweat and blood, in frustration, ennui, broken homes, smashed ideals, illness and insanity. We have the most wonderful hospitals, the most fabulous prisons, the best equipped and highest paid army and navy, the speediest bombers, the largest stockpile of atom bombs, yet never enough of any of these items to satisfy the demand. Our manual workers are the high-est paid in the world; our poets the worst. . . ."

And Miller gives this answer, letting Krishnamurti say it:

> The world problem is the individual problem; if the individual is at peace, has happiness, has great tolerance, and an intense desire to help, then the world problem as such ceases to exist. You con-sider the world problem before you have considered your own problem. Before you have established peace and understanding in your own hearts and in your own minds you desire to establish peace and tranquility in the minds of others, in your nations and in your states; whereas peace and understanding will only come when there is understanding, certainty and strength in yourselves.

To place the individual before the state, whether the Russian state or the American state, is the first need of modern man. To interpret Miller, man is like the common soldier on the battlefield; he can know nothing of the battle at large or of its causes; he can know only the fifty feet or so in his immediate vicinity; within that radius he is a man responsible for himself and his fellows; beyond that he is powerless. Modern life, having made everyone state conscious, has destroyed the individual. America has as few individuals today as Russia, and as many taboos to keep the individual from coming to life as the USSR. First, we have contaminated the idea of society; second, we have contaminated the idea of community. Miller writing about his little community at Big Sur frowns on the idea of community itself. "To create community—and what is a nation, or a people, without a sense of community—there must be a common purpose. Even here in Big Sur, where the oranges are ready to blossom forth, there is no common purpose, no common effort. There is a remarkable neighborliness, but no community spirit. We have a Grange, as do other rural communities, but what is a 'Grange' in the life of man? The real workers are outside the Grange. Just as the 'real men of God' are outside the Church. And the real leaders out-side the world of politics."

"We create our fate," says Miller. And better still: "Forget, forgive, renounce, abdicate." And "scrap the past instantly." Live the good life in-stantly; it's now or never, and always has been.

Miller is "irresponsible" as far as officials and popular politics go, or as far as common church morality goes, and as far as literary manners go. But he is not a poseur, he has no program, yet he has a deep and pure sense of morality. I would call him a total revolutionary, the man who will settle for nothing less than "Christmas on earth." In his remarkable study of Rim-baud, a prose-poem of one hundred and fifty pages called *The Time of the Assassins,* Miller discourses on the spiritual suicide of modern youth.

I like to think of him as the one who extended the boundaries of that only partially explored domain. Youth ends where manhood begins, it is said. A phrase without meaning, since from the beginning of history man has never enjoyed the full measure of youth or known the limitless possibilities of adulthood. How can one know the splendor and fullness of youth if one's energies are consumed in combating the errors and falsities of parents and ancestors? Is youth to waste its strength unlocking the grip of death? Is youth's only mission on earth to rebel, to destroy, to assassinate? Is youth only to be offered up to sacrifice? What of the *dreams* of youth? Are they always to be regarded as follies? Are they to be populated only with chimeras? . . . Stifle or deform youth's dreams and you destroy the creator. Where there has been no real youth there can be no real manhood. If society has come to resemble a collection of deformities, is it not the work of our educators and preceptors? Today, as yesterday, the youth who would live his own life has no place to turn, no place to live his youth unless, retiring into his chrysalis, he closes all apertures and buries himself alive. The conception of our mother the earth being "an egg which doth contain all good things in it" has undergone a profound change. The cosmic egg contains an addled yolk. This is the present view of mother earth. The psychoanalysts have traced the poison back to the womb, but to what avail? In the light of this profound discovery we are given permission . . . to step from one rotten egg into another. . . . Why breed new monsters of negation and futility? Let society scotch its own rotten corpse! Let us have a new heaven and a new earth!—that was the sense of Rimbaud's obstinate revolt.*

Miller calls for an end to revolt once and for all. His message is precisely that of Whitman, of Rimbaud, of Rilke: "Everything we are taught is false"; and "Change your life." As a writer Miller may be second- or third-rate or of no rating at all; as a spiritual example he stands among the great men of our age. Will this ever be recognized? Not in our time probably.

The Rimbaud book ends with a Coda, a little recital of the literature of despair which has surrounded us for a hundred years. Listen to it.

Rimbaud was born in the middle of the nineteenth century, October 20th, 1854, at 6:00 A.M., it is said. A century of unrest, of materialism, and of "progress," as we say. Purgatorial in every sense of the word, and the writers who flourished in that period re-

* Henry Miller, *The Time of the Assassins.* Copyright 1946, 1949, © 1956 by New Directions Publishing Corporation. Reprinted by permission of New Directions Publishing Corporation.

flect this ominously. Wars and revolutions were abundant. Russia alone, we are told, waged thirty-three wars (mostly of conquest) during the eighteenth and the nineteenth centuries. Shortly after Rimbaud is born his father is off to the Crimean War. So is Tolstoy. The revolution in 1848, of brief duration but full of consequences, is followed by the bloody Commune of 1871, which Rimbaud as a boy is thought to have participated in. In 1848 we in America are fighting the Mexicans with whom we are now great friends, though the Mexicans are not too sure of it. During this war Thoreau makes his famous speech on Civil Disobedience, a document which will one day be added to the Emancipation Proclamation. . . . Twelve years later the Civil War breaks out, perhaps the bloodiest of all civil wars. . . . From 1874 until his death in 1881 Amiel is writing his *Journal Intime* . . . which . . . gives a thoroughgoing analysis of the moral dilemma in which the creative spirits of the time found themselves. The very titles of the books written by influential writers of the nineteenth century are revelatory. I give just a few . . . *The Sickness unto Death* (Kierkegaard), *Dreams and Life* (Gérard de Nerval), *Les Fleurs du Mal* (Baudelaire), *Les Chants de Maldoror* (Lautréamont), *The Birth of Tragedy* (Nietzsche), *La Bête Humaine* (Zola), *Hunger* (Knut Humsun), *Les Lauriers Sont Coupés* (Dujardin), *The Conquest of Bread* (Kropotkin), *Looking Backward* (Edward Bellamy), *Alice in Wonderland, The Serpent in Paradise* (Sacher-Masoch), *Les Paradis Artificiels* (Baudelaire), *Dead Souls* (Gogol), *The House of the Dead* (Dostoevski), *The Wild Duck* (Ibsen), *The Inferno* (Strindberg), *The Nether World* (Gissing), *A Rebours* (Huysmans). . . .

Goethe's *Faust* was not so very old when Rimbaud asked a friend for a copy of it. Remember the date of his birth is October 20th, 1854 (6:00 A.M. Western Standard Diabolical Time). The very next year, 1855, *Leaves of Grass* makes its appearance, followed by condemnation and suppression. Meanwhile *Moby Dick* had come out (1851) and Thoreau's *Walden* (1854). In 1855 Gérard de Nerval commits suicide, having lasted till the remarkable age of 47. In 1854 Kierkegaard is already penning his last words to history in which he gives the parable of "The Sacrificed Ones." Just four or five years before Rimbaud completes *A Season in Hell* (1873), Lautréamont publishes his celebrated piece of blasphemy, another "work of youth," as we say, in order not to take these heartbreaking testaments seriously. . . . By 1888 Nietzsche is explaining to Brandes that he can now boast three readers: Brandes, Taine, and Strindberg. The next year he goes mad and remains that way until his death in 1900. Lucky man! From 1893 to 1897 Strindberg is experiencing a *crise* . . . which he describes with magisterial effects in *The Inferno*. Reminiscent of Rimbaud is the title of another of his works: *The Keys to Paradise*. In 1888 comes

Dujardin's curious little book, forgotten until recently. . . . By this time Mark Twain is at his height, *Huckleberry Finn* having appeared in 1884, the same year as *Against the Grain* of Huysmans. . . . By the fall of 1891 Gissing's *New Grub Street* is launched. It is an interesting year in nineteenth-century literature, the year of Rimbaud's death. . . .

What a century of names! . . . Shelley, Blake, Stendhal, Hegel, Fechner, Emerson, Poe, Schopenhauer, Max Stirner, Mallarmé, Chekhov, Andreyev, Verlaine, Couperus, Maeterlinck, Madame Blavatsky, Samuel Butler, Claudel, Unamuno, Conrad, Bakunin, Shaw, Rilke, Stefan George, Verhaeren, Gautier, Léon Bloy, Balzac, Yeats. . . .

What revolt, what disillusionment, what longing! Nothing but crises, breakdowns, hallucinations and visions. The foundations of politics, morals, economics, and art tremble. The air is full of warnings and prophecies of the debacle to come—and in the twentieth century it comes! Already two World Wars and a promise of more before the century is out. Have we touched bottom? Not yet. The moral crisis of the nineteenth century has merely given way to the spiritual bankruptcy of the twentieth. It is "the time of the assassins" and no mistaking it. . . .*

Rimbaud is indeed the symbol of the death of modern poetry. This seer, this visionary deserts poetry at the age of eighteen to make money, by gunrunning, even by slave-trading, ending with a death-bed conversion. His is a life of slander, beginning with the motto "Death to God" chalked on the church and ending with extreme unction and the money belt under the bed. I think the message of Rimbaud to Miller is the death of poetry, the death of history. The whole romantic agony of the nineteenth century is summed up in this adolescent genius, a curse laid on us. Miller obliterates the curse; he pronounces the benediction over Rimbaud, over the death of poetry, over the death of civilization itself but with a side-splitting laugh without an iota of animosity in it. Miller leads us away from the charnel house of nineteenth-century poetry; he does not even recognize the existence of twentieth-century poetry. For poetry has lost its significance, its relevance, and even its meaning in our time. To begin again it must repair to the wilderness, outside society, outside the city gates, a million miles from books and their keepers. Almost alone of the writers of our time Henry Miller has done this; I would guess that his following is enormous and that it is just beginning to grow. Like Nietzsche, like Lawrence, his word somehow spreads abroad and somehow cleanses the atmosphere of the mind of its age-old detritus of tradition, its habits of despair, its hates.

One word more: at the close of his beautiful clown story, "The Smile at the Foot of the Ladder," Miller talks about the clown, the hero of so much of the best contemporary literature.

> Joy is like a river [says Miller], it flows ceaselessly. It seems to me that this is the message which the clown is trying to convey to us, that we should participate through ceaseless flow and movement, that we should not stop to reflect, compare, analyze, possess, but flow on and through, endlessly, like music. This is the gift of surrender, and the clown makes it symbolically. It is for us to make it real.
>
> At no time in the history of man has the world been so full of pain and anguish. Here and there, however, we meet with individuals who are untouched, unsullied, by the common grief. They are not heartless individuals, far from it! They are emancipated beings. For them the world is not what it seems to us. They see with other eyes. We say of them that they have died to the world. They live in the moment, fully, and the radiance which emanates from them is a perpetual song of joy.*

And Miller is certainly one of these who have died to the world, like the clown. The ponderous absurdities of modern literature and the world it perpetuates dissolve in the hilarities of this almost unknown American author; this poet who dissociates himself from the so-called modern age and whose one aim is to give literature back to life. There are not many of these emancipated beings left in our world, these clowns and clairvoyants, celebrants of the soul and of the flesh and of the still-remaining promise of America. And of these few great souls the greatest is—the Patagonian.

* Henry Miller, *The Smile at the Foot of the Ladder,* Copyright 1948 by Henry Miller. Reprinted by permission of New Directions Publishing Corporation.

RICHARD WRIGHT

****

As dean of modern black writers, Wright has been both re-
pudiated and praised by those who have followed. The story of his
early life is most completely told in his autobiographical *Black Boy*
(1945) and, fictionally, in some of the stories in *Uncle Tom's
Children* (1938); his complete life is revealed in sympathetic detail in Constance Webb's *Richard Wright: A Biography* (New York,
1968). Much of the better writing about him has appeared in
European periodicals (Wright lived in France from 1946 until his
death in 1960), but an exception is Robert Bone's brief *Richard
Wright* (Minneapolis, Minn., 1969). Writings which seem to me
helpful, though not always objective, are Nelson Algren, "Remem-
bering Richard Wright," *Nation,* CXCII (January 28, 1961), p. 85;
James Baldwin, "Alas, Poor Richard," *Nobody Knows My Name*
(New York, 1961); "The Survival of Richard Wright," *Reporter,*
XXIV (March 16, 1961), pp. 52–55; Maurice Charney, "James
Baldwin's Quarrel with Richard Wright," *American Quarterly,* XV
(Spring 1963), pp. 65–75; Nick Aaron Ford, "The Ordeal of

Richard Wright," *College English,* XV (November 1953), pp. 87–94; Gerald Green, "Back to Bigger," *Kenyon Review,* XXVIII (Winter 1966), pp. 521–536; Nathan A. Scott, "Search for Beliefs," *University of Kansas City Review,* XXIII (October and December 1956), pp. 19–24, 131–139; and Henry F. Winslow, "Richard Nathaniel Wright: Destroyer and Preserver," *Crisis,* LXIX (March 1962), pp. 149–163.

RICHARD WRIGHT'S BLUES

Ralph Ellison

****

If anybody ask you
   who sing this song,
Say it was ole [Black Boy]
   done been here and gone.[1]

As a writer, Richard Wright has outlined for himself a dual role: to discover and depict the meaning of Negro experience; and to reveal to both Negroes and whites those problems of a psychological and emotional nature which arise between them when they strive for mutual understanding.

Now, in *Black Boy,* he has used his own life to probe what qualities of will, imagination and intellect are required of a Southern Negro in order to possess the meaning of his life in the United States. Wright is an important

---

[1] Signature formula used by blues singers at conclusion of song.

writer, perhaps the most articulate Negro American, and what he has to say is highly perceptive. Imagine Bigger Thomas projecting his own life in lucid prose, guided, say, by the insights of Marx and Freud, and you have an idea of this autobiography.

Published at a time when any sharply critical approach to Negro life has been dropped as a wartime expendable, it should do much to redefine the problem of the Negro and American Democracy. Its power can be observed in the shrill manner with which some professional "friends of the Negro people" have attempted to strangle the work in a noose of newsprint.

What in the tradition of literary autobiography is it like, this work described as a "great American autobiography"? As a non-white intellectual's statement of his relationship to Western culture, *Black Boy* recalls the conflicting pattern of identification and rejection found in Nehru's *Toward Freedom*. In its use of fictional techniques, its concern with criminality (sin) and the artistic sensibility, and in its author's judgment and rejection of the narrow world of his origin, it recalls Joyce's rejection of Dublin in *A Portrait of the Artist*. And as a psychological document of life under oppressive conditions, it recalls *The House of the Dead,* Dostoievsky's profound study of the humanity of Russian criminals.

Such works were perhaps Wright's literary guides, aiding him to endow his life's incidents with communicable significance; providing him with ways of seeing, feeling and describing his environment. These influences, however, were encountered only after these first years of Wright's life were past and were not part of the immediate folk culture into which he was born. In that culture the specific folk-art form which helped shape the writer's attitude toward his life and which embodied the impulse that contributes much to the quality and tone of his autobiography was the Negro blues. This would bear a word of explanation:

The blues is an impulse to keep the painful details and episodes of a brutal experience alive in one's aching consciousness, to finger its jagged grain, and to transcend it, not by the consolation of philosophy but by squeezing from it a near-tragic, near-comic lyricism. As a form, the blues is an autobiographical chronicle of personal catastrophe expressed lyrically. And certainly Wright's early childhood was crammed with catastrophic incidents. In a few short years his father deserted his mother, he knew intense hunger, he became a drunkard begging drinks from black stevedores in Memphis saloons; he had to flee Arkansas, where an uncle was lynched; he was forced to live with a fanatically religious grandmother in an atmosphere of constant bickering; he was lodged in an orphan asylum; he observed the suffering of his mother, who became a permanent invalid, while fighting off the blows of the poverty-stricken relatives with whom he had to live; he was cheated, beaten and kicked off jobs by white employees who disliked his eagerness to learn a trade; and to these objective circumstances must be added the subjective fact that Wright, with his sensitivity, extreme shyness and intelligence, was a problem child who rejected his family and was by them rejected.

Thus along with the themes, equivalent descriptions of milieu and the perspectives to be found in Joyce, Nehru, Dostoievsky, George Moore and Rousseau, *Black Boy* is filled with blues-tempered echoes of railroad trains, the names of Southern towns and cities, estrangements, fights and flights, deaths and disappointments, charged with physical and spiritual hungers and pain. And like a blues sung by such an artist as Bessie Smith, its lyrical prose evokes the paradoxical, almost surreal image of a black boy singing lustily as he probes his own grievous wound.

In *Black Boy,* two worlds have fused, two cultures merged, two impulses of Western man become coalesced. By discussing some of its cultural sources I hope to answer those critics who would make of the book a miracle and of its author a mystery. And while making no attempt to probe the mystery of the artist (who Hemingway says is "forged in injustice as a sword is forged"), I do hold that basically the prerequisites to the writing of *Black Boy* were, on the one hand, the microscopic degree of cultural freedom which Wright found in the South's stony injustice, and, on the other, the existence of a personality agitated to a state of almost manic restlessness. There were, of course, other factors, chiefly ideological; but these came later.

Wright speaks of his journey north as

> . . . taking a part of the South to transplant in alien soil, to see
> if it could grow differently, if it could drink of new and cool rains,
> bend in strange winds, respond to the warmth of other suns, and
> perhaps, to bloom. . . .

And just as Wright, the man, represents the blooming of the delinquent child of the autobiography, just so does *Black Boy* represent the flowering —cross-fertilized by pollen blown by the winds of strange cultures—of the humble blues lyric. There is, as in all acts of creation, a world of mystery in this, but there is also enough that is comprehensible for Americans to create the social atmosphere in which other black boys might freely bloom.

For certainly, in the historical sense, Wright is no exception. Born on a Mississippi plantation, he was subjected to all those blasting pressures which in a scant eighty years have sent the Negro people hurtling, without clearly defined trajectory, from slavery to emancipation, from log cabin to city tenement, from the white folks' fields and kitchens to factory assembly lines; and which, between two wars, have shattered the wholeness of its folk consciousness into a thousand writhing pieces.

Black Boy describes this process in the personal terms of *one* Negro childhood. Nevertheless, several critics have complained that it does not "explain" Richard Wright. Which, aside from the notion of art involved, serves to remind us that the prevailing mood of American criticism has so thoroughly excluded the Negro that it fails to recognize some of the most basic tenets of Western democratic thought when encountering them in a black skin. They forget that human life possesses an innate dignity and mankind an innate sense of nobility; that all men possess the tendency to dream and the compulsion to make their dreams reality; that the need to be ever dissatisfied and the urge ever to seek satisfaction is implicit in the human organism; and that all men are the victims and the beneficiaries of the goading, tormenting, commanding and informing activity of that imperious process known as the Mind—the Mind, as Valéry describes it, "armed with its inexhaustible questions."

Perhaps all this (in which lies the very essence of the human, and which Wright takes for granted) has been forgotten because the critics recognize neither Negro humanity nor the full extent to which the Southern community renders the fulfillment of human destiny impossible. And while it is true that *Black Boy* presents an almost unrelieved picture of a personality corrupted by brutal environment, it also presents those fresh, human responses brought to its world by the sensitive child:

> There was the *wonder* I felt when I first saw a brace of mountain-like, spotted, black-and-white horses clopping down a dusty road . . . the *delight* I caught in seeing long straight rows of red and green vegetables stretching away in the sun . . . the faint, cool kiss of *sensuality* when dew came on to my cheeks . . . the vague *sense of the infinite* as I looked down upon the yellow, dreaming waters of the Mississippi . . . the echoes of *nostalgia* I heard in the crying strings of wild geese . . . the *love* I had for the mute regality of tall, moss-clad oaks . . . the hint of *cosmic cruelty* that I *felt* when I saw the curved timbers of a wooden shack that had been warped in the summer sun . . . and there was the *quiet terror* that suffused my senses when vast hazes of gold washed earthward from star-heavy skies on silent nights. . . .[2]

And a bit later, his reactions to religion:

> Many of the religious symbols appealed to my sensibilities and I responded to the dramatic vision of life held by the church, feeling that to live day by day with death as one's sole thought was

[2] Italics mine.

to be so compassionately sensitive toward all life as to view all men as slowly dying, and the trembling sense of fate that welled up, sweet and melancholy, from the hymns blended with the sense of fate that I had already caught from life.

There was also the influence of his mother—so closely linked to his hysteria and sense of suffering—who (though he only implies it here) taught him, in the words of the dedication prefacing *Native Son,* "to revere the fanciful and the imaginative." There were also those white men—the one who allowed Wright to use his library privileges and the other who advised him to leave the South, and still others whose offers of friendship he was too frightened to accept.

Wright assumed that the nucleus of plastic sensibility is a human heritage: the right and the opportunity to dilate, deepen and enrich sensibility —democracy. Thus the drama of *Black Boy* lies in its depiction of what occurs when Negro sensibility attempts to fulfill itself in the undemocratic South. Here it is not the individual that is the immediate focus, as in Joyce's *Stephen Hero,* but that upon which his sensibility was nourished.

Those critics who complain that Wright has omitted the development of his own sensibility hold that the work thus fails as art. Others, because it presents too little of what they consider attractive in Negro life, charge that it distorts reality. Both groups miss a very obvious point: That whatever else the environment contained, it had as little chance of prevailing against the overwhelming weight of the child's unpleasant experiences as Beethoven's Quartets would have of destroying the stench of a Nazi prison.

We come, then, to the question of art. The function, the psychology, of artistic selectivity is to eliminate from art form all those elements of experience which contain no compelling significance. Life is as the sea, art a ship in which man conquers life's crushing formlessness, reducing it to a course, a series of swells, tides and wind currents inscribed on a chart. Though drawn from the world, "the organized significance of art," writes Malraux, "is stronger than all the multiplicity of the world; . . . that significance alone enables man to conquer chaos and to master destiny."

Wright saw his destiny—that combination of forces before which man feels powerless—in terms of a quick and casual violence inflicted upon him by both family and community. His response was likewise violent, and it has been his need to give that violence significance which has shaped his writings.

What were the ways by which other Negroes confronted their destiny?

In the South of Wright's childhood there were three general ways: They could accept the role created for them by the whites and perpetually resolve the resulting conflicts through the hope and emotional cartharsis of

Negro religion; they could repress their dislike of Jim Crow social relations while striving for a middle way of respectability, becoming—consciously or unconsciously—the accomplices of the whites in oppressing their brothers; or they could reject the situation, adopt a criminal attitude, and carry on an unceasing psychological scrimmage with the whites, which often flared forth into physical violence.

Wright's attitude was nearest the last. Yet in it there was an all-important qualitative difference: it represented a groping for *individual* values, in a black community whose values were what the young Negro critic, Edward Bland, has defined as "pre-individual." And herein lay the setting for the extreme conflict set off, both within his family and in the community, by Wright's assertion of individuality. The clash was sharpest on the psychological level, for, to quote Bland:

> In the pre-individualistic thinking of the Negro the stress is on the group. Instead of seeing in terms of the individual, the Negro sees in terms of "races," masses of peoples separated from other masses according to color. Hence, an act rarely bears intent against him as a Negro individual. He is singled out not as a person but as a specimen of an ostracized group. He knows that he never exists in his own right but only to the extent that others hope to make the race suffer vicariously through him.

This pre-individual state is induced artificially—like the regression to primitive states noted among cultured inmates of Nazi prisons. The primary technique in its enforcement is to impress the Negro child with the omniscience and omnipotence of the whites to the point that whites appear as ahuman as Jehovah, and as relentless as a Mississippi flood. Socially it is effected through an elaborate scheme of taboos supported by a ruthless physical violence, which strikes not only the offender but the entire black community. To wander from the paths of behavior laid down for the group is to become the agent of communal disaster.

In such a society the development of individuality depends upon a series of accidents, which often arise, as in Wright's case, from conditions within the Negro family. In Wright's life there was the accident that as a small child he could not distinguish between his fair-skinned grandmother and the white women of the town, thus developing skepticism as to their special status. To this was linked the accident of his having no close contacts with whites until after the child's normal formative period.

But these objective accidents not only link forward to these qualities of rebellion, criminality and intellectual questioning expressed in Wright's work today. They also link backward into the shadow of infancy where environment and consciousness are so darkly intertwined as to require the skill of a psychoanalyst to define their point of juncture. Nevertheless, at the age of four, Wright set the house afire and was beaten near to death by his frightened mother. This beating, followed soon by his father's desertion of the family, seems to be the initial psychological motivation of his quest for a new identification. While delirious from this beating Wright was haunted "by huge wobbly white bags like the full udders of a cow, suspended from the ceiling above me [and] I was gripped by the fear that they were going to fall and drench me with some horrible liquid. . . ."

It was as though the mother's milk had turned acid, and with it the whole pattern of life that had produced the ignorance, cruelty and fear that has fused with mother-love and exploded in the beating. It is significant that the bags were of the hostile color white, and the female symbol that of the cow, the most stupid (and, to the small child, the most frightening) of domestic animals. Here in dream symbolism is expressed an attitude worthy of an Orestes. And the significance of the crisis is increased by virtue of the historical fact that the lower-class Negro family is matriarchal; the child turns not to the father to compensate if he feels mother-rejection, but to the grandmother, or to an aunt—and Wright rejected both of these. Such rejection leaves the child open to psychological insecurity, distrust and all of those hostile environmental forces from which the family functions to protect it.

One of the Southern Negro family's methods of protecting the child is the severe beating—a homeopathic dose of the violence generated by black and white relationships. Such beatings as Wright's were administered for the child's own good; a good which the child resisted, thus giving family relationships an undercurrent of fear and hostility, which differs qualitatively from that found in patriarchal middle-class families, because here the severe beating is administered by the mother, leaving the child no parental sanctuary. He must ever embrace violence along with maternal tenderness, or else reject, in his helpless way, the mother.

The division between the Negro parents of Wright's mother's generation, whose sensibilities were often bound by their proximity to the slave experience, and their children, who historically and through the rapidity of American change stand emotionally and psychologically much farther away, is quite deep. Indeed, sometimes as deep as the cultural distance between Yeats' *Autobiographies* and a Bessie Smith blues. This is the historical background to those incidents of family strife in *Black Boy* which have caused reviewers to question Wright's judgment of Negro emotional relationships.

We have here a problem in the sociology of sensibility that is obscured by certain psychological attitudes brought to Negro life by whites.

The first is the attitude which compels whites to impute to Negroes sentiments, attitudes and insights which, as a group living under certain definite social conditions, Negroes could not humanly possess. It is the identical mechanism which William Empson identifies in literature as "pastoral." It implies that since Negroes possess the richly human virtues credited to them, then their social position is advantageous and should not be bettered; and, continuing syllogistically, the white individual need feel no guilt over his participation in Negro oppression.

The second attitude is that which leads whites to misjudge Negro passion, looking upon it as they do, out of the turgidity of their own frustrated yearning for emotional warmth, their capacity for sensation having been constricted by the impersonal mechanized relationships typical of bourgeois society. The Negro is idealized into a symbol of sensation, of unhampered social and sexual relationships. And when *Black Boy* questions their illusion they are thwarted much in the manner of the occidental who, after observing the erotic character of a primitive dance, "shacks up" with a native woman—only to discover that far from possessing the hair-trigger sexual responses of a Stork Club "babe," she is relatively phlegmatic.

The point is not that American Negroes are primitives, but that as a group their social situation does not provide for the type of emotional relationships attributed them. For how could the South, recognized as a major part of the backward third of the nation, nurture in the black, most brutalized section of its population, those forms of human relationships achievable only in the most highly developed areas of civilization?

Champions of this "Aren't-Negroes-Wonderful?" school of thinking often bring Paul Robeson and Marian Anderson forward as examples of highly developed sensibility, but actually they are only its *promise*. Both received their development from an extensive personal contact with European culture, free from the influences which shape Southern Negro personality. In the United States, Wright, who is the only Negro literary artist of equal caliber, had to wait years and escape to another environment before discovering the moral and ideological equivalents of his childhood attitudes.

Man cannot express that which does not exist—either in the form of dreams, ideas or realities—in his environment. Neither his thoughts nor his feelings, his sensibility nor his intellect are fixed, innate qualities. They are processes which arise out of the interpenetration of human instinct with environment, through the process called experience; each changing and being changed by the other. Negroes cannot possess many of the sentiments attributed to them because the same changes in environment which, through experience, enlarge man's intellect (and thus his capacity for still greater change) also modify his feelings; which in turn increase his sensibility, i.e., his sensitivity, to refinements of impression and subtleties of emotion. The extent of these changes depends upon the quality of political and cultural freedom in the environment.

Intelligence tests have measured the quick rise in intellect which takes place in Southern Negroes after moving north, but little attention has been paid to the mutations effected in their sensibilities. However, the two go hand in hand. Intellectual complexity is accompanied by emotional complexity; refinement of thought, by refinement of feeling. The movement north affects more than the Negro's wage scale; it affects his entire psychosomatic structure.

The rapidity of Negro intellectual growth in the North is due partially to objective factors present in the environment, to influences of the industrial city and to a greater political freedom. But there are also changes within the "inner world." In the North energies are released and given *intellectual* channelization—energies which in most Negroes in the South have been forced to take either a *physical* form or, as with potentially intellectual types like Wright, to be expressed as nervous tension, anxiety and hysteria. Which is nothing mysterious. The human organism responds to environmental stimuli by converting them into either physical and/or intellectual energy. And what is called hysteria is suppressed intellectual energy expressed physically.

The "physical" character of their expression makes for much of the difficulty in understanding American Negroes. Negro music and dances are frenziedly erotic; Negro religious ceremonies violently ecstatic; Negro speech strongly rhythmical and weighted with image and gesture. But there is more in this sensuousness than the unrestraint and insensitivity found in primitive cultures; nor is it simply the relatively spontaneous and undifferentiated responses of a people living in close contact with the soil. For despite Jim Crow, Negro life does not exist in a vacuum, but in the seething vortex of those tensions generated by the most highly industrialized of Western nations. The welfare of the most humble black Mississippi sharecropper is affected less by the flow of the seasons and the rhythm of natural events than by the fluctuations of the stock market; even though, as Wright states of his father, the sharecropper's memories, actions and emotions are shaped by his immediate contact with nature and the crude social relations of the South.

All of this makes the American Negro far different from the "simple" specimen for which he is taken. And the "physical" quality offered as evidence of his primitive simplicity is actually the form of his complexity. The American Negro is a Western type whose social condition creates a state which is almost the reverse of the cataleptic trance: Instead of his consciousness being lucid to the reality around it while the body is rigid, here it is the body which is alert, reacting to pressures which the constricting forces of Jim Crow block off from the transforming, concept-creating activity of the brain. The "eroticism" of Negro expression springs from much the same conflict as that displayed in the violent gesturing of a man who attempts to express a complicated concept with a limited vocabulary; thwarted ideational energy is converted into unsatisfactory pantomime, and his words are burdened with meanings they cannot convey. Here lies the source of the basic ambiguity of *Native Son,* wherein in order to translate Bigger's complicated feelings into universal ideas, Wright had to force into Bigger's consciousness concepts and ideas which his intellect could not formulate. Between Wright's skill and knowledge and the potentials of Bigger's mute feelings lay a thousand years of conscious culture.

In the South the sensibilities of both blacks and whites are inhibited by the rigidly defined environment. For the Negro there is relative safety as long as the impulse toward individuality is suppressed. (Lynchings have occurred because Negroes painted their homes.) And it is the task of the Negro family to adjust the child to the Southern milieu; through it the currents, tensions and impulses generated within the human organism by the flux and flow of events are given their distribution. This also gives the group its distinctive character. Which, because of Negroes' suppressed minority position, is very much in the nature of an elaborate but limited defense mechanism. Its function is dual: to protect the Negro from whirling away from the undifferentiated mass of his people into the unknown, symbolized in its most abstract form by insanity, and most concretely by lynching; and to protect him from those unknown forces *within himself* which might urge him to reach out for that social and human equality which the white South says he cannot have. Rather than throw himself against the charged wires of his prison he annihilates the impulses within him.

The pre-individualistic black community discourages individuality out of self-defense. Having learned through experience that the whole group is punished for the actions of the single member, it has worked out efficient techniques of behavior control. For in many Southern communities everyone knows everyone else and is vulnerable to his opinions. In some communities everyone is "related" regardless of blood-ties. The regard shown by the group for its members, its general communal character and its cohesion are often mentioned. For by comparison with the coldly impersonal relationships of the urban industrial community, its relationships are personal and warm.

Black Boy, however, illustrates that this personal quality, shaped by outer violence and inner fear, is ambivalent. Personal warmth is accompanied by an equally personal coldness, kindliness by cruelty, regard by malice. And these opposites are as quickly set off against the member who gestures toward individuality as a lynch mob forms at the cry of rape. Negro leaders have often been exasperated by this phenomenon, and Booker T.

Washington (who demanded far less of Negro humanity than Richard Wright) described the Negro community as a basket of crabs, wherein should one attempt to climb out, the others immediately pull him back.

The member who breaks away is apt to be more impressed by its negative than by its positive character. He becomes a stranger even to his relatives and he interprets gestures of protection as blows of oppression—from which there is no hiding place, because every area of Negro life is affected. Even parental love is given a qualitative balance akin to "sadism." And the extent of beatings and psychological maimings meted out by Southern Negro parents rivals those described by the nineteenth-century Russian writers as characteristic of peasant life under the Czars. The horrible thing is that the cruelty is also an expression of concern, of love.

In discussing the inadequacies for democratic living typical of the education provided Negroes by the South, a Negro educator has coined the term *mis-education*. Within the ambit of the black family this takes the form of training the child away from curiosity and adventure, against reaching out for those activities lying beyond the borders of the black community. And when the child resists, the parent discourages him; first with the formula, "That there's for white folks. Colored can't have it," and finally with a beating.

It is not, then, the family and communal violence described by *Black Boy* that is unusual, but that Wright *recognized* and made no peace with its essential cruelty—even when, like a babe freshly emerged from the womb, he could not discern where his own personality ended and it began. Ordinarily both parent and child are protected against this cruelty—seeing it as love and finding subjective sanction for it in the spiritual authority of the Fifth Commandment, and on the secular level in the legal and extralegal structure of the Jim Crow system. The child who did not rebel, or who was unsuccessful in his rebellion, learned a masochistic submissiveness and a denial of the impulse toward Western culture when it stirred within him.

Why then have Southern whites, who claim to "know" the Negro, missed all this? Simply because they, too, are armored against the horror and the cruelty. Either they deny the Negro's humanity and feel no cause to measure his actions against civilized norms; or they protect themselves from their guilt in the Negro's condition and from their fear that their cooks might poison them, or that their nursemaids might strangle their infant charges, or that their field hands might do them violence, by attributing to them a superhuman capacity for love, kindliness and forgiveness. Nor does this in any way contradict their stereotyped conviction that all Negroes (meaning those with whom they have no contact) are given to the most animal behavior.

It is only when the individual, whether white or black, *rejects* the pattern that he awakens to the nightmare of his life. Perhaps much of the South's regressive character springs from the fact that many, jarred by some casual crisis into wakefulness, flee hysterically into the sleep of violence or the coma of apathy again. For the penalty of wakefulness is to encounter ever more violence and horror than the sensibilities can sustain unless translated into some form of social action. Perhaps the impassioned character so noticeable among those white Southern liberals so active in the Negro's cause is due to their sense of accumulated horror; their passion—like the violence in Faulkner's novels—is evidence of a profound spiritual vomiting.

This compulsion is even more active in Wright and the increasing number of Negroes who have said an irrevocable "no" to the Southern pattern. Wright learned that it is not enough merely to reject the white South, but that he had also to reject that part of the South which lay within. As a rebel he formulated that rejection negatively, because it was the negative face of the Negro community upon which he looked most often as a child. It is this he is contemplating when he writes:

> Whenever I thought of the essential bleakness of black life in America, I knew that Negroes had never been allowed to catch the full spirit of Western civilization, that they lived somehow in it but not of it. And when I brooded upon the cultural barrenness of black life, I wondered if clean, positive tenderness, love, honor, loyalty and the capacity to remember were native to man. I asked myself if these human qualities were not fostered, won, struggled and suffered for, preserved in ritual from one generation to another.

But far from implying that Negroes have no capacity for culture, as one critic interprets it, this is the strongest affirmation that they have. Wright is pointing out what should be obvious (especially to his Marxist critics) that Negro sensibility is socially and historically conditioned; that Western culture must be won, confronted like the animal in a Spanish bullfight, dominated by the red shawl of codified experience and brought heaving to its knees.

Wright knows perfectly well that Negro life is a by-product of Western civilization, and that in it, if only one possesses the humanity and humility to see, are to be discovered all those impulses, tendencies, life and cultural forms to be found elsewhere in Western society.

The problem arises because the special condition of Negroes in the United States, including the defensive character of Negro life itself (the "will toward organization" noted in the Western capitalist appears in the Negro as a will to camouflage, to dissimulate), so distorts these forms as to render their recognition as difficult as finding a wounded quail against the brown and yellow leaves of a Mississippi thicket—even the spilled blood blends with the background. Having himself been in the position of the quail—to expand the metaphor—Wright's wounds have told him both the question and the answer which every successful hunter must discover for himself: "Where would I hide if *I* were a wounded quail?" But perhaps that requires more sympathy with one's quarry than most hunters possess. Certainly it requires such a sensitivity to the shifting guises of humanity under pressure as to allow them to identify themselves with the human content, whatever its outer form; and even with those Southern Negroes to whom Paul Robeson's name is only a rolling sound in the fear-charged air.

Let us close with one final word about the blues: Their attraction lies in this, that they at once express both the agony of life and the possibility of conquering it through sheer toughness of spirit. They fall short of tragedy only in that they provide no solution, offer no scapegoat but the self. Nowhere in America today is there social or political action based upon the solid realities of Negro life depicted in *Black Boy;* perhaps that is why, with its refusal to offer solutions, it is like the blues. Yet in it thousands of Negroes will for the first time see their destiny in public print. Freed here of fear and the threat of violence, their lives have at least been organized, scaled down to possessable proportions. And in this lies Wright's most important achievement: He has converted the American Negro impulse toward self-annihilation and "going-under-ground" into a will to confront the world, to evaluate his experience honestly and throw his findings unashamedly into the guilty conscience of America.

RALPH ELLISON

****

A trustworthy introduction to Ellison can be found in James
A. Emanuel and Theodore L. Grass's *Dark Symphony: Negro
Literature in America* (New York, 1968), in Robert L. Bone's
The Negro Novel in America (New Haven, Conn., 1958; revised,
1965), and perhaps best in his own *Shadow and Act* (New York,
1964). Marcus Klein presents a balanced extended discussion of
his writing in *After Alienation: American Novels in Mid-Century*
(Cleveland, Ohio, 1964), and shorter studies include Jonathan
Baumbach's "Nightmare of a Native Son," *Critique,* VI (Spring
1963), pp. 48–65, Raymond M. Olderman's "Ralph Ellison's
Blues," *Wisconsin Studies in Contemporary Literature,* VII (Summer 1966), pp. 142–159, and Richard Kostelanetz's "The Politics of
Ellison's Booker: *Invisible Man* as Symbolic History," *Chicago Review,* XIX (November 2, 1967), pp. 5–26. Ellison speaks of him-
self with dignity in "A Very Stern Discipline," *Harper's Magazine,*
CCXXXIV (March 1967), pp. 76–95.

RALPH ELLISON AND THE AMERICAN COMIC TRADITION

Earl H. Rovit

****

The most obvious comment one can make about Ralph Ellison's *Invisible Man* is that it is a profoundly comic work. But the obvious is not necessarily either simple or self-explanatory, and it seems to me that the comic implications of Ellison's novel are elusive and provocative enough to warrant careful examination both in relation to the total effect of the novel itself and the American cultural pattern from which it derives. It is generally recognized that Ellison's novel is a highly conscious attempt to embody a particular kind of experience—the experience of the "outsider" (in this case, a Negro) who manages to come to some sort of temporary acceptance, and thus, definition, of his status in the universe; it is not so generally recognized that *Invisible Man* is an integral link in a cumulative chain of great American creations, bearing an unmistakable brand of kinship to such

From Earl H. Rovit, "Ralph Ellison and the American Comic Tradition," *Wisconsin Studies in Contemporary Literature,* Volume I, Number 1 (© 1967 by the Regents of the University of Wisconsin), pp. 34–42.

seemingly incongruous works as *The Divinity School Address, Song of Myself, Moby-Dick,* and *The Education of Henry Adams.* But the latter proposition is, I think, at least as valid as the former, and unless it is given proper recognition, a good deal of the value of the novel will be ignored.

First it should be noted that Ellison's commitment to what Henry James has termed "the American joke" has been thoroughly deliberate and undisguised. Ellison once described penetratingly the ambiguous *locus* of conflicting forces within which the American artist has had always to work: "For the ex-colonials, the declaration of an American identity meant the assumption of a mask, and it imposed not only the discipline of national self-consciousness, it gave Americans an ironic awareness of the joke that always lies between appearance and reality, between the discontinuity of social tradition and that sense of the past which clings to the mind. And perhaps even an awareness of the joke that society is man's creation, not God's." This kind of ironic awareness may contain bitterness and may even become susceptible to the heavy shadow of despair, but the art which it produces has been ultimately comic. It will inevitably probe the masks of identity and value searching relentlessly for some deeper buried reality, but it will do this while accepting the fundamental necessity for masks and the impossibility of ever discovering an essential face beneath a mask. That is to say, this comic stance will accept with the same triumphant gesture both the basic absurdity of all attempts to impose meaning on the chaos of life, and the necessary converse of this, the ultimate significance of absurdity itself.

Ellison's *Invisible Man* is comic in this sense almost in spite of its overtly satirical interests and its excursions into the broadly farcical. Humorous as many of its episodes are in themselves—the surreal hysteria of the scene at the Golden Day, the hero's employment at the Liberty Paint Company, or the expert dissection of political entanglements in Harlem—these are the materials which clothe Ellison's joke and which, in turn, suggest the shape by which the joke can be comprehended. The pith of Ellison's comedy reverberates on a level much deeper than these incidents, and as in all true humor, the joke affirms and denies simultaneously—accepts and rejects with the same uncompromising passion, leaving not a self-cancelling neutralization of momentum, but a sphere of moral conquest, a humanized cone of light at the very heart of the heart of darkness. *Invisible Man,* as Ellison has needlessly insisted in rebuttal to those critics who would treat the novel as fictionalized sociology or as a dramatization of archetypal images, is an artist's attempt to create a *form.* And fortunately Ellison has been quite explicit in describing what he means by *form;* in specific reference to the improvisation of the jazz-musician he suggests that form represents "a definition of his identity: as an individual, as member of the collectivity, and as a link in the chain of tradition." But note that each of these definitions of identity must be individually exclusive and mutually contradictory on any logical terms. Because of its very pursuit after the uniqueness of individuality, the successful definition of an individual must define out the possibilities of generalization into "collectivity" or "tradition." But herein for Ellison in his embrace of a notion of fluid amorphous identity lies the real morality and humor in mankind's art and men's lives—neither of which have much respect for the laws of formal logic.

At one time during the novel when Ellison's protagonist is enthusiastically convinced that his membership in the Brotherhood is the only effective means to individual and social salvation, he recalls these words from a college lecture on Stephen Dedalus: "Stephen's problem, like ours, was not actually one of creating the uncreated conscience of his race, but of creating the *uncreated features of his face.* Our task is that of making ourselves individuals. The conscience of a race is the gift of its individuals who see, evaluate, record. . . . We create the race by creating ourselves and then to our great astonishment we will have created something far more important: We will have created a culture. Why waste time creating a conscience for something that doesn't exist? For, you see, blood and skin do not think!" This is one of the most significant passages in the novel, and one which must be appreciated within the context of the total form if the subtle pressure of that form is to be adequately weighed. And this can be done only if the Prologue and the Epilogue are viewed as functional elements in the novel which set the tempo for its moral action and modulate ironically upon its emergent meanings.

The Prologue introduces the narrator in his underground hibernation musing upon the events of his life, eating vanilla ice-cream and sloe gin, listening to Louis Armstrong's recording, "What Did I Do to Be so Black and Blue?" and trying to wrest out of the confusions of his experiences some pattern of meaning and/or resilient core of identity. The next twenty-five chapters are a first-person narrative flashback which covers some twenty years of the protagonist's life ending with the beginning, the hero's descent into the underground hole. The concluding Epilogue picks up the tonal patterns of the Prologue, implies that both meaning and identity have been discovered, and dramatically forces a direct identification between the narrator and the reader. Ostensibly this is another novel of the initiation of a boy into manhood—a *Bildungsroman* in the episodic picaresque tradition. The advice of the literature teacher has been realized; the hero has created the features of his face from the malleable stuff of his experience. He who accepts himself as "invisible" has ironically achieved a concrete tangibility, while those characters in the novel who seemed to be "visible" and substantial men (Norton, Brother Jack, and even Tod Clifton) are discovered to be really "invisible" since they are self-imprisoned captives of their own capacities to see and be seen in stereotyped images. However, to read the novel in this way and to go no further is to miss the cream of the jest and the total significance of the whole form which pivots on the ironic fulcrum of the blues theme introduced in the Prologue and given resolution in the Epilogue. As in all seriously comic works the reader is left not with an answer, but with a challenging question—a question which soars beyond the novel on the unanswered notes of Armstrong's trumpet: "What did I do to be so black and blue?"

For the protagonist *is* finally and most comically *invisible* at the end of the novel; he has learned that to create the uncreated features of his face is at best a half-value, and at worst, potentially more self-destructive than not to strive after identity at all. For Ellison ours is a time when "you prepare a face to meet the faces that you meet"—a time when we have learned to shuffle and deal our personalities with a protean dexterity that, as is characterized through Rinehart, is a wholesale exploitation of and surrender to chaos. After the narrator's fall into the coalpit he discovers that his arrogantly naive construction of personality is nothing more than the accumulated fragments in his briefcase: the high-school diploma, Bledsoe's letter, Clifton's dancing doll, Mary's bank, Brother Tarp's iron. And most ironically, even these meager artifacts—the fragments he has shored against his ruin—represent not him, but the world's variegated projections of him. The narrator learns then that his educational romance is a farcical melodrama of the most garish variety; the successive births and rebirths of his life (his Caesarean delivery from college, his birth by electronics at the factory hospital, the christening by the Brotherhood) were not the organic gestations of personality that he idealized so much as they were the cold manipulations of artificial insemination. His final acceptance of his invisibility reminds us of the demand of the Zen Master: "Show me the face you had before you were born."

However, we must note also that this acceptance of invisibility, of amorphous non-identity, is far from a resignation to chaos. The protagonist has successfully rebelled against the imposition of social masks whether externally (like Clifton's) or internally (like Brother Tarp's) bestowed; his is not a surrender of personality so much as a descent to a deeper level of personality where the accent is heavier on possibilities than on limitations. The 1,369 glowing light bulbs in his cellar retreat attest to the increased power and enlightenment which are positive gains from his experience, as well as to the strategic advantages of his recourse to invisibility. The literature teacher unwittingly pointed out the flaw in his exhortation even as he declaimed it: "Blood and skin do not think!" For to think is to be as much concerned with analysis as it is with synthesis; the ironic mind tears radiant unities apart even as it forges them. Accordingly Ellison's narrator assumes the ultimate mask of facelessness and emphasizes the fluid chaos which is the secret substance of form, the dynamic interplay of possibilities which creates limitations. The narrator is backed into the blank corner where he must realize that "the mind that has conceived a plan of living must never lose sight of the chaos against which that pattern was conceived." In accepting himself as the Invisible Man he assumes the historic role which Emerson unerringly assigned to the American poet; he becomes "the world's eye"— something through which one sees, even though it cannot itself be seen.

And here it may be fruitful to investigate briefly the peculiar relationship of Emerson's work to Ellison (whose middle name is propitiously Waldo). In the recently published excerpt from a novel in progress, "And Hickman Arrives," Ellison has his main character, Alonzo Zuber, Daddy Hickman, make some complementary remarks about Emerson, "a preacher . . . who knew that every tub has to sit on its own bottom." Daddy Hickman, a Negro preacher ("Better known as GOD'S TROMBONE"), is vividly characterized as a wise and shrewd virtuoso of the evangelical circuit who might not unfairly be taken as a modern-day Emerson, preaching eloquently the gospel of humanity. These facts may be significant when we remember that Emerson's work is given short shrift as rhetorical nonsense in *Invisible Man* and his name is bestowed upon a character whose minor function in the novel is to be a self-righteous hypocrite. This shift in attitude may indicate that Ellison has come to realize that there are some major affinities binding him to his famous namesake, and, more important, it may enable us to understand more clearly the remarkable consistency of the American struggle to create art and the relatively harmonious vision which these unique struggles have attained.

Superficially there would seem to be little to link the two men beyond the somewhat labored pun of their names and Ellison's awareness of the pun. The one, an ex-Unitarian minister of respectable, if modest, Yankee background, whose orotund explorations in autobiography gave fullest form to the American dream—whose public pose attained an Olympian serenity and optimistic faith which have caused him to be associated with a wide range of sentimentalities from Mary Baker Eddy to Norman Vincent Peale; the other, an Oklahoma City Negro, born in 1914, ex-Leftist propagandist and editor, who would seem to have belied the Emersonian prophecy of individualism and self-reliance by the very title of his novel, *Invisible Man*. The one, nurtured by the most classical education that America had to offer; the other, a rapt disciple of jazzmen like Charlie Christian and Jimmy Rushing who has attributed to their lyric improvisations his deepest understanding of aesthetic form. The one, white and given to the Delphic utterance; the other, black and adept in the cautery of bitter humor. But in their respective searches for identity, in their mutual concern with defining the possibilities and limitations which give form and shape to that which is human, the poet who called man "a golden impossibility" and the novelist who teaches his protagonist that life is a latent hive of infinite possibilities draw close together in their attempts to find an artistic resolution of the contrarieties of existence.

"Only he can give, who has," wrote Emerson; "he only can create, who is." Experience is the fluxional material from which these all-important values and identities are created, and Emerson's great essays are processive incantations whose ultimate function is to bring identity into being, even as they chant the fundamental fluidity of all forms spontaneously and eternally merging into other forms. When we remember that Emerson once wrote: "A believer in Unity, a seer of Unity, I yet behold two," it may be worth a speculation that the Emerson behind the triumphant artifices of the *Essays* was not a terribly different person from the Invisible Man in the coalpit whose submersion into the lower frequencies had given him an entree to the consciousnesses of all men. This awareness of the absurdity of meaning (and the potential meaningfulness of chaos) is at the heart of Emerson's delight in paradox, his seeming inconsistencies, his "dialogistic" techniques, his highly functional approach to language. "All symbols are fluxional," he declaimed; "all language is vehicular and transitive and is good for conveyance not for homestead." Thus Melville's attempted criticism of Emerson in *The Confidence Man* misses widely the mark; Emerson isn't there when the satire strikes home. Melville, who above all of Emerson's contemporaries should have known better, mistook the Olympian pasteboard mask for a reality and misread the eloquent quest for identity as a pretentious melodrama. For, as Constance Rourke recognized, Emerson is one of our most deft practitioners of the American joke, and the magnitude of his success may be measured by the continued effectiveness of his disguises after more than a hundred years.

But again we must return to the *form* of *Invisible Man* to appreciate how deeply involved Ellison's work is with the most basic American vision of reality. Although it is probably true as some critics have pointed out that the dominating metaphor of the novel—the "underground man" theme— was suggested by Dostoevsky and Richard Wright, it is for our purposes more interesting to note a similar metaphor in Hart Crane's poem, "Black Tambourine":

> The interests of a black man in a cellar
> Mark tardy judgment on the world's closed door.

Gnats toss in the shadow of a bottle,
And a roach spans a crevice in the floor.

. . . .

The black man, forlorn in the cellar,
Wanders in some mid-kingdom, dark, that lies,
Between his tambourine, stuck on the wall,
And, in Africa, a carcass quick with flies.*

Invisible Man achieves an expert evocation of that "mid-kingdom," that *demi-monde* of constant metamorphosis where good and evil, appearance and reality, pattern and chaos are continually shifting their shapes even as the eye strains to focus and the imagination to comprehend. The Kafka-esque surrealism of the novel's action, the thematic entwinement of black-white and dark-light, and the psychic distance from the plot-development which the use of the Prologue and the Epilogue achieves posit the moral center of the novel in that fluid area where experience is in the very process of being transformed into value. The narrator, the author, and the reader as well are caught in the "mid-kingdom" which seems to me to be the characteristic and unavoidable focus of American literature. For this mid-kingdom, this unutterable silence which is "zero at the bone," seems to me to be the one really inalienable birthright of being an American. Some Americans following Swedenborg named it "vastation"; others gave it no name and lamented the dearth of an American tradition within which the artist could work; at least one commissioned the sculptor, St. Gaudens, to incarnate it in a statue. One way of attempting to describe the sense of being within this mid-kingdom can be most dramatically seen in "The Castaway" chapter of *Moby-Dick* were Pip is left floundering in the boundless Pacific. And although the techniques of approaching the experience have been richly various, the experience itself, an incontrovertible sense of absolute metaphysical isolation, can be found at the core of the most vital American creations.

"American history," writes James Baldwin in *Notes of a Native Son,* is "the history of the total, and willing, alienation of entire peoples from their forebears. What is overwhelmingly clear . . . is that this history has created an entirely unprecedented people, with a unique and individual past." The alienation, of course, is more than sociological and ideological; it seeps down into the very depths whence the sureties of identity and value are wrought; and it imprisons the American in this mid-kingdom where the boundaries—the distance from the tambourine on the wall to the carcass quick with flies—cannot be measured in either years or miles. The American seeking himself—as an individual, a member of the collectivity, a link in the chain of tradition—can never discover or create that identity in fixed restrictive terms. The past is dead and yet it lives: note Ellison's use of the narrator's grandfather, the yams, the techniques of the evangelical sermon. Individuals are frozen in mute isolation, and yet communication is possible between them: the Harlem riot, the way the narrator listens to music. Ellison's novel is the unique metaphor of his own thoroughly personal experience, and yet it makes a fitting link in the chain of the American tradition.

That Ellison and his narrator are Negroes both is and is not important. From the severe standpoint of art the racial fact is negligible, although there are doubtless areas of meaning and influence in *Invisible Man* which sociological examination might fruitfully develop. From the viewpoint of cultural history, however, the racial fact is enormously provocative. It is strikingly clear that contemporary American writing, particularly the writing of fiction, is dominated by two categories of writers: members of religious and racial minorities, and writers who possess powerful regional heritages. Both groups have an instinctive leasehold within the boundaries of the "mid-kingdom"; the Negro, the Catholic, the Jew, and the Southerner share the immediate experience of living on the razor's edge of time, at the very point where traditions come into desperate conflict with the human need to adapt to change. And, of equal importance, both groups—in varying degrees—are marked out on the contemporary scene as being "different"; both groups cannot avoid the terrible problem of identity, because it is ever thrust upon them whether they like it or not. These are the conditions which in the American past have nourished our spasmodic exfoliations of significant literary activity: the great "Renaissance" of the 1840s and '50s, the Twain-James-Adams "alliance" of the late nineteenth century, the post-World War One literary florescence from which we have just begun to break away. But the Lost Generation was the last generation which could practise the necessary expatriation or "fugitivism" in which these factors—the disseverance from the past and the search for identity—could operate on non-minority or non-regional American writers. Thus Ralph Ellison—and contemporaries like Saul Bellow, Flannery O'Connor, and William Styron—are *inside* the heart of the American experience by the very virtue of their being in some way "outsiders." Like Emerson, himself a royal inhabitant of the mid-kingdom over a century ago, they are challenged to create form, or else succumb to the enveloping chaos within and without.

And the answers which they arrive at—again as with Emerson—are answers which cannot be taken out of the context of their individually achieved forms without being reduced to platitude or nonsense. Form, the creation of a radical, self-defining metaphor, is the one rational technique which human beings have developed to deal adequately with the basic irrationality of existence. The answer which *Invisible Man* gives to the unanswerable demands which life imposes on the human being has something to do with human limitation and a good deal to do with freedom; it has something to do with hatred, and a good deal more to do with love. It defines the human distance between the tambourine and the carcass and it accepts with wonder and dignity the immeasurable gift of life. The black man in the cellar transforms his isolation into elevation without denying the brute facts of existence and without losing his ironic grip on the transiency of the moment. The amorphous ambiguity of the mid-kingdom is for a timeless instant conquered and made fit for habitation. Perhaps tragedy teaches man to become divine, but before man can aspire to divinity, he must first accept completely the responsibilities and limitations of being human. The American experience, cutting away the bonds of tradition which assure man of his humanity, has not allowed a tragic art to develop. But there has developed a rich and vigorous comic tradition to which *Invisible Man* is a welcome embellishment, and it is this art which promises most as a healthy direction into the future.

SAUL BELLOW

****

When the essay printed here was first published, Saul Bellow had not yet written *Henderson the Rain King* (1959), *Herzog* (1964), or the recent *Mr. Sammler's Planet* (1970), which have extended, if not increased, his reputation; but what is said here seems to go so directly to matters of central importance that it could not be omitted; see also what Leslie A. Fiedler has to say of Bellow in "No! In Thunder," *Esquire,* LIV (September 1960), pp. 76–79. The larger canon of writings by Bellow is sensibly examined, briefly in Jack Ludwig's *Recent American Novelists* (Minneapolis, Minn., 1962), and at greater length in Chester E. Eisinger's *Fiction of the Fifties* (Chicago, 1963), Marcus Klein's *After Aliena-tion: American Novels in Mid-Century* (Cleveland and New York, 1964) and Howard M. Harper's *Desperate Faith* (Chapel Hill, N.C., 1967), which may together make up the most satisfactory examination of contemporary fiction now available; but see also Earl H. Rovit's *Saul Bellow* (Minneapolis, Minn., 1967). Bellow is in mid-career, so that the definitive words on his writing have not been spoken, but he shows promise of becoming a major figure of post-World War II fiction. Those who have written briefly but with some authority about him include Robert Alter, "The Stature of Saul Bellow," *Midstream,* X (December 1924, pp. 3–15; Malcolm Bradbury, "Saul Bellow and the Naturalist Tradition," *Review of English Literature,* IV (1963), pp. 80–92; Albert J. Guerard, "Saul Bellow and the Activists," *Southern Review,* III (July 1967), pp. 582–596; Richard Poirier, "Bellow to Herzog," *Partisan Review,* XXXII (Spring 1965), pp. 264–271; and Stanley Trachtenburg, "Saul Bellow's *Luftmenschen:* The Compromise with Reality," *Critique,* IX (Summer 1967), pp. 37–61. Four books, each tough enough to be quarreled with, also speak of Bellow in some detail: Peter M. Axthelm's *The Modern Confessional Novel* (New Haven, Conn., 1967), Jonathan Baumbach's *The Landscape of Nightmare* (New York, 1965), David D. Galloway's *The Absurd Hero in American Fiction* (Austin, Tex., 1966), and Ihab Hassan's *Radical Innocence* (Princeton, N.J. 1961). There is also a collection of good critical essays in *Saul Bellow and the Critics* (New York, 1967), by Irving Malin.

SAUL BELLOW

Leslie A. Fiedler

****

WITH the publication of *Seize the Day,* Saul Bellow has become not merely a writer with whom it is possible to come to terms, but one with whom it is *necessary* to come to terms—perhaps of all our novelists the one we need most to understand, if we are to understand what the novel is doing at the present moment. Bellow has endured the almost ritual indignities of the beginning fictionist: his first novel a little over-admired and read by scarcely anyone; his second novel once more critically acclaimed, though without quite the thrill of discovery, and still almost ignored by the larger public; his third novel, thick, popular, reprinted in the paper-backs and somewhat resented by the first discoverers, who hate seeing what was exclusively theirs pass into the public domain; and now a fourth book: a collection of stories, most of which have appeared earlier, a play, and a new novella.

Reprinted by permission from *Prairie Schooner,* Autumn 1957. Copyright 1957 by the University of Nebraska Press.

Suddenly, the novelist whom we have not ceased calling a "young writer" (it is a habit hard to break and the final indignity) is established and forty, a part of our lives and something for the really young to define themselves against. But it has become clear that he will continue to write, that he is not merely the author of a novel or two, but a *novelist;* and this in itself is a triumph, a rarity in recent American literary history and especially among the writers with whom we associate Bellow. We think of the whole line of Jewish-American novelists, so like him in origin and aspiration, of Daniel Fuchs and Henry Roth and Nathanael West, those poets and annalists of the thirties who did not survive their age, succumbing to death or Hollywood or a sheer exhaustion of spirit and subject. Or we think of Bellow's own contemporaries, the *Partisan Review* group, urban Jews growing up under the threat of failure and terror, the depression and Spain and the hopelessly foreseen coming of war. We remember, perhaps, Isaac Rosenfeld or H. J. Kaplan or Oscar Tarcov or Delmore Schwartz or even Lionel Trilling, who had also to be twice-born, committed first to Stalinism and then to disenchantment, but who were capable of using imaginatively only the disenchantment. And remembering these, we recall beginnings not quite fulfilled, achievements which somehow betrayed initial promises. Certain short stories remain in our minds (flanked by all those essays, those explanations and rejoinders and demonstrations of wit): Kaplan's "The Mohammedans," Rosenfeld's "The Pyramids," Schwartz's "In Dreams Begin Responsibilities," Trilling's "The Other Margaret"; but where except in *The Dangling Man* and *The Victim* and *Augie March* do the themes and motifs of the group find full novelistic expression?

We must begin to see Bellow, then, as the inheritor of a long tradition of false starts and abject retreats and grey inconclusions. There is a sense in which he fulfills the often frustrated attempt to possess the American imagination and to enter the American cultural scene of a line of Jewish fictionists which goes back beyond the post-war generation through Ben Hecht and Ludwig Lewisohn to Abe Cahan. A hundred, a thousand one-shot novelists, ephemeral successes and baffled eccentrics stand behind him, defining a subject: the need of the Jew in America to make clear his relationship to that country in terms of belonging or protest—and a language: a speech enriched by the dialectic and joyful intellectual play of Jewish conversation.

Bellow's own story is, then, like the archetypal Jewish dream a success story; since, like the standard characters in the tales of my grandfather (socialist though he was!), the novelist, too, has "worked himself up in America." Bellow's success must not be understood, however, as exclusively his own; for he emerges at the moment when the Jews for the first time move into the center of American culture, and he must be seen in the larger context. The background is familiar enough: the gradual breaking up of the Anglo-Saxon domination of our imagination: the relentless urbanization which makes rural myths and images no longer central to our experience; the exhaustion as vital themes of the Midwest and of the movement from the provinces to New York or Chicago or Paris; the turning again from West to East, from our own heartland back to Europe; and the discovery in the Jews of a people essentially urban, essentially Europe-oriented, a ready-made image for what the American longs to or fears he is being forced to become.

On all levels in the years since World War II, the Jewish-American writer feels imposed on him the role of being The American, of registering his experience for his compatriots and for the world as The American Experience. Not only his flirtation with Communism and his disengagement, but his very sense of exclusion, his most intimate awareness of loneliness and flight are demanded of him as public symbols. The southerner and the Jew, the homosexual out of the miasma of Mississippi and the ex-radical out of the iron landscape of Chicago and New York—these seem the exclusive alternatives, contrasting yet somehow twinned symbols of America at mid-century. *Partisan Review* becomes for Europe and *Life* magazine the mouthpiece of intellectual America, not despite but because of its tiny readership and its specially determined contributors; and in Saul Bellow a writer emerges capable of transforming its obsessions into myths.

He must not, however, be seen only in this context. His appearance as the first Jewish-American novelist to stand at the center of American literature is flanked by a host of matching successes on other levels of culture and sub-culture. What Saul Bellow is for highbrow literature, Salinger is for upper middlebrow, Irwin Shaw for middle middlebrow and Herman Wouk for lower middlebrow. Even on the lowbrow levels, where there has been no such truce with antisemitism as prosperity has brought to the middle classes, two young Jews in contriving Superman have invented for the comicbooks a new version of the Hero, the first purely urban incarnation of the most ancient of mythic figures. The acceptance of Bellow as the leading novelist of his generation must be paired off with the appearance of Marjorie Morningstar on the front cover of *Time*. On all levels, the Jew is in the process of being mythicized into the representative American.

There is a temptation in all this to a kind of assimilation with the most insipid values of bourgeois life in the United States. It is to Bellow's credit that he has at once accepted the full challenge implicit in the identification of Jew with American, and yet has not succumbed to the temptation; that he has been willing to accept the burden of success without which he might have been cut off from the central subject of his time; and that he has accomplished this without essential compromise. In *Augie March,* which is the heart of his work (though technically not as successful as *The Victim* or *Seize the Day*), he has risked the final absurdity: the footloose Jewish boy, harried by urban machiavellians, the picaresque *schlimazl* out of Fuchs or Nathanael West, becomes Huck Finn; or, if you will, Huck is transformed into the footloose Jewish boy. It is hard to know which way of saying it gives a fuller sense of the absurdity and importance of the transaction. The point is, I think, that the identification saves both halves of the combination from sentimental falsification: Huck Finn, who has threatened for a long time to dissolve into the snubnosed little rascal, barefoot and overalled; and the Jewish *schlimazl,* who becomes only too easily the liberals' insufferable victim, say, Noah Ackerman in Irwin Shaw's *The Young Lions.*

The themes of Saul Bellow are not, after all, very different from those of the middlebrow Jewish novelists in step with whom he has "worked himself up"; but in treatment they become transformed. Like Wouk or Shaw, he, too, has written a War Novel: a book about the uncertainty of intellectual and Jew face to face with a commitment to regimentation and violence. But unlike Wouk and Shaw, Bellow has not merely taken the World War I novel of protest and adulterated it with popular front pieties. His intellectual is not shown up like Wouk's Keefer; his Jew does not prove himself as brave and brutal as his antisemitic buddies like Shaw's Ackerman or Wouk's Greenspan, whose presumable triumphs are in fact abject surrenders. The longing to relinquish the stereotyped protest of the twenties, no longer quite believed in, is present in Bellow's *Dangling Man,* but present as a *subject:* a temptation to be confronted, not a value to be celebrated.

Dangling Man is not an entirely successful book; it is a little mannered, a little incoherent, obviously a first novel. But it is fresh beyond all expectation, unlike any American war book before or since; for Bellow has realized that for his generation the war itself is an anticlimax (too foreknown from a score of older novels to be really lived), that their real experience is the waiting, the dangling, the indecision before the draft. His book therefore ends, as it should, with its protagonist about to leave for camp and writing in his journal: "Hurray for regular hours! And for the supervision of the spirit! Long live regimentation!" In the purest of ironies, the slogans of accommodation are neither accepted nor rejected, but suspended.

Similarly, in *The Victim* Bellow takes up what is, perhaps, the theme *par excellence* of the liberaloid novel of the forties: antisemitism. In proletarian novels, though many were written by Jews, this was a subject only peripherally treated; for the Jew in the Communist movement, Judaism was the enemy, Zionism and the Jewish religion the proper butt of satire and dissent. But Hitler had made a difference, releasing a flood of pious protests against discrimination; from Arthur Miller's *Focus* to John Hersey's *The Wall,* via *Gentlemen's Agreement, The Professor's Umbrella,* etc., Jew and

Gentile alike took up the subject over and over. In a time when the Worker had been replaced by the Little Man as a focus for undiscriminating sympathy, the Little Jew took his place beside the Little Negro, the Little Chinese, the Little Paraplegic as a favorite victim. Even what passed for War Novels were often merely anti-antisemitic fictions in disguise, the war itself being treated only as an occasion for testing a Noble Young Jew under the pressure of ignorant hostility.

In the typical middlebrow novel, it was seldom a real Jew who was exposed to persecution; rather some innocent gentile who by putting on glasses mysteriously came to look Jewish or some high-minded reporter only pretending to be a Jew. In part what is involved is the commercial necessity for finding a gimmick to redeem an otherwise overworked subject; but in part what is at stake is surely a confusion in the liberal, middlebrow mind about what a Jew is anyhow: a sneaking suspicion that Jew-baiting is real but Jews are imaginary, just as, to the same mind, witch-hunting is real but witches only fictions.

In Bellow's book about antisemitism, *The Victim*, once more the confusion becomes the subject. It is Asa Leventhal, not the author, who is uncertain of what it means to be a Jew, because he does not know yet what it is to be a man; and neither he nor his author will be content with the simple equation: the victim equals the Jew, the Jew the victim. In *The Victim*, Jew and antisemite are each other's prey as they are each other's beloved. At the moment when the Jew in general, when the author himself as well as his protagonist, have moved into situations of security, however tenuous, inflicting injury in their scramble to win that security, Bellow alone among our novelists has had the imagination and the sheer nerve to portray the Jew, the Little Jew, as victimizer as well as victim. Allbee may be mad, a pathological antisemite and a bum, but his charge that Leventhal's success was achieved somehow at his expense is not utter nonsense. It is the necessary antidote to the self-pity of the Jew, one part of the total ambiguous picture. In the slow, grey, low-keyed exposition of *The Victim*, Leventhal's violence and his patience, his desire to exculpate himself and his sense of guilt, his haunting by the antisemite he haunts, become for us truths, part of our awareness of our place as Jews in the American scene.

As *The Victim* in Bellow's most specifically Jewish book, *Augie March* (in this, as in all other respects, a reaction from the former) is his most generally American. Its milieu is Jewish American, its speech patterns somehow moulded by Yiddish, but its theme is the native theme of *Huckleberry Finn:* the rejection of power and commitment and success, the pursuit of a primal innocence. It is a strangly non-Jewish book in being concerned not with a man's rise but with his evasion of rising; and yet even in that respect it reminds us of *David Levinsky,* of the criticism of David implicit in the text and entrusted to the Socialist characters. It is as if David had been granted a son, a grandson, to try again—to seek a more genuine Americanism of non-commital. Certainly, Bellow's character is granted a symbolic series of sexual successes to balance off the sexual failures of Cahan's protagonist. But the socialism of Cahan does not move his descendant; it has become in the meanwhile Soviet Communism, an alternative image of material success, and has failed; so that there is left to Augie only the denial of the values of capitalism without a corresponding allegiance, a desire to flee success from scene to scene, from girl to girl, from father to father—in favor of what? The most bitter of Happy Endings as well as the most negative, the truly American Happy Ending: no reunion with the family, no ultimately happy marriage, no return to the native place—only a limitless disponsibility guarded like a treasure. It is, of course, the ending of *Huckleberry Finn,* an ending which must be played out as comedy to be tolerable at all; but unlike Twain, Bellow, though he has found the proper tone for his episodes, cannot recapture it for his close. *Augie,* which begins with such rightness, such conviction, does not know how to end; shriller and shriller, wilder and wilder, it finally whirls apart in a frenzy of fake euphoria and exclamatory prose.

Seize the Day is a pendant and resolution to *Augie March.* Also a study of success and failure, this time it treats them in contemporary terms rather than classic ones, reworking directly a standard middlebrow theme. Call it "The Death of a Salesman" and think of Arthur Miller. It is the price of failure in a world dedicated to success that Bellow is dealing with now; or more precisely, the self-consciousness of failure in a world where it is not only shameful but rare; or most exactly of all, the bitterness of success and failure become pawns in the deadly game between father and son. Bellow is not very successful when he attempts to deal with the sentimental and erotic relations that are the staples of the great European novels; his women tend to be nympholeptic projections, fantasies based on girls one never had; and his husbands and wives seem convincing only at the moment of parting. But he comes into his own when he turns to the emotional transactions of males inside the family: brother and brother, son and father—or father-hating son and machiavellian surrogate father. It is the muted rage of such relationships that is the emotional stuff of his best work; and in *Seize the Day,* it is the dialogues of Tommy and his old man, Tommy and the sharper Tamkin that move us, prepare us for Tommy's bleakest encounter: with himself and the prescience of his own death.

But how, we are left asking, has Bellow made tragedy of a theme that remains in the hands of Arthur Miller sentimentality and "good theatre"? It is just this magical transformation of the most travestied of middlebrow themes which is Bellow's greatest triumph. That transformation is in part the work of style, a function of language. Bellow is in no sense an experimental writer; the scraps of avant-garde technique which survive in *The Dangling Man* are purged away in *The Victim;* yet he has managed to resist the impulse to lifeless lucidity which elsewhere has taken over in a literature reacting to the linguistic experiments of the twenties. There is always the sense of a living voice in his prose, for his books are all dramatic; and though this sometimes means a deliberate muting of rhetoric for the sake of characterization, it just as often provides occasions for a release of full virtuosity. Muted or released, his language is never dull or merely expedient, but always moves under tension, toward or away from a kind of rich, crazy poetry, a juxtaposition of high and low style, elegance and slang, unlike anything else in English except *Moby Dick,* though at the same time not unrelated in range and variety to spoken Yiddish.

Since Bellow's style is based on a certain conversational ideal at once intellectual and informal, dialogue is for him necessarily a distillation of his strongest effects. Sometimes one feels his characters' speeches as the main events of the books in which they occur; certainly they have the impact of words exchanged among Jews, that is to say, the impact of actions, not merely overheard but *felt,* like kisses or blows. Implicit in the direction of his style is a desire to encompass a world larger, richer, more disorderly and untrammelled than that of any other writer of his generation; it is this which impels him toward the picaresque, the sprawling, episodic manner of *Augie March.* But there is a counter impulse in him toward the tight, rigidly organized, underplayed style of *The Victim:* and at his best, I think, as in *Seize the Day,* an ability to balance the two tendencies against each other: hysteria and catalepsy, the centrifugal and the centripetal in a sort of perilous rest.

But the triumphs of Bellow are not mere triumphs of style; sometimes indeed they must survive the collapse of that style into mannerism, mechanical self-parody. Beyond an ear, Bellow possesses a fortunate negative talent: a constitutional inability to dissolve his characters into their representative types, to compromise their individuality for the sake of a point. It is not merely that his protagonists refuse to blur into the generalized Little People, the Victims of sentimental liberalism; but that they are themselves portrayed as being conscious of their struggle against such debasement. That struggle is, indeed, the essence of their self-consciousness, their self-definition. Their invariable loneliness is felt by them and by us not only as a function of urban life and the atomization of culture, but as something *willed:* the condition and result of their search to know what they are.

More, perhaps, than any other recent novelist, Bellow is aware that the collapse of the proletarian novel, which marks the starting place of his own art, has meant more than the disappearance of a convention in the history of fiction. With the disappearance of the proletarian novel as a form there has taken place the gradual dissolution of the last widely shared definition of man: man as the product of society. If man seems at the moment extraordinarily lonely, it is not only because he finds it hard to communicate with his fellows, but because he has lost touch with any overarching definition of himself.

This Bellow realizes; as he realizes that it is precisely in such loneliness, once man learns not to endure but to *become* that loneliness, that man can rediscover his identity and his fellowship with others. We recognize the Bellow character because he is openly what we are in secret, because he is us without our customary defenses. Such a protagonist lives nowhere except in the City; he camps temporarily in boardinghouses or lonely hotels, sits by himself at the corner table of some seedy restaurant or climbs backbreaking stairways in search of another whose existence no one will admit. He is the man whose wife is off visiting her mother or has just left him; the man who returns to find his house in disorder or inhabited by a squalid derelict; the man who flees his room to follow the funeral of someone he never knew.

He is essential man, man stripped of success and belongingness, even of failure; he is man disowned by his father, unrecognized by his son, man without woman, man face to face with himself, which means for Bellow face to face not with a fact but a question: "What am I?" To which the only answer is: "He who asks!" But such a man is at once the Jew in perpetual exile and Huck Finn, in whom are blended with perfect irony the twin American beliefs that the answer to all questions is always over the next horizon and that there is no answer now or ever.

NORMAN MAILER

****

As novelist, journalist, politician, or political gadfly, Norman
Mailer is often reported on—in an interview in *Playboy*, XV
(January 1968), pp. 69–84, or the *Paris Review*, No. 31 (Winter-
Spring 1964), pp. 28–35. Joseph Blotner writes of him in *The
Political Novel in America* (Austin, Tex., 1966), Howard M.
Harper, Jr., in *Desperate Faith* (Chapel Hill, N.C., 1967), and
Michael Millgate in *American Social Fiction* (Edinburgh, 1964);
Lionel Trilling speaks of "The Radical Moralism of Norman
Mailer," in *The Creative Present* (New York, 1963). Essays which
concentrate on his literary achievement include Charles I. Glicks-
berg's "Norman Mailer: The Angry Young Novelist in America,"
Wisconsin Studies in Contemporary Literature, I (Winter 1960),
pp. 25–34, Frederick J. Hoffman's "Norman Mailer and the Heart
of the Egg," *Wisconsin Studies in Contemporary Literature*, I (Fall
1960), pp. 5–12, Irving Howe's "A Quest for Peril," *Partisan Review*, XXVII (Winter 1960), pp. 143–148, Norman Podhoretz's
"Norman Mailer: The Embattled Vision," *Partisan Review*, XXVI

(Summer 1959), pp. 371–391, George A. Schrader's "Norman Mailer and the Despair of Defiance," *Yale Review,* LI (Winter 1962), pp. 267–280, and Brom Weber's "A Fear of Dying," *Hollins Critic,* II (1965), pp. 1–11.

THE BLACK BOY LOOKS
AT THE WHITE BOY

James Baldwin

****

I walked and I walked
Till I wore out my shoes.
I can't walk so far, but
Yonder come the blues.
　　　　　—Ma Rainey

I first met Norman Mailer about five years ago, in Paris, at the home of
Jean Malaquais. Let me bring in at once the theme that will repeat itself
over and over throughout this love letter: I was then (and I have not
changed much) a very tight, tense, lean, abnormally ambitious, abnormally
intelligent, and hungry black cat. It is important that I admit that, at the

time I met Norman, I was extremely worried about my career; and a writer who is worried about his career is also fighting for his life. I was approaching the end of a love affair, and I was not taking it very well. Norman and I are alike in this, that we both tend to suspect others of putting us down, and we strike before we're struck. Only, our styles are very different: I am a black boy from the Harlem streets, and Norman is a middle-class Jew. I am not dragging my personal history into this gratuitously, and I hope I do not need to say that no sneer is implied in the above description of Norman. But these are the facts and in my own relationship to Norman they are crucial facts.

Also, I have no right to talk about Norman without risking a distinctly chilling self-exposure. I take him very seriously, he is very dear to me. And I think I know something about his journey from my black boy's point of view because my own journey is not really so very different, and also because I have spent most of my life, after all, watching white people and outwitting them, so that I might survive. I think that I know something about the American masculinity which most men of my generation do not know because they have not been menaced by it in the way that I have been. It is still true, alas, that to be an American Negro male is also to be a kind of walking phallic symbol: which means that one pays, in one's own personality, for the sexual insecurity of others. The relationship, therefore, of a black boy to a white boy is a very complex thing.

There is a difference, though, between Norman and myself in that I think he still imagines that he has something to save, whereas I have never had anything to lose. Or, perhaps I ought to put it another way: the things that most white people imagine that they can salvage from the storm of life is really, in sum, their innocence. It was this commodity precisely which I had to get rid of at once, literally, on pain of death. I am afraid that most of the white people I have ever known impressed me as being in the grip of a weird nostalgia, dreaming of a vanished state of security and order, against which dream, unfailingly and unconsciously, they tested and very often lost their lives. It is a terrible thing to say, but I am afraid that for a very long time the troubles of white people failed to impress me as being real trouble. They put me in mind of children crying because the breast has been taken away. Time and love have modified my tough-boy lack of charity, but the attitude sketched above was my first attitude and I am sure that there is a great deal of it left.

To proceed: two lean cats, one white and one black, met in a French living room. I had heard of him, he had heard of me. And here we were, suddenly, circling around each other. We liked each other at once, but each was frightened that the other would pull rank. He could have pulled rank on me because he was more famous and had more money and also because he was white; but I could have pulled rank on him precisely because I was black and knew more about that periphery he so helplessly maligns in *The White Negro* than he could ever hope to know. Already, you see, we were trapped in our roles and our attitudes: the toughest kid on the block was meeting the toughest kid on the block. I think that both of us were pretty weary of this grueling and thankless role, I know that I am; but the roles that we construct are constructed because we feel that they will help us to survive and also, of course, because they fulfill something in our personalities; and one does not, therefore, cease playing a role simply because one has begun to understand it. All roles are dangerous. The world tends to trap and immobilize you in the role you play; and it is not always easy—in fact, it is always extremely hard—to maintain a kind of watchful, mocking distance between oneself as one appears to be and oneself as one actually is.

I think that Norman was working on *The Deer Park* at that time, or had just finished it, and Malaquais, who had translated *The Naked and the Dead* into French, did not like *The Deer Park*. I had not then read the book; if I had, I would have been astonished that Norman could have expected Malaquais to like it. What Norman was trying to do in *The Deer Park,* and quite apart, now, from whether or not he succeeded, could only —it seems to me—baffle and annoy a French intellectual who seemed to me essentially rationalistic. Norman has many qualities and faults, but I have never heard anyone accuse him of possessing this particular one. But Malaquais' opinion seemed to mean a great deal to him—this astonished me, too; and there was a running, good-natured but astringent argument between them, with Malaquais playing the role of the old lion and Norman playing the role of the powerful but clumsy cub. And, I must say, I think that each of them got a great deal of pleasure out of the other's performance. The night we met, we stayed up very late, and did a great deal of drinking and shouting. But beneath all the shouting and the posing and the mutual showing off, something very wonderful was happening. I was aware of a new and warm presence in my life, for I had met someone I wanted to know, who wanted to know me.

Norman and his wife, Adele, along with a Negro jazz musician friend, and myself, met fairly often during the few weeks that found us all in the same city. I think that Norman had come in from Spain, and he was shortly to return to the States; and it was not long after Norman's departure that I left Paris for Corsica. My memory of that time is both blurred and sharp, and, oddly enough, is principally of Norman—confident, boastful, exuberant, and loving—striding through the soft Paris nights like a gladiator. And I think, alas, that I envied him: his success, and his youth, and his love. And this meant that though Norman really wanted to know me, and though I really wanted to know him, I hung back, held fire, danced, and lied. I was not going to come crawling out of my ruined house, all bloody, no, baby, sing no sad songs for *me*. And the great gap between Norman's state and my own had a terrible effect on our relationship, for it inevitably connected, not to say collided, with that myth of the sexuality of Negroes which Norman, like so many others, refuses to give up. The sexual battleground, if I may call it that, is really the same for everyone; and I, at this point, was just about to be carried off the battleground on my shield, if anyone could find it; so how could I play, in any way whatever, the noble savage?

At the same time, my temperament and my experience in this country had led me to expect very little from most American whites, especially, horribly enough, my friends: so it did not seem worthwhile to challenge, in any real way, Norman's views of life on the periphery, or to put him down for them. I was weary, to tell the truth. I had tried, in the States, to convey something of what it felt like to be a Negro and no one had been able to listen: they wanted their romance. And, anyway, the really ghastly thing about trying to convey to a white man the reality of the Negro experience has nothing whatever to do with the fact of color, but has to do with this man's relationship to his own life. He will face in your life only what he is willing to face in his. Well, this means that one finds oneself tampering with the insides of a stranger, to no purpose, which one probably has no right to do, and I chickened out. And matters were not helped at all by the fact that the Negro jazz musicians, among whom we sometimes found ourselves, who really liked Norman, did not for an instant consider him as being even remotely "hip" and Norman did not know this and I could not tell him. He never broke through to them, at least not as far I know; and they were far too "hip," if that is the word I want, even to consider breaking through to him. They thought he was a real sweet ofay cat, but a little frantic.

But we were far more cheerful than anything I've said might indicate and none of the above seemed to matter very much at the time. Other things mattered, like walking and talking and drinking and eating, and the way Adele laughed, and the way Norman argued. He argued like a young man, he argued to win: and while I found him charming, he may have found me exasperating, for I kept moving back before that short, prodding forefinger. I couldn't submit my arguments, or my real questions, for I had too much to hide. Or so it seemed to me then. I submit, though I may be wrong, that I was then at the beginning of a terrifying adventure, not too unlike the conundrum which seems to menace Norman now:

"I had done a few things and earned a few pence"; but the things I had written were behind me, could not be written again, could not be repeated. I was also realizing that all that the world could give me as an artist, it had, in effect, already given. In the years that stretched before me, all that I could look forward to, in that way, were a few more prizes, or a lot more, and a little more, or a lot more money. And my private life had failed—had failed, had failed. One of the reasons I had fought so hard, after all, was to wrest from the world fame and money and love. And here I was, at thirty-two, finding my notoriety hard to bear, since its principal effect was to make me more lonely; money, it turned out, was exactly like sex, you thought of nothing else if you didn't have it and thought of other things if you did; and love, as far as I could see, was over. Love seemed to be over not merely because an affair was ending; it would have seemed to be over under any circumstances; for it was the dream of love which was ending. I was beginning to realize, most unwillingly, all the things love could not do. It could not make me over, for example. It could not undo the journey which had made of me such a strange man and brought me to such a strange place.

But at that time it seemed only too clear that love had gone out of the world, and not, as I had thought once, because I was poor and ugly and obscure, but precisely because I was no longer any of these things. What point, then, was there in working if the best I could hope for was the Nobel Prize? And *how,* indeed, would I be able to keep on working if I could never be released from the prison of my egocentricity? By what act could I escape this horror? For horror it was, let us make no mistake about that.

And, beneath all this, which simplified nothing, was that sense, that suspicion—which is the glory and torment of every writer—that what was happening to me might be turned to good account, that I was trembling on the edge of great revelations, was being prepared for a very long journey, and might now begin, having survived my apprenticeship (but had I survived it?), a great work. I might really become a great writer. But in order to do this I would have to sit down at the typewriter again, alone—I would have to accept my despair: and I could not do it. It really does not help to be a strong-willed person or, anyway, I think it is a great error to misunderstand the nature of the will. In the most important areas of anybody's life, the will usually operates as a traitor. My own will was busily pointing out to me the most fantastically unreal alternatives to my pain, all of which I tried, all of which—luckily—failed. When late in the evening or early in the morning, Norman and Adele returned to their hotel on the Quai Voltaire, I wondered through Paris, the underside of Paris, drinking, screwing, fighting —it's a wonder I wasn't killed. And then it was morning, I would somehow be home—usually, anyway—and the typewriter would be there, staring at me; and the manuscript of the new novel, which it seemed I would never be able to achieve, and from which clearly I was never going to be released, was scattered all over the floor.

That's the way it is. I think it is the most dangerous point in the life of any artist, his longest, most hideous turning; and especially for a man, an

American man, whose principle is action and whose jewel is optimism, who must now accept what certainly then seems to be a gray passivity and an endless despair. It is the point at which many artists lose their minds, or commit suicide, or throw themselves into good works, or try to enter politics. For all of this is happening not only in the wilderness of the soul, but in the real world which accomplishes its seductions not by offering you opportunities to be wicked but by offering opportunities to be good, to be active and effective, to be admired and central and apparently loved.

Norman came on to America, and I went to Corsica. We wrote each other a few times. I confided to Norman that I was very apprehensive about the reception of *Giovanni's Room,* and he was good enough to write some very encouraging things about it when it came out. The critics had jumped on him with both their left feet when he published *The Deer Park*—which I still had not read—and this created a kind of bond, or strengthened the bond already existing between us. About a year and several overflowing wastebaskets later, I, too, returned to America, not vastly improved by having been out of it, but not knowing where else to go; and one day, while I was sitting dully in my house, Norman called me from Connecticut. A few people were going to be there—for the weekend—and he wanted me to come, too. We had not seen each other since Paris.

Well, I wanted to go, that is, I wanted to see Norman; but I did not want to see any people, and so the tone of my acceptance was not very enthusiastic. I realized that he felt this, but I did not know what to do about it. He gave me train schedules and hung up.

Getting to Connecticut would have been no hassle if I could have pulled myself together to get to the train. And I was sorry, as I meandered around my house and time flew and trains left, that I had not been more honest with Norman and told him exactly how I felt. But I had not known how to do this, or it had not really occurred to me to do it, especially not over the phone.

So there was another phone call, I forget who called whom, which went something like this:

N: Don't feel you have to. I'm not trying to bug you.

J: It's not that. It's just—

N: You don't really want to come, do you?

J: I don't really feel up to it.

N: I understand. I guess you just don't like the Connecticut gentry.

J: Well—don't you ever come to the city?

N: Sure. We'll see each other.

J: I hope so. I'd like to see you.

N: Okay, till then.

And he hung up. I thought, I ought to write him a letter, but of course I did nothing of the sort. It was around this time I went South, I think; anyway, we did not see each other for a long time.

But I thought about him a great deal. The grapevine keeps all of us advised of the others' movements, so I knew when Norman left Connecticut for New York, heard that he had been present at this or that party and what he had said: usually something rude, often something penetrating, sometimes something so hilariously silly that it was difficult to believe he had been serious. (This was my reaction when I first heard his famous running-for-President remark. I dismissed it. I was wrong.) Or he had been seen in this or that Village spot, in which unfailingly there would be someone—out of spite, idleness, envy, exasperation, out of the bottomless, eerie, aimless hostility which characterizes almost every bar in New York, to speak only of bars—to put him down. I heard of a couple of fist-fights, and, of course, I was always encountering people who hated his guts. These people always mildly surprised me, and so did the news of his fights: it was hard for me to imagine that anyone could really dislike Norman, anyone, that is, who had encountered him personally. I knew of one fight he had had, forced on him, apparently, by a blowhard Village type whom I considered rather pathetic. I didn't blame Norman for this fight, but I couldn't help wondering why he bothered to rise to such a shapeless challenge. It seemed simpler, as I was always telling myself, just to stay out of Village bars.

And people talked about Norman with a kind of avid glee, which I found very ugly. Pleasure made their saliva flow, they sprayed and all but drooled, and their eyes shone with that blood-lust which is the only real tribute the mediocre are capable of bringing to the extraordinary. Many of the people who claimed to be seeing Norman all the time impressed me as being, to tell the truth, pitifully far beneath him. But this is also true, alas, of much of my own entourage. The people who are in one's life or merely continually in one's presence reveal a great deal about one's needs and terrors. Also, one's hopes.

I was not, however, on the scene. I was on the road—not quite, I trust, in the sense that Kerouac's boys are; but I presented, certainly, a moving target. And I was reading Norman Mailer. Before I had met him, I had only read *The Naked and The Dead, The White Negro,* and *Barbary Shore*—I think this is right, though it may be that I only read *The White Negro* later and confuse my reading of that piece with some of my discussions with Norman. Anyway, I could not, with the best will in the world, make any sense out of *The White Negro* and, in fact, it was hard for me to imagine that this essay had been written by the same man who wrote the novels. Both *The Naked and The Dead* and (for the most part) *Barbary Shore* are written in a lean, spare, muscular prose which accomplishes almost exactly what it sets out to do. Even *Barbary Shore,* which loses itself in its last half (and which deserves, by the way, far more serious treatment than it has received) never becomes as downright impenetrable as *The White Negro* does.

Now, much of this, I told myself, had to do with my resistance to the title, and with a kind of fury that so antique a vision of the blacks should, at this late hour, and in so many borrowed heirlooms, be stepping off the A train. But I was also baffled by the passion with which Norman appeared to be imitating so many people inferior to himself, i.e., Kerouac, and all the other Suzuki rhythm boys. From them, indeed, I expected nothing more than their pablum-clogged cries of *Kicks!* and *Holy!* It seemed very clear to me that their glorification of the orgasm was but a way of avoiding all of the terrors of life and love. But Norman knew better, had to know better. *The Naked and The Dead, Barbary Shore,* and *The Deer Park* proved it. In each of these novels, there is a toughness and subtlety of conception, and a sense of the danger and complexity of human relationships which one will search for in vain, not only in the work produced by the aforementioned coterie, but in most of the novels produced by Norman's contemporaries. What in the world, then, was he doing, slumming so outrageously, in such a dreary crowd?

For, exactly because he knew better, and in exactly the same way that no one can become more lewdly vicious than an imitation libertine, Norman felt compelled to carry their *mystique* further than they had, to be more "hip," or more "beat," to dominate, in fact, their dreaming field; and since this *mystique* depended on a total rejection of life, and insisted on the fulfillment of an infantile dream of love, the *mystique* could only be extended into violence. No one is more dangerous than he who imagines himself pure in heart: for his purity, by definition, is unassailable.

But *why* should it be necessary to borrow the Depression language of deprived Negroes, which eventually evolved into jive and bop talk, in order to justify such a grim system of delusions? Why malign the sorely menaced sexuality of Negroes in order to justify the white man's own sexual panic? Especially as, in Norman's case, and as indicated by his work, he has a very real sense of sexual responsibility, and, even, odd as it may sound to some, of sexual morality, and a genuine commitment to life. None of his people, I beg you to notice, spend their lives on the road. They really become entangled with each other, and with life. They really suffer, they spill real blood, they have real lives to lose. This is no small achievement; in fact, it is absolutely rare. No matter how uneven one judges Norman's work to be, all of it is genuine work. No matter how harshly one judges it, it is the work of a genuine novelist, and an absolutely first-rate talent.

Which makes the questions I have tried to raise—or, rather, the questions which Norman Mailer irresistibly represents—all the more troubling and terrible. I certainly do not know the answers, and even if I did, this is probably not the place to state them.

But I have a few ideas. Here is Kerouac, ruminating on what I take to be the loss of the garden of Eden:

> At lilac evening I walked with every muscle aching among the lights of 27th and Welton in the Denver colored section, wishing I were a Negro, feeling that the best the white world had offered was not enough ecstasy for me, not enough life, joy, kicks, darkness, music, not enough night. I wished I were a Denver Mexican, or even a poor overworked Jap, anything but what I so drearily was, a "white man" disillusioned. All my life I'd had white ambitions. . . . I passed the dark porches of Mexican and Negro homes; soft voices were there, occasionally the dusky knee of some mysterious sensuous gal; and dark faces of the men behind rose arbors. Little children sat like sages in ancient rocking chairs.

Now, this is absolute nonsense, of course, objectively considered, and offensive nonsense at that: I would hate to be in Kerouac's shoes if he should ever be mad enough to read this aloud from the stage of Harlem's Apollo Theater.

And yet there is real pain in it, and real loss, however thin; and it *is* thin, like soup too long diluted; thin because it does not refer to reality, but to a dream. Compare it, at random, with any old blues:

> Backwater blues done caused me
> To pack my things and go.
> 'Cause my house fell down
> And I can't live there no mo'.

"Man," said a Negro musician to me once, talking about Norman, "the only trouble with that cat is that he's white." This does not mean exactly what it says—or, rather, it *does* mean exactly what it says, and not what it might be taken to mean—and it is a very shrewd observation. What my friend meant was that to become a Negro man, let alone a Negro artist, one had to make oneself up as one went along. This had to be done in the not-at-all-metaphorical teeth of the world's determination to destroy you. The world had prepared no place for you, and if the world had its way, no place would ever exist. Now, this is true for everyone, but, in the case of a Negro, this truth is absolutely naked: if he deludes himself about it, he will die.

This is not the way this truth presents itself to white men, who believe the world is theirs and who, albeit unconsciously, expect the world to help them in the achievement of their identity. But the world does not do this—for anyone; the world is not interested in anyone's identity. And, therefore, the anguish which can overtake a white man comes in the middle of his life, when he must make the almost inconceivable effort to divest himself of everything he has ever expected or believed, when he must take himself apart and put himself together again, walking out of the world, into limbo, or into what certainly looks like limbo. This cannot yet happen to any Negro of Norman's age, for the reason that his delusions and defenses are either absolutely impenetrable by this time, or he has failed to survive them. "I want to know how power works," Norman once said to me, "how it really works, in detail." Well, I know how power works, it has worked on me, and if I didn't know how power worked, I would be dead. And it goes without saying, perhaps, that I have simply never been able to afford myself any illusions concerning the manipulation of that power. My revenge, I decided very early, would be to achieve a power which outlasts kingdoms.

II

When I finally saw Norman again, I was beginning to suspect daylight at the end of my long tunnel, it was a summer day, I was on my way back to Paris, and I was very cheerful. We were at an afternoon party, Norman was standing in the kitchen, a drink in his hand, holding forth for the benefit of a small group of people. There seemed something different about him, it was the billigerence of his stance, and the really rather pontifical tone of his voice. I had only seen him, remember, in Malaquais' living room, which Malaquais indefatigably dominates, and on various terraces and in various dives in Paris. I do not mean that there was anything unfriendly about him. On the contrary, he was smiling and having a ball. And yet—he was leaning against the refrigerator, rather as though he had his back to the wall, ready to take on all comers.

Norman has a trick, at least with me, of watching, somewhat ironically, as you stand on the edge of the crowd around him, waiting for his attention. I suppose this ought to be exasperating, but in fact I find it rather endearing, because it is so transparent and because he gets such a bang out of being the center of attention. So do I, of course, at least some of the time.

We talked, bantered, a little tensely, made the usual, doomed effort to bring each other up to date on what we had been doing. I did not want to talk about my novel, which was only just beginning to seem to take shape, and, therefore, did not dare ask him if he were working on a novel. He seemed very pleased to see me, and I was pleased to see him, but I also had the feeling that he had made up his mind about me, adversely, in some way. It was as though he were saying, Okay, so now I know who *you* are, baby.

I was taking a boat in a few days, and I asked him to call me.

"Oh, no," he said, grinning, and thrusting that forefinger at me, *"you* call me."

"That's fair enough," I said, and I left the party and went on back to Paris. While I was out of the country, Norman published *Advertisements for Myself,* which presently crossed the ocean to the apartment of James Jones. Bill Styron was also in Paris at that time, and one evening the three of us sat in Jim's living room, reading aloud, in a kind of drunken, masochistic fascination, Norman's judgment of our personalities and our work. Actually, I came off best, I suppose; there was less about me, and it was less venomous. But the condescension infuriated me; also, to tell the truth, my feelings were hurt. I felt that if that was the way Norman felt about me, he should have told me so. He had said that I was incapable of saying "F——you" to the reader. My first temptation was to send him a cablegram which would disabuse him of that notion, at least insofar as one reader was concerned. But then I thought, No, I would be cool about it, and fail to react as he so clearly wanted me to. Also, I must say, his judgment of myself seemed so wide of the mark and so childish that it was hard to stay angry. I wondered what in the world was going on his mind. Did he really suppose that he had now become the builder and destroyer of reputations?

And of *my* reputation?

We met in the Actors' Studio one afternoon, after a performance of *The Deer Park*—which I deliberately arrived too late to see, since I really did not know how I was going to react to Norman, and didn't want to betray myself by clobbering his play. When the discussion ended, I stood, again on the edge of the crowd around him, waiting. Over someone's shoulder, our eyes met, and Norman smiled.

"We've got something to talk about," I told him.

"I figured that," he said, smiling.

We went to a bar, and sat opposite each other. I was relieved to discover that I was not angry, not even (as far as I could tell) at the bottom of my heart. But, "Why did you write those things about me?"

"Well, I'll tell you about that," he said—Norman has several accents, and I think this was his Texas one—"I sort of figured you had it coming to you."

"Why?"

"Well, I think there's some truth in it."

"Well, if you felt that way, why didn't you ever say so—to me?"

"Well, I figured if this was going to break up our friendship, something else would come along to break it up just as fast."

I couldn't disagree with that.

"You're the only one I kind of regret hitting so hard," he said, with a grin. "I think I—probably—wouldn't say it quite that way now."

With this, I had to be content. We sat for perhaps an hour, talking of other things and, again, I was struck by his stance: leaning on the table, shoulders hunched, seeming, really, to roll like a boxer's, and his hands moving as though he were dealing with a sparring partner. And we were talking of physical courage, and the necessity of never letting another guy get the better of you.

I laughed. "Norman, I can't go through the world the way you do because I haven't got your shoulders."

He grinned, as though I were his pupil. "But you're a pretty tough little mother, too," he said, and referred to one of the grimmer of my Village misadventures, a misadventure which certainly proved that I had a dangerously sharp tongue, but which didn't really prove anything about my courage. Which, anyway, I had long ago given up trying to prove.

I did not see Norman again until Provincetown, just after his celebrated brush with the police there, which resulted, according to Norman, in making the climate of Provincetown as "mellow as Jello." The climate didn't seem very different to me—dull natives, dull tourists, malevolent policemen; I certainly, in any case, would never have dreamed of testing Norman's sanguine conclusion. But we had a great time, lying around the beach, and driving about, we began to be closer than we had been for a long time.

It was during this Provincetown visit that I realized, for the first time, during a long exchange Norman and I had, in a kitchen, at someone else's party, that Norman was really fascinated by the nature of political power. But, though he said so, I did not really believe that he was fascinated by it as a possibility for himself. He was then doing the great piece on the Democratic convention which was published in *Esquire,* and I put his fascination down to that. I tend not to worry about writers as long as they are working —which is not as romantic as it may sound—and he seemed quite happy with his wife, his family, himself. I declined, naturally, to rise at dawn, as he apparently often did, to go running or swimming or boxing, but Norman seemed to get a great charge out of these admirable pursuits and didn't put me down too hard for my comparative decadence.

He and Adele and the two children took me to the plane one afternoon, the tiny plane which shuttles from Provincetown to Boston. It was a great day, clear and sunny, and that was the way I felt: for it seemed to me that we had all, at last, reestablished our old connection.

And then I heard that Norman was running for mayor, which I dismissed as a joke and refused to believe until it became hideously clear that it was not a joke at all. I was furious. I thought, You son of a bitch, you're copping out. You're one of the very few writers around who might really become a great writer, who might help to excavate the buried consciousness of this country, and you want to settle for being the lousy mayor of New York. *It's not your job.* And I don't at all mean to suggest that writers are not responsible to and for—in any case, always for—the social order. I don't, for that matter, even mean to suggest that Norman would have made a particularly bad Mayor, though I confess that I simply cannot see him in this role. And there is probably some truth in the suggestion, put forward by Norman and others, that the shock value of having such a man in such an office, or merely running for such an office, would have had a salutary effect on the life of this city—particularly, I must say, as relates to our young people, who are certainly in desperate need of adults who love them and take them seriously, and whom they can respect. (Serious citizens may not respect Norman, but young people do, and do not respect the serious citizens; and their instincts are quite sound.)

But I do not feel that a writer's responsibility can be discharged in this way. I do not think, if one is a writer, that one escapes it by trying to become something else. One does *not* become something else: one becomes nothing. And what is crucial here is that the writer, however unwillingly, always, somewhere, knows this. There is no structure he can build strong enough to keep out this self-knowledge. What *has* happened, however, time and time again, is that the fantasy structure the writer builds in order to escape his central responsibility operates not as his fortress, but his prison, and he perishes within it. Or: the structure he has built becomes so stifling, so lonely, so false, and acquires such a violent and dangerous life of its own, that he can break out of it only by bringing the entire structure down. With a great crash, inevitably, and on his own head, and on the heads of those closest to him. It is like smashing the windows one second before one asphyxiates; it is like burning down the house in order, at last, to be free of it. And this, I think, really, to touch upon it lightly, is the key to the events at that monstrous, baffling, and so publicized party. Nearly everyone in the world—or nearly everyone, at least, in this extraordinary city—was there: policemen, Mafia types, the people whom we quaintly refer to as "beatniks," writers, actors, editors, politicians, and gossip columnists. It must be admitted that it was a considerable achievement to have brought so many unlikely types together under one roof; and, in spite of everything, I can't help wishing that I had been there to witness the mutual bewilderment. But the point is that no politican would have dreamed of giving such a party in order to launch his mayoralty campaign. Such an imaginative route is not usually an attribute of politicians. In addition, the price one pays for pursuing any profession, or calling, is an intimate knowledge of its ugly side. It is scarcely worth observing that political activity is often, to put it mildly, pungent, and I think that Norman, perhaps for the first time, really doubted his ability to deal with such a world, and blindly struck his way out of it. We do not, in this country now, have much taste for, or any real sense of, the extremes human beings can reach; time will improve us in this regard; but in the meantime the general fear of experience is one of the reasons that the American writer has so peculiarly difficult and dangerous a time.

One can never really see into the heart, the mind, the soul of another. Norman is my very good friend, but perhaps I do not really understand him at all, and perhaps everything I have tried to suggest in the foregoing is false. I do not think so, but it may be. One thing, however, I am certain is *not* false, and that is simply the fact of his being a writer, and the incalculable potential he as a writer contains. His work, after all, is all that will be left when the newspapers are yellowed, all the gossip columnists silenced, and all the cocktail parties over, and when Norman and you and I are dead. I know that this point of view is not terribly fashionable these days, but I think we *do* have a responsibility, not only to ourselves and to our own time, but to those who are coming after us. (I refuse to believe that no one is coming after us.) And I suppose that this responsibility can only be discharged by dealing as truthfully as we know how with our present fortunes, these present days. So that my concern with Norman, finally, has to do with how deeply he has understood these last sad and stormy events. If he has understood them, then he is richer and we are richer, too; if he has not understood them, we are all much poorer. For, though it clearly needs to be brought into focus, he has a real vision of ourselves as we are, and it cannot be too often repeated in this country now, that, where there is no vision, the people perish.

JAMES BALDWIN

****

The question asked by Howard M. Harper, Jr., "James Baldwin—Art or Propaganda?" in *Desperate Faith* (Chapel Hill, N.C., 1967), has been variously answered, at some length by Robert A. Bone in *The Negro Novel in America* (New Haven, Conn., 1958; revised, 1965), more briefly by Robert Coler in "Baldwin's Burden," *Partisan Review*, XXXI (Summer 1964), pp. 409–16, Marvin Elkoff in "Everybody Knows His Name," *Esquire*, LXII (August 1964), pp. 59–64, James Finn in "James Baldwin's Vision," *Commonweal*, LXXVIII (July 26, 1963), pp. 447–449, Stephen Spender, "James Baldwin: Voice of a Revolution," *Partisan Review*, XXX (Spring 1963), pp. 256–260, and Edward A. Watson, "The Novels and Essays of James Baldwin: Case Book on a 'Lover's War' with the United States," *Queens Quarterly*, LXXII (Summer 1965), pp. 385–402. But the verdict is not yet in, nor have all the right voices been heard, on whether Baldwin has indeed sacrificed, and with what effect, his talent as an artist in order to further social and racial causes.

BLACK BOYS AND NATIVE SONS

Irving Howe

****

James Baldwin first came to the notice of the American literary public not through his own fiction but as author of an impassioned criticism of the conventional Negro novel. In 1949 he published in *Partisan Review* an essay called "Everybody's Protest Novel," attacking the kind of fiction, from *Uncle Tom's Cabin* to *Native Son,* that had been written about the ordeal of the American Negroes; and two years later he printed in the same magazine "Many Thousands Gone," a tougher and more explicit polemic against Richard Wright and the school of naturalistic "protest" fiction that Wright represented. The protest novel, wrote Baldwin, is undertaken out of sympathy for the Negro, but through its need to present him merely as a social victim or a mythic agent of sexual prowess, it hastens to confine the Negro to the very tones of violence he has known all his life. Compulsively reenacting and magnifying his trauma, the protest novel proves unable to transcend it. So choked with rage has this kind of writing become, it cannot

445

show the Negro as a unique person or locate him as a member of a community with its own traditions and values, its own "unspoken recognition of shared experience which creates a way of life." The failure of the protest novel "lies in its insistence that it is [man's] categorization alone which is real and which cannot be transcended."

Like all attacks launched by young writers against their famous elders, Baldwin's essays were also a kind of announcement of his own intentions. He wrote admiringly about Wright's courage ("his work was an immense liberation and revelation for me"), but now, precisely because Wright had prepared the way for all the Negro writers to come, he, Baldwin, would go further, transcending the sterile categories of "Negro-ness," whether those enforced by the white world or those defensively erected by the Negroes themselves. No longer mere victim or rebel, the Negro would stand free in a self-achieved humanity. As Baldwin put it some years later, he hoped "to prevent myself from becoming *merely* a Negro; or even, merely a Negro writer." The world "tends to trap and immobilize you in the role you play," and for the Negro writer, if he is to be a writer at all, it hardly matters whether the trap is sprung from motives of hatred or condescension.

Baldwin's rebellion against the older Negro novelist, who had served him as a model and had helped launch his career, was not of course an unprecedented event. The history of literature is full of such painful ruptures, and the issue Baldwin raised is one that keeps recurring, usually as an aftermath to a period of "socially engaged" writing. The novel is an inherently ambiguous genre: it strains toward formal autonomy and can seldom avoid being a public gesture. If it is true, as Baldwin said in "Everybody's Protest Novel," that "literature and sociology are not one and the same," it is equally true that such statements hardly begin to cope with the problem of how a writer's own experience affects his desire to represent human affairs in a work of fiction. Baldwin's formula evades, through rhetorical sweep, the genuinely difficult issue of the relationship between social experience and literature.

Yet in *Notes of a Native Son,* the book in which his remark appears, Baldwin could also say: "One writes out of one thing only—one's own experience." What, then, was the experience of a man with a black skin, what *could* it be in this country? How could a Negro put pen to paper, how could he so much as think or breathe, without some impulsion to protest, be it harsh or mild, political or private, released or buried? The "sociology" of his existence formed a constant pressure on his literary work, and not merely in the way this might be true for any writer, but with a pain and ferocity that nothing could remove.

James Baldwin's early essays are superbly eloquent, displaying virtually in full the gifts that would enable him to become one of the great

American rhetoricians. But these essays, like some of the later ones, are marred by rifts in logic, so little noticed when one gets swept away by the brilliance of the language that it takes a special effort to attend their argument.

Later Baldwin would see the problems of the Negro writer with a greater charity and more mature doubt. Reviewing in 1959 a book of poems by Langston Hughes, he wrote: "Hughes is an American Negro poet and has no choice but to be acutely aware of it. He is not the first American Negro to find the war between his social and artistic responsibilities all but irreconcilable." All but irreconcilable: the phrase strikes a note sharply different from Baldwin's attack upon Wright in the early fifties. And it is not hard to surmise the reasons for this change. In the intervening years Baldwin had been living through some of the experiences that had goaded Richard Wright into rage and driven him into exile; he too, like Wright, had been to hell and back, many times over.

II

Gawd, Ah wish all them white folks was dead.

The day *Native Son* appeared, American culture was changed forever. No matter how much qualifying the book might later need, it made impossible a repetition of the old lies. In all its crudeness, melodrama and claustrophobia of vision, Richard Wright's novel brought out into the open, as no one ever had before, the hatred, fear and violence that have crippled and may yet destroy our culture.

A blow at the white man, the novel forced him to recognize himself as an oppressor. A blow at the black man, the novel forced him to recognize the cost of his submission. *Native Son* assaulted the most cherished of American vanities: the hope that the accumulated injustice of the past would bring with it no lasting penalties, the fantasy that in his humiliation the Negro somehow retained a sexual potency—or was it a childlike good-nature?—that made it necessary to envy and still more to suppress him. Speaking from the black wrath of retribution, Wright insisted that history can be a punishment. He told us the one thing even the most liberal whites preferred not to hear: that Negroes were far from patient or forgiving, that they were scarred by fear, that they hated every moment of their suppression even when seeming most acquiescent, and that often enough they hated us, the decent and cultivated white men who from complicity or neglect shared in the responsibility for their plight. If such younger novelists as Baldwin and Ralph Ellison were to move beyond Wright's harsh naturalism and toward more supple modes of fiction, that was possible only because

Wright had been there first, courageous enough to release the full weight of his anger.

In *Black Boy,* the autobiographical narrative he published several years later, Wright would tell of an experience he had while working as a bellboy in the South. Many times he had come into a hotel room carrying luggage or food and seen naked white women lounging about, unmoved by shame at his presence, for "blacks were not considered human being anyway. . . . I was a non-man. . . . I felt doubly cast out." With the publication of *Native Son,* however, Wright forced his readers to acknowledge his anger, and in that way, if none other, he wrested for himself a sense of dignity as a man. He forced his readers to confront the disease of our culture, and to one of its most terrifying symptoms he gave the name of Bigger Thomas.

Brutal and brutalized, lost forever to his unexpended hatred and his fear of the world, a numbed and illiterate black boy stumbling into a murder and never, not even at the edge of the electric chair, breaking through to an understanding of either his plight or himself, Bigger Thomas was a part of Richard Wright, a part even of the James Baldwin who stared with horror at Wright's Bigger, unable either to absorb him into his consciousness or eject him from it. Enormous courage, a discipline of self-conquest, was required to conceive Bigger Thomas, for this was no eloquent Negro spokesman, no admirable intellectual or formidable proletarian. Bigger was drawn —one would surmise, deliberately—from white fantasy and white contempt. Bigger was the worst of Negro life accepted, then rendered a trifle conscious and thrown back at those who had made him what he was. "No American Negro exists," Baldwin would later write, "who does not have his private Bigger Thomas living in the skull."

Wright drove his narrative to the very core of American phobia: sexual fright, sexual violation. He understood that the fantasy of rape is a consequence of guilt, what the whites suppose themselves to deserve. He understood that the white man's notion of uncontaminated Negro vitality, little as it had to do with the bitter realities of Negro life, reflected some ill-formed and buried feeling that our culture has run down, lost its blood, become febrile. And he grasped the way in which the sexual issue has been intertwined with social relationships, for even as the white people who hire Bigger as their chauffeur are decent and charitable, even as the girl he accidentally kills is a liberal of sorts, theirs is the power and the privilege. "We black and they white. They got things and we ain't. They do things and we can't."

The novel barely stops to provision a recognizable social world, often contenting itself with cartoon simplicities and yielding almost entirely to the nightmare incomprehension of Bigger Thomas. The mood is apocalyptic, the tone superbly aggressive. Wright was an existentialist long before he heard the name, for he was committed to the literature of extreme situations both through the pressures of his rage and the gasping hope of an ultimate catharsis.

Wright confronts both the violence and the crippling limitations of Bigger Thomas. For Bigger white people are not people at all, but something more, "a sort of great natural force, like a stormy sky looming overhead." And only through violence does he gather a little meaning in life, pitifully little: "he had murdered and created a new life for himself." Beyond that Bigger cannot go.

At first *Native Son* seems still another naturalistic novel: a novel of exposure and accumulation, charting the waste of the undersides of the American city. Behind the book one senses the molding influence of Theodore Dreiser, especially the Dreiser of *An American Tragedy* who knows there are situations so oppressive that only violence can provide their victims with the hope of dignity. Like Dreiser, Wright wished to pummel his readers into awareness; like Dreiser, to overpower them with the sense of society as an enclosing force. Yet the comparison is finally of limited value, and for the disconcerting reason that Dreiser had a white skin and Wright a black one.

The usual naturalistic novel is written with detachment, as if by a scientist surveying a field of operations; it is a novel in which the writer withdraws from a detested world and coldly piles up the evidence for detesting it. *Native Son,* though preserving some of the devices of the naturalistic novel, deviates sharply from its characteristic tone: a tone Wright could not possibly have maintained and which, it may be, no Negro novelist can really hold for long. *Native Son* is a work of assault rather than withdrawal; the author yields himself in part to a vision of nightmare. Bigger's cowering perception of the world becomes the most vivid and authentic component of the book. Naturalism pushed to an extreme turns here into something other than itself, a kind of expressionist outburst, no longer a replica of the familiar social world but a self-contained realm of grotesque emblems.

That *Native Son* has grave faults anyone can see. The language is often coarse, flat in rhythm, syntactically overburdened, heavy with journalistic slag. Apart from Bigger, who seems more a brute energy than a particularized figure, the characters have little reality, the Negroes being mere stock accessories and the whites either "agit-prop" villains or heroic Communists whom Wright finds it easier to admire from a distance than establish from within. The long speech by Bigger's radical lawyer Max (again a device apparently borrowed from Dreiser) is ill-related to the book itself: Wright had not achieved Dreiser's capacity for absorbing everything, even the most recalcitrant philosophical passages, into a unified vision of things. Between Wright's feelings as a Negro and his beliefs as a Communist there is hardly a genuine fusion, and it is through this gap that a good part of the novel's unreality pours in.

Yet it should be said that the endlessly repeated criticism that Wright caps his melodrama with a party-line oration tends to oversimplify the novel, for Wright is too honest simply to allow the propagandistic message to constitute the last word. Indeed, the last word is given not to Max but to Bigger. For at the end Bigger remains at the mercy of his hatred and fear, the lawyer retreats helplessly, the projected union between political consciousness and raw revolt has not been achieved—as if Wright were persuaded that, all ideology apart, there is for each Negro an ultimate trial that he can bear only by himself.

Black Boy, which appeared five years after *Native Son,* is a slighter but more skillful piece of writing. Richard Wright came from a broken home, and as he moved from his helpless mother to a grandmother whose religious fanaticism (she was a Seventh-Day Adventist) proved utterly suffocating, he soon picked up a precocious knowledge of vice and a realistic awareness of social power. This autobiographical memoir, a small classic in the literature of self-discovery, is packed with harsh evocations of Negro adolescence in the South. The young Wright learns how wounding it is to wear the mask of a grinning niggerboy in order to keep a job. He examines the life of the Negroes and judges it without charity or idyllic compensations—for he already knows, in his heart and bones, that to be oppressed means to lose out on human possibilities. By the time he is seventeen, preparing to leave for Chicago, where he will work on a WPA project, become a member of the Communist party, and publish his first book of stories called *Uncle Tom's Children,* Wright has managed to achieve the beginnings of consciousness, through a slow and painful growth from the very bottom of deprivation to the threshold of artistic achievement and a glimpsed idea of freedom.

III

Baldwin's attack upon Wright had partly been anticipated by the more sophisticated American critics. Alfred Kazin, for example, had found in Wright a troubling obsession with violence:

> If he chose to write the story of Bigger Thomas as a grotesque crime story, it is because his own indignation and the sickness of the age combined to make him dependent on violence and shock, to astonish the reader by torrential scenes of cruelty, hunger, rape, murder and flight, and then enlighten him by crude Stalinist homilies.

The last phrase apart, something quite similar could be said about the author of *Crime and Punishment;* it is disconcerting to reflect that few novelists, even the very greatest, could pass this kind of moral inspection. For the novel as a genre seems to have an inherent bias toward extreme effects, such as violence, cruelty and the like. More important, Kazin's judgment rests on the assumption that a critic can readily distinguish between the genuine need of a writer to cope with ugly realities and the damaging effect these realities may have upon his moral and psychic life. But in regard to contemporary writers one finds it very hard to distinguish between a valid portrayal of violence and an obsessive involvement with it. A certain amount of obsession may be necessary for the valid portrayal—writers devoted to themes of desperation cannot keep themselves morally intact. And when we come to a writer like Richard Wright, who deals with the most degraded and inarticulate sector of the Negro world, the distinction between objective rendering and subjective immersion becomes still more difficult, perhaps even impossible. For a novelist who has lived through the searing experiences that Wright has there cannot be much possibility of approaching his subject with the "mature" poise recommended by highminded critics. What is more, the very act of writing his novel, the effort to confront what a Bigger Thomas means to him, is for such a writer a way of dredging up and then perhaps shedding the violence that society has pounded into him. Is Bigger an authentic projection of a social reality, or is he a symptom of Wright's "dependence on violence and shock?" Obviously both; and it could not be otherwise.

For the reality pressing upon all of Wright's work was a nightmare of remembrance, everything from which he had pulled himself out, with an effort and at a cost that is almost unimaginable. Without the terror of that nightmare it would have been impossible for Wright to summon the truth of the reality—not the only truth about American Negroes, perhaps not even the deepest one, but a primary and inescapable truth. Both truth and terror rested on a gross fact which Wright alone dared to confront: that violence is central to the life of the American Negro, defining and crippling him with a harshness few other Americans need suffer. "No American Negro exists who does not have his private Bigger Thomas living in the skull."

Now I think it would be well not to judge in the abstract, or with much haste, the violence that gathers in the Negro's heart as a response to the violence he encounters in society. It would be well to see this violence as part of an historical experience that is open to moral scrutiny but ought to be shielded from presumptuous moralizing. Bigger Thomas may be enslaved to a hunger for violence, but anyone reading *Native Son* with mere courtesy must observe the way in which Wright, even while yielding emotionally to

Bigger's deprivation, also struggles to transcend it. That he did not fully succeed seems obvious; one may doubt that any Negro writer could.

More subtle and human than Baldwin's criticism is a remark made
some years ago by Isaac Rosenfeld while reviewing *Black Boy:* "As with
all Negroes and all men who are born to suffer social injustice, part of
[Wright's] humanity found itself only in acquaintance with violence, and in
hatred of the oppressor." Surely Rosenfeld was not here inviting an easy acquiescence in violence; he was trying to suggest the historical context, the
psychological dynamics, which condition the attitudes all Negro writers
take, or must take, toward violence. To say this is not to propose the condescension of exempting Negro writers from moral judgment, but to suggest
the terms of understanding, and still more, the terms of hesitation for making a judgment.

There were times when Baldwin grasped this point better than anyone
else. If he could speak of the "unrewarding rage" of *Native Son,* he also
spoke of the book as "an immense liberation." Is it impudent to suggest that
one reason he felt the book to be a liberation was precisely its rage, precisely the relief and pleasure that he, like so many other Negroes, must have
felt upon seeing those long-suppressed emotions finally breaking through?

The kind of criticism Baldwin wrote was very fashionable in America
during the post-war years. Mimicking the Freudian corrosion of motives
and bristling with dialectical agility, this criticism approached all ideal
claims, especially those made by radical and naturalist writers, with a weary
skepticism and proceeded to transfer the values such writers were attacking
to the perspective from which they attacked. If Dreiser wrote about the
power hunger and dream of success corrupting American society, that was
because he was really infatuated with them. If Farrell showed the meanness
of life in the Chicago slums, that was because he could not really escape it.
If Wright portrayed the violence gripping Negro life, that was because he
was really obsessed with it. The word "really" or more sophisticated equivalents could do endless service in behalf of a generation of intellectuals
soured on the tradition of protest but suspecting they might be pygmies in
comparison to the writers who had protested. In reply, there was no way to
"prove" that Dreiser, Farrell and Wright were not contaminated by the false
values they attacked; probably, since they were mere mortals living in the
present society, they were contaminated; and so one had to keep insisting
that such writers were nevertheless presenting actualities of modern experience, not merely phantoms of their neuroses.

If Bigger Thomas, as Baldwin said, "accepted a theology that denies
him life," if in his Negro self-hatred he *"wants* to die because he glories in
his hatred," this did not constitute a criticism of Wright unless one were prepared to assume what was simply preposterous: that Wright, for all his emo-

tional involvement with Bigger, could not see beyond the limitations of the character he had created. This was a question Baldwin never seriously confronted in his early essays. He would describe accurately the limitations of Bigger Thomas and then, by one of those rhetorical leaps at which he is so gifted, would assume that these were also the limitations of Wright or his book.

Still another ground for Baldwin's attack was his reluctance to accept the clenched militancy of Wright's posture as both novelist and man. In a remarkable sentence appearing in "Everybody's Protest Novel" Baldwin wrote: "our humanity is our burden, our life; we need not battle for it; we need only to do what is infinitely more difficult—that is, accept it." What Baldin was saying here was part of the outlook so many American intellectuals took over during the years of a post-war liberalism not very different from conservatism. Ralph Ellison expressed this view in terms still more extreme: "Thus to see America with an awareness of its rich diversity and its almost magical fluidity and freedom, I was forced to conceive of a novel unburdened by the narrow naturalism which had led after so many triumphs to the final and unrelieved despair which marks so much of our current fiction." This note of willed affirmation was to be heard in many other works of the early fifties, most notably in Saul Bellow's *Adventures of Augie March.* Today it is likely to strike one as a note whistled in the dark. In response to Baldwin and Ellison, Wright would have said (I virtually quote the words he used in talking to me during the summer of 1958) that only through struggle could men with black skins, and for that matter, all the oppressed of the world, achieve their humanity. It was a lesson, said Wright with a touch of bitterness yet not without kindness, that the younger writers would have to learn in their own way and their own time. All that has happened since, bears him out.

One criticism made by Baldwin in writing about *Native Son,* perhaps because it is the least ideological, remains important. He complained that in Wright's novel "a necessary dimension has been cut away; this dimension being the relationship that Negroes bear to one another, that depth of involvement and unspoken recognition of shared experience which creates a way of life." The climate of the book, "common to most Negro protest novels . . . has led us all to believe that in Negro life there exists no tradition, no field of manners, no possibility of ritual or intercourse, such as may, for example, sustain the Jew even after he has left his father's house." It could be urged, perhaps, that in composing a novel verging on expressionism Wright need not be expected to present the Negro world with fullness, balance or nuance; but there can be little doubt that in this respect Baldwin did score a major point: the posture of militancy, no matter how great the need for it, exacts a heavy price from the writer, as indeed from everyone else. For "Even the hatred of squalor/Makes the brow grow stern/Even anger against injustice/Makes the voice grow harsh. . . ." All one can ask, by way of reply, is whether the refusal to struggle may not exact a still greater price. It is a question that would soon be tormenting James Baldwin, and almost against his will.

IV

In his own novels Baldwin hoped to show the Negro world in its diversity and richness, not as a mere specter of protest; he wished to show it as a living culture of men and women who, even when deprived, share in the emotions and desires of common humanity. And he meant also to evoke something of the distinctiveness of Negro life in America, as evidence of its worth, moral tenacity and right to self-acceptance. How can one not sympathize with such a program? And how, precisely as one does sympathize, can one avoid the conclusion that in this effort Baldwin has thus far failed to register a major success?

His first novel, *Go Tell It on the Mountain,* is an enticing but minor work: it traces the growing-up of a Negro boy in the atmosphere of a repressive Calvinism, a Christianity stripped of grace and brutal with fantasies of submission and vengeance. No other work of American fiction reveals so graphically the way in which an oppressed minority aggravates its own oppression through the torments of religious fanaticism. The novel is also striking as a modest *Bildungsroman,* the education of an imaginative Negro boy caught in the heart-struggle between his need to revolt, which would probably lead to his destruction in the jungles of New York, and the miserly consolations of black Calvinism, which would signify that he accepts the denial of his personal needs. But it would be a mistake to claim too much for this first novel, in which a rhetorical flair and a conspicuous sincerity often eat away at the integrity of event and the substance of character. The novel is intense, and the intensity is due to Baldwin's absorption in that religion of denial which leads the boy to become a preacher in his father's church, to scream out God's word from "a merciless resolve to kill my father rather than allow my father to kill me." Religion has of course played a central role in Negro life, yet one may doubt that the special kind of religious experience dominating *Go Tell It on the Mountain* is any more representative of that life, any more advantageous a theme for gathering in the qualities of Negro culture, than the violence and outrage of *Native Son.* Like Wright before him, Baldwin wrote from the intolerable pressures of his own experience; there was no alternative; each had to release his own agony before he could regard Negro life with the beginnings of objectivity.

Baldwin's second novel, *Giovanni's Room,* seems to me a flat failure. It abandons Negro life entirely (not in itself a cause for judgment) and focuses upon the distraught personal relations of several young Americans adrift in Paris. The problem of homesexuality, which is to recur in Baldwin's fiction, is confronted with a notable candor, but also with a disconcerting kind of sentimentalism, a quavering and sophisticated submission to the ideology of love. It is one thing to call for the treatment of character as integral and unique; but quite another for a writer with Baldwin's background and passions to bring together successfully his sensibility as a Negro and his sense of personal trouble.

Baldwin has not yet succeeded—the irony is a stringent one—in composing the kind of novel he counterposed to the work of Richard Wright. He has written three essays, ranging in tone from disturbed affection to disturbing malice, in which he tries to break from his rebellious dependency upon Wright, but he remains tied to the memory of the older man. The Negro writer who has come closest to satisfying Baldwin's program is not Baldwin himself but Ralph Ellison, whose novel *Invisible Man* is a brilliant though flawed achievement, standing with *Native Son* as the major fiction thus far composed by American Negroes.

What astonishes one most about *Invisible Man* is the apparent freedom it displays from the ideological and emotional penalties suffered by Negroes in this country—I say "apparent" because the freedom is not quite so complete as the book's admirers like to suppose. Still, for long stretches *Invisible Man* does escape the formulas of protest, local color, genre quaintness and jazz chatter. No white man could have written it, since no white man could know with such intimacy the life of the Negroes from the inside; yet Ellison writes with an ease and humor which are now and again simply miraculous.

Invisible Man is a record of a Negro's journey through contemporary America, from South to North, province to city, naive faith to disenchantment and perhaps beyond. There are clear allegorical intentions (Ellison is "literary" to a fault) but with a book so rich in talk and drama it would be a shame to neglect the fascinating surface for the mere depths. The beginning is both nightmare and farce. A timid Negro boy comes to a white smoker in a Southern town: he is to be awarded a scholarship. Together with several other Negro boys he is rushed to the front of the ballroom, where a sumptuous blonde tantalizes and frightens them by dancing in the nude. Blindfolded, the Negro boys stage a "battle royal," a free-for-all in which they pummel each other to the drunken shouts of the whites. Practical jokes, humiliations, terror—and then the boy delivers a prepared speech of gratitude to his white benefactors. At the end of this section, the boy dreams that he has opened the briefcase given him together with his scholarship to a

Negro college and that he finds an inscription reading: "To Whom It May Concern: Keep This Nigger-Boy Running."

He keeps running. He goes to his college and is expelled for having innocently taken a white donor through a Negro gin-mill which also happens to be a brothel. His whole experience is to follow this pattern. Strip down a pretense, whether by choice or accident, and you will suffer penalties, since the rickety structure of Negro respectability rests upon pretense and those who profit from it cannot bear to have the reality exposed (in this case, that the college is dependent upon the Northern white millionaire). The boy then leaves for New York, where he works in a white-paint factory, becomes a soapboxer for the Harlem Communists, the darling of the fellow-travelling Bohemia, and a big wheel in the Negro world. At the end, after witnessing a frenzied race riot in Harlem, he "finds himself" in some not entirely specified way, and his odyssey from submission to autonomy is complete.

Ellison has an abundance of that primary talent without which neither craft nor intelligence can save a novelist: he is richly, wildly inventive; his scenes rise and dip with tension, his people bleed, his language sings. No other writer has captured so much of the hidden gloom and surface gaiety of Negro life.

There is a great deal of superbly rendered speech: a West Indian woman inciting men to resist an eviction, a Southern sharecropper calmly describing how he seduced his daughter, a Harlem streetvendor spinning jive. The rhythm of Ellison's prose is harsh and nervous, like a beat of harried alertness. The observation is expert: he knows exactly how zootsuiters walk, making stylization their principle of life, and exactly how the antagonism between American and West Indian Negroes works itself out in speech and humor. He can accept his people as they are, in their blindness and hope:—here, finally, the Negro world does exist, seemingly apart from plight or protest. And in the final scene Ellison has created an unforgettable image: "Ras the Destroyer," a Negro nationalist, appears on a horse dressed in the costume of an Abyssinian chieftain, carrying spear and shield, and charging wildly into the police—a black Quixote, mad, absurd, pathetic.

But even Ellison cannot help being caught up with *the idea* of the Negro. To write simply about "Negro experience" with the esthetic distance urged by the critics of the fifties, is a moral and psychological impossibility, for plight and protest are inseparable from that experience, and even if less political than Wright and less prophetic than Baldwin, Ellison knows this quite as well as they do.

If *Native Son* is marred by the ideological delusion of the thirties, *Invisible Man* is marred, less grossly, by those of the fifties. The middle section of Ellison's novel, dealing with the Harlem Communists, does not ring quite true, in the way a good portion of the writings on this theme during the post-war years does not ring quite true. Ellison makes his Stalinist figures so vicious and stupid that one cannot understand how they could ever have attracted him or any other Negro. That the party leadership manipulated members with deliberate cynicism is beyond doubt, but this cynicism was surely more complex and guarded than Ellison shows it to be. No party leader would ever tell a prominent Negro Communist, as one of them does in *Invisible Man:* "You were not hired [as a functionary] to think"—even if that were what he felt. Such passages are almost as damaging as the propagandist outbursts in *Native Son.*

Still more troublesome, both as it breaks the coherence of the novel and reveals Ellison's dependence on the post-war *Zeitgeist,* is the sudden, unprepared and implausible assertion of unconditioned freedom with which the novel ends. As the hero abandons the Communist Party he wonders, "Could politics ever be an expression of love?" This question, more portentous than profound, cannot easily be reconciled to a character who has been presented mainly as a passive victim of his experience. Nor is one easily persuaded by the hero's discovery that "my world has become one of infinite possibilities," his refusal to be the "invisible man" whose body is manipulated by various social groups. Though the unqualified assertion of self-liberation was a favorite strategy among American literary people in the fifties, it is also vapid and insubstantial. It violates the reality of social life, the interplay between external conditions and personal will, quite as much as the determinism of the thirties. The unfortunate fact remains that to define one's individuality is to stumble upon social barriers which stand in the way, all too much in the way, of "infinite possibilities." Freedom can be fought for, but it cannot always be willed or asserted into existence. And it seems hardly an accident that even as Ellison's hero asserts the "infinite possibilities," he makes no attempt to specify them.

Throughout the fifties Richard Wright was struggling to find his place in a world he knew to be changing but could not grasp with the assurance he had felt in his earlier years. He had resigned with some bitterness from the Communist Party, though he tried to preserve an independent radical outlook, tinged occasionally with black nationalism. He became absorbed in the politics and literature of the rising African nations, but when visiting them he felt hurt at how great was the distance between an American Negro and an African. He found life in America intolerable, and spent his last fourteen years in Paris, somewhat friendly with the intellectual group around Jean-Paul Sartre but finally a loner, a man who stood by the pride of his rootlessness. And he kept writing, steadily experimenting, partly, it may be, in response to the younger men who had taken his place in the limelight and partly because he was a dedicated writer.

These last years were difficult for Wright, since he neither made a true home in Paris nor kept in imaginative touch with the changing life of the United States. In the early fifties he published a very poor novel, *The Outsider,* full of existentialist jargon applied but not really absorbed to the Negro theme. He was a writer in limbo, and his better fiction, such as the novelette "The Man Who Lived Underground," is a projection of that state.

In the late fifties Wright published another novel, *The Long Dream,* which is set in Mississippi and displays a considerable recovery of his powers. This book has been attacked for presenting Negro life in the South through "old-fashioned" images of violence, but one ought to hesitate before denying the relevance of such images or joining in the criticism of their use. For Wright was perhaps justified in not paying attention to the changes that have occurred in the South these past few decades. When Negro liberals write that despite the prevalence of bias there has been an improvement in the life of their people, such statements are reasonable and necessary. But what have these to do with the way Negroes feel, with the power of the memories they must surely retain? About this we know very little and would be well advised not to nourish preconceptions, for their feelings may well be closer to Wright's rasping outbursts than to the more modulated tones of the younger Negro novelists. *Wright remembered,* and what he remembered other Negroes must also have remembered. And in that way he kept faith with the experience of the boy who had fought his way out of the depths, to speak for those who remained there.

His most interesting fiction after *Native Son* is to be found in a posthumous collection of stories, *Eight Men,* written during the last 25 years of his life. Though they fail to yield any clear line of chronological development, these stories give evidence of Wright's literary restlessness, his often clumsy efforts to break out of the naturalism which was his first and, I think, necessary mode of expression. The unevenness of his writing is highly disturbing: one finds it hard to understand how the same man, from paragraph to paragraph, can be so brilliant and inept. Time after time the narrative texture is broken by a passage of sociological or psychological jargon; perhaps the later Wright tried too hard, read too much, failed to remain sufficiently loyal to the limits of his talent.

Some of the stories, such as "Big Black Good Man," are enlivened by Wright's sardonic humor, the humor of a man who has known and released the full measure of his despair but finds that neither knowledge nor release matters in a world of despair. In "The Man Who Lived Underground" Wright shows a sense of narrative rhythm, which is superior to anything in his full-length novels and evidence of the seriousness with which he kept working.

The main literary problem that troubled Wright in recent years was that of rendering his naturalism a more terse and supple instrument. I think he went astray whenever he abandoned naturalism entirely: there are a few embarrassingly bad experiments with stories employing self-consciously Freudian symbolism. Wright needed the accumulated material of circumstance which naturalistic detail provided his fiction; it was as essential to his ultimate effect of shock and bruise as dialogue to Hemingway's ultimate effect of irony and loss. But Wright was correct in thinking that the problem of detail is the most vexing technical problem the naturalist writer must face, since the accumulation that makes for depth and solidity can also become very tiresome. In "The Man Who Lived Underground" Wright came close to solving this problem, for here the naturalistic detail is put at the service of a radical projective image—a Negro trapped in a sewer; and despite some flaws, the story is satisfying both for its tense surface and elasticity of suggestion.

Richard Wright died at 52, full of hopes and projects. Like many of us, he had somewhat lost his intellectual way, but he kept struggling toward the perfection of his craft and toward a comprehension of the strange world that in his last years was coming into birth. In the most fundamental sense, however, he had done his work: he had told his contemporaries a truth so bitter, they paid him the tribute of trying to forget it.

V

Looking back to the early essays and fiction of James Baldwin, one wishes to see a little further than they at first invite:—to see past their brilliance of gesture, by which older writers could be dismissed, and past their aura of gravity, by which a generation of intellectuals could be enticed. After this hard and dismal decade, what strikes one most of all is the sheer pathos of these early writings, the way they reveal the desire of a greatly talented young man to escape the scars—and why should he not have wished to escape them?—he had found upon the faces of his elders and knew to be gratuitous and unlovely.

Chekhov once said that what the aristocratic Russian writers assumed as their birthright, the writers who came from the lower orders had to pay for with their youth. James Baldwin did not want to pay with his youth, as Richard Wright had paid so dearly. He wanted to move, as Wright had not been able to, beyond the burden or bravado of his stigma; he wanted to enter the world of freedom, grace, and self-creation. One would need a heart of stone, or be a brutal moralist, to feel anything but sympathy for this desire. But we do not make our circumstances; we can, at best, try to remake them. And all the recent writing of Baldwin indicates that the wishes of his youth could not be realized, not in *this* country. The sentiments of humanity which had made him rebel against Richard Wright have now driven him back to a position close to Wright's rebellion.

Baldwin's most recent novel *Another Country* is a "protest novel" quite as much as *Native Son,* and anyone vindictive enough to make the effort, could score against it the points Baldwin scored against Wright. No longer is Baldwin's prose so elegant or suave as it once was; in this book it is harsh, clumsy, heavy-breathing with the pant of suppressed bitterness. In about half of *Another Country*—the best half, I would judge—the material is handled in a manner somewhat reminiscent of Wright's naturalism: a piling on of the details of victimization, as the jazz musician Rufus Scott, a sophisticated distant cousin of Bigger Thomas, goes steadily down the path of self-destruction, worn out in the effort to survive in the white man's jungle and consumed by a rage too extreme to articulate yet too amorphous to act upon. The narrative voice is a voice of anger, rasping and thrusting, not at all "literary" in the somewhat lacquered way the earlier Baldwin was able to achieve. And what that voice says, no longer held back by the proprieties of literature, is that the nightmare of the history we have made allows us no immediate escape. Even if all the visible tokens of injustice were erased, the Negroes would retain their hatred and the whites their fear and guilt. Forgiveness cannot be speedily willed, if willed at all, and before it can even be imagined there will have to be a fuller discharge of those violent feelings that have so long been suppressed. It is not a pretty thought, but neither is it a mere "unrewarding rage"; and it has the sad advantage of being true, first as Baldwin embodies it in the disintegration of Rufus, which he portrays with a ferocity quite new in his fiction, and then as he embodies it in the hard-driving ambition of Rufus' sister Ida, who means to climb up to success even if she has to bloody a good many people, whites preferably, in order to do it.

Another Country has within it another novel: a nagging portrayal of that entanglement of personal relationships—sterile, involuted, grindingly rehearsed, pursued with quasi-religious fervor, and cut off from any dense context of social life—which has come to be a standard element in contemporary fiction. The author of *this* novel is caught up with the problem of communication, the emptiness that seeps through the lives of many cultivated persons and in response to which he can only reiterate the saving value of true and lonely love. These portions of *Another Country* tend to be abstract, without the veined milieu, the filled-out world, a novel needs: as if Baldwin, once he moves away from the Negro theme, finds it quite as hard to lay hold of contemporary experience as do most other novelists. The two pulls upon his attention are difficult to reconcile, and Baldwin's future as a novelist is decidedly uncertain.

During the last few years Baldwin has emerged as a national figure, a leading intellectual spokesman for the Negroes, whose recent essays, as in *The Fire Next Time,* reach heights of passionate exhortation unmatched in modern American writing. Whatever his ultimate success or failure as a novelist, Baldwin has already secured his place as one of the two or three greatest essayists this country has ever produced. He has brought a new luster to the essay as an art form, a form with possibilities for discursive reflection and concrete drama which makes it a serious competitor to the novel, until recently almost unchallenged as the dominant literary genre in our time. Apparently drawing upon Baldwin's youthful experience as the son of a Negro preacher, the style of these essays is a remarkable instance of the way in which a grave and sustained eloquence—the rhythm of oratory, but that rhythm held firm and hard—can be employed in an age deeply suspicious of rhetorical prowess. And in pieces like the reports on Harlem and the account of his first visit South, Baldwin realizes far better than in his novels the goal he had set himself of presenting Negro life through an "unspoken recognition of shared experience." Yet it should also be recognized that these essays gain at least some of their resonance from the tone of unrelenting protest in which they are written, from the very anger, even the violence Baldwin had begun by rejecting.

Like Richard Wright before him, Baldwin has discovered that to assert his humanity he must release his rage. But if rage makes for power it does not always encourage clarity, and the truth is that Baldwin's most recent essays are shot through with intellectual confusion, torn by the conflict between his assumption that the Negro must find an honorable place in the life of American society and his apocalyptic sense, mostly fear but just a little hope, that this society is beyond salvation, doomed with the sickness of the West. And again like Wright, he gives way on occasion to the lure of black nationalism. Its formal creed does not interest him, for he knows it to be shoddy, but he is impressed by its capacity to evoké norms of discipline among its followers at a time when the Negro community is threatened by a serious inner demoralization.

In his role as spokesman, Baldwin must pronounce with certainty and struggle with militancy; he has at the moment no other choice; yet whatever may have been the objective inadequacy of his polemic against Wright a decade ago, there can be no question that his refusal to accept the role of protest reflected faithfully some of his deepest needs and desires. But we do not make our circumstances; we can, at best, try to remake them; and the arena of choice and action always proves to be a little narrower than we had supposed. One generation passes its dilemmas to the next, black boys on to native sons.

"It is in revolt that man goes beyond himself to discover other people, and from this point of view, human solidarity is a philosophical certainty." The words come from Camus; they might easily have been echoed by Richard Wright; and today one can imagine them being repeated, with a kind of rueful passion, by James Baldwin. No more important words could be spoken in our century, but it would be foolish, and impudent, not to recognize that for the men who must live by them the cost is heavy.